AFRICA

controlling processes:
division of → Africa export of
labor rubber tree due to
lack of knowledge of
making rubber

AFRICA

AFRICA

VOLUME 4

THE END OF COLONIAL RULE: NATIONALISM AND DECOLONIZATION

Edited by

Toyin Falola

Carolina Academic Press

Durham, North Carolina

Library of Congress Cataloging-in-Publication Data

Africa / edited by Toyin Falola.
   p.   cm.
Includes bibliographical references and index.
ISBN 0-89089-768-9 (v. 1) — ISBN 0-89089-769-7 (v. 2) —
ISBN 0-89089-770-0 (v. 3) — ISBN 0-89089-202-4 (v. 4) —
1. Africa — History — To 1884. I. Falola, Toyin.

DT20 .A61785 2000
960 — dc21
                               00-035789

Carolina Academic Press
700 Kent Street
Durham, North Carolina 27701
Telephone (919) 489-7486
Fax (919) 493-5668
E-mail: cap@cap-press.com
www.cap-press.com

Printed in the United States of America

For Dr. Kassahun Checole and the Africa World Press

Contents

Preface and Acknowledgments

This text is intended to introduce Africa to college students and the general public. Volumes 3 and 4 both cover the entire period of colonial rule in Africa during the twentieth century. These two interrelated volumes meet the requirements of history and culture-related courses in most schools. Moreover, they address major issues of interest to the general public. The choice of topics is dictated both by relevance and the need to satisfy classroom requirements.

Volume 3 examines the colonial period from its initial foundation in the 1880s up until the outbreak of the Second World War in 1939. Among the issues examined in Volume 3 are those relating to the colonial imposition, the changes introduced by Europeans, the reactions of Africans to these changes, and the main historical events within each African region during this period.

Volume 4 continues with the discussion of the colonial period, focusing on the themes of change and freedom. The volume presents, in a simplified manner, various aspects of African history and culture from the period of World War II to the time that African countries became free of European rule. Important themes are identified in the first part, all revolving around issues of reforms and colonial disengagement. The aim in this section is to present the broad picture of Africa in the last decades of colonial rule. As to be expected, the theme of nationalism is dominant. Four chapters are devoted to the analysis of nationalism, including the contributions by women, which have generally been ignored. These were also the years of reforms, when Africa actually began to see significant changes. Various chapters are devoted to the reforms and other social aspects that received major attention at the time, notably health, business, and education. The authors pay attention to the role of Africans in initiating some of these changes. In the second part, the themes are analyzed chronologically, focusing on each region in turn. The final part reflects on what colonialism meant for Africa, both during European rule period and since independence. The concluding chapters prepare the reader to understand contemporary Africa, which is covered in Volume 5, the last in the series.

The choice of the various authors was primarily based on their competence as teachers in the explanation of history to college students and beginners, as well as their skill in synthesizing a large body of data and ideas. Among the notable pedagogical features of this volume are chapter abstracts to orient readers to the objectives and ideas of each chapter, ideas organized into various themes, review questions to help students test their knowledge of the main ideas of the chapter, and suggestions for additional reading materials to facilitate advanced research.

I am grateful to all the contributors, students, and readers who have helped in various ways to make the book readable for a diverse audience. Dr. Ann O'Hear and Ms. Jennifer Spain made many suggestions regarding style and intelligibility. Sam Saverance prepared the final maps and illustrations. Friends, associates, and students gave me access to their photo albums to make selections that have improved the overall presentation of the book. Two artists, Professor Dele Jegede and Chris Adejumo, as well as Jeff Rowe of Austin Prints and Tim Colton of Carolina Academic Press, were helpful with comments on cover illustrations.

Toyin Falola
Frances Higginbothom Nalle Centennial Professor in History
The University of Texas at Austin

List of Illustrations
and Maps

Notes on the Authors

Edmund Abaka completed his Ph.D. in history in 1998 at York University, Toronto, Canada. He is currently an Assistant Professor of History at the University of Miami, Florida. He is the author of a number of articles: "Kola Nut" (*Cambridge History of Food and Nutrition*, 2000); "Eating Kola: The Pharmacological and Therapeutic Significance of Kola Nuts" (*Ghana Studies*, 1998); with J. B. Gashugi, "Forced Migration from Rwanda: Myths and Realities" (*Refuge*, 1994); and with Samuel Woldu, "The International Context of the Rwandan Crisis" (*Refuge*, 1994). He has completed a manuscript entitled "Kola in God's Gift: The Asante and Gold Coast Kola Industry c. 1815–1950," as well as a number of entries for the forthcoming *Encyclopedia of African History*.

G. Adebayo is a Professor of History at Kennesaw State University, Georgia. He is the author of *Embattled Federalism: A History of Revenue Allocation in Nigeria* (1993) and a co-author of *History of West Africa* (1983) and *Culture, Politics and Money among the Yoruba* (2000). He has contributed essays to various journals, including the *Journal of African History*, the *International Journal of African Historical Studies*, *History in Africa*, the *Journal of Modern African Studies*, and the *Journal of the Georgia Association of Historians*. He is a member of the editorial boards of *African Economic History* and *Nigerian Journal of Economic History*. He has taught in many institutions in Africa, Europe, and Canada. He presently teaches African and world history at Kennesaw State University, where he served as Assistant Director of International Programs and now helps organize the Georgia consortium of universities involved in academic and other activities in West Africa.

Adeleke Adeeko is an Associate Professor of English at the University of Colorado, Boulder. His *Proverbs, Textuality, and Nativism in African Literature* was published in 1998. He has published articles on African and African American literature. He is currently completing a book project, tentatively titled "Black Thunder," on slave rebellions and black literature in the Caribbean, Africa, and the United States.

Saheed Adejumobi obtained his Ph.D. in African history at the University of Texas at Austin, where he also taught in the Center for African and African American Studies as an assistant instructor. He specializes in African intellectual history, researching and writing on indigenous and transnational cultural forms, popular culture, and identity politics. He has degrees from the University of Lagos, Nigeria, and the University of Oregon, Eugene.

Julius Adekunle holds a Ph.D. degree from Dalhousie University, Halifax, Nova Scotia. He has taught at Tennessee State University, Nashville and at Dalhousie and St. Mary's Universities, Halifax. He is currently an Assistant Professor of African History and the Caribbean and the Director of the Graduate Program at Monmouth University, West Long Branch, New Jersey. His work on the precolonial history of Nigerian Borgu is being revised for publication. He has published articles in *Anthropos, Ife: Annals of Cultural Studies*, and *African Economic History*. He has won many academic awards, including the Judith M. Stanley Fellowship for Improvement in Teaching at Monmouth University.

Funso Afolayan holds a Ph.D. in African History from Obafemi Awolowo University, Ile Ife, Nigeria. In addition to his research publications in Africa, Europe, and the United States, he is a co-author of *Yoruba Sacred Kingship: A Power Like That of the Gods*. Among the many books to which he has contributed are *Yoruba Historiography*; *Warfare and Diplomacy in Precolonial Nigeria*; *Dilemmas of Democracy in Nigeria*; *The Historical Encyclopedia of World Slavery*; *Culture and Society in Yorubaland*; *War and Peace in Yorubaland*; and *African Democracy in the Era of Globalization*. He has held research and teaching positions at Obafemi Awolowo University, Ile Ife, Nigeria; in the Department of Religions at Amherst College; and in the Department of History and African and Afro-American Studies Program at Washington University in St. Louis. He currently teaches African and world history at the University of New Hampshire, Durham, where he is an Associate Professor of African History and the African Diaspora.

Kwabena Akurang-Parry is an Assistant Professor of History at Shippensburg University, Shippensburg, Pennsylvania. He received his Ph.D. in African history from York University, Toronto, Canada, in 1998. His research interests include slavery and colonial rule in Ghana, the impact of abolition on gender and labor in colonial Ghana, the indigenous press in colonial West Africa, and colonial Ghana and the two World Wars. Apart from several publications in edited works, his articles have appeared or are forthcoming in *Slavery and Abolition, Ghana Studies, Refuge, History in Africa, African Economic History*, and the *International Journal of African History Studies*. His poems have appeared in *Okike* and *Ufahamu*.

Gloria Chuku, Ph.D., teaches African History and World Civilization from 1500 at South Carolina State University, Orangeburg. She has taught in three Nigerian colleges: the Federal College of Education, Umunze; Abia State University, Uturu; and Imo State University, Owerri. She has also taught at the University of Memphis in the United States. Dr. Chuku specializes in African and African women's history and gender studies. She is the recipient of many academic awards and distinctions. She was a Visiting Scholar in the James S. Coleman African Studies Center at the University of California at Los Angeles from 1999 to 2000 and a Research Scholar in the Council for the Development of Economic and Social Science Research in Africa (CODESRIA) at the Gender Institute, Dakar, Senegal, in 1995. Dr. Chuku's articles have appeared in *Women in World History, African Economic History*, and *UFAHAMU*, and she has contributed several entries to the forthcoming *Encyclopedia of African History*. She is currently revising her Ph.D. dissertation for publication, to be titled "Gender and the Changing Role of Women in Igbo Economy, 1900–1970."

J. I. Dibua holds a Ph.D. in History from the University of Benin, Nigeria. He has published numerous articles in various international journals and contributed chapters to books. He has taught at the Edo State (now Ambrose Alli) University, Ekpoma, Nigeria; the University of Benin, Benin City, Nigeria; North Carolina State University, Raleigh, NC; and North Carolina Central University, Durham, North Carolina. He is currently an Associate Professor of African and African Diaspora History at Morgan State University, Baltimore, Maryland.

Toyin Falola, Ph.D., editor of the series, is the Frances Higginbothom Nalle Centennial Professor in History at the University of Texas at Austin. He is the author of numerous articles and books, most recently *The Culture and Customs of Nigeria* (2001) and *Nationalism and African Intellectuals* (2001). A teacher at numerous institutions in various countries since the 1970s, he is the recipient of the 2000 Jean Holloway Award for Teaching Excellence at the University of Texas at Austin.

E. G. Iweriebor is a graduate of the University of Ibadan, Nigeria. He obtained his Ph.D. from Columbia University, New York. He specializes in colonial and contemporary Nigerian and African intellectual history and the history of contemporary African political and economic development. He has published several articles and is a commentator on current affairs in Nigerian newspapers. His current research is in contemporary economic history, with special reference to endogenous innovative responses to economic crisis, technological developments, and the growth of autocentric perspectives and actions among Nigerian entrepreneurs. His books include *Radical Politics in Nigeria, 1945–1950: The Significance of the Zikist Movement* (1996); *The Age of Neo-Colonialism in Africa* (1997); and, with Dr. Martin Uhmoibhi, *UN Security Council: The Case for Nigeria's Membership* (1999). He taught at the Department of History at the University of Ilorin, Nigeria, and was the first Chair of the Department of African Studies at Manhattanville College, Purchase, New York. He is currently an Associate Professor in the Department of Black and Puerto Rican Studies at Hunter College, New York.

Alusine Jalloh is an Associate Professor of History and the founding director of the Africa Program at the University of Texas at Arlington. His recent publications include *African Entrepreneurship: Muslim Fula Merchants in Sierra Leone* (1999); *Islam and Trade in Sierra Leone* (1997); and *The African Diaspora* (1996).

dele jegede obtained his Ph.D. from Indiana University, Bloomington. Currently a Professor of Art History at Indiana State University, Terre Haute, he has published extensively on various aspects of the traditional, contemporary, and popular arts of Africa. His recent publications include *Five Windows into Africa* (2000) and *Contemporary African Art: Five Artists, Diverse Trends* (2000). In 2000, he curated two major art shows, "Contemporary African Art" at the Indianapolis Museum of Art and "Women to Women: Weaving Cultures, Shaping History" at Indiana State University. Artist, art critic, cartoonist, and art historian, dele jegede has held many solo exhibitions and participated in numerous group shows.

Christian Jennings, M.A., is a doctoral student at the University of Texas at Austin, specializing in East African and environmental history. In addition to this textbook chapter, he has contributed several entries to the forthcoming *Encyclopedia of African History*.

Chima J. Korieh teaches African History at Central Michigan University. He holds degrees from the University of Nigeria, the University of Helsinki, Finland and the University of Bergen, Norway. He is currently completing his

Ph.D. dissertation at the University of Toronto. He is the recipient of many academic awards and distinctions, including the Rockefeller African Dissertation Internship Award and the Australian Overseas Postgraduate Research Award. He was the Jacob Jimeson Teaching Fellow at Hartwick College in New York, 2001–2002. He has published journal articles and book chapters.

George Ndege holds a Ph.D. from West Virginia University. He is an Assistant Professor in the Department of History at Saint Louis University. He is the author of many articles and essays in journals, books, and encyclopedias, most recently in the *Journal of Asian and African Studies*; the *Scandinavian Journal of Development Alternatives and Area Studies*; *Economic History of Kenya*; *Ethnicity, Nationalism and Democracy in Africa*; the *Encyclopedia of African History*; and the *Worldmark Encyclopedia of National Economies*. He has taught at Moi and Maseno Universities in Kenya. His monograph on the medical history of Kenya in the twentieth century is being prepared for publication.

Ugo Nwokeji holds a Ph.D. from the University of Toronto. He is an Assistant Professor in the History Department and in the Institute for African American Studies at the University of Connecticut, Storrs. He is also a Research Associate at the DuBois Institute for Afro-American Research at Harvard University, Cambridge. With David Eltis, he is creating a database of the nineteenth-century slave trade. Dr. Nwokeji has published many articles, including "African Conceptions of Gender and the Slave Traffic" in *William and Mary Quarterly* (2001); "The Atlantic Slave Trade and Population Density: A Historical Demography of the Biafran Hinterland" in the *Canadian Journal of African Studies* (2000); "Slave Emancipation Problematic: Igbo Society and the Colonial Equation" in *Comparative Studies in Society and History* (1998); and, with David Eltis, "Characteristics of Captives Leaving the Cameroons for the Americas, 1822–1837" in the *Journal of African History* (forthcoming). He has recently been a Fellow at the Gilder Lehrman Center for the Study of Slavery, Resistance, and Abolition at Yale University and a Visiting Scholar at the Center for Modern Oriental Studies, Berlin.

Apollos O. Nwauwa is Assistant Professor of African History at Bowling Green State University, Bowling Green, Ohio. Dr. Nwauwa has previously taught at Edo State University, Ekpoma, Nigeria, and at Rhode Island College and Brown University, both in Providence, Rhode Island. His scholarly works include *Imperialism, Academe, and Nationalism: Britain and University Education for Africans, 1860–1960* (1997). He has contributed many chapters to books and articles to journals such as *Anthropos*; *Cahiers D'Études Africaines*; *Africa Quarterly*; *Asian and African Studies*; *History in Africa*; the *Canadian Journal of African Historical Studies*; the *Ife Journal of History*; and the *International Journal of African Studies*.

Chidiebere Nwaubani is with the History Department at the University of Colorado at Boulder. He was previously a faculty member at Imo State University, Okigwe, Nigeria. He holds degrees from the universities of Ilorin, Ibadan, and Toronto. A recipient of many academic awards and distinctions, he was a Visiting Fellow of the British Academy in the summer of 1997. He has published in several journals on subjects including the philosophy of history, the history of the Igbo, British decolonization in Africa, and the political economy of contemporary Africa. His latest book, *The United States and Decolonization in West Africa, 1950–1960*, was published in 2001.

Adebayo Oyebade obtained his Ph.D. in history from Temple University, Philadelphia. He is currently an Associate Professor of History at Tennessee State University. He co-edited *Africa After the Cold War: The Changing Perspectives on Security* (1998) and is currently completing a book-length manuscript on the United States's strategic interests in West Africa during World War II. He has authored chapters on African history and published scholarly articles in such journals as *African Economic History* and the *Journal of Black Studies*. He has also received scholarly awards including Fulbright and Ford Foundation research grants.

Steve Salm is completing his Ph.D. in history and is a William S. Livingston Fellow at the University of Texas at Austin. He has performed fieldwork in several West African countries, focusing on twentieth century urban history and culture. He has received a number of awards and fellowships for his work, including the Jan Carleton Perry Prize for his M.A. thesis, a dissertation fellowship, and a University of Texas at Austin Thematic Fellowship on Urban Issues. He has given many guest lectures, presented research papers at various conferences, and published chapters and articles on a wide range of topics such as gender, youth, music, literature, alcohol, and popular culture. His writings have appeared in *Africa Today, African Economic History,* the *Encyclopedia of African History*, and other publications. His book *The Culture and Customs of Ghana* was published in 2002.

Bessie House Soremekun is an Associate Professor in the Department of Political Science and the Executive Director and Founder of the Minority Business Program at Kent State University. Her research has focused primarily on economic and political development in Africa and the United States. She has published numerous scholarly articles, book chapters, and book reviews. Her works have appeared in *Africa Today; African Urban and Rural Studies; Africa: Rivista Trimestrale*; the *Journal of the African Society of International and Comparative Law*; the *Ohio Journal of Economics and Politics*; and the *International Journal of African Historical Studies*. She is the author of *Class Development and Gender Inequality in Kenya, 1963–1990* (1990) and the co-editor of *African Market Women and Economic Power: The Role of Women in African Economic Development* (1995). Her book *Confronting the Odds: African-American Entrepreneurship in Cleveland, Ohio* is forthcoming.

Olufemi Vaughan holds a doctorate in politics from the University of Oxford and is currently an Associate Professor in both the Department of Africana Studies and the Department of History at the State University of New York, Stony Brook. His publications in African studies have appeared in many edited volumes and in journals such as *African Affairs*; the *Journal of Commonwealth and Comparative Politics*; the *Journal of Asian and African Studies*; the *International Journal of Politics*; and *Culture and Society*. He is the author of *Nigerian Chiefs: Traditional Power in Modern Politics, 1890s–1990s* (2000) and a co-editor of *Legitimacy and the State in Twentieth Century Africa* (1993). Vaughan is a recipient of the State University of New York's President and Chancellor's Award for Excellence in Teaching.

Introduction

Toyin Falola

This volume examines the last years of colonial rule in Africa from 1930 until the various African countries obtained their independence. A number of major developments characterized this period. First, changes continued as before as the colonial governments initiated a number of reforms after World War II. For instance, in the British colonies, the idea of economic planning was introduced in order to improve education and social services. One notable outcome of this was the creation of the first set of universities in sub-Saharan Africa. In the French colonies, the use of forced labor was abolished in 1946 and there was an increase in opportunities to demand reforms. Africans, too, continued to be innovative and to retain various aspects of their past that they found useful to their survival. Chapters 5 to 16 of this volume examine the leading issues and changes of the post-1939 era.

The second development was decolonization—the transfer of power to Africans. Colonialism crumbled as nationalism intensified. African elites found themselves acting as the representatives of their people and holding meetings with European officers who had previously ignored them. Where the colonial powers indicated that they were not ready to leave Africa, the African freedom fighters used violence as a strategy. Whereas the anticolonial protests of the early years had involved only a small number of Africans, after 1939, various social classes and segments of the population became involved. Chapters 1 to 4 capture the phases of decolonization after 1939.

The regional chapters (17–22) provide details on the struggles to regain freedom. Whereas many countries became free by the 1960s, the process was long and difficult in Namibia, South Africa, and the Portuguese-speaking countries of Mozambique and Angola. Apartheid crumbled in the 1990s, bringing the decolonization era to a close.

Background to 1939

In volume three of this series, the major events of the colonial period were discussed in detail. As shown in the previous volume, Euro-African relations changed after 1885. In contrast to the long-established relations based on trade, Europe conquered Africa and used its people as labor to produce materials for export. Within a period of twenty years, the continent was divided and shared by invading European powers. By 1901, a new map of Africa had been created, with only Ethiopia and Liberia able to escape control by Europeans. Africa then entered a period of colonial rule in the first half of the twentieth century. Thus, the history of Africa prior to 1939 was comprised of the following major issues:

The Partition

A handful of European countries, including Britain, France, Germany, Portugal, Spain, Italy, and Belgium, divided Africa among themselves. At the Berlin Conference in 1884–1885, they made arrangements to determine "spheres of interests" and minimize conflicts in the process of taking over the continent. With modern rifles and machine guns, the aggressive European powers were able to defeat many African nations.

Colonial Rule and Changes

In the early part of the twentieth century, seven colonial empires and systems were created. When Germany lost World War I, it lost its African colonies, thereby reducing the number of empires and systems to six. Some systems involved a direct form of government with European officials in power who were aided by a large number of African subordinates. Where traditional kings and chiefs were co-opted, a system of "indirect rule" operated. Irrespective of the political systems of the colonies, the objective was the same: Africa would serve the economic interests of Europe. Colonial rule was exploitative and racist.

This period witnessed a number of changes, both positive and negative. African nations were reduced to about fifty colonies with new boundaries that did not necessarily respect the interests of Africans. Previous rulers lost their powers. European officers were able to finance the various colonial administrations with money from taxation and dues on trade. Western education, thanks to the missionaries, spread in many areas. African land and labor were used to produce export crops, minerals were exploited by foreign companies, big foreign firms controlled trade, and low prices were paid for African products. Everywhere, the goal was to transfer wealth from Africa to Europe. Although Europe had passed through an industrial revolution, Africa did not see many gains in terms of the transfer of technology or industries.

African Responses

Africans responded in various ways to the partition and colonial rule. They did not want to be colonized by Europeans, and they struggled in vain to avoid this. When conquest became a reality, early forms of cooperation or nationalism sought the means to humanize the colonial systems. A number of kings and chiefs who derived benefits from the colonial systems pursued a strategy of accommodation with the colonial officers. For those, such as traders, who sought gains from the new export economy, creating retail stores was a way of making money. Those with education could serve in subordinate positions and make small salaries.

Revolt was the choice of those who had little to gain from the system or who wanted improved opportunities. The experience of colonial domination and exploitation united many Africans, as many citizens of the same country began to talk as if they had a common destiny. Nationalism became a source of identity— to unite colonized peoples against colonial rule and to build a set of cultural and political values to create a common future.

However, protest was not organized on any continental level. The Europeans had already divided Africa into many colonies, and nationalist expression tended to be confined to each country. Even within each country, as colonial policies divided the people, anticolonial nationalism was also expressed along ethnic lines. It acquired a racial divide as well: whites (European colonizers) against blacks (Africans). Thus, it was common for European officers to dismiss African freedom fighters as anti-white or as representatives of ethnic, rather than national or continental, interests. This can be seen in the Europeans' attitude toward the Mau Mau protesters in Kenya and the freedom fighters in Algeria.

The End of Colonial Rule

The events that brought European rule in Africa to an end are discussed in this volume. By 1951, it was clear that European rule would soon be over. In the 1960s, many African countries obtained their independence. However, a few countries where Africans endured long periods of struggles, deprivations, and warfare had to wait for much longer. Namibia became independent only in 1990. The apartheid policy in South Africa did not end until the early 1990s. With the end of apartheid in South Africa, the struggles for independence came to an end. The leading issues in the decolonization process include the following:

Demands for Reforms

The expression of nationalism up to 1939 focused on various demands for reforms and changes to improve people's lives, provide more social and educational services, and create jobs. In the 1940s, the elite and the masses began to come together to create mass movements that took radical positions. Trade unions and political parties became combative. Underlining the various demands was the strong belief that colonial rule was oppressive and that Africans would never make progress as long as they were under European rule. In the nationalists' view, colonial rule had brought disaster and ruin. They complained that Africans had been humiliated, had lost their land, and were denied social amenities and economic opportunities.

Before 1939, anticolonial protests took the form of defending rights to land, seeking the inclusion of Africans in legislative councils, and creating a role for the African educated elites who were excluded from local government. Christianity, too, became involved in nationalist struggles. Mission schools edified many Africans in the hope of converting them to Christianity. As Africans sought more education, including higher education, their demand was expressed in nationalist terms. Educated Africans became the leaders of ethnic associations and political parties, mastered and used Western skills against the colonizers, and provided the leadership for social movements. As the Christian elites became acculturated to

Western ways of life, they acquired ideas and values with which to criticize colonial regimes. The church also preached the doctrines of equality before God and the need for social justice. Although the church fell far short of putting into these doctrines into practice, Africans were able to use the ideas and the language in anticolonial arguments. Africans even established their own separatist churches as a form of protest to assert African identity, gain leadership, and redefine Christianity to accept a number of traditional practices condemned by foreign missions.

Impact of World War II

About two million Africans were recruited as soldiers to fight on the Allied side during World War II. These soldiers imbibed the anti-Hitlerian propaganda of the war years, especially as it stressed the need to fight for freedom, justice, and equality. In addition, the soldiers expected gratitude for their military duties. Disappointed by the colonial government's failure to reward them, many turned against the colonial governments. The experience of the war led African soldiers to reject ideas about white superiority and to question colonial domination. The political parties of the postwar years were able to recruit large numbers of ex-soldiers.

The deteriorating economic conditions of the war years instigated rural-urban migrations and competition for scarce resources in the cities. Many young people lived in crowded areas and had no jobs. The peasants were called upon to produce more materials to meet war needs. The worsening conditions fueled anger and anticolonial resentment.

World War II ended with Britain and France in weakened positions. The United States became a superpower with an interest in expanding its influence in Africa; it was, therefore, unwilling to see the continuation of European rule. Africans, too, formed radical opinions during the war. It became more and more difficult for the European powers to use force to suppress radicalism.

Another outcome of the war was the establishment of the United Nations (UN) to replace the League of Nations. Although the UN was controlled by Western powers, African nationalists quoted some of its anticolonial statements and hoped to obtain support from the organization. Anticolonial statements were made by UN representatives from countries such as the Soviet Union, which had no colonies in Africa, and African leaders saw the UN as a forum in which to criticize the European powers. Articles 62 and 73 of the UN Charter appealed to African leaders because they involved freedom and human rights. Article 62 sought recommendations on how to promote fundamental freedom and human rights, while Article 73 entreated member nations to support the development of self-government in all parts of the world.

Pan-Africanism

Help came from outside as well. Marcus Garvey, W.E.B. DuBois, and Henry Sylvester-Williams were the leading names in the Pan-Africanist movement which sought to unite all blacks in Africa and the African diaspora and to end colonial domination and all forms of racial injustice. Sylvester-Williams convened the first meeting of Pan-Africanists in London in 1900 in order to free Africans from the encroaching power of Europe. W.E.B. DuBois took up the challenge thereafter and was active in organizing Pan-Africanist meetings and calling attention to the plight of Africans under colonial rule. His message spread in the United States, Europe, Latin America, and the Caribbean. He and others organized a series of political campaigns against colonial rule and wrote many essays and books to highlight the achievements of Africans in their long history in order to build pride among black people and show that Africans were capable of governing themselves. Marcus Garvey, too, was famous, although he was more practically oriented in calling for the return of black people to Africa and the creation of conditions conducive to developing economic power. In 1936, when Italy invaded Ethiopia, the event energized Pan-Africanists all over the world and intensified anticolonial sentiments.

In 1945, emerging African leaders and representatives of trade unions, students' associations, and youth leagues joined others at a Pan-Africanist congress in Manchester. This was the largest Pan-Africanist gathering in history. Members demanded independence for Africa and passed resolutions to fight for it. Various statements made during and after the meeting revealed the goals of Pan-Africanism—to serve as an instrument of black unity and provide a platform to criticize all forms of colonial and racial domination of black peoples. In 1963, shortly after many African countries had become independent, the Organization of African Unity (OAU) was established to continue fighting for some of the goals of Pan-Africanism.

Transfer of Power

The transfer of power from Europeans to Africans began to occur mainly after 1945. School teachers, market women, civil servants, students, and others, each with different interests but with the common goal of attaining independence, came together in various associations to fight for independence. Radical religious organizations, trade unions, and political parties became assertive in their calls for an end to European rule. A new generation of leaders emerged with greater determination to fight the colonial officers.

After 1945, in areas where they did not have large numbers of European settlers, France and Britain began a gradual process of withdrawal. Reforms were made in various aspects of society, and a series of constitutional changes transferred power to Africans. If the European powers thought that the reforms would serve as concessions to pacify Africans, they were mistaken. The nationalists kept asking for more and would be satisfied only by independence.

In countries such as Algeria, Kenya, South Africa, and others with large numbers of white settlers, the struggle for independence took a violent turn. As white settlers refused to yield to the demands for independence, both Africans and settlers took to violence. In South Africa and Southern Rhodesia (now Zimbabwe), power was actually given to the white settlers. In the Portuguese colonies, the struggle was bitter, as the Portuguese simply refused to accept the right of Africans to govern themselves. Guerrilla wars became common, and the freedom fighters succeeded after bitter and prolonged encounters.

Independence was not won by all African countries at the same time. Before 1950, Egypt, Liberia, and Ethiopia were already free. During the 1950s, Libya, Morocco, Tunisia, the Sudan, Morocco, Ghana, and Guinea attained their freedom. In the 1960s, thirty-one countries gained their independence. In the 1970s, the five Portuguese-speaking colonies became free. Zimbabwe ended its struggles in 1980 and Namibia became free in 1990.

Beyond Colonial Rule

The relationship between Africa and Europe did not end with the independence of African nations. As power was being transferred to Africans, the European powers were putting in place a series of policies to protect themselves and to secure a transition from the exercise of power based on direct control to the indirect exercise of power known as neocolonialism. Colonial legacies became a feature of the contemporary era. Independence enabled Africans to take partial control of their countries, but the new leaders had to cope with the challenges of underdevelopment, political instability, and dependence on the former colonial masters.

As Volume 5 shows, postcolonial Africa has witnessed profound changes and great calamities. A history of contradictions has begun to unfold: the colonial powers left, but their legacies remain; Africans are now in power, but many leaders abuse their power; development occupies an important place in government policies, but the continent gets poorer; and while the state continues to function, political institutions decay. Until African countries solve their economic and political problems, many of their citizens will continue to regard the struggle for independence as incomplete.

PART A

AFRICA IN THE YEARS OF DECOLONIZATION

Chapter 1

Trends and Patterns in African Nationalism

Ehiedu E. G. Iweriebor

This chapter examines the movement that sought to liberate Africa from colonial domination, overthrow European colonial governments, and achieve independence. The focus is on the evolution of African nationalism, especially the emergence of mass nationalism and the drive to independence between the 1940s and the 1960s. This struggle, though countered by the colonialists' divisive actions and the creation of disabling conditions for postcolonial development, ultimately resulted in a major victory. It created the opportunity for African peoples to, once again, be acknowledged as a history-making people. African independence was, therefore, a major contribution to the global quest for freedom.

* * *

Introduction

African nationalism involved the collective effort of many anticolonial African groups. These included groups that were political, ideological, cultural, and labor-related. Their purpose in working together was to overthrow European colonial domination, achieve independence, and build new nation-states out of the various peoples and societies that comprised the European colonial territories. While the focus here is on the period of the concerted drive toward independence between the 1940s and the 1960s, African struggles for freedom from European colonial domination started much earlier. This later phase was a culmination of all previous struggles.

The first section of this chapter outlines the emergence of African nationalism in the context of the imposition and consolidation of European colonial domination from the late nineteenth century onward. The political, economic, and cultural forces that this domination set in motion are noted. The exploitative and oppressive conditions generated various protests and freedom struggles; these included political, ideological, cultural, and economic resistance. The colonial enterprise also motivated the human and social forces, the educated elite, the intelligentsia, the labor unions, various social and cultural groups, and the activated masses to fight against colonialism. This led to the growth of various proto-nationalist pressure groups and movements whose political and ideological activities formed the seedbed of incipient anticolonial nationalism from the late nineteenth century to the late 1920s.

African nationalism continued to grow from the early 1930s onward. Other developments, global and internal, laid the groundwork for the rise of militant mass nationalism from the 1940s to the 1960s. The catalytic events of the 1930s and 1940s included the world depression; the formation of African social, cultural, and labor groups; the rise of a new nationalist intelligentsia and more militant movements; and the Italo-Ethiopian conflict. These issues, examined in the second section, created the conditions in which the African freedom movements evolved, matured, and became more focused and directed toward the achievement of independence. World War II (1939–1945) also had a decisive impact on the course of political developments in Africa. The conditions which led to the emergence of mass nationalism in the postwar period are outlined in the third section. The fourth section examines the drive to independence in the different regions which used various practical strategies as dictated by their conditions. Whatever their different strategies and paths to independence, all regions had to contend with the colonizers' objective to retain indirect control after independence.

The conclusion highlights the forces that contributed to the emergence and maturation of the struggles for freedom and independence. It emphasizes the significance of the political and ideological concepts and practical strategies African freedom movements used and the challenges they faced politically and practically in their long struggles for the recovery of political independence.

Background:
European Colonial Domination and the Origins of African Nationalism

The Imposition of European Colonial Domination

European colonial domination over Africa was established in the early twentieth century. Colonies were established in an especially frenzied fashion after the Berlin Conference of 1884–1885 by seven imperial powers: Britain, France, Germany, Italy, Belgium, Portugal, and Spain.[1] The European quest for colonies in Africa followed the decline of the profitability of the slave trade. The abolition of the slave trade coincided with the development of a need for steady supplies of raw materials and markets for Europe's expanding industries. The initial European commercial strategy, known as free trade imperialism, was to establish commercial relations with African societies as suppliers of raw materials and market outlets. This attempt to structure African societies into producers of raw materials and importers of manufactured goods did not quite succeed. This was primarily because these societies still had their sovereignty; therefore, European traders,

---

1. For the imposition of colonial domination and African resistance, see Adu Boahen, ed., *UNESCO General History of Africa VII: Africa under Colonial Domination, 1880–1935* Abridged Edition, (Paris: UNESCO, 1989), Chapters 2–10;1–19.

Africa, 1914.

merchants, companies, cultural agents, and missionaries had to operate partly on terms imposed by sovereign African leaders and societies.

However, the imperative of Europe's industrial production and capitalist economic calculations could not tolerate relations of equality and equal exchange with African societies. This was the context and impetus of the European movement for the colonization of Africa. Equipped with superior military technology provided by industrial development and spurred politically by inter-European power struggles for preeminence, the aspirant European imperialists embarked on the colonization of Africa. In the confrontation between European forces and African forces—even though African societies in different parts of the continent valiantly resisted—the imperial forces ultimately won; and in the late nineteenth and early twentieth centuries, they imposed colonial domination over all of Africa except Ethiopia and Liberia.

Thereafter, the European imperial powers began establishing the political and administrative machinery to facilitate the realization of colonialism's basic objective, that is, the exploitation of African resources for European industrial production, economic development, and prosperity. The various administrative systems that the European powers established reflected their national administrative traditions, their imperial ideologies, and the conditions they met in African societies. Whatever their formal differences, they were all bureaucratic, authoritarian colonial state systems which were organized to extract resources and labor to build the administrative, social, and physical infrastructures needed to facilitate economic exploitation. In practice, Africans experienced colonial domination through forced labor, low wages, heavy taxation, land expropriation, social segregation, racial discrimination in employment and services, racist colonial education, and the vassalization and diminution of the traditional political leaders and institutions. It was these oppressive and exploitative colonial political, administrative, cultural, and economic institutions and processes that generated the African human and social forces that began the quest for freedom in various spheres of life: political, social, economic, cultural, and religious. This culminated in the emergence of African nationalism and the eventual attainment of independence.

The Emergence of African Nationalism, 1880s–1920s

African nationalism was part of the broader struggles of African peoples for political, economic, cultural, and religious freedom from European colonial domination.[2] The movement for political freedom, or nationalism, did not initially emerge as a fully formed movement. It went through various phases and struggles over different aspects of life affected by colonialism. African nationalism can be defined as the movement that sought to overthrow European colonial domination, achieve independence, and build new nation-states out of the peoples who composed the colonial territories. The aim of building new nation-states is analytically important, as it distinguishes postcolonization nationalist freedom struggles from the resistance struggles of the precolonial African societies against the imposition of colonial domination. The African societies that faced colonial pressures and subsequent military invasions included organically different political and social entities organized as empires, kingdoms, chiefdoms, and decentralized societies (the so-called stateless societies). They struggled to resist the colonial invasions, maintain their political sovereignty, and retain the precolonial political and social order.

On the other hand, African nationalist movements were struggles for freedom in the postcolonization phase, occurring specifically within the new colonial territories. As the ruling global, political, and social entities of the era were nations and nation-states, not surprisingly, African freedom movements also aimed to achieve power and independence as new nations. Hence, the nationalist struggles for inde-

---

2. For the emergence and development of African nationalism, see Thomas Hodgkin, *Nationalism in Colonial Africa* (New York: New York University Press, 1957); J. Ayo Langley, *Ideologies of African Liberation, 1856–1970: Documents on Modern African Political Thought from Colonial Times to the Present* (London: Rex Collings, 1979); Basil Davidson, *Africa in Modern History: The Search for a New Society* (Harmondsworth: Penguin Books, 1978); Basil Davidson, *Modern Africa: A Social and Political History* 2nd ed. (New York: Longman, 1989).

pendence and the objective of building new nation-states were products partly of living in new colonial territories and partly of the global prevalence of nation-states as the dominant political forms of the time. Consequently, the historiography of African nationalism attempts to identify the resistance of precolonial African societies as primary resistance and the African nationalism of the postcolonization phase as secondary resistance, implying they shared substantively similar goals. This is misleading. While African nationalists undoubtedly derived inspiration and examples from the anticolonial resistance to the imposition of colonial domination, postcolonization African nationalism was a new and substantively different movement which aimed not to restore the old political order, but to win independence for the colonized territories and to transform these territorial shells into new political and cultural communities, that is, postcolonial nation-states.

Thus, it is common for those who subscribe to a Hamitic view of African history to believe that external impulsion was required for the development of nationalism. This, again, is misleading. The primary and irreducible fact about African nationalism is that it was an internally generated, internally organized, and internally directed movement for freedom. Nationalists struggled against powerful imperialist forces that expected to keep their colonies permanently. The colonizers did not believe that African colonial territories could emerge as nations. They perceived and treated people within their territories as distinct, incompatible, and unrelated "tribes" who were so culturally different that they could not possibly form nations. In this context, the chief achievement of the African nationalists was to perceive their colonial territories as potential nations, struggle to achieve independence, and, in the process, create the ideological, cultural, and political consciousness that aided in converting the colonial territorial shells into vital new political-cultural communities. In the light of this fact, the significance ascribed to external ideas in the development of African nationalism has to be reduced. Struggles for freedom originated from a variety of conditions: the actual responses of Africans to the experiences of colonial oppression and exploitation, Africans' desire for freedom, their ideological formulations, their psychological motivations, and their practical nationalist activities. Hence, African nationalism was the product of the imaginative conceptions and practical struggles of Africans for freedom—not the result of copied ideas or external stimulation.

African nationalism evolved in different phases between the 1880s and the attainment of independence. Three main phases of the freedom struggles may be distinguished according to the following time periods: 1880s–1920s, 1930s–1940s, and 1940s–1960s.

The period from the 1880s to the 1920s saw the emergence of the nationalist intelligentsia and the rise of early protest movements in political, economic, cultural, and religious spheres. The early manifestations of African anticolonial resistance included pressure group protests against specific abuses such as forced labor, administrative malfeasance, and racial discrimination.

In terms of the development of colony-wide or territorial nationalism, while various groups such as farmers, workers, market women, traders, and youth and community associations organized the protection and advancement of their own group interests and thereby contributed to the general stream of nationalism, it was the nationalist intelligentsia that played the decisive coordinating role which converted these discrete and diverse movements into territorial ones. The members of the intelligentsia were products of the colonial or Western educational systems. They rebelled against education for subservience, detached themselves in varying degrees from colonial ideological acculturation, and began to raise the banner of freedom. These members of the intelligentsia were often economically and professionally independent and included lawyers, surveyors, merchants, traders, doctors, newspaper publishers, and employed groups such as teachers, clerks, and labor union leaders.

The members of this small educated elite were very politically and socially active. They struggled for political and social change through frameworks of ideas and ideological constructs. For instance, to the colonial views about African inferiority and the necessity for African subjection and external guidance, the intelligentsia counterposed and propagated ideas of cultural nationalism, political capacity, self-determination, independence, and nationhood. Petitions, the press, organizational activity, and other methods were used to disseminate these views.

The intelligentsia were responsible for bringing together and mobilizing the various nationalist groups, articulating and propagating nationalist ideas, and formulating preliminary visions of postcolonial nation-building. They spearheaded the formation of political pressure groups, cultural nationalist associations, and broad nationalist parties and movements. Thus, they provided the general leadership for the freedom movement, and some of them went on to become leaders of the independent nation-states. Examples include Gamal Nasser of Egypt, Habib Bourguiba of Tunisia, Ben Bella of Algeria, Nnamdi Azikiwe of Nigeria, Kwame Nkrumah of Ghana, Jomo Kenyatta of Kenya, Milton Obote of Uganda, Julius Nyerere of Tanzania, Kamuzu Banda of Malawi, Felix Houphouet-Boigny of the Ivory Coast, Leopold Sedar Senghor of Senegal, Sékou Touré of Guinea-Conakry, Robert Mugabe of Zimbabwe, Samora Machel of Mozambique, Amilcar Cabral of Guinea-Bissau, Agostinho Neto of Angola, and Nelson Mandela of South Africa.

The intelligentsia evolved historically and ideologically throughout the colonial period. Some of its members were moderate reformist nationalists who preferred a nonmilitant strategy of struggle, advocated gradual change and negotiations with the colonial powers, and even accepted colonialist ideas of postindependent African development. Others evolved into radical nationalists, advocating radical strategies of struggle which included politicized strikes, civil disobedience, and armed insurrection. They often broached ideas of national liberation as a composite of political independence and social and economic revolution. Yet, despite their political and ideological differences, the members of the intelligentsia were united by ideas of African freedom and independence.

The early protest movements focused on ameliorating conditions of political disempowerment, economic exploitation, social oppression, and cultural denigration. They campaigned for the protection of land rights, the expansion of educational facilities and opportunities, civil and political rights, participation in colonial political institutions and processes, and the dignity and integrity of indigenous leaders and political institutions. They campaigned against forced labor, heavy taxation, and colonial racism, and and also against their vassalization, misuse, corruption, and diminution as adjuncts of the colonial authorities.

This small group of elites spearheaded the early expressions of nationalist resistance and organization in the form of cultural and religious nationalism. Cultural nationalism was an attempt by the intelligentsia to assert the integrity, validity, and normalcy of African culture, practices, values, and institutions such as languages, orature (i.e., the literature of predominately oral societies),

dance, music, cuisine, style of dress, historical achievements, and social and political thought. Religious nationalism asserted the validity of indigenous religions. In the non-Muslim parts of Africa, African Christians also attempted to
establish independent churches under African control. In Muslim parts of
Africa, such as Egypt, Morocco, Somalia, and Tunisia, Islam and syncretic, indigenous, Islamic cultural forms provided coherent and unified cultural and religious traditions which the nationalists used to defend their social order and
cultural heritage.

Major cultural and religious nationalists included Simon Kimbangu of the
Belgian Congo; Nehemiah Tile of South Africa; Edward Blyden of Liberia, Sierra
Leone, and Nigeria; Casely Hayford and Mensah Sarbah of the Gold Coast; Patri-
arch Campbell and Mojola Agbebi of Nigeria; and others.

Cultural and religious nationalist activities were also important in the psychological re-empowerment of the colonized. Nationalist attempts at cultural and religious rebirth provided the colonized with the cultural resources and psychological confidence to organize nationalist movements, challenge colonial certitudes,
and struggle for freedom and independence.

The intelligentsia also spearheaded the formation of the early political pressure
groups, associations, and later nationalist parties and movements. The early political pressure groups and movements in North Africa included the Wafd of Egypt
(1918); the Young Tunisian Party and the Destour (1920) of Tunisia; and the Etoile
Nord Africain (the North African Star) formed by a group of Algerian migrants in
France in 1926. In West Africa, these movements included the Aborigines Rights
Protection Society of the Gold Coast (1897); the People's Union in Lagos (1908);
the Nigerian National Democratic Party in Nigeria (1923); and the interterritorial
nationalist movement—the National Congress of British West Africa (1920) which
embraced nationalists from Nigeria, the Gold Coast, Gambia, and Sierra Leone.
Another expression of regional Pan-Africanism was the West African Students
Union which was formed in London in 1925 by students led by Nigerian Ladipo
Solanke. It was also in the 1920s that the militant Pan-Africanism of Marcus Garvey spread through the establishment of Garvey's Universal Negro Improvement
Association in various parts of Africa, especially West and South Africa.

In South Africa, African political nationalism was partially stimulated by
Britain's withdrawal and the assumption of power by British and Boer settlers
under the Union Constitution of 1910. The new white power structure began to
systematically deprive Africans of political, civil, social, and economic rights and
impose wide-ranging racially discriminatory laws and policies. This systematic
deprivation was epitomized by the Land Act of 1913 which reserved eighty-seven
percent of the land for whites and thirteen percent of the land for the African majority. These developments led to the emergence of organized African political activity as expressed in the South African Native National Congress, formed in
1912, which later became the African National Congress in 1923. Led by Pixley
Seme, John Jabavu, John Dube, and Sol Plaatje, the Congress campaigned against
the removal of political and civil rights and economic and social discrimination.

In general, the early African nationalist groups can be described as reformist.
This is because they demanded gradual reform of defective aspects of the colonial
systems. Their demands included the review of expropriatory land policies, the
maintenance of civil liberties, a universal franchise, African representation in
colonial legislative and executive councils, the liberalization of colonial rule, the

Figure 1.1. Marcus Garvey.

abolition of racial discrimination in employment and social relations, the maintenance of traditional institutions, and the provision of mass education. Thus, while
the early nationalist groups were still dominated by the elite and by elite concerns
and had not yet evolved into mass movements as they would after World War II,
they also championed the social causes of other groups like workers, farmers,

traders, market women, and youth and advocated policies that would have mass consequences and ultimately undermine colonial power.

The Gestation and Growth of African Nationalism, 1930s–1940s

During the second phase of the African freedom struggles, in the 1930s and the 1940s, African nationalism was affected by developments in the colonial political economy, internal developments in the colonies, and other events within and outside Africa.

The nature of nationalism began to change in the early 1930s. This was partly due to the Great Depression and its impact, the emergence of a new generation of young militant nationalists and youth movements, the growth of social, cultural, ethnic, and community associations, the Italo-Ethiopian conflict of 1935–1941, and World War II and its simultaneously destabilizing and liberating effects.[3]

In the economic sphere, by the 1920s, African economies and their production patterns had been structured in such a way that they exported their primary commodities to Europe and imported manufactured goods. This meant that Africa had been effectively integrated into the global capitalist commercial network. As a result, African economies began to be subjected to the economic cycles of the Western world. Consequently, when the crash of 1929 occurred and set off the Great Depression, Africa was automatically affected. The demand for Africa's primary commodities, mineral and agricultural, fell precipitously and the impact of this was felt in the export and import dependent sectors. At the same time, the importation of manufactured goods and items like soap, medicines, sugar, oil, rice, bicycles, cars, trucks, and other goods on which the colonies now depended was severely affected. The consequences of this massive economic contraction in African colonies included the closure of import and export companies, the disruption of distributive networks, a reduction in plantation production, and a reduced demand for the products of peasant and large-scale farmers. These developments all generated unemployment, hardship, deprivation, and general impoverishment, leading to labor and social protests which the colonial governments tried to contain.

Although labor organization and action was still in its incipient phase during this period, labor activism did occur. For example, workers organized strikes in the mines in Sierra Leone, Guinea, and the Gold Coast in the 1920s and in the copperbelt of Northern Rhodesia in the period from 1935 to 1940. This led to colonial repression, but labor consciousness and activism continued to evolve. Various social, community, self-help, ethnic, and economic interest groups also emerged to protect and advance their interests.

In the political sphere, three important events took place. The first was the emergence of a new, young intelligentsia and of youth nationalist movements. Most members of this intelligentsia had been born in the early colonial period and

---

3. For the political and economic developments of this period, see Boahen, ed., *UNESCO General History of Africa VII*: chapters 14, 22–27; Davidson, *Modern Africa*, 47–95; Kevin Shillington, *History of Africa* rev. ed., (New York: St, Martins Press, 1995), 347–62.

received their early education and socialization in colonial schools. As they matured, these young Africans often found the political movements, activities, and ambitions of their elders too reformist, too gradualist, too inadequately focused on independence, and therefore too "tame" and generally unsatisfactory as challenges to colonialism. They consequently adopted a more militant stance and a populist orientation, becoming more focused on speedy political reform and advancement toward some form of self-rule. The vehicles they created were energetic youth political movements. Among them were the Gold Coast Youth Conference led by J. B. Danquah (1930), I.T.A. Wallace-Johnson's West African Youth League (1935), the Nigerian Youth Movement (1934), and Habib Bourguiba's New Destour of Tunisia (1934). These movements directly demanded self-government and pushed their demands militantly. They also began mobilizing the people, which gradually led to the expansion of nationalism beyond the elite, a development which intensified after World War II.

The Italo-Ethiopian crisis of 1935–1941 intensified the political militancy of the youth and anticolonial nationalism. The Italians had invaded and occupied Ethiopia following an incident in 1934 in which the Ethiopians attacked an Italian garrison. For the Italians, this was a godsend, an event with which to redeem their national "honor" which had been sullied by Ethiopia's decisive defeat of Italian forces at the Battle of Adowa in 1896 during the Scramble for Africa. It was also an opportunity for the Italians to satisfy the fascist objectives of imperial expansion. Despite militant protest and the actions of the League of Nations, the Italians occupied Ethiopia between 1935 and 1941.

This event had a great impact on African political consciousness and the growth of nationalism. It generated massive anti-imperialist and anticolonial sentiments throughout the African world, both within the continent and in the African diaspora in the Americas and Europe. This was because Ethiopia, Liberia, and Haiti were seen by African and black nationalists as islands of African freedom and independence and as exemplars of the African political capacity for self-rule in a sea of white colonial domination. From different parts of Africa and the black world including the U.S., Britain, and the West Indies, Africans provided funds, arms, ammunition, and other support for the Ethiopian resistance. This was a classic expression of practical Pan-Africanism. Partly as a result of this mobilization, Pan-African sentiments, views, and activities spread beyond the elite to the masses of Africans.

All these developments aroused a mass political consciousness and made the nationalist intelligentsia and their movements more geared to political militancy. This was aided by the third major political event of this period: World War II.

The Emergence of Mass Nationalism:
Conditions and Constraints

The period after World War II saw the emergence of mass nationalism, the intensification of freedom struggles, labor agitation, popular protests, and armed struggles in some colonies. In other colonies, constitutional struggles and negotiations between nationalists and colonial authorities preceded the restoration of African independence. These developments were facilitated by a number of factors, including the emergence and maturation of the nationalist intelligentsia; the impact of World War II; the economic prostration of the imperial countries; the weakening of the political and moral confidence of the imperial powers; the formation of broader nationalist parties and movements; and the activation, incorporation, and participation of the masses in the nationalist struggles for independence.[4]

During World War II, European colonial powers intensified their exploitation of African human, agricultural, and mineral resources for the furtherance of the war. Large numbers of Africans were recruited into colonial armies and served in various parts of the world including Africa, Europe, and Asia. For instance, the British recruited 280,000 people from East Africa and 167,000 from West Africa. The French conscripted over 100,000 from West Africa alone. Thus, between these two colonial powers, nearly 500,000 Africans were recruited.

The war also required the increased production of export crops such as cocoa, palm products, rubber, timber, peanuts, iron ore, and coal. This intensified demand led to the construction or expansion of railroads, seaports, and airfields and the general expansion of economic activities in the African colonies. The labor for these activities was sometimes forced or involuntarily procured through colonial chiefs. The recruitment of soldiers, expansion of raw materials production, and construction of physical infrastructure generated employment opportunities and a small economic boom in the colonies. They also led to rapid urbanization by means of migration to towns where, despite all the economic activities, employment was still inadequate and social facilities, health care, and housing infrastructures were largely unavailable. Thus, those attracted to the opportunities in the town actually faced social deprivation and hardship. This situation was exercabated by a shortage of food due to the focus on production of export crops and restrictions on the use of foreign exchange for the importation of consumer goods on which the colonized had become dependent. Consequently, there were shortages of foods and basic necessities like soap, oils, sugar, salt, and medicines in the urban centers and even rural areas. This situation led to scarcities and price inflation. Faced with these hardships, the people, especially the growing labor unions, organized popular protests and strikes. Labor activism expanded rapidly after the war.

In fact, after the war ended in 1945 and for the next few years, there were numerous strikes in various parts of Africa. These included the 1945 General Strike in Nigeria; the railway worker's strike in French West Africa in 1946; the mine and railway workers strike in Zambia in 1945; the strikes in Tanganyika in 1947; the coal miners strike in Enugu, Nigeria in 1949, in which twenty-one miners were killed; and several others in Kenya and Sierra Leone. There were also popular protests by the laboring classes, a prominent example being the Gold Coast demonstrations of 1948 during which protesters were killed. These actions often elicited colonial repression, but they also often won some concessions—no matter how small and grudging—from the colonial states which, in the postwar situation, were concerned about mobilizing African people and resources to pay for the reconstruction of their devastated societies. The strikes revealed the emergence of the working class as a powerful social and political force that would play a significant part in the postwar freedom struggles.

---

4. For developments during and after World War II, see Davidson, *Modern Africa,* 62–95; Shillington, *History of Africa,* 364–2.

The war experience and postwar activities of the returning ex-servicemen also contributed to the growth of political consciousness and political militancy that fed into the nationalism of the period. These soldiers had seen service across the world; they had seen free and independent peoples, and they had seen Japan, a powerful non-European country, fighting against Europeans. They had also observed the nationalist freedom struggles in places like India, Pakistan, Ceylon, and Burma. All these experiences stimulated their desire for freedom.

In the actual theaters of war, they saw European soldiers and officers express normal human fear and saw them killed by African soldiers fighting in opposing armies. Thus, they began to see Europeans as normal human beings and not as superior or invincible beings, as they had been constructed and projected in the colonies. Also, living in European countries the soldiers saw all classes of Europeans: the unemployed, the poor, the middle classes, and the upper classes. This helped to destroy the erroneous impression that all Europeans were rich and authoritative as they seemed in the colonies. Lastly, the war itself, along with its destructiveness and savagery, raised questions about the alleged superiority of the Europeans who had clearly demonstrated their inability to resolve their conflicts without recourse to war. Taken together, these experiences were profoundly liberating psychologically, intellectually, and politically for the war veterans and the colonized in general. Consequently, when the soldiers returned home and began to face hardships due to the failure of the colonial governments to provide jobs and the promised entitlements, they often joined the nationalist movements and adopted a militant approach.

Internationally, the Atlantic Charter's declaration for the right of all peoples to determine the governments they will live under, the formation of the United Nations and its anticolonial orientation, and the emergence of the U.S. and the Soviet Union as superpowers with their own national political and economic agendas for global ascendancy—which differed from those of the European colonial powers—all helped to create a context in which the direct colonialism of the European variety began to seem less tolerable.

The nationalist forces of this period mobilized the labor movements, peasant farmers, war veterans, youth, market women, traders, and other interest groups with grievances against the colonial system. By attempting to advance and incorporate the social concerns of these groups and reaching out to various groups in different parts of the country, these political parties enlarged the ideological platforms of the nationalist struggles and became mass nationalist movements. These activities led to the expansion of the scope of nationalism in terms of territorial reach and social composition, which now became broader and more representative of the populace. Thus, even though they were still led by the reformist intelligentsia, mass nationalist movements were emerging. The nationalists used the enlarged constituency to intensify their struggles for political independence.

Impediments to the Struggle for Independence

Although this period saw more concerted direct freedom struggles, it did not see a painless or one-way drive to independence. It saw all the twists and turns of major historical events, including heightened organization and forward movement; but it also saw uncertainties, hesitations, and deliberately-generated reactionary forces. In the anticolonial nationalist movement, this was exemplified by the emergence of competing political currents of divisive and subversive natures, including all manner of regional, ethnic, and religious movements. This often happened when a pan-territorial nationalist movement had become better organized and emerged as the ascendant political force and, therefore, a more formidable challenge against the colonial state. Ethnic, sectional, and religious groups that had no previous political agenda or direct involvement in the nationalist struggles were "suddenly" manufactured and brought into the political scene to compete against the pan-territorial nationalist movements and leaders. Since territorial national consciousness was still inchoate and evolving, it was easy to mobilize the primordial parochialisms of ethnicity, sectionalism, and religion against the broader nationalist movements. These new anti-national forces constituted major obstacles to the drive to unfettered independence. Indeed, they became constraints on the movements and to the postindependence nation-building processes.

A second profound challenge in the period leading up to independence was caused by counter-nationalist actions and by the terms of independence set by the colonial powers. On the one hand, the primary colonial powers in Africa, Britain and France, were shaken and weakened politically, economically, and morally by World War II. This removed the imperialist certitudes and confidence of the period of colonial conquest, domination, and consolidation up to the early 1930s. Weakened by the war, these imperial powers now directed their attention to the economic and social reconstruction of their devastated nations. Therefore, for them, the colonies became extremely important as sources of primary commodities, agricultural and mineral, for capital accumulation for national economic and social reconstruction.

This led the colonial powers, during the negotiations for independence, to insist on and require the protection of their economic interests by the maintenance of the African societies as captive suppliers of raw materials and importers of manufactured goods. The territorial nationalist movements and the mobilized masses were geared toward the recovery of independence as the all-consuming passion and fundamental concern. However, these groups were somewhat less focused on regaining total freedom—not only political, but also economic, social, and cultural. They therefore paid less than adequate attention to the full terms for the recovery of political independence. Hence, the colonial powers were able to create and insist on conditions in which African states won political independence without economic freedom. The African states were to pay a heavy price for this oversight. This was the origin of the neocolonial condition under which African states won independence but found themselves in conditions of economic dependency.

Despite these challenges, there is no question that the recovery of independence was an important victory and historic achievement for African peoples. It was a major contribution to the growth of freedom globally.

The Drive to Independence

As noted earlier, the period from the 1940s onward saw the rise of mass nationalist movements and focused nationalist struggles, which led to the emergence of numerous free African states in the 1960s—an era which can be rightly called the age of African political independence. However, as African countries were colonized at different times and nationalist movements emerged at different times, they also achieved their independence at different times.[5] This section outlines the main highlights of the drive to independence in selected countries chronologically, beginning with the earliest victories in North Africa.

North Africa

The first major African colony to achieve independence was Egypt in 1922. This followed the struggles of the various secular and religious nationalist and protest groups which eventually formed a nationalist party, the Wafd, in 1918 under Zaghlul Pasha. Yet this independence was only nominal, since Britain had set conditions that made it the effective ruler of Egypt even though Egyptians now formally governed their state. This continued until the 1940s, when there was a revival of Egyptian nationalism. It was best illustrated by the coup d'etat led by Colonel Gamal Abdel Nasser in 1952. The senior officer whom the young military nationalists installed as head of government, General Naguib, was removed in 1954. Colonel Gamal Nasser assumed leadership and expressed a radical nationalism that was strongly resented by the Western powers such as Britain, the U.S., France, and the new state of Israel. These powers came into conflict with Nasser. They sought to destroy him, the independence which he had shown, and the national pride which he had generated. Seeking to defend their revolution and to promote their nation's economic development, the Egyptians became allies of the Soviet Union, which provided them with military and economic support. Determination to destroy the Egyptian revolutionary government led to an invasion by Israeli forces, supported by Britain and France, in November 1956. While Egypt suffered considerable losses, it resisted valiantly and, hurt by international denunciations of their unprovoked aggression, the aggressors withdrew. Thereafter, Egypt emerged as a truly independent state.

Libya was the second North African colony to achieve independence. Libya was a former Italian colony, and arguments arose among the major powers over who should assume UN trusteeship over it after World War II. Britain and the U.S. made their interests known during these deliberations. The British, working with the aristocracy, granted Libyan independence in 1951 under King Idris, head of the Sanusiyya Brotherhood. This was clearly a compromised, incomplete, and unsatisfactory independence. Libyan middle-class nationalists campaigned for fuller independence and political modernization, which was partially realized in 1969, when young military nationalists under Colonel Muammar Gaddafi overthrew King Idris, established effective independence, and initiated a populist, Islam-based social revolution.

In Morocco, which was occupied by many French settlers and administered through the indirect rule system, the upsurge of nationalism was partly due to an

---

5. For exhaustive discussions of the drive to independence in the various regions and countries of Africa, see Ali Mazrui, *UNESCO General History of Africa, VIII: Africa since 1935* (Paris: UNESCO, 1999), Chapters 5–10; Davidson, *Modern Africa* 101–64; Shillington, *History of Africa*, 373–397; Richard Olaniyan, *African History and Culture* (Lagos: Longman, 1982), 81–110; Ehiedu Iweriebor, *Radical Politics in Nigeria, 1945–1950: The Significance of the Zikist Movement* (Zaria: Ahmadu Bello University Press, 1996).

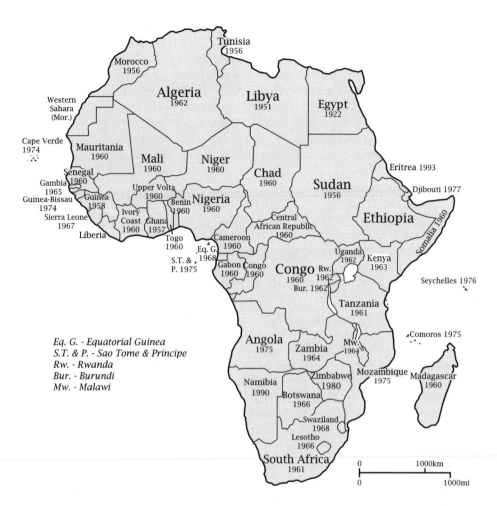

African nations, with dates of independence.

informal alliance of Sultan Mohammed and the nationalist forces led by the Istiqlal (Independence) Party (1943). The French, enraged by the sultan's alliance with the nationalists, deposed the sultan and exiled him to Madagascar. However, the sultan's popularity continued to soar, and France returned him after being pressured by the Algerian liberation war. Morocco became independent in 1956.

In Tunisia, the nationalist struggle, led by Habib Bourguiba and the Neo-Destour Party, grew stronger after the war. The movement received mass support from both urban and rural people who felt that independence was necessary for social betterment. The French, in typical fashion, resorted to oppression and violence. The Neo-Destour Party was banned in 1952, Bourguiba was detained, and attempts were made to destroy the trade unions. These actions stiffened Tunisian nationalist resolve and led to an armed struggle. Although organized by small groups, the struggle was sufficiently effective that the French brought in a large army. Due to the strength of the resistance and pressures on France in its other colonies in Africa and Asia, France was compelled to negotiate with Bourguiba and the Neo-Destour Party. In 1956, Tunisia won her independence.

The fiercest struggle for independence in North Africa took place in Algeria, as the French established it as a settler colony and considered it a province of France. The settlers, who were over one million strong by 1945, also received the best land, from which Algerians were expelled. Much land was also devoted to the cultivation of grapes for wine. This reduced the land available for food crops and made food supplies inadequate and expensive. All these conditions, combined with the settlers' intransigence, forced the Algerians to resort to armed struggle. Beginning in 1945, Algerian reformist nationalists campaigned unsuccessfully for civil, political, and social rights. Consequently, young nationalists formed the National Liberation Front (FLN). Led by war veterans like Ahmed Ben Bella, the FLN launched an armed struggle in 1954 and won mass support. The French eventually mobilized a large army that checkmated the FLN in battle but did not defeat it. The FLN's popularity remained strong. The stalemate in the war, despite the French massive military presence, convinced the French of the need to negotiate. The settlers, feeling betrayed, engaged in terrorist acts in France, convincing Charles de Gaulle to negotiate seriously with the FLN. A cease-fire was declared in March 1962. After elections, which the FLN won resoundingly, Algeria became independent in July 1962.

West Africa

In British West Africa, there was a fairly common pattern in the advancement toward independence from the 1940s onward. Following nationalist agitation, the colonialists usually formulated constitutions that were often rejected by nationalists as inadequate, because they provided insufficient room for African "participation" in government. After further struggles and negotiations, "responsible" government was often conceded to the nationalists before independence was eventually won.

The first British West African colony to win independence was the Gold Coast in 1957. Independence was preceded by efforts of a reformist nationalist movement, the United Gold Coast Convention (UGCC), which was founded in 1946 by Dr. J. B. Danquah. The UGCC was a conservative and moderate elite party which was temperamentally, ideologically, and politically out of tune with the radicalized political attitudes of the times. The party was eventually displaced by a radical nationalist party, the Convention People's Party (CPP), led by Kwame Nkrumah, the UGCC's former secretary. Nkrumah had studied in the United States and was influenced by Marcus Garvey's militant Pan-Africanist ideas and activities. Nkrumah had had a distinguished Pan-African career in London and was involved in the Pan-African Conference in Manchester in 1945. The CPP had a populist political and ideological orientation, and it expanded to embrace the working class, the war veterans, the youth, the market women (traders), and even the unemployed youth derisively described by the elite as "Singlet Boys," referring to the inexpensive V-necked T-shirts they commonly wore. With this broad social base, the CPP became a formidable challenge to the colonial authorities who blamed the political, economic, and social challenges of any organized group on CPP incitement. Consequently, following the violent general strike of 1950, Nkrumah was imprisoned. This merely increased his popularity and his reputation as a committed and fearless radical nationalist. In the 1951 elections, the CPP won resoundingly, gaining most of the seats in the legislature. Nkrumah was released and became a leader of government business. He led the Gold Coast to

Figure 1.2. Kwame Nkrumah of Ghana.

independence in 1957. The country's name was later changed to Ghana, in honor of the great empire of ancient Ghana.

The next colony to gain its independence was Nigeria. Its most important nationalist movement in the years after World War II was the National Council of Nigeria and Cameroon (NCNC), which was founded in 1944 at the instigation of younger activists who were tired of their elders debilitating intra-elite conflicts and of the neglect of the colonial enemy. It was led by veteran nationalist Herbert Macaulay and a younger militant reformist nationalist, Nnamdi Azikiwe. The NCNC spread nationalism across Nigeria. It mobilized the labor movement, war veterans, ethnic communities, town associations, social and cultural clubs, market women, other women's groups, urban elites, and politicized youths. Its Pan-Nigerian Tour of 1946, which took it to virtually all the provinces of colonial

Figure 1.3. Dr. Nnamdi Azikiwe of Nigeria.

Nigeria, was the most extensive effort to propagate nationalism in the history of colonial Nigeria. Another major nationalist movement, which aided the expansion of Nigerian nationalism and added a dimension of radical militancy to the nationalist struggle, was the Zikist Movement, founded in 1946. This was the primary radical political movement of the early postwar period. It gradually transformed itself from a Pan-Nigerian militant nationalist movement into a radical populist, socialist-oriented movement. The Zikists used a strategy of "positive action," which included politicized strikes, civil disobedience, and sabotage. Its militant agitations, along with the NCNC's struggles, compelled the colonial government to draft a constitution in 1951. New regional parties emerged under this constitution: the Northern Peoples Congress (NPC) in the North and the Action Group in the West. The emergence of these sectional parties weakened the Pan-Nigerian drive to independence, as their sectionalist claims had to be accommodated. This undoubtedly delayed Nigeria's progress toward independence. Eventually, after several constitutional conferences, all the parties agreed on Nigeria's freedom, and the country became independent in October of 1960.

Sierra Leone, after similar constitutional struggles from the 1950s onward, became independent in 1961, led by the Sierra Leone Peoples Party (SLPP). Gambia, led by the People's Progressive Party (PPP), was the last British colony in West Africa to gain its independence, which was achieved in 1965.

French West Africa

The path to independence in the French West and Equatorial (Central) African territories was complicated by the French doctrine of assimilation and the French view of the colonies as being part of a Greater France that would ultimately be assimilated into French culture and society. While some African politicians subscribed to these views, others began to organize the political movements that eventually led to independence.

The major political movement in these territories was the Rassemblement Democratique Africain (RDA), formed in Bamako, French Soudan (Mali), in 1946. It was an inter-territorial movement that covered French West and Equatorial Africa. It was led by Felix Houphouet-Boigny of the Ivory Coast, Mamadou Konate of Mali, Leopold Senghor of Senegal, Sékou Touré of French Guinea, and Barthelemy Boganda of Central Africa (Ubangi Shari). The RDA struggled for basic political and civil rights such as the right to form trade unions, establish newspapers, form political parties, and end forced labor. French settlers and businessmen, supported by the French government, reacted strongly against this upsurge of African nationalism and tried to destroy the RDA.

The RDA continued the struggle, however, and demanded that French West Africa (with eight territories) and French Equatorial Africa (with four territories) emerge as two federated states with strong central governments. The French refused, since it was clear that such federations with large populations and territories would be difficult to control. In 1956, under the *loi cadre* or enabling law, the French transferred power from the central capitals in Brazzaville and Dakar to the individual territories that then controlled local affairs. This action weakened the drive to federation and encouraged the growth of territorial nationalism—both of which suited France's objectives.

Despite this setback, African nationalists continued the struggle, while France remained determined to prevent full independence. In 1958, the French president, General Charles de Gaulle, came up with the idea of a French Community under which the twelve territories would be given self-governments and responsiblity for local affairs like education, health, and agriculture. France would remain responsible for such critical areas as finance, defense, and foreign affairs.

This plan proved attractive to some African nationalists. Those who accepted the plan would vote "yes" and become autonomous republics within the community; those who opposed the plan would vote "no" and become fully independent nations while losing all French support. De Gaulle campaigned extensively for the "yes" vote and largely succeeded; all the colonies except one voted for the plan. French Guinea, led by the radical nationalist and labor leader Sékou Touré and his well organized political party, the PDG, voted "no." The French reaction was swift and spiteful. The French removed all mechanical and electrical fixtures, typewriters, tables, chairs, and file cabinets. They also stopped all aid in hopes of crippling the new state.

But Guinea survived with support from the new government of Ghana and the Soviet Union. Guinean independence came in 1958 in spite of French tantrums, and it affected the course of political developments in the region. Soon, all the countries that had voted "yes" demanded independence. By 1960, all had gained independence, but the countries remained under the indirect control of France, as they had all signed agreements giving France supervision over their finances and foreign and military affairs, thereby creating a situation of neocolonialism. By the mid-1960s, all the West African colonies had become independent states. The Portuguese colonies were the only exception.

East and Central Africa

In the British East and Central African colonies of Tanganyika, Uganda, Kenya, Nyasaland, and Southern and Northern Rhodesia, struggles for independence were complicated by the presence of European and Asian minority settlers. Together, these settlers controlled much of the best land and much of the economic life of the colonies. The European settlers also saw themselves as potential political successors to the colonial powers. Nevertheless, African movements for freedom emerged.

The first colony to recover its independence was Tanganyika. Its early proto-nationalist group was the Tanganyika African Association (TAA), which struggled for political and civil rights. In the postwar period, the TAA supported a general strike of the port workers, teachers, and salt and sisal workers. It also had close links with African cooperative societies, farmers, and pastoralists. The TAA was succeeded by a broader-based nationalist movement, the Tanganyika African National Union (TANU), formed in 1954 and led by the modest but astute and effective leader, Julius Nyerere. TANU established its presence across the country and applied the Nkrumaist strategy of positive action which served to increase activism. It attracted repressive responses from the colonial government, which banned TANU in eleven districts in 1958.

This merely increased the party's popularity. Nyerere also exploited Tanganyika's status as a UN trusteeship territory to advance the goal of independence. He sent proposals to a visiting UN delegation in 1954 and visited the UN headquarters to make his case. With TANU established as the uncontested nationalist party, the colonial government, in a classic display of colonialist bad faith, deployed the divide-and-rule tactic of promoting a so-called "multiracial" constitution which was intended to dilute TANU's power at the district and national levels. But this ploy failed; in the parliamentary elections of 1958, under the "multiracial" constitution, TANU won decisively, capturing all the African seats and some European and Asian seats. In 1961, Tanganyika won its independence.

In 1964, Tanganyika and Zanzibar formed the loose political union of Tanzania. This was after the island of Zanzibar recovered her independence from the British in 1963 and the African majority there carried out a military revolution that overthrew the Arab sultan. The new Tanzanian union was a testimony to Nyerere's commitment to Pan-African unity.

Uganda's path to independence was complicated by the heightened level of political, cultural, and religious divisions in the colony. In addition to the continued existence of precolonial entities, especially Buganda, whose king had received

Figure 1.4. Dr. Julius Nyerere of Tanzania.

special treatment as a junior partner and collaborator with the British, the colony was afflicted with religious divisions and conflicts that impeded united action by nationalist politicians. These included differences between Muslims and Christians and between Catholics and Protestants. Thus, the nationalist parties that emerged in the 1950s, the Uganda National Congress (UNC) and the Democratic Party (DP), were sectional groups, even though the UNC had a broader national base. They could not agree on a form of government for postindependence-Uganda. Yet, in any event, the UNC—which had become the Uganda Peoples Congress (UPC) led by Milton Obote—aligned with the Bugandan royalist party to lead Uganda to independence in 1962. This compromise could not last long, however. The King and Kingdom of Buganda had been granted the right to operate a separate government distinct from the national government (in effect, a state within a state). This was clearly a recipe for future political conflict. Not surprisingly, as the government of Obote became more powerful, it dislodged the leadership and Kingdom of Buganda. Thus, Uganda achieved independence with major unresolved political and administrative problems.

The Kenyan struggle for independence involved a peasant armed struggle and negotiations between moderate African nationalists and the British government. The armed faction, known as Mau Mau, was led by the Kenya Land and Freedom Army and was a reaction against the economic exploitation and social deprivation perpetrated by the large European settlers who had expropriated African lands and turned the Kikuyu, Meru, and Embu into landless "squatters" and low-paid wage laborers so as to prevent African peasant farmers from competing with the settlers. This led to violent protests beginning in the 1940s, including labor strikes and the destruction of farm buildings, crops, and livestock intended to scare white farmers into leaving the country. As revolutionary actions intensified in the 1950s, the colonial government declared a State of Emergency, arrested well-known African nationalists, including Jomo Kenyatta, and brought in British troops. The Mau Mau struggles continued, though the movement suffered significant losses, and the British detention of Africans in concentration camps weakened the movement militarily. Yet the force of the resistance persuaded the British to accept the principle of majority rule. The State of Emergency was lifted in 1959, and the British negotiated with two new African parties, the Kenya African National Union (KANU) led by Jomo Kenyatta and the Kenyan African Democratic Union (KADU) founded by the radicals Oginga Odinga and Tom Mboya. Kenya became independent in 1963 under the moderate leadership of Kenyatta, its economic and social problems unresolved.

In the Central African colonies of Nyasaland, Northern Rhodesia, and Southern Rhodesia, the British and the white settler population attempted to prevent the emergence of African nationalism, majority rule, and independence by creating a large, rich, settler-dominated Central African Federation in 1956. This was used to entrench discriminatory laws and the disempowerment of Africans. The colonialist hope of African acquiescence and depoliticization was not realized. Instead, African political activism was reactivated and concerted struggles began. These were led in Nyasaland by the Nyasaland African National Congress, later the Malawi Congress Party under the physician and nationalist Dr. Kamuzu Banda, and in Northern Rhodesia by the Northern Rhodesia African National Congress, later the Zambia African National Congress led by Harry Nkumbula. Both parties intensified their struggles through strikes, demonstrations, and protests, which persuaded the British to accept the inevitability of independence. Following constitutional conferences, Nyasaland (Malawi) and Northern Rhodesia (Zambia) became independent in 1964.

In Southern Rhodesia, where Africans were faced with a determined white settler regime, the nationalist struggle was led by the African National Congress and later the Zimbabwe African National Union and the Zimbabwe African People's Union. These groups continued their struggles beyond the 1960s, and their full story belongs to the second wave of African nationalism.

The other Central African territories, including the Belgian Congo, Rwanda, and Urundi, were Belgian colonies. The Belgians did not expect or plan that these colonies would become independent in the foreseeable future. In the Congo, Belgium's primary colony, Africans had experienced the full weight of colonial depredations: economic exploitation, cultural domination, and racial discrimination. There was no political progress, and Africans worked only in the lowest levels of the civil service.

The small African intelligentsia of teachers, clerks, priests, and traders began to demand political liberalization and an end to racial discrimination. The Belgians responded with repression and then tried to channel the rising African activism into political participation in elections for town councils in the major cities. The elections spurred African political activity and the formation of numerous, mostly regional, parties such as the ABAKO of the Bakongo led by Joseph Kasavubu, the CONAKAT of Katanga led by Moise Tshombe, and the MNC (Congolese National Movement) led by Patrice Lumumba which, although locally based, attempted to develop a colony-wide following. In this state of political and popular activation, popular protests exploded in Leopoldville in 1959 and included attacks on colonial institutions, Catholic missions, and European property. The Belgian government, shaken by these events, negotiated with the nationalists, and Congo became independent in 1960, with the conflict between regionalism and centralism unresolved.

The UN-mandated territories of Rwanda and Burundi, which has been under Belgian control, gained their independence in 1962. Accumulated intergroup antipathies, partly historical and partly fostered by colonial divide-and-rule policies, led to conflicts after independence.

Southern Africa

In southern Africa, the colonies included South Africa, the British protectorates of Basutoland, Bechuanaland, and Swaziland, and the UN Trusteeship Territory of South West Africa. The nationalist struggles in South Africa, as noted earlier, began early in the twentieth century. However, due to the British transfer of power to the settlers and the subsequent emergence of the apartheid state in 1948, the African struggles continued through the 1990s, when democratic majority rule was finally established. The character and strategies of the struggles changed during this long period. The details of these struggles and those of South West Africa against the white South African state belong to the second wave of African nationalism, from the 1960s to the 1990s.

In the case of Bechuanaland, Basutoland, and Swaziland, the British assumption was that they would ultimately be absorbed by South Africa. Yet the emergence of the apartheid state and its vigorous and unapologetic repression of the African majority, brutally manifested in the Sharpeville massacre of 1960, changed British political calculations. Thereafter, political parties emerged in the territories, and negotiations led to the achievement of independence by Bechuanaland (Botswana) and Basutoland (Lesotho) in 1966 and by Swaziland in 1968.

Conclusion

The struggles of the various nationalist movements led to the achievement of independence by about forty African countries by the late 1960s. It has been shown that African nationalism began with political, economic, cultural, and religious protests by groups like the intelligentsia, laborers, farmers, traders, market women, and youth. These subsequently gelled into colony-wide nationalist movements led by the nationalist intelligentsia. The freedom movements derived their ideas from internal responses to colonial domination and from external sources including Pan-Africanism, Western liberalism, and Marxist radicalism. But the primary intellectual and ideological achievement of the nationalist intelligentsia was that, though they logically accepted Western ideas of the nation-state as the organizational form of postindependence polities, their nationalist assumptions and conceptions of the possibilities of nationhood differed fundamentally from the colonizers' assumptions and expectations. The colonizers saw and administered their colonies as incompatible agglomerations of discrete "tribal" entities that could not possibly emerge as nations. It was the nationalists who envisioned the fusion, political and cultural, of the various precolonial societies into coherent nation-states. Equally crucially, these African freedom movements that had organized colony-wide campaigns against colonialism began to arouse a common consciousness of colonial oppression and to infuse these colonial territorial shells with the cultural, social, and emotive aspects of nationhood.

As the imperial powers also had their designs, they countered the nationalist upsurge with violent repression and containment strategies. They created fissiparous social and political forces (ethnic, sectional, and religious) and disabling economic conditions that affected the freedom struggles and constrained the future of Africa. But the forceful pull of freedom compelled the nationalists to proceed to independence with these disabilities and without adequate preparation or vigilance, probably hoping to address the challenges of nationhood subsequently. Yet, limited as political independence was, the struggle was hard fought and hard won; and its historic significance in the annals of global struggles for human freedom should not be minimized. Frantz Fanon summarizes the extent and limits of any generation's understanding of the context and resources for its struggles:

> Each generation must out of relative obscurity discover its mission, fulfil it, or betray it. In underdeveloped countries the preceding generations have both resisted the work of erosion carried out by colonialism and also helped in the maturing of the struggles of today. We must rid ourselves of the habit...of minimizing the actions of our fathers or of feigning incomprehension...They fought as well as they could, with the arms that they possessed then.[6]

Review Questions

1. What is African nationalism and how did it evolve during the early phase of colonialism between the 1880s and 1920s?
2. Identify the various groups that contributed to the emergence of African nationalism and assess their relative contributions.
3. What forces and developments affected the growth of nationalism during the interwar years?
4. What internal and external factors contributed to the emergence of mass nationalism in the post-World War II period? How was this new mass nationalism expressed?
5. Describe in detail the struggles for independence in one region of Africa with particular attention to movements, strategies, leaders, and responses of the colonial states.

Additional Reading

Davidson, Basil. *Modern Africa: A Social and Political History*. New York: Longman, 1989.

Hodgkin, Thomas. *Nationalism in Colonial Africa*. New York: New York University Press, 1957.

---

6. Frantz Fanon, *The Wretched of the Earth* (New York: Grove Press, 1968), 206–7.

Boahen, Adu, ed. *UNESCO General History of Africa, VII: Africa under Colonial Domination, 1880–1935.* Paris: UNESCO, 1990.

Mazrui, Ali, ed. *UNESCO General History of Africa VIII: Africa Since 1935.* Paris: UNESCO, 1999.

Chapter 2

Pan-Africanism

J. I. Dibua

Pan-Africanism grew out of the appalling experiences of slavery among both continental Africans and those who were forcibly dispersed from the continent. It was a reaction to the shared feelings of brotherhood and unity among people of African descent all over the world. The movement became more systematized and formalized in the twentieth century. During this period, there were two clearly discernible phases in the Pan-African movement. The first phase, largely characterized by romanticism and idealism, was dominated by diasporan Africans, and lasted until 1945. The second phase, which lasted from 1945 to 1963, was dominated by continental Africans. One of the main catalysts for the development of this phase was the Italian invasion of Ethiopia in 1935–1936. This phase associated Pan-Africanism with the liberation of the African continent from European imperialism. It also was concerned with the promotion of African unity. The formation of the Organization of African Unity (OAU) in 1963, in certain respects, marked the culmination of this phase.

Pan-Africanism is one of the most momentous and unifying developments that has occurred during the historical experience of peoples of African descent all over the world. The injustices, inhumanity, exploitation, and racism associated with the European slave trade, European imperialism in Africa, and racism in the Americas created a collective feeling of resentment among people of African descent all over the world. It also fostered the desire and determination to struggle against oppression and degradation. Pan-Africanism can, therefore, be seen as a collective effort on the part of African peoples worldwide to promote unity and solidarity of people of African descent, and to liberate them from various forms of European domination and oppression. Although the most visible aspect of Pan-Africanism is manifested on the political front, it is a multifaceted approach that includes political, economic, cultural, and religious aspects in the struggle for the unification, rehabilitation, and regeneration of peoples of African descent in all parts of the world.

Most scholars agree that the origin of Pan-Africanism can be traced to the era of the European slave trade when enslaved Africans, whether en-route to the New World or already in the New World, grieved and longed to unite with their kin on the African continent. This implies that the origin of Pan-Africanism is related to the activities of African descendants in the diaspora. Michael Williams, however, has argued that the origin of Pan-Africanism can equally be traced to the African continent during the period of the slave trade. Africans in Africa who lost relatives and members of their ethnic groups to slavery "manifested a pristine desire for Pan-African unity by grieving for their relatives' safe return to Africa." This perspective points to a Pan-Africanism that was characterized by mutual duality originating from the dispersion of Africans as well as from those who were dispersed.[1] Nevertheless, the most visible players in the Pan-African movement up to World War II were Africans in the diaspora. After World War II, continental Africans started acting in much more visible roles in the Pan-African movement, and the eradication of colonial rule from all parts of Africa became one of their major concerns.

This chapter is mainly concerned with the post-World War II Pan-African movement in Africa that culminated in the formation of the Organization of African Unity (OAU) in 1963. Although, as has already been pointed out, Pan-Africanism was manifested in various dimensions, the main concern here is with the political and institutional aspects of the movement, especially in the form of the organization of congresses/conferences. In order to situate the discussion in a proper historical perspective, I will begin with a brief examination of the Pan-African movement before World War II and will examine the immense significance of the Italian invasion of Ethiopia in 1935–1936 for the Pan-African movement.

* * *

Pan-Africanism before World War II

One of the earliest manifestations of Pan-Africanism was the expression of a desire to emigrate to Africa. Although the best known cases of emigration involved the establishment of Sierra Leone and Liberia, the movements responsible for the creation of these countries, were not really part of the Pan-Africanist movement. White-dominated groups championed the establishment of these settlements—the Abolitionist movement in Britain in the case of Sierra Leone and the American Colonization Society in the case of Liberia. These organizations were not moved by Pan-Africanist sentiments but saw the formation of the territories as a way of getting rid of the free blacks in their societies. On the other hand, the nineteenth-century emigration efforts by prominent blacks like Paul Cuffe, Martin Delany, and Henry McNeal Turner were motivated largely by Pan-Africanist sentiments.

Perhaps the best known Pan-Africanist advocate who espoused the emigration sentiment was Marcus Garvey. Although his movement has been unfairly portrayed as being primarily concerned with the "Back to Africa" philosophy, Garvey was not just an emigrationist; he was thoroughly Pan-Africanist. His United Negro Improvement Association (UNIA) was committed to the promotion of the unity of people of African descent in all parts of the world, the restoration of the dignity of the black person, the economic empowerment of black individuals, and liberation from all vestiges of colonialism. According to Vincent Thompson,

> Garvey's programme included four principles which are among the guiding light of contemporary Pan-Africanism: first, the common destiny of all Africans and the need for continental unity as a prerequisite for deal-

---

1. Michael Williams, "The Pan-African Movement," in *Africana Studies: A Survey of Africa and the African Diaspora*, Second Edition, ed. Mario Azevedo (Durham, NC: Carolina Academic Press, 1998), 170.

ing with the numerous problems; second, the "Negro or African personality", third, the repudiation of all foreign rule and control and the eradication of all its vestiges which are retarding the growth of African man; and, fourth, social change including cultural regeneration and reactivation of the world's cultures.[2]

The various business enterprises of Garvey's movement, including the Black Star Shipping Line, the *Negro World*—the fiery and uncompromising newspaper of the movement—and the annual congresses Garvey organized in New York from 1920 onward, were avenues for the attainment of these objectives. Garvey's charisma, his organizational and oratorical skills, and the popularity and effectiveness of the *Negro World* in both exposing the degradation of black folk and mobilizing African peoples all over the world in the struggle against racism and colonial domination, caused him to be viewed as a serious foe by imperialist forces. The effectiveness of Garvey's Pan-Africanist ideals and anti-colonial sentiments were such that his movement and the *Negro World* were banned in British colonies. Nevertheless, branches of the UNIA were formed in various cities in the United States and in different parts of the Caribbean and Africa. All this turned him into a marked man. It is therefore not surprising that various attempts were made to silence him. However, despite Garvey's imprisonment and eventual deportation from the United States in the late 1920s, the impact of his movement was such that its ideals remained the focal points for various Pan-Africanist organizations.

Prior to World War II, Pan-Africanism was also manifested in the convening of Pan-African conferences. The first such conference was convened by the Caribbean lawyer, Henry Sylvester-Williams, and it took place in London in 1900. The achievements of this conference were modest. It is nevertheless significant that for the first time, a meaningful attempt was made to bring people of African descent (although most of the participants came from Europe and the New World) together to discuss their common fate and to foster the idea of cooperation and unity among them. The conference was able to draw attention to the evils of European imperialism and racism directed against African peoples. In addition, it promoted a genuine interest in African history and culture. This congress laid the pattern for future conferences that were to become an important feature of the Pan-African movement in the period leading up to the formation of the OAU.

The next Pan-African congresses were those organized by W.E.B. DuBois. Between 1919 and 1927, he organized four congresses which met in various Western nations. The opportunity for the 1919 Pan-African congress was provided when the National Association for the Advancement of Colored People (NAACP) sent DuBois to Paris in December 1918 to investigate reports of discrimination against and maltreatment of black soldiers in the United States army who were stationed in France. He was also to ensure that African interests were addressed at the impending Versailles Peace Conference. DuBois equally intended to use this opportunity to revive the Pan-African congresses. But on the advice of the United States government, the French government sought to prevent him from holding a congress. However, through the assistance of Blaise Diagne, the Senegalese deputy in the French parliament, the French authorities allowed him to organize his con-

---

2. Vincent Bakpetu Thompson, *Africa and Unity: The Evolution of Pan-Africanism* (London: Longman, 1969), 38.

gress with the understanding that there would be no sharp criticism of the colonial governments. The resolutions of this congress, which was held in February 1919, were therefore rather timidly moderate. Among other things, the resolutions demanded the improvement in the living conditions of Africans and peoples of African descent; the abolition of some harsh aspects of the colonial system, like corporal punishment and forced labor; the provision of access to education; protection from land expropriation and economic exploitation; and the gradual involvement of Africans in the administration of their territories, especially at the local level.

The resolutions of the next three congresses were equally moderate. They reiterated the demands of the 1919 congress, demanding absolute equality for people of all races, access to education in the widest sense, tolerance of all forms of society, however different from one's own, and local self-government for "backward groups" which, over time, would develop into complete self-government. Thus the main preoccupation of these congresses was the reform of the colonial system. The idea of self-determination was not an immediate or serious concern. Although during this period, Garvey's movement was gaining a great deal of popularity in the African continent, disagreements between Garvey and DuBois and the opposition from liberal white supporters of the Pan-African congresses prevented Garvey from being invited to attend these congresses. This was in spite of the attempts by some of his supporters to secure his invitation. Yet the limitations of Garveyism notwithstanding, the immense popularity of his movement, his emphasis on the empowerment of the common black folk, his uncompromising attitude toward racism and colonial exploitation, and his solid Pan-Africanist credentials would have complemented the goals of these congresses. DuBois believed in an intellectual-led gradualist Pan-African movement while Garvey believed in a radical, mass-based movement that, if necessary, should not discount the use of force to achieve the liberation of African colonies. The feud between DuBois and Garvey made the Pan-Africanist movement split into two rival camps, the radical camp (led by Garvey and the UNIA) and the moderate camp (led by DuBois).[3]

Continental Africans equally formed some Pan-African organizations. The National Congress of British West Africa (NCBWA) and the West African Students Union (WASU) were two of the most significant ones. Although restricted to West Africa, both organizations were transterritorial and transnational. The NCBWA, which was founded in 1920 through the efforts of Joseph Casely-Hayford of Ghana and Akiwande Savage of Nigeria, had as one of its aims the promotion of unity among the people of British West Africa. The NCBWA demanded the reform of the colonial system and that educated Africans gain more access to the institutions of government. In line with the spirit of Pan-Africanism, the NCBWA further advocated the establishment of a West African university and a West African court of appeal; they also resolved to set up a West African Press Union. On the other hand, the WASU, which was established in Britain in 1925 through the untiring efforts of Ladipo Solanke, had among its aims the provision of a hostel for students of African descent; the presentation to the world of a true picture of African life and philosophy, thereby showing African contributions to

---

3. Adekunle Ajala, *Pan-Africanism: Evolution, Progress and Prospects* (London: Andre Deutsch, 1973), 7.

world civilization; and the promotion of a spirit of goodwill, better understanding, and brotherhood between all persons of African descent. WASU also collaborated with various Pan-African organizations and maintained contacts with Pan-Africanists like Garvey and his wife, Amy Garvey. Nevertheless, as was the case with the Pan-African congresses, the anticolonial politics of the NCBWA and WASU were moderate and broadly concerned with the reform of the colonial system and not the immediate termination of colonial rule.

The Pan-Africanist movement before World War II was generally infused with romanticism and was more concerned with transcontinental collaboration and unity. It was against racism but believed that Africans had to undergo a process of education in the Western system of government and that power should gradually be devolved to them. The movement's immediate concern was with reform and not termination of the colonial system. Thus while during this period, Pan-Africanism spoke to the issue of cooperation and unity, it did not, save for Marcus Garvey's UNIA, develop a perception of Pan-Africanism as a serious and fundamental instrument for the liberation of the African continent from European imperialism. The Italian invasion of Ethiopia in 1935, however, radicalized the movement, bringing to the forefront the liberation aspect of Pan-Africanism, which came to full fruition in the post-World War II period.

Italian Invasion of Ethiopia, 1935–1936

Prior to the Italian invasion of Ethiopia there had been a considerable decline in the momentum of Pan-Africanism. The jailing and deportation of Garvey led to the virtual collapse of the UNIA. After 1927, DuBois did not organize any other Pan-African congress. But the invasion of Ethiopia led to an upsurge in the Pan-African movement, marking a turning point in the development of Pan-Africanism. It made Pan-Africanism uncompromisingly committed to the liberation of African countries from the clutches of European colonialism. This commitment to liberation reached its peak at the Manchester Pan-African Congress of 1945. Incidentally, it was in the area of liberation that Pan-Africanism would achieve its greatest success.[4] The invasion of Ethiopia had this far-reaching impact for a number of reasons.

Ethiopia had immense symbolic, sentimental, and even religious importance for black people all over the world. As the only country that was able to escape European conquest during the partitioning of Africa, decisively repulsing the Italian attempt to colonize it at the Battle of Adowa in 1896, independent Ethiopia became a source of pride and hope for millions of Africans all over the world. The independence of Ethiopia symbolized the aspirations of a future Africa, one free from the shackles of European imperialism. Moreover, for the vast majority of

---

4. See Edem Kodjo and David Chanaiwa, "Pan-Africanism and Liberation," in *UNESCO General History of Africa: vol. VIII: Africa since 1935* eds. Ali A. Mazrui and C. Wondji (Paris: UNESCO, 1999), 744–66.

Figure 2.1. Emperor Haile Selassie of Ethiopia.

Africans in the diaspora, Ethiopia represented their heritage and was a source of identity as exemplified in the use of the name "Ethiopia" to prefix many diasporan institutions, especially cultural and religious ones. Furthermore, for the Rastafarians, Ethiopia had religious significance: they deified Emperor Haile Selassie and adopted his previous title, Ras Tafari. In short, "Ethiopia had great appeal among African peoples and . . . historically the consciousness of the Ethiopian heritage had inspired a redemptive ideology which continued as a recurring force of identity and solidarity in Africa and the diaspora."[5]

The timid way in which the European countries reacted to the invasion and the lame-duck reaction of the League of Nations further helped to bring into sharp focus the evils of European imperialism in Africa as well as the danger posed by fascism. The reaction of the League also helped to convince many Africans that, contrary to the belief of some of the moderate Pan-Africanists, the League of Nations was not in a position to defend the interests of Africans. Moreover, many Africans came to see it as an institution that existed to defend the imperial interests of European nations. Africans all over the world therefore came to the conclusion that they should take their fate into their own hands and that the only way to defend Africa's interest was through the eradication of colonialism from the African continent. The struggle to free Ethiopia from Italian occupation was seen as the first step toward the attainment of this goal, and it became the rallying point of Pan-Africanists.

The invasion provoked a massive reaction among blacks all over the world. They launched various activities aimed at putting an end to the Italian occupation. Mass rallies were organized, Ethiopian liberation funds were launched, and organizations devoted to pursuing the Ethiopian cause were formed. Furthermore, blacks all over the world volunteered to enlist in the Ethiopian liberation

---

5. Joseph E. Harris and Slimane Zeghidour, "Africa and Its Diaspora since 1935," in Mazrui and Wondji, *Africa since 1935*, 709.

army. Public demonstrations were held in various African countries and in the diaspora while newspaper editorials and articles supportive of the Ethiopian cause
were written. For instance, the Baltimore-based *Afro-American*, one of the leading black newspapers in the United States, consistently tried to rally blacks behind
the Ethiopian cause. In Nigeria, an Abyssinian Association that included many
prominent individuals was formed to mobilize people in support of the Ethiopian
cause. The United States government proclaimed its neutrality and prohibited
Americans from participating in the war, even though many African-Americans
expressed eagerness to join the Ethiopian army. Despite the ban on participation,
two African-American pilots, Hubert Julian and John Robinson, still went to
Ethiopia to join in the war effort.[6]

A number of organizations aimed at providing moral and material support to
Ethiopia emerged in the United States. One of these organizations was the Friends
of Ethiopia (FOA), which was organized by Willis Huggins, an African-American
teacher. The FOA organized joint fund-raising programs with the International
African Friends of Ethiopia in London. Within a year, the FOA had branches in
nineteen states and 106 cities. In 1937, the Ethiopian World Federation (EWF)
was formed under the leadership of Malaku Bayen, Emperor Haile Selassie's emis-
sary to the Western hemisphere. The organization was committed both to instill-
ing black pride in the black world and to the creation of a United States of Africa.
In the same year and under the leadership of Max Yergan, an African-American,
the International Committee on Africa (ICA) was formed. The ICA was transformed into the Council on African Affairs (CAA) in 1941. The objectives of this
organization included the promotion of the political liberation of African countries; the advancement of the social and economic well-being of Africans through
the dissemination of relevant and current information and facilitation of training
for Africans in Europe and America; and the arrangement of mutual exchanges of
visits and cooperation among African people.[7]

There was equally widespread condemnation of the attack by Africans in
Britain. WASU, for example, joined forces with other African organizations to condemn the attack. WASU saw the invasion as a racial war, and the organization's
opposition to all forms of European imperialism in Africa was heightened. From
September 1935, WASU started holding weekly religious services to "invoke divine
intervention" in the conflict. In the following month, it launched an Ethiopian Defence Fund to raise money to defend the people of Ethiopia against the Italian invasion. For WASU, the invasion brought into sharp focus the need for greater unity
among people of African descent, and it showed the need for a "Black United
Front" against the common front presented by European imperialism.[8]

In 1936, C.L.R. James and a number of blacks in Britain came together to
form the International African Friends of Ethiopia (IAFE). The following year,
this organization joined forces with other pro-Ethiopian groups and individuals
to form the International African Service Bureau (IASB). The new organization
was designed to promote the political, economic, and educational empowerment
of blacks in Britain and it successfully married local issues with the Ethiopian cri-

---

6. Ibid., 709.
7. Ibid., 709–14.
8. Hakim Adi, *West Africans in Britain 1900–1960: Nationalism, Pan-Africanism and
Communism* (London: Lawrence & Wishart, 1998), 67–70.

sis. The IASB published a paper known as *International African Opinion*, and the wide appeal of this paper gave the organization a number of followers and sympathizers outside Britain. In 1944, the IASB aligned with twelve other active black welfare, students', and political organizations to transform itself into the Pan-African Federation (PAF). This federation published a journal known as *Pan-Africa* through which Pan-African sentiments were disseminated throughout the black world. The objectives of the PAF were to promote the well-being and unity of African peoples and peoples of African descent throughout the world; to demand the independence of Africans and other subject races from the domination of powers proclaiming sovereignty and trusteeship over them; and to secure equality of rights for African peoples and the total abolition of all forms of racial discrimination. In short, the invasion of Ethiopia became a "catalyst which united many Afro-Americans, West Indians and Africans residing in Britain."[9]

The PAF included among its leading members Kwame Nkrumah and Jomo Kenyatta (who were to play pivotal roles in the politics of decolonization in Africa) as well as George Padmore, C.L.R. James, and Peter Abrahams, who organized the Manchester Pan-African Congress of 1945. This congress was to radically transform the nature of the Pan-African movement and anticolonial politics in Africa. The opportunity to organize this conference was created when the British Trades Union Congress invited representatives of labor from the colonies, mainly Africa and the West Indies, to a conference of the World Federation of Trade Unions (WFTU) in February 1945. The PAF used the opportunity to invite these labor representatives to a conference in Manchester at which it was decided that a Pan-African congress should be convened in October 1945, coinciding with the next WFTU meeting.

A "Special International Conference Secretariat" was set up to prepare for the Pan-African congress. The members of this body included Dr. Peter Milliard of British Guiana, chairman, T. R. Makonnen of Ethiopia, treasurer, George Padmore of Trinidad and Kwame Nkrumah of the Gold Coast, joint secretaries, Peter Abraham of South Africa, publicity secretary, and Jomo Kenyatta of Kenya, assistant secretary. By August 1945, arrangements for the conference had been finalized and the agenda was generally approved.

The Manchester Pan-African Congress

This congress was unique in a number of ways. It was the first one attended and dominated by people from the colonies, including Africa. The congress was attended by over 200 delegates from the black world. DuBois and Milliard jointly chaired the conference on the first day, but in recognition of the contributions that DuBois had made to the Pan-African movement, he was made the chair for the rest of the conference. The conference went beyond the realm of idealism that had characterized the previous congresses. It jettisoned the moderate tone of the previous congresses and adopted a more militant and radical stance. It was uncompromisingly committed to the total liberation of Africa from foreign economic and

---

9. Thompson, *Africa and Unity*, 31–3.

political control. It clearly warned that if the Europeans were still determined to rule their African colonies by force, Africans would have no other choice than to use force to achieve their freedom. Thus for the first time Pan-Africanism was linked to African nationalism, and the need for well-organized and coordinated liberation movements as a *sine qua non* for African liberation was stressed. It was recognized that the liberation of Africa was a necessary step toward the restoration of the dignity of the black man and the promotion of African unity.

Most of the resolutions of the congress centered on the abolition of European imperialism in Africa. In their declaration to the colonial powers, the delegates stated their belief in peace but made it abundantly clear that if the colonial powers were "still determined to rule mankind by force, then Africans, as a last resort, may have to appeal to force in the effort to achieve freedom." They then went on to demand "autonomy and independence; so far and no further than it is possible in this 'One World' for groups of people to rule themselves subject to inevitable world unity and freedom." It was emphasized that the struggle for political power by colonial and subject peoples was "the first step towards, and the necessary prerequisite to, complete social, economic and political emancipation."[10] The delegates called upon the urban and rural masses and the intellectuals and professionals of Africa to unite and organize themselves effectively so that independence might be won. The Congress further demanded the immediate abolition of all racial and other discriminatory laws; the abolition of forced labor and the introduction of equal pay for equal work; the freedom of speech, press, association, and assembly; and the right of every man and woman over the age of twenty-one to vote and be voted for.

The Manchester Pan-African Congress can be seen as the greatest moment of the Pan-African movement. According to Kwame Nkrumah, the congress "provided the outlet for African nationalism and brought about the awakening of African political consciousness."[11] Pan-Africanism and nationalism now became a mass movement of Africans for Africans. In assessing the impact of the Manchester Pan-African Congress on the development of Pan-Africanism, Edem Kodjo and David Chanaiwa wrote that

> By the end of the…Congress, pan-Africanism finally had been turned into a mass ideology of Africa, by Africans and for Africans. It had grown from a reformist, protest ideology for the peoples of African descent in the New World into a nationalist ideology for the continental liberation of Africa. The global pan-Africanism of DuBois, the militant self-determination and self-reliance of Garvey, and the cultural restoration of Cesaire had then become integral elements of African nationalism.…The constitutions of all nationalist movements included pan-Africanist clauses.[12]

The Manchester Congress marked a turning point in the Pan-African movement. It propelled the movement from the realm of idealism into the realm of practical politics in which Pan-Africanism was now effectively associated with the demand

---

10. Ibid., 58–60.
11. Quoted in Ajala, *Pan-Africanism: Evolution, Progress and Prospects*, 11.
12. Kodjo and Chanaiwa, "Pan-Africanism and Liberation," 746.

for the total liberation of the African continent from European imperialism. The movement now placed its emphasis on ending colonialism on the continent as the first step toward the achievement of the Pan-African goal. In place of the global Pan-Africanism that had previously characterized the movement, primacy was now placed on promoting unity within the African continent as the necessary stepping stone toward global Pan-Africanism.

In line with the Manchester Conference's emphasis on liberation as a necessary condition for the eventual unity of the African countries, a number of West African students in Britain came together to establish the West African National Secretariat (WANS) in December 1945. WANS had Wallace Johnson as its chairman and Nkrumah as its secretary-general. The organization was expected to be the nerve center for directing and coordinating the struggle against imperialism in West Africa. It aimed to work with nationalist organizations in West Africa to build unity in order to realize the dream of creating "a West African Front for a united West African National Independence." The organization saw itself as the vanguard in the struggle not only for "absolute independence for all of West Africa" but also for uniting West Africa as "one country."[13] Toward this end, WANS convened the West African National Congress of August 1946, which pledged to promote the concept of a West African federation as a first step toward the ultimate achievement of a United States of Africa. Although this organization was extremely active, it had a short life span. It collapsed after Nkrumah, the energetic secretary-general of the movement, departed for the Gold Coast in 1947 to assume the position of secretary-general of the United Gold Coast Convention (UGCC). It was not until 1957 that there was a revival of the Pan-African movement. This time the movement was geared mainly to the promotion of African unity and the spirit behind this new phase of Pan-Africanism was Nkrumah.

Kwame Nkrumah and the
New Pan-Africanism

Between 1957 and 1958, Nkrumah dominated the Pan-African movement, working tirelessly toward the realization of a United States of Africa. After leading Ghana to political independence in March 1957, Nkrumah stated that the independence of Ghana would not be complete unless it was linked with the total liberation of the African continent from colonial domination. Nkrumah then devoted his energy and the resources of Ghana to the eradication of colonialism from the continent and the promotion of African unity. He did this through the provision of material assistance and the convening of conferences.

In pursuance of these goals, Nkrumah convened two conferences in Ghana in 1958, marking the formal launching of the Pan-African movement on African soil. The first was the Conference of Independent African States, held in Accra in April 1958. This conference was attended by the leaders of the eight independent African states (Ghana, Ethiopia, Libya, Liberia, Morocco, Tunisia, Sudan, and

---

13. Adi, *West Africans in Britain 1900–1960*, 128–31.

the United Arab Republic (Egypt). The conference aimed at discussing issues of common interest and working out policies covering political, economic, social, and cultural matters. Among other things, the conference was to discuss the continuing problem of colonialism in Africa, exchange views on foreign policy and the relationship of African countries with the United Nations and other international regional bodies, discuss ways of promoting economic cooperation among African states, formulate ways of promoting cultural exchange among African countries, and discuss the establishment of permanent machinery for consultation on foreign policy. This conference was a demonstration of the transformation of Pan-Africanism from the realm of idealism to that of pragmatism.

The resolutions of this conference were moderate in terms of their attitudes to a strong union among African states. But the conference did advance the cause of Pan-Africanism by proclaiming unity and cooperation among the independent African states in such areas as foreign policy, the fight against colonialism, and economic, cultural, and technical developments. In terms of foreign policy, the heads of state resolved "to pursue a common foreign policy with a view to safeguarding the hard-won independence, sovereignty and territorial integrity of the participating States." They went on to express their determination to "assert a distinctive African Personality which will speak with a concerted voice" in the area of foreign policy.[14] They condemned the continued presence of colonialism in Africa, declared their solidarity with the just struggle for self-determination by colonial subjects, and resolved to offer all possible assistance to nationalist movements in their struggle to achieve self-determination and independence for their territories. A non-voting status was accorded to the representatives of the Algerian National Liberation Front, which was engaged in an armed struggle for political independence from French colonial rule. They condemned racism and apartheid in South Africa and called on the United Nations to intensify its efforts at combating and eradicating this ignoble and inhuman practice. They resolved to cooperate with one another in safeguarding their independence, sovereignty, and territorial integrity, and in their economic, technical, and scientific developments with a view to raising the standard of living of their citizens. Toward this end they agreed to set up a Joint Economic Research Commission. Foreign ministers and other ministers or experts from the states were to meet from time to time to study and deal with particular problems of common concern to the African states. The Conference of Independent African States was to be reconvened every two years.[15]

The second conference that was held in 1958, the All African People's Conference (AAPC), was more radical and in many respects similar to the 1945 Manchester Pan-African Congress. This conference, which was held in Accra in December 1958, was attended by over 300 representatives of political parties from all over Africa. In his opening address, Nkrumah reminded the participants that there were four hurdles that had to be crossed before the final objective of Pan-Africanism could be achieved. The hurdles were the attainment of freedom and independence by every African state; the consolidation of that freedom and independence; the creation of unity and community between African states; and the economic and social reconstruction of Africa.[16] The resolutions of this conference

---

14. Thompson, *Africa and Unity*, 345.
15. For a complete reproduction of the resolutions, see Ibid., 342–50.
16. Ajala, *Pan-Africanism: Evolution, Progress and Prospects*, 17–8.

were less restrained than those of the conference of the heads of states. The views of this conference with regard to the eradication of colonialism and the promotion of Pan-Africanism were uncompromisingly radical.

In the case of the struggle against imperialism, the conference, among other things, vehemently condemned colonialism and imperialism in whatever shape or form; deplored the continued political and economic exploitation of Africans by imperialist Europeans and stated that the exploitation should cease forthwith; and enjoined independent African states to pursue, in their international policy, principles that would expedite and accelerate the independence and sovereignty of all dependent and colonial African territories. The conference declared "its full support to all fighters for freedom in Africa, to all those who resort to peaceful means of non-violence and civil disobedience as well as to all those who are compelled to retaliate against violence to attain national independence and freedom for the people."[17] This stance on liberation is particularly significant because it reaffirmed the radical anticolonial position of the 1945 Manchester Pan-African Congress.

The conference gave its full backing to the goals of Pan-Africanism and African unity by calling for the creation of a commonwealth of African states. In this regard, the conference made the following resolutions: it endorsed Pan-Africanism and the desire for unity among African peoples; declared that its ultimate objective was the evolution of a commonwealth of free African states; called upon the independent states of Africa to lead the peoples of Africa toward the attainment of this objective; and expressed the hope that the day would dawn when the first loyalty of African states would be to an African commonwealth. Thus, the AAPC unlike the conference of heads of states unreservedly endorsed Nkrumah's desire for a strong African union. Since the delegates were representatives of political parties and not heads of state, they did not have the considerations, interests, and restraints of the heads of state.

With regard to the international boundaries of African countries, the AAPC denounced the artificial boundaries drawn by the imperialist powers to divide the people of Africa; demanded for the abolition or adjustment of such frontiers at an early date; and called upon independent African states to support a permanent solution to the boundary problem based upon the true wishes of the people. In addition, the conference called for the establishment of a permanent secretariat to organize the All African People's Conference on a permanent basis. This secretariat was also to help in promoting understanding and unity among peoples of Africa, accelerate the liberation of Africa from imperialism and colonialism, mobilize world opinion against the denial of political rights and fundamental human rights to Africans, and develop the feeling of community among the peoples of Africa with the object of the emergence of a United States of Africa.[18]

Apart from the radical nationalist and Pan-Africanist resolutions of the AAPC, the conference significantly affected the pace of decolonization struggles, especially in those territories where nationalist activities had been lukewarm, like the Belgian Congo. Due to the extremely harsh and inhumane policies of the Belgian colonial authority, nationalism had been unable to attain a firm footing in

---

17. Thompson, *Africa and Unity*, 352.
18. For a complete reproduction of the resolutions, see Ibid., 350–8.

Figure 2.2. William Tubman of Liberia.

this territory. Based on the resolutions of the conference, Patrice Lumumba, one of the Congolese delegates, returned home determined to effect the liberation of his country from Belgian colonial domination. At a rally held on December 28, 1958, Lumumba, citing the resolutions of the Accra conference, demanded independence as a right for the Congolese people. He declared that his objective was the unity and organization of the Congolese people in order to improve their lot. The Belgian authorities were jolted out of their previous complacency and in a panic hastily arranged a decolonization process, the outcome of which plunged the Congo into serious political turmoil that was unfortunately to claim the life of Lumumba.

After the 1958 conferences, Nkrumah initiated steps that he hoped would lead to the eventual realization of a commonwealth of African states. On November 23, 1958, after talks in Accra between Nkrumah and Sékou Touré, the Prime Minister of the newly independent Guinea, the leaders announced that the two countries had decided to form a union, which would constitute the nucleus of a Union of West African States. Both countries agreed to adopt a Union flag and harmonize their policies in the areas of defense, foreign affairs, and economic affairs. In May 1959, during a state visit to Guinea by Nkrumah, both leaders not only reaffirmed the friendship, fraternity, and solidarity between the two countries, they produced a draft constitution for the Union of Independent African States. This draft was to be submitted to the governments of independent African states and those countries that would soon achieve their political independence, for their consideration.

In reaction to the proposed union between Ghana and Guinea and the draft constitution for a Union of Independent African States prepared by the two countries, President Tubman of Liberia decided to convene a meeting of the heads of state of Liberia, Ghana, and Guinea. This meeting, which took place at Sanniquellie, Liberia, in July 1959, discussed issues like African unity, liberation struggles, racial discrimination in South Africa, nuclear tests in the Sahara, and a future conference of independent African states. Although Nkrumah and Sékou

Early pan-Africanist organizations up to the OAU.

Touré insisted that concrete decisions should be taken regarding the nature and specific form that African unity should take, Tubman was of the opinion that such far-reaching and intricate decisions could not be taken until most African states had become independent. Nevertheless, the leaders agreed to the formation of "the Community of Independent African States" with a view to achieving unity among independent African states. Each member state of the community was to maintain its own national identity and constitutional structure. In addition, each member accepted the principle of non interference in the internal affairs of other members. The community was to set up an economic council, a cultural council, and a scientific and research council. Membership was open to any independent African state. The conference resolved to assist, foster, and speed up the liberation of dependent African territories. It was proposed that a special conference of independent African states and non independent states which had dates fixed for independence should be held in 1960 to write a charter which would help to achieve the ultimate goal of unity between independent African states.

Both the Ghana-Guinea Union and the Sanniquellie meeting marked a further advance in the Pan-African movement. They clearly put the issue of African unity on the table at a point when the majority of African states were on the verge of attaining political independence. In certain significant respects, the union and the Sanniquellie meeting set the tone for the conferences and debates that occurred between 1960 and 1963 regarding the form that African unity should take.

Pan-Africanist activities flourished in 1960, the year in which the majority of African countries attained their political independence. Among the Pan-African activities of this year were the second AAPC and Independent African States conferences. The first Pan-Africanist activity to be organized was the second All African Peoples Conference, held in Tunis in January. While emphasizing the political, economic, and cultural aspects of Pan-Africanism, the conference stressed the need for African unity. The conference fixed the objectives of Pan-Africanism as follows: promotion of understanding and unity among the peoples of Africa; development of a feeling of one community among the African people; acceleration of the liberation of Africa from imperialism and colonialism; mobilization of world opinion in support of African liberation; and intensification of efforts toward the emergence of a United States of Africa. With regard to the struggle for Algeria's independence, which was to be one of the issues that caused cleavages in the Pan-African movement, the conference called on all independent African states to recognize the provisional government of Algeria and give material, financial, and military assistance to the Algerian liberation movement. Furthermore, the conference demanded the withdrawal of soldiers from other French African territories fighting on the side of the French imperialist forces against the Algerian liberation fighters.

The second Conference of Independent African States held at Addis Ababa in June 1960 was not as widely attended as had been anticipated. Although invitations were extended to countries that were already independent and those countries whose dates for independence had been fixed, most countries under French colonial rule did not attend. At the conference there was general agreement on the need for African countries to establish some form of unity. But the nature of this unity was greatly in dispute. Ghana, supported by Guinea, pushed for a political union and urged that the Sanniquellie declaration be used as the basis for the achievement of a union of African states. The opposing group, led by Nigeria and Ethiopia, was against this type of strong union but favored cooperation in the economic field while moving gradually toward some form of loose political cooperation. In the words of Maitama Sule, the leader of the Nigerian delegation:

> (W)e must not be sentimental: we must be realistic. It is for this reason that we would like to point out that at this moment the idea of forming a Union of African States is premature. On the other hand we do not dispute the sincerity and indeed the good intentions of those people that advocate it. But we feel that such a move is too radical—perhaps too ambitious—to be of any lasting value.[19]

Nigeria and the other members of this group therefore advocated a gradual and functional approach to African unity. This difference was to characterize the approaches to African unity in subsequent Pan-African conferences.

---

19. Quoted in Ibid., 167.

Nevertheless, there was consensus on the need for more economic cooperation among African countries, the need to eradicate of colonialism from the continent, and the need to remove the apartheid system from South Africa. Although
there was consensus over supporting the Algerian liberation movement, the conference failed to explicitly recognize the Algerian provisional government as
Ghana and Guinea demanded. Instead it recommended that France and Algeria
should enter into negotiations.

After the Addis Ababa Independent African states meeting, two major blocs,
representing the differing positions on African unity, emerged. These blocs were
later to be known as the Casablanca group, representing the radical perspective,
and the Monrovia group, representing the moderate/conservative perspective.[20]
The Casablanca group emerged from a conference that was held in Morocco in
January 1961. The conference was attended by the heads of state of Ghana,
Guinea, Mali, Morocco, and the United Arab Republic, including a representative
of the Algerian provisional government and the foreign minister of Libya. One of
the main issues discussed at the conference was the Congo crisis. Contrary to the
stand of the Brazzaville conference, where delegates praised the role the United
Nations (UN) was playing in the crisis, this group was highly critical of the UN's
role. With regard to Pan-Africanism, the conference decided on the establishment
of an effective form of cooperation in the economic, social, and cultural fields. It
was resolved to create an African consultative assembly as soon as conditions permitted. This consultative assembly was to be made up of representatives of every
African state and was to meet periodically. In the interim, the conference recommended the setting up of a political committee, an economic committee, a cultural
committee, and a Joint African high command. To ensure effective cooperation
among these organizations, a liaison office was to be established and to be en-
trusted with the organization of a meeting of experts.

Meanwhile, as a practical way of demonstrating their commitment to Pan-
African unity, the heads of state of Ghana, Mali, and Guinea announced the formation of the Ghana-Guinea-Mali Union in December 1960. The union was to
make it possible for them to harmonize and coordinate their policies on important foreign affairs, as well as promote cooperation in the economic and monetary fields. In April 1961, they published a "Charter for the Union of African
States" and changed the name of their union to "the Union of African States".
They regarded this union as the nucleus of a United States of Africa.

The Monrovia group emerged from the conference of heads of state that
was held in Liberia in May 1961. The conference was ostensibly convened to
bridge the gulf that was emerging in the Pan-African movement and work out
ways of fashioning an acceptable form of African unity. However, most members of the Casablanca group refused to attend the conference, partly because of
the failure to invite the Algerian provisional government. The conservative and
moderate groups dominated the conference. This was clearly reflected in the
resolutions that were passed regarding the issue of African unity. It was emphasized that what African states needed was not a political union but unity of as-
piration and cooperation in various fields. Other resolutions were: absolute

---

20. There was a third group (the Brazzaville group) made up mainly of ex-French
colonies. This group took a conservative stand and was later to merge with the Monrovia
group.

equality and sovereignty of African states; non interference in the internal affairs of other states; respect for the sovereignty of each state and its inalienable right to existence; and promotion of cooperation based upon tolerance, solidarity, and good-neighborliness, periodical exchange of views, and non acceptance of any leadership.

The delegates urged the Algerian provisional government and the French government to expedite an agreement that would put an end to the war of liberation and grant independence to Algeria. In the case of the Congo crisis, the delegates reaffirmed their belief in the ability of the UN to effectively resolve the situation. It was decided that another conference to be attended by all African heads of state would be held in Lagos, in January 1962.

Although the Lagos conference, which was held in January 1962, was expected to bridge the gap between the competing groups, this was blocked by the refusal of members of the Casablanca group to attend. They based their refusal on the fact that arrangements for the conference were made without input from their group and that the representatives of the Algerian provisional government were not invited. In fact, this failure to invite the representatives of Algeria even caused disagreement within the Monrovia group, leading to the refusal of three members of this group (Tunisia, Libya, and the Sudan) to attend the conference. As a result, no North African country was represented at the conference.

The Lagos conference resolved to set up an Inter-African and Malagasy Organization. It adopted in principle a draft charter, which was to become the charter of the organization. This draft charter stressed the need for greater economic cooperation among member states, as well as cooperation in areas like education, culture, politics, and foreign affairs. It stressed the equality of all sovereign African states and non interference in the internal affairs of member states. The charter was to be submitted to all the governments for detailed comments and subsequently considered by a committee of representatives of all the governments concerned. The committee was expected to meet within three months and incorporate all the comments in a revised charter to be submitted to the next conference of heads of state. The documents produced by this committee became known as the Lagos Charter.

By now, the two distinct blocs within the Pan-African movement, the Casablanca group and the Monrovia group, had definitely emerged. Each of these groups had its own idea about the form that African unity should take as articulated in their respective charters. Paradoxically, the events that were to lead to the demise of these two groups and the subsequent formation of a body representing all African countries started at the Lagos conference. This was largely due to the statesmanlike efforts of Emperor Haile Selassie of Ethiopia.

Formation of the
Organization of African Unity

In the midst of some of the divisive speeches at the Lagos conference and the reactions from members of the Casablanca group, Emperor Haile Selassie decided to act as a unifier. In the conciliatory speech he delivered at the Lagos conference, he said that:

Ethiopia is committed to the principle of political unity among African states—indeed, we believe that we all are, and that we differ only in our assessment of the speed with which this most desirable of goals can be attained. The task now is to devise the means whereby this basic agreement may be most rapidly advanced.... Ethiopia considers herself a member of one group only—the African group.... We contend, accordingly, that no wider and unbridgeable gap exists between the various groupings which have been created. It is our belief, to the contrary, that a close and careful analysis of the policies adopted by the African nations today on a wider range of questions emphasises, not the differences among them, but the larger number of views which they share in common. We urge that this conference use this as its starting point, that we emphasise and lay stress on the areas of similarity and agreement rather than upon whatever disagreements and differences may exist among us.[21]

After the Lagos conference, Emperor Haile Selassie devoted much of his energy toward convening a meeting of all African heads of state at Addis Ababa during which the issue of African unity would be discussed. At the same time, some members of the two opposing camps started adopting a more conciliatory approach and calling on all African heads of state to sink their differences for the sake of African unity. State visits between African heads of state and bilateral meetings at which the issue of African unity was discussed were intensified. Haile Selassie was determined to hold a meeting of African heads of state in Ethiopia in 1963. He invited all African leaders to the proposed conference and dispatched his foreign minister, Ato Ketema Yifru, on a mission to these countries in order to work out the details of the conference with them. These efforts finally resulted in general agreement, and so the conference was fixed for May 1963.

The meeting of the heads of state was preceded by that of the foreign ministers, which began at Addis Ababa on May 15, 1963. The meeting had the responsibility of producing a draft charter and an agenda for the forthcoming summit of the heads of state. But because of disagreements between ministers from states belonging to the opposing camps, the foreign ministers were unable to agree on a draft charter, although they were able to draw up a comprehensive agenda. When the summit began on May 22, 1963, there was a fear that the disagreement might hinder the formation of a united organization. Nkrumah and some other members of the Casablanca bloc insistently demanded a stronger union of African states while most members of the Monrovia bloc were strongly opposed to such a strong union.

However, the passionate opening address of Emperor Haile Selassie set the tone for a compromise. He emphasized that Africa needed a united platform on which Africans could collaborate in solving Africa's problems, settle inter-African disputes, promote common defense and economic and social programs, and speak with one voice to the rest of the world. As a result, he emphasized that "this conference cannot close without adopting a single African organisation.... If we fail in this, we will have shirked our responsibility to Africa and to the people we lead. If we succeed, then and only then, will we have justified our presence

---

21. Quoted in Thompson, *Africa and Unity*, 175; see also Ajala, *Pan-Africanism: Evolution, Progress and Prospects*, 48.

here."[22] One of the most difficult issues that confronted the conference was the form that African unity should take. Nkrumah insisted on a continental union government but this received only scant support. By May 25th, however, the charter of a proposed organization had been prepared, debated, and accepted by the summit. The African leaders decided to form an organization which was titled the Organization of African Unity (OAU). With the formation of this organization, the Casablanca and Monrovia blocs ceased to exist.

This organization was not the type of union government advocated by Nkrumah but a loose association of states in line with the stand of the conservative group. The OAU was a child of compromise although the nature of the organization was generally closer to the position of the conservative group. This was to be expected because the Monrovia group was larger than the Casablanca group. The nature of the organization notwithstanding, the fact that all African countries were able to come together in a single organization marked some form of victory for Pan-Africanism. The objectives of the OAU were the promotion of unity and solidarity among African states and peoples; the achievement of a better life for the peoples of Africa; the defence of their sovereignty, territorial integrity and independence; the eradication of all forms of colonialism from Africa; and the promotion of international cooperation.

The principles of the organization included the sovereign equality of member-states; non interference in the internal affairs of states; respect for the sovereignty and territorial integrity of each state and for its inalienable right to an independent existence; and peaceful settlement of disputes by negotiation, mediation, conciliation, or arbitration. There was also a commitment to the policy of non alignment with regard to all major power blocs.

Conclusion

Pan-Africanism grew out of the gruesome and inhuman experiences of slavery that led to the forced dispersion of a large number of Africans from the mother continent. There were two clearly discernible phases in the growth of the Pan-African movement. The first phase, in the period before World War II, was dominated by Africans in the diaspora and characterized by a great deal of idealism and romanticism. The two leading protagonists of Pan-Africanism during this period were W.E.B. DuBois, with his Pan-African congresses, and Marcus Garvey, who adopted a more radical and multifaceted approach to African unity.

The Italian invasion of Ethiopia in 1935–1936 set in motion forces that led to the second phase of Pan-Africanism. This phase was much more radical and adopted a pragmatic approach to African unity. Continental Africans dominated it and they emphasized liberation from colonialism and the promotion of continental cooperation and unity. This phase successfully linked Pan-Africanism with African liberation and nationalism. Although it was very successful in its liberation agenda, the same cannot be said in terms of its promotion of African unity. The quest for continental unity was bedeviled by a number of divisions resulting

---

22. Quoted in C.O.C. Amate, *Inside the OAU: Pan-Africanism in Practice*, (New York: St. Martins Press, 1986), 56–7.

in the formation of antagonistic blocs. Nevertheless, the fact that the various blocs were eventually able to compromise and come together to form the OAU can be regarded as some form of victory for the Pan-African movement. Unfortunately, as a product of compromise, the OAU was a rather deformed child from its birth, and it negated some of the hopes and aspirations of genuine and committed Pan-Africanists.

Review Questions

1. Explain the term Pan-Africanism. Identify and analyze the two broad phases of the Pan-African movement.
2. Discuss the impact of the Italian invasion of Ethiopia on the development of Pan-Africanism.
3. Critically examine the achievements and failures of the Pan-African movement in the period between 1945 and 1963.
4. Examine the contributions of Kwame Nkrumah and Emperor Haile Selassie to the development of Pan-Africanism.

Additional Readings

Ajala, Adekunle. *Pan-Africanism: Evolution, Progress and Prospects*. London: Andre Deutsch, 1973.

Amate, C.O.C. *Inside the OAU: Pan-Africanism in Practice*. New York: St. Martin's Press, 1986.

Clarke, John Henrik, ed. *Marcus Garvey and the Vision of Africa*. New York: Vintage Books, 1974.

Esedebe, Olisanwuche. *Pan-Africanism: The Idea and Movement, 1776–1963*. Washington, D.C.: Howard University Press, 1982.

Geiss, Imanuel. *The Pan-African Movement: A History of Pan-Africanism in America, Europe and Africa*. New York: Africana Publishing Company, 1974.

Legum, Colin. *Pan-Africanism: A Short Political Guide*. Greenwood Press, 1965.

Padmore, George *Pan-Africanism or Communism*. Garden City, NY: Doubleday, 1971.

Thompson, Vincent Bakpetu. *Africa and Unity: The Evolution of Pan-Africanism*. London: Longman, 1969.

Chapter 3

Africa and World War II

Kwabena O. Akurang-Parry

We all overseas soldiers are coming back home with new ideas. We have been told what we fought for. That is "freedom." We want freedom, nothing but freedom.[1]

This chapter examines Africa and World War II. It briefly discusses the political and economic conditions in Africa on the eve of the war, positing that two major events, the Great Depression and the Italian invasion of Ethiopia in 1935, moved African nationalism from reformism to revolution and affected African responses to the colonial powers' war efforts. The chapter also explores how wartime colonial policies were geared toward supporting the war. The nature of mobilization, recruitment, and African responses are examined, stressing the roles of African rulers and the Western-educated elites in the war effort. It highlights the Africans' participation in the various theaters of war and explains why demobilization led to discontent. Lastly, the chapter examines the effects of the war on Africa, concluding that it increased the pace of anticolonialism.

* * *

Introduction:
The War and Africa

World War II was a paradoxical turning point in the relationship between the European colonial powers and colonized Africans. The exigencies of the war forced the colonial powers to intervene more in their African colonies, while the war's cumulative effects compelled the colonial powers to relinquish their grasp on those colonies. Many aspects of World War II and Africa remain to be fully understood. During World War I, battles took place in several colonies, namely in Togoland, Cameroon, German West Africa, and German East Africa. In contrast, during World War II, Ethiopia and North Africa were the only places where fighting occurred. Despite this difference, World War II had farther-reaching consequences for Africa.

This chapter will examine Africa and World War II. It will explore the state of Africa on the eve of the war, wartime colonial policies, the mobilization and re-

---

1. Quoted in Basil Davidson, *Modern Africa* (New York: Longman, 1983), 60.

cruitment of Africans, and African responses and contributions to the war effort. The chapter also examines the participation of Africans in the theaters of the war, demobilization and discontent, and the effects of the war on African societies, politics, and economies.

Africa Before the Outbreak of War

On the eve of World War II, two major developments which had their seeds in international events were affecting Africa: the Depression of the 1930s and the Italian invasion of Ethiopia in 1935. Both events redefined the relationship between the colonial powers and their African colonies. The effects of the Depression animated African resistance to colonial rule. New forms of resistance—for example, cocoa holdups in the Gold Coast—were used to call attention to the ways the Depression was harming African economies and affecting societies.

The impact of the Great Depression on colonial economies and the ensuing African responses forced Britain and France, the major colonial powers, to reexamine their respective colonial policies. As a result, Britain and France introduced economic policies that were geared toward achieving two things: the maximization of the economic exploitation of their colonies and the removal of the looming shadows of African disaffection and resistance.

The Italian invasion of Ethiopia coincided with a shift in African nationalism from reformist protests to revolutionary quests to overthrow colonial rule. The event was a defining moment in the relationship between colonized Africa and the European colonial powers for two reasons. First, Ethiopia symbolized African independence in the face of European domination. Secondly, though Ethiopia was a member of the League of Nations, Britain and France remained silent regarding the Italian invasion.

Thus, the Italian aggression against Ethiopia accelerated the forceful articulation of anticolonialism and vigorous campaigns against white domination and racism in Africa and the African Diaspora. Indeed, the Pan-African movement associated the Italian occupation of Ethiopia with systemic white racism and domination. The fact that the war occurred when it did undoubtedly stalled the quest to end European colonialism in Africa. There is no doubt, as some African historians have maintained, that but for the outbreak of World War II in 1939 African independence would have emerged from seeds sown by the Depression and the brazen Italian occupation of Ethiopia.

Wartime Colonial Policies
and African Responses

The official news of the possibility of a war filtered down to all levels of African society. The intensified anxiety brought about frantic preparations for war in the colonies in support of the colonial powers. In the Gold Coast, for example, by the time Britain declared war on Germany on September 4, 1939, the colonial state had prepared for the defense of the colony.[2]

As the possibility of war simmered in Europe in the late 1930s, France and Britain increasingly warned their African colonies about German aggression and fascism. For example, a spate of telegrams from the Colonial Office in London to Governor Arnold Hodgson in the Gold Coast revealed the possibility of a German invasion of Africa to reconquer the African territories that Germany had lost in the course of World War I. Added to this was the suggestion that the French and British colonies flanking the former German colonies would be affected if Germany was allowed to reconquer its African colonies. Also, Africans were informed that Hitler would unleash political and economic havoc in Africa. Africans came to accept this view: Hitler and Mussolini's racist tirades against people of color conveyed to Africans the necessity of supporting the Allied powers.

The means of spreading propaganda included local newspapers, radio, mobile cinemas, churches, schools, pamphlets, and information service departments. To reach the African population, propaganda was broadcast in local languages. In British West Africa, loudspeakers were placed at vantage points, including markets, lorry parks, and stores, to entice people to listen to wartime news. The use of these agencies successfully disseminated anti-German propaganda to a large audience. In most British and French colonies, the Western-educated elites articulated anti-German propaganda. Overall, as in World War I, propaganda served two main goals: first, it was used to demonize Germany, and secondly, anti-German anxieties facilitated military recruitment and prepared Africans for wartime hardships and demands.

To minimize cost and concentrate resources on the war, the colonial powers established policies that sought to make the colonies self-sufficient. The collapse of France in 1940 meant that Britain had to go to great lengths to maximize its economic and human resources to sustain the war. Thus, Britain's external trade with the colonies and the production of raw materials were further fine-tuned toward profitability and the emerging wartime needs. Furthermore, colonial governments were encouraged to increase taxation and local borrowing to assist in the war effort.[3] One method was to decrease consumption by increasing prices of consumer goods so that Africans would have enough money to pay taxes. In some African colonies like Kenya and Uganda, prewar imports were reduced by one half.[4]

Production of specific raw materials for the war effort was intensified, especially when Japan gained control of southeast Asia in 1941. In Nigeria, for example, conscripted labor was used to mine tin. Overall, colonial governments engaged in bulk purchasing. Britain established ministries of supply, food, shipping, and economic warfare which were mandated to obtain all the supplies that Britain would need to prosecute the war.

---

2. Wendell P. Holbrook, "British Propaganda and the Mobilization of the Gold Coast War Effort, 1939–1945," *Journal of African History* 26 (1985), 347–8.

3. Gilbert A. Sekgoma, "The Second World War and the Sierra Leone Economy: Labor Employment and Utilization, 1939–45," in Africa and the Second World War, ed., David Killingray and Richard Rathbone (London, 1986), 232–3.

4. Michael Cowen and Nicholas Scott, "British Imperial Economic Policy During the War," in Africa and the Second World War, ed., Killingray and Rathbone, 20–39.

Figure 3.1. Wartime propaganda, Gold Coast, 1942.

To ensure that raw materials could be bought at lower prices than before the war, the British government decided to buy raw materials in bulk. Consequently, state marketing controls were organized to assist in purchasing raw materials. For example, in West Africa, the West African Cocoa Control Board (WACCB), which became the West African Produce Control Board (WAPCB) in 1942, was established. It exported oilseeds, palm oil, and cocoa and WAPCB purchased cocoa at fixed prices. In East Africa, the Sisal Growers Association monopolized the sisal trade.

Given the increasing prewar militancy against colonial rule, overall African responses to the war effort were encouraging for the colonists. Newspapers and radios dedicated their resources to disseminating information about the war. For example, the *Gold Coast Times* gave regular commentaries on the war and called for recruitment. However, the coexistence of active and passive attitudes toward the war was inevitable. For example, the Western educated elites championed the Allied war efforts, but, at the same time, some of them remained indifferent to colonial military recruiting drives. Some African chiefs became active recruiting agents, others exhibited a passive stance, and still others exhibited spirited resistance to recruitment.

Mobilization, Recruitment, and Theaters of the War

Labor mobilization and the military recruitment of Africans were crucial elements of World War II. Apart from other types of wartime propaganda, patriotic songs encouraged recruitment. In the Gold Coast, recruiting bands played drums and sang what became a popular refrain in Akan.

Barima ehh yen ko ooh!
Barima ehh yen ko ooh!
Yen ko East Africa, Barima
Besin, na yen ko![5]

Brave men and warriors let us go [enlist]!
Brave men and warriors let us go [enlist]!
Let us go to East Africa and Burma
Come, let us go [enlist]!

The song includes a pun on *barima* (brave man or warrior), which sounds like Burma, a major theater of war in Asia where African soldiers were needed to fight the Japanese. Warrior traditions that underscored the accolade *barima* and its association with recruitment for the Burma campaign accounted for some of the success that recruiting agents achieved in the Akan-speaking areas of the Gold Coast.

Just as in World War I, incentives in the form of wages, remuneration, and gifts played enticing roles in African responses to recruitment. However, coercion formed the main means of recruitment. The colonial authorities made concerted efforts at conscripting; district commissioners and military and police personnel were directly involved. African rulers, the main recruiting agents, used their labor recruiting capacities to enforce enlistment in the army. For their part, the Western educated elites capitalized on their roles as opinion leaders and public pressure groups to fuel public enthusiasm.

Colonial recruitment drives in World War II experienced more problems than those during World War I. The intensity of the buildup toward anticolonialism in the interwar years frustrated the efforts of recruiters. Some Africans came to be-

---

5. Interview with Oheneba Kwasi Akurang, Mamfe Akuapem, June 16, 1997. I conducted interviews and collected oral histories of the war for a manuscript on the Gold Coast and World War II.

Africa and World War II.

lieve that they were being recruited to fight in a white man's war. This belief was truer in the white-settler colonies of Southern Africa than in the nonwhite regions of West Africa. In the former, the economic impoverishment, land alienation, and disenfranchisement, which underscored the racial stratification of society, presented barriers to recruitment. Some members of the African intelligentsia assiduously questioned why they should defend the very countries that had imposed colonial rule over them.

Furthermore, by the outbreak of the hostilities in 1939, African economies were more developed than they had been at the time of World War I. This was a result of the European colonizers' forceful intervention in African economies during the interwar period, which was aimed at compensating for economic losses during World War I. Consequently, until the Depression of the 1930s, various sectors of the colonial economy, including cash-crop production, mining, porterage services, and petty trading had attracted a large number of Africans. Additionally, clerical and teaching jobs were becoming available not only in the urban centers, but also in rural areas bordering urban centers. This was truer in the non-settler

West African colonies than in the settler colonies of East and Southern Africa. However, in the settler colonies, migrant labor, although very exploitative and demanding, served as an alternative to enlistment. Thus, other avenues of employment limited military and labor recruitment efforts.

Lastly, the labor recruiting capacities of African rulers had been considerably weakened by the exigencies of colonial rule. In the Northern Territories of the Gold Coast, for example, chiefs had played crucial roles in labor and military recruiting drives during World War I. In contrast, during World War II, the colonial authorities realized that the chiefs were no longer effective recruiting agents. In other parts of Africa, for instance, in French West Africa, African rulers encountered difficulties in recruitment, because the French had failed to honor promises made to recruits during World War I. Therefore, Africans used the outcome of World War I as a reason to reject enlistment. In spite of these problems, however, the colonial authorities succeeded in recruiting large numbers of Africans, although in most cases recruitment fell short of anticipated numbers.

Overall, the French succeeded in recruiting about eighty thousand African troops. Out of this number, an estimated twenty thousand perished in action or were murdered by Nazi troops during the German invasion of France in May of 1940. Following the French military reversal at the hands of Nazi Germany in 1940, Britain was forced to increase the recruitment of Africans. In East and Central Africa, the British conscripted 280,000 men and organized them into fighting brigades. Of this number, Tanganyika supplied eighty-six thousand men, of whom 2,538 perished in the course of the war.

The Gold Coast, Nigeria, Sierra Leone, and the Gambia provided 167,000 men. These were divided into seven brigades—three Nigerian, two from the Gold Coast, and one each from the Gambia and Sierra Leone. Most of these brigades engaged in active service[6] and provided support services as drivers, carriers, cooks, and launderers. Compulsory service rules and regulations were used to draft skilled men such as drivers, mechanics, and dispensers for the medical corps.

Apart from the French West African forces that fought in the European theaters of war, African troops were instrumental in driving out the fascist Italian army from East Africa in battles that spanned across Ethiopia and Somaliland. Africans also participated in the North African theaters of war and were decisive in Britain's protection of its strategic position in Egypt against the Italian and German armies. With the help of African brigades, the British vanquished Italo-German forces in late 1942.[7] In Asia, African contingents fought the Japanese in Burma. Thus, African soldiers and auxiliary workers played decisive roles in the war, roles that are consistently omitted from, or treated inconsequentially in, Western accounts and public celebrations of the war.

Africans contributed material and financial resources to the war efforts and produced local food staples to feed soldiers. They contributed funds to purchase munitions for the colonial powers. African labor went into the development of the infrastructure constructed to ease the movement of troops and equipment. It is possible that no event during the colonial period was comparable to the war-embroiled European colonizers' optimization of African human and natural resources.

---

6. Davidson, *Modern Africa*, 58.
7. Ibid., 58.

Figure 3.2. Colonial police, British colonies.

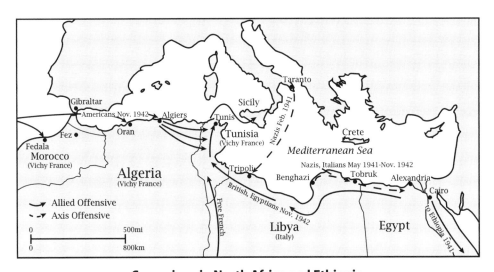

Campaigns in North Africa and Ethiopia.

Demobilization and Discontent

In the aftermath of World War II, the demobilization of African soldiers constituted a watershed of discontent and led to anticolonial activism. Demobilized soldiers realized that wartime promises were not being kept by colonial governments. Salaries and pensions were not regularly paid. In some cases, demobilized soldiers were kept in barracks for long periods before being allowed to return to their homes.

After years of fighting for the European colonizers, African soldiers returned home to find the same conditions that existed before the war. In most colonies, the conditions were worse as a result of wartime exploitation. The participation of African soldiers in the war opened new windows through which to view social inequalities and warped ideologies of domination. Thus, the war had expanded the intellectual and political horizons of the demobilized soldiers. In Nigeria, the Gold Coast, Kenya, and South Africa, demobilized soldiers played active roles in the rising tide of nationalist movements. In these and other colonies, the pace of anticolonialism was accelerated by the fiscal demands of ex-servicemen, including demands for pay and pensions, but also by the intensity of their political activism.

For instance, in February 1948, Gold Coast ex-servicemen marched to the Osu Castle, the seat of the colonial government, to demand their end-of-service benefits. They were asked to leave, but they refused. The colonial forces open fired on them, killing two and injuring many others. This incident, coupled with popular protest over prevailing economic conditions, led to spontaneous revolt in all corners of the colony. Lasting seventeen days, the revolts led to the death of twenty-nine people. In additions, 237 more people were injured, and there was an estimated two million pounds of property damage. This forced the British authorities to institute a commission to investigate the causes of the revolt and to make recommendations. Among other things, the Watson Commission recommended increasing the African participation in government by enlarging the Legislative Council. Undoubtedly, the 1948 revolt propelled the Gold Coast toward independence like no other single incident in the postwar period.

The Effects of the War on Africa

World War II had significant effects on all sectors of African societies. As noted, Africans' direct association with the theaters of World War I was more pronounced than in World War II, and despite this fact, World War II had a more decisive and long-lasting impact on Africa. These effects arose from local and international situations during and after the war.

Social and Political Effects

The war affected African social structures and families. Labor mobilization and military recruitment took men away from their homes and from society for long periods of time. Many of the soldiers died in the course of the war. For example, about one-quarter of the eighty-thousand Africans recruited by the French perished. Among those who returned home, a large number were afflicted with physical disabilities from injuries they had sustained. Additionally, in French West Africa, some soldiers suffered psychological trauma from racist treatment in Nazi camps. No major study has been done to ascertain the effects of the war on African social structures and families. There is no doubt, however, that the conditions of those married women who lost their husbands in the war, or whose husbands returned home physically and emotionally disabled, were exacerbated. In the Western world, governments and ex-servicemen associations have continued to cater to both the emotional and financial needs of those who participated in wars and their families. Such associations exist in Africa, but unlike those in the West, they exist only as poignant, sad reminders of the neglect of the African ex-servicemen.

The strains of the war in areas of colonial economic exploitation put additional demands on rural peoples. In Northern Nigeria and East Africa, for example, the stress on tin and sisal production decreased the labor available for the production of local staple crops. In addition, forced labor and military recruitment in the Northern Territories of the Gold Coast created mass migrations that affected the sources of labor for certain agricultural regions. Added to wartime shortages of imported food, such as rice and flour, local staple food shortages in both rural and urban Africa became common. Overall, rural-urban migration resulted from rural instability. As living conditions became worse and family bonds loosened, rural dwellers began to flood to the towns and cities in search of new opportunities.

Beginning in 1940, the European-settler production economy of Kenya was given a boost by the demand for beef and maize to feed African troops and Italian prisoners quartered in East Africa. Additionally, the demand for raw materials that were no longer obtainable in Asia due to the Japanese occupation, such as sisal, stimulated production in Kenya.[8] In the midst of the economic boom and transformation, rural Kenyans were turned into landless peasants. Dispossessed of their lands, a large number of Kikuyus and members of other ethnic groups migrated to Nairobi in search of economic opportunities. Wherever this occurred, it was not only males that left in large numbers. Young females also migrated to avoid the constraints of rural poverty that were exacerbated further by the demands of patriarchy.

The impact of rural-urban migration during the war continued into the postwar period, although it varied from place to place. Overall, rural-urban migration weakened the bonds supporting the traditional family structures in rural areas that served as repositories of normative African ways of life. Rural-urban migration affected urban Africa in many ways. In Nairobi, Dakar, Johannesburg, Lagos, and Accra, for example, the large influxes of rural migrants led to housing and environmental problems. Slums developed, resulting in outbreaks of disease and violence. Additionally, scarce urban social amenities like water and electricity were stretched to their limits. The lack of employment for unskilled migrants led them to commit crimes in order to survive.

----

8. See, for example, John Lonsdale, "The Depression and the Second World War in the Transformation of Kenya," in *Africa and the Second World War*, ed., Killingray and Rathbone, 97–142.

However, there were also positive benefits resulting from rural-urban migration in the postwar period. The population increase in the urban setting provided the mass support for nationalism, as impoverished yet enthusiastic, optimistic, and unemployed youths placed their enormous political support and social capital behind nationalist parties and groups. Also, by leaving their traditional, ethnic rural environments for towns and cities teeming with heterogenous populations, rural migrants began to blend new values that cut across boundaries of ethnicity, language, and religion. These social variables became crucial to the cohesion of independence movements and to the vitality for nation-building in the post-war independent Africa. Overall, the population increase in the urban areas of Africa during the war quickened the velocity of anticolonial struggles in Africa.

In some parts of Africa, the already-weakened position of African rulers, which resulted from colonial rule and the increasing importance of the Western educated elites as opinion leaders, became weaker still. As agents of military recruitment, African rulers bore the complaints not only of their subjects, but also of the colonial authorities. Those chiefs who became active agents of recruitment benefitted from the patronage of the colonial state but suffered the complaints of their subjects, who were angered by the colonists' forced recruitment strategies. In the Gold Coast, for example, the African rulers of Akyem Abuakwa had to deal with insurgent commoner resistance to recruitment. At the same time, African rulers who demonstrated varying forms of resistance to colonial recruitment policies were subjected to colonial officials' paternalistic indignation.

As noted, ex-servicemen became crucial cogs in the wheels of anticolonialism after the war. We have already cited the case of the Gold Coast to show ex-servicemen's discontent and resentment against the colonial authorities as it was expressed in 1948. Indeed, whether Gold Coast nationalist leaders such as anticolonialist Kwame Nkrumah capitalized on this popular revolt is a matter of contention. What is certain is that the 1948 revolt was a radicalizing, even revolutionary, political action. Africans used the 1948 revolt to define their local grievances as functions of colonial rule, and they envisioned political independence as a prerequisite for economic and material improvements. It must be stressed that the use of the term "riots" in colonial reports and extant literature to qualify the events of 1948 is one of the patronizing Eurocentric accounts of Africa which tends to obscure rather than illuminate the context, motivation, and goals of the participants.

The war led to increased Western activities in Africa. In Senegal and the Gold Coast, for example, airstrips were built to assist the Allies with the transport of soldiers and goods to North Africa and the Middle East. As a result, the populations of European and American settlers in Africa increased during the war. Forced labor was used to build the infrastructure and to construct living quarters for personnel and soldiers. This put additional strains on the colonies, whose economic and human resources were already being exploited to the limit.

The war increased the role of the United States in Africa. With the fall of France early in the war, the British war effort was sustained by the United States. While Anglo-American cooperation benefitted Britain, it also posed a number of problems. For one thing, the British authorities believed that the Anglo-American partnership might undermine British colonial rule; for another, the British authorities realized that the Americans were interested in controlling vital resources in Africa. In West Africa, Anglo-American bases developed at Freetown, Dakar, and

Accra. In Liberia, the American authorities harnessed the production of rubber for the war effort. The need for vital mineral resources extended American interests to the rich Congolese-Angolan mineral region. The wartime interests in the strategic minerals in the Congolese-Angolan region would extend into the postindependence period, unleashing problems of neocolonialism and political instability in the region.

The war weakened the colonial resolve of the two major colonial powers, France and Britain. Germany's defeat of France in 1940 was a major blow to French pride and imperialism. Britain sustained the Allied war effort to the end, but the story would have been different had it not been for America's material and financial contribution and direct military participation. Thus, by the end of the war, Britain and France were no longer dominant world powers. This, combined with the fact that both countries were war-weary, meant that they could no longer define the destinies of their colonies alone. The interests of the Americans, the Russians, and their respective African colonies would determine the forces of change or continuity. As the history shows, the latter prevailed.

The emergence of the United States and the Soviet Union as the two major powers in the postwar period further weakened the tottering efforts of the colonial powers to maintain their colonies. The United States was in favor of free trade around the world and, therefore, was wary of colonial interests that involved tariffs and protectionism. The Soviet Union espoused anticolonialism, a position that stemmed from the Russian Revolution of 1917 and its socialist principles. Thus, the two most dominant major powers were anticolonial—at least as far as their strategic interests in Africa were concerned.

Coupled with the anticolonial positions of the United States and the Soviet Union, certain events resulting from the Second World War offered not only African, but Asian and Caribbean colonies as well, opportunities to agitate for independence. One of these opportunities was the Atlantic Charter of 1941. Agreed upon by Prime Minister Churchill of Britain and President Roosevelt of the United States, the charter supported self-determination for all peoples and nations. Africans seized this principle in their struggles for independence. Further, the formation of the United Nations in 1945 enabled colonized peoples to use its General Assembly as a platform for attacking colonialism. This resulted in the success of Asian nationalism, leading to the independence of India and Pakistan in 1947. In the end, African nationalists used the precedent of Asian independence to agitate for their own independence.

Economic Effects

The war had both positive and negative effects on Africa, but the negative effects outweighed the positive ones. The impacts varied from colony to colony, based on the degree of colonial involvement in the war and African responses. Like the social and political effects of the war, the economic effects helped to encourage the march toward independence.

While forced labor was closely tied to colonial economies, World War II led to the construction of forced labor regimes, even in areas where they did not previously exist. In West, East, and North Africa, forced labor was used to build airstrips to transport goods, soldiers, and barracks to house troops. Thus, forced labor, which had been associated with rural Africa for much of the colonial period, was transposed onto the urban scene. Forced labor was also used in the production of raw materials. In Northern Nigeria, for example, about ten thousand workers were forced to mine tin under appalling, unsanitary conditions. Africans in the Congo, where forced labor was conducted in the most inhuman conditions, were forcibly recruited to increase rubber production. In Tanganyika, the colonial government facilitated forced labor recruitment for sisal production on farms owned by white settlers.[9]

During the war, there were frequent problems stemming from inadequate shipping space. The naval blockade of the high seas and the need to export materials for the war effort limited the shipment of export cash crops and imported goods. The significance of this was twofold. First, gluts of cash crops decreased their export prices and, hence, affected the fortunes of African farmers and middlemen. Secondly, the decrease in the quantity of imported goods forced prices up, especially in urban areas where dependencies on imported goods had developed. Additionally, wartime inflation increased the amount of money in circulation. This, coupled with limited quantities of imported goods, further increased prices. In addition, African economies were increasingly dominated by expatriate firms during the war. Monopolies allowed these firms to hoard imported goods, creating artificial shortages that sent the prices of imported goods soaring. The prewar purchasing power of Africans was thereby reduced, significantly affecting trading patterns.

Colonial governments also enacted stringent taxation policies aimed at maximizing revenue in support of the imperial war effort. Methods of tax collection were intensified, ironically, at a time when the prices of cash crops were declining. In some areas, like the Akuapem region of the Gold Coast, people became hostile toward tax collectors, increasingly seeing them as agents of alien rule.[10]

The emphasis placed on the production of specific raw materials to support the war effort stimulated African economies, as did the production of cotton and sisal in Kenya, for example. However, it is necessary to stress that it was the white settler farmers who gained in this instance. In parts of West Africa, the wartime scarcity of consumer goods stimulated African farmers to produce staple foods for the urban markets.[11] Thus, despite wartime economic hardships, some African farmers were able to make money by increasing food production for local markets.

It was not only the production of agricultural raw materials but also the need for industrial goods and munitions that stimulated South Africa's economy. The industrial base of South Africa, which rested on the discovery of gold and diamonds in the last quarter of the nineteenth century, enabled South Africa to provide manufactured goods for the Allied powers. Overall, the manufacturing output of South Africa increased by 166 percent, and its industrial labor force shot up fifty-three per cent—an increase of 125,000 laborers, including nineteen thousand whites.[12] Thus, it can be argued that for South Africa, the second, and perhaps most important, industrial revolution occurred during the war.

---

9. John D. Hargreaves, *Decolonization in Africa* (New York: Longman, 1996), 55–6.
10. Interview with Oheneba Kwasi Akurang, Mamfe Akuapem, June 16, 1997.
11. Hargreaves, *Decolonization in Africa*, 56.
12. Ibid., 56.

Conclusion

Africans' participation in World War II was inevitable; once the European powers committed to war, their African colonies became inextricably involved. World War II was a major watershed in the history of European colonial rule in Africa. The war drew Africa into European political conflicts and harnessed African resources for the European colonial powers. Like the First World War, African contributions to the war were substantial. The war had an enormous impact on African societies and economies. The colonial powers, especially Britain, maximized their colonial resources to conduct the war. One of the major effects of World War II on Africa was that both local and international outcomes charted new paths toward African independence from colonial rule.

Review Questions

1. Discuss the contributions of Africans to the war efforts of the Allies during the Second World War.
2. What were some of the methods of anti-German propaganda in Africa during World War II? Why did some African states and societies believe the anti-German propaganda? What were its effects?
3. Discuss the effects of the war on Africa. In your opinion, which of the effects were most crucial to independence movements in Africa?

Additional Reading

R.T. Kerslake. *Time and the Hour: Nigeria, East Africa, and the Second World War*. London, 1997.
Timothy S. Oberst. *Cost of Living and Strikes in British Africa c.1939–1948: Imperial Policy and the Impact of the Second World War*. Ann Arbor, Michigan, 1991.

Chapter 4

Radical Nationalism and Wars of Liberation

Adebayo Oyebade

The post-World War II period witnessed the intensification of nationalist movements in Africa. A new era of mass protest began in which nationalists were uncompromising in their demands for independence. This radical movement replaced the gradualist and reformist elite agitation of the pre-World War II era. Where the colonial power resisted peaceful protests and resorted to violent suppression of nationalist activities, African nationalists had no alternative but to resort to armed struggle. This chapter examines wars of national liberation in the colonies where they occurred.

* * *

A small elite class largely shaped the character of African nationalism before World War II. The nationalist protest movement in these years was in the hands of a small educated elite that formed conservative groups, such as the National Congress of British West Africa (NCBWA), to demand small advances. These educated elites did not often agitate for an end to European rule. They accepted the colonial status quo, asking only for modest changes in the system that would accommodate their own agenda. Their immediate demand was, therefore, not independence for the colonies, but partnership with Europeans in the colonial project in the hope that political power would eventually be transferred to them. In their modest agitation, they did not seek a mass following or support. Elite nationalism in the pre-World War II period thus lacked radicalism, populist support, and participation.

The character of African nationalism changed after World War II. A major shift occurred from the gradualist and reformist agitation of the elite to a radical and uncompromising mass protest movement. The debilitating legacies of the prewar Great Depression and of the war itself contributed to this shift in the dynamics of nationalism. In the postwar period, nationalist leaders and organizations were no longer willing to accommodate the colonial system but were ready to do away with it entirely. This new class of leaders also projected nationalist politics beyond elite circles into the popular arena.

In a number of places, mostly settler colonies, the new nationalist agenda for radical change did not sit well with the colonizing power. Peaceful protests, and in many places civil disobedience, did not achieve any forward movement toward national self-determination. In such colonies, radical nationalism culminated in prolonged and brutal wars of liberation. The purpose of this chapter is to examine these armed liberation struggles, drawing examples from different regions of the continent.[1]

Labor Militancy and the Rise of Radical Nationalism

The colonial system established a new type of labor force in Africa which was hitherto unknown. In many territories, the colonial economy was organized so that African producers lost control over their own labor and were forced to work in the mines or on settlers' farms for wages. Most of these workers had been up-rooted, and the source of their livelihood as independent farmers or artisans was removed. Many, particularly in settler colonies, were migrants employed on a contract basis. These workers faced many constraints. Apart from being grueling, the working conditions were often dangerous, leading to injuries, chronic ill-nesses, and sometimes even death. Railway and mine workers worked in ex-tremely perilous situations. In addition to these dismal conditions, wages were often low, despite the escalating cost of urban living.

The biting effects of the depression and the vicissitudes of World War II, which included forced labor in some colonies, aggravated the suffering of African workers. Rural-urban migration induced by rural poverty swelled the wage labor force in the towns and increased workers' numerical strength. The discontent of increasing numbers of wage-workers helped to strengthen organized workers' groups and radicalize labor unionism. In urban areas, these unions championed workers' demands for better wages and improved working conditions.

Strikes were the chief instrument for labor demands, and these became more common after 1945 in many colonies. They were championed by the radical labor unions. In those colonies in which colonial powers had given some latitude to labor union activities, and where workers' demands were met with less state vio-lence, unions flourished and were better able to achieve their goals. The restric-tions placed on labor unions in some colonies did not mean that labor activity was dormant in those places. Workers often broke the rules to embark on strikes, and in such cases the consequence was violent colonial repression. When the workers in the South African gold mines went on strike in 1946, it was violently repressed by the police. Despite repression, workers' movements remained strong. The 1945 railroad and mine workers' strike in Northern Rhodesia demonstrated this fact, as it helped to build labor power.

More than ever, workers in the post-World War II period were better able to organize against colonial governments. In urban areas such as Dakar, Lagos, Accra, Kampala, Nairobi, Mombasa, and Dar es Salaam, successful strikes were held by various segments of the workforce—in the railways, mines, transport in-dustry, docks, post and telegraph services, and government services. Some strikes were sporadic and brief but still effective. Others were highly organized and longer lasting, involving coalitions of unions. One of the most successful strikes was the almost two month-long nationwide general strike in Nigeria in 1945, in-

---

1. The discussion here excludes South Africa, which is treated in chapters 21 and 22.

volving workers of various types, including civil servants.[2] A similar general strike occurred in Tanganyika (now Tanzania) in 1957, beginning in Dar es Salaam and spreading inland along the railroad. French West Africa saw a strike by railway workers in 1947 that lasted for about four months. These successful strikes further enhanced labor power.

The postwar shift from the elite-dominated politics to radical, mass nationalist parties was intricately interwoven with growing labor radicalism. In the burgeoning workers' movement, the new class of nationalist leaders who sought mass support saw a means through which they could reach the masses. They also saw participants in the labor movement as useful collaborators in the struggle against the colonialists. Nationalist leaders thus turned toward this radical segment of the society, courted it, and succeeded in incorporating it into the anticolonial movement. The workers, who had their own axe to grind with the colonial authorities, were receptive to joining with the political class in order to achieve their own goals. Thus, mine workers in Northern Rhodesia threw the weight of their union behind the nationalist struggle for independence.

In many parts of Africa, labor union leaders played significant roles in the politics of national independence. In Guinea, the man who led the country to independence and became the nation's first president, Sékou Touré, achieved political prominence as a labor leader. In Sierra Leone, nationalist leader Siaka Stevens, who also became the nation's president, was a labor leader. Tom Mboya, a Kenyan labor leader, was one of the leaders of the Kenya African National Union (KANU), a mass nationalist political party. The prominent Nigerian radical labor leader Michael Imodu was involved in the Nigerian struggle for independence.

Nationalist leaders in turn supported the actions of the labor unions. Both Kwame Nkrumah of the Gold Coast (later Ghana) and Nnamdi Azikiwe of Nigeria had strong ties with the labor movement and always supported workers' agitation. For instance, Nkrumah's Convention People's Party (CPP) threw its support behind the Gold Coast strike of January 1950. Colonial authorities blamed Azikiwe for the Nigerian general strike of 1945.

Armed Struggle and National Liberation Wars

The coalition between the radical wing of the labor movement and the mass-oriented nationalist organizations increased the momentum of nationalism in the years after World War II. The state's response in some colonies was to resist the growing demand for radical change. The inevitable result here was violent confrontation between the nationalists and the colonial authorities.

---

2. A total of 31,000–33,000 people were said to be involved in the month-long strike. See Frederick Cooper, *Decolonization and African Society: The Labor Question in French and British Africa* (Cambridge: Cambridge University Press, 1996), 134–6, for details of the strike. See also Wale Oyemakinde, "The Nigerian General Strike of 1945," *Journal of the Historical Society of Nigeria* 7 (1975): 693–710.

Such confrontations occurred in settler colonies where minority European colonists held considerable political and economic power and influence to the detriment of the majority African group. In many of these settler colonies, such as Kenya, the colonial government succeeded in checking the political power of settlers, although they granted them the privileges they wanted. In the case of a colony like Southern Rhodesia (later Zimbabwe), however, the settlers achieved political control. The anticolonial struggle in settler colonies was invariably a battle fought on two fronts. Both the colonizing European power and the settlers stood between the nationalists and independence.

Guerrilla War in French North Africa: Algeria

Algeria's bloody war for independence, from 1954 to 1962, exemplified nationalist agitation culminating in the successful overthrow of the colonial order. Algeria was an important part of the French Empire, whose provinces were recognized as *départements* of the metropolis. The colony included a large number of European settlers, the *colons*. By the early 1950s, close to a million of these settlers lived in Algeria. Though a minority, the *colon* population constituted the privileged class and exercised a good measure of political and economic power. Determined to take the reins of power from France, the settlers would prove an obstacle to Algerian nationalism.

As settlers, the French immigrants harbored the idea that they owned Algeria and acted in accordance with that idea. From about 1850, African landownership was systematically reduced by settler appropriation of the most fertile lands in the country. By 1890, the settlers owned about 3,520,000 acres of Algerian land; and by 1940, the amount increased to about 5,940,000 acres.[3] By the end of World War II, about one-third of the best Algerian land was in the hands of the settlers. For Algerians, the result of this was a shortage of land for their own use. Many of them, displaced from their land, had to seek work in urban centers; others were forced to work on settler farms.

The settlers also held considerable political power in Algeria. In partnership with the settlers, the French colonial authority governed according to a very repressive and virulently racist colonial system. African demands for change were often met with colonial violence and repression. The settlers in particular were vehemently opposed to any colonial reforms to make life better for the indigenous population. The settlers continued to enjoy a privileged position in every area of life while denying Algerians the most basic rights.

As in other parts of Africa, the nationalist movement in Algeria gathered momentum after World War II. Decades of peaceful protests had not moved Algeria any closer to political independence. Indeed, the peaceful campaigns of Algerian nationalists had always been countered by colonial repression. Nationalist leaders now came to acknowledge the failure of passive resistance and sought a change in

---

3. Basil Davidson, *Modern Africa: A Social and Political History* (London: Longman, 1994), 119.

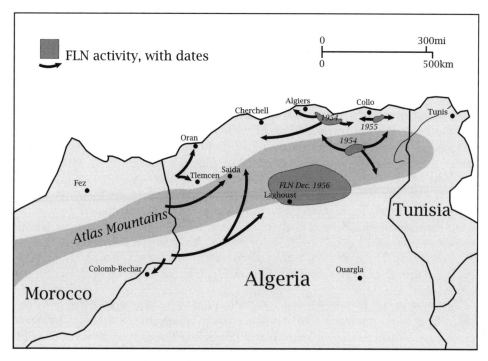

FLN activity, with dates

The war for independence in Algeria.

strategy. The violent and brutal French repression of the May 8, 1945 Algerian uprising helped to radicalize nationalism. The uprising, particularly at Sétif and Guelma, claimed the lives of about a hundred Europeans, many of whom were brutally murdered. The reaction of the French authorities was swift and devastating. About forty-five thousand Algerians were slaughtered in retribution; many more were arrested, condemned to death, or jailed.

The determination to adopt a more militant anticolonial strategy was first reflected in the creation of a clandestine revolutionary body, the Special Organization (Organisation Spéciale, or OS) in 1947. This body, led by militant nationalists like Ahmed Ben Bella, who had fought gallantly in the French army against the Axis powers during World War II, aimed at fomenting a revolution in Algeria. By 1949, it had recruited as many as 1,500 fighters for this purpose. However, the French smashed the movement in 1950, and many of its leaders were imprisoned.

The War of Independence

The formal resumption of armed struggle, however, came in 1954, when the various nationalist factions united to form the National Liberation Front (Front de Liberation Nationale, or FLN), which proclaimed a war of national liberation. The FLN was formed by a core group of nine young revolutionary nationalists, often referred to as the *chefs historiques* of the Algerian revolution. Among them was Ahmed Ben Bella, who would become the first president of independent Algeria. The war began on November 1, 1954, when guerrilla fighters launched attacks in several parts of Algeria. Earlier, for the purpose of the war, the revolutionaries had divided the country into six (initially five) military zones called *wilayas*, each headed by a colonel.

At its beginning, the war was a modest one in which rural guerrillas launched bomb attacks and assaults against specific targets, including public buildings, communication systems, and Algerians in the service of the colonial government. The war hardly touched the *colon* population. Indeed, the guerrilla fighters, the *mujahids*, deliberately refrained from attacking settler communities.

However, the war intensified in the middle of 1955 when, on August 20, FLN guerrillas committed violent acts against civilians, especially the *colons*. Frustrated that the settlers who were opposed to Algeria's independence had not been touched by the revolution, the guerrillas launched a series of major attacks on civilian communities. The most devastating attack was launched against a small town called El-Halia, a suburb of Philippeville. Here, an estimated 123 people were massacred, including seventy-one *colons*.[4] The response of the French authority was to send a combined force of police, army, and settler vigilantes against the insurgents. The result was a counter massacre of about twelve thousand Algerians, according to FLN accounts.[5] This incident transformed an insurrection into a total war.

Despite its sophisticated weaponry, the FLN army was initially able to successfully contain the formidable French army of about 200,000 men. The Algerian masses rallied to the revolution, and through volunteer recruitment, the FLN was able to build an army of about fifteen thousand guerrilla fighters. However, by 1956, the FLN army was being thoroughly pounded by French forces. Meanwhile, the escalation of the war necessitated the restructuring of the FLN military command for its effective execution. In August 1956, the guerrilla forces were restructured into a National Liberation Army (Armée de Libération Nationale, or ALN). In the following months, the ALN stepped up its guerrilla campaign, often targeting the European civilian population. Beginning in late September 1956, urban guerrillas carried the revolution to the Algerian capital in the so-called Battle of Algiers. For several months, guerrillas planted bombs in public places in the city, killing numerous Europeans. Through arrests, interrogation by torture, and the murder of suspected guerrillas, the French authorities were finally able to contain the bloody terrorist acts by the summer of 1957, by which time most of the guerrillas had been arrested. Although the brutal French crackdown on the revolutionaries during the Battle of Algiers severely weakened the movement, it nevertheless brought the Algerian struggle to international attention.

During the rest of the war, the ALN was never able to win a significant military victory, although it continued to resist. The French consistently held the upper hand in the war for a number of reasons. First, the French army was overwhelmingly superior in terms of weaponry. The French forces consisted of highly mobile armored units and paratroop regiments, both of which were armed with modern equipment. The ALN, on the other hand, was short of sophisticated arms and often had to rely on obsolete weapons. Secondly, the French army was numerically stronger than the ALN. The French withdrawal from Indochina, following its defeat at Dien Bien Phu in 1954, together with the declarations of Moroc-

---

4. See John Ruedy, *Modern Algeria: The Origins and Development of a Nation* (Bloomington: Indiana University Press, 1992), 163.

5. Ibid., 163.

can and Tunisian independence in 1956 meant that Paris had more forces available for the Algerian War. By 1958, the French boasted of about half a million troops in Algeria.

France's upper hand in the war by late 1956 forced many FLN leaders to seek refuge outside the country, particularly in Tunisia. The leadership of the revolution thus became divided between the exiled political leaders, the "externals," and the revolutionaries within, the "internals." Despite this division, the movement's political leaders outside the country continued to influence the revolution. The French attempted to block cross-border assistance, particularly the supply of weapons from Tunisia. To this end, the two hundred mile Morice Line, an electrified barbed-wire fence, was erected in September 1957 along the Algerian side of the border with Tunisia. Over a million land mines were laid along the fence, and troops were concentrated along the border to police it.

The superior firepower capability and anti-guerrilla strategy of the French proved very effective in weakening the FLN. The movement had also lost many of its leaders who had been killed, arrested, or exiled. For example, the French jailed Ben Bella in October 1956, and he remained in jail until the end of the war. Along with four of his compatriots, he had been captured when French forces hijacked his plane in northern Algeria. By the spring of 1958, the French were basically in control of the war, and the battlegrounds were restricted to the Morice Line.

However, despite its apparent inability to stem the tide of military defeat, the FLN continued to enjoy mass support. Many Algerians had been driven into the arms of the revolutionaries due to the French's indiscriminate arrests of people suspected to be insurgents. Such people were often brutally treated, many ending up dead or in jail. Thus, the popular support for the liberation war among Algerians remained steadfast. This posed a problem for the French, who had expected FLN defeat on the battlefield to end all opposition. The French could not translate triumph on the battlefield into political victory.

In metropolitan France itself, sharp divisions began to arise over the unending war. As the Algerian resistance continued, the war became increasingly unpopular among many Frenchmen. Both the human and the material costs of the war were becoming repugnant to many people. The sheer brutality on both sides—especially France's counterinsurgency tactics involving mass arrests, torture, and the murder of suspected insurgents—turned public opinion against the war. There was a general disillusionment about the war, a feeling that France was not going to win politically. International pressure was also put on Paris to negotiate a peaceful end to the war.

General Charles de Gaulle and the End of the Algerian War

A new factor entered the situation in 1958 when Charles de Gaulle became the French president. He thought it politically expedient to end the war, and thus he entered into negotiations with the FLN. His initial strategy in negotiating a diplomatic end to the war was not to accede to the demand for Algeria's independence, but to further integrate the country with France and preserve French suzerainty over it. De Gaulle seemed not to have adequately grasped the depth of the Algerian desire for self-determination. His plan was unacceptable to the nationalists. They rejected it, and the talks broke down.

By 1959, de Gaulle was convinced that a military solution would not resolve the Algerian crisis. With the stability of France itself threatened by division over the war and by settler terrorism, he began to take steps to grant Algeria its independence. Sensing de Gaulle's apparent inclination to give in to the FLN demand for Algeria's independence, the settlers launched an uprising in Algiers in January 1960, but this fizzled out after a week due to de Gaulle's masterly handling of the situation. Another settler uprising occurred in February 1961, this time in collusion with disgruntled French generals in Algeria who were unhappy with de Gaulle's intention to abandon the war. During the uprising, which lasted until late April, Algiers was taken over by the putschists. The coup was masterminded by the Secret Army Organization (Organisation Armée Secrete; OAS), an organization formed in 1961 by hard-line *colons*. Again, de Gaulle was able to quash the rebellion, removing the last stumbling block to negotiating the end of the Algerian war.[6]

Meanwhile, the FLN had already begun to make its own plans for Algerian self-government. On September 19, 1958, it created the Provisional Government of the Algerian Republic (Gouvernement Provisoire de la République Algérienne, or GPRA), headed by Ferhat Abbas. The formation of this body was motivated by the FLN's quest for international recognition and also by a desire to demonstrate Algeria's ability to govern itself to the world. Although internal divisions racked the FLN, beginning in 1961, it participated in negotiations with the French government that culminated in the Evian Agreements signed on March 18, 1962. Among other things, the agreements recognized Algerians' right to self-determination and called for a referendum on the question of independence.

Meanwhile, in the final months preceding independence, as negotiations proceeded between the French government and the GPRA, the OAS conducted a frenzied campaign of renewed violence designed to derail the process. However, this did not achieve the desired result, and the march toward independence gathered momentum. In accordance with the Evian Agreements, a referendum was held on July 1, 1962, in which an overwhelming majority of Algerians voted for independence. On July 3rd, independence was proclaimed with Ben Bella (now released from a French jail) appointed as the first president.

Having failed in their last bid to prevent Algerian independence, and fearful of reprisals for their bloody opposition to the revolution, the *colons* began to flee from the country in large numbers before independence was declared. By July 1st, about half a million of them had fled the country, and 300,000 more were to follow.[7] By the end of 1962, the settler population had shrunk to just about thirty thousand, comprised of mainly the old and the poor who were unable to move.[8]

The Algerian revolution proved to be one of the most costly wars of national independence in Africa in terms of human and material loss. On the Algerian side, at the conclusion of the war, over one million people had lost their lives. The physical devastation of the country was also enormous. Farms were destroyed, forests were burned, villages were razed to the ground, and cities lost much of

---

6. For a comprehensive analysis of the OAS opposition to De Gaulle, see Alexander Harrison, *Challenging De Gaulle: The OAS and the Counterrevolution in Algeria, 1954–1962* (New York: Praeger, 1989).

7. *Le Monde*, September 6, 1962.

8. See Ruedy, *Modern Algeria*, 185.

their infrastructure. For the French, the war was the longest and most bitter struggle against colonial self-determination in its imperial history.

Peasant Revolt in British East Africa: Kenya

In Kenya, decades of repression, exploitation, racism, and disregard for the plight and demands of Africans by the British colonial power found expression in the early 1950s in violent anticolonial protests. This radical nationalism was best exemplified by the Mau Mau rebellion against settler domination and the colonial authorities in central Kenya from 1952 to 1956. Although the uprising was unsuccessful, it had repercussions for Britain's imperial future in Kenya.

The background to the Mau Mau uprising can be found in the changes that attended the transformation of Kenya into a settler colonial state. Perhaps the most significant change was the land appropriation by the colonial government for European settlement. To facilitate this, starting in the late nineteenth century, the colonial government introduced a number of measures including the 1896 Land Acquisition Act and the Land Ordinances of 1902 and 1915. In the process of transferring land to Europeans, the state played the facilitating role of an agent. Under the 1915 Land Ordinance, which created native reserves—that is, land reserved for Africans—the colonial governor could still remove lands from the reserves for European use.

The land appropriation displaced many Kenyans, leaving them landless. The minority group of white settlers owned the most fertile lands in the country and continued to pressure the state for further appropriation of suitable reserve land for their benefit. Africans, especially in the central province, saw their economic future devastated in the absence of land. Moreover, cultivation of the chief export crops, such as coffee and pyrethrum, was exclusively preserved for Europeans. Many Africans had no alternative but to live on European land as squatters and work on settler farms, meeting settler labor demands. Some migrated to urban centers in search of wage labor. Whether they worked for Europeans or took jobs in urban centers, the wages of Africans were often meager. Africans were also burdened by colonial taxation, designed to raise revenue and, at the same time, induce Africans to work for European farmers.

Not only did they possess exclusive economic privileges, but the Europeans also held sole political control. Kenyans had little or no say in the administration of the affairs of their country, and Europeans, particularly settlers, had no intention of sharing political power with them. As in British West Africa, the colonial state treated the agitating Kenyan educated elite with disdain, viewing them as troublemakers out to exploit the masses of the people for their own selfish political ends. The settlers also aimed at frustrating African nationalism.

Europeans were also racist in their relations with Africans. They saw Africans as inferior and treated them as such. Racial discrimination was rampant in practically all spheres of Kenyan life—housing, education, employment, and public service.

The alterations in traditional economic and political systems as a result of the imposition of colonial rule were a major source of discontent for Kenyans. Despite African agitation for change, the colonial state remained insensitive and unwilling to budge. As a result of this unwillingness, an African anticolonial protest movement began to emerge in the early 1920s. In 1920, the Young Kikuyu Association (YKA), led by Harry Thuku, was formed. It was succeeded in 1926 by the Kikuyu Central Association (KCA). The Kenya African Union (KAU) emerged in 1944 with Jomo Kenyatta as its most prominent leader. The KAU was the first modern political organization in Kenya.

The crystallization of opposition, however, did not lead the colonial state to effect any significant policy change. The British authorities remained opposed to changes. Many nationalist leaders found themselves in detention for protesting against colonial policies and agitating for reform.

The British had clearly failed to recognize the widespread discontentment among Kenyans and the deep-rooted nature of their demands for change. The direct result of this was the escalation and radicalization of the African protest movement. In the years following the end of World War II, anticolonial protests began to find expression in sporadic violent disturbances in many parts of Kenya. There were attacks on European landowners and agents of the colonial government by landless peasants and other discontented elements. The state, in turn, responded to these disturbances with violent repression. By 1952, the colonial government had banned all avenues for the expression of grievances by Africans. Antigovernment activities, including those of the Mau Mau, greatly intensified underground. The colonial governor was forced to proclaim a state of emergency in October 1952.

The Mau Mau Uprising

The Mau Mau revolt can be seen as a direct reaction to the continued intransigence of the colonial state with regard to African demands. Mau Mau was an ethnically based peasant movement consisting mainly of the Kikuyu, a major ethnic group in Kenya that had suffered particularly under British colonial rule. The primary aim of the movement was land recovery. The great majority of the insurgents were landless peasants; in addition, there were some who had previously had access to land as squatters on European farms but had lost it as a result of the 1937 Resident Laborer Ordinance, which sent them to the reserves.

However, beyond its immediate concern for economic reform, Mau Mau had a broader nationalist, anticolonial outlook. It viewed foreign domination in all its ramifications as evil and detrimental to African progress. Foreign domination was seen as the cause of land loss, rural and urban unemployment and poverty, racial denigration of Africans, and other evils. The emergence of Mau Mau was, therefore, also a direct challenge to the exploitative, oppressive, and racist colonial system. The uprising was a struggle for African self-determination in Kenya.

The main targets of the uprising were Europeans, both colonial officials and settlers. The settlers were particularly hated. They had not only appropriated much of Kenya's fertile land, but they had also become the major stumbling block to any change aimed at improving the conditions of Africans. The Mau Mau fighting force, the "Land and Freedom Army," took to the forests of Mount Kenya and the Aberdare Mountains and began to operate from there. The guerrilla fighters systematically attacked settler farms and eliminated Europeans, but they did not limit their opposition to Europeans. Traitors—that is, Kenyans

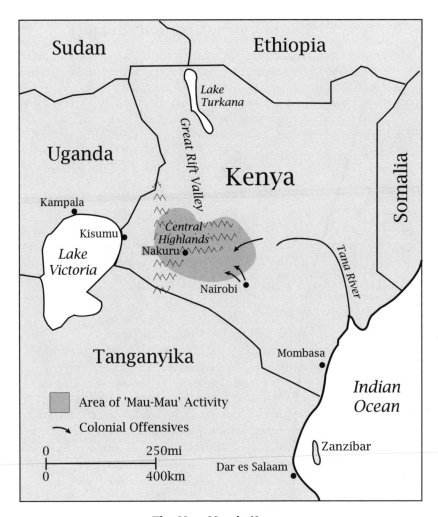

The Mau-Mau in Kenya.

known to have cooperated with the Europeans or to be opposed to Mau Mau—
were also targeted.

The British colonial authorities once again failed to appreciate the depth of
the African discontentment. Instead, the authorities denounced the movement as
evil and barbaric. The authorities viewed the uprising as totally unwarranted, and
the insurgents as a tool in the hands of unscrupulous educated political agitators.
Indeed, the colonial authorities believed that Mau Mau was connected, at least in
some informal way, to the largely Kikuyu nationalist party, the KAU, under Jomo
Kenyatta. The Corfield Report, a government-commissioned study of the Mau
Mau, described Kenyatta as "the chief architect" of the movement.[9] In November
1952 he was charged with Mau Mau offenses.[10] His alleged complicity in the re-

9. F. D. Corfield, *Historical Survey of the Origins and Growth of Mau Mau* (London:
Her Majesty's Stationery Office, 1960), 219.

10. Ibid., 316.

Table 1 Emergency Statistics to the End of 1956

	Killed	Captured Wounded	Captured in Action	Arrested	Surrendered
Terrorist Casualties	11,503	1,035	1,550	26,625	2,714

Security Forces Casualties			Killed	Wounded
European			63	101
Asian			3	12
Africa			101	1,469
Loyal Civilians				
European			32	26
Asian			26	26
African			1,819	916

Source: F. D. Corfield, *Historical Survey of the Origins and Growth of Mau Mau* (Corfield Report) (London: Her Majesty's Stationery Office, 1960), 316.

bellion earned him a seven-year jail term in 1953. Given the government's view of the Mau Mau insurgents as a criminal gang, "wholly evil in its conception,"[11] the government refused to acknowledge the legitimate demands of the guerrillas.

The state's response was to marshal a 100,000-strong counterforce to quell the uprising.[12] Despite this formidable force, the state was unable to contain the guerrilla onslaught until the end of 1953. By early 1954, however, Mau Mau had begun to suffer devastating military defeats. Large numbers of its fighters and suspected supporters were herded into detention camps. The colonial forces used captured Mau Mau soldiers to penetrate the strongholds of the remaining resisters. Colonial forces also cut off food supplies to the guerrillas in the forest. Mau Mau's loss of the military initiative by 1954 began to have a telling effect on the rebellion. Support for the struggle, even among the Kikuyu, rapidly dwindled as a result of mass arrests of all those suspected of harboring sympathy for the movement. With the capture of one of the most revered Mau Mau generals, Dedan Kimathi, at Nyeri on October 21, 1956, the uprising collapsed.[13]

The human and material costs of the uprising were huge. According to the Corfield Report, the financial cost to the government exceeded £55 million by the end of June 1959.[14] The report also detailed the human cost, as seen in Table 1.

The failure of the Mau Mau uprising can be attributed to a number of factors. First, the movement could not match the opposing colonial force in terms of either weaponry or numbers. The "Land and Freedom Army" simply lacked enough weapons to face the well-equipped colonial forces.

Secondly, Mau Mau lacked the support necessary to make it a mass organization. It remained largely a peasant movement with the bulk of its fighting force

---

11. Ibid., 7–8.
12. Davidson, *Modern Africa*, 150.
13. Wunyabari O. Maloba, *Mau Mau and Kenya: An Analysis of a Peasant Revolt* (Bloomington: Indiana University Press, 1993), 96.
14. Corfield, *Historical Survey*, 316.

composed of displaced rural people, squatters, and urban unemployed.[15] It was also primarily a Kikuyu movement, gaining little support from other Kenyan ethnic groups apart from neighbors such as the Embu and the Meru. Loyalty to the movement was obtained through mass oath-taking, but this alienated many people, particularly those to whom the practice was foreign.

The successful British propaganda that painted Mau Mau as evil and barbaric alienated the Christian-trained African educated elite and other professional people. Outside Kenya, left-wing and liberal-minded elements, particularly in Europe, who recognized the evils of imperialism and the legitimacy of opposition to it by the oppressed still could not bring themselves to endorse a movement generally categorized as barbaric.[16] This was exactly the intention of the colonial state when it inundated the media with reports of alleged atrocities committed by the guerrillas. Unfortunately, Mau Mau did not possess an effective apparatus to counter the colonial government's propaganda.

Thirdly, Mau Mau was incapable of providing the kind of informed leadership necessary to lead a successful nationalist revolution. As it was largely a peasant movement, its leadership consisted of men who lacked formal education, and were thus unable to project a clear ideological platform on which to base their struggle against colonial imperialism. The movement did not possess the intellectual wherewithal to build an effective propaganda machine through which it could mobilize support for a clearly defined anticolonial struggle. Instead, it resorted to archaic traditionalism as a way of building support and solidarity. As we have seen, oath-taking alienated many people who might otherwise have thrown their support behind the movement.

The failure of the Mau Mau uprising had a devastating impact on the Kikuyu. In the aftermath of Mau Mau, the Kikuyu were regarded by the British with deep suspicion and mistrust. The arrest, detention, and imprisonment of the Kikuyu was not limited to those directly linked with the movement. Retribution against the Kikuyu people in general was widespread, including the expulsion of many of them from major urban centers like Nairobi.

Perhaps the greatest legacy of Mau Mau was that it helped foster the desire for a united Kenyan nation. It aroused national feelings among Kenyans that intensified the struggle for independence. Although a military failure, the uprising forced the British to move from their rigid position of refusing to attend to African demands to a position of policy reform. Gradually, the colonial authorities conceded the inevitability of Kenyan independence, which was achieved in December 1963.

National Liberation Wars in Portuguese Southern Africa: Angola and Mozambique

Angola and Mozambique were Portuguese colonies in southern Africa, and both of them suffered from a particularly backward, severe, and exploitative form of colonial rule. Indeed, Portuguese colonial rule in Africa was the worst form of imperialism. Relatively underdeveloped itself, Portugal lacked the industrial base,

---

15. See Maloba, *Mau Mau and Kenya.*
16. Ibid., 10–11.

the economic power, and the political will to develop its colonies. Its colonial policy was based on a system of economic exploitation backed by brutal, absolute rule and political repression.

As in other settler colonies, Portugal's colonial system was characterized by land expropriation for the use of white settlers. The settler population was substantial in both colonies, increasing tremendously after World War II. In Mozambique, the white population numbered 97,200 in 1960.[17] The figure was far greater in Angola in the same year—about 200,000.[18] This increase in settler population led to the widespread practice of forceful seizure of land for European occupation. In Mozambique, the colonial state enacted laws that not only severely limited African landownership, but also induced Africans through taxation to provide labor for settler farms and plantations. Indeed, in order to ensure adequate amounts of cheap labor, the colonial authority set up a system of forced labor known as *chibalo*. Through this system, Africans were made to produce export cash crops like coffee, maize, beans, wheat, and cotton on European plantations. The vast majority of Africans who remained unassimilated into Portuguese culture, the *indigenas,* were subject to this forced labor.

Under Portuguese colonial rule, Africans had virtually no political or civil rights. The *indigenas* were not only subject to forced labor, but also to other brutal colonial policies. The few assimilated Africans, the *assimilados*, though entitled to some privileges, lacked real political rights. For Africans generally, opportunities were severely limited in all areas of life. The colonial authority restricted access to education, health care, and other social services. For instance, in Mozambique as late as 1960, children attending school numbered about 400,000 out of a school-age population of about three million. Even then, only one percent of the children enrolled in school were in high school; those in the first three grades accounted for about ninety percent of the total.[19] Mobility in the economic sector and the state bureaucracy was also curtailed; only Europeans could attain top-level positions. In addition, the colonial government severely restricted all avenues of political and nationalist expression. Ethnic associations, labor unions, and other African organizations—where they were allowed to exist at all—were rigidly controlled. Protests and other forms of resistance to colonial rule were often violently repressed.

Portuguese colonial repression and intransigence toward African demands for self-determination in Angola and Mozambique were to make armed struggle inevitable. The blocking of African avenues of expression led to the emergence of underground revolutionary organizations. In Angola, the Party of the United Struggle of Africans of Angola (Partido da Luta Unida dos Africanos de Angola, or PLUS) was formed in 1953, and it became the earliest nationalist movement to demand self-determination. Similar nationalist organizations emerged later in Mozambique; they included the National Democratic Union of Mozambique (Uniao Democratica Nacionale de Moçambique, or UDENAMO), the Mozam-

---

17. Thomas H. Henriksen, *Mozambique: A History* (London: Rex Collings, 1978), 135.

18. Americo Boavida, *Angola: Five Centuries of Portuguese Exploitation* (Richmond, VA: LSM Information Center, 1972), 47.

19. Allen Isaacman and Barbara Isaacman, *Mozambique: From Colonialism to Revolution, 1900–1982* (Boulder, CO: Westview Press, 1983), 51.

bique African National Union (MANU), and the National African Union of Independent Mozambique (Uniao Nacionale Africana de Moçambique Independente, or UNAMI). As a result of the intensification of the nationalist struggle, confrontations between Africans and the colonial authority increased. If the nationalist organizations initially hoped for change by peaceful means, this expectation was soon dashed as a result of Portugal's intolerance of opposition and resort to brutal repression. The revolutionary movements saw no other option in this circumstance besides armed struggle.

The War of Independence in Angola

The Angolan War of Independence began in February 1961, when the Popular Movement for the Liberation of Angola (Movimento Popular de Libertação de Angola, or MPLA) began a military campaign to end Portuguese rule. The MPLA had been formed in December 1956, when PLUS merged with other nationalist organizations under the leadership of Antonio Agostinho Neto. But the MPLA was only one of three revolutionary movements dedicated to Angolan independence. It was joined in the nationalist struggle by the National Front for the Liberation of Angola (Frente Nacional de Libertação de Angola, or FNLA), founded by Holden Roberto in 1962. A third group, the National Union for the Total Independence of Angola (União Nacional para a Independência Total de Angola, or UNITA), led by Jonas Savimbi, emerged in 1966 to join the armed confrontation.

In response to the liberation war, the Portuguese mounted vicious military and political campaigns against the nationalist movements and their guerrilla armies. By the end of 1961, African casualties had already reached about fifty thousand, and another 500,000 Africans had fled to Zaire.[20] Portugal's brutal repression ensured that the nationalists did not make significant progress in the war. At best, they were only able to achieve a stalemate.

Portugal's superior military power was not solely responsible for the inability of the guerrillas to make much headway. Also significant was the lack of unity among the members of the nationalist movements. In terms of military strategy, the movements unnecessarily dissipated energy by not making a concerted effort. Each movement had its own military wing and fought the Portuguese on its own terms. Ethnic and regional divisions also characterized the movements, as each derived support from particular ethnic groups or regions. The MPLA was popular among the Mbundu, who formed its main support base. The FNLA, on the other hand, derived its main support from the Kongo. UNITA's support base was among the Ovimbundu.

Ideological and political differences also divided the nationalist movements. The MPLA professed the merits of Marxism and had links with the Soviet Union and Cuba. UNITA initially found ideological support from China but soon turned to South Africa and the United States. The FNLA, which derived support from Zaire, espoused a liberal, laissez-faire belief. Rivalry among the main leaders, each of whom had a personal agenda, also contributed to the division between the movements. Thus, although the common goal of these nation-

---

20. Boavida, *Angola: Five Centuries of Portuguese Exploitation*, 31.

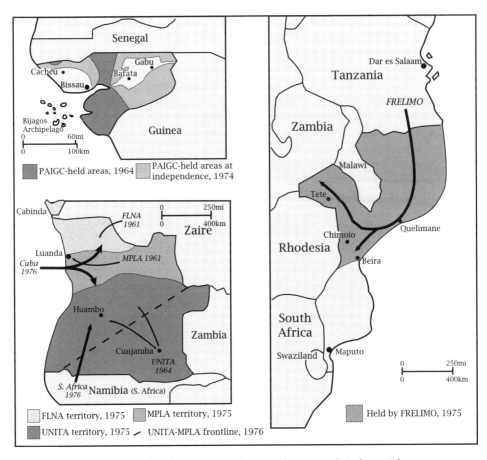

Wars of liberation in Angola, Mozambique, and Guinea-Bissau.

alist movements was to overthrow Portuguese colonial rule, from the outset they were deeply divided and failed to present a common front. These divisions were to plague postindependent Angola and eventually launch the country into a civil war.

The War of Independence in Mozambique

As the liberation war raged in Angola, Mozambican nationalists also rose in armed struggle in late 1964 to overthrow Portuguese colonial rule. The liberation war began when guerrillas of the Front for the Liberation of Mozambique (Frente de Libertação de Moçambique, or FRELIMO) launched an attack on the Portuguese administrative headquarters at Chai in the Cabo Delgado Province on September 25th. The signal for a determined, anticolonial struggle had been the formation of FRELIMO, Mozambique's main nationalist organization, on June 25, 1962. FRELIMO emerged from the merging of the three existing nationalist groups—UDENAMO, MANU, and UNAMI—for the purpose of organizing effective opposition to the colonial regime.[21] The leadership of the unified organization fell to a militant nationalist, Eduardo Mondlane.

Mozambican nationalists resorted to guerrilla war against the Portuguese. FRELIMO courted mass support and aimed especially at incorporating the peasantry into the struggle. The Portuguese responded to the war with a combination of military offensives to cripple the guerrillas and diplomatic initiatives to obtain support and assistance from Western countries. To launch an effective counterinsurgency campaign, Portugal progressively increased its colonial army which, in the early 1970s, boasted of more than seventy thousand men (as compared with four thousand in 1961).[22] Apart from increasing its fighting force, Portugal obtained military assistance and financial aid from its North Atlantic Treaty Organization (NATO) partners, principally the United States. It also sought Western recognition and diplomatic support for its policy of preserving its colonial empire. The West readily provided Portugal much of the requested assistance, especially when Lisbon's diplomacy redefined the conflict in Cold War terms. Portugal projected FRELIMO and other nationalist movements, like the Angolan MPLA, as Soviet-controlled Communist organizations that would help increase the Kremlin's influence in Africa.

FRELIMO, however, was not without international support. The United Nations accorded it recognition and granted the guerrillas observer status in the UN. Much of FRELIMO's weaponry came from China and the Soviet Union, and other assistance came from the Warsaw Pact countries. Within the African continent, the nationalist movement received the endorsement of the Organization of African Unity (OAU) and the support of states like Tanzania, Zambia, and Algeria.

FRELIMO had its own problems; it was not immune to internal division, ideological differences, or power struggles. When Mondlane was assassinated in February 1969 by a letter bomb, evidence implicated a dissenting group within the organization's Central Committee.[23] The committee's election of Samora Machel to the organization's presidency over Vice President Uria Simango reflected this division.

End of Colonial Rule in Angola and Mozambique

For the nationalists in Angola and Mozambique, an event in Portugal itself furthered their cause. On April 25, 1974, the Portuguese armed forces overthrew the dictatorship of Prime Minister Marcelo Caetano. This act had been caused, in part, by the cost of human and material resources of the liberation wars. The Mozambican war in particular had produced much discontent within the Portuguese armed forces. In spite of Western support for Portugal, the Mozambican guerrillas steadily gained ground. By the middle of 1974, it was apparent that the Portuguese colonial army was unable to defeat the guerrillas, and the military balance was beginning to change in favor of the guerrilla fighters. The Portuguese army's war weariness was, therefore, a factor in the April coup.

---

21. An important source of information on the formation of FRELIMO is Eduardo Mondlane, *The Struggle for Mozambique* (Harmondsworth, England: Penguin, 1969).

22. Ibid., 102.

23. Isaacman and Isaacman, *Mozambique: From Colonialism to Revolution*, 98.

The overthrow of the fascist regime and the emergence of a new government in Lisbon marked the beginning of the end for Portugal's colonial empire. The new regime promptly began to negotiate a peaceful end to Portuguese colonial rule in Africa. After the talks, Lisbon agreed to a transfer of power to the Angolan and Mozambican nationalists. In Angola, negotiations led to the signing of the Alvir Agreement in January 1975. In this agreement, three nationalist movements, the MPLA, the FNLA, and UNITA, agreed to form a transitional government and conduct elections that would usher in independence in November 1975. Angola's independence was finally granted on November 11, 1975. In Mozambique, negotiations toward independence had led to the formation of a transitional government on September 20, 1974. Independence was declared in Mozambique on June 25, 1975.

National Liberation Wars in Southern Africa: Southern Rhodesia and Namibia

As in other settler colonies, the nationalist struggles in Southern Rhodesia[24] and Namibia were violent. In the case of Southern Rhodesia, a self-governing British Crown Colony since 1924, the settlers who held power would not share it with a black majority without a fight. Namibia was a victim of racist South African colonization, and it too had to endure a liberation war to be free. The armed struggle in both colonies was long and brutal, lasting almost two and half decades in Namibia.

Southern Rhodesia

Settler power in Southern Rhodesia was very pronounced. White settlers, whose population had increased tremendously after World War II though they still constituted a small minority, held dominant economic and political power in the colony. With a population of about 158,000 in 1953,[25] the settlers, who constituted less than five percent of the colony's population, owned about half of the land and had established farms. The 1930 Land Apportionment Act, approved by Britain, further entrenched the racial division of land. Africans, largely uncompensated for their land losses, were forced by tax requirements to work in the colony's mines and to provide cheap labor for settler farms. In the post World War II period, the settlers prospered economically, acquired considerable political power, and enjoyed privileged status. This was achieved at the expense of the majority black population, which was relegated to a second-class position by racist, discriminatory policies.

Naturally, Africans felt discontented with the colonial status quo, which not only disenfranchised them and denied them basic rights and opportunities, but also allowed the growth of a settler hegemony that racially subordinated blacks.

---

24. Southern Rhodesia became simply "Rhodesia" when Northern Rhodesia became independent in 1964 as Zambia.
25. Howard Simon, *Zimbabwe: A Country Study* (Uppsala, Sweden: Scandinavian Institute of African Studies, 1979).

Anticolonial sentiments, which had begun to emerge in the 1920s, gathered momentum after 1945. A number of African nationalist parties emerged and began to ask for Southern Rhodesian independence under African majority rule. As African opposition to the settler control of the colony increased, the settlers intensified their repressive measures against the nationalists. African nationalist organizations opposed to colonial rule, such as the National Democratic Party (NDP) established in 1960, were outlawed. The colonial government adamantly refused to yield to demands for self-determination.

From the early 1960s onward, two main political organizations began to dominate the African nationalist struggle in Southern Rhodesia. The Zimbabwe African People's Union (ZAPU), strong among the Ndebele, was founded in December 1961 and led by one of the early prominent nationalists, Joshua Nkomo. The other nationalist party, the Zimbabwe African National Union (ZANU), was founded in August 1963. Marxist in orientation, this movement was founded by a breakaway group from ZAPU led by Ndabaningi Sithole and Robert Mugabe, and it was comprised of those who yearned for a more radical approach. Although divided by ideological and ethnic cleavages, both nationalist parties aimed for the same goal: national independence under African majority rule. The colonial government would not tolerate nationalist activities and soon had both organizations banned. The result was a clandestine, anticolonial movement in Southern Rhodesia. But the nationalists were encouraged in their struggle against colonialism by the attainment of independence by the neighboring states of Malawi (formerly Nyasaland) in July 1964 and Zambia (formally Northern Rhodesia) in October of the same year.

Settler Rule in Southern Rhodesia

The white settlers, who had long enjoyed a privileged position in Africa, did not wish to be swept by the winds of change down the social ladder. They did not merely oppose the nationalists; they also wanted full independence to put Southern Rhodesia under their absolute control. In March 1962, the settlers formed a racist, white supremacist party called the Rhodesian Front (RF). The white electorate, fearing the onslaught of black nationalism, voted this party into power in December. By 1964, a new RF leader, Ian Douglas Smith, became the prime minister. Smith headed a white minority government determined to stem the tide of African nationalism, consolidate white supremacy, and reduce the African population to a permanently subservient position. However, the Labour government in Britain, learning from the bloody Mau Mau rebellion in Kenya, demanded that the minority regime implement significant constitutional changes that would guarantee political rights for blacks. The British government consistently refused the settlers' demand for Southern Rhodesian independence under their control. In response to London's refusal to grant independence without a guarantee of black majority rule, the Smith regime went ahead anyway and declared Southern Rhodesia independent of Britain on November 11, 1965. This Unilateral Declaration of Independence (UDI), essentially a rebellion against Britain, severed all relations with London.

Beyond refusing to recognize the illegal Southern Rhodesian state, Britain proved unwilling or unable to take any decisive action against the white supremacist government. Although the United Nations refused to recognize the purportedly independent state and imposed on it selective economic sanctions, the sanctions proved ineffective. One reason was that the sanctions regime was not honored by many states, including South Africa (also a white supremacist state), Portugal, and the United States. Covert trading activities by many Western business interests also helped reduce the effect of the sanctions. The supremacist regime was able to hold the reins of power and block any attempt to effect change that would accommodate black political participation.

The Liberation War

With the failure of sanctions and the ready use of repression by the minority government against the anticolonial movement, by the late 1960s the nationalists were fully persuaded that only armed struggle could bring down the government. The government, determined to destroy African nationalism, continued to persecute black political organizations, detain nationalist leaders, and enact new laws designed to broaden and further consolidate settler power and privilege.

In 1966, an armed struggle forged by radical nationalist organizations, principally ZAPU and ZANU, began modestly and with limited success. However, by the early 1970s, these movements, especially those led by ZANU with its military wing, the Zimbabwe African National Liberation Army (ZANLA), began to launch successful guerrilla attacks on the government. The guerrilla war intensified in the mid-1970s with exiled guerrillas operating from their bases in Zambia and Mozambique. Particularly after its liberation from Portuguese colonialism in 1974, Mozambique afforded the guerrillas, especially ZANU forces, an effective operational base. In order to provide a more formidable challenge to the settler government, the Patriotic Front (PF), a combined ZANU/ZAPU military force, was formed in 1976. By 1978, the guerrillas had claimed control of a considerable part of Southern Rhodesia.

From Rhodesia to Zimbabwe

Southern Rhodesia was internationally isolated under the minority government. After the successful liberation wars in Angola and Mozambique, Portugal was no longer in a position to continue to aid the white regime. Meanwhile, the PF escalated its guerrilla warfare, which was proving to be very successful. The long, weary war, a war the white government knew it could not win, helped to persuade the government to agree to negotiations with the nationalists. Also fearing that the war could invite the intervention of the Soviet Union and the Eastern bloc, Britain and the United States began to urge the Smith government to negotiate with the Africans. In 1979, the minority regime negotiated a political arrangement with moderate African politicians. This arrangement enfranchised blacks and allowed for some measure of power sharing. However, the arrangement still preserved much of the whites' privileges. Under this so-called "internal settlement," elections were held in which a moderate black politician, Bishop Abel Muzorewa, emerged as prime minister of a coalition government composed of his party and the RF.

The radical nationalists of ZANU and ZAPU, however, refused to accept the coalition government. Indeed, Muzorewa was widely denounced in African circles as a puppet of the white supremacist regime. The PF continued its armed struggle, and Anglo-American prodding eventually persuaded the government to accept full black majority rule. Consequently, in 1980, the government and the major black political leaders signed the Lancaster House agreement providing for black majority rule. In the election that followed, the first free election in Southern Rhodesia, the Zimbabwe African National Union-Patriotic Front (ZANU-PF), as ZANU was now known, swept the polls, defeating ZAPU. Mugabe, the ZANU-PF leader, became the prime minister, and Southern Rhodesia became independent on April 18 under the name of Zimbabwe.

Namibia

In Namibia, the colonial power was not a European nation; it was white-ruled, racist South Africa. During World War I, the South Africans had occupied Namibia, and their control of the erstwhile German colony was confirmed in 1920 when the League of Nations designated it a "mandated territory." This meant that the League mandated South Africa to administer Namibia, then called South West Africa, on its behalf. In essence, then, South Africa held Namibia in trust. As a "mandated territory" it was supposed to eventually move toward self-rule. But in all practical senses, Namibia was a South African colony. South Africa never intended to lose control of its *de facto* colony. After World War II, South Africa refused the UN demand that it relinquish control of Namibia.

By the 1970s, decolonization was already a strong force in the entire southern region, and the Namibians were not to be left out of the struggle for self-determination. Nationalist organizations that had begun to emerge in the 1950s were dedicated to protesting South Africa's rule and demanding independence. In 1960, a number of these organizations merged to form the South West Africa People's Organization (SWAPO) under the leadership of activists such as Sam Nujoma.

In the beginning, Namibian nationalists adopted a peaceful method of protest. They challenged the South African occupation of their country in the UN. This was unsuccessful. Although the UN voted to terminate its mandate and transfer the administration of the colony to the Council for South West Africa, South Africa refused to withdraw from the country. It continued to subject Namibians to racist laws under its apartheid policy and to other unjustifiable oppression in the form of forced labor and low wages.

Resort to Armed Struggle

The refusal of South Africa to surrender its mandate left the nationalists with no other option than to embark on an armed struggle. SWAPO guerrillas began to launch campaigns against the South African authorities and their occupying forces in 1966. Guerrilla bases were established in Zambia and later in Angola. In this war of national liberation, the nationalists were able to acquire mass support.

Meanwhile, the armed struggle was complemented by international pressure. SWAPO, the main force in the liberation war, gained both UN and OAU recognition as the sole representative of the Namibian people. In 1971, the International Court of Justice (ICJ) ruled South Africa's administration of Namibia illegal and called for its withdrawal. South Africa, however, remained adamant, ignored international opinion, and responded to the guerrilla war with violent attempts to suppress SWAPO. Some nationalist leaders were arrested, and some, like Sam Nujoma, were forced into exile.

The attainment of independence by Namibia's northern neighbor, Angola, in 1975 was a significant blow to South African power in the region. Now governed by the Marxist-oriented MPLA, Angola offered a sanctuary for Namibian nationalists and an important base for the guerrillas. South Africa, in retaliation, began incursions into Angola designed to destabilize the MPLA government. These incursions, however, were unsuccessful, and South Africa's aggression ceased after its humiliating defeat in 1988 by Cuban-backed Angolan forces.

Namibia's Independence

The decisive military defeat of South Africa in Angola proved to be a turning point in the Namibian struggle for independence. Since 1975, Angola had been defended by the Cuban military against its civil war foe, UNITA, which was backed by South African forces. Defeated in Angola and realizing it could not win the guerrilla war in Namibia, South Africa decided in 1988 to sue for a negotiated end to the war. This decision was also precipitated by international pressure and a declining economy as a result of the war. However, South Africa tied any peace agreement and negotiations for Namibian independence to the withdrawal of Cuban forces from Angola. After negotiations, Cuba agreed to withdraw its troops from Angola, and South Africa accepted a UN plan for Namibia's independence. A preindependence general election under UN supervision followed in November 1989. In this election, SWAPO emerged victorious; its leader, Nujoma, became the first president of independent Namibia. With independence declared on March 21, 1990 in Namibia, the curtain on colonialism in Africa was drawn.

Armed Struggle in Portuguese
West Africa: Guinea-Bissau

All the colonies in West Africa obtained political independence without much violence; the exception was Portuguese Guinea (now Guinea-Bissau). Like the other Portuguese colonies, Portuguese Guinea was forced onto the path of armed struggle to liberate itself from colonial rule. An anticolonial movement began to gather momentum in the early 1950s when nationalist leaders embarked on organizing urban protests against colonial policies through unions. The nationalist leaders soon realized that the strategy of urban protest and union agitation would not achieve any change in Portugal's colonial policy. Indeed, the rise of the protest movement had heightened Portugal's intolerance of nationalist sentiments and galvanized it to more repressive measures. For instance, the August 1959 strike by dock workers, masterminded by nationalists, was violently suppressed by the colonial authorities, resulting in the death of at least fifty Africans and the wounding of many more.[26] Lisbon's use of its repressive machine in this "massacre of Pidjiguiti quay" was a major factor in convincing the nationalists of the futility of urban protest. In the circumstance of Portugal's recalcitrance, armed struggle became inevitable in Portuguese Guinea.

---

26. See Patrick Chabal, *Amilcar Cabral: Revolutionary Leadership and People's War* (Cambridge: Cambridge University Press, 1983), 56.

The force behind Portuguese Guinea's liberation struggle was the African Party of Independence for Guinea and Cape Verde (Partido Africano da Independencia da Guiné e Cabo Verde, or PAIGC). This movement was founded in September 1956 by a Cape Verdean nationalist, Amilcar Lopes Cabral, and a few other fellow nationalists. Cabral, an agronomist by profession, nurtured the organization. As its secretary-general, he gave it the leadership that made it one of the most successful anticolonial movements in Africa.

The War of Independence

The Angolan liberation war provided encouragement to the Guinean nationalists. Cabral himself had worked closely with the MPLA at the beginning of its armed struggle against the Portuguese. Realizing the futility of protest by the urban working class, Cabral and the PAIGC saw the need for a mass movement involving rural people. Accordingly, the PAIGC began a campaign of turning the rural population into a politically conscious class. Its aim was to bring ideological cohesion to the diverse rural population and, thus, create a strong mass movement to challenge the Portuguese.

Due to Portugal's repression of any kind of anticolonial agitation, in late 1959, the PAIGC established its headquarters outside the country in Conakry, Guinea.[27] Over the next three years, it struggled to politically mobilize the countryside for a military campaign against the Portuguese. This was a very difficult task given the profound political unawareness of rural dwellers. Unlike the situation in Angola and Mozambique, Portuguese colonial rule really was not very well entrenched in the Guinean countryside, and its effects on rural people were relatively small. For instance, there was no large-scale land appropriation or peasant displacement, and forced labor was minimal. Even before the rise of nationalist agitation, Portuguese colonial repression was not very profound. Thus, the prevailing political condition in the countryside was not favorable for mass mobilization. The PAIGC, nevertheless, succeeded in incorporating villagers into the struggle. By 1962, an armed struggle had begun, initially on a small scale in the south of the country, but soon escalating into a full-scale guerrilla war.

Portugal's counterinsurgency was as brutal as it was in Angola and Mozambique. Lisbon's military buildup in Portuguese Guinea commenced immediately after the liberation war in Angola broke out in 1961. In order to suppress the PAIGC's activities in the countryside, Portugal increased its military force from one thousand in 1961 to over thirteen thousand in 1963.[28] However, despite superior Portuguese military power, the PAIGC was able to liberate a large part of the country from Portugal's control between 1964 and 1974.

It should be noted that, although the PAIGC was the main nationalist movement and the most successful in the military field, others were involved in the armed struggle. There were also movements abroad, mostly operating from Senegal. One of these Dakar-based organizations, which was able to exert some influence inside Guinea, was the Guinea Liberation Movement (Movimento de Liber-

---

27. Guinea is not to be confused with Portuguese Guinea. Guinea was a former French colony bordering Portuguese Guinea in the south and in the east.
28. Quoted in Chabal, *Amilcar Cabral*, 56.

tação da Guine, or MLG). In 1961, the PAIGC attempted to form a united front that would accommodate the other nationalist movements, and toward this end the United Front of the Liberation of Guinea and Cape Verde (Front Uni de Libération de la Guinée et du Cap Vert, or FUL) was founded. However, this organization failed to achieve its purpose, and the PAIGC remained the main nationalist movement recognized as the representative of the Guinean and Cape Verdean people. In the struggle, it was able to achieve some level of international support. It was recognized by the OAU, and outside Africa, the Soviet Union and the Communist East European countries gave it substantial military support. Cabral's diplomatic acumen also ensured that the PAIGC received some level of Western support, mainly from Scandinavia.

Portuguese Guinea and Cape Verde's Independence

Having consolidated its power in the liberated areas, and encouraged by international recognition, the PAIGC proclaimed a unilateral declaration of independence on September 24, 1973. Portugal's recognition of the country's independence followed only after a 1974 coup that removed the fascist Lisbon regime. Meanwhile, independence for Cape Verde came on July 5, 1975. Although guerrilla activities never took place in Cape Verde, many of its inhabitants had been part of the PAIGC's liberation war. However, the envisaged political union between Guinea-Bissau and Cape Verde never materialized.

Conclusion

In a number of African colonies, the road to independence, though not exactly smooth, was devoid of large-scale bloodshed. For others, those with considerable white settler populations, independence was not to come easily. Nationalists who had hoped to use peaceful protest as a vehicle for change soon found that passive resistance was ineffective. They realized, instead, that peaceful campaigns resulted in more colonial repression and strengthened the will of the colonial authorities to destroy nascent nationalism.

In settler colonies, the nationalists' resort to armed struggle was inevitable. If the colonizing authority used violence to perpetuate colonial rule, the nationalists replied with more violence to liberate their countries. Unlike nationalists elsewhere, nationalists in settler colonies faced challenges both from the colonial authority and the settlers. In most places, the necessary wars of liberation were long and vicious, entailing enormous losses of life, destruction of property, and untold human hardship. Yet armed struggle succeeded in liberating the colonies in the end.

Critical to the success of armed struggle was mass support for the liberation movements. This was amply demonstrated in the Algerian war. Despite superior European military power, mass support for the Algerian revolutionaries sustained the momentum of resistance that made the war unwinnable for the French. Lack of mass support, on the other hand, partly accounted for the collapse of the Mau Mau revolt in Kenya. Since the liberation wars were protracted and bitter, they left a lasting legacy where they were fought: they discouraged neocolonial relationships with erstwhile colonial masters.

Review Questions

1. How do you define a settler colony? What role did settlers play in the struggle for independence in those colonies?
2. Assess the role of President Charles de Gaulle of France in the Algerian Revolution.
3. Why was the Mau Mau rebellion in Kenya a military failure? In what way did the rebellion contribute to the nationalist struggle in Kenya?
4. What event in Portugal in April 1974 facilitated the collapse of its imperial empire in Africa?
5. What was UDI? Assess settler rule in Southern Rhodesia.

Additional Reading

Buijtenhuijs, Robert. *Essays on Mau Mau*. Leiden: African Studies Centre, 1982.

Chabal, Patrick. *Amilcar Cabral: Revolutionary Leadership and People's* War. Cambridge: Cambridge University Press, 1983.

Cilliers, J. K. *Counter-Insurgency in Rhodesia*. London: Croom Helm, 1985.

Handyside, Richard, ed. *Revolution in Guinea: Selected Texts by Amilcar Cabral*. New York: Monthly Review Press, 1969.

Hayes, Patricia, et al. *Namibia under South African Rule: Mobility and Containment, 1915–46*. Athens: Ohio University Press, 1988.

Henriksen, Thomas H. *Revolution and Counterrevolution: Mozambique's War of Independence, 1964–1974*. Westport, CT: Greenwood Press, 1983.

Horne, Alistair. *A Savage War of Peace: Algeria, 1954–1962*. New York: Penguin Books, 1987.

Hutchinson, Martha Crenshaw. *Revolutionary Terrorism: The FLN in Algeria, 1954–1962*. Stanford, CA: Hoover Institution Press, 1978.

Isaacman, Allen, and Barbara Isaacman. *Mozambique: From Colonialism to Revolution, 1900–1982*. Boulder, CO: Westview Press, 1983.

Leys, Colin, and John S. Saul. *Namibia's Liberation Struggle: The two-edged Sword*. Athens: Ohio University Press, 1995.

Marcum, John A. *The Angolan Revolution*. Cambridge: Mass., MIT Press, 1978.

Martin, David, and Phyllis Johnson. *The Struggle for Zimbabwe: The Chimurenga War*. New York: Monthly Review Press, 1981.

Wolfers, Michael, and J. Bergerol. *Angola in the Front Line*. London: Zed Press, 1983.

Wunyabari O. Maloba. *Mau Mau and Kenya: An Analysis of Peasant Revolt*. Bloomington: Indiana University Press, 1993.

Chapter 5

Women Under Colonial Rule

Bessie House Soremekun

This chapter examines the impact of colonial rule on the roles and status of women in African societies. Although the discussion provides a general overview of the continent, specific references are made to women in Kenya, Tanzania, Nigeria, Côte d-Ivoire (Ivory Coast), Zimbabwe, and South Africa. The major goal of the analysis is to provide an examination of the political, economic, cultural, and social impact of colonialism on African societies with particular attention to women. The chapter assesses the extent to which African women experienced a change in their roles and status with regard to the previous sexual division of labor, the agricultural and urban sectors of the economy, and political roles.

European expansionist efforts and subsequent colonization processes had profound effects on African societies. The Berlin Conference of 1884–1885 allowed for the formal division of African states between the major European colonial powers who had several centuries earlier initiated a struggle for control over the people, land, and resources of the African continent. The "Scramble for Africa" by European countries culminated in the formal establishment of colonial enclaves throughout the continent by Britain, Italy, France, Belgium, Germany, Portugal, and Spain.[1]

The purpose of this chapter is to discuss the impact of colonial rule on the roles and status of women in African societies. The goal is to provide the reader with a general overview of how colonialism affected African women while providing specific examples from several countries. The first section provides an examination of colonial rule in Africa with particular emphasis on the factors that motivated European expansionist efforts as well as a discussion of how European powers administered their overseas territories. The second section analyzes the gendered impact of colonialism by providing a deconstruction of gender which clearly explicates how women's roles and status were affected in different spheres of society including the sexual division of labor, the agricultural realm, the urban economy, commercial activities, and the political realm. The third section assesses African women's responses to the political order. Here, the data indicate that women were very much engaged in political discourse and, in some instances, political violence, to achieve a positive change in their status. They were actively involved in the ongoing struggle for self-determination. Conclusions are presented in the final section.

* * *

---

1. Peter J. Schraeder, *African Politics and Society: A Mosaic in Transformation* (Bedford: St. Martin's Press, Boston, 2000), 88.

Reconstructing the Colonial Experience in Africa

Motivations of European Powers

European interest in Africa predated the formal establishment of its colonial empires. Portugal was the first European country to penetrate the coast of West Africa. Prince Henry the Navigator (1434) and Vasco de Gama (1497–1499) aided Portugal in extending its influence around the Cape of Good Hope into the Indian Ocean.[2] Portugal was motivated by numerous factors in its quest to extend its influence and power, such as a desire to expand its economic and military capabilities;[3] an interest in spreading Christianity;[4] a need to decrease the influence and power of the Arab traders who had hitherto exercised control over Portugal's overland access to the expanding gold trade in West Africa and the trade in silk and spices with Asia;[5] as well as a need to stake a claim in West Africa before other European competitors such as the Dutch, the Danes, the French, and the British could establish spheres of influence.[6] Ultimately, the Portuguese achieved success as they built several coastal forts from which they were able to participate in a lively and profitable trade in gold and ivory. In the seventeenth century, Portugal also became a participant in the expanding slave trade.[7]

Peter Schraeder has emphasized that, at the end of the fifteenth century, slavery was regarded by Europeans as a "legitimate and necessary tool of political-military and economic expansion."[8] Hence, four major trade networks were established to transport slaves to various regions of the world. These included the trans-Saharan slave trade, the Atlantic slave trade, the Red Sea slave trade, and the Swahili Coast slave trade. Although the Atlantic slave trade was controlled by European countries, the trans-Saharan, Red Sea, and Swahili coast trade activities were dominated by the Islamic World. As the "Scramble for Africa" intensified, European countries developed strategies by which they could make their expansionist dreams become reality by effectively occupying African territories.[9] According to William Tordoff,

> The partition of Africa was precipitated by the ambition of King Leopold II of the Belgians to absorb the whole of the Congo basin into a personal empire and the annexation by Germany, in 1883–1885, of the Cameroons, East Africa, Southwest Africa, and Togoland, thereby projecting the rivalry of the European powers into Africa. The Berlin Conference of 1884–1885,

---

2. Schraeder, *African Politics and Society*, 88; John McCormick, *Comparative Politics in Transition*, 2nd., ed., (Orlando, FL: Harcourt Brace and Company, 1998); William Tordoff, *Government and Politics in Africa*, 3rd., ed., (Bloomington, IN: Indiana University Press, 1997).
3. Schraeder, *African Politics and Society*, 88.
4. Ibid., 88.
5. Ibid., 88.
6. William Tordoff, *Government and Politics in Africa*, 29.
7. Schraeder, *African Politics and Society*, 89.
8. Ibid., 89.
9. Ibid., 89.

Figure 5.1. Five women, one carrying a child on her back, picking pyrethrum flowers, Kenya.

by recognizing the existence of a "Congo Free State," was the signal for France and Britain to extend their sphere of influence, preliminary to creating new colonies and protectorates. The boundaries between one colony and another were often drawn arbitrarily, with scant regard for traditional allegiance; thus, the Bakongo were split between the French Congo, the Belgian Congo and Angola.[10]

European colonization processes were also affected by the notion of racial supremacy, which supported ideas of the "white man's burden" and European control over people characterized as backward, inferior, and uncivilized. The growing needs of the capitalist world economy also necessitated a constant supply of raw materials to be used to enhance development in European industries. By the onset of World War I, seven colonial powers exercised control over the African continent with the exception of Ethiopia and Liberia. The largest empires, however, were controlled by the French and the British. The French Empire included four administrative regions: French West Africa, French Equatorial Africa, the Maghreb (Algeria, Tunisia, and Morocco), and various overseas departments and territories such as Réunion and Mayotte. The British Empire stretched as far north as Egypt and all the way down to South Africa. It included colonies in East, West, and southern Africa.[11]

Smaller empires were established by Portugal and Belgium. These empires were mainly located in Central and southern Africa. Belgium's influence was largely centered in central Africa while southern Africa became a major focus for

---

10. Tordoff, *Government and Politics in Africa*, 29–30.
11. Ibid.; Schraeder, *African Politics and Society*, 94, 96.

Portugal adding to its control over the territories of Guinea-Bissau in West Africa and the smaller island areas of Principe, São Tomé, and Cape Verde. Germany lost its colonies when it was defeated in World War I. Germany's colonies were given to other colonial powers as League of Nations mandates. Italy's defeat in World War II resulted in the loss of its colonial territories in Eritrea and Libya. Italy was, however, allowed to oversee a trusteeship mandated by the United Nations over Italian Somaliland during the 1950s. The smallest European empire in Africa was established by the Spanish.[12]

Administrative Policies of the Colonial Powers

Lord Lugard, a well-known British administrator in colonial Africa, described the mission of the British in the following way:

> The British Empire.... has only one mission—for liberty and self-development on no standardized lines, so that all may feel that their interests and religion are safe under the British flag. Such liberty and self-development can be best secured to the native population by leaving them free to manage their own affairs through their own rulers, proportionately to their degree of advancement, under the guidance of the British staff, and subject to the laws and policy of the administration.[13]

Although some degree of variation existed in anglophone Africa with regard to how Britain administered its overseas colonies, there seems to be a general consensus among scholars that the principle of "indirect rule" was institutionalized. Primary emphasis was placed on elevating the role of indigenous political institutions such as councils and chiefs in the overall governance process.[14] According to D. A. Low and R. C. Pratt,

> In all the various types of local rule to which the term was applied, the local administration was entrusted to those native chiefs and headmen whose position was rooted in custom and who thus commanded the loyalty of the people. In contrast to any system of "direct rule," either through British officers or through Africans appointed without reference to local traditional claims to authority, "indirect rule" meant the appointment of traditional tribal chiefs as agents of local rule, the use in local government of those men whom the people were accustomed to obey. This principle of native administration was exceedingly influential throughout British Africa in the inter-war period.[15]

---

12. Schraeder, *African Politics and Society,* 97.

13. Lord Lugard, "Principles of Native Administration" in *Problems in the History of Colonial Africa: 1860–1960,* ed. Robert O. Collins, (Englewood Cliffs, NJ: Prentice-Hall, Inc. 1970) 88.

14. D.A. Low and R.C. Pratt, "British Colonial Policy and Tribal Rulers," in Collins *Problems in the History of Colonial Africa: 1860–1960,* 151.

15. Ibid., 151.

French colonial rule can best be characterized as a "direct rule" in which administrative subdivisions were established in each colony. In this system, Africans who were loyal to France were provided with lower level administrative appointments while French officials reported directly to the highest levels of the administration. The concept of *assimilation* was important to the maintenance of this system of administration as indigenous Africans were encouraged to *assimilate* into French culture and were rewarded for their ability to do so. In order to *assimilate*, they had to "become more French than the French," as they learned to speak fluent French, became Christians, completed a high school education, and purchased property. In return for this, they were presented with the possibility, at least in theory, of attaining French citizenship. Africans who were successful in their bid to become *assimilated* into French culture were referred to as évolués (evolved or civilized individuals).[16]

In the colonial territories governed by Belgium and Portugal, the idea of *assimilation* was also important in terms of encouraging indigenous Africans to understand and utilize the cultural traditions and ideas of the European colonialists. Hence, Belgium and Portugal, like France, sought to develop a privileged group of évolués. While the French used the criterion of complete acculturation as a prerequisite for Africans to become full members of the French community, the British did not offer Africans the possibility of attaining social equality with them. The Portuguese social policy encouraged different racial groups to interact via cohabitation and marriage. Although Africans with Portuguese blood were valued, they were never considered to be equal to pure Portuguese colonialists.[17]

The Sexual Division of Labor

It is difficult to assess the roles and status of African women without placing the analysis within the context of the precolonial sexual division of labor. With respect to this division of labor, different cultural expectations were held of men and women in African societies with regard to the tasks that they were assigned. Much differentiation existed between men and women in regard to their work in the family unit, their social life, and various types of rituals. Beyond this, there was also a physical separation or demarcation between the two sexes as husbands and wives had different or separate living quarters, separate initiation ceremonies, and different roles to perform in the agricultural sector of the economy.[18] Felix K. Ekechi has described the sexual division of labor in the following way:

In Africa, men and women traditionally performed different roles, generally defined along sex or gender lines. Hence in the agricultural sphere,

---

16. Schraeder, *African Politics and Society*, 97–8; Tordoff, *Government and Politics in Africa*, 32–3.

17. Schraeder, *African Politics and Society*, 98; See also Vincent B. Khapoya, *The African Experience: An Introduction*, 2nd ed., (Upper Saddle River, NJ: Prentice-Hall, Inc., 1998), 124–5.

18. Bessie House-Midamba and Felix K. Ekechi, *African Market Women and Economic Power: The Role of Women in African Economic Development* (Westport, Connecticut: Greenwood Press, 1995), xv.

Figure 5.2. Kenyan woman cutting vegetables as another watches.

certain activities were (and still are) defined as men's or women's work. Thus, while women's work on the farm included the planting and weeding of crops, as well as "carrying the harvest home," men were responsible for clearing the brush and preparing the farm for planting. In the case of yams, men were solely responsible for stalking them. On the whole, "The men help with the heavier parts of the farm work.... But there are months when they have little if nothing to do in the farms whereas all year round, though particularly in the wet season, the women are occupied in weeding, planting, [and] tending crops.[19]

Amongst the Kikuyu ethnic group in Kenya, a sexual division of labor also existed with regard to the performance of tasks in the agricultural sector and to society in general. For example, men performed the heavy work in home building; cultivated and cleared the brush; cut the trees; pruned the banana plants; tended the cattle, sheep, and goats; were involved in hunting and warfare, and built roads and bridges. Women, in contrast, cut and carried grass for thatching, prepared the ground for sowing, harvested the crops, ground corn and millet, and made pottery and clothes. Men and women planted different crops, were responsible for performing different stages in the process of brewing beer, and traded in different types of products. Kikuyu men typically traded in livestock while women traded in grains.[20]

During the precolonial period among the Baule of Côte d'Ivoire (Ivory Coast), men were very dominant actors in the cultivation of yams while women

---

19. Ibid., 42.
20. Jomo Kenyatta, *Facing Mt. Kenya* (New York: Vintage Books, 1965), 53–5.

Figure 5.3. Women cutting early rose potatoes for planting.

exercised more control over the production of cloth and developed strategies to intercrop cotton in the yam fields. Women also spun the thread that was then presented to the men to weave. Colonialism negatively affected the status of the women because the eventual manufacture and importing of thread, which was encouraged by the Europeans, led to a decreased need for women to spin the thread. With the subsequent decision to develop cotton into a cash crop that would be controlled by the men, the sexual division of labor between men and women was severely disrupted. Additionally, women's land rights deteriorated, and they also lost the control they had exercised previously in the area of production. Consequently, women were forced to become workers on land that was now owned by African men.[21]

Thus, it is widely acknowledged that in the African context, women and men had their own respective spheres with attendant duties and responsibilities. Yet, these spheres did vary according to ethnicity, geography, and time period. Although the roles of men and women were to a large degree complementary in nature, African society was characterized by male dominance.[22] "Though women had a substantial measure of economic independence and a voice in political affairs in many parts of the continent, they were not dominant, as some have said, and they were not equal."[23]

African women's central role in agriculture has been discussed by a number of writers who have suggested that they were responsible for seventy to eighty per-

---

21. Tordoff, *Government and Politics in Africa*, 44.
22. Nancy J. Hafkin and Edna G. Bay, *Women in Africa: Studies in Social and Economic Change* (Stanford, CA: Stanford University Press, 1976), 7–8.
23. Ibid., 8.

cent of the agricultural work performed on the continent. Ester Boserup's land-mark book, *Woman's Role in Economic Development,* provided quantitative data with regard to the actual work input of men and women in African agricultural processes. These data indicated that women's agricultural work in cultivator families was usually greater than that of the men, and that women usually worked more days than men in farm activities, even though in some instances, their work shifts were shorter.[24]

Kenya was declared a protectorate by the British in 1895, and by 1920 the territory had been brought under British control except for a ten-mile coastal strip of land. One of the major goals of the British colonialists was to establish Kenya as a major supplier of raw materials to be used in British industries. Hence, the development of a "cash crop economy" became a fundamental component of British rule. Some of the main crops produced for export included hides, cotton, sisal, tea, and coffee. In fact, by 1920, coffee was the number one cash crop in Kenya, and potatoes and maize were important cash crops from the beginning of settler farming in the colony.[25]

Another major goal of the British involved a large-scale reallocation of land from the hands of Africans to Europeans. "By the 1930s, much of the temperate hill country around Nairobi had become the 'White Highlands.' More than 6 million acres of land—Maasai pasture and Kikuyu and Kamba farms—were stolen. African communities were often displaced to increasingly overcrowded reserves. Laborers, mostly Kikuyu migrants from the reserves, worked for the new European owners, sometimes on lands that they had once farmed for themselves."[26] Therefore, several simultaneous processes were underway, including the transformation of Kenya from a subsistence-based agricultural economy to one based on the development of cash crops for export. Also important was the alienation of the Kikuyu from their land and the ensuing economic deprivation that the Kikuyu and other groups experienced as they lost control of their economic resources. African discontent with the strategies utilized by the Europeans, as well as the continual forced removals of African squatters from their land, intensified as increasing gaps emerged between Africans based on class, religion, and ideology. All of these factors ultimately set the stage for the Mau Mau struggle.[27] It is indeed quite remarkable that little, if any, consideration was given to the role and position of women in these contestations over power and access to scarce resources. As Catherine Coquery-Vidrovitch has so clearly articulated,

> Generally, the colonial administration ignored women, and for a long time development "experts," African and foreign, did as well. The colonizers focused on men, from whom they demanded a tax in silver and compulsory cash-cropping, privileging men's entry into the monetary

24. Ester Boserup, *Woman's Role in Economic Development* (London: George Allen and Unwin Ltd., 1970), 21–22.

25. Bessie House-Midamba, *Class Development and Gender Inequality in Kenya, 1963–1990.* (Lewiston, NY: Edwin Mellen Press, 1990), 33–35.

26. Jeffress Ramsay, *Global Studies: Africa,* 8th ed., (Guilford, CT: Dushkin/McGraw-Hill, 1999), 112.

27. Ibid.

economy. Cash-crop production was a determining factor in keeping men on the land while profoundly changing how the land was worked.[28]

Several scholars have posited that the imposition of colonial rule in African societies had deleterious effects on the status and equality that women had achieved during the precolonial era. For example, in the Kenyan context, the Europeans did not support the continuation of precolonial women's farming systems. This was particularly disempowering for women, who had exercised a central role in the agricultural sector where they provided about seventy to eighty percent of all agricultural labor. In some cases, Europeans prevented women from performing certain functions in this sector, especially for work that was linked to the cash-crop economy.[29]

Margot Lovett, Sharon Stichter, and Jeanne Henne have provided interesting assessments of the development of the gender gap in the agricultural sector in Kenya as a result of Britain's emphasis on the development of the cash-crop economy. According to these authors, four major strategies lowered the status that Kenyan women had achieved in the precolonial era. The first strategy involved the use of colonial taxation, imposing a poll tax on African families in order to force them to produce for the export-oriented sector. Concomitantly, some modifications were made in terms of the sexual division of labor. This led to a situation in which the workload of women actually increased in some cases in the agricultural sector, while unmarried men were recruited to work in heavy construction, on the plantations, in the mines, or road building. In support of this argument, Jeanne Henne has pointed out that the colonial focus on developing economic surpluses meant that higher taxes would be levied by the colonial government. Hence, indigenous Kenyans were increasingly called upon to produce cash crops as taxes were put on food. As this process continued, Kenyan women, of necessity, provided the labor in the countryside.[30]

With regard to the second strategy, because Europeans believed that cultivation should be performed by men and that men would have more success in this area than women, they did not encourage female farming systems to continue. Gradually, male farming systems replaced female farming systems. Additionally, men were often taught to use modern techniques to enhance their cultivation of agricultural products while women continued to rely on traditional strategies. For example, men used animal and mechanical power as women continued to rely on hoe culture. Men also used ploughs and trucks. Men rode bicycles as women continued to carry headloads. Eventually, the status of men improved as women's status and power deteriorated. These developments led to a situation in which

---

28. Catherine Coquery-Vidrovitch, *African Women: A Modern History*, (Boulder, CO: Westview Press, 1997), 63.

29. House-Midamba, *Class Development and Gender Inequality in Kenya, 1963–1990*, 35.

30. Margot Lovett, "Gender Relations, Class Formation, and the Colonial State in Africa," in *Women and the State in Africa*, ed. Jane L. Parpart and Kathleen A. Staudt (Boulder, CO: Lynne Rienner Publishers, 1989): 37; Sharon B. Stichter, "Women and the Labor Force in Kenya, 1895–1964," Discussions Paper No. 258, Institute for Development Studies, University of Nairobi, 1977, 3–9; Jeanne K. Henne, "Women in the Rural Economy: Past, Present, and Future," in *African Women South of the Sahara*, edited by Margaret Jean Hay and Sharon Stichter, (London: Longman Group Ltd., 1984), 1–18.

women's interest in agriculture decreased, and they left the agricultural sector if their husband's income permitted it.[31]

Thirdly, a large labor gap emerged that corresponded to the changing gender dynamics in the agricultural sector. This gap intensified because it was precisely in the area of cash-crop production that men were taught to use modern methods. The cash-crop sector benefited enormously from research and governmental investment. In contrast, no government support or research efforts were provided for women in the production of their crops. New farming technologies were thus utilized in the male sector, while females continued to use traditional methods of production that yielded lower productivity than the newer methods of the men. Sharon Stichter noted that the sexual division of labor was ultimately modified in such a way that women performed the unskilled tasks while men performed the skilled work. The colonial state used agricultural training centers and government farms where young men, many of whom were the sons of chiefs, were provided with the means to learn how to use the new technology. Missions and settlers imparted knowledge to young men of how to handle tools and these men later introduced the new skills and techniques into their various communities. Therefore, state practice in this area assisted in determining that the Africans who would benefit from cash-crop production would be African men.[32]

Fourthly, women were not allowed to participate in state-land reform programs as members of the advisory groups organized in connection with the allocation of land rights in Western Kenya. These programs were designed to develop land tenure systems under which men were awarded title deeds. Because women were not awarded title deeds to land, they did not possess the collateral that would have helped them qualify later for bank loans or to move into marketing or retail trade activities in significant numbers. Thus, the process of individualizing land in the colonial era had negative effects on women.[33]

Kenya was and still is a patrilineal society where inheritance passes through the male line. Colonial state policy exacerbated the gap between men and women by developing a policy of land ownership in which males would be granted land rights under the Swynnerton Plan. Although the plan was developed in large measure as a solution for the stagnation that had developed in the agricultural sphere, the plan also made provisions for the consolidation of land with high agricultural potential and the awarding of land to individual household heads. The land under consideration included the entire Central Province area including Embu and Meru, Nyanza Province and Kericho, Nandi, Elgeyo, West Suk, and the Taita Hills.[34]

The implementation of the Swynnerton Plan in 1954 exerted a negative impact on the position of Kenyan women. Women's economic position deteriorated with the imposition of land consolidation strategies. Thus, traditional user rights systems in which women had been accorded access to the land in the precolonial period were transformed into systems in which men had almost exclusive rights to land

31. Boserup, *Woman's Role in Economic Development*, 53–55; House-Midamba, *Class Development and Gender Inequality in Kenya, 1963–1990*, 37.

32. Lovett, "Gender Relations, Class Formation, and the Colonial State in Africa," 60; House-Midamba, *Class Development and Gender Inequality in Kenya, 1963–1990*, 38.

33. Lovett, "Gender Relations, Class Formation, and the Colonial State in Africa", 60.

34. Henne, "Women in the Rural Economy," 12–4; House-Midamba, *Class Development and Gender Inequality in Kenya, 1963–1990*, 39.

Figure 5.4. Tanzanian woman with heavy load strapped to her back.

ownership. Additionally, men were in charge of the most profitable cash crops such as tea, maize, and high-producing dairy cattle. The higher levels of profit that were generated in these areas led to an inequitable situation in which men earned more than women, and the economic gap between men and women continued to grow.[35]

---

35. House-Midamba, *Class Development and Gender Inequality in Kenya, 1963–1990,* 39–40.

In South Africa as well, the sexual division of labor widened during the colonial period. Men were increasingly sent to work on the railroads and in the mines during the nineteenth century and later to accommodate the growing needs of capitalist economic expansionist processes. During this time, women stayed behind and nurtured their families. Yet their workloads often increased. Most women were illiterate. "Colonial law did not help matters by promoting marital authority—recognizing the family head as the sole owner of goods whose value had been created by women. Protected by colonial officers and missionaries, men were also the first to benefit from the technical innovations they gradually introduced."[36]

The Development of the Urban Economy and the Quest for African Labor

The newly created export-oriented economies in African societies required additional sources and inputs of labor. Increasing numbers of African men were recruited to enhance productivity. The gender gap between men and women was very pronounced in the developing urban centers and on agricultural plantations. Only a few jobs were available for women during the colonial era. Moreover, although some women worked on European plantations on a seasonal basis, these were women who lived in areas close to the plantations. Although both men and women usually received only limited economic compensation for their labor, women's wages were still much less than those of males.[37]

Carolyne Dennis has argued that wage employment in Africa was determined largely on the basis of gender. The first wage employment was created by European administrators and companies and was considered to be the purview of men in both skilled and unskilled labor positions. Women were left in the household economy to nurture their children in order to reproduce workers needed for the growing capitalist world economy. In some Islamic countries and in the Sahel region of West Africa, women were also discouraged from participating in the public realm because of religious and cultural beliefs. In other parts of the continent, women's lower level of access to education also served as a barrier to attaining jobs in the formal sector of the economy. Hence, over time, women were eventually only able to acquire jobs that were low paying, required minimal education and training, and had few prospects for career advancement.[38]

While Kenya was colonized by the British, Tanzania was initially ruled by the Germans, from 1885 until World War I. After Germany was defeated in the war, Tanzania officially became the British mandated territory of Tanganyika under the aegis of the League of Nations. Following World War II and the establishment

---

36. Coquery-Vidrovitch, 60.
37. Jeanne Koopmen, "Women in the Rural Economy: Past, Present, and Future," in Hay an Stichter, *African Women South of the Sahara*, edited by Margaret Jean Hay and Sharon Stichter, 18–19.
38. Carolyne Dennis, Women in African Labour History, *Journal of Asian and African Studies*, 22, 1–2, (1988): 128–129.

Figure 5.5. An African woman in modern and traditional attire.

of the United Nations, mandates became trust territories.[39] In Kenya and Tanganyika (now known as Tanzania), systems of forced labor were instituted by the colonialists when Africans rebelled against the often harsh and cruel working conditions they had to endure and the low levels of remuneration they received. In Kenya, young African males were forced to work on European plantations, on railroads, and in state-owned mines. A complex system of migratory labor also developed where African men would agree to abide by contracts for six months to two years. Their low wages barely kept them alive. Tanzanian migrants were also forced to work on European plantations during the 1920s and 1930s, and they left their homes in order to earn money to pay their taxes and meet other requirements of basic survival. They went to work on sisal and other plantations. They were employed by the settler population in Tanzania, but this was small in comparison to that of Southern Rhodesia and Kenya at that time. The migrant labor

---

39. Susan Geiger, *TANU Women: Gender and Culture in the Making of Taganyikan Nationalism, 1955–1965* (Portsmouth: Heinemann, 1997), 6.

system had a disruptive effect on the household unit, especially in the case of married couples, as men were forced to leave their households in order to earn wages.[40]

Only four major roles emerged for women in urban centers during the colonial period. These roles were housewives, sellers of cooked food, prostitutes, and brewers of illegal beer. By the mid-1950s, the three most lucrative jobs open to Tanzanian women were beer-brewing, fish selling, and prostitution. Women also earned money by cutting and selling firewood and selling various types of food such as cakes, fritters, coconut ice, and beans to workers. Hence, only a minuscule number of Tanzanian women were employed in the formal sector of the economy. Many of these positions required education and special training. By 1952, African women comprised about six percent of the regular workforce and three percent of the casual workforce.[41]

The main objective of the settler administration and the British South Africa Company was to develop the farming and mining sectors in southern Zimbabwe (former Southern Rhodesia). Several strategies were initiated by the government to accommodate the needs of white farmers and miners as Bulawayo became the mining capital and the center of the country's railroad system. Salisbury became the administrative center of the country. Most of the employees in these developing urban centers were men. In 1926, for example, 11,962 African men had jobs in the urban sector of the economy in comparison with only 139 African women. An additional sixty-four women were employed as domestic workers in suburban areas in the north.[42]

In South Africa, in the early years, only men were employed to work in the mines. During the 1920s, for example, most of the employees were white or colored men. Women were negatively affected by many factors such as racial discrimination, sexual stereotypes regarding the capabilities of women, and legal restrictions on apprenticeships. Consequently, black women were unable to acquire highly paid, semiskilled work. By 1917, about six thousand females worked in the Cape Colony, almost all of them white. A law was passed in 1930 providing local authorities with the power to expel any women who could not demonstrate that they had residency in certain city areas. This factor led to a situation in which many black women were forced to serve as domestic servants in jobs that had earlier been largely performed by white and colored women. Black women did acquire more work in factories during World War II (in the western Cape area) as they replaced white women who moved into other areas of work.[43]

40. Geiger, *TANU Women*, 21; House-Midamba, *Class Development and Gender Inequality in Kenya, 1963–1990*, 40.

41. Ibid., 34.

42. Teresa A. Barnes, *We Women Worked So Hard: Gender, Urbanization and Social Reproduction in Colonial Havare, Zimbabwe, 1930–1956*, (Portsmouth: Heinemann, 1999), 4–5.

43. Coquery-Vidrovitch, *African Women*, 131.

Women's Involvement in Trade

African women have been involved in commercial activities in western, eastern, central, and southern African states. Although the market women of West Africa are legendary and well known, recent studies indicate that women in other parts of the continent were also actively involved in trade. For example, Claire Robertson's work on Kikuyu women demonstrated that they participated in trade as early as the mid-nineteenth century. Their trade activities focused primarily on staple food items such as beans, vegetables, and maize.[44]

Colonialism affected women's trade activities in different ways. In the case of Yoruba market women in southwestern Nigeria, Toyin Falola has noted that colonial and postcolonial penetration did not in any way diminish Yoruba women's important role in trade activities. Colonialism did, however, have a negative impact on Kikuyu women in Kenya and Igbo market women in Southeastern Nigeria. Igbo market women experienced a new reality when palm oil became commercialized under colonial rule in the 1830s. Many Igbo women gained wealth as a result of their participation in the palm produce and cassava trades. The expansion of trade in the colonial period, however, led to the declining significance of women in the economy as men seized opportunities to reduce women's dominance in the palm oil trade by using more advanced types of transportation. In Kenya, Kikuyu traders were negatively impacted by the loss of their land to the Europeans and by policies that tended to provide more support for the development of European firms and the commercial activities of East African Indians.[45]

Women's Political Responses

African women have participated in the politics of their societies for long periods of time. Nevertheless, serious discussions about the pivotal role of women in African nationalist movements have been conspicuously absent from many studies. In some of the more recent literature, however, Africanist feminist scholars have sought to deconstruct women's roles in the political realm. In so doing, they have demonstrated that, contrary to some previous stereotypes regarding women's perceived passivity in societal affairs, women were actively engaged in

---

44. Toyin Falola, "Gender, Business, and Space Control: Yoruba Market Women and Power" in *African Market Women and Economic Power: The Role of Women in African Economic Development,* edited by Bessie House-Midamba and Felix K. Ekechi, Westport, CT, Greenwood Press, 1995: 27–28; Claire Robertson, "Comparative Advantage: Women in Trade in Accra, Ghana, and Nairobi, Kenya" in *African Market Women and Economic Power: The Role of Women in African Economic Development,* edited by Bessie House Midamba and Felix K. Ekechi, Westport, CT, Greenwood Press, 1995, 105.

45. Felix K. Ekechi, "Gender and Economic Power: The Case of Igbo Market Women in Eastern Nigeria," in *African Market Women and Economic Power: The Role of Women in African Economic Development,* edited by Bessie House-Midamba and Felix K. Ekechi, Westport, CT: Greenwood Press, 1995: 45–46; Falola, "Gender, Business, and Space Control," 27–8; Robertson, Comparative Advantage: Women in Trade in Accra, Ghana, and Nirobi, Kenya, 105.

Figure 5.6. A Muslim woman.

the struggle for change. Kikuyu women, for example, were an integral part of all aspects of the nationalist struggle in Kenya and were major participants in the Mau Mau struggle. Their involvement in Mau Mau was influenced by several major issues such as the use of the forced labor of children and women on coffee estates and road projects initiated by the Kenyan government; the takeover of Kikuyu land by the British; the detention of Harry Thuku; and the irreconcilability between the Europeans and the Kikuyu on the issue of female circumcision.[46]

A large number of Kikuyu (approximately 1.5 million) lost their homes during the Emergency period. In *Kikuyu Women, the Mau Mau Rebellion and Social Change in Kenya*, Cora Ann Presley demonstrated that Kikuyu women participated in large numbers in almost all aspects of the war engaged in by the Land and Freedom Army. Women fought alongside Kikuyu men and some were sent to prison. They gained political power through both formal and informal means. Women sang protest songs about the policies of the government, the chiefs, and the retainers who used force to control their labor. Women left the male-controlled Kikuyu Central Association and developed the Mumbi Central Association. Many Kikuyu women who helped to establish this organization were considered to be "subversives" by the Kenyan government and were subsequently incarcerated like their male counterparts.[47]

---

46. House-Midamba, Gender, Democratization, and Associational Life in Kenya, in Africa Today, 43, 3, (July–September 1996), 294.

47. Elkins, Forest War No More, 1; Cora Ann Presley, *Kikuyu Women, The Mau Mau Rebellion, and Social Change in Kenya,* (Boulder: Westview Press, 1992) 107–122; 123–150; House-Midamba, Gender, "Democratization, and Associational Life in Kenya," 294.

In neighboring Tanzania, women were equally engaged in the political struggles and contestations over power and resources. The women of the Pare highlands area of Tanzania are particularly noteworthy in this regard. The large-scale
involvement of Pare women in the political realm was influenced by occurrence of
tax riots in Pare District during the 1940s. The riots developed after members of
the Pare District Council took the advice of a British district officer and decided
to implement a graduated income tax. In 1942–1943, the graduated income tax
was imposed on the populace by nine male chiefs in conjunction with a poll tax
which was already in place. The extra money was earmarked for development
projects in the Pare District.[48]

Many people were confused over the exact procedures regarding the assessment and collection of taxes. They demanded more information about the basis
of the tax assessments, the name, and the form of the new tax. The traditional
chiefs responded by implementing the tax without any changes. In response to
this, thousands of men took action by marching to the district headquarters in
Same and declaring that they intended to stay there until the tax was eliminated.
Although various meetings were held between the representatives of the people,
the native authorities, and the colonial administrators, no solution was found.
Eventually, after several months had passed, women marched to the district headquarters to support the men. The women insisted either that the colonialists provide a settlement, allowing the men to return home, or that the men should im-
pregnate the women. They also threatened to stay with their husbands in Same
because their separation from them had disrupted their households.[49]

When national officials came to Pare in 1946 at the request of the local district
officer, the women began to throw stones at them. When the conflict continued to
escalate, the chiefs gave in. Although they still maintained that a new tax was justified, they agreed to develop a new way to assess the amount to be collected. More
than two thousand of the citizens in Pare paid their taxes in the nearby district of
Kilimanjaro in 1946 in an effort to show that, although they were willing to pay
their taxes, they did not like the form or the manner in which they had been as-
sessed in Pare District. In 1947, the graduated tax idea was abolished although the
poll tax was increased. Although some progress was subsequently made in expanding popular representation in decision-making processes at the district level for the
citizenry, it did not lead to direct political participation by the women.[50]

Nigerian women have an impressive history of political activity. Felix K.
Ekechi has noted that the women of southern Nigeria were involved in collective
political action during the precolonial period. They used various strategies, such
as participating in traditional dances and songs as well as the "sitting on" strategy
used as a form of political protest and social commentary. One of the most successful political protests by Nigerian women was the women's war of 1929 in
Eastern Nigeria. The major reason for the women's protest was the policy of direct taxation introduced by the British in 1928. Women were also unhappy with
the policy of indirect rule imposed by the colonialists. The coalescence of political
and economic forces ultimately ignited the fire of dissatisfaction. One part of the

---

48. Jean O'Barr, "African Women in Politics," in Hay and Stichter, *African Women
South of the Sahara*, 145.
    49. Ibid., 145–6.
    50. Ibid., 145–6.

**Figure 5.7. An elite woman — Western education enabled
women to respond to new opportunities.**

problem was the insistence by the British on the use of a tax roll on which the
names of the taxpayers would be listed in addition to the number of wives in each
household and details of livestock.[51]

Although the British were able to collect the taxes without major problems in
1928, they were not as successful the following year largely because of a rumor
that women were going to be taxed as well. A number of forces converged to lay
the groundwork for the women's war. Women were experiencing a marked decline in the price paid to them for various types of palm products, and this led to
increased economic discontent among them. Many of the women were already
helping their husbands to pay their taxes, and the threat to tax the women, cou-

---

51. Felix Ekechi, "Perceiving Women as Catalysts," *Africa Today*, 43, 3, (July–September 1996), 243.

pled with the decrease in their income from palm products, increased their unhappiness and despair.[52]

The immediate factor that precipitated the women's war of 1929 was the decision by Chief Okugo of Oloko in the Aba Division to send a certain Mark Emerewa to take the tax census. The tax count continued successfully until Emerewa came to the compound of one Ojim, where he encountered Nwanyeruwa, one of the wives of Ojim. A disturbance erupted when Emerewa inquired of Nwanyeruwa how many people lived in the household unit and the number of animals that they owned. The woman reacted in a hostile manner and asked Emerewa if her own mother had also been included in his count. Thereafter, "some pushing and kicking" occurred and the woman ran out and informed a group of women who were attending a meeting close by. After hearing what had transpired, they came over to "sit on" Emerewa and Chief Okugo and sent messengers with palm leaves to women in nearby areas, who sent the message on to other villages.[53] To quote Ekechi,

> The women's revolt was characterized by violence against colonial agents and institutions, the symbols of colonial oppression and exploitation. Attacks were directed principally at warrant chiefs, native courts, and European factories. Warrant chiefs were beaten, and their houses (for example, Chief Okugo's) were looted and razed to the ground. Also, many colonial courthouses, European factories, and court messengers' houses were ransacked and destroyed. To the women, these facilities symbolized colonial oppression and exploitation, although some repudiated the destruction of houses and "the raiding of stores [as] part of their program for securing redress on the tax question."[54]

Conclusion

This chapter has examined the multifarious roles of African women during the colonial period. The main goal has been to explain how colonialism affected the status and authority that women had achieved in the precolonial era. The data indicate that colonialism severely impacted women in virtually every aspect of life. In many ways, women's status and power declined during the colonial period. Yet, women did not stand by idly. They were actively engaged in various attempts to change this inequitable situation, and, along with their male counterparts, they used whatever means were available to them to gain control over the future development of their societies.

---

52. Ibid., 243.
53. Ibid., 243.
54. Ibid., 243.

Review Questions

1. What factors motivated Europeans to colonize Africa?
2. How did the Europeans administer their colonies?
3. Define the sexual division of labor in Africa and explain how it was affected by colonialism.
4. What types of political strategies did African women use to promote political change in their societies?
5. Describe women's commercial and economic activities during the colonial period.

Additional Reading

Coquery-Vidrovitch, Catherine. *African Women: A Modern History*. Boulder, CO: Westview Press, 1997. English translation.

Hay, Margaret Jean, and Sharon Stichter. *African Women South of the Sahara*. London: Longman, 1984.

House-Midamba, Bessie. *Class Development and Gender Inequality in Kenya, 1963–1990*. Lewiston, NY: Edwin Mellen Press, 1990.

House-Midamba, Bessie, and Felix K. Ekechi, eds. *African Market Women and Economic Power: The Role of Women in African Economic Development*. Westport, CT: Greenwood Press, 1995.

Schraeder, Peter. *African Politics and Society: A Mosaic in Transformation*. Bedford St. Martin's Press, Boston, 2000.

Chapter 6

Women and Nationalist Movements

Gloria I. Chuku

Most of the major works on African nationalism have either omitted or assigned a minimal role to the activities of women in the struggles. Contrary to the notion portrayed in such works, African women played active roles in the continent's nationalist movements. Through deductive reasoning, this chapter discusses the different roles of African women in the continent's path to independence under the following headings: women and the colonial situation; women in cultural nationalism; women in labor movements and rural resistance; women in political protests and armed struggles; and powerful women nationalists.

* * *

Studies of African nationalist movements seldom give evidence of any active participation by women. They tend to concentrate on the activities of men, while the roles played by women are, by and large, relegated to the background. Most of the major works[1] on African nationalism have either omitted or assigned a minimal role to the activities of women in the struggles. Such works not only fail to reveal the historical development of women's involvement in the key issues and events of nationalist movements but also neglect to mention the achievements and sacrifices of these women. As one scholar puts it,

---

1. Basil Davidson, *Modern Africa: A Social and Political History* (London: Longman, 1998); Norrie MacQueen, *The Decolonization of Portuguese Africa: Metropolitan Revolution and the Dissolution of Empire* (London: Longman, 1997); Robert O. Collins et al., eds., *Historical Problems of Imperial Africa* (Princeton, NJ: Markus Wiener Publishers, 1996); A. A. Boahen, ed., *UNESCO General History of Africa vol. V11: Africa under Colonial Domination, 1880–1935*, abridged ed. (Berkeley: University of California Press, 1990); John D. Hargreaves, *Decolonization in Africa* (London: Longman, 1988); Shula Marks and Stanley Trapido eds., *The Politics of Race, Class, and Nationalism in Twentieth Century South Africa* (London: Longman, 1987); Ali Mazrui, *Nationalism and New States in Africa from About 1935 to the Present* (Nairobi: Heinemann, 1984); Ayodele Langley, *Pan-Africanism and Nationalism, 1940–1945* (Oxford: Clarendon Press, 1972); Robert Rotberg, *The Rise of Nationalism in Central Africa* (Cambridge, MA: Harvard University Press, 1966); Henry Wilson, *Origins of West African Nationalism* (London: Macmillan, 1969); Hans Kohn, *African Nationalism in the Twentieth Century* (Princeton, NJ: Van Nostrand, 1965); and Thomas Hodgkin, *Nationalism in Colonial Africa* (New York: New York University Press, 1957).

women emerge only as nameless supporting characters in a play dominated by men. Nationalist literature fails to confront the issue of women's
participation either as freedom fighters joining the men in the forests or as
supporters in the local communities working clandestinely to keep the
fighters supplied with information, food, and firearms.[2]

Women's anticolonial protests and wars are called "riots" in colonial records to
downplay their importance. Those who fought in the forests along with men were
represented in both colonial records and Africanist works as lovers or prostitutes
serving the fighting men. Primarily because of their concentration on male roles in
their own societies, colonial administrators were largely insensitive to the roles of
African women in political struggles and therefore hardly mentioned these
women's activities in their records.

Unfortunately, this trend has continued and is reflected in literary works by
Africans on African colonial and decolonization experiences. For example, one of
the celebrated literary works depicting indigenous response to the colonial situation in an African society virtually omitted the role of women and gave credit
only to the men.[3] Similarly, another literary work on an African people's liberation struggle against colonialism mentioned only one woman, one who had joined
the freedom fighters in the forest out of love for one of the fighters rather than out
of any sincere political commitment.[4] Donald Barnett claims that women fled to
the forest in Kenya to escape the hardship of the reserves. He admits that once in
the forest, they helped in the struggle, but argues that they were more concerned
with personal safety and survival than with political will and commitment.[5] As
Kathy Santilli rightly observes, men's accounts emphasize women's roles in the
forest as mistresses and the use of their sexuality to aid the forest fighters.[6] Sexual
roles and tactics may have been used, as we shall see later, but the problem is with
the possible exaggeration that leaves readers with a distorted view of female participation in African nationalist struggles.

The distortion and/or omission of the indispensable contributions of women
to the African nationalist movements may result from data that have been almost
exclusively provided by males, whether Europeans or Africans. These sources
have created the false idea that nationalist movements and politics in Africa were
mainly male concerns. Yet we now know that any investigation of the dynamics
of nationalism in Africa is incomplete without a consideration of women's roles.
Herein lies the contribution of this chapter.

African women played pivotal roles in the continent's nationalist struggles, in
organizing anticolonial activities, and in disseminating nationalist ideas. They
participated in the nationalist revolutions in diverse ways. Women's involvement
and degree of participation in the nationalist movements were primarily deter-

---

2. Jean O'Barr, "Introductory Essay," in *Passbook Number F. 47927: Women and Mau
Mau in Kenya*, ed. Muthoni Likimani, (London: Macmillan, 1985), 6.

3. Chinua Achebe, *Things Fall Apart*, expanded ed. (Oxford: Heinemann, 1996).

4. Ngugi wa Thiong'O, *A Grain of Wheat*, revised ed. (Athens, OH: Heinemann,
1986).

5. Donald Barnett and K. Njama, *Mau Mau From Within* (New York: Monthly Review
Press, 1966), 151.

6. Kathy Santilli, "Kikuyu Women in the Mau Mau Revolt: A Closer Look," *UFA-
HAMU*, 8 (1977): 143–59.

mined by the colonial situation. In other words, the various kinds of nationalist movements, as well as the period in which they occurred, provided the contexts within which women acted. For example, there were the early and relatively non-violent movements in the West African states of Ghana, Nigeria, and Sierra Leone; there were also early movements in the former French West African colonies and in East and Central Africa. In addition, there were nationalist movements in the entrenched settler colonies of Kenya, Algeria, and Zimbabwe where violent struggle was necessary. A later wave of more self-consciously socialist movements led to intense fighting in Guinea-Bissau, Angola, and Mozambique. Nationalist activity in South Africa was greatly prolonged because of harsh repression by the apartheid government. Thus, the colonial situation in Algeria, Angola, Guinea-Bissau, Kenya, Mozambique, Namibia, South Africa, and Zimbabwe made armed resistance inevitable.

In some places, women's roles involved the organization of rural resistance, cultural nationalism, religious protests, labor movements, and political protests. Elsewhere, especially in the settler colonies where independence was achieved through wars of liberation, women participated actively not only by writing protest letters and organizing strikes, boycotts, and demonstrations, but also in the wars as combatants.

Through synthesis, this chapter discusses the different roles of African women in the continent's path to independence under the following headings: women and the colonial situation; women in cultural nationalism; women in labor movements and rural resistance; women in political protests and armed struggles; and powerful women nationalists.

Women and the Colonial Situation in Africa

The colonial situation in Africa was characterized primarily by political and economic domination. Under the international division of trade, African colonies were compelled to produce agricultural products badly needed for industries in Europe in exchange for surplus industrial products. In some colonies, especially where Europeans settled, European plantation agriculture was introduced. Plantation agriculture required large acreage of land, which the various colonial administrations did not hesitate in seizing from indigenous people.

Africa, as Ester Boserup has observed, was a region whose farming was dominated by females.[7] Therefore, women suffered the most from land impoverishment resulting from the European land alienation policy. Not only did the women lose their farmlands, but they inherited the burden of providing food for their families and for local consumption. In Kenya, the British colonial government introduced the Crown Land Act in 1902, which alienated the indigenous people from their farmlands. The Kiambu District of Kenya lost about sixty thousand acres of Southern Kiambu—the most fertile area, with a population of around

---

7. Ester Boserup, *Women's Role in Economic Development* (London: Allen and Unwin, 1970).

eleven thousand Kikuyu—to the European settlers.[8] Women bore the burden of producing for local economies and for the colonial export trade. Coupled with the problem of land alienation was the policy of confining Africans to particular regions of the continent; for example, Africans were removed to reserves in South Africa and underwent "villagization"[9] in Kenya.

Forced labor and poor wages were other characteristics of the colonial situation that directly affected African women. Colonial export production in Africa was labor-intensive. The commercialization of agriculture through the introduction of cash crops altered the customary gender division of labor in ways that were mostly disadvantageous to women. Although men participated in export production, it was the women who bore the greatest burden. In addition, while men were taught how to grow new cash crops such as cocoa and coffee and how to use improved technologies to achieve higher quality and increased production, women continued to grow food crops for the family and for local consumption with crude and time-consuming indigenous techniques. Furthermore, while men had the opportunity to move into the wage economy by working in mines, on plantations, in construction, or in towns, most women remained in the rural areas, often assuming the responsibilities of their absent menfolk. Women's workloads increased considerably. In the Zambian copper belt, for example, wives were required to perform their customary domestic services for their husbands in town, although they were unable to claim any share of their husbands' incomes. Women played a major role in organizing rural activities; managing and working on farms; and producing such cash crops as tea, cotton, coffee, and cocoa, despite the fact that the British and French usually identified men as the farm owners.

In some settler colonies, women also worked on European plantations. For example, in colonial Kenya, women were extensively used as seasonal laborers in coffee picking or harvesting. On these plantations, women were subjected to unfair labor practices. Some of them suffered from beatings, rape, detention, withholding of wages, and physical coercion during recruitment. The issue of women's labor was a major focus of Harry Thuku's anticolonial campaigns in Kenya, campaigns that made him a hero to Kikuyu women but a threat to the British colonial government. We shall see later how his arrest and detention resulted in one of the most famous women's uprisings in all of colonial Africa.

Certain colonial policies were specifically directed against women. In many colonies, women were prevented from migrating to the cities either by statute, as in Zambia (then Northern Rhodesia); by the dynamics of apartheid, as in South Africa; and/or by the difficulty of finding housing and employment. This policy was primarily intended to keep women in rural production and thereby maintain

---

8. Audrey Wipper, "Kikuyu Women and the Harry Thuku Disturbances: Some Uniformities of Female Militancy," *Africa* 59, 3 (1989): 309; and Cora Ann Presley, "The Mau Mau Rebellion, Kikuyu Women, and Social Change," *Canadian Journal of African Studies* 22, 3 (1988): 505.

9. The British colonial government, to isolate or cut off the civil population or the "passive wing" of support to the Mau Mau fighters in the forest, adopted a ""villagization" policy. For more information, see Presley, "The Mau Mau Rebellion," 503–4; Presley, "Kikuyu Women in the Mau Mau Rebellion" in *In Resistance: Studies in African, Caribbean, and Afro-American History,* ed. Gary Y. Okihiro (Amherst: University of Massachusetts, 1986), 53–70; and Presley, "Kikuyu Women, Culture, and Nationalist Movement in Colonial Kenya," *African Studies Journal* 6 (1981): 1–9.

local economies. In mining areas such as Zambia and Zimbabwe (Southern Rhodesia), indigenous rural authorities had the power to send those who defied such restrictions back to the villages. This joint interest of colonial officials and traditional authorities in legally controlling women has been closely documented.[10] In 1930 and 1937, South African legislators passed laws that began controlling women's movement to the cities.

The few women who ventured into the cities suffered from discriminatory restrictions on their economic advancement. At times, they had no access to wage employment. They were also discouraged from running independent businesses. For example, women beer brewers in Nairobi (Kenya) were subjected to harassment, arrest, fines, and imprisonment. There were also plans in Nairobi to demolish homes of female prostitutes and banish them from the city's streets. It is, therefore, not surprising that this group of women played an active role in Harry Thuku's revolt of the 1920s, because they felt that their rights had been disregarded or their sphere invaded. Women in Durban, South Africa, responding to restrictions on domestic beer brewing and to government support of municipal beer halls, invaded and burned beer halls and clashed with police. A similar ban was placed on local gin brewing in Nigeria, which the British colonial government labeled "illicit."[11]

Africans who found themselves in the wage economy were offered wages that were not commensurate with the amount of work they did. The wages were so poor that, after paying taxes, a man had virtually nothing left to support his family. This situation exacerbated the burden of women as household managers and even turned some of them into the sole breadwinners for their families. At times, local authorities were used to organize compulsory communal labor for the colonial government and the settler community.

Western education and new skills were made available primarily to males. Men gained some access to important resources such as money, skills, land, and education—all resources that were less available to women. As Claire Robertson suggests, colonial education was not only economically dysfunctional for women, but it also prepared them for subordination.[12] Contributing to the dysfunction of women's education was the discrimination against them in access to wage jobs.

Men also gained political advantages as customary sources of female power were ignored or undermined. There were, for example, all-male native authorities in almost all the colonies. Studies of the impact of colonialism on women's political institutions and authority in several African societies have concluded that much of the basis of women's former power collapsed under the rule of colonial administrators who, blinded by their Victorian ethos, failed to notice its pres-

10. Julia Wells, *We Now Demand! The History of Women's Resistance to Pass Laws in South Africa* (Johannesburg: Witwatersrand University Press, 1993); Judy Kimble and Elaine Unterhalter, "'We Opened the Road for You, You Must Go Forward': ANC Women's Struggles, 1912–1982," *Feminist Review,* 12 (1982): 11–35.

11. See Iris Berger, "Women in East and Southern Africa," in *Women in Sub-Saharan Africa,* ed. Iris Berger and E. Frances White (Bloomington: Indiana University Press, 1999), 48; and Gloria I. Chuku, "The Changing Role of Women in Igbo Economy, 1929 to 1985," (Ph.D. Thesis, Department of History, University of Nigeria, 1995).

12. Claire Robertson, "Women's Education and Class Formation in Africa, 1950–1980," in *Women and Class in Africa,* ed. Claire Robertson and Iris Berger (New York: Africana Publishing Company, 1986), 110.

ence.[13] Colonialism altered women's positions in their societies. It particularly affected their ability to participate in local government. Women were acutely aware of the threats that colonial policies, especially alienation and exclusion, posed to their social status. Thus, as W. O. Maloba rightly observes, Angolan women saw the fight against colonialism as the first step toward their own emancipation.[14]

Taxation was a most sensitive issue in colonial Africa, and it sparked widespread demonstrations by women. Taxation issues stimulated protests by Yoruba market women in 1908 (against the water rate tax); protests in the 1930s and 1940s in Lagos; the 1940s protests in Abeokuta; the Igbo women's war; the Anlu Rebellion in Cameroon; and the general tax riots in Tanzania. In 1945, the Pare women of northern Tanzania marched to the district headquarters to voice their opposition to new taxes that were seen as disruptive to family and agricultural life.[15] There were demonstrations against the 1910 and 1934 poll taxes in Kenya and the hut-tax war in Sierra Leone. In Usumbura, Burundi in the late 1950s, Muslim women organized an effective revolt against a special tax on single women.[16] Women demonstrated against taxation not only because it was new to most African societies, but also because taxation adversely affected the family resources that African women managed. The burden of male taxation alone was becoming so unbearable for women who were household managers that plans or rumors of the extension of taxation to women caused widespread revolts and demonstrations in different parts of Africa.

Another source of resentment against colonial rule was the low price of exports compared with the ever-increasing cost of imported goods. Women, as the backbones of local economies and major producers of exports, felt the impact most. The effects of world recessions and the depression of the 1920s and 1930s were devastating to women and their economic resources. The unequal exchange relations that characterized the international division of trade between Europe and Africa made Africans—especially women—most vulnerable. There were cases when African producers withheld their crops due to poor prices; but such protests did not last long since Africans could not consume raw materials before they were processed.

Conflicts were seen most clearly at the level of local government, where the colonial system directly impinged on women's daily lives. African women's

13. A. Lebeuf, "Women in Political Organization," in *Women of Tropical Africa*, ed. D. Paulme (Berkeley: University of California Press, 1971), 93–119; B. Awe, "The Iyalode in the Traditional Yoruba Political System," in *Sexual Stratification: A Cross Cultural View*, ed. A. Schlegel (New York: Columbia University Press, 1977), 140–60; Judith Van Allen, "'Sitting on a Man': Colonialism and the Lost Political Institutions of Igbo Women," *Canadian Journal of African Studies* 6, 2 (1972): 165–82; Mona Etienne and Eleanor Leacock, eds., *Women and Colonization: Anthropological Perspectives* (New York: Praeger, 1980); LaRay Denzer, "Yoruba Women: A Historiographical Study," *International Journal of African Historical Studies* 27, 1 (1994): 1–39; and Gloria Chuku, "The Militancy of Nigerian Women since the Colonial Period: Evolution and Transformation," *UFAHAMU* 26, 1 (1998): 55–76.

14. Wunyabari O. Maloba, *Mau Mau and Kenya: An Analysis of a Peasant Revolt* (Bloomington: Indiana University Press, 1993). Also see Stephanie Urdang, *Fighting Two Colonialisms: Women in Guinea-Bissau* (New York: Monthly Review Press, 1979).

15. Jean O'Barr, "Pare Women: A Case of Political Involvement," *Rural Africana*, 29 (1975–1976): 121–34.

16. Nancy Rose Hunt, "Domesticity and Colonialism in Belgian Africa: Usumbura's *Foyer Social*," *Signs* 15, 3 (1990): 447–74.

Figure 6.1. Reflections through prayer. Muslim women praying about peace, social order, political stability and prosperity.

strongest hostility was, therefore, not necessarily directed against the Europeans but against their local agents: chiefs, headmen, court clerks, indigenous police, and labor recruiters who often abused their power by exploiting women. While women, being among the most vulnerable members of African societies, had to shoulder a disproportionate share of government-imposed burdens, some men acted as collaborators who cooperated with and profited from the colonial regime. As wives, mothers, farmers, and traders, women were already overburdened with demands on their time and energy. As additional burdens were placed on them, they lost much of their power. Even though women disliked the colonial government, which was insensitive to or ignorant of their institutions, rights, and aspirations, it was the actions of the local agents that upset them most. Thus, in Igboland, Nigeria, women's wrath fell on the warrant chiefs, tax collectors, and native court messengers. The Kikuyu women ridiculed the chiefs and taunted the *askaris* (native police); and the Kom women of Cameroon rejected the native courts and set up their own. Since women had lost faith in the formal channels for settling grievances, they resorted to informal channels.

Women in Cultural Nationalism

The role of women in cultural nationalism during the colonial period could earn them the title of "cultural crusaders" for African values and heritage. Most of the early political and nationalist activities of African women were centered on

cultural survival. As Felix Ekechi put it, African women were champions of cultural nationalism who challenged European pretensions of cultural hegemony.[17]
In Nigeria (in Igbo and Ibibio areas), women carried out protest movements as
early as the 1840s and 1860s in response to what Ekechi calls "missionary iconoclasm." Christian missions were preaching against time-honored African institutions, like polygyny and other societal customs and practices, such as the killing
of twins. In 1864, west and east of the River Niger, Igbo women inspired by the
spirit-medium called *Odesoruelu*, "Restorer of Traditional Life," traveled from
town to town preaching a message of peace and cultural renewal as well as calling
for a return to the days before Christianity. They were also concerned by the
spread of new diseases, such as smallpox and influenza, believed to have been
brought by the missionaries.[18]

African women used their religious power as an instrument of anticolonial resistance. Some of them founded independent African churches as a means of
breaking away from European domination. There was the case of Beatrice Kim-
parita of the Congo, whose religious organization was a mixture of Christianity
and messianism. She preached an anti-Catholic Christianity rooted in the Kongo
cultural heritage. To her, Africans were the fathers of Christianity, Jesus Christ
was born in Sao Salvador, and the Congo was the Holy Land. Pedro IV of Portugal burned her as a heretic, along with her unborn child, at the age of twenty-four
years. Iris Berger, in her study of spirit mediums in East Africa, concludes that
spirit-medium cults provided a new, militant form of organized resistance against
the Europeans.[19] Other important examples of women in traditional religious
movements included Alice Lichina in Kenya, the Nyabingi of the Kenya-Uganda
border, and Magoi's healing/possession movement in Renamo areas of Mozambique, which mobilized antigovernment forces against the exploitation of rural
people. Nehanda (1862–1898) of Shonaland (Zimbabwe) used her religious
movement to preach resistance against Cecil Rhodes's massive land expropria-
tions for the British South Africa Company in the 1890s. With Kagubi, another
great priest of the period, Nehanda was able to mobilize the Shona people in their
first war of liberation, which began in 1896 and was led by Mkwati, the greatest
of the religious chiefs preaching unity between the Shona and Ndebele peoples.
Nehanda became a formidable war chief, operating from a Musaka fortress with
well-organized troops. She was captured by the British in December 1897 and
later executed and buried in a place kept secret to avoid its becoming a site of
worship.[20]

In the 1920s in southeastern Nigeria, female demonstrators were characterized as bands of women dancers preaching desirable reforms. These included the

---

17. Felix K. Ekechi, "Historical Women in the Fight for Liberation," in *The Feminization of Development Processes in Africa*, ed. V. U. James and J. I. Etim (Westport, CT:
Praeger, 1999), 196.
18. Ibid., 97–9; and Ekechi, "Perceiving Women as Catalysts," *Africa Today* 43, 3
(1996): 240.
19. Iris Berger, "Rebels or Status-Seekers? Women as Spirit Mediums in East Africa," in
Women in Africa: Studies in Social and Economic Change, ed. Nancy Hafkin and Edna Bay
(Stanford: Stanford University Press, 1976), 157–81.
20. Catherine Vidrovitch-Coquery, *African Women: A Modern History*, trans. Beth
Gillian Raps [Social Change in Global Perspective] (Boulder, CO: Westview of Harper
Collins, 1997), 44.

Nwabiala (in Igboland) and the *Obanjili* (in Ibibioland). The women, moving, singing, and dancing in groups or bands of fifty to three hundred, protested against the poor sanitary conditions of many compounds, the introduction of coinage, the introduction of cassava and men's participation in its cultivation, girls wearing dresses, the corrupt practices of native courts, and the high prices of certain food items. The women wanted the restoration of the old ways, especially the observance of their customs.[21] A similar mass movement operated in Ibibioland in 1927 and 1928, the "Spirit Movement." In this movement, the women accused Christian missionaries of undermining some of their cultural practices and values. The "Spirit Movement" crystallized into the first independent indigenous church in Ibibioland, the *Oberi Okaime Mission,* with its own language, script, calendar, and hierarchy. By 1938, it had expanded to Bamenda in Cameroon.[22] Similarly, women played important roles in the foundation and leadership of the Aladura churches that appeared in Yorubaland in the 1930s.[23]

The response of Kenyan women to the female circumcision controversy, which became a matter of official concern in the 1920s and 1930s, also fell within the paradigm of cultural resistance to colonialism. In 1956, clitoridectomy was officially banned. The passing, defiance, and enforcement of the ban took place during the Mau Mau rebellion. The issue of female circumcision added fuel to the growing nationalism among the Kikuyu women who saw the attack on clitoridectomy as an attempt by the European missionaries to destroy the integrity of Kenyan culture. Women, as well as men, left the churches, removed their children from the mission schools, and established independent primary schools. At the height of this move toward independence in education and religion came the founding of Githunguri School, almost entirely funded and built by women.[24] In the early and mid-1920s in the Herschel District of the Cape in South Africa, rural Christian women organized and sustained boycotts of local shops and schools in protest against male migration, taxation, land registration, and limitations placed on polygyny.

21. Chuku, "The Militancy of Nigerian Women," 60–61; Nina Mba, *Nigerian Women Mobilized: Women's Political Activity in Southern Nigeria, 1900–65* (Berkeley: University of California Press, 1982), 68; Nigerian National Archives (NNA) Enugu, CSE 3/17/15, File No B15 44/25, "Anti-Government Propaganda by Women-Dancers in Owerri, Onitsha and Ogoja Provinces, 1925; NNA Enugu, ONPROF 7/12/92, File No. OP391, "Movement of Bands of Women Dancers Proclaiming Ideas of Desirable Reforms, 1925–26; and NNA Enugu, AWA80A, "Women Dancers Preaching Ideas of Desirable Reforms, 1925–26."

22. NNA Enugu, CALPROF 3/1/209, File No CP245 vol.1, "Disturbances at Ibibio by Mission Youth Reported, "Spirit Movement at Enyong and Ikot Ekpene Division, Report of 1928; M. N. Noah, "The Role, Status and Influence of Women in Traditional Times: The Example of the Ibibio of Southeastern Nigeria," *Nigeria Magazine* 54, 4 (1985): 27; and Chuku, "The Militancy of Nigerian Women," 61–2.

23. Aladura churches provide the opportunity for African women to blend their African beliefs and cultural heritage with some Christian traditions. The African cultural heritage is preserved as some Christian European cultural traits are rejected.

24. Presley, "Kikuyu Women in the Mau Mau Rebellion," 55–56; Presley, "Kikuyu Women, Culture, and the Nationalist Movement," 1–2; and Lynn M. Thomas, "'Ngaitana (I will circumcise myself)': The Gender and Generational Politics of the 1956 Ban on Clitoridectomy in Meru, Kenya" in *Gendered Colonialisms in African History*, ed. Nancy Rose Hunt, T. P. Liu and Jean Quataert (Oxford: Blackwell Publishers, 1997), 16–41.

Women in Rural Resistance and Labor Movements

African women played an active part in rural resistance and labor movements during the colonial period. In Egypt, as Afaf Marsot puts it, "veiled gentlewomen of Cairo" paraded the streets shouting slogans for independence and freedom from foreign occupation, organized strikes, demonstrations, and boycotts of British goods and wrote petitions protesting British actions in their country.[25] These women went to the rural areas, side by side with the men, to cut the telephone wires and disrupt the railroad. Some of their names, such as Shafika Mohammed, Hamida Khalil, Sayeda Hassan, Fahima Riad, and Aisha Omar, are known. However, hundreds of poor women lost their lives without anyone being able to trace their identities.[26] The works of Iris Berger have demonstrated that South African women, for example, have a history of participation in working-class struggles that dates back to their involvement in the Industrial and Commercial Workers' Union and the Women Workers' General Union of the 1920s, as well as to the garment and textile workers' organization of the 1930s.[27] In the early 1930s, thousands of white and colored women in these newly expanding industries went on strike in an effort to stave off wage cuts resulting from the depression and to gain some control over their wages and working conditions. The leaders included Johanna and Hester Cornelius, Anna Scheepers, Dulcie Hartwell, and Bettie du Toit. These women succeeded in unionizing large numbers of semi-skilled and unskilled workers, among them female candy and tobacco workers, milliners, and food and canning workers. There were also spontaneous uprisings by South African women in Natal in the late 1950s. For example, in the second half of the 1950s, trade union women formed a large number of the organizers of the Federation of South African Women, which led the protests against passes for women. In the Bafarutshe reserve near the Botswana border, women incited a virtual civil war against anyone who cooperated in the distribution of passes. In 1956, more than two thousand women demonstrated in Pretoria against the migrant labor system and rigid government controls. Female industrial workers in South Africa, many of them household heads, were heavily involved in labor protests during the intensive organizing that followed the Durban strikes of 1973.

Women's working conditions in Kenya, especially in European coffee plantations, generated widespread protest. The protests of the East African Association (EAA) between 1913 and 1923 focused on the coercion of women workers. Women voiced their grievances through temporary work stoppages and strikes. In

---

25. Afaf L. Marsot, "The Revolutionary Gentlewomen in Egypt," in *Women in the Muslim World*, ed. Lois Beck and Nikki Keddie (Cambridge, MA: Harvard University Press, 1978), 269.

26. N. El-Saadawi, *The Hidden Face of Eve: Women in the Arab World* (London: Zed Press, 1980), 176; and Kumari Jayawardena, *Feminism and Nationalism in the Third World* (London: Zed Books, 1986), 53.

27. Iris Berger, "Women in East and Southern Africa," in Berger and White, *Women in Sub-Saharan Africa*, 47–56; Iris Berger, *Threads of Solidarity: Women in South African Industry, 1900–1980* (Bloomington: Indiana University Press, 1992); and Berger, "Sources of Class Consciousness: South African Women in Recent Labor Struggles," in Robertson and Berger, *Women and Class in Africa*, 216–35.

1947, women also organized labor strikes over the conditions on the coffee estates. Women of the Fort Hall District in Kenya participated in what was termed the "Revolt of the Women," a protest against a scheme to compel women to construct terraces on their farms for soil conservation. In Senegal, females played active roles in organized labor protests. For example, in the post-World War II railroad strike, women not only supported the strikers but also marched from Thies to Dakar to press for the strikers' demands. Women played active roles in the Watchtower Movement in Katanga, which was of great significance in the Manono miners' strike of 1941. Guinean women also justified Sékou Touré's faith in them by collaborating in the famous strike of 1953. While the strike was in effect, women traders refused to sell chicken, eggs, and fresh milk to the French while feeding strikers for free. Peasant women contributed rice for the strikers. With active women's support, the strikers were able to hold on for seventy-three days, seriously weakening the French colonial government.[28]

In Nigeria, women were active in organizing anticolonial protest demonstrations. The well-known Igbo women's war of 1929 is a case in point. Thousands of Igbo and Ibibio women, concerned that they would be taxed and angry at corrupt warrant chiefs for implementing unpopular government policies amidst a continuous fall in the price of exports and an ever-increasing rise in import prices, rebelled against the warrant chiefs, native courts, and European factories. Warrant chiefs were beaten and their houses looted; many court houses, European factories, and court messengers' houses were ransacked and destroyed. These facilities, to the women, symbolized colonial oppression and exploitation. The women demanded, among other things, the deposition and prosecution of the corrupt warrant chiefs and the abolition of taxation. They demanded that all white men go back to their country. More than one hundred women were killed or wounded in the clashes, and property damage was estimated at more than sixty thousand pounds. Some remarkable successes were achieved in the deferral of the taxation of women; the removal and prosecution of notorious and corrupt warrant chiefs; the establishment of a new system of local government acceptable to the people; and the inclusion of women in the local administration as members of native courts and even as warrant chiefs.[29]

The Lagos Market Women Association (LMWA) of Nigeria, under the able leadership of Alimotu Pelewura, protested colonial authority through petitions, meetings, boycotts, and demonstrations from 1908 to the 1940s. Some of these are discussed in the section on Pelewura as one of the heroines of Africa's nationalist movements. However, I must not fail to mention the great support the strikers in the 1945 General Strike received from the LMWA. The women involved

28. E. Frances White, "Women in West and West-Central Africa," in Berger and White, Women in Sub-Saharan Africa, 112; John Higginson, "Liberating the Captives: Independent Watchtower as an Avatar of Colonial Revolt in Southern Africa and Katanga, 1908–1941," Journal of Social History 26, 1 (1992): 55–80; Sembene Ousmane, God's Bits of Wood, trans. Francis Price (Oxford: Heinemann, 1995); Margarita Dobert, "Liberation and the Women of Guinea," Africa Report 15 (October 1970): 26–8.

29. Chuku, "The Militancy of Nigerian Women; Chuku, "The Changing Role of Igbo Women;" Ekechi, "Perceiving Women as Catalysts; Mba, Nigerian Women Mobilized; Report of the Commission of Inquiry Appointed to Inquire into the Disturbances in the Calabar and Owerri Provinces, December, 1929 (Lagos: Government Printer, 1930); and Aba Commission of Enquiry: Minutes of Evidence (Lagos: Government Printer, 1930).

contributed to the Workers' Relief Fund and kept food prices low in solidarity with the strikers.[30]

A major protest in Cameroon was popularly known as the Anlu Women's Uprising. The uprising started in April 1958, when seven thousand Kom women staged a series of mass demonstrations in Bamenda Province. On July 8, 1958, about two thousand women marched to the weekly market eight miles away, closed the market and the mission school, and blocked the roads with stones. On November 22, about two thousand women entered the government station at Bamenda after a thirty-eight-mile march of a day and a half protesting the summoning for interrogation of four of their leaders. The women generally were rebelling against the rumored introduction of taxation on women; the premature enforcement of a new contour-farming regulation to check soil erosion; the government neglect of their claims of crop damage against the Fulani; and the rumor that the government was selling their land. With the backing of almost all the Kom women, the Anlu movement declared that it was in control and demanded that there should be no more use of courts, schools, churches, or hospitals by the people and that all strangers — Hausa, Fulani, and European — should leave. Using Anlu, a sanctioning device traditionally employed by women to punish rule-breakers, the Kom women rendered the paramount chief and his executive council powerless, unseated the ruling party (the Kameruns National Congress) and helped to get the Kameruns National Democratic Party into power following the 1959 elections.[31]

This was not the first time women had unseated a ruling authority. They had done the same among the Yoruba of Nigeria in the 1940s. Any encroachment upon or abrogation of women's rights — be it by chiefs, agricultural officers, colonial administrators, or even the head of state — met with righteous indignation and stiff resistance. On November 29–30, 1947, more than ten thousand women led by Funmilayo Ransome-Kuti mounted an all-night vigil outside the palace of the *alake* (king) of Egbaland to protest against taxation and the activities of the Ogboni chiefs and tax collectors. Further, women's demonstrations of July 27–28, 1948 resulted in the abdication of Alake Ademola II.[32]

30. Cheryl Johnson, "Grass Roots Organizing: Women in Anticolonial Activity in Southern Nigeria," *African Studies Review* 2, 3 (1982): 137–157; Johnson, "Class and Gender: A Consideration of Yoruba Women during the Colonial Period," in Robertson and Berger, *Women and Class in Africa*, 237–54; and Johnson, "Madam Alimotu Pelewura and the Lagos Market Women," *Tarikh* 7, Ic (1981): 1–10.

31. Robert E. Ritzenthaler, "Anlu: A Women's Uprising in the British Cameroons," in *Collective Behavior,* ed. Raph H. Turner and Lewis M. Killian, 2nd ed. (Englewood Cliffs, NJ: Prentice-Hall, 1972), 399–404.

32. C. Johnson-Odim and Nina Emma Mba, *For Women and the Nation: Funmilayo Ransome-Kuti of Nigeria* (Urbana: University of Illinois Press, 1997); and N. Mba, "Olufunmilayo Ransome-Kuti," in *Nigerian Women in Historical Perspective*, ed. B. Awe (Lagos: Sankore Publishers, 1992), 135–48.

Figure 6.2. Funmilayo Ransome-Kuti of Nigeria. Her son, Fela Anikulapo-Kuti, became one of Africa's most talented musicians and a revolutionary artist.

Women in Political Protests and Armed Struggles

Contrary to accepted ideas, African women played active roles in the political protests and armed struggles that facilitated the decolonization process. Women expressed their political sentiments through major political parties and local resistance movements in both urban and rural areas. In Egypt, women's political demonstrations occurred on four occasions in 1919 during the nationalist upsurge in which all classes participated. Egyptian women were organized by many of the wives of the Wafd founders. Middle-class women were seen protesting for the first time in public. Egyptian women had to break cultural and religious constraints to protest openly in public. In the Ivory Coast (Côte d'Ivoire), the Baule women in particular played an important and very active role in the country's struggle for independence. The national party relied heavily on women's support. In 1949, the women marched on the prison of Grand-Bassam to liberate political prisoners. Many were maimed or injured in the violent encounter with colonial troops.

Women in Tanzania also proved to be a formidable force used by Julius Nyerere to make the Tanganyika African National Union (TANU) a credible and
successful nationalist movement. The Ngoma women's dance groups were transformed into highly politicized networks for the exchange of information and
ideas, for the publicizing of TANU values and marches, and for fundraising for
the party. As vehicles for nationalist mobilization, women's dance associations
undertook house-to-house canvassing to mobilize communities and neighborhoods for mass rallies. Women brought to the party the sense of trans-ethnic,
Swahili-speaking urban community that informed their nationalism. They raised
money locally and pawned their jewelry for Nyerere's trips abroad in connection
with his court case in 1958, for party headquarters' expenses, and for staff
salaries. They purchased TANU membership cards and also mobilized people to
buy them as a way of helping the party raise funds. Women housed TANU leaders
during rallies. In fact, they saw in TANU not only an opportunity to gain national
independence, but also a means to struggle against male domination. Sudanese
women participated in their country's nationalist movement first through the
local Communist Party and later through larger nationalist movements. The
Women's League and its successor, the Women's Movement, as vehicles of political and nationalist mobilization, started among urban women and later spread to
workers and peasants in the northern part of the country.

In Nigeria, where the nationalist movement was centered on electoral struggles, women's organizations, such as that of market women, were key supporters
of political parties during elections. Market women's support became a leading
factor in a party's control of an area. The women were active in endorsing and financing candidates, extracting promises, and generally participating in the political process. The Lagos Market Women Association, for example, provided many
of the members of the Nigerian National Democratic Party (NNDP) of Herbert
Macaulay, the father of Nigerian nationalism. The LMWA also contributed gen-
erously to the party. Women leaders such as Funmilayo Ransome-Kuti and Margaret Ekpo attended constitutional conferences held in London where they presented not only the interests and aspirations of Nigerian women but also those of
the masses. Sierra Leonean women institutionalized their participation in politics
both during and after the nationalist period.

In Guinea (in former French West Africa), the nationalist movement acquired
a more socialist ideology and had a greater commitment to the political importance of women. Women played a direct role in Sékou Touré's rise to power. They
gave money and provided communication links among the revolutionaries, and
their leader participated in policy formation. Like the leaders of nationalist movements in Angola and Mozambique, Touré recognized the vital role of Guinean
women in the country's independence movement. During the 1964 elections,
when tension between the country's French-backed conservatives and Touré's followers exploded in fierce street brawls, women collected rocks and carried them
to the men who threw them at French soldiers.

The role of Empress Taytu and thousands of other Ethiopian women in their
country's nationalist war with Italy has been well documented.[33] The logistics of

---

33. Chris Prouty, *Empress Taytu and Menelik II: Ethiopia, 1883–1910* (London:
Ravens Educational and Development Services, 1986).

military campaigns were heavily dependent on the thousands of women who carried on their backs that which could not be loaded on a mule. Women cooked for the soldiers, retrieved the dead, attended to the wounded, and maintained the supply line for the fighters. All these activities facilitated Ethiopia's victory in the Battle of Adowa in 1896, which freed the country from the threat of European colonial domination. The Front for the Liberation of Mozambique (FRELIMO) and the Popular Movement for the Liberation of Angola (MPLA) both recognized the role of women and included them in their fights for independence. Women proved their worth in Mozambique and Angola by participating in mass mobilization for popular support, contributing supplies for the soldiers, and even taking part in combat. They experienced a role transformation as a result of the nationalist struggles. In the Angolan revolution of the 1970s, for example, women were organized into local committees to support the guerrilla armies and protect and defend themselves from Portuguese attacks. They also received military training, primarily to defend liberated areas. Some of them, like Josina Machel, were combatants, fighting side by side with men, thereby transforming the definition of the role of women from that of homemakers on the land to that of fighters and strategists on battlefields. The Organization of Angolan Women (OMA) contributed a great deal to the fight.[34]

Algerian women were both participants in and victims of the protracted guerrilla war of independence between Algeria and France. In the seven-year war (1956–1962), Algerian women moved from their usual home-centered social roles into the world of urban and rural guerrilla warfare. Women turned the veil into a tool of action. On missions to urban areas to deliver messages or to accompany male nationalists as carriers, women discarded the veil and adopted Western dress and mannerisms. When stopped, they put on the veil and voluminous dress of traditional Algerian women to conceal what they were carrying. Whether they joined the struggle as members of guerrilla cells operating in urban centers, left for the mountains where battles took place, or lived in strategic rural areas, Algerian women were all drawn into the war by their very location and their conviction that the struggle was a national cause that would help to liberate them. Their activities were extensive and varied. While about twenty percent of urban women joined the National Liberation Front (FLN), 77.9 percent of the total female population that participated in the war were rural women who joined the National Liberation Army (ALN). In the mountainous war fronts, women were nurses and first aid attendants treating the wounded. They also acted as weapon carriers, cooks, liaison agents, and fighters (moudjahidat). The moudjahidat threw bombs at civilian targets or attacked policemen and collaborators or traitors. They also did fund-raising, performed liaison work, collected food and medical supplies, and purchased weapons. Women provided an underground network of sanctuaries, worked in intelligence, and served as guides. They provided moral support to the fighters and resisters and took care of families and children left behind by those at the front, in prison, or in detention camps. As Marnia Lazreg describes it, their militancy was built upon a tradition dating back to the heroic period of Islamic history when women fought alongside men and was sustained by the mem-

34. Judith Van Allen, "African Women, Modernization, and National Liberation," in Women in the World: A Comparative Study, ed. Lynne B. Iglitzin and Ruth Ross (Santa Barbara: Clio Books, 1976), 46, 48–50.

ory of the first forty years of colonial rule and women's marginalization by a social order that used them as the cornerstone of merciless ideological warfare.[35] Algerian women were not only fighting to liberate their country from French colonial rule, but also to free themselves of certain cultural and religious constraints
that undermined their status in society.

The African Party of Independence for Guinea and Cape Verde (PAIGC)
pushed out the Portuguese in 1974 after fighting a guerrilla war for eleven and
half years (1963–1974) under Amilcar Cabral. Many women, like Bwetna, joined
PAIGC before their husbands and helped to mobilize them and convince them of
the need to join the struggle against the Portuguese. Guerrilla camps were established in the forest filled with men and women who had come from the villages;
some trained as guerrilla fighters, others carried out supporting tasks. Women organized the cooking and transport of food to those who were in the forest, passing through dangerous terrain. The women in the villages felt responsible for providing the guerrillas with food and other supplies. Many women were shot for
refusing to cooperate with the Portuguese. Many defied them at the cost of their
lives. Women gathered information on the movements of Portuguese troops.
Some were trained to fight. Women were potentially a formidable revolutionary
force. It was the women who were the easiest to mobilize, and their participation
in the struggle was rewarded. At least two of the five member-elected council,
both at the village sector and the regional level, had to be women. Some councils
had more than two female members; one council, for example, had four. Some
councils had female presidents or vice presidents. Women came out en masse and
participated actively in the liberation struggle because, as Stephanie Urdang puts
it, they knew they were fighting "two colonialisms."[36]

Women were very much involved in the Mau Mau rebellion in Kenya. Mau
Mau was a revolt by African peasants against the economic, political, and cultural conditions imposed on them by the British colonial regime. It was an armed
expression of the African nationalist movement in Kenya. War broke out on October 20, 1952 between the British and the Mau Mau freedom fighters. Women
were active in every aspect of the Mau Mau movement and performed tasks vital
for the continuance of the struggle. Women acted as "gangs" in the forests and as
participants in the rural network, providing information and supplies. The Land
and Freedom Army sought out women to act as spies, scouts, messengers, and as
couriers for food and armaments, because they were less closely watched and had
greater freedom of movement than men. It was reported that a group of 220
women in Nairobi was responsible for delivering guns, ammunition, and food to
the Mountain Kenya forest fighters. They also secured information about government strategies. One Wamuju Muceri was assigned to discern the best time and
method of staging the escape of certain Mau Mau prisoners from Nairobi Prison,
and she executed this task successfully. Mohamed Mathu successfully organized a
three-day boycott of the camp food in Embakasi Detension Camp in 1954 by

---

35. Marnia Lazreg, *The Eloquence of Silence: Algerian Women in Question* (New York:
Routledge, 1994). See also David C. Gordon, *Women of Algeria: An Essay on Change*, Harvard Middle Eastern Monograph Series, 19 (Cambridge, MA: Harvard University Press,
1968); and Frantz Fanon, *Studies in Dying Colonialism* (New York: Monthly Review Press,
1965).

36. Urdang, *Fighting Two Colonialisms*.

passing notes from prison to prison via the female detainees who collected eating utensils after each meal. Women frequently hid warriors in their huts for long periods of time. Women were also valued as seducers of the enemy. Prior to the Emergency, they used sexual favors and bribes to win government officials and others to the side of the Mau Mau movement. The home guard recruited women left on the reserves as warriors and guards. In the forest, women were responsible for cooking and cleaning, hauling water, and knitting sweaters. They carried baggage whenever the forest units changed camps. They cared for the wounded in makeshift hospitals.

Women's massive participation in Mau Mau contributed to the psychological and military successes of the movement. They served as seers, blessing and cleansing the warriors. They determined propitious times and places for raids. The women seers helped maintain the morale of the forest fighters by sanctioning the fighters' actions. One woman seer purified over one hundred fighters in a traditional ceremony. Women performed crucial roles in oath-taking ceremonies that bonded the fighters and the other Mau Mau participants in a common cause. Wives persuaded their husbands to take the oath and were very militant. In fact, women were described as "the eyes and ears of Mau Mau."[37] They recruited for Mau Mau. Women in the reserves organized themselves into Mau Mau support groups for the regular provision of the supplies essential for sustained resistance. Perhaps the most crucial area of women's involvement in Mau Mau was in helping maintain the supply line of the organization. The rebellion could not have lasted for seven years without the information, food, clothing items, medicine, and guns that flowed from the towns and reserves into the forest. The government's forced "villagization" program was instrumental in the eventual military defeat of the Mau Mau revolt, because it cut off the forest fighters from their support in the reserves. This attests to the central role of women from the reserves in the struggle.

A few women took part in actual combat as forest fighters. Some of them even attained high ranks in the force. For example, reference has been made to one Wanjiru Wambogo as a female colonel and to one Wanguiwa Gikuyi as a female *askaris* (soldiers or freedom fighters) captured while fighting.

Women, like men, were captured, tortured, and incarcerated in detention camps and jails and forced into barbed wire-enclosed villages during the Mau Mau Emergency. They were beaten and sexually molested by tribal retainers. Their activities carried the same penalty as those of the forest fighters. For example, beginning in 1953, possessing arms and ammunition, providing supplies, and consorting with armed men were offenses punishable by death. One Miriam Muthoni was said to have been caught with a pistol and sentenced to death; though this was later commuted, she remained in detention as late as 1960. Of the eighty-four Mau Mau loyalists killed in the Lari massacre of March 26, 1953, two-thirds were women. At the end of the Emergency in 1956, of 27,841 Kikuyu in detention camps, 3,103 were women. In fact, Kamiti prison was reserved for "hard core" Mau Mau women, some of whom were not released until 1960. Women's roles in Mau Mau, therefore, were as multifaceted as the revolt itself.[38]

---

37. Presley, "The Mau Mau Rebellion," 508 quoting a British colonial official.

38. For more information, see Maloba, *Mau Mau and Kenya*; Likimani, *Passbook Number F. 47927*; Cora Ann Presley, *Kikuyu Women, The Mau Mau Rebellion, and Social*

Women's roles in the antiapartheid movement were so vital that without them, as Nancy Van Vuuren asserts, "the movement would have been but a shell."[39] Without women, there would have been no mass movement. Women protested against the apartheid regime through their numerous organizations, such as the African National Congress Women's League, the Women Leaders of the Colored and Indian Communities, the Federation of South African Women, Black Sash, the Women of the South African Institute of Race Relations, and the Women of the Congress of Democrats and the Communist Party. Black Sash, for example, was a multiracial organization of women that opposed the apartheid laws. It stands as an important example of how South African women found ways to resist the dominant political culture. South African women resisted by initiating protests, often joining men in opposing repressive conditions. Thus, while the official, recognized leadership of the antiapartheid movement was male, the unofficial leadership was female.

Identifiable Nationalist Heroines

There are thousands and even millions of nationalist heroines, both identifiable and non-identifiable, whose commitment to the challenge of decolonization processes contributed to the achievement of independence by various African states. A few of the more powerful of them are discussed here.

Empress Taytu (Taitou), wife of Emperor Menelik II (1844–1913) of Ethiopia, played a pivotal role in Ethiopia's wars of resistance against Italy. She was unusually well educated, in Ge'ez and Amharic. She was an influential and powerful woman who was likened to Catherine the Great of Russia or Christiana of Sweden. Through her uncompromising attitude toward the Wuchale Treaty, which would have recognized the political domination of Ethiopia by Italy, Taytu, using insulting words, persuaded Menelik to reject the treaty and go to war against Italy. She also took to the battlefield against Italian troops. Taytu and other Ethiopian women made remarkable contributions that facilitated the victory of their country over Italy at the Battle of Adowa in 1896. This was a decisive victory, securing the independence of Ethiopia from European colonialism until 1935, when Italy invaded the country.

Mary Muthoni Nyanjiru is remembered for her role in the Harry Thuku uprising in Kenya in 1922. Thuku was arrested and imprisoned because of his campaigns against the colonial government's pass law (*kipande*), the forced labor of women and girls, the hut and poll taxes, and poor wages. On March 16, 1922, about eight thousand men and women gathered at the prison in Nairobi demand-

---

Change in Kenya (Boulder, CO.: Westview Press, 1992); Presley, "Kikuyu Women in "The Mau Mau' Rebellion;" Presley, "The Mau Mau Rebellion, Kikuyu Women;" Presley, "Kikuyu Women, Culture, and Nationalist Movement;" Santilli, "Kikuyu Women in the Mau Mau Revolt;" J. M. Kariuki, *Mau Mau Detainee* (London: Oxford University Press, 1975); Barnett and Njama, *Mau Mau from Within*; and Carl Rosberg and John Nottingham, *The Myth of Mau Mau,* (New York: Frederick A. Preager, 1966).

39. Nancy Van Vuuren, *Women against Apartheid: The Fight for Freedom in South Africa, 1920–1975* (Palo Alto, CA: R and E Research Associates, 1979).

ing Thuku's release. Disappointed with the way men were handling the situation, women began to curse and taunt them. Mary, acting as the spokesperson, pulled her dress over her shoulder and called the men cowards who should exchange their trousers for dresses. At this, hundreds of women trilled their *ngemi* (Kikuyu ululation) in approbation, and chaos ensued. The police responded by shooting at the crowd, killing twenty-eight people including Mary and wounding several others. Thuku was deported to Kismayu and some reforms were made to modify the labor policy and rescind the tax increases. Other powerful Kenyan women nationalists included Florence Wangui Kiguru, a woman leader as well as a member of the African Advisory Council, who fought over separate areas for Europeans, Asians, and Africans and ensured security in Nairobi and Rebecca Njeri, a woman leader of Mau Mau and a close associate of Jomo Kenyatta, who had a vitriolic tongue and incited all the hate she could against the Europeans.

Queen Mother Yaa Asantewaa of Asante mobilized the Asante regiments and led them into battle against the British, who had exiled King Prempeh I after the colonial conquest in 1900. She assembled almost fifty thousand Asante for a siege of Kumasi that lasted for two months. She is said to have spit on the British officer who arrested her. Though it was no match for British military power, Yaa Asantewaa's bravery remains an inspiration to Asante women and girls.

Madam Alimotu Pelewura was the leader of the Lagos Market Women Association (LMWA), an association with more than eight thousand members. Under her leadership, the LMWA recorded its period of greatest anticolonial resistance in Nigeria. She led the women in their 1908 protest against the imposition of a water rate; in 1932 over the rumor of the taxation of women; in the mid-1930s against the relocation of Ereko Market; in 1940 against the income tax ordinance; and in the 1940s against the food and price control instituted by A. P. Pullen. Pelewura was so popular among the women and such a threat to the colonial administration in Lagos that the colonial government offered to put her on its payroll in exchange for her enlisting the support of the market women for price control. She rejected the offer and even refused a salary of one hundred pounds a month. Due to the women's petitions and demonstration, the government deregulated the price of food items. Pelewura also participated in political and labor movements. She was, for example, one of the speakers at a public rally for Michael Imodu, the leader of the 1945 strikes. She mobilized the women to support Herbert Macaulay's party, the NNDP, both numerically and financially. Other powerful Nigerian women nationalists included Funmilayo Ransome-Kuti, Nwanyeruwa, and Margaret Ekpo. Nwanyeruwa, of the famous participants in Aba women's war of 1929 in Igboland, was the heroine of heroines. She played a major role in precipitating the revolt and emerged as a leading advocate of nonviolence during the demonstrations.

Huda Sharawi (1882–1947) of Egypt was educated at home in French, Turkish, and Arabic, and she was widely read. She organized Egyptian women to demonstrate during the 1919 agitation. She collected women's signatures for a petition to the British high commissioner condemning the shooting of demonstrators and exiling of Egyptian leaders. The petition read:

We the women of Egypt, mothers, sisters, and wives of those who have been the victims of British greed and exploitation, deplore the brutal, barbarous actions that have fallen upon the Egyptian nation. Egypt has com-

mitted no crime except to express her desire for freedom and independence.[40]

Nancy Steele was the most dynamic force in the National Congress of Sierra
Leone Women (the women's wing of the ruling All People's Congress), founded in
1968, and probably the most militant figure to emerge in the Sierra Leone nationalist movement and Sierra Leone politics. As an organizing secretary and co-
founder of the Women's Congress, Nancy demonstrated strong and determined
leadership which earned her the admiration of her many followers.

Djamila Boupacha and Djamila Bouhired are some of the identifiable heroines in the Algerian war of liberation against the French. Bouhired, as a liaison
agent of Saadi Yacef (one of the commanders of the liberation network), was
wounded, arrested, subjected to torture several times, and condemned to death
for bombing a restaurant and killing many French civilians. The death sentence
was commuted, but Bouhired remained in prison from 1958 until the end of the
revolution. She was named by *El-Moudjahid* (an organ of the FLN) as the best-
known Algerian woman concerned with the Algerian revolution. Her name became a household word. Boupacha, a French-educated woman, was accused of
throwing a bomb at a café near the University of Algiers. She was tortured with
electric shocks, cigarette burns, kicks, and, most humiliating of all, she was penetrated with the neck of a bottle. She remained in prison until 1962. Boupacha was
a resolute and insistent militant who never denied her allegiance to the FLN. She
became an international figure, with her picture and stories of her deeds spread
over popular magazines and newspapers.

A number of women attained prominence at the head of resistance movements in South Africa. Some of them were Manye Maxeke, Molly Wolton, Zainurissa (Cissie) Gool, Josie Mpama, Florence Matomela, Mary Mafekeng, Liz
Abrahams, and Frances Baard. Manye Maxeke was the head of the ANC Bantu
Women's Organization. She was one of the organizers of the 1913 anti-pass
demonstrations in the Orange Free State. She was also one of the original
founders and one of the three leaders of the ANC in the 1920s. She led demonstrations in Johannesburg in the first half of the 1920s. She campaigned to have
women replace men as domestic workers and led delegations to meet with Prime
Minister Botha. She opened an employment office for women. Molly Wolton was
one of the three leaders of the Communist Party in the early 1930s who organized
the Unemployment Workers Union in 1931 and held meetings, multiracial
marches, and demonstrations throughout 1931 and 1932. She was arrested while
telling women to demand equal pay for equal work in factories and on farms and
to demand the abolition of all pass laws for men and women. Zainurissa Gool
spoke at a 1931 rally at Cape Town in support of the extension of the franchise to
colored and African women. She was elected as the first president of the National
Liberation League in 1937. She was also elected president of the Non-European
United Front, which was founded in 1938 and demanded the repeal of all racial
laws. Gool was one of the two female members of the reformed Political Bureau
of the Communist Party. Josie Mpama was the first African woman leader in the
Communist Party. Florence Matomela was a treason trial defendant who helped

---

40. Elizabeth Fernea and B. Q. Bezirgan, eds., *Middle Eastern Muslim Women Speak*
(Austin, TX: Texas University Press, 1977), 193–196.

revive the ANC Women's League in the Eastern Cape. She was also the leader of the Food and Canning Workers' Union in the Eastern Cape and was held in solitary confinement in 1963. Mary Mafekeng, Liz Abrahams, and Frances Baard rose to responsible positions in the Federation of South African Women, the organization that led the massive women's anti-pass demonstrations in the 1950s.[41]

Conclusion

Women were a formidable force in Africa's nationalist movements. Their anticolonial activities and nationalist struggles were linked to a number of issues such as cultural survival, judicial control, land ownership, education, and political and economic control. Through their concerted resistance to colonial government policies that affected them directly or indirectly, African women proved very effective in achieving results. An important aspect of the women's solidarity lies in the dictum that "in unity lies strength." African women were the unofficial leaders of African nationalism. Unfortunately, women's contributions to Africa's independence have not been adequately acknowledged or rewarded by heads of government in postcolonial Africa.

Review Questions

1. In what ways did the colonial situation in Africa affect African women?
2. To what extent is it correct to refer to African women as cultural nationalists and crusaders for African values and heritage?
3. How did women voice their protests against low wages, labor discrimination, and poor working conditions in colonial Africa?
4. Discuss the role of African women in political protests and armed struggles during the colonial period.

---

41. For more information on nationalist heroines in Africa, see Johnson-Odim and Mba, *For Women and the Nation*; Felix K. Ekechi, "Historical Women in the Fight for Liberation," in James and Etim, *The Feminization of development Processes in Africa*, 95–112; Susan Geiger, "Tanganyikan Nationalism as Women's Work': Life Histories, Collective Biography and Changing Historiography," *Journal of African History* 37 (1996): 465–478; Jacklyn Cock, *Women and War in South Africa* (Cleveland, OH: The Pilgrim Press, 1993); Cherryl Walker, *Women and Resistance in South Africa*, 2nd ed. (New York: Monthly Review, 1992); Awe, *Nigerian Women*; Stella A. Effah-Attoe and S.O. Jaja, *Margaret Ekpo: Lioness in Nigerian Politics* (Abeokuta: ALF Publications, 1993); T. Cleaver and Marion Wallace, *Namibia: Women in War* (London: Zed Books, 1990); Prouty, *Empress Taytu*; Kwame Arhin, "The Role of Akan Women" in *Female and Male in West Africa*, ed. Christine Oppong (London: Allen & Unwin, 1983), 91–98; Cheryl Johnson, "Madam Alimotu Pelewura and the Lagos Market Women," in *Tarikh* 7, 1c(1981): 1–10; Van Vuuren, *Women against Apartheid*; Filomina Chioma Steady, *Female Power in African Politics: The National Congress of Sierra Leon,* Munger Africana Library Notes, no. 31 (CA: California Institute of Technology, 1975); and Hilda Bernstein, *For Their Triumph and for Their Tears: Conditions and Resistance of Women in Apartheid South Africa* (Cambridge, MA: Internal Defence and Aid Fund, 1975).

5. Write short notes on any three of the major nationalist heroines discussed in the text.

Additional Reading

Berger, I. and E. White. *Women in Sub-Saharan Africa*. Bloomington: Indiana University Press, 1999.

Mba, Nina. *Nigerian Women Mobilized: Women's Political Activity in Southern Nigeria, 1900–65*. Berkeley: University of California Press, 1982.

Presley, C. A. *Kikuyu Women, The Mau Mau Rebellion, and Social Change in Kenya*. Boulder, Westview Press, 1992.

Prouty, Chris. *Empress Taytu and Menelik II: Ethiopia, 1883–1910*. London: Ravens Educational and Development Services, 1986.

Urdang, Stephanie. *Fighting Two Colonialisms: Women in Guinea-Bissau*. New York: Monthly Review Press, 1979.

Walker, C. *Women and Resistance in South Africa*. 2nd ed. New York: Monthly Review Press, 1992.

Chapter 7

African Economies in the Years of Decolonization

G. Ugo Nwokeji

This chapter describes the economies of the African countries that underwent decolonization from the 1940s through the 1960s. Its organizing principle is economic change. Although political developments were far more dramatic than economic changes, in comparison to the colonial period, the years of decolonization were a period of boom and growth. These developments took shape in the context of rapid political developments, environmental factors, sweeping global trends, and changing colonial policies. The controlled marketing of commodities, development planning, import substitution industrialization, and Africanization chiefly characterized the economy during this period. Industry, commerce, agriculture, and transport are examined in some detail.

* * *

Impact of Decolonization on African Economies

From the long-run historical perspective, the half-century or so of African decolonization is a fleeting moment in the African economic experience. However, the period challenges us with complexity and chronological disjuncture. Decolonization spanned the late 1940s through the 1950s in most countries in East, West, and Central Africa, but was only experienced in much of southern Africa in the 1960s through the 1990s. This chapter deals with the continent apart from Southern Africa. Effectively, therefore, the colonial systems under consideration are those of Britain and France. The organizing principle of this account is economic change.

Analyses of the colonial economy usually take one of three approaches. One presents the essential economic data and analyzes processes of the pre-decolonization period without offering similar data and analysis for the decolonization era, or otherwise fails to discuss the data in the context of decolonization. The other approach focuses on the decolonization period, but rather than analyze economic indicators, it uses anecdotal evidence to establish the roots of neocolonialism. Thus, neither approach provides much essential data on, or analysis of, the economy during decolonization. A third approach provides such data but avows that decolonization did not mark a discontinuity in the economic experience enough to warrant serious analysis.[1] Yet, economic historical analysis grounded in the context of decolonization is necessary for a clearer understanding of the era itself and the subsequent economic development of the continent.[2]

The Context of Decolonization

Analysis must begin with an outline of the context of decolonization. One defining element of the period was the nature of the stakes. Although explicit debate about the economy was rare among contemporaries, decolonization was essentially an intense discourse about economic control. The imperial powers had vested interests in the colonial economy and would not voluntarily relinquish them. This situation was anticipated by Adam Smith nearly two hundred years before with respect to the British colonies in the Americas. "To propose that Great Britain should voluntarily give up all authority over her colonies...would be to propose such a measure as never was and never will be adopted, by any nation in the world."[3] The Europeans had to leave Africa long before they had expected to leave. The stage for struggle was set in the timing of decolonization.

The colonial powers emerged from World War II with a severe economic crisis, and they envisaged the colonies as the lynchpins of their postwar economic recovery and development. Colonies were indeed extremely useful, and this was not a convenient period for the willing "transfer of power" to colonial peoples. Pressures from elsewhere—internationally and within the colonies—forced the colonial powers to reassess their African enterprise, but once the course of decolonization had been embarked upon, colonial powers focused on how best to salvage, protect, and perpetuate their economic interests—the primary purpose of colonialism. They were up against an ambitious and often self-serving African political elite, which had come to see political control as the avenue to economic power. At its barest essentials, "decolonization" thus represented negotiations about control of the postcolonial political economy.

A second defining feature of the decolonization era was economic growth. The purchasing power of the populace grew markedly. Peasants sold more produce for better prices on the world market. Expanding cities, import substitution industrialization, service industries, transport, and commercial infrastructure boosted the populations of wage-laborers and blue-collar and clerical workers. Improving educational opportunities increased the numbers of the white collar

---

1. The first approach is represented by Claude Ake, *A Political Economy of Africa*, Ibadan, Longman, 1981; John Sender and Sheila Smith, *The Development of Capitalism in Africa*, London, Methuen, 1986; the second by Segun Osoba, "Transition to Neo-Colonialism" in *Britain and Nigeria: Exploitation or Development?*, ed Toyin Falola, London, Zed, 1987; and the third by Ralph Austen, *African Economic History*, London, James Currey, 1987.

2. Exceptions include D.K. Fieldhouse, *Black Africa 1945–80: Economic Reconstruction and Arrested Development*, Allen and Unwin, London, 1986; Peter Kilby, "Manufacturing in Colonial Africa," in *Colonialism in Africa, Volume 4. The Economics of Colonialism*, eds. P. Duigan and L.H. Gann Cambridge, University Press, 1975.

3. Adam Smith, *Wealth of Nations Vol. 2*, New York, The Modern Library,1966, 112–3.

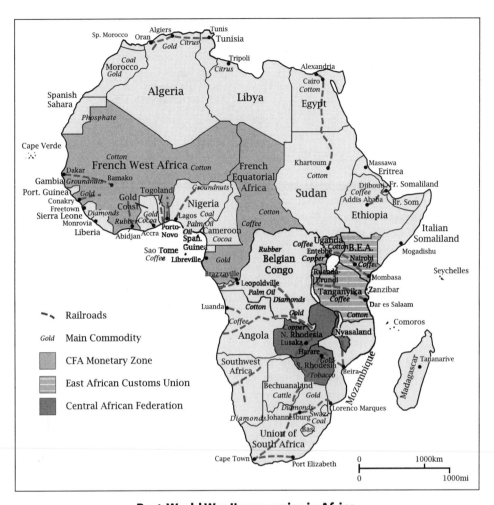

Post-World War II economies in Africa.

population as well. The <u>political elite</u> gained concessions, receiving a boost from an Africanization policy that pursued the infusion of African personnel into the private and public sectors and their increasing control of state institutions.

One hallmark of African economies in the era of decolonization was development planning. The imperial powers were more willing than ever to invest in the colonies. The British established the Colonial Development and Welfare (CDW) program in 1939 and the French launched the Fonds d'Investiment pour le Développment Economique et Social (FIDES) in 1946, the former as a ten-year plan. The era of decolonization saw the colonial powers allotting unprecedented sums of money to development expenditure, much of it now in the form of outright grants as opposed to the earlier loans. The stated purpose of development planning was colonial self-sufficiency and the pursuit of welfare programs. The development plans' essential components were, however, import substitution industrialization and especially the development of primary commodity production. The aid component of the programs did not really take off until the 1950s, however. The development plans aimed to make the colonies more profitable to their colonizers as hard currency earners and producers of consumer goods, which the colonizers would have had to buy on the international market in foreign exchange. This was the purpose of the British Colonial Development Corporation (CDC), established in 1947. The programs were based on reformist ideas informed by the desire to impose European value systems on African attitudes toward work and capital.[4]

The French invested much more than the British, about 350 billion francs in their sub-Saharan African colonies between 1947 and 1955. Between 1946 and 1964, French public investment in Africa amounted to an estimated eight billion U.S. dollars, many times that of Britain. Although much of this money returned to France through French experts' salaries, the massive investment indicated the importance of the colonies to France during decolonization. Britain, on the other hand, took some £140 million from the colonies between 1945 and 1951 under the CDW program while investing only forty million pounds.[5] Still, if France benefited less from its colonial imports than Britain, French manufacturers, like their British counterparts, found protected markets in the colonies.

The development and welfare programs were thus meant to tie African countries to the metropolises. In 1951, the French narrowed the objective of FIDES and explicitly devoted the fund to increasing "agricultural production in the perspective of a European community." The fund, therefore, effectively became the counterpart of the British Overseas Food Corporation (OFC) established in 1948, with an investment of some 270 billion francs between 1947 and 1952. The OFC and the CDC were to initiate and finance productive efforts, but they concentrated on primary production and mostly on strategic commodities. Summarizing his ministry's achievements at the end of 1948, the British colonial secretary, Arthur Creech Jones, "put the 'export drive' first, 'dollar earnings' second, and social programs in Africa and the West Indies thirteenth."[6]

Decolonization was marked by some expansion but no major initiatives or restructuring. Production levels rose due to a greater exploitation of labor (quantitative improvement), but not productivity, which reflects efficiency levels (qualitative improvement). The ability of African producers to capitalize on a worldwide boom in these years ensured some economic growth, but development, that is, improvement in the quality of life, remained elusive. The following outline of sectorial activities shows that the decolonization-era African economies did not undergo transformation.

Industry

Industrialization during the earlier colonial period concentrated on such areas as electric power generation, soft drink plants, soap, furniture, and cigarette factories, brickworks, printing presses, oil mills, saw mills, flour mills, textile mills, and breweries, in different combinations in various colonies. During

---

4. Fred Cooper, *Decolonization and African Society: The Labor Question in French and British Africa*, Cambridge, Cambridge University Press, 1996, 176–7.

5. For the French, see Richard Joseph, "The Gaullist Legacy: Patterns of French Neocolonialism," *Review of African Political Economy*, no. 6, 1976, 6; and for the British, see Fieldhouse, *Black Africa*, 6.

6. This information in this paragraph is taken from Cooper, 120, 204–6.

decolonization, the industries producing these items slowly expanded and proliferated, and others emerged that provided for a wider range of consumer and
some capital goods, such as rubber goods, metal doors, confectionery, beverages,
concrete and precast concrete, paints, shoes, stationery, tiles, plywood, and plas-
tics. There were also bicycle and truck assembly plants. No one colony had industries producing all these items. Gains were quite modest. Small power-driven
rice mills proliferated in the Gold Coast in the 1940s.[7] Sales of soap manufactured in Unilever's factory in Lagos rose from 4,400 tons in 1937 to 10,643 in
1946, marking the beginning of a massive expansion that characterized the era
of decolonization.[8] Manufacturing generally remained small-scale in the
colonies.

Manufacturing

Two reasons account for this. The first is that the big trading companies,
which dominated the economies of colonial West Africa especially, had little interest in engaging in industrial ventures. Although the largest of them, the British
United Africa Company (UAC), had owned a Lagos soap factory since 1923 and
had started or inherited one small manufacturing plant or another since 1939, in
the Gold Coast, Kenya, and especially Nigeria, it either discontinued manufacturing in short order or assumed a minority role and transferred responsibility to
other principals. It also drafted plans for establishing manufacturing enterprises,
which, apart from the Lagos brewery that came into existence in 1949, generally
failed to materialize.[9] Peter Kilby has observed that European trading firms had
no incentive to engage in manufacturing and were powerful enough to oppose it.
Although the firms abandoned this strategy in the 1950s, due to increasing competition in the import market, manufacturing accounted for less than two percent
of national income in the Gold Coast and Nigeria, the two biggest and richest
countries of British West Africa, as late as 1957.[10]

One reason for this is that industrialization before and during decolonization
was shaped more by governmental policy than by market forces. For example, an
Industrial Management Board was established in Kenya during World War II to
promote manufacturing and extend its range. East African Industries Limited was
established at the end of the war to produce detergents, soap, and margarine.
Other firms set up subsidiaries, and European and Asian businessmen started
companies, especially in the Nairobi area. The Industrial Advisory Council,
founded by the British in 1948 to license firms in scheduled industries, was largely
ineffective. There was only a small number of scheduled industries to start with.
Further, "there was no overall plan or direction of the location of industry, [and]
excess capacity resulted in some sectors, including paper, cement and oil refin-
ing."[11] This is not surprising. The colonial state that shaped African industrializa-

---

7. Sender and Smith, *Development of Capitalism*, 11.
8. Fieldhouse, *Black Africa*, 10.
9. Fieldhouse, *Merchant Capital and Economic Decolonization: The United Africa
Company 1929–1987*, Oxford, Oxford University Press, 1994, 299–307.
10. Kilby, "Manufacturing."
11. Peter Lionel Wickens, Cape Town, Oxford University Press, 189, 213.

tion was, in fact, averse to it. Colonial officers espoused their primary responsibility in terms of

> advancing African welfare, that is, with raising money incomes and providing more medical facilities, schools and roads. It was their judgement that...this could best be brought about by encouraging African producers to grow crops for sale to the export market.

Besides, manufacturing entailed a net loss in the public revenue that would otherwise accrue from tariffs on imports.[12] If state intervention failed to facilitate significant development in the manufacturing sector, it also failed to achieve equitable allocation of industries throughout the colonies. The distribution of industrial manufactures was extremely uneven among and within colonies and regions. Such towns and cities as Lagos, Dakar, Nairobi, and Abidjan dominated the industrial sector.

Import Substitution

The pace of import substitution industrialization accelerated during the 1950s with the attainment of self-government. Besides simply appeasing African politicians, some European trading firms, such as the UAC and the Société Commerciale de l'Ouest Africain (SCOA), saw economic sense in getting involved in manufacturing at this juncture. They restructured their operations by entering manufacturing and construction in response to increasing competition in the import trade. Between 1954 and 1955 and 1960 and 1961, the proportion of SCOA's turnover from construction increased from 11.5 percent to twenty-three percent and that from technical and industrial activities from three percent to ten percent. Another reason for the expansion of import-substitution industrialization was the interest of the indigenous political leaders in achieving rapid industrialization. European firms rushed to establish import-substitution industries before the nationalists did, even when profit prospects were slim.[13] By the end of the colonial period, the mass market for such consumer goods as bicycles, radio sets, soap, knives, needles and thread, buttons, kettles, mirrors, electrical supplies, folding chairs, enamelware, construction materials, matches, and lanterns were "beginning to be supplied by a large-scale, modern domestic industry." However, many consumer goods and the vast majority of capital goods continued to be imported.[14] In the final analysis, industrialization remained focused on the most rudimentary consumer products. Rather than lead to true industrialization, import-substitution industrialization increased the technological dependence of African countries on Western countries more than ever before. Since the African economies were producers of primary products (basically raw materials), the absence of an industrial base precluded these countries' ability to serve as significant markets for one another's commodities. Structural impediments aside, colonial trade policy generally discouraged the growth of international trade among African countries and encouraged the production of primary commodities for export.

---

12. Kilby, 492.
13. Fieldhouse, *Black Africa*, 10-1, 19.
14. Sender and Smith, *Development of Capitalism*, 12, 13.

Commerce

The structural integration of the colonies into the economies of their former colonizers ensured that colonial commerce during decolonization continued to be biased toward the metropolises. This situation resulted from the imperial powers' neo-mercantilist policies that entailed a measured application of tariffs and quotas and from their control of monetary systems. Specifically, the imperial powers restricted the export to the colonies of metropolitan manufactures that would earn foreign exchange elsewhere, built credits from marketing board surpluses, established currency pools to channel all colonial dollar earnings to the metropolises, and bulk-purchased commodities to keep prices down in the metropolitan markets. These measures were most strictly applied during World War II and continued into the decolonization years as the imperial powers relied on the colonies for recovery.

Trade in Primary Products

Forecasts that immediate postwar shortfalls in world primary product supply were temporary and manageable were too optimistic. They did not address the great increase in the consumption of primary products, especially by the U.S., which developed additional demands for strategic stockpiles. Thus, the U.S. was taking in an increasing share of a reduced general supply, despite increasing prices. This development further drove up prices by an average of sixty percent and tilted the terms of trade in favor of primary producers until 1948, when a downward spiral in demand and prices set in for the next seven years. Yet the outbreak of the Korean War in the mid-1950s started another cycle of boom. By the end of 1952, the boom had cooled, and prices did not revert to pre-Korean War levels for much of the remainder of the decade.[15]

Colonial mercantilism ensured that the increasing exportation of primary products meant growing demand for metropolitan manufactures. France supplied eighty percent of imports into black Africa and Algeria and absorbed seventy-five percent of their exports by 1949.[16] Imports from France rose one hundred percent between 1949 and 1955, and exports to the country rose by 115 percent during the same period. In 1959, the French colonies received the following products as percentages of total French exports: ninety-five percent vegetable oils, 85.5 percent sugar, 83.6 percent cotton textiles, 78.8 percent clothing, and 92.2 percent of soap. These goods did not come from France's more competitive industries, but the French could not sell them elsewhere; they were selling the goods, along with some capital goods, to the colonies at higher prices than the colonies could have bought them elsewhere.[17] This practice ensured that France, rather than the colonies, was the main beneficiary of the commodity boom. To check the foreign exchange crisis that began during World War II, Britain and France ceased the

---

15. J.W.F. Rowe, *Primary Commodities in International Trade*, Cambridge, Cambridge University Press, 1965, 96–98, 104–6.

16. Joseph, "Gaulist Legacy."

17. Fieldhouse, *Black Africa*, 6, 13, 15.

free conversion of their currencies into others until the early 1950s. Britain required its colonies to cover sterling issues with one hundred percent reserve deposits in London. Rather than putting affected colonial earnings to colonial use,
Britain used them to shore up the sterling. The French adopted a more liberal
monetary policy, establishing a single monetary zone for its Equatorial and West
African colonies, the Coloniale françaises d'Afrique (CFA) franc, which could be
freely exchanged with the differently valued metropolitan French franc. This measure promoted inter-African trade within the French zone, but trade between the
countries in this zone and with other countries was another matter. Trade between French Cameroon and Sierra Leone, for instance, would take a back seat to
trade between Cameroon and France on the one hand and trade between Sierra
Leone and the United Kingdom on the other. At any rate, such inter-African trade
followed the rules that governed the trade between the imperial powers.

One other way in which Britain exercised control over colonial trade was
through the bulk-purchasing of export commodities via produce-marketing boards.
The system started as a way of cushioning Britain during World War II. The colonial authorities designated certain organizations to buy export produce from
African producers below world market prices. In many colonies, trading firms
played this role, but in Kenya, it was the Farmers Association, the organ of white
farmers, which received full prices for its members' produce but paid lower prices
to African farmers. The ostensible purpose of the marketing boards was to stabilize
and guarantee producer prices and to pressure farmers to produce food. The main
beneficiary was, however, the colonial empire. Marketing boards replaced middlemen, but they did not offer the competitive environment that middlemen provided.
They thus undermined producers' control of their marketing options. The system
controlled inflation and made the price difference between producer and world
prices available to the colonial power as war loans. Thus, African producers were
forced to pay a part of Britain's deficit in its trade with the U.S. The system prevented producers from meeting increasing taxation demands and prices for imported goods. Although the method guaranteed and stabilized returns for African
producers, they received only a small portion of the world market value of their
products. The West African Produce Control Board, which replaced the West
African Cocoa Control Board in 1942, was an instant success for Britain, making a
profit of $8.7 million between 1941 and 1942 in spite of unfavorable wartime ship-
ping and regulatory conditions. The British government retained the system after
the war to serve the same purpose during Britain's postwar recovery. Separate commodity boards were established in Britain's West African colonies in 1947. By this
time, the role of the marketing board as "a ready-made instrument for taxing farmers, enriching [indigenous politicians] and financing their political activities," observed by Gavin Williams in the Nigerian case, was also possible elsewhere.[18]

The French system was different, but it was based on neo-mercantilist principles similar to those that marked the British system of bulk-purchasing. Certain
French consumers of African produce did enter into bulk-purchasing arrangements with African producers, and French colonial goods enjoyed tariff preferences in the French metropolitan market, but the thrust of French official policy

---

18. Gavin Williams, "Marketing without and with Marketing Boards: The Origins of
State Marketing Boards in Nigeria," *Review of African Political Economy* (no. 34, 1985),
4–15.

resided in allocating to international buyers African commodities equal in value to French imports from such buyers. The French then reimbursed the colonies in francs or French manufactured goods. In this way, the French avoided paying foreign exchange for France's imports. An essential difference between the British and French systems was that African consumers bore the entire cost in the British system, while African and French consumers shared the cost in the French system. In both systems, however, bulk purchase ensured the metropolis access to the primary produce of its colonies while being shielded from the severe and persistent American competition. America had access only to the portion that the metropolises made available to the world market. African primary producers could not, therefore, take full advantage of the economic boom.

The 1950s were even worse than the 1940s for African producers. Despite dramatic increases in exports induced by the Korean War from 1950 to 1951, the prices of African exports were in steady decline from the mid-1950s onward. Africa shared with other developing regions a trade gap estimated at $1200 million.[19] These developments, along with political pressures from the U.S. and African nationalists, forced the imperial powers to reassess the future of their African colonies. Beginning in 1952, when the boom occasioned by the Korean War had waned and the imperial countries were on the path to postwar recovery, there were small-scale attempts to relax restrictive trade policies, encourage inter-African trade, and diversify colonial economies. The Central African Federation (of Northern and Southern Rhodesia and Nyasaland) provided for the free movement of persons and capital goods and introduced a common tariff, a common currency, and common economic policies. The Federation fostered an intra-regional trade that accounted for a quarter of all trade of the region. The East African customs union involving Kenya, Tanganyika, Uganda, and Zanzibar provided for a common tariff and common currency. The performance of these trade areas was extremely uneven. In the East African union, Kenya (especially the sectors dominated by whites) benefitted most, while Tanganyika benefited least. In the Central African Federation, Southern Rhodesia was the main beneficiary. Northern Rhodesia benefited least, because the Federation did little more than facilitate a long-established movement of labor and did not significantly affect the market due to poverty levels and Northern Rhodesia's remoteness from the centers of production. This union appears to have been counterproductive, for it accounted for only eight percent of total trade, even less than the African level during the 1950s, which, at ten percent, was already too low.[20]

Poor Diversification

Also unimpressive were attempts at diversifying colonial economies. One component of diversification was the promotion of import-substitution industrialization already discussed above; the other—attempts to diversify the export commodities—will be discussed under agriculture. Diversification did not only involve agricultural products. Liberia, Sierra Leone, Rhodesia, Nyasaland, and

19. J.A.C. Brown, "A Brief Survey of Prospects for African Exports of Agricultural Products" in *African Primary Products and International Trade,* ed I.G. Stewart and H.W. Ord, Edinburgh, University Press, 1964.

20. Wickens, 211-2.

French Equatorial Africa also exported mineral products. This phenomenon was most pronounced in Liberia, where diamonds and iron ore accounted for 42.2 percent of all exports between 1951 and 1956, and in Rhodesia and Nyasaland, where precious stones (principally copper) accounted for as much as 54.1 percent of all exports between 1950 and 1957.[21] The liberalization of imperial trade was faster in the British sphere, where trade between Britain and its colonies had fallen by a quarter in 1960 from its 1945 levels. By contrast, it had fallen only five percent in the French sphere.[22]

Foreign Domination

Any discussion of commerce during the decolonization era must consider how the European firms, which dominated commerce, responded to the prospect of African rule. There is a tendency among economic historians to see the firms as largely unconcerned with the prospect of decolonization, seamlessly adapting to the new situation by restructuring their operations. This interpretation emanates from the premise that independence posed no serious threat to European firms.[23] These firms did indeed make successful transitions and generally enjoyed the goodwill of African politicians who began to take political control in the 1950s. Still, European commercial firms did try, at least in British West Africa, to influence the other political actors, particularly colonial officials, during decolonization.[24] They pursued a public relations offensive aimed at the mass media and society at large. The firms under the umbrella of the Association of West African Merchants (AWAM) also employed a strong London lobby to pursue their case. They demanded increased representation in the legislature, special consultation in public policy formulation, and constitutional and extra-constitutional guarantees of institutionalized roles in the postindependence dispensation.

Officialdom insisted on a compromise that took the new realities of post-World War II politics into account and sought to make the European business lobby link its interests to those of the capitalist-oriented African nationalists rather than constitute a parallel political movement, as the lobby planned at one point. By early 1950, the colonial secret intelligence community had known for some time that "certain firms were indeed willing to keep a larger European staff than was commercially justifiable in order to permit their members to participate in the work of the legislature."[25] European businesses had become so deeply in-

---

21. These figures are from Ake, *Political Economy of Africa*, Table 3.4.
22. Wickens, 210.
23. For this view, see Austen, *African Economic History*, 211-6, and especially Fieldhouse, *Black Africa* and *Merchant Capital*.
24. For the Gold Coast, see S.E. Stockwell, "Political Strategies of British Business during Decolonization: The Case of the Gold Coast/Ghana, 1945–57," *Journal of Imperial and Commonwealth History*, 23, 2 (1995): 277–300, and for Nigeria, see G. Ugo Nwokeji, "An Abortive Attempt to 'Hijack' Decolonization: European Traders, Colonial Officers, and Nationalists in Nigeria," 23rd conference of the Canadian Association of African Studies, Peterborough, Ontario, Canada, May 1995; and A. Olukoju, "Anatomy of Business-Government Relations: Fiscal Policy and Mercantile Pressure Group Activity in Nigeria, 1916–1933," *African Studies Review*, 38, 1 (1995): 23–50.
25. PRO/CO 537/5789/30453/11 1950: See memo of a meeting with AWAM representatives.

volved in politics that the 1949 visit of UAC's managing director, Frank Samuel, to West Africa may have actually been intended to gauge the political situation and consult with British authorities, notwithstanding his ostensible intention of assessing the impact of swollen shoot disease in cocoa. That same year, the holder of the newly created office of chief public relations officer of the UAC visited the Colonial Office to inquire about the extent to which "the British commercial interests in West Africa would be consulted in regard to the forthcoming constitutional changes."[26] The European firms did not get all they wanted, but in Nigeria and, even more so, in the Gold Coast, they achieved greater representation in the legislatures during the 1950s.[27] One of the measures the European firms embraced in their effort to restructure was an accelerated Africanization of their staff, a process that the major firms had begun before the 1950s. The firms were, therefore, more politically aware and involved than is often claimed.

The commercial sector thus felt the tremors of decolonization. Developments in this sector show clearly that the colonial powers were no longer interested in keeping the colonies in their classic forms. In British West Africa, Britain intervened to check European business' attempts to hijack decolonization. The imperial powers were committed to decolonization for reasons broader than simple developments in the economic sector. Yet the result of colonial commercial policy was that the colonies' economies became more dependent than ever at the end of the colonial period. Africans were now more dependent on commodity exports and were consuming more foreign-made goods than ever before.

Agriculture

Although hardly mentioned in the decolonization discourse, agriculture continued to be the mainstay of the colonial economies. The imperial states promoted the production of primary commodities for export through tariffs and quotas and the allocation of the bulk of colonial capital flow to such production, which ensured that the capital was repatriated in the form of primary commodities sent to the metropolises.[28] For example, the British East African Agricultural and Forestry Research Organization was formed in 1948 to tap into CDW funds. It was a direct offshoot of the East African Agricultural Institute at Amani, Tanganyika, established in 1927. The organization's mandate was to undertake research in areas where longer-term work than provided by the various territories' departments of agriculture and forestry was necessary or were common to all the territories or where the pooling of highly specialized equipment and officers was necessary. The organization worked closely with the East African Veterinary Research Organization. Financed by the colonial governments of Kenya, Tanganyika, Uganda, and Zanzibar in conjunction with the British government through Colonial Development and Welfare funds, these organizations established laboratories, experimental farms, and plantations. The general policy of the

---

26. PRO/CO 537/4645/33539/231/1949: Gorsurch to the Nigerian Governor, 6 Aug. 1949.
27. The foregoing analysis is from Nwokeji, "Abortive Attempt."
28. Ake, *Political Economy of Africa*, 28.

Figure 7.1. Cattle market.

two organizations was decided by the East African Agricultural and Fisheries Research Council, with the aim of effecting centralized planning in the region.

Market forces also helped shape the agricultural sector. The sector experienced
great volatility during the period—two major booms in the years up to 1948 and
1950–1951 and slumps occasioned by an oversupply of commodities. Cocoa sold
for £430 a ton in 1954 but for only £209 in 1956; copper sold for £351 a ton in
1955 but only £197 in 1958; groundnuts sold for fifty-eight pounds a ton in 1956
but only sixty pounds in 1958; and cotton sold for fifty-three pence a pound in
1956 but only thirty-two pence in 1958.[29] In addition, some crops suffered attacks
by pests, although many of these attacks were localized and did not cause major
damage. The year 1947 was bad for cotton in Egypt and Sudan. Egyptian output
had fallen from 412,000 metric tons in 1940 to 300,000 metric tons. That of
Sudan fell from sixty-eight thousand metric tons in 1944 to forty thousand metric
tons. Output soon rebounded, however, with Egypt registering 400,000 metric
tons in 1948 and Sudan 100,000 metric tons in 1950.[30] The problem that arose
from swollen shoot disease in cocoa during the late 1940s was more widespread.
Inevitably, this disease affected the world cocoa supply and attracted the attention
of the colonial powers. The disease led to the outright destruction of affected trees,
and West African farmers resisted this in what amounted to anticolonial protests.

Importance of Agriculture

Notwithstanding these and other problems, agriculture remained the most
important sector of the economy, not only in providing foreign exchange but also

---

29. Arthur Hazlewood, *The Economy of Africa*, London, Oxford University Press,
1961, 16.
30. Wickens, 185.

Figure 7.2. Moving peanuts for export in Senegal. The economy was based on production for export.

in providing food for the population. It also employed the vast majority of Africans, despite a growing trend toward urbanization. The boom occasioned by the Korean crisis of the early 1950s varied by commodity. During the period, Africa supplied twenty-four percent of the world supply of oilseeds, a level never attained since. World consumption of sugar, which was produced by Mauritius, Mozambique, and Reunion, doubled during the 1950s as tea production in East Africa tripled. Simultaneously, Africa's share of the world coffee supply rose from seventeen percent to twenty-four percent, mainly at the expense of Latin America. French West Africa, the Congo, Ruanda-Urundi, Uganda, Kenya, and Ethiopia were the main beneficiaries. North Africa benefited from increased consumption of citrus fruits, and Côte d'Ivoire, Western Cameroon, Mozambique, Somalia and the Canary Islands from substantial increases in banana consumption. Liberia's export of rubber increased by two-thirds, and Côte d'Ivoire, Gabon, the Gold Coast, and Nigeria benefited from substantial increases in timber exports.[31] Yet farmers' handsome returns from the world market presented their own problems,

31. Brown, "Brief Survey," 3–6.

the most important of which was a disincentive to produce food crops for the growing urban populations. The colonial powers took measures to compel farmers to produce foodstuffs. This was one of the avowed functions of the marketing boards, which capped producer prices in British West Africa to discourage firms from concentrating wholly on producing export commodities.

Despite its impressive performance, agriculture remained narrowly based. This was in part a function of geography. The forest and secondary forest regions of West Africa produced palm products while the Sahel produced peanuts and leather and the highland savanna of East Africa produced coffee and cotton. Cocoa came mainly from the forest regions of the Gold Coast, Nigeria, Côte d'Ivoire, and Cameroon. The narrow agricultural base also resulted from the failure of the imperial powers to modernize agriculture sufficiently to overcome basic climatic problems. The export bases of African economies from that of Egypt, whose main export (raw cotton) accounted for eighty-five percent of the country's annual exports between 1950 and 1954, to that of Sierra Leone, whose most important export commodity (palm oil) accounted for only 34.5 percent of the country's annual exports between 1950 and 1957.

On the whole, the period of decolonization witnessed some diversification in the export sector. In 1938, wine accounted for as much as 48.9 percent of Algeria's total exports, and citrus fruits and iron ore for only 2.5 percent and 5.6 percent, respectively; but between 1950 and 1957, the value of wine had declined to 39.7 percent, while the values of citrus fruits and iron ore had increased to 5.6 percent and 6.8 percent, respectively. Earnings were spread fairly evenly among Nigeria's major exports in 1956–1958; palm oil and palm kernels accounted for £33,393,000, groundnuts (including palm oil and cake) for £30,267,000, and cocoa for £25,605,000. Even in the Gold Coast, where cocoa alone had accounted for eighty percent of export earnings in 1939, the share of this commodity in all exports had fallen to 67.9 percent between 1950 and 1954. The diversification trend can quite easily be overemphasized, because in many cases certain export crops merely replaced others, resulting in changes in the composition of export commodities rather than diversification.[32]

Problems

Despite the importance and expansion of agriculture during decolonization, the economic sector did not witness any significant structural developments. The grandiose schemes of the CDW, FIDES, and allied programs failed monumentally due to poorly understood environmental factors and the failure of African resettlement schemes.[33] The most dramatic scheme was the French Office du Niger, intended to produce raw cotton. By 1961, the project had gulped forty-four billion francs, fifty-six percent of French West Africa's total allocation to agriculture, but had resulted in the cultivation of only forty-eight thousand hectares of land, almost one billion francs per one thousand hectares, and had produced only one thousand of the projected 300,000 tons of raw cotton.[34] Further, there were no

---

32. The figures quoted on diversification are from Ake, *Political Economy of Africa*, 51–3.
33. Austen, *African Economic History*, 208–9.
34. Fieldhouse, *Black Africa*, 13–4.

Table 1 Export Economies Mainly Dependent on a Single Commodity, 1950–1954*

Country & Item	Total Value (in millions of national currency)	Main Commodity	Value of Main Commodity	Value of Main Commodity as Mean % of Yearly Total
Egypt	789	Raw Cotton	669.8	85
Ethiopia	541.8	Coffee	310.9	56.3
Gambia	14.4	Groundnuts	13.1	91
Gold Coast	451.8	Cocoa	308.1	67.9
Sudan	216	Raw Cotton	146.9	67.2

*Figures for Ethiopia are for 1951–1954.
Source: Calculated from Claude Ake, *A Political Economy of Africa*, Ibadan, Longman, 1981, Table 3.3.

changes in land tenure that merit any discussion. It was during this era of rapid expansion that the unbalanced economic growth that Claude Ake has pungently

Table 2 Semi-Diversified Export Economies, with Selected Principal Products, 1950–1957 (Millions of national currency)

Country & Item	Total Value of All Exports	Mean Yearly Value	Mean % of Total Exports
Algeria	129,102		
Citrus Fruits		8,310	5.6
Wine		57,687	39.7
Iron Ore		9,987	6.8
Phosphates & Chemical Fertilizers		2,129	1.5
*Liberia**	39		
Rubber		30.2	76.3
Iron Ore		4.8	13.2
Palm Kernels		1.7	4.3
French Equatorial Africa	11,653		
Coffee		628	5.4
Raw Cotton		4,297	36.9
Wood & Wood Products		3,831	32.9
Diamonds		398	3.4
*Rhodesia & Nyasaland***	145.8		
Copper (& other precious stones)		80.1	54.1
Tobacco		104.2	16.9
Sierra Leone	10.2		
Palm Kernels		3.5	34.5
Iron Ore		2.8	27.8
Uncut & Unworked Diamonds		1.5	14.4

*Figures for 1951–1956 only.
**Figures for 1950–1958.
Source: Adapted from Claude Ake, *A Political Economy of Africa*, Ibadan, Longman, 1981, Table 3.4.

highlighted in his *Political Economy of Africa* became most pronounced. By 1958, the increase in total agricultural production was lagging behind population growth.[35] In addition, better conditions during boom periods did not affect all farmers: only those involved in the production of export commodities benefited from the improvement. Further, if farming in the countryside was so alluring, then

---

35. Wickens, 209.

Figure 7.3. Street-side petty trade.

why did young people continue to migrate to cities? Social factors, in particular: the need to escape the oppression of rural elders and colonial *covée* labor were, of course, major push factors. Yet there were economic reasons as well. The city did not offer many avenues out of poverty. The poor conditions of and pay for city workers were sources of deep-seated discontent, and city workers became reliable allies of the nationalist elite.

Transport

Few new major initiatives were launched in the sphere of transport, in spite of the Colonial Development and Welfare program. Changes took the form of expansion and, in some areas, the upgrading of existing facilities as the colonial states responded to the expansion of the export sector. The improvements in infrastructure, however, gave Africans the opportunity to travel more frequently and quickly than ever before, exchanging goods, services, and ideas with greater frequency and intensity.

Railroads

The subsector that saw the least development in facilities was the railroads. The first railroad in Africa dates back to 1882, when the French started work on the St. Louis-Dakar Line. The first British railroad was the Lagos-Abeokuta Line begun in 1896. By the beginning of World War II, the African rail systems—such as they were—had been constructed. French West Africa had only 3,772 kilometers of single-track, one-meter gauge railroads. Even then, the railroads did not provide an integrated system; they were simply parallel lines that connected the seaports with the sources of export commodities. In spite of its stunted growth, however, the rail subsector remained the most important. It continued to carry the bulk of export commodities to their points of shipment, provided the largest single employer in many colonies, and played an important role in colonial life. Of some 241,700 wage earners in French West Africa in 1947, as many as twenty thousand were railroad employees.[36] Railroad workers became important elements in nationalist anticolonial agitation. Some of the more notable actions in which they were involved were the Lagos general strike of 1945, the successful Tanganyika general strike of 1947, and the strike by the railroad workers of French West Africa in 1947. This last lasted for 160 days, making it the longest strike in colonial Africa.

Seaports

There was far more noticeable change in infrastructure in the seaports. The major seaports, which were built at railroad terminals to facilitate the shipment of colonial produce, continued to serve primarily this purpose during the decolonization era. Ports had a multiplier effect on the economy by generating service industries, such as lodging, catering, maintenance, and construction, and by facilitating the growth of virtually all other sectors. Whatever manufacturing—in-

---

36. Information on French West Africa is from Jean Suret-Canale, "The French West African Railway Workers's Strike, 1947–1948," in *African Labor History*, eds. Peter C.W. Gutkind et al, Beverly Hills, Sage, 1978, 129.

cluding assembly and processing—existed was concentrated in port areas, not only because of the markets these areas provided, but also because proximity to ports significantly reduced the cost of moving equipment and products. It was no wonder, therefore, that most of the fastest growing hubs were port cities. The economic expansion of the era increased, and concomitant increases in export commodity production and colonial demands for metropolitan manufactured goods tremendously expanded freight volumes. For example, the total freight passing through Nigerian ports quadrupled between 1914 and 1954. Growing international trade led to a restructuring of port facilities. In French West Africa, port management was separated from railroad management and made autonomous. There was also a general trend toward the concentration of facilities. The concentration of ports increased; diffused, multiple and small ports made way to fewer, upgraded, larger ones in such cities as Dar es Salaam, Mombasa, Lagos, and Port Harcourt. Port concentration fostered economies of scale in freight handling through the use of sophisticated equipment. In Nigeria, for instance, this meant a reduction from fourteen customs ports in 1914 to seven in 1954, when the Nigerian Ports Authority was established. By 1950, Lagos and Port Harcourt ports accounted for eighty percent of all traffic, with Lagos alone accounting for sixty-three percent. The other ports essentially ceased to attract international freight and became feeder ports.[37] In spite of these developments, however, seaport infrastructure in most countries remained inadequate at the end of the colonial period.

Motor roads

The subsector that experienced the most development was motor roads. Considerable resources from CDW and FIDES went to motor roads, which enhanced interregional trade within territories and encouraged the growth of indigenous transport entrepreneurs.[38] An ILO source reports that in 1947, French West Africa had 101,000 kilometers of roads, Nigeria 42,232, the Gold Coast 13,058, and Tanganyika 39,280. The number of licensed motor vehicles in the Gold Coast increased from 3,287 in 1923 to 35,268 in 1957, and in Tanganyika, the number of privately owned motor vehicles increased from 5,175 in 1938 to 38,893 in 1962.[39]

Aviation

The novel element in the transport sector was aviation, which expanded from the few military bases built during World War II. Expansion during the 1940s was slow. The 1950s witnessed a proliferation of aviation facilities, and by independence, airports had become widespread. While they had some economic benefits, they were also among the white elephant projects embarked upon by emergent African leaders.

---

37. B.O. Ogundana, "Seaport Development in Colonial Nigeria," in *Topics on Nigerian Social and Economic History*, eds. I.A. Akinjogbin and S.O. Osoba, Ile-Ife, Nigeria, University of Ife Press, 1980.
38. Austen, *African Economic History*, 207.
39. Cited by Sender and Smith, *Development of Capitalism*, 14.

Although the economies expanded during decolonization, they lacked structural character in the sense that the various sectors did not complement one another. If the economy of this era was not on the path toward development, it has been used to account for the breathtaking political changes that decolonization represented. The political changes have been attributed to the economic boom that raised African expectations but failed to satisfy them. While the economic expansion suited the aspirations of Africans, it set the stage for the struggle for control that ensued.

Economy and the Politics of Decolonization

It is possible to state that, before World War II, the growth of African economies was a bonus rather than the outcome of economic policy and that long-term plans for self-sufficiency and development were out of the question. Whether or not African nationalists believed that the colonial powers had long-term plans for the self-sufficiency of the colonies in the postwar period, these nationalists understood that colonial powers catered primarily for their own economic well-being. Decolonization thus included a competition for economic space between Africans and expatriates, but for clear historical reasons, this aspect of the struggle never took center stage. African leaders came to accept that political control was easier to achieve and defined their priorities accordingly. Even the most forceful spokesman of the era, Kwame Nkrumah of the Gold Coast, explicitly prioritized the realization of the "political kingdom" over the "economic kingdom". Political control per se was not the ultimate purpose of colonialism; economic domination was. If the establishment of European political control ensured economic domination, the removal of that control would not automatically translate to economic freedom. Calculations about the postcolonial period shaped African economies during decolonization and helped to push political developments far ahead of economic change.

After World War II, the imperial powers, which had banked on the colonies for their postwar recovery, were opposed to decolonization. Pressures from African nationalists, the postwar slump in commodity prices, and the success of the imperial powers' recovery programs encouraged them to relinquish the colonies. Whether decolonization was seen as a voluntary "transfer of power" on the part of a colonial power or a forced one, the economy takes a central role. If the imperial powers voluntarily relinquished their colonies, what economic considerations informed that action? If, on the other hand, they were forced to relinquish their colonies, what measures did they take to secure their long-term interests in their colonies? D.K. Fieldhouse denies that there was a deliberate scheme to replace colonialism "by some form of neocolonialist domination," and even suggests that such a scheme was unnecessary.[40]

The British case shows that there was indeed a deliberate scheme to establish a neocolonialist system. The colonial powers looked to reform the colonies into

---

40. See Fieldhouse, *Black Africa* and *Merchant Capital*.

neo-colonies after realizing that classical colonialism had been rejected and could no longer guarantee the benefits for which colonies had been acquired. By December 1947, the British Colonial Office had prepared a plan to shepherd the colonies toward neocolonialism. The memorandum outlining this plan noted that the appearance of a politically conscious colonial intelligentsia "has upset our calculations and disturbed the even tenor of political development among the slow moving masses [and produced] a real need for a policy of cooperation with this class." Noting that the group was "one of the most important vehicles of culture and thought between the Western world and Africa," the document recommended, "(1) the incorporation of this class in a realistic way in the social, political and economic scheme; [and] (2) the education of this class for their high calling as leaders and eventually rulers of their own people."[41] A committee was constituted to implement this policy.

Classical colonialism had become obsolete, but colonies were still useful. The worst of the postwar economic crisis may have been over by 1952, but the colonial powers still needed cheap raw materials and food. Keeping the colonies was out of the question, given pressures from African nationalists and the U.S. In "transferring" power, the colonizers made no serious effort to transform the economies of the colonies into self-sustaining, development-oriented systems; rather, they worked hard to transform the colonies into neo-colonies. The relatively large public investment of this period was a way to guarantee huge returns for Western enterprises "increasingly organized within transnational corporate structures."[42] The CDW and FIDES funds went overwhelmingly into the development of export commodities. The primary purpose of the political engineering of the 1950s was to make independent Africa useful to the imperial powers rather than to ensure a well-governed and development-oriented continent. The colonial powers did not invest so massively simply to prevent the African countries from falling into the economic abyss. After all, when it suited them, the colonial powers did not shy away from abrupt withdrawal, leaving a chaotic situation behind, as Britain did in Palestine in 1947, France in Indo-China in 1954, and Portugal in Mozambique and Angola during the 1970s. The independence negotiations and timetables that occupied colonial powers in the 1950s were means to facilitate the political and economic engineering involved in the process of shaping colonies into neo-colonies.

Conclusion

Although political change clearly outpaced economic development, the two forces reinforced each other. Expansion of the economies facilitated population movements into areas of intensive economic activity, concentrating people in the in cities—closer to the seats of colonial administration and centers of intense po-

---

41. Quoted by G. Ugo Nwokeji, "Britain's Response to Post-Second World War Colonial Crisis, 1947–50: Findings and Reflection from the Nigeria Research," *Frankfurter Afrikanistische Blätter* 6 (1994): 76–7.

42. Basil Davidson, *Africa in Modern History: The Search for a New Society*, Middlesex, England, Penguin, 1978, 205–206.

litical discourse and propaganda. Former peasants, who now became miners, railroad laborers, factory workers, and artisans, experienced capitalistic exploitation firsthand and came under the direct influence of nationalist propagandists. They could translate their critique of the colonial dispensation to their families in the countryside. In this manner, more and more Africans came to express their political views in "modern" terms.

The economic boom of the decolonization era had only a limited impact on the well-being of Africans.[43] The boom raised expectations that turned out to be unfulfilled "and dramatized the inequalities and the exploitative character of the colonial situation." Per capita production in Africa was falling after 1958, when that of the rest of the world was rising.[44] While postindependent African leaders contributed to the continent's economic malaise, the imperial powers were equally culpable. The kinds of African leaders they encouraged and favored, if not chose, the political frameworks they fostered, and their continuing exploitation of African countries in the international market contributed to the story of mismanagement and misdirected energies that has marked Africa's postindependence experience.

Review Questions

1. What economic forces favored decolonization?
2. What was the role of produce marketing boards both for the colonies and the metropolitan countries?
3. Is it correct to say that the European powers granted independence to their African colonies because they were no longer economically beneficial to the metropolitan countries?

Additional Reading

Claude Ake. *A Political Economy of Africa.* Ibadan: Longman, 1981.
Fred Cooper. *Decolonization and African Society: The Labor Question in French and British Africa.* Cambridge: Cambridge University, 1996, 176–77.
D.K. Fieldhouse. *Black Africa 1945–80: Economic Reconstruction and Arrested Development.* Allen and Unwin: London, 1986.
Alusine Jalloh and Toyin Falola, eds. Black Business and Economic Power. Rochester, NY: University of Rochester Press, 2002.

---

43. Ake, *Political Economy of Africa*, 71.
44. Wickens, 209.

Chapter 8

African Business

Alusine Jalloh

This chapter examines African business during the European colonial era from 1900 to the 1950s. It begins with a discussion of the various trading groups, including Africans, Europeans, Asians, and Lebanese, that comprised the colonial business community. Regional differences in the colonial economic environment, including those between western and southern Africa, are discussed. The study also examines African entrepreneurial success, business organization and management, and challenges. The chapter concludes with an assessment of the colonial impact on African business, highlighting both advantages and disadvantages of colonial rule.

* * *

European colonization started well before the nineteenth century, but it proceeded at an accelerated pace during the 1880s, when Britain and France gained much of the territory of Africa. The partition of the continent formed part of a renewed upsurge of European domination in the world. African territories could now be directly controlled from the metropolis. By 1900, European colonial rule was entering a period of consolidation. This was greatly aided when, in the early twentieth century, the steamship and telecommunications industries brought the European metropolis much closer to their African colonies. World War II was both a political and an economic watershed in Africa. Before this time, the development of African private enterprise had been slowed not only by the general economic climate but also by a number of specific problems that had smaller impacts on non-African business groups. Indigenous entrepreneurship was largely confined to traditional activities in which European firms had no commercial interest—like the internal trade in foodstuffs and cash-crop production or the less profitable small-scale commercial ventures that composed the lowest stratum of the European-dominated trading hierarchy. Beginning in the early 1940s, however, the economic environment improved for all types of business, while many of the constraints formerly experienced by African entrepreneurs began to ease and new business opportunities emerged. By the late 1950s, European colonial rule had entered the phase of decolonization, which led to the independence of most African territories in the 1960s.

This chapter is divided into three sections. The first describes the business community in colonial Africa, focusing on the indigenous population. The second section examines indigenous business from 1900 to the late 1950s. The third section assesses the colonial impact on African business.

Figure 8.1. African traditional market.

The Business Community
in Colonial Africa

In colonial Africa, the business community was a composite entity. Not only was it differentiated in terms of the groups involved, but also in terms of size and specialization. Africans were only one element in the multiethnic and multinational business population, which included Europeans, Lebanese, Arabs, African Americans, and Indians. Colonial businesses could be classified on the basis of their scale of operations, using the term "merchant" for large-scale operators and "traders" for smaller ones. On the basis of this classification, merchants tended to be expatriates, mainly Europeans, while indigenous entrepreneurs dominated the small-scale businesses category.

Africans ran both wholesale and retail businesses in which the scale of trade ranged from small to large. Some of the large-scale indigenous entrepreneurs came from well-established merchant families like the Dantata in northern Nigeria and the Allie family in Sierra Leone. Others included traditional rulers such as kings, chiefs, and religious leaders in colonies like Sudan, Kenya, the Belgian Congo, and Sierra Leone. They enjoyed certain advantages because of their office and social status, which also often provided resources for business. Among African retailers, there were hawkers, market stall owners, and owners of large, small, and multiple shops. African business entrepreneurs included two sets of people. There were those whose commercial activities were oriented toward profit with a view toward expansion and capital accumulation, and there was a group that saw entrepreneurship primarily as a source of a steady income, or "living." Overall, whether by choice or necessity, the vast majority of Africans who were engaged in business in colonial Africa ran small-scale enterprises, earning only enough to support the household to which they belonged and to replenish their business stocks.[1]

The colonial business community was also differentiated through participation in the import or the export trade. Some African enterprises found it easier to engage in the import trade while occasionally, during periods of economic boom, entering the export trade. There was also specialization according to merchandise: textiles, kola nuts, palm produce, miscellaneous European merchandise, or minerals. Many African businesses concentrated on merchandise trading.

Within the colonial business community, the relationship among participants of diverse nationalities and specialities can be represented by a pyramid. Its broad base was comprised of the large number of African petty traders. Many of these traders, especially in West Africa, were women who played a major role in market and other kinds of trade, trade in processed food and a host of other petty trading activities. Above this level came the middle-rank businesses that included a small number of African merchants, the Lebanese, the Indians, and the smaller European firms. At the apex of the pyramid were the big European companies like the United Africa Company (UAC), Paterson, Zochonis and Company (PZ), G. B. Ollivant and Company (GBO), the Société Commerciale de l'Ouest Africain (SCOA), the Compagnie Française de l'Afrique Occidentale (CFAO, or the French Company), and the African and Eastern Trade Corporation. These big expatriate businesses traded in various items including produce, provisions, and manufactured goods. They had their head offices in Europe and operated in various African countries, especially in West Africa. European trading companies had long-established commercial links with various West African economies.[2]

According to one group of scholars, some indigenous entrepreneurs in colonial Africa, as in Angola, were "compradors," that is, individuals or groups who willingly operated as the local representatives or agents of foreign capitalists, sometimes mediating between the latter and the local groups. Earning their profits through the supply of auxiliary services for foreign business interests, "comprador" entrepreneurs facilitated their countries' continued subordination to outside influences, thereby perpetuating national economic dependency and underdevelopment.[3]

The colonial business community operated in an environment of marked regional variation in Africa, especially in relation to the opportunities and constraints experienced by indigenous entrepreneurs. In West Africa, which had a long history of indigenous entrepreneurship, there were no European settler territories. This allowed indigenous entrepreneurs to achieve greater business success. In contrast, eastern and southern Africa had settler colonies that significantly shaped the local business environment and greatly constrained indigenous entrepreneurship.

In West Africa, the European powers, once in control, were primarily concerned with structuring the territories they had acquired in such a way as to meet

---

1. See M. Kilson, *Political Change in a West African State: A Study of the Modernization Process in Sierra Leone* (Cambridge, MA: Harvard University Press, 1966).

2. See A. G. Hopkins, *An Economic History of West Africa* (London: Longman, 1973).

3. The term "comprador" was originally a Portuguese word used to describe the native representatives of Portuguese trading companies operating in various parts of Asia. See also Paul Kennedy, *African Capitalism* (Cambridge: Cambridge University Press, 1988).

the needs of various European interest groups, including trading companies. The main aim of the colonial governments was to encourage peasant cash-crop production on a much wider scale, thus promoting new kinds of export production. Large numbers of coastal Africans were already accustomed to a money economy and had accumulated financial resources from earlier production. This was evident in the oil-palm producing areas of the southern Gold Coast and Niger Delta. In inland areas where cash-crop farming was less established, the colonial governments used various measures, including the imposition of hut taxes, to increase local participation in the colonial economy.

In much of southern and eastern Africa, previous indigenous contact with European commerce had been relatively limited. Unlike West Africa, the colonial environment in these regions was greatly influenced by white settlers and by the presence of mining companies whose owners set out to exploit valuable mineral deposits—especially those in Northern Rhodesia (present-day Zambia), Southern Rhodesia (present-day Zimbabwe), and South Africa. The main priority of colonial governments was not to encourage peasant cash-crop production but to promote a large-scale migrant labor force whose members would seek employment in the European-owned mines, plantations, and factories. To achieve this goal, colonial governments adopted stringent measures to incorporate the indigenous societies into the colonial and world economy. These included land alienation, discrimination, taxation, and the imposition of legal restrictions on the scope and types of economic activity Africans were permitted to pursue.[4]

An important feature of African business in colonial Africa was the ethnic trading diaspora that resulted from the mostly voluntary migration of Africans to communities where they formed ethnic minorities. This phenomenon dates back several centuries and has been seen in many areas of the continent. Most of the current interdisciplinary research has focused on ethnic minority migrant communities in West Africa. Often, the African migrant communities were involved in chain migration from their homelands to their host countries. But the migration of Africans from different areas of the continent to towns and cities in search of profit did not lead to a dissolution of their social ties with their homelands. Many of them returned home periodically to reinforce their kinship links, and they also sent remittances to their kinsmen. The African migrants had widely extended kinship networks that reached all the way to their homelands. These kinship networks were an important aspect of the organizational structure of the internal and cross-boundary trading of indigenous groups in colonial Africa.

Both within and outside the trading diaspora, a patron-client relationship existed between wealthy African merchants and their clientele. In many of the West African diaspora communities, like those of the Fula in Sierra Leone, patrons provided their clients with free food and lodging. Some Fula patrons also obtained immigration documents for their customers and gave them opportunities to acquire commercial skills as assistants in the patrons' various trading undertakings. Eventually, patrons would provide their clients with credit in cash or goods with which to launch their own trading careers. In keeping with their Islamic faith, the recipients repaid the cash at their convenience without *riba* (usury). Fula clients often reciprocated with labor and loyalty which was not remunerated, tran-

---

4. See Ralph Austen, *African Economic History* (London: James Currey, 1987).

scended commerce, and had significance in politics and in the social domain. They would also give their patrons gifts at social events like child-naming ceremonies.

Wealthy African merchants also offered accommodation to their kinsmen and to other newcomers. They provided the new immigrants with free lodging at below-market prices until the boarders could save enough money to start their own trading enterprises. Often the landlords protected their tenants' rights and were accountable for their clients' actions toward others. This patron-client relationship facilitated the entry of many newcomers into the commerce of colonial cities like Freetown, Accra, Lagos, Ibadan, and Nairobi. Some even attempted to link their prosperity to their landlords by marrying their daughters. The landlords also served as cross-cultural brokers, encouraging trade between the host society and the ethnic trading diaspora.

In the African business community, not only was wealth (which included cash, property, and livestock) a status symbol, but it was also an avenue for social mobility, especially in the ethnic trading diaspora. A study of the Fula in Sierra Leone showed that some of the earlier immigrants came from aristocratic backgrounds but that the vast majority came from the lowest social stratum in their homelands, especially in Guinea. Commerce provided the only opportunity for them to become wealthy and achieve social recognition in their host country. An industrious unknown could, through hard work, the accumulation of capital, marriage, kinship, and a bit of luck, work his way into the respectable upper level of the Fula merchant group. Personal achievement led to social mobility and produced a society in which there was a constant filtering of members in and out of the middle and upper merchant groups. The traditional Fula class divisions based on ascriptive values were weak among the Sierra Leonean-born Fula and the new Fula immigrants. The evidence also suggests, however, that many successful Fula merchants remembered their humble origins and were willing to help worthy young Fula achieve the same upward social and economic mobility.

Commercial networking across generational lines was also an important aspect of the African business community in colonial Africa. For example, such networking existed in several ethnic diaspora trading groups in West Africa, such as that of the Hausa in Ibadan. Factors like kinship ties, limited formal credit options, the need for start-up capital, intergenerational business continuity, the necessity for clients to support commercial activities like business expansion, and trading competition from other ethnic groups led many West African immigrants, including the Fula, to develop extensive commercial networks in their host countries. Such networks also often served the social and political activities of the mercantile immigrants in their local communities.[5]

5. See Alusine Jalloh, "The Fula Trading Diaspora in Colonial Sierra Leone," in *The African Diaspora*, ed. Alusine Jalloh and Stephen E. Maizlish (College Station, TX: Texas A & M University Press, 1996), 22–38.

Colonial Rule and African Business, 1900–1950s

In their search for profits in colonial Africa, Africans pursued diverse trading activities. They wanted to spread their business risks, increase profits, and provide kinsmen with employment. Despite strong competition from European firms and foreign traders like the Lebanese, Africans demonstrated business leadership and an ability to respond to market opportunities effectively. Also, they were able to position themselves in key sectors of the colonial economy, including the motor transport business, livestock trade, commercial agriculture, and mining. Not only do these sectors reveal African internal and external business activities, they provide important examples of successful African entrepreneurship in the colonial era.

The motor transport business was perhaps one of the best examples of African entrepreneurial success in the colonial era. Beginning in the late 1920s, cheaper European-introduced motor transport and an expanding road network led to the emergence of the motor transport business as a profitable venture. African entrepreneurs entered the motor transport business as they sought diversification in the expanding colonial economy.

Motor transport had several advantages, including the opening of the African hinterlands to commerce and to economic opportunities. It also helped link indigenous producers in the rural areas with consumers in the urban centers. Producers were aided in marketing their merchandise, as they could choose from a wider range of potential buyers. Motor transport contributed to internal specialization and the division of labor, which further resulted in lower retail prices for food and other consumer goods produced for the local market.

The motor transport business included passenger and goods transportation and the import and retail sale of motor vehicles. The passenger transportation business included the use of trucks, minivans, and taxis which operated mainly in urban areas with expanding multiethnic populations. Goods were mainly transported by trucks between the urban and rural areas. The goods transported included cattle, merchandise, and produce such as coffee and palm kernels. Africans imported motor vehicles from Europe, North America, and Asia, although most of the imported cars and trucks were British and American made. The largest buyers of motor vehicles included African business owners and professionals who were concentrated in colonial cities.

African entrepreneurs in the motor transport business came from diverse economic backgrounds, including the merchandise trade, commercial agriculture, and the livestock trade. Many African businessmen, especially Muslims, did not borrow capital from Western banks to finance their business activities in the motor transport sector because of their objection to repayment of loans with interest, which contravenes the Islamic ban on *riba*. Instead, they accumulated capital through various trading sources, including the merchandise trade and the livestock business. Some accumulated capital through savings from various menial occupations, including those of domestic servants, housekeepers, shop boys, or watchmen (night security guards). Prominent African entrepreneurs in the colonial transport business included Agibu Jalloh in Sierra Leone and Aminu Dantata in Nigeria.

Figure 8.2. Agibu Jalloh.

Africans had extensive consanguineous and affinal kinship networks in the motor transport business, and these were a major reason for their success. Wealthy African businessmen employed their sons, sons-in-law, brothers, brothers-in-law, nephews, cousins, and grandsons as drivers; they were crucial to the success of the business and as apprentices. The apprentices played an important role in collecting fares from passengers and advertising in the highly competitive "lorry parks" in colonial cities. Perhaps the biggest advantage of the kinship-centered employment approach was that it reduced operating costs, since kinsmen were often underpaid or received deferred payment. It also minimized losses through theft by drivers who were responsible for collecting the daily proceeds. The profitability of commercial passenger vehicles was largely dependent on the honesty of drivers in reporting earnings, since, unlike the situation in advanced industrial societies, there were no money meters to verify daily takings. Theft by unscrupulous drivers could be a serious problem in the passenger transport business. As an incentive to encourage drivers to report full earnings, some African entrepreneurs, like the Fula, offered their drivers oral business deals. These deals were such that the drivers would assume ownership of the vehicle after the purchase price had been paid and a negotiated amount of profit had been realized on the investment within a certain period of time. This was quite successful in helping drivers become business partners rather than exploiters of owners.

Kinship ties to mechanics who did vehicle repair and maintenance also reduced the operating costs of African entrepreneurs in the motor transport business. The vast majority of indigenous mechanics were concentrated in colonial cities like Freetown and Lagos, where they owned auto repair shops. Having an honest mechanic was crucial to profitability, since drivers often would connive with mechanics to fleece an owner for alleged vehicle repairs. Frequent garage visits by drivers led to the bankruptcy of many vehicle owners, since they spent money on fixing problems (many invented) and lost income when the vehicle was off the road. Vehicle repair was costly to owners, and unscrupulous mechanics made it even costlier by suggesting unnecessary repairs. Frequent maintenance of vehicles was essential in this industry because of the poor condition of the roads, especially in the rainy season, and the age of the vehicles. Perhaps the most common problem was the need to replace shock absorbers. Given the frequency with which broken parts had to be replaced and the fact that most spare parts were imported and expensive, African businessmen grappled with large and costly maintenance overheads. European businesses like UAC Motors dominated the import and retail of spare parts.[6]

Internally, African entrepreneurs were highly successful in the cattle trade and its related butchering business. In West Africa, this business success was exemplified by the Fula, who had a long history of entrepreneurship. In Sierra Leone, for example, the cattle trade benefitted greatly from Fula capital, initiative, and experience; it was virtually integrated with the Fula, who were responsible for raising, purchasing, transporting, and distributing cattle. Apart from high beef prices, the success of the Fula could be attributed to five factors. First, they controlled most of the supply networks originating in the Republic of Guinea and the northern province of Sierra Leone, especially in the Koinadugu and Bombali districts. Secondly, they controlled most of the retail distribution networks through extensive kinship connections in the colony. Thirdly, the employment of kinsmen made their operations cost-effective. Fourthly, they had the ability to transport large numbers of cattle legally or by smuggling across the Guinea-Sierra Leone border to the major markets in Sierra Leone, such as Freetown, the capital city. Finally, the favorable economic environment in colonial Freetown, which offered many employment and business opportunities, attracted a large beef-consuming population that expanded the meat market. This high public demand was complemented by large government contracts for the supply of meat.

Prominent among the Fula cattle entrepreneurs in the colonial era was Alhaji Momodu Allie of Sierra Leone. During a business career lasting from 1904 through 1948, Alhaji Allie developed an elaborate commercial organization with three dimensions: the purchase of cattle from Guinea and the Sierra Leone interior, the supply of meat to Freetown consumers and the British colonial administration, and the investment of business profits in real estate in Freetown. The cornerstone of Alhaji Allie's entrepreneurial success was the butchering business. Essential to a successful butchering enterprise was a stable supply of cattle. Alhaji Allie obtained most of his cattle from Futa Jalon, an important area for the West

---

6. See Alusine Jalloh, "The Fula and the Motor Transport Business in Freetown, Sierra Leone," *African Economic History* 26 (1998): 63–81.

Figure 8.3. Alhaji Momodu Allie.

African cattle trade. In addition to employing Fula to purchase cattle, Alhaji Allie had eighteen *warehs* (cattle ranches) in Freetown where he kept his cattle before they were slaughtered. From a management perspective, Alhaji Allie is an example of the owner-centered decision-making approach of most African entrepreneurs in the colonial economy. He made all the management decisions, including how many cattle to purchase, how much credit to give to customers, whom to give credit to, and where to invest his business profits. This business centralization resulted from the belief that commercial details should be kept secret within the family or kinship group. Through his butchering business, Alhaji Allie developed extensive commercial and social networks that brought him vast wealth and prestige in Freetown, far away from Senegal, his homeland. He was the wealthiest butcher in colonial Sierra Leone and was recognized by the multiethnic population and the colonial administration as a member of the merchant elite.[7]

Many of the characteristics of Fula cattle trading in Sierra Leone were similar to those of other West African cattle trading groups. Like the Fula, the Hausa cattle traders in Ibadan, for example, conducted their business within the frameworks of indigenous institutions. All cattle sales were on credit and based on informal arrangements. There were no signed documents, no use of bank loans, and no resort to courts to settle debt default or business problems. The entire organization of the Hausa cattle trade, like that of the Fula in Sierra Leone, was indigenous. Wealthy Hausa cattle dealers, like their counterparts in Freetown, dominated the local community economically and politically.[8]

In external trade, Africans tried to achieve business success but faced many obstacles, especially in trade involving products like cocoa, coffee, palm kernels, and groundnuts. It is estimated that the real value of West African exports rose approximately fifteen-fold between 1900 and the late 1950s. During the 1930s, African farmers in several West African countries, including Ghana and Nigeria, tried to establish companies with the intention of securing alternative and direct

---

7. See Alusine Jalloh, "Alhaji Momodu Allie: Muslim Fula Entrepreneur in Colonial Sierra Leone," in *Islam and Trade in Sierra Leone*, ed. Alusine Jalloh and David E. Skinner (Trenton, N J: Africa World Press, 1997), 65–86.

8. See Abner Cohen, *Custom and Politics in Urban Africa : A Study of Hausa Migrants in Yoruba Towns* (Berkeley: University of California Press, 1969).

outlets for the sale of African produce in the United States or Europe. Such business initiatives, which were largely unsuccessful, were mainly motivated by the belief that Africans were being cheated by the big European companies. In Ghana, indigenous entrepreneurs like Tete Ansah helped to organize African businessmen in order to compete more effectively with European companies like the UAC and regain some of the economic initiative for African farmers and traders. This was to be achieved by the founding banks financing African businesses, establishing limited liability companies that would buy farmers' produce and ship it directly to the United States and Europe independently of big European companies, and establishing cooperative buying facilities and stores.[9]

In their search for profits in colonial Africa, African business people, whether engaged in external or internal trade, faced many challenges. Of these challenges, five were most important. First, European colonial officials displayed attitudes varying from indifference, reluctance, and the provision of assistance to downright hostility and discrimination in dealing with indigenous business interests. Colonial rulers relied on a wide range of legal and bureaucratic measures, as well as economic controls like foreign exchange restrictions, to consolidate and protect European commercial interests at the expense of the indigenous business population. In the period prior to the outbreak of World War II, colonial legal and administrative restraints were applied systematically and comprehensively in eastern and southern Africa more than in West Africa. The most widely used restraint involved the requirement that African traders purchase government licenses. Sometimes the cost of a license alone was sufficient to prevent Africans from entering business, given the low value of their likely turnover in relation to the license fee. Also, the issue of licenses frequently involved a variety of rules relating to eligibility, the particular activities for which licenses were valid, and the areas where licensed traders were entitled to operate.

In Zambia, for example, Africans were prohibited from operating stores in towns, except in African locations. Restrictions were also imposed on the kind of goods Africans were allowed to sell so that their trade would not impinge on that of European storekeepers. Local people were also forbidden to register companies on their own land. This resulted in most kinds of business being more or less prohibited for Africans during the greater part of the colonial period. In effect, government power was often used to create or enhance monopolistic tendencies and interests. The exercise of discriminatory state power was highly advantageous to certain European business interests. These strategies were more pronounced in eastern and southern Africa than in the western region of the continent.

Secondly, African entrepreneurs were faced with the superior competition presented by foreign (mainly European) capital. Africans were generally ill-prepared to cope with this competition and received little government protection against it. The most important advantage of some of the large European firms was access to a plentiful supply of capital; this was not usually available to local entrepreneurs. This capital gave the European businesses crucial advantages in such sectors as the produce trade, gold mining, and the timber business. Unlike European firms, African entrepreneurs lacked the opportunity to establish direct, easy access to overseas companies like shippers, manufacturers, merchant suppliers, or other firms. European companies could afford to operate offices in the metropolitan countries. They enjoyed informal contacts with firms in Africa and overseas, and they were sometimes formally linked through mergers and company agreements. Through these connections, the expatriate firms enjoyed ease of access to information, markets, and supplies. European-based companies normally preferred to deal with large orders and established customers with whom they shared certain national and cultural bonds. Furthermore, the large European firms enjoyed substantial economies of scale which gave them several advantages, including the possibility of obtaining discounts from overseas suppliers.[10]

Thirdly, the colonial policy of encouraging non-African immigrant minorities to settle and adopt intermediate business roles between African farmers and workers and big European commercial interests also adversely impacted African entrepreneurship. In eastern and central Africa this intermediate position was dominated by Asians, who became established in Kenya, Uganda, Tanzania, Malawi, and Zambia. In most of these colonies, the Asians enjoyed advantages over their African rivals, including commercial experience, government support, a network of business contacts, start-up capital, and internal group solidarity. In West Africa, the vast majority of the non-African immigrants were Lebanese and Syrians who became established in colonies like Senegal, Sierra Leone, Guinea, the Ivory Coast, Ghana, and Nigeria. There was also a sizable Indian business population. These foreign traders established themselves as retailers and wholesalers of imported goods. As in East and Central Africa, they enjoyed certain advantages unavailable to African entrepreneurs, such as access to credit, government contracts, and import quotas.[11]

Fourthly, African business was constrained by the unfair practices of European banks. Indigenous entrepreneurs were often discriminated against and charged higher fees for services compared with European clients. During the economic crisis of the 1930s, African entrepreneurs found European banking interests indifferent to their problems. Some banks made secret preferential agreements with the large European trading firms. Often, banks refused to provide loans or overdraft facilities to the vast majority of African customers, who were much more dependent on loan capital to expand their businesses than were foreign companies. African entrepreneurs usually had great difficulty in obtaining the collateral needed to secure bank loans. Not only was land owned communally, but few Africans owned modern houses in the early colonial period. Indeed, the widespread tendency for indigenous entrepreneurs to invest in real estate probably resulted as much from the problems of providing security for loans as from the desire to achieve financial security and social status. By denying Africans basic services, the banks effectively reduced overall competition in the colonial economy and held back African enterprise. The banks' preference was to serve the European businesses, with whom they shared certain common perceptions about Africans.[12]

---

10. See P. T. Bauer, *West African Trade: A Study of Competition, Oligopoly and Monopoly in a Changing Economy* (London: Routledge, 1954).

11. See M. Mamdani, *Politics and Class Formation in Uganda* (London: Heinemann, 1976); and H. L. van der Laan, *The Lebanese Traders in Sierra Leone* (The Hague: Mouton, 1975).

12. See Endre Stiansen and Jane I. Guyer, eds. *Credit, Currencies and Culture: African Financial Institutions in Historical Perspective* (Stockholm: Nordiska Afrikainstitutet, 1999).

Lastly, the African desire for Western education contributed to the underdevelopment of indigenous entrepreneurship in the colonial period. For many Africans, education appeared to offer a much more promising avenue for future wealth and power than business enterprise. Lucrative employment with promotion prospects in the bureaucracy, the professions, and big European companies all depended on educational attainments. Salaried employment seemed much more secure than business enterprise as a path to personal advancement. In Sierra Leone, for example, many chiefs, and others who possessed the means to do so, like the Krios, increasingly invested their wealth not in business ventures but in education for their sons, nephews, and other kinsmen. This channeling of economic resources into education, in the hope that this would pave the way for kinsmen to eventually attain high bureaucratic, professional, or political positions, represented a serious deterrent to long-term capital accumulation and business growth.[13]

The Colonial Impact on African Business

European colonial rule brought both benefits and problems for African businesses. Africans were able to establish themselves quite successfully in a few areas of modern business like motor transport. However, colonial rule left behind a weak African business class alongside a foreign, mainly European, domination of key sectors of the African economy, especially overseas commerce. The main purpose of acquiring colonies in Africa was to secure profitable trade for the metropolitan countries. While indigenous entrepreneurs lost overall commercial power relative to the big European trading companies, it did not mean that African business people went into uninterrupted decline or that they were all reduced to petty trading. Indigenous capital did make considerable advances in both trading and production, especially beginning in the early 1940s. Africans made significant gains from their participation in the export trade during the colonial era. However, African entrepreneurial activities were still concentrated in agriculture and commerce in the late 1950s.

On the positive side, colonial rule brought modern forms of transport that helped create an enabling infrastructure for African entrepreneurship. Beginning in the 1920s, modern transport played an important role in opening the African hinterlands to business opportunities. Colonial investments in roads, railroads, and seaports led to the incorporation of most African regions into the expanding world economy. African entrepreneurs could now produce for and sell to a much wider market than had hitherto been possible. Also, African transport owners successfully ran small haulage firms, buses, taxis, and trucks, especially from the mid-1940s onwards. During World War II, many Africans were taught to drive while serving in the British army. Such skills were easily transferred to the transport business in the years of post-war prosperity. The spread of modern forms of transport quickly reduced freight costs, thereby accelerating the expansion of the money economy and cash-crop production.

---

13. See Arthur T. Porter, *Creoledom: A Study of the Development of Freetown Society* (London: Oxford University Press, 1963).

Secondly, the introduction of European banking and a uniformly accepted portable currency in both notes and coin expanded and improved the African business environment. This facilitated the growth of both internal trade and overseas commerce. In West Africa, European currencies replaced long-established local currencies like cowries, Kissy pennies, and gold dust. In British West Africa the issuance of coin was, at first, a monopoly of the Bank of West Africa, and profits from it accrued to the metropolitan power, not to the colonies in which it circulated. Therefore, the West African Currency Board was established as the source of coinage and was also given the power to issue notes, which were first issued in 1916. In French West Africa, the Banque de l'Afrique Occidentale was founded in 1901 by decree and charged with control over all types of banking operations and currency issuing.

Thirdly, colonial rule produced a relatively stable political-legal order, which was essential for the successful operation of business enterprises. African entrepreneurs benefitted from the increased security by expanding and increasing their participation in both short-term and long-term commercial ventures. The relatively stable environment helped pave the way for the colonial expansion of the modern market economy by removing the constraints to the development of the export sector, which was dependent on agriculture. The European aim was to expand the market economy. Africans, by accepting European-introduced market opportunities and creating others for themselves, ensured that export production and trade expanded. By the late 1950s, the colonial economy began to acquire important new elements, including a substantial public sector and modern manufacturing.

On the negative side, European colonial rule led to a number of disadvantages for African business, including those discussed above. Colonial rule restricted African entrepreneurship through trade licensing, credit restrictions, the introduction of statutory marketing monopolies granted only to non-African traders, and the banning of African cultivation of cash crops like coffee. These colonial policies were most pronounced in settler colonies like Kenya, South Africa, and Zimbabwe.

Secondly, until World War II, there was a failure in most African colonies to seriously consider the development of manufacturing. Even after the war, manufacturing was concentrated in certain processing industries only. In the 1950s, the major European trading companies began to switch their local capital into manufacturing. This diversification into industrial investment by the European companies was, in part, a response to increasing competitive pressures, since it was becoming much easier at this time for smaller companies to enter trade on a profitable basis. Also, during this period, Indian and Lebanese entrepreneurs in East and West Africa transferred some capital into manufacturing. In contrast to these other groups, Africans did not have the capital to undertake any significant manufacturing activity.

Thirdly, the failure of colonial governments to provide direct assistance to, and protection for, African business owners significantly slowed the growth of indigenous entrepreneurship. The colonial governments had a preference for European commercial interests, particularly the big trading companies. Although formally neutral in commercial matters, in practice the colonial administrations preferred to deal with a few established expatriate companies like the UAC.

Conclusion

This chapter has examined various African business activities during the European colonial period between 1900 and the 1950s. It has shown that, despite many challenges, Africans were able to achieve business success. The study has also shown that colonial rule provided a number of benefits for African business. Such benefits included an improvement in the economic environment through the introduction of rail, sea, and road transportation. On the other hand, colonial rule severely constrained African entrepreneurship through both state and private European business practices.

Review Questions

1. Describe the business community in colonial Africa.
2. Describe African business organization and management in the colonial era.
3. Discuss the achievements of African entrepreneurs during the colonial period.
4. In what ways did European colonial rule impede African entrepreneurship?
5. Evaluate the impact of colonialism on African business.

Additional Reading

Austen, Ralph. *African Economic History*. London: James Currey, 1987.

Crowder, M. *West Africa under Colonial Rule*. London: Hutchinson, 1976.

Curtin, P. D. *Cross-Cultural Trade in World History*. Cambridge: Cambridge University Press, 1984.

Fieldhouse, D. K. *Black Africa 1945–1980: Economic Decolonization and Arrested Development*. London: Allen and Unwin, 1986.

Hill, Polly. *Studies in Rural Capitalism in West Africa*. Cambridge: Cambridge University Press, 1970.

Hopkins, A. G. *An Economic History of West Africa*. London: Longman, 1973.

Illife, John. *The Emergence of African Capitalism*. Minneapolis: University of Minnesota Press, 1983.

Jalloh, Alusine. *African Entrepreneurship: Muslim Fula Merchants in Sierra Leone*. Athens, OH: Ohio University Press, 1999.

Jalloh, Alusine, and David E. Skinner, eds. *Islam and Trade in Sierra Leone*. Trenton, NJ: Africa World Press, 1997.

Kennedy, Paul. *African Capitalism*. Cambridge: Cambridge University Press, 1988.

Mamdani, M. *Politics and Class Formation in Uganda*. London: Heinemann, 1976.

Meillassoux, C., ed. *The Development of Indigenous Trade and Markets in West Africa*. Oxford: Oxford University Press, 1971.

Munro, J. F. *Africa and the International Economy, 1800–1960*. London: J. M. Dent, 1976.

Zeleza, T. *A Modern Economic History of Africa*. Vol. 1. Dakar: CODESRIA, 1993.

Chapter 9

Educational Policies and Reforms

Apollos O. Nwauwa

This chapter discusses the colonial educational policies and reforms of European colonialists in Africa from 1939 through 1960. It examines how and why the abysmally slow progress of reforms of the pre-1939 era gave way to more sweeping changes during the post-1939 period. These dramatic changes included the rapid expansion of educational facilities—primary, secondary, and tertiary—especially the establishment of universities, the revision of curricula and syllabi, and the new nationalist reorientation of the philosophy of education. The discussion begins with the pre-1939 educational policies involving missionary education, government involvement, "adaptation," and African responses. The chapter then focuses on the extraordinary wartime and postwar changes that accompanied nationalism and the politics of decolonization.

* * *

What at present time is wanted is not anybody highly trained, but an ordinary individual with some training...to be unable to take part in local life and local habits of thought. We do not want the Divisional Commander nor even the Platoon Leader. What is wanted is not even the Sergeant but something—which we are more likely to get—on the level of the Lance Corporal; i.e., men just a little removed from the common ruck who will be able to spread a bit of the leaven among the unresponsive lump.[1]

If ever the historian required a simple, crude, yet effective and pithy statement of the core of the philosophy of colonial education in Africa, J. E. W. Flood of the British Colonial Office provided it in the quotation above. Educational policies and practices in colonial Africa were hardly in consonance with the needs of the African peoples. Rather, they were dictated by financial parsimony, administrative necessity, and the racist predispositions of the various colonial powers. From the start, colonial education for Africans "was rarely seen in pedagogical terms either by its dispensers or by its clients."[2] It was intended to serve the interests of both

---

1. Public Records Office, CO 847/3/2 J.E.W. Flood to Hans Vischer, *Colonial Office Notes*, 2 October 1933. This was Flood's response to African demands for higher education in the 1930s.
2. David Ruddell, "Class and Race: neglected determinants of colonial 'adapted education' policies," *Comparative Education*, Volume 18, No.3, (1982), pp. 293–4.

Christian missionaries and the colonial governments who funded it and was never correlated to the assumptions of the "civilizing mission." While missionaries used it as an instrument for the effective conversion of Africans to Christianity, colonial governments saw education as a means of socially and politically controlling their subjects. For African recipients, however, Western education remained an important vehicle for upward social mobility and access to the powers akin to those of the colonizers. Nevertheless, education was offered to Africans in strictly regulated doses. Persistent African demand for reform and expansion of the educational system before 1939 was ignored. The negligible changes Europeans opted to introduce were strictly dictated by selfish imperial objectives until the outbreak of World War II, when the concomitant "winds of change" pushed them toward reform. Essentially, this chapter will focus on the pre- and post-war colonial educational policies and reforms as they correlated to the larger questions of nationalism and the politics of decolonization.

In the Western world, education has always been seen as a lever for social, economic, and political advancement. In Africa during the colonial era, however, European rulers conceived the purpose of education in a different light. Initially, colonial government shied away from providing facilities for education. It was European missionaries who championed the cause of education in Africa, primarily for the promotion and proselytization of their various faith and sects. The first attempts at providing formal European-style schooling were made by the Portuguese in the middle of the sixteenth century with little success. It was not until the nineteenth century that actual foundations for Western education were laid by missionaries from Britain, France, and, later, America. However, "stringent budgets, limited personnel, and unhealthful working conditions" frustrated missionary efforts.[3] Despite their shortcomings, mission schools, modeled after metropolitan institutions, became the cornerstones of future educational systems, as the cases of Fourah Bay College in Sierra Leone and Achimota College in Ghana demonstrated. Generally, technical education was de-emphasized, partly because missionaries did not have the resources and expertise to support such effort but mostly because colonial administrations direly needed clerks.

With the formal establishment of colonial rule, Western education began to fulfill economic as well as administrative needs for colonial authorities. There arose a great demand for indigenous auxiliaries to fill subordinate positions in the colonial service. African subordinates were cheaper than expatriates. As missionaries began to experience increasing difficulties in financing education, due in part to expanded operations resulting from increased numbers of European settlers and traders in the colonial territories, they called upon their home governments for more support.[4] Soon it became clear that missionary bodies alone could no longer bear the burden of education in Africa. Consequently, colonial powers began to provide more financial support and to formulate educational policies through agencies such as advisory committees and commissions of inquiry. However, these policies still catered to narrow imperial objectives.

---

3. L. Gray Cowan, James O'Connell and David G. Scanlon, eds., *Education and Nation-Building in Africa*, (New York: Frederick A. Praeger, 1965), p. 4.

4. Bob W. White, "Talk about School: Education and the Colonial Project in French and British Africa (1860–1960)," *Comparative Education*, Volume 32, No.1, (1996), p. 11.

The new interest in education before 1939 has been explained in varying terms. First, there was increasing international concern about the problems of colonial education; the League of Nations mandate system had insisted that colonial powers reassess their educational plans for Africans. Secondly, interest grew in reaction to the tide of criticisms from the Phelps-Stokes Commission's report relating to the curricula of colonial schools.[5] Thirdly, there was a growing recognition among Europeans of the value of African agricultural exports following the end of World War I. "Not only were African territories becoming more profitable, but they were also increasing in geo-political importance."[6] Despite these new policy statements by European colonizers, their actual implementation was left to the discretion of the various colonial governments and religious bodies. As a result, there were variations in practice, partly because of a lack of coordination and largely because of budgetary constraints. Great Britain and France were the two colonial powers that devised understandable colonial education policies.

Reforms and Changes Before 1939

Following the end of the First World War, colonial powers began to show more interest in the education of their African subjects. The French policy of assimilation, which sought to absorb Africans into the French culture and way of life, implied that the education of Africans should be a priority. However, like the British, the Portuguese, and the Belgians, missionaries—not government—established the first schools in the French African colonies. It was in 1922 that the French Government issued a decree limiting missionary involvement in education. Under this law, "the establishment of a new school in the colonies required government permission, government-certified teachers, a government curriculum and the exclusive use of French as the language of instruction."[7] Since the majority of the teachers were French, the use of African languages would have been very difficult in any case. Indeed, "students were prevented, on pain of punishment, from expressing themselves in their mother tongues within school premises."[8] Educational curricula at all levels were heavily Europeanized. Thus, early enough, the French imperial government had full control of educational development in its colonies despite missionary participation.

France vigorously pursued the idea of cultural universalism, which sought to unify her dependents through the French language and culture. Essentially, three main features characterized French colonial education in Africa. The first was the widespread use of the French language. Although, in some instances, France permitted the short-term use of indigenous languages in order to meet immediate teaching needs such as health education and morality, the ultimate goal of instruc-

---

5. See L. J. Lewis, ed., *Phelps-Stokes Reports on Education in Africa, 1922 and 1924* (London: Oxford University Press, 1962). The Phelps-Stokes Commission, which visited Africa between 1920 and 1924, originated from the United States but included British as well African educators.

6. White, "Talk about School," 11.

7. Ibid., 11.

8. Ansu Datta, *Education and Society: A Sociology of African Education*, (New York: St. Martin's Press, 1984), 18.

tion was the mastery of the French language. The second feature was the limitation on enrollment based on estimates of job vacancies for graduates. This was intended to forestall the disillusionment and disorientation faced by educated but unemployed youths. The third element was the dualism in the French colonial school system where, on the one hand, African schools were intended to educate the masses, and, on the other hand, European schools were more selective, concentrating on educating African elites that could eventually fill the lower cadres of the colonial civil service.[9]

The British involvement in formal education in Africa came later and was hardly as visible as that of the French. Unlike the French, the British Government encouraged the operations of the missionaries, giving them full administrative freedom and financial grants. Such posture relieved Britain of the responsibility of policy formulation and the implementation of colonial education. Later, however, a dual system of education emerged whereby mission schools existed alongside state schools. Strong pressure, especially from white settlers, forced Britain to begin to invest more in education in its colonial territories. In 1923, the Colonial Office formed an advisory committee on native education that was later renamed the Advisory Committee on Education in the Colonies (ACEC). The memorandum issued by ACEC in 1925 constituted the first authoritative articulation of British educational policy in the colonies. The hallmark of the memorandum was the statement on the need for adaptation:

> Education should be adapted to the mentality, aptitudes, occupation and traditions of the various peoples conserving as far as possible all sound and healthy elements in the fabric of their social life.[10]

Nevertheless, Africans were suspicious of adaptation as formulated by the British. For one thing, it was not clear "how the aptitudes of Africans were decided without implying racial stereotypes."[11] Furthermore, it was also befuddling how African abilities were measured. Who would measure them? What was the purpose of this education? Indeed, Africans viewed such adaptation as an attempt to provide them with second-rate education and to condemn them to subordinate positions in the colonial service. Thus, Walter Rodney observed, "Colonial schooling was education for subordination, exploitation, the creation of mental confusion and the development of underdevelopment."[12] Similarly, Ruddell has argued that the goal of colonial education was for "social control, socialization, and the reinforcing of existing social institutions—invariably those of the ruling class."[13]

The Belgian and Portuguese colonial efforts in African education were characterized by the principles of European authority and African subordination.

9. White, "Talk about Schools," 11–12. See also Victor Uchendu, *Education and Politics in Tropical Africa*, (New York: Conch Publishers, 1979), 4.

10. Uchendu, *"Education and Politics,"* 4.

11. Apollos O. Nwauwa, *Imperialism, Academe and Nationalism: Britain and University Education for Africans, 1860–1960*, (London: Frank Cass, 1997), 54.

12. Walter Rodney, *How Europe Underdeveloped Africa*, (London: Bogle-L'Ouverture Publications, 1972), 264. See also John Karefah Marah, "Educational Adaptation and Pan-Africanism: Developmental Trends in Africa," *Journal of Black Studies*, Vol. 17, No. 4, (1987): 460–81.

13. Ruddell, "Class and Race," 294.

Thomas Hodgkin describes the Belgian educational policy as Platonism, because it was "primarily concerned with the transmission of certain unquestioned and unquestionable moral values, and intimately related to status and function."[14] The Portuguese educational philosophy was very similar to that of the French, especially in their view of the school as the vehicle for the spread of Portuguese language and culture. The purpose was to create a civilization that was essentially non-African in character. However, while the French endeavored to produce an African elite inspired by French values, the Portuguese educational policy aimed at preserving the elite status in the hands of the Portuguese.

Contradictions and Limitations

Every colonial education policy produced its own contradictions which, in turn, provoked differing political protests by African elite. Beginning in 1925, Africans challenged British policy of educational adaptation, refusing to accept formal education "that was adapted to the colonial society." They demanded a direct "transplant" of metropolitan educational standards, which they did not get. Instead, metropolitan standards and educational adaptations were redefined and reinterpreted by territorial governments to perpetuate colonial domination.[15]

The educational institutions provided to Africans before 1939 were quantitatively and qualitatively deficient. Heavy stress was placed on primary education, which would train the African subordinates—the clerks, messengers, typists, and artisans—that were sorely needed by the colonial service. For instance, in the whole of East Africa by 1937, only Makerere College offered full secondary education; Kenya had only two junior secondary schools, which were run by missionaries. Since the number of secondary schools was so small, only a few Africans made it into schools. In the whole of French West Africa, the French provided education for seventy-seven thousand pupils out of at least fifteen million in 1938.[16] That the British colonies on average did better in terms of the provision of educational institutions owed a lot to the missionary initiates rather than the British government. However, while Ghana, Nigeria, Uganda, and Sierra Leone were, on average, better off educationally, Kenya, Tanganyika, the Central African territories, and South Africa were almost neglected. Even within the same colony there were serious variations in opportunity, because the respective colonial governors controlled policies and practices. In many colonies, only Africans who lived in or near the principal towns were given the opportunity for education; those in the so-called remote areas were denied education due to the lack of facilities for training. This unevenness in educational opportunities also reflected patterns of economic exploitation, since those educationally neglected regions, such as the Northern Territories in the Gold Coast and Southern Sudan, were areas that did not offer the colonial rulers any immediate products for export.

14. Thomas Hodgkin, *Nationalism in Colonial Africa*, (New York: New York University Press, 1957), 52.
15. Uchendu, *Education and Politics*, 3; See also Rodney, *How Europe Underdeveloped Africa*, 264.
16. Rodney, *How Europe Underdeveloped Africa*, 364.

In spite of their dismally small numbers and dubious quality, by 1939, primary and secondary schools were firmly established by the different colonial powers. One major problem in all this was the absence of tertiary (university) institutions. In the whole of West Africa, only Fourah Bay College in Sierra Leone awarded degrees. This happened under an affiliation arrangement (1874) with Durham University in England. However, Fourah Bay's degrees were only in theology and classics. Several colleges, all founded in the 1920s and including Yaba Higher College in Lagos, Nigeria, Achimota College in the Gold Coast, Gordon College in the Sudan, and the Higher College of East Africa at Makerere, Uganda awarded higher certificates that were not full-fledged degrees. Consequently, Africans who desired full university degrees had to go overseas to complete the degree programs, if they could afford it. European colonialists consistently ignored the persistent African demand for the establishment of universities in Africa.[17]

European objections to the provision of university facilities in Africa could also be explained in terms of administrative convenience, financial parsimony, and racial prejudice. The British consolidation of the indirect rule policy as an ideal administrative mechanism became antithetical to the idea of universities in Africa. Since indirect rule relied largely on African traditional chiefly rulers, there was no room for university educated Africans. Indeed, it was the indirect rule policy that now began to dictate the content and pace of African education. The diminutive pre-1939 reforms and changes were predicated upon the principles and practice of the indirect rule system. Thus, Lord Hailey aptly concluded that, overall, the British educational policy in Africa had "in truth been…an effort to implement the view held of the place which the African should occupy in the social economy [of the colonial state]."[18] Educated Africans were expected to occupy subordinate positions that did not require university educations. Given the costs involved, European governments were not ready to use their taxpayers' money to establish universities in Africa. Furthermore, there was some doubt, particularly among the British, as to whether Africans were intellectually capable of benefitting from university education.

Sometimes, European opposition to universities in Africa was rationalized with the argument that since primary and secondary schools (which would supply the students for universities) were still in their embryonic stages, it would be foolish to build universities. The development of educational institutions was perceived in the form of a pyramid that should build its layers successively. By 1939, however, imperial opinions became fluid and shifting, and some colonial officials like Governor George Mitchell of Uganda were now arguing that the university should be built simultaneously with primary and secondary schools, because progress in one stage depended on progress in other stages.[19] It was clear that a change of attitude on the university question was beginning to manifest itself not

17. Beginning with James Africanus Horton in the 1860s and Edward Wilmot Blyden in the 1870s, both in Sierra Leone, through J.A. Casely Hayford in the 1920s in the Gold Coast and Nnamdi Azikiwe in the 1930s in Nigeria, African educated elements pleaded with imperial Britain to establish universities in Africa. They reasoned that a university situated in Africa would enable Africans to study at home instead of overseas to minimize the enormity of the impact of cultural alienation.

18. Lord Hailey, *An African Survey*, (London: Oxford University Press, 1938), 1208.

19. Public Records Office, CO 822/99/20 "A Governor's Views on Education in East Africa: Thinks University Should Come First", Extract from the *East African Standard*, (18 August 1939). Mitchell argued that the university should be seen as the roots and trunk of

only in colonial governments but also in metropolitan governments. Although not a full-fledged university, it was partly this shifting attitude that accounted for the use of imperial funds (British tax-payers' money) for the establishment of Makerere Higher College in East Africa in 1938.

The administrative policy of the French, Portuguese, and Belgians, which sought to assimilate a tiny number of educated Africans into the metropolitan way of life, was such that Africans were expected to be trained overseas in the rich cultures of their colonial overlords. One of the major arguments by African intelligentsia in favor of the provision of university facilities in Africa revolved around adaptation. They wanted education to be adapted to the African environment and "to the inherent necessities of the race."[20] Ironically, the African argument for adaptation was analogous to the British opposition against universities in Africa. Be that as it may, adaptation, which fitted the British indirect rule system almost perfectly, ran counter to the French assimilation, Portuguese *civilizado*, and Belgian *evolues* administrative principles. Under this arrangement, there was little or no attempt to establish universities.

War, Neo-Colonialism, and Reforms, 1939–1950

Three major processes characterized colonial education between 1939 and 1950: massive expansion at all levels, the provision for technical and professional instruction, and increased Europeanization of the curricula. This was the period of unprecedented policy shift among European colonizers in favor of more educational opportunities for Africans. Imperial policy-makers began to acknowledge the connection between education and the forces of social change, especially in the areas of economic and political development. It was now believed that education should not only target the youth but the whole community if the social improvement of the colonial peoples was to be realized. The pyramidal imagery, or layered institutional development, was abandoned in favor of the spontaneity of a volcano. In its 1940 report, the British ACEC argued that, like a volcano, which "built up its cone in all stages at once," university development should advance simultaneously with both primary and secondary education.[21] Furthermore, education should not only be geared toward the production of clerks, messengers, and interpreters, but also toward the training of individuals who would be the future leaders of their communities. In 1944, the ACEC warned that the past practice of educating only a handful of the population had led to serious dislocation in African societies. The committee argued that since Africans would be the chief agents in their own improvement, they should be educated for that role. Furthermore, the intensity of post-war nationalism dictated that the colonialists reposi-

the educational tree, the pursuit of knowledge the sap, and the schools the branches, foliage, and flowers.

20. Edward Blyden to Governor Hennessy of Sierra Leone, 9 December 1872, *The West African University*, (Freetown: Negro Printing Office, 1872), 11.

21. Public Records Office, CO 847/18/9 *Report of the ACEC Sub-Committee on the Recommendation of West African Governors' Conference*, (December 1940).

tion themselves for the eventuality of decolonization. Thus, in reality, educational reforms were intended to strengthen the empire.

As the war raged, the British continued to make rapid changes to their educational policy in Africa. Mass education became vital, and equal emphasis was placed on the education of adults and the training of youth.[22] However, mass education required a substantial improvement not only in the quality but also in the number of primary and secondary schools. It was also under this liberal imperial posture on colonial education that the idea of founding universities in Africa became attractive to policy makers in London. Shortly after the war, money became available for education under the Colonial Development and Welfare Acts; this gave Africans and colonial governments new hope.[23] In Kenya, for instance, a ten-year development plan budgeted an expenditure of £15,500,000 of which £2,400,000 was for education. Although quite low by reasonable standards, this was an important improvement as compared to the previous period.

The European change of attitude toward African education can be properly understood within the context of the war and the "winds of change" blowing over Europe and Africa. Most importantly, it must be understood as a "new deal" intended to pacify the colonies and stave off possible outbursts of radical nationalism. The West Indian riots of 1938–39 were a wake-up call for Britain, adding to their growing apprehension that if reforms and changes were not instituted at once, Africans might follow suit. Furthermore, Lord Hailey's survey of the social and political conditions in British African colonies submitted to Parliament in 1939 was not particularly encouraging.[24] It was recognized that increasing roles should be given to educated Africans in the political, economic and social affairs of the colonies. Additionally, pressures from the critics of empire within Britain—especially the Fabians and their charges that Britain was running a "slummy" empire—resulted in a reevaluation of colonial policies, including those regarding education. From a slightly different standpoint, it was now considered quite dangerous to continue to deny Africans access to university education in Africa, which forced them to take advantage of American universities and be exposed to their radicalizing social and political ideas.[25] The war had humbled the colonial powers, particularly with the Nazi defeat of France in 1940, and both Britain and France were only capable of maintaining the status quo in their colonies. Consequently, favors and bribes had to be offered to the colonial peoples not only to keep the peace and retain their loyalty and support, but also to prove to critics of the empire that, even in the midst of war, the welfare of the colonial subjects remained a top priority.

It was based on this belief that the Colonial Development and Welfare Acts (CD and WA) of 1940 and 1945; designed to improve the social conditions of the

---

22. *Advisory Committee on Education in the Colonies, Mass Education in African Society*, (London: HMSO, 1944) as cited in Cowan et.al. eds., *Education and Nation-Building in Africa*, pp.7–8.

23. W.E.F. Ward and L.W. White, *East Africa: A Century of Change, 1870–1970*, (New York: Africana Publishing Corporation, 1971), 248–9.

24. See Hailey, *African Survey*.

25. For British apprehensions on the impact of American education on Africans, see Apollos O. Nwauwa, "The British Establishment of Universities in Tropical Africa: A Reaction Against the Spread of American Radical Influence", *Cahiers D'Études Africaines*, vol. 130, no. XXXIII-2, (1993), 247–74.

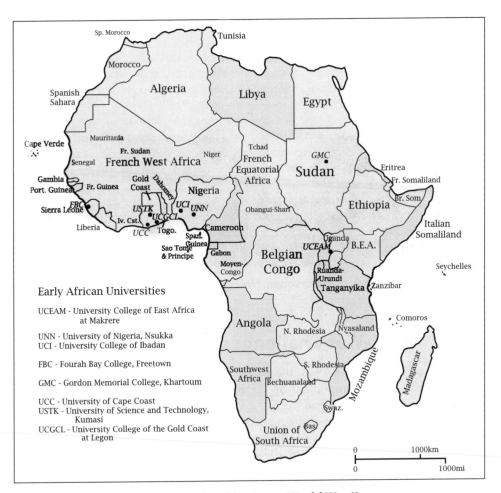

Sp. Morocco
Tunisia
Morocco
Spanish
Sahara
Algeria
Libya
Egypt
Cape Verde
Mauritania
Fr. Sudan
Niger
Tchad
GMC
Eritrea
Senegal
French West Africa
French
Equatorial
Africa
Sudan
Fr. Somaliland
Gambia
Port. Guinea
Fr. Guinea
Gold
Coast
Dahomey
Nigeria
Br. Som
FBC
Sierra Leone
USTK
UCGCL
UCI
UNN
Obangui-Shari
Ethiopia
Iv. Cst.
UCC
Togo.
Cameroon
Italian
Somaliland
Spa.
Guinea
Sao Tome
& Principe
Gabon
Moyen-
Congo
Belgian
Congo
UCEAM
Uganda
B.E.A.
Seychelles
Ruanda-
Urundi
Tanganyika
Zanzibar
Angola
N. Rhodesia
Nyasaland
Comoros
Southwest
Africa
Bechuanaland
S. Rhodesia
Mozambique
Madagascar
Swaz.
Bas.
Union of
South Africa

Early African Universities

UCEAM - University College of East Africa
    at Makrere

UNN - University of Nigeria, Nsukka
UCI - University College of Ibadan

FBC - Fourah Bay College, Freetown

GMC - Gordon Memorial College, Khartoum

UCC - University of Cape Coast
USTK - University of Science and Technology,
    Kumasi
UCGCL - University College of the Gold Coast
    at Legon

0   1000km
0   1000mi

Education in Africa, post-World War II.

colonial peoples, were passed by British Parliament without filibusters. These acts allocated funds for the expansion of educational facilities in Africa, including the establishment of universities. Finally, it has been argued that the expansion of educational facilities in Africa during the war was a necessary precondition for "self-government" as suggested by the British Secretary of State for the Colonies, Malcolm MacDonald. With the CD and WA funds now available, the Colonial Office began to undermine the opposition of British officials in the colonies toward universities. Feeling that the war years remained "an ideal period to prepare for the post-war social, economic and political transformation of the colonial empire,"[26] London quickly set in motion the course of events that culminated in the creation of universities in Africa.

---

26. Nwauwa, *Imperialism, Academe and Nationalism*, 207.

Figure 9.1. Main tower, University of Ibadan, Nigeria.

Post-War Challenges and Responses

Soon after the war, in 1945, the two authoritative commissions on higher education in the colonies appointed by the British Government—the Asquith Commission for all the colonies and the Elliot Commission for West Africa—submitted their reports. The highlight of the reports was the unanimous recommendation for the immediate establishment of universities in Africa. Both reports produced instant results with the founding, in 1948, of three university colleges in Africa—the University College of East Africa at Makerere, the University College of Ibadan in Nigeria, and the University College of the Gold Coast at Legon—and the reorganization of Fourah Bay College in Sierra Leone into a composite college.[27] New imperial challenges in the postwar (1945–1950) years dictated that educational reforms and changes were imperative and should be rapidly pursued, no matter how unprecedented. The effects of the over-expansion of the African educated elite no longer troubled British colonial officials as was the case before 1939. There was now a conscious effort to expand the class of educated Africans as the likelihood of "self-government" loomed. Indeed, the spontaneous development of educational facilities at all levels had become vital as an effective means of creating African educated "compradors" who would collaborate with and sustain British interests in the colonies in the event of the sudden disintegration of the empire.

In French territories, just before the outbreak of the Second World War, the highest education available to most Africans was the École William Ponty in Dakar, Senegal, a teacher-training college with a three-year medical course. Ponty's educational system "was a compromise between the assimilationist aim of forming highly selected elites who could be considered Frenchmen, [*sic*] and that

---

27. The composite college offered some form of degree courses and middle-level training of a polytechnic nature. It took almost ten years before Fourah Bay College could attain university college status.

of filling the short-term needs of the administration."[28] Admissions into this college, like similar institutions in British Africa, depended on the number of middle-level positions the colonial administration needed to fill. It is not surprising that many political leaders of the post-war era in the French territories attended Ponty; even before the outbreak of World War II, many educated (assimilated) Africans, such as Leopold Senghor of Senegal, had begun to react against French cultural assimilation and to assert the value of African culture and tradition. In Ivory Coast and Guinea, French-educated Africans developed interests in African history and culture and began a vigorous revival of traditional theater and dancing. Senghor's concept of negritude soon became the hallmark nationalist slogan in French African territories.

Transplantation and Adaptation

No sooner had the new schools and universities been established than African nationalists became appalled that the institutions were African only in their location. In terms of their curricula, standards, and academic culture, these universities were transplantations of similar institutions in Europe. Whether to confuse the colonial subjects or mystify their imperial systems, European curricula were imposed without reference to African conditions. In any case, it has been argued elsewhere that the unprecedented post-war progress in colonial education, followed by the transplantations of foreign academic models, values, and curricula, were intended to prepare both the colonial rulers and the colonized peoples for possible decolonization.[29] In other words, it was a calculated effort on the part of Europeans to position themselves well for a neo-colonial role should the post-war winds of change sweep them out of power in Africa, placing Africans in charge.

At the end of the war, a grateful France granted French citizenship to all inhabitants of French colonies. A policy of complete assimilation was implemented, integrating the educational systems of her African colonies with those of France.[30] For instance, there were six years of primary school taught entirely in French, which included a curriculum identical to that in France and culminated with a certificate of primary studies (CEP). Those who obtained their CEPs were admitted to the six-year secondary school, or *lycée*, utilizing the traditional French curriculum; and those who passed *lycée* were eligible to enter the university. Educational facilities were rapidly expanded, while scholarships were given to bright students to study in French schools and universities. Soon, an increasing number of university educations became available for the first time, particularly in 1953, when an institution of higher learning in Dakar was granted university status within the French university system. Mass education, as well as the unrestricted

28. J.A. Ballard, "The Colonial Phase in French West Africa", J.F. Ade Ajayi and Ian Espie, eds., *A Thousand Years of West African History*, (Ibadan: University of Ibadan Press, 1965, reprinted 1979), 453.

29. Nwauwa, *Imperialism, Academe and Nationalism*, 105–34.

30. Ballard, "The Colonial Phase in French West Africa," 453. France was very grateful to their African colonial subjects for their unflinching support during the German blitzkrieg and occupation during the war and wanted to reform her colonial policy to take more responsibility in the social, economic, and political development of her colonies.

provision of higher learning for Africans, became the focus of post-war reform. However, French post-war educational reforms called for more integration and assimilation into France than adaptation of the system to African culture and tradition. African children continued to be indoctrinated and taught about the achievement of "Our ancestors, the Gauls."[31] African nationalists in French territories, themselves educated and assimilated, would later pick their fight with France and begin to push for adaptation and Africanization.

Similarly, the British ensured that the new educational institutions, particularly the university colleges, conformed to British academic curricula, standards, and models. Syllabi for African schools were crafted in England as were examination questions. The content of colonial education and the reality of Africa continued to be quite incongruous. Thus, on a hot afternoon in a tropical African school, as Rodney has noted,

> a class of black shining faces would listen to their geography lesson on the seasons of the year—spring, summer, autumn, and winter. They would learn about the Alps and the river Rhine but nothing about the Atlas Mountains of North Africa or the river Zambezi.[32]

The British ensured that African children:

> memorized the names of obscure English plants and the wives of Henry VIII....The stress on the Bible in religious education left little time for an understanding of the traditional beliefs and rituals of the African peoples.[33]

This was alienation and indoctrination, pure and simple, through the medium of colonial instruction.

To Africans, the European idea of adaptation remained suspect. The dubious intent of the British indirect rule system had been the training of Africans for subordinate positions in the colonial service, and this resulted in African apprehension for the European brand of adaptation in education. Although it is true that initially the African educated elite clamored for the academic standards of the colonial rulers, this had resulted largely from European denigration of local diplomas and certificates awarded by African institutions. African recipients of these qualifications endured untold discrimination in employment, salary, and promotion. For instance,

> a Yaba trained doctor was a 'medical assistant' on salary scale of £120 rising to £400 after fifteen years' service whereas a doctor trained in the United Kingdom was a 'medical officer' on a salary scale of £400 to £720, though both might be performing similar duties.[34]

The only logical explanations for this discrepancy were racism and European assumptions that educational accomplishments in Europe were greater than those in the colonies. Overseas education, therefore, became the hallmark of academic qualification, and Africans began to move abroad for education. Those who could

---

31. Datta, *Education and Society*, 18.
32. Rodney, *How Europe Underdeveloped Africa*, 271.
33. Datta, *Education and Society*, 18.
34. Eric Ashby, *Universities: British, Indian, African*, (Cambridge, Massachusetts: Harvard University Press, 1966), 196. Yaba was the acronym for Nigerian Higher College at Yaba, Lagos.

not afford overseas education called upon Europeans to "transplant" their own academic models to Africa. Thus, with impunity, the British imposed their models on the new African educational institutions. Indeed, many African students bragged about the foreign traditions of their institutions. In its early years, for instance, the students of the University College of Ibadan, Nigeria, proudly referred to their institution as "the University of London situated at Ibadan for purposes of convenience."[35] Alienation and indoctrination yielded dividends for the colonialists, as African students became suspicious of all forms of educational adaptation and, sometimes, of the Africanization of curricula, standards, and personnel.

Nationalism and Africanization

The colonial system created a new stratification pattern in African societies with a thin layer of modern elite at the top. The elite were themselves products of Western education. Fully aware of their exalted position in the colonial state, these elite began to demand a larger share of political power. The continued efforts of European officials to alienate the emergent African elite from the political process produced radical anticolonial movements that saw their ultimate goal as the wrestling of political power from Europeans. In short, alienation produced nationalism. Education was the vital tool through which the effective communication with and mobilization of the masses could be achieved. To achieve their objectives, African nationalists had to reconfigure their elitist stature and enlist the support of the African masses. Thus, Kwame Nkrumah of the Gold Coast, Sékou Touré of Guinea, Nnamdi Azikiwe of Nigeria, Julius Nyerere of Tanganyika, and many other leaders placed a high premium on the role of education and the masses in the nationalist movements. Not only was education seen as good in and of itself, it was also considered to be the best "means of bringing about economic development and cultural self-assertion" to the colonized peoples.[36] Consequently, mass education became the centerpiece of nationalist educational policy and reform.

Once African nationalists seized the initiative and began to demand independence, they realized that Africanization of the colonial structures and institutions was the only purposeful way to articulate their positions and dislodge colonialism. The need for reform and Africanization in the educational system became a *sine qua non* to the nationalist slogan. In light of this, the expansion of educational facilities and reorientation of the educational curricula and philosophy remained paramount. This involved increasing the number of primary, secondary, and technical schools and universities as well as raising the consciousness of the masses about the value of modern education. To leave education to expand at its own pace "without any proper guidance of direction, without intelligent stimulation," the nationalists insisted, "would be clearly irresponsible and positively unsuitable for the needs of Africa today."[37] One of the most enduring demands of

---

35. Chukwuemeka Ike, *University Development in Africa: The Nigerian Experience*, (London: Oxford University Press, 1976), 1.

36. Datta, *Education and Society*, 22.

37. "Proposals for an Education Policy for the Western Region, Nigeria, 1952" in Cowan et.al. (eds.), *Education and Nation-Building in Africa*, 141.

nationalists was that the colonial regimes stop withholding funds for education; rather, they should devote a much larger percentage of government budgets to mass education.

Nonetheless, the need to create a national spirit and identity through the schools clashed with the existing use of foreign teachers, foreign language, and foreign control of education. School curricula had been little adapted to African conditions and values, and church schools remained under the control of foreign priests. Education could not be made relevant to Africa so long as it was under the control of foreigners—missionaries or colonialists. However, given the relatively cheap and efficient educational administration of the religious bodies, African nationalists shied away from pressing for complete nationalization of their school systems. Consequently, the Africanization of education could not be completed.

Once the nationalists began to take the mantle of power in their respective territories, they pressed for more reforms and further expansion of the educational system. Although the number of primary school pupils had tripled in the Gold Coast by 1946–1951, the new African majority in government continued to push for more expansion, so that by 1957 there were more than half a million children enrolled in primary school classes. Similar expansion occurred in secondary schools and teacher-training classes. When it came to power in the Western Region of Nigeria in 1951, the first major step taken by the Action Group Government of Obafemi Awolowo was a plan for universal primary education (UPE) in the region. Some of these changes, however, stemmed from the pressures of public opinion. The masses had begun to view education as the panacea for not only material benefits but also higher standards of living. In some cases, the nationalists were forced to offer universal, free primary education even when they could not realistically afford it. As a result, the UPE schemes were soon abandoned.

African leaders saw education as the key to technological modernization, an effective tool for imparting a sense of African dignity, and a means of promoting political integration. The need to overcome the "colonial mentality" by creating a new sense of confidence in African tradition and heritage constituted a major concern for the emergent African elite. The propagation of this new sense of African mentality fell within the professional ambit of teachers and, hence, for the nationalists, the political future of Africa depended upon a reorientation of the educational system. Adaptation and Africanization were no longer suspect, as they became the bedrock of nationalist educational philosophy and policy. As a result, the Western system of education devised by colonial administrations had to be adapted to the needs and desires of the African peoples and the changing times. School curricula were to be Africanized to place more emphasis on the study of African history, ethnography, and vernacular languages and literature. The curricula, standards, and syllabi of the new educational institutions, including the university colleges in the Gold Coast, Nigeria, Uganda, and Sierra Leone, came under a barrage of criticism.

Nnamdi Azikiwe's dissatisfaction with the British elitist traditions of the University College at Ibadan partly led to his establishment of the University of Nigeria, Nsukka in 1960, based on American models.[38] Similarly, Nkrumah's opposition to the practices of the University College of the Gold Coast at Legon

---

38. Azikiwe was the first African Governor-General and President of Nigeria between 1960 and 1966. He was educated in the United States and, not surprisingly, he became enamored of American educational system.

Figure 9.2.   A woman graduating from an African university. The vigorous attention on the education of women did not come until after 1960.

culminated in the founding of the University of Cape Coast and the University of Science and Technology at Kumasi in 1961. While Azikiwe was appalled that Ibadan had no courses in agriculture, domestic science, engineering, business administration, or education, Nkrumah insisted, "a University must relate its activities to the needs of the society in which it exists."[39] Ironically, however, while Azikiwe and Nkrumah preached adaptation and Africanization, they flirted with

---

39. *Daily Graphic*, (Accra Gold Coast: 30 May 1953).

foreign standards—American and Soviet systems. In the end, a complex combination of factors, including ethnic and regional squabbles, placed educational expansion and changes at the forefront of nation building in the emergent independent states, culminating in the proliferation of educational institutions, especially those of higher education.

Conclusion

The educational policies of the colonial powers prior to World War II were dictated purely by both administrative convenience and the view Europeans held of the role of the educated African under colonial rule. For the British, the indirect rule policy, which placed high premium on chiefs rather than the educated elites, continued to frustrate African demands for educational expansion and reform. Adaptation, as articulated by the British, was intended to keep Africans undereducated and, therefore, less competitive for the colonial service positions. It was believed that complete education would "spoil" Africans by turning them into agitators and nationalists. Similarly, for the French, the Portuguese, and the Belgians, the policy of assimilation and paternalism provided education to a select few whom they would use in the administration of their colonies. War exigencies and the need to retain the loyalty and support of their African subjects forced Britain and France to initiate liberal educational changes and reforms. Not only was expansion encouraged in primary and secondary levels of education, efforts were placed in high gear toward the establishment of universities in Africa. At the end of the war, a grateful France not only expanded the facilities for education in her colonies but also encouraged more Africans to proceed to France for education on scholarships.

The nationalists, who had been inspired by the events and aftermath of the war, began to press not only for greater expansion of educational facilities but also insisted on the need for adaptation and Africanization. As they prepared to take over power from Europeans, they resolved that the only effective way to decolonize the minds of Africans revolved around Africanization and a reorientation of the inherited colonial educational system. However, since African nationalists were also products of Western education and its attendant alienation, their efforts became quite arduous. When independence came in 1960, nationalist leaders were determined to revise the inherited colonial educational structures as they began to relate the standards, curricula, and content of education to the realities of African needs and desires. The extent to which they succeeded remains to be evaluated.

Review Questions

1. Discuss the educational objectives of missionaries and European colonial regimes in Africa. In what ways did these objectives coincide with those of the Africans?
2. Compare and contrast Africans' rejection of adaptation as it was formulated by the British in 1925 and their demand for adaptation and Africanization in the postwar period.

3. Account for the dramatic reforms and changes in colonial education in the postwar years.

Additional Reading

Cowan, L. Gray, James O'Connell, and David G. Scanlon, eds. *Education and Nation-Building in Africa*. New York: Frederick A. Praeger, 1965.

Datta, Ansu. *Education and Society: A Sociology of African Education*. New York: St. Martin's Press, 1984.

Nwauwa, Apollos O. *Imperialism, Academe and Nationalism: Britain and University Education for Africans, 1860–1960*. London: Frank Cass, 1997.

White, Bob W. "Talk about School: Education and the Colonial Project in French and British Africa (1860–1960)." *Comparative Education*, 32, 1, 1996.

Chapter 10

Social and Religious Changes

Julius O. Adekunle

This chapter analyzes social and religious changes in Africa from the out-break of World War II in 1939 to independence. During the war, the provision of social amenities was slow, but at its conclusion in 1945, significant changes took place in the areas of education, health, urbanization, and religion. The analysis of these changes is based on the policies and activities of the colonial powers and the responses of the Africans, especially the educated elite who provided leadership for their various communities. This chapter examines the role of Christian missionaries in evangelizing as well as providing Western education for Africans. Closely interwoven with colonial economic policy was the provision of social services such as education, transportation, communication, and health. During World War II, social issues did not constitute a priority for the colonial authorities, but from 1945 onward, economic realities and an increase in nationalist activities compelled the colonial powers to pay more attention to the provision of social services. The chapter concludes that, in spite of the slowness of provision and the inadequacy of social services during the colonial period, some lasting and desirable changes took place.

* * *

Colonial Economy and Social Services

Underlying the European colonization of Africa was the belief in the superiority of Western civilization and the desire to exploit the African economy. The Europeans considered Africans to be backward socially, economically, politically, and technologically. The Africans, therefore, needed to be civilized. Looming in the background of this self-imposed civilizing mission were economic interests. Instead of establishing industries in Africa, the Europeans transported raw materials such as palm oil, palm kernels, ivory, cocoa, coffee, cotton, sisal, rubber, and minerals such as gold, uranium, copper, tin, and lead to Europe. While African resources were exploited to meet the needs of Europe's industrialization, no corresponding developments took place in Africa. European exploitation of Africans was exacerbated by the economic depressions of the interwar years during which time the colonial authorities failed to promote programs that benefited Africans

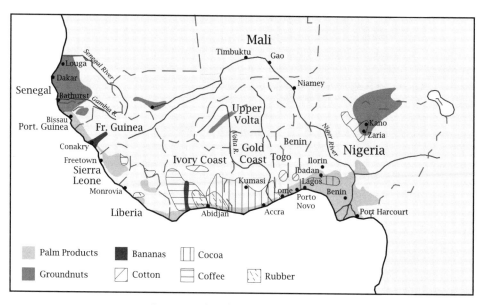

Crop production in West Africa.

or stimulated lasting social growth. For instance, despite the intensive use of forced or cheap human labor, colonial governments provided few health facilities, accepted a low standard of education, and constructed very few motor roads. African participation in government was almost nonexistent.

The reorientation of the African economy from food to cash crops not only drove Africans to supply what the Europeans wanted but also forced them to look for wage labor that would enable them to pay taxes. This situation adversely affected the African economy as well as the close-knit traditional social system. The movement of migrant workers to urban centers for wage labor led to the underdevelopment of the rural areas. Since the migrant workers did not receive an education or learn industrial skills, many of them could earn only enough to pay their taxes and found it difficult to improve their living standards. Significant changes, however, took place after World War II due to the pressure that the African nationalist leaders put on the colonial governments. For instance, more roads and railways were constructed, more schools were established, and more urban centers developed as a result of industrialization. Whether initiated by African nationalists or the colonial powers, the provision of social services improved during the period of decolonization after World War II.

Christianity grew rapidly during the colonial period, but to prevent religious conflicts and to ensure the success of colonial administration, the colonial powers did not permit evangelical work to be performed in Muslim-dominated areas. The experience of the British in Nigeria and the French in North and West Africa showed how religious conflicts could disrupt colonial administration. The growth of Islam and its civilization combined with colonial attitudes made it difficult for Christianity to penetrate into Muslim areas. The absence of Christian missionaries made the provision of Western education in Muslim-controlled areas quite inadequate. In Nigeria, while the Fulani and Hausa in the north received Islamic education, Christian education flourished in the south among the Edo, Igbo, and

Yoruba. Educational and religious differences have continued to create social and political problems for Nigeria.

Similar educational and social problems occurred in the Portuguese-controlled colonies of Angola and Mozambique. In Angola, Protestant missions evangelized and constructed hospitals, dispensaries, and schools. Although, by European standards, the services were limited and the number of hospitals and schools was small when compared with the population of Angola, the missionaries' contributions were impressive. In Mozambique, however, the Protestants had some difficulties, primarily because of the Muslim factor. The Portuguese government even closed down the Protestant hospitals and schools between 1919 and 1930, accusing them of providing inadequate services.[1]

Pre-1939 Development

Between 1914 and 1918, when World War I was fought, the colonial powers concentrated on the production of weapons and neglected the importation of commodities. After the war, the series of economic depressions that occurred worldwide made it difficult for the European powers to provide, or Africans to enjoy, economic and social services. This led the European firms in Africa to downsize their workforces and reduce wages for unskilled and semiskilled workers. For example, in the Nigerian tin mines, workers' weekly wages fell from six to seven shillings in 1928 to three shillings and six pence in 1937.[2] Throughout Africa, social inequality and widespread unemployment provoked Africans to express their frustration and desperation in the form of demonstrations, protests, and strikes. In West Africa, groups of workers organized strikes in both the French and British colonies. Strikes were organized in French West Africa in cities such as Conakry (1919), Porto Novo (1923), and Lomé (1933) and in British West Africa in countries such as Sierra Leone (1919, 1920, 1926, 1935, and 1937), the Gambia (1921 and 1929), the Gold Coast (1924 and 1930), and Nigeria (1920).[3] In spite of the widespread strikes, trade unions had not yet come into being. Trade unionism was a post-World War II phenomenon.

In North and West Africa, the French established some small-scale industries, but very little was produced or exported. However, the French did improve transportation and communication with the construction of roads and the introduction of motor vehicles, trains, and air travel. While these programs were intended to boost the French economy, they also helped to promote social growth in France's North African colonies. General Lyautey, the French Resident of Morocco (1912–1925), promoted education for the Africans in order to win support for the French government. He allowed French medical doctors to provide health care for the Muslims who had not yet submitted to French rule in order to gain

---

1. James Duffy, *Portuguese Africa* (Cambridge, MA: Harvard University Press, 1959), 126–9.

2. A. G. Hopkins, *An Economic History of West Africa* (London: Longman, 1973), 257.

3. Ibid., 257–8.

their favor.[4] In contrast, the French did not pay sufficient attention to the social and economic growth of their West African colonies, which were regarded primarily as purveyors of raw materials.[5]

In the Sudan, the over-reliance on a single cash crop, cotton, further complicated economic problems. Due to a series of crop diseases and locust invasions, cotton production fell and government revenue dropped. Faced with stringent financial conditions, the government reduced workers' salaries by thirty percent[6] and left the cotton farmers to grapple with more serious social and economic problems. In Northern Rhodesia (modern Zambia), copper had been mined before colonialization began,[7] but major exploitation was delayed until the Mufulira and Nchanga Mines were reopened in 1933 and 1939, respectively.[8] Until the mines were reopened, workers had to find alternative means of survival, and the government was forced to pare down social services in health and education.[9]

The Portuguese colonies experienced the worst economic and social conditions. Due to internal political and industrial vicissitudes in Portugal, little attention was devoted to political and social changes in Africa. For example, an African Education Commission was established under the aegis of the Phelps-Stokes Fund, and, in its report, the Commission indicated that Angola and Mozambique were not advanced in education because few schools existed, teaching was inadequate, and the government did not provide enough funds to improve the situation.[10] In 1932, when Antonio de Oliveira Salazar emerged as the prime minister of Portugal, Portuguese policies and administration became even worse. Salazar drastically reduced government expenditure, and he neither invested in Africa nor attracted investors to it. James Duffy, however, believed that Salazar's stringent measures pulled Angola from bankruptcy in the 1920s and set an economic pattern that carried both Angola and Mozambique through the depression of the 1930s. In both colonies, the Portuguese subsidized development projects mainly by using foreign capital.[11]

---

4. Robin Bidwell, "French North Africa," in *The Cambridge Encyclopedia of Africa,* ed. Roland Oliver and Michael Crowder (Cambridge: Cambridge University Press, 1981), 178–9.

5. Michael Crowder, "French Black Africa," in *Cambridge Encyclopedia of Africa,* ed. Oliver and Crowder, 179–81.

6. P. M. Holt and M. W. Daly, *A History of the Sudan: From the Coming of Islam to the Present Day,* 5th ed. (London: Pearson Education Limited, 2000), 121.

7. Cecil Rhodes has been credited with the development of the copper belt region. In 1891, his British South Africa Company extended its charter to the northern Zambezi River. As a result, the whole region came under company rule.

8. There were four mines: Roan Antelope, Mufulira, Rhokana, and Nchanga. They all began operation in the 1920s. While Roan Antelope and Mufulira were controlled by the Rhodesian Selection Trust, the British-owned Anglo-American Corporation of South Africa controlled Rhokana and Nchanga. R. E. Baldwin, "The Northern Rhodesian Economy and the Rise of the Copper Industry," in *An Economic History of Tropical Africa,* vol. 2, ed. Z. A. and J. M. Konczacki, (London: Frank Cass, 1977), 60–70.

9. John D. Hargreaves, *Decolonization in Africa* (London: Longman, 1988), 35.

10. The small number of schools was associated with the fact that the Portuguese did not take the education of the African seriously. They believed that Christian morality and instruction in how to work was what the African needed. This presumption emanated from the European perspective that the African was lazy and incapable of understanding Western education. Duffy, *Portuguese Africa,* 258–60.

11. Duffy, *Portuguese Africa,* 332–3.

Angola and Mozambique could not establish economic relations with other European countries, because the Portuguese dominated their export and import trade between 1938 and 1955.[12] In both colonies, forced labor (*chibaro*) was imposed when inadequate numbers of migrant workers were available on the sugar and coffee plantations.[13] Cotton became the predominant crop, which African farmers could grow and sell only to the Portuguese; with world competition and low market prices, the farmers could not earn much from the crop. In the midst of misery, and as a means of resistance, farmers sang anticolonial songs, and urban centers grew as a result of population movement in search of wage labor.[14] According to Zbigniew A. Konczacki, the Portuguese administration "differed significantly from the mature colonialism evolved by Britain, France and even Belgium."[15] This is not to exonerate the other colonial powers, because all of them exploited Africans.

Social changes occurred in Somalia, because the Italians devoted attention to the welfare of their subjects by providing dispensaries in the rural areas and hospitals in the urban centers. In 1939 they established schools for training hospital workers. As in other colonies, Christian missions provided education for the people. Initially, Somali and Italian children attended the same schools, but that changed in 1929, when educational facilities expanded and the student population in elementary schools increased from 1,390 in 1930 to 1,776 in 1939.[16]

Owing to the rapid growth of white settler and Asian trading communities in Kenya in the 1920s, conflicts occurred over land, labor, and taxation. In their determination to control trade, the white settlers acquired the fertile land and exploited Africans through cheap labor. The British colonial government became aware of the growing economic and racial tension and tried to curtail the powers of the white settlers, but it did very little to improve the social and economic conditions of Africans. As farmers, the Kikuyu (the largest ethnic group in Kenya) were the most adversely affected by the appropriation of land. The insensitivity of the colonial government to the people's socioeconomic frustration led to the formation of the Kikuyu Central Association (KCA) in the 1920s, through which protests were organized against the colonial imposition of taxation, the acquisition of land, and the use of forced labor.[17]

By the outbreak of World War II in 1939, Africans had demonstrated to their colonial authorities that they would not tolerate exploitation or the building of European capitalism at their expense. Their resistance, however, lacked coordination and articulation until after World War II, when education, nationalism, trade

---

12. Peter Wickins, *Africa, 1880–1980: An Economic History* (Cape Town: Oxford University Press, 1986), 129.

13. David Birmingham, "Portuguese Africa," *Cambridge Encyclopedia of Africa*, ed. Oliver and Crowder, 190.

14. For more information, see Allen Isaacman, *Cotton Is the Mother of Poverty: Peasants, Work, and Rural Struggle in Colonial Mozambique, 1938–1961* (Berkeley, CA: Heinemann, 1996).

15. Zbigniew A. Konczacki, "Portugal's Economic Policy in Africa: A Reassessment," in *Economic History of Tropical Africa*, vol. 2, ed. Konczacki and Konczacki, 71–87.

16. I. M. Lewis, *The Modern History of Somaliland: From Nation to State* (New York: Frederick A. Praeger, Publishers, 1965), 97.

17. Wunyabari O. Maloba, *Mau Mau and Kenya: An Analysis of a Peasant Revolt* (Bloomington: Indiana University Press, 1993), 1–4.

unionism, and international influences came into play and compelled colonial governments to develop social programs for Africans.

Africans and World War II

The end of World War II heralded a new phase in the social and political history of Africa. Between 1939 and 1945, colonial economic exploitation continued, and a substantial number of Africans went to the war front. The important role of Africans in World War II should not be ignored; many of them were drafted to fight on the side of their colonial masters. In West Africa, the British mobilized about 700,000 soldiers from their various colonies.[18] Participation in the war exposed the Africans to new experiences in warfare and in social and interracial relations. Africans' perceptions of their colonial masters changed after exposure to the physical weaknesses and vulnerability of the Europeans. They found that the Europeans were not as invincible as they had thought them to be, and this fact erased the aura of European superiority. On their return, the ex-servicemen brought with them new ideas about freedom and self-rule.

The wartime reports of the ex-servicemen, in addition to worldwide opposition to colonialism, inspired Africans to demand social change and an end to colonialism. The concept of self-rule as enunciated in the Atlantic Charter respected the right of all peoples to choose the form of government under which they would live.[19] Once the Atlantic Charter was issued in 1941, African soldiers expected better social and economic lives. No immediate changes took place. Realizing that the colonial masters had not met their social and economic expectations, the veterans collaborated with the educated elite to form the vanguard in the decolonization struggles. The combined efforts gave a stimulus to nationalism, which became an indispensable instrument for achieving self-rule and for establishing nation-states.

After 1945, the colonial powers began to introduce social changes. A combination of factors made the changes possible. The role of ex-servicemen, the increasing pressure from the nationalists, the growth of education, and the urban population made the colonial authorities rethink their positions and policies toward Africans. In both western and eastern Africa, people flocked to urban centers for employment. The period of decolonization (1945–1960) witnessed an intensified nationalist struggle and saw more people enjoying social amenities. It was an era of hope and great expectations, when Africans expressed their desire to take control of the social and political affairs of their states. In view of the strength of African demands, colonial authorities were compelled to provide more employment opportunities, to construct more elementary and secondary schools, and to increase health facilities and services. Education began to have a liberating influence; the more Africans that became educated within and outside the conti-

---

18. Vincent B. Khapoya, *The African Experience: An Introduction*, 2nd ed. (Upper Saddle River, NJ: Prentice Hall, 1998), 158.

19. Basil Davidson, *Let Freedom Come: Africa in Modern History* (Boston: Little, Brown and Company, 1978), 197.

nent, the more they put pressure on their colonial masters. The educated elite organized mass movements and led the crusade for colonialism's termination. They won the support of the masses by emphasizing the weakness of colonialism and the inadequate social amenities it had provided. The period of decolonization became one of political and social advancement for Africans.

The increase in the European demand for raw materials after World War II accelerated the processes of economic growth and social change. Great demand for products such as cocoa, cotton, palm oil, sisal, groundnuts, and coffee increased the economic prosperity of many Africans. Even though the real income of agricultural workers was low, general economic growth provided opportunities for social change.[20] In West and East Africa, William Tordoff identified a number of social and economic groups, with specific interests, that supported the nationalists in pressuring the colonial authorities for greater social changes. These groups were the traditional rulers, professionals (doctors and lawyers), teachers, clerks, small merchants, Westernized Africans, urban workers, petty traders, and cash-crop farmers.[21] Forming powerful social and economic associations, the groups provided a base from which the nationalists could articulate their demands. Anticolonial sentiments spread beyond the educated elite to the farmers and the urban unemployed. According to Tordoff,

> Peasant farmers—consisting [of] the bulk of the population in virtually all African states—together with urban workers and the unemployed, were the "ordinary" people who looked for an improvement in their standard of living, better health care and increased educational opportunities for their children.[22]

The growth of education and the economy became a dynamic source of social change and political transformation. The more education Africans received, the stronger was their power of opposition against the unfavorable policies of the colonial governments.

Colonial governments took some measures to revitalize the economy in order to increase social services. In Northern Rhodesia (Zambia), the exploitation of copper mines increased in the 1950s when operations began at new sites, such as the Rhodesian Selection Trust mine in 1956 and Bancroft in 1957.[23] In West Africa, the British established marketing boards in the Gold Coast and Nigeria to

---

20. Elliot J. Berg, "Real Income Trends in West Africa, 1939–1960," in *Economic Transition in Africa*, ed. Melville J. Herskovits and Mitchell Harwitz (London: Routledge and Kegan Paul, 1964), 199–238.

21. William Tordoff, *Government and Politics in Africa*, 2nd ed. (Bloomington: Indiana University Press, 1984), 43–4.

22. Ibid., 44.

23. Northern Rhodesia experienced a rapid growth of copper production after World War II. Production increased from 138, 000 tons in 1934 to 379,000 tons in 1954. Agricultural production also increased. The growth in production was due to the increase in the price of copper. It should be noted, however, that the growth benefited only the European mining companies and not the African miners, who were paid meager wages and whose standards of living remained poor. For a long time, the copper mining industry dominated the economy of Northern Rhodesia. Baldwin, "The Northern Rhodesian Economy and the Rise of the Copper Industry," 60–70.

stabilize prices for cash crops and farmers' incomes. While the boards helped maintain social and economic standards for the farmers through price stabilization and subsidies, the government provided scholarship funds and sponsored educational programs. For example, the Ghana Educational Trust successfully established and funded some secondary and teacher training colleges through the reserve funds from the cocoa industry. The funds provided by the Ghana Cocoa Marketing Board were used to construct the Akuafo (Farmers) Hall at the University of Ghana.[24]

In Kenya and Southern Rhodesia, noticeable social changes occurred only among the white settlers. The appropriation of land by the white settlers in North Africa, Kenya, and Southern Rhodesia led to the relocation of Africans, creating more social, political, and economic problems. For Africans, land was not only their livelihood; it was sacred. In no other place was the struggle over land more vigorous than in Kenya, where the white settlers prevented progress and social change for Africans because the settlers appropriated land and controlled the economy. In order to maintain their superior positions, privileges, and standards of living, the settlers frustrated the efforts of the British colonial administration to provide social amenities for the people of Kenya. In the 1950s, the settlers, aiming to consolidate their hold on the land and economy, won some concessions from the government that resulted in intensified African protests. Land remained important to the Kikuyu farmers, as it was to the Maasai cattle keepers, but it was the former who provided leadership for the uprising that erupted in 1952, during which the British arrested and imprisoned Jomo Kenyatta. Further protests by the farmers erupted over Kenyatta's imprisonment. An armed peasant uprising broke out with the goal of reclaiming the land. The rebellion spread fast and continued for several years. While the British described the farmers as rebels and called them Mau Mau, the people called themselves land and freedom fighters. Although they were ultimately subdued in 1955, the Kikuyu had demonstrated that the British needed to evolve a new land policy and set in motion a process of social changes for the people of Kenya.

The Growth of Urbanization and Trade Unions

World War II drained the economic and technological resources of the Western world, giving rise to stringent colonial measures in Africa. For example, low production levels in Europe led to the scarcity and high prices of imported goods in Africa. As part of their recovery measures, expatriate firms downsized their workforces (leading to a high rate of unemployment), reduced wages, and squeezed out African merchants. Due to lack of capital and the monopoly of trade by foreign companies, African merchants suffered economic defeat. All of these conditions relegated farmers, urban workers, and small-scale business people to a lower standard of living. Workers in urban and industrial centers

---

24. F. K. Buah, *West Africa since A. D. 1000* (London: Macmillan, 1977), 142.

formed strong trade unions through which they expressed their discontent in riots and strikes.

Urbanization

Industrialization was a key to modernization and urbanization. The growth of industrial centers, the development of commerce, and the improvement in transportation greatly increased the urban population. Cities such as Accra in the Gold Coast, Dakar in Senegal, Dar es Salaam in Tanganyika, Khartoum in Sudan, Lagos and Kano in Nigeria, Nairobi in Kenya, and Salisbury in Nyasaland witnessed increases in population. During the process of decolonization in the 1950s, improvements in educational and industrial infrastructure encouraged workers in the rural areas to gravitate to urban centers. While rural economies remained largely subsistent, Africans moved to cities in order to take advantage of growing industries and job opportunities in mining centers. The urban centers and new towns became attractive places for young people who wanted to escape the strict control and discipline of elders and have a taste of independent life. In Nigeria, the textile factories, flour mills, tire plants, bicycle factories, cotton gins, and cement and asbestos factories attracted workers to cities such as Lagos, Ibadan, Enugu, Port Harcourt, Kaduna, and Kano. Between 1921 and 1952 in eastern Nigeria, four cities increased in population by seventy percent as a result of trade, industrialization, and mining.[25]

One effect of industrialization, education, and urbanization was the emergence of a type of social stratification that had not existed in preindustrial times. In the copper belt in Kenya, the Europeans occupied supervisory positions over African miners and workers, thereby increasing the urban problems of racial and social division. Violence erupted, not only due to political grievances, but also because of social inequality and the insufficiency of essential amenities. Another development was the emergence of an African middle class composed of merchants who were able to acquire wealth through trading or establishing small businesses. The Yoruba call this group the *olowos* (the wealthy) to differentiate them from the *mekunnus* (the commoners). The gap between the two groups widened as the wealthy went on to attain higher social statuses and refused to intermingle with the less privileged.

Urbanization had some positive impacts. Cities attracted immigrants who wanted to enjoy freedom and social advancement.[26] The immigrants adapted themselves to better housing, pipe-borne water, education, and health services. Some were self-employed in tailoring, barbering, and crafts in which little capital was required. Capital formation was made possible by profits from industrial and mining jobs as well as from self-employment. Such profits were either expended on housing projects in the rural areas or used to begin new businesses. In this respect, urbanization fostered the gradual economic and social development of the rural areas.

Urbanization permitted the spread of Western languages and dress. The urbanized and educated assumed a new status, because they were able to speak the

25. Toyin Falola, *The History of Nigeria* (Westport, CT: Greenwood Press, 1999), 79.
26. Wallerstein, Immanuel, *Africa: The Politics of Independence* (New York: Vintage Books, 1986), 34–5.

colonial language, which was considered a symbol of elite status. Being exposed to Western culture, urban dwellers saw the need for social changes more than rural dwellers, who had little access to government services. Through visits to their villages, workers passed on new ideas from the cities.

Urban societies became stratified into the administrative or professional bourgeoisie, the sub-elite, and the workers or the urban proletariat. Membership in these groups depended largely on individual effort and achievement rather than birth.[27] Unlike the rural dwellers, city dwellers enjoyed banking services and other services such as the radio and the post office.

The enjoyment of city life did not obliterate traditional ethnic affiliation. A network of ethnic, economic, and social associations emerged to provide necessary support for new immigrants. In Nigeria, the Igbo and Yoruba formed such ethnic associations. In the Gold Coast, sixty-one ethnic associations existed in Sekondi and Takoradi in the 1950s.[28] Similarly, the urban areas of French Equatorial Africa hosted various ethnic and racial organizations.[29]

There were some problems associated with industrialization and urbanization. Overcrowding, the spread of diseases, prostitution, and a high crime rate characterized city life. More often than not, the populations of the urban centers were predominantly male, and divorce became rampant as a result of married men migrating to the city and abandoning their wives. This weakened traditional social relations and values.

Trade Unions

In the process of decolonization, political agitation accompanied social and economic changes. Workers, whether self-employed, earning wages, or salaried, wanted improvements in their earning levels in order to raise their standards of living. Africans expressed their dissatisfaction with the unfavorable social and economic policies of the colonial authorities, and they expressed their reactions in different ways. They formed trade unions; voluntary organizations; and ethnic, social, and economic associations, especially in urban and industrial centers. Since the people in the rural areas were predominantly farmers, urban centers became attractive to migrant workers, even though most of them had not acquired the industrial skills or education necessary to secure good jobs.

Nationalists and trade unionists worked together to demand improvements in people's social conditions. The cooperation of nationalists and trade unionists strengthened the nationalists in their political struggle and enabled the trade unionists to promote a wider awareness of the social desires of workers. The economic situation in Africa after World War II prompted the formation of strong

---

27. A. Adu Boahen, *African Perspectives on Colonialism* (Baltimore: Johns Hopkins University Press, 1987), 105.

28. E. Franklin Frazier, "The Impact of Colonialism on African Social Forms and Personality," in *Africa in the Modern World*, 5th impression, ed. Calvin W. Stillman, (Chicago: University of Chicago Press, 1967), 75.

29. Jean-Paul Lebeuf, "Centres Urbains d'Afrique Equatoriale Française," *Africa* 23 (October 1953): 285–97.

trade unions with large memberships. The table below shows the number of workers and trade unions in different parts of Africa, explaining why nationalists allied with them in demanding social changes.

Trade Unionists in Africa in 1947

Table 1			
Territory	Number of Wage Earners	Percentage of Total Population	Number of Trade Unionists
French West Africa	350,000	2.0	70,000
French Equatorial Africa	190,000	4.2	10,000
French Cameroons	125,000	4.0	35,000
Nigeria (and British Cameroons)	500,000	1.5	150,000
Gold Coast	200,000	4.5	150,000
Sierra Leone	80,000	4.0	20,000
Gambia	5,000	2.5	1,500
Belgian Congo (and Ruanda-Urundi)	1,000,000	8.5	6,000
Uganda	280,000	4.0	1,500
Kenya	450,000	8.0	32,000
Tanganyika	400,000	6.0	400
British Somaliland	2,000	0.3	Nil
Somalia	25,000	2.0	3,700
Zanzibar	5,000	4.0	900
Northern Rhodesia	250,000	13.0	50,000
Nyasaland	120,000	24.0	1,000
Southern Rhodesia	530,000	24.0	Nil
Sudan	200,000	2.0	100,000

Source: Thomas Hodgkin, *Nationalism in Colonial Africa*, New York: New York University Press, 1957, 118.

The numerous trade unions demanded better crop prices for farmers and higher wages or salaries for unskilled and skilled workers. In some cases, trade unions did not act in isolation from each other; they combined their efforts as partners in the struggle. For example, industrial and farmers' unions acted jointly with public workers in transport and communication to embark on strike actions. Workers had organized strikes in the interwar years, but these became more frequent after World War II. Strikes occurred in Nigeria (1945), Madagascar (1947), French West Africa (1947), the Ivory Coast (1947), Senegal (1947–1948), Guinea and Dahomey (1949–1950), and Kenya (1952). These examples show that the late

1940s and early 1950s could be regarded as a period of strikes and labor unrest which served as wake up calls for the colonial authorities, inducing them to pay attention to the Africans' social and economic conditions. The frequent and often serious strikes threatened colonial governments and demonstrated that the power of African workers to resist obnoxious colonial policies could not be underestimated.

The strike of 1945 was one of the most successful work actions in Nigerian history, not only because approximately thirty-three thousand railway workers and civil servants participated, but also because Michael Imoudou (leader of the railway workers' union), Herbert Macaulay, and Nnamdi Azikiwe (political nationalists) organized it. Because it was a national strike, G. C. Whiteley, the acting governor, described it as "a political weapon" and he admitted that

> There is little more I can do in the way of positive action to end the strike....[The] mood of the people in Lagos in general is such that there are few lengths short of violence to which they would not go to secure greatly increased wages. With a population which is largely either uneducated or semi-educated, among which an anti-European Press has considerable license, it is of no use to appeal to reason.[30]

The strikes and riots led the anticolonial press, founded by Nigerians, to express nationalistic opinions and to demand social change.[31] The newspapers involved included the *Lagos Weekly Record*, the *Nigerian Chronicle*, the *Nigerian Pioneer*, the *Nigerian Times*, and the *West African Pilot*. Until his death in 1946, Macaulay remained the foremost nationalist leader, a role that earned him the title of "Father of Nigerian Nationalism."

In the Gold Coast, economic problems such as the monopoly of trade by foreign companies, the high prices of goods, and the destruction of diseased cocoa trees led to the emergence of powerful and dynamic movements that put pressure on the colonial government for social changes. Cocoa farmers disagreed with the British over low prices for their products, and World War II veterans expressed their displeasure at not being employed in government jobs. As a result of the government's inertia, riots broke out as the people decided to boycott all European goods, and, led by ex-servicemen, they marched to Government House on February 28, 1948. Disturbances and looting occurred. The police opened fire and killed two of the rioters. The government arrested and imprisoned Dr. Kwame Nkrumah and some members of his Convention People's Party (CPP) and appointed the Coussey Committee to investigate the riots. Its report was implemented in the Coussey Constitution of 1951.

Trade union and political party relations were common in French colonies. In Guinea, Sékou Touré, who led his country to independence, had been a trade union leader. In French Cameroon, while the main political party, the Union des Populations du Cameroun (UPC), initially worked with the leading trade union, the Union des Syndicats Confédérés du Cameroun, the relationship became strained in 1955 when the French prohibited the UPC.[32] The relationship be-

---

30. As quoted in Frederick Cooper, *Decolonization and African Society: The Labor Question in French and West Africa* (Cambridge: Cambridge University Press, 1996), 135.
31. Boahen, *African Perspectives on Colonialism*, 68.
32. Tordoff, *Government and Politics in Africa*, 54–5.

tween trade unions and political parties strengthened the nationalists' effort in mobilizing the people, thus creating more political and economic awareness.

Wage discrimination and racial segregation forced people in South Africa into separate social groups. As in Kenya, the white minority in South Africa controlled the economy and dictated government policies. In 1942, the government prohibited strikes by Africans, but because of depressed wages and harsh social, living, and working conditions, including inadequate transportation and housing, the African Mineworkers Union led about fifty thousand African miners in a strike action.[33] By the 1950s, when the apartheid policy had been fully implemented, two main groups of trade unions had emerged: the Trade Union Council of South Africa, comprising seventy affiliated unions with 191,063 members, and the South African Confederation of Labour, with thirty affiliated unions and 155,000 members.[34] In 1956, the government passed the Industrial Coalition Act, which restricted certain skilled jobs to white workers, and the South African Garment Workers Union embarked on a strike. These actions brought together workers and associations to fight in a common cause. Black workers organized widespread protests later, especially in 1987 when 250,000 members of the Black National Union of Mineworkers staged a three-week strike.[35]

Christianity, Education, and the African

Islam was introduced to several parts of Africa long before Christianity, but by the end of the nineteenth century, Christian missionaries had become agents of European imperialism in Africa. Christianity did not seek to tolerate African traditional religions; it aimed to replace them. While Islam condoned some aspects of African culture, Christianity condemned them. Christianity grew under the protection of the colonial administrators, but it competed with Islam. The growth of African independent churches strengthened evangelical work, because their activities were closely associated with the process of decolonization. Both Christianity and Islam were effective in relegating to the background, but not completely displacing, African traditional religions.

While colonial control encouraged the replacement of African religions with Christianity in some areas, it did not permit Christian influence to spread to Muslim-dominated regions. This was to prevent religious conflict and to avoid upheavals that would disrupt the colonial political process. Lord Lugard, the governor-general of Nigeria, set up an indirect rule system in the Muslim-dominated north and prevented Christian missionaries from operating there. Subsequent governors followed the same approach, thereby creating a wide gap between the educational achievements of the southern and northern regions.

---

33. Leo Kuper, "African Nationalism in South Africa, 1910–1964," in *The Oxford History of South Africa, 1879–1966*, vol. 2, ed. Monica Wilson and Leonard Thompson (New York: Oxford University Press, 1971), 454–5.

34. Alex Hepple, *South Africa: A Political and Economic History* (New York: Frederick A. Praeger, Publishers, 1966), 241–5.

35. For more information, see M. Horrel, *South African Trade Unionism* (Johannesburg: South African Institute of Race Relations, 1961).

Figure 10.1. Priest of traditional religion.

Figure 10.2. African masquerade festival.

From all indications, Western education, colonialism, and Christianity interacted very closely in Africa. The provision of Western education stemmed from European needs. Because the colonial government, trading companies, Christian mis-

Figure 10.3. Church in Côte d'Ivoire.

Figure 10.4. Mosque in Côte d'Ivoire.

sions, and hospitals needed trained workers, education became necessary to produce the workforce. While Christian missionaries saw Western education as a
means of evangelizing Africans, colonial administrators regarded it as a "civilizing
mission," and European merchants considered it as a means of achieving their eco-

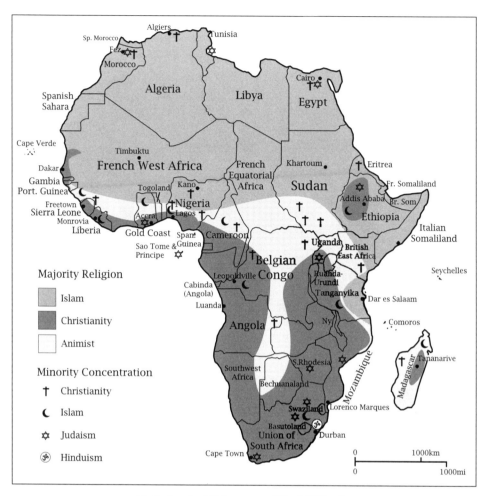

Religion in Africa, post-World War II.

nomic goals.[36] As pioneers of Western education, the Christian missionaries taught and preached mostly in the non-Muslim areas. The narrow curriculum consisted of reading the Bible, writing simple English words, and solving simple arithmetical problems. Gradually, an educated group emerged and provided a cheap labor force for the colonial administration and expatriate firms. The central government did not give these early beneficiaries of Western education any important positions or assignments; they merely served as messengers or interpreters. Thus, the educational system was designed to help the Europeans achieve their objectives of producing Africans who would serve the needs of colonial administration.

Christianity changed the beliefs of Africans and replaced traditional religions, but Western education has not been able to completely displace the indigenous system of education; the two systems of education have different values, focuses, and emphases. At first, it was difficult to separate Christianity from Western education. Education became an instrument for evangelizing Africans. To receive ed-

---

36. Wallerstein, *Africa: The Politics of Independence*, 37.

Figure 10.5. Wedding ceremony in progress.

Figure 10.6. An African modern family. Christianity and western education promoted monogamous marriages.

ucation and enjoy its benefits, an African had to convert to the new faith. The presence and impact of the Christian missionaries in providing education and health services was felt in both the urban and the rural areas.

Rather than the colonial authorities, it was the Christian missionaries who pioneered the provision of education for the Africans. The British and French colonial governments wanted to prevent the emergence of an African educated class that would compete with the Europeans in public and private employment. The colonial governments, however, assisted the missionaries as need arose. In their colonies, the British appointed boards of education to regulate finances and to oversee educational institutions. Educational standards were better in British West Africa than in East Africa for two reasons. First, there were more missionaries in the west than in the east. Secondly, there were more white settlers in East than in West Africa. Whites received better educations than indigenous Africans. The people of Kenya, for example, remained uneducated and were treated as servants by the white settlers and Indians who dominated the colony. In 1940, a West African soldier in Kenya recorded that:

> The educational standard of the natives is very low. One hardly gets one out of a hundred to speak any form of English, whether pidgin or proper.... It is surprising to see that the knowledge of the English language is so scanty in a country like Kenya, where so many white settlers live. When one considers the highly limited opportunities for Africans in this part of the continent one would thank goodness for the privileges one enjoys on the West Coast.[37]

Given that Kenya and Nigeria were both colonized by the British, similar educational development in the colonies might have been expected. But the white settlers enjoyed the advantages of colonization, and Kenyans were deprived of social services. In Nigeria, the government constructed more schools because of higher numbers of applicants after World War II. Higher education improved with the founding of University College, Ibadan, in 1948 and the Nigerian College of Arts, Science, and Technology in 1952. A major period of change in education began when southwestern Nigeria adopted the policy of universal primary education in 1954; the east followed suit in 1957. The provision of free education and facilities ultimately led to considerable investment by the British government under the Colonial Development and Welfare Acts.[38]

In Nigeria, the expansion of primary education in the west and east created a wide gap between the northerners and southerners. Owing to the lack of trained manpower in the north, southerners were transferred to the north to fill positions in government offices and factories, but they experienced hard times, and, indeed, many of them died in the Kano riots of 1953. Although Christianity and Western education had penetrated the Middle Belt, the educational system in northern Nigeria remained largely below the southern standard. The inadequacy of Western education partly explains why northern Nigeria did not achieve self-government in 1957. All of these problems suggested that the colonial government needed to per-

---

37. As cited in G. O. Olusanya, *The Second World War and Politics in Nigeria, 1939–1953* (Lagos: Evans Brothers Limited, 1973), 95, quoting from *West African Pilot*, December 6, 1940.

38. Cooper, *Decolonization and African Society*, 213.

mit the missionaries to spread Western education in the north, realizing that substantial non-Muslim populations lived in the north as well as in the Middle Belt.[39]

The growth of higher education in British West Africa has been linked to the expansion of Achimota College in the Gold Coast and Yaba College in Nigeria. Founded in 1925 by Governor Sir Gordon Guggisberg, Achimota College grew during the interwar years to become the main source of higher education for British West Africa as a whole after World War II. The enrollment of pupils in elementary schools rose from 299,705 in 1951 to 595,538 in 1957 in the Gold Coast,[40] while the number of students in Achimota College increased from 208 to 317 in one year (1957).[41]

In Nigeria and the Gold Coast, education helped produce a core of nationalist leaders and enhanced the process of social change. Dr. Kwame Nkrumah, educated in the United States and imbued with Pan-African ideas, became one of the foremost nationalist leaders in the Gold Coast. Nkrumah and other educated nationalists, such as J. B. Danquah and K. A. Busia, pressed the British government for social changes as well as asking for "self-government now." After leaving the United Gold Coast Convention (UGCC) because of political and ideological differences with its leaders, Nkrumah built a popular base by collaborating with the trade unions, local societies, and associations that drew their membership from farmers, traders, and other interest groups.[42] With this strong base, Nkrumah formed the Convention People's Party (CPP) and used his newspapers, such as the *Accra Evening News* (founded in 1948), *Morning Telegraph*, and *Daily Mail* as the official mouthpieces of the party.[43] Following a general strike organized by the Trade Union Congress in 1950, the British colonial government jailed Nkrumah, but he was subsequently released in 1951 to become the leader of government business. Nkrumah embarked on development programs that made social progress possible in the areas of road construction and education.

Like other social services, education developed slowly in French West Africa. The colonial administration did not enforce primary education for all children. Very few people attended school, and standards were poor. Furthermore, information in schools was transmitted, very largely, in French as dictated by the policy of *assimilation*. Only Qur'anic schools escaped the general rule, because the French wanted to avoid religious conflict with the Muslims.[44] By 1954, only about one thousand rural Senegalese had graduated from elementary schools. The few French Africans who received educations in Dakar or Paris were limited not only in their political activities, but also in their opportunities to struggle for social justice.

The Belgians in the Congo demonstrated their lack of interest in educating Africans by confining financial support to elementary schools. Since the Belgians

---

39. Kenneth Kirkwood, *Britain and Africa* (Baltimore: Johns Hopkins University Press, 1965), 131.

40. F. Agbodeka, *The Rise of Nation States: A History of the West African Peoples 1800–1964* (London: Thomas Nelson, 1965), 166.

41. Ibid. 167.

42. John Darwin, *Britain and Decolonization: The Retreat from Empire in the Post-war World* (New York: St. Martin's Press, 1988), 176–9.

43. A. B. Assensoh, *African Political Leadership* (Malabar, FL: Krieger Publishing Company, 1998), 91.

44. Claude Wauthier, *The Literature and Thought of Modern Africa: A Survey* (New York: Frederick A. Praeger Publishers, 1967), 35.

did not plan to decolonize immediately following World War II, they refused to provide higher education for Africans except for those who chose to be trained as Catholic priests. These circumstances severely inhibited the development of nationalism and the struggle for social change. For any meaningful transfer of power to occur, the Belgians had to improve the economic, social, and educational standards of the Congolese.[45] In one of his speeches, Patrice Lumumba, a leading nationalist (later the prime minister), realizing the importance of education to the political struggles of the Congolese, called on the Belgians to set up a system of education that would prepare the way for democratic government at independence.[46] Moise Tshombe, a successful businessman who turned to politics and became the leader of the Conakat Party, had received only a high school education.[47] Only a few people received higher education. At independence, this lack of education, together with political inexperience, created untold problems that culminated in chaos and led to the arrest and murder of Patrice Lumumba in 1961.[48]

Through their colonial development and welfare scheme, the Italians in Somaliland embarked on programs that fostered social change. In addition to the three elementary schools that were established in 1942 at Hargeisa, Berbera, and Burao, seven more were opened in 1945. Furthermore, public health services increased in rural areas and a training school for nurses was founded in 1945. The government provided financial assistance to nineteen private Qur'anic schools where Arabic and arithmetic were taught, and by 1950, concrete plans had been made to introduce secondary education.[49] The scope of agricultural services expanded with experimentation with new crops and fertilizers. By the end of 1949, Somali nationalism had begun to grow, with nationalists asking for more social changes.

When the apartheid policy came into full force in South Africa in 1948, it became impossible for the indigenous Africans to enjoy equal social rights with whites. In 1949, a commission was established to investigate appropriate conditions for African education. The commission's recommendation that all education be transmitted in the mother tongue was heavily criticized as favoring the provision of an inferior and limited type of education for Africans. Based on the commission's report, the Bantu Education Act was passed in 1953.[50] The act withdrew control of education from missionaries. Separate schools were established for the blacks where they were taught, in Bantu languages, only the skills that would make them permanent subordinates of the whites. While African students were removed from the white universities, separate colleges were established for each racial group. Because the government provided fewer schools for Africans,

45. George Martelli, *Leopold to Lumumba: A History of the Belgian Congo 1877–1960* (London: Chapman and Hall Ltd., 1962), 217.
46. Jean Van Lierde, ed., *Lumumba Speaks: The Speeches and Writings of Patrice Lumumba, 1958–1961* (Boston: Little, Brown and Company, 1963), 71–9.
47. Crawford Young, *Politics in the Congo: Decolonization and Independence* (Princeton, NJ: Princeton University Press, 1965), 300–2.
48. For more information on the life and death of Lumumba, see Thomas Kanza, *The Rise and Fall of Patrice Lumumba: Conflict in the Congo* (London: Penguin Books, 1972).
49. Lewis, *The Modern History of Somaliland*, 132–3.
50. David Welsh, "The Growth of Towns, " in *Oxford History of South Africa*, ed. Wilson and Thompson, 221–227; and Kevin Shillington, *History of Africa*, revised edition (New York: St. Martin's Press, 1995), 404.

the number of white students in universities by 1969 was sixty-eight thousand, while the number of Africans was four thousand.[51]

Overall, however, Western education became one of the important means of empowerment for Africans, enabling them to participate in colonial administration, to prepare for independence, and to participate in global affairs in the postindependence era. For Africans, investment in education has yielded positive dividends in the political, economic, and social spheres.

Higher Education

Before World War II, institutions of higher education were sparse in Africa. With the exception of Fourah Bay College in Sierra Leone, Achimota College in the Gold Coast, and Yaba Higher College in Nigeria, people in African colonies had no access to higher education. The process of expanding higher education in West Africa began in 1943, when the British government set up two commissions. The first, headed by Walter Elliot and including some Africans, was to investigate, recommend, and report on the organization and provision of higher education facilities in British West Africa. The second, headed by Justice Asquith, emphasized the need for the establishment of universities in West Africa to enable students to study in their own environments.[52] This led the Nigerian intelligensia not only to demand an institution that would be of higher status than Yaba College, but also to petition the British government to establish the proposed University of West Africa in Nigeria. Their reasons included the higher number of potential students and higher standard of education in Nigeria than in the Gold Coast. The Church Missionary Society (CMS) Yoruba Mission supported the university in Nigeria. The Walter Elliot Commission did not produce a unanimous report. While the majority report supported two universities, one in Nigeria and the other in the Gold Coast, the minority report recommended a single university college to be located in Nigeria.[53] Understandably, the minority report was rejected in the Gold Coast and Sierra Leone. The Creoles of Sierra Leone opposed a unitary university, because it would reduce the status of Fourah Bay College. Ultimately, the British established two university colleges in 1948, one in Ibadan (Nigeria) and the other in Accra (Gold Coast).

From 1903 to 1944, the French system of education reflected a "civilizing mission" and a policy of *assimilation* that aimed to fully integrate Africans into French culture. This led to a uniform system of education both in the colonies and in metropolitan France. The top French government officials met in Brazzaville in 1944 to discuss political and social plans for the colonies. Some important recommendations made at the Brazzaville Conference of 1944 included the abolition of forced labor, an increase in the number of teachers, and the establishment of higher institutions to enable Africans to participate in administration. As Michael

---

51. Robin Hallett, *Africa since 1875* (London: Heinemann, 1980), 672.

52. Apollos O. Nwauwa, *Imperialism, Academe and Nationalism: Britain and University Education for Africans 1860–1960* (London: Frank Cass, 1997), 162–3.

53. For the names of the members of the commission, see Nwauwa, *Imperialism, Academe and Nationalism*, 159 and 163–5.

Crowder indicated, "the social and economic recommendations of Brazzaville were eventually embodied in the Fonds d'Investissement pour le Développement Économique et Social (FIDES) that helped transform the social and economic development of the colonies."[54]

The Belgians also adopted the approach of integrating Africans into the European educational system. They provided elementary and secondary education, but those who proceeded to higher institutions would have diplomas and certificates equivalent to those earned in Belgium. Unlike the British and French, the Belgians did not send Africans to Belgium for higher education. Rather, they trained them in Africa, where they made available some technical and higher education. This might seem to be a creditable approach; however, of the thirteen million people in the Congo at independence, only sixteen had graduated from the university; this reveals that the Belgians did not, in reality, implement their lofty educational policy.[55]

Spain and Portugal established schools simply to assimilate Africans into their respective cultures. Higher education did not constitute a social priority, since the colonial powers did not anticipate self-government for their colonies. This policy retarded the progress of the colonies and created problems for inexperienced African leaders at independence.

Health Services

Some important changes occurred in the provision of health services. As in education, both the colonial administrations and the Christian missions provided health services to Africans. The Catholic, Anglican, Methodist, and Baptist missions established clinics or hospitals in West African colonies, while the Catholics were particularly active in East, Central, and southern Africa. The primary objective of these missions was to gain converts by establishing clinics, dispensaries, and maternity centers in rural areas. The various colonial governments built hospitals in urban centers in order to maintain the health of the workforce. In Nigeria, the Sudan Interior Mission (SIM) established its Eye Hospital and Orthopaedic Hospital in 1942. In 1957, the British established university teaching hospitals in Lagos, Ibadan, and Zaria to promote medical research and to train African doctors and nurses who would provide health services in both urban and rural areas. Between 1951 and 1960, the number of hospitals in Nigeria grew from 157 to over three hundred.[56] Given the growth of population in industrial centers, the prevention of the spread of diseases, the promotion of sanitary behavior, and the establishment of clinics where the sick could be treated became important considerations. In contrast to Nigeria and the Gold Coast, health services in Sierra Leone and the Gambia remained inadequate because of their small size and economic conditions.

Although the health department of the Portuguese government in Mozambique built hospitals and dispensaries and trained nurses in order to eradicate dis-

---

54. Michael Crowder, *West Africa under Colonial Rule* (Evanston, IL: Northwestern University Press, 1968), 500–1.

55. K. A. Busia, *Purposeful Education for Africa* (The Hague: Mouton, 1969), 24–5.

56. Falola, *History of Nigeria*, 78.

eases, the Catholic and Protestant missionaries provided most of the health care. The missionaries staffed their dispensaries and maternities in various parts of Mozambique with well-trained nurses.[57] The collaboration between the colonial and Christian authorities, even though it was directed toward specific goals, inevitably benefited Africans.

Africans benefited significantly from the changes in health care after World War II, when the control of epidemic diseases generally reduced the death rate. Populations also grew, because male rural migrant laborers, largely responsible for the spread of diseases, received treatment. The British government even became concerned about the rate of population growth in British colonies, as the colonial secretary indicated in 1948:

> We apply better health arrangements only to be faced with a population problem of appalling dimensions. We have to feed that increased population while they employ agricultural methods and ways of living hopelessly inadequate for such numbers....We cannot pursue development schemes fast enough to absorb all the rising generation in useful wage-employment.[58]

Overall, the improvement in health services can be regarded as one of the major social changes in colonial Africa after World War II. Western medicine ultimately replaced traditional healing methods. Even if the number of hospitals and clinics did not adequately serve the African population, the Europeans had introduced Africans to Western medicine.

Conclusion

While the rhetoric of social change produced by the Europeans was meant to portray them as providing adequate amenities and services, Africans felt dissatisfied, cheated, and exploited. Africans expected more rapid and more widespread social changes after World War II, given the enormous economic benefits that the Europeans derived from Africa. Social change depended largely on the effective and efficient working of provisions in communication, transportation, employment, education, and health. From the African perspective, Africa possessed the economy on which the provision of social amenities was based.

Social change can be understood in the context of African needs and the willingness of colonial governments to satisfy them. The colonial governments, however, provided social services that largely favored the Europeans. Social services, in theory, should have been evenly distributed. However, while Africans labored, the Europeans reaped the benefits. Rural areas did not feel the immediate impact of the social changes that took place after World War II. They continued to experience low standards of living, poor educational provisions, and inadequate

---

57. Eduardo Mondlane, "Mozambique," in *Africa in the Modern World*, 5th impression, ed. Calvin W. Stillman, (Chicago: University of Chicago Press, 1967), 242.

58. Quoted in John Iliffe, *Africans: The History of a Continent* (Cambridge: Cambridge University Press), 241–2.

health services. However, discernible social and religious changes became more widespread beginning in the 1950s, when nationalists and trade unionists pushed harder and won concessions from the colonial authorities.

Review Questions

1. Discuss the factors that brought about social changes in Africa after World War II.
2. Why did the colonial authorities prevent the Christian missionaries from operating in Muslim-dominated areas?
3. Explain the interaction between colonialism, Christianity, and Western education.
4. How did trade unions become instruments of social change in colonial Africa?
5. Why was educating an African important to the colonial authorities, Christian missionaries, and European merchants?
6. What role did African elites play in demanding social change during the colonial period?

Additional Reading

Boahen, A. Adu. *African Perspectives on Colonialism*. Baltimore: Johns Hopkins University Press, 1987.

Falola, Toyin. *The History of Nigeria*. Westport, CT: Greenwood Press, 1999.

Holt, P. M., and M. W. Daly. *A History of the Sudan: From the Coming of Islam to the Present Day*, 5th ed. London: Pearson Education Limited, 2000.

Iliffe, John. *Africans: The History of a Continent*. Cambridge: Cambridge University Press, 1995.

Isaacman, Allen. *Cotton Is the Mother of Poverty: Peasants, Work, and Rural Struggle in Colonial Mozambique, 1938–1961*. Berkeley, CA: Heinemann, 1996.

Maloba, Wunyabari O. *Mau Mau and Kenya: An Analysis of a Peasant Revolt*. Bloomington: Indiana University Press, 1993.

Tordoff, William. *Government and Politics in Africa*, 2nd ed. Bloomington: Indiana University Press, 1984.

Chapter 11

Chieftaincy Structures and State Formation

Olufemi Vaughan

This chapter examines the struggles of traditional rulers, chiefs, modernizing elites, and European administrators over the meaning of indigenous political authority in colonial Africa. Drawing from the theory and practice of the direct rule and indirect rule systems, it contends that the competing notions of indigenous political authorities were critical for the European colonizing project and for the opposition mounted by modernizing elites against imperial rule during decolonization. Marked by elite claims to democracy and development, the modernizing elites, drawing from chieftaincy institutions and reconstructed ethnic identities, intensified the process of elite formation during this critical period. While the reforms of the modernizing elites formally marginalized chiefs from state institutions, the politics of decolonization, with the imperative of mobilizing deeply divided societies, paradoxically, incorporated chiefs into emerging ethno-regional alliances. These colonial distortions were important ideological platforms on which important aspects of African collective action were later grafted.

* * *

It is now widely accepted that chieftaincy structures and the contested meaning of tradition were essential ingredients in the strategies of colonial administration and control in Africa. The interaction between chieftaincy, colonialism, and local communities was shaped by trends in colonial policies, the perspective of European colonial functionaries, imperial economic interests, rapidly changing social conditions, and the role of traditional and modern elites in the political transformation of local communities.

This chapter charts the multiple dimensions of indigenous political authorities and the conflicting ideologies that sustained local governance from the imposition of colonialism in the late nineteenth century to the introduction of modern political institutions during the decolonization process in the 1950s. Specifically, I analyze two major questions in the historiography of colonialism and chieftaincy in Africa. First, in the context of local governance, I examine the implications of the French, Portuguese, and Belgian applications of the direct rule system for the shifting role of chieftaincy in their African colonies. Second, I show how the interaction between conflicting applications of the indirect rule system and chieftaincy structures transformed political and social relations in British Africa from the inception of colonial rule to the period of decolonization. The general trends and

Figure 11.1. A West African king. Their traditional power began to decline after 1945, although they continue to retain their symbolic significance.

contrasting patterns of the interaction between chieftaincy, colonialism, and decolonization are illustrated by examples from the British colonies of Nigeria, Ghana, Uganda, Kenya, Nyasaland, and South Africa; the French colonies of Upper Volta and Dahomey; the Portuguese colonies of Angola, Mozambique and Guinea-Bissau; and the Belgian Congo. Both conceptual trends and illustrative references will show that at the core of this important subject of colonial control lies the rapidly shifting status of traditional rulers, chiefs, and elders in the unfolding drama of colonialism and decolonization.

The transformation of chieftaincy structures was thus contingent on the encroaching forces of modernization and colonial imperatives, especially in late colonialism when African societies were under considerable sociopolitical and economic stress. Despite these rapidly shifting political, social, and economic conditions, chieftaincy thrived because colonial administrators, traditional chiefs, and the emerging modernizing elite adapted the legitimating ideologies of traditional culture to the unfolding structures of colonialism and decolonization.[1] Furthermore, while the modern local government and liberal democratic structures that were imposed by the French and the British in the 1950s undermined chieftaincy institutions, chiefs still managed to retain their political significance by projecting themselves as custodians of cherished local values amidst rapid social change.[2] In short, chieftaincy institutions were transformed in the context of the new questions of governance and development, an issue further complicated by

---

1. Kofi Busia, *The Position of the Chief in the Modern Political System of the Ashanti*, (London: Oxford University Press, 1951).
2. Lucy P. Mair, "The African Chiefs Today," *Africa* 28 (1958).

the dominant interests of traditional chiefs, the Western-oriented African elites, and colonial administrators who sought to co-opt chieftaincy structures for legitimation and mobilization purposes within rapidly shifting political dispensations.

From Direct Rule to Decolonization

In theory, the French system of direct rule made a concerted effort to undermine African chieftaincy structures, by establishing *chefs de canton*, in a reorganization of local communities of fairly similar population and territory, under the influence of local French agents. Within a rigid, hierarchical colonial structure, a central colonial government led by the governor-general created policies that were implemented in all local government jurisdictions throughout France's West African colonial territories. This hierarchical system drew from the French metropolitan political culture of republicanism, which favored uniformity while shunning administrative innovations and minimizing diversity in sociopolitical experiences. The political arrangements gave French colonial administrators considerable power to use traditional rulers, chiefs, and elders in specific functions sanctioned by colonial circulars. Yet chiefs in French colonies generally lacked official authority in civil and criminal cases as well as in budgetary and administrative matters. Thus, French historian Jean Suret-Canale notes that while the chief had no real power at the inception of colonial rule, he:

> had many trying duties. He was the *commandant*'s general factotum. He was responsible for collecting taxes, supplying the requisitions of labour, supervising forced labour and the compulsory planting of cash crops. After the First World War, he had to accommodate and feed the envoys or representatives of the various administrations when they were on tour with their entourage! He had to entertain agents or representatives from the chief town of the *cercle*, pay a literate secretary and keep up an armed band of agents to carry out his orders.[3]

However, there is a clear distinction between the theory of imperial rule and colonial administrative practice. In other words, imposing novel colonial rules is one thing; implementing these rules in the context of the underlying sociopolitical arrangements and the exigencies of imperial interests is something altogether different. The implementation of French direct rule in complex societies required the manipulation of local communities, rulers, potentates, and elders. More importantly, given the gross inadequacy of the French administrative structure in West Africa, colonial policy had to adjust to evolving sociopolitical conditions and imperial demands. Suret-Canale notes:

> Such a policy of direct administration carried to its extreme presupposed a large number of European personnel, but the 1914–18 war restricted their numbers and afterwards financial difficulties prevented them from

---

3. Jean Suret-Canale, "The Futa-Djalon Chieftaincy," in *West African Chiefs: Their Changing Status under Colonial Rule and Independence*, New York: eds. Michael Crowder and Obaro Ikime (Africana Publishing Corporation, 1970) 90.

Problem w/ European personnel & to implement rules

being very much increased. Finally, the growing instability of the European personnel (the average period of service in one station is [sic] usually less than one year), their lack of specialization (administrators were sent indiscriminately and successively from Guinea to Niger, from Mauritania to Dahomey or from Madagascar to Tahiti) and their ignorance of local languages made it inevitable to fall back on native intermediaries.[4]

The severe limitation of the direct rule system, coupled with the rapid social change of the interwar period thus forced senior administrators in Paris to adapt general colonial policies to shifting local sociopolitical and economic conditions. These rapidly evolving conditions led to a less paternalist strategy of colonial rule in which the French co-opted sections of the African political elite as junior partners in the colonial administrative system. Known as the policy of *association*, this pragmatic policy was in fact apparent as early as August 1917 when Governor-General Van Vollenhoven instructed his subordinates to selectively integrate aspects of chieftaincy into the colonial administrative system. Van Vollenhoven, however, underscored the subordinate role of chiefs in this new administrative arrangement. He noted that chiefs would:

 have no real power of any kind, for there are not two authorities in the *cercle*, French authority and native authority. There is only one. The *commandant de cercle* alone is in command; he alone is responsible. The native chief is only an instrument, an auxiliary.[5]

This rapid transformation of the rigid direct rule system to the more pragmatic policy of *association* was vividly illustrated in the administration of colonial Upper Volta and Dahomey. With only one French administrator for every six thousand Mossi subjects, the Mogho Naba (the Mossi king) and his chiefs succeeded in retaining considerable influence throughout the colonial era. In fact, during the stewardship of Governor General Merleau-Ponty, French administrators were instructed to embrace the king and his chiefs and to utilize them to advance French objectives. After the initial failure of a rigid application of direct rule, the Mogho Naba and his chiefs emerged as critical intermediaries between French administrators and local communities.[6] Drawing from official reports that identified the Mogho Naba as an important agent of French colonial rule in the early twentieth century, anthropologist Elliott Skinner noted:

The Mogho Naba helped Blaise Diagne, first African Deputy of Senegal, to recruit thousands of Mossi for World War I. When the Upper Volta became a colony in 1919 the new Governor Hesling sought help from the Mogho Naba to create in Ouagadougou a capital worthy of the territory. And when in the early 1920s, the Governor implemented Saurrat's plans in Upper Volta it was to the Mogho Naba and his chiefs that he looked for labour to grow and export the expected thousands of tons of cotton. The Mogho Naba also helped the administration to recruit from "reser-

---

4. Ibid., 89.
5. Ibid., 86.
6. Elliot Skinner, "The Changing Status of the 'Emperor of the Mossi' under Colonial Rule and since Independence," in Crowder and Ikime, *West African Chiefs*, 80–98.

voir of man-power" that was Mossi country 6,000 workers for the Tries-Kayes railway, renewable every six months; and under the same conditions to furnish 2,000 labourers to build the railways in the Ivory Coast.[7]

The relative success of this policy notwithstanding, the enhanced status of the Mogho Naba and his vassals was in fact a distortion of the traditional role of the king and chiefs in Mossi society. With the growing perception that the King and his chiefs were auxiliaries of a highly authoritarian, illegitimate, and extractive colonial regime, the indigenous political structure was seen as an integral part of a corrupt colonial system. This development compromised the legitimacy of the king and the chiefs as intermediaries between the colonial authorities and local people during the transitional process of decolonization.

Similarly, in the Yoruba kingdom of Ketu in colonial Dahomey, where the *oba* (king) of Ketu, the *alaketu*, unlike the Mogho Naba, was relegated to the mere status of local head chief, the *alaketu* was recognized only as a government functionary. Thus, rejecting the monarchical traditions of the Ketu people, French administrators insisted that the alaketu could only transmit orders from the administrator to village chiefs in his *canton*; present young men before the commission for military recruitment; conduct censuses of the local population to facilitate obligatory labor and taxation; and assist in the arrest of criminals.[8] Furthermore, beyond interventions in minor local disputes, the alaketu could not preside over civil or criminal cases. All accused persons were tried in the *tribunal de subdivision* and in the *tribunal de cercle*, both of which were presided over by the European *commandant de cercle* or his European deputies. As *chef de canton*, the alaketu was entitled to a monthly salary, and could be disciplined for "misbehavior, carelessness or any other offense punishable in the civil service."[9]

This policy came to an abrupt end immediately after World War II, when the emergent Dahomian modernizing elites, along with their counterparts in other parts of Africa, insisted on decolonization. Extolling French republican traditions, the decolonization process marginalized monarchical and chieftaincy institutions in Dahomey.[10] More importantly, because the direct rule system had weakened indigenous political structures, French political traditions were superficially deployed as important institutions during this critical period of transition. Indeed, as President de Gaulle's government retained considerable influence in the decolonization process, African nationalists found themselves outmaneuvered by the French authorities. Thus, the attainment of independence entrenched neocolonial relations as most newly independent francophone African states accepted political, military, and economic directives from their erstwhile colonial rulers. Important political, economic, and cultural linkages were not only retained between the metropolis and the former colonies, but government decisions had to receive the approval of the French government immediately after independence.

---

7. Ibid., 102.
8. I. A. Asiwaju, "The Alaketu of Ketu and the Onimeko of Meko: The Changing Status of Two Yoruba Rulers under French and British Rule," in Crowder and Ikime, *West African Chiefs*.
9. Ibid., 152.
10. Ibid., 154.

Similarly, following the failure of a brutal direct rule system, the Portuguese and Belgian colonial authorities embraced chiefs and elders as agents of the colonial state. For example, in the administrative reorganization of the early 1920s, the Belgian colonial authorities required African subjects to return to the rural areas from which they were deemed to have come in the first place, and insisted that as "tribal" people Africans had to be under the control of "tribal" political institutions. Moreover, given this alleged tribal orientation, Africans could only be recognized as peasants and could only be temporarily designated as migrant workers.[11] This colonial arrangement was reinforced by draconian ordinances, a dehumanizing system of forced labor, and a rigid social hierarchy that recognized a small Western-oriented African elite as favored colonial subjects worthy of only limited legal rights. Portuguese and Belgian colonialism insisted that for the masses of "uncivilized" African "natives," local administration was essentially mediation between field officers and the village headmen.[12] Thus, with the exception of the centralized political structures of the Bakongo in Angola and the Fula in Guinea, native policy was "systematized in the late 1920s and put under the charge of the local state, its functionaries being the *chefes de posto* (district officers) and the *negedores* (administrative chiefs). In time, there evolved hierarchies of African chiefs from the senior *regulos* to the junior *cabos*."[13] Yet, because of the excessive extraction of the colonial economy, local people saw chiefs as intermediaries in a highly corrupt system.

In the struggle for independence in Belgian and Portuguese Africa, the Western-oriented nationalists, like their French counterparts (operating under different circumstances), had to strike a balance between their commitment to the radical political transformation of society and the appropriation of the practices, symbols, and structures of traditional culture under the control of chiefs and elders. In the political arrangement that unfolded, especially in the lusophone colonies of Angola, Mozambique, and Guinea-Bissau during the wars of liberation, nationalists of varying ideological orientations clashed with local chiefs and elders. Conversely, as the potential inheritors of state power, the nationalists also had to cooperate with the chiefs to form movements of local power and patronage; and in cases where they supported radical liberation movements, the chiefs emerged as supporters of radical nationalist resistance.[14]

From Indirect Rule to Decolonization

The British adopted the indirect rule system as a strategy of local administration in the colonial territories of West, East and South Africa. Initially imposed to administer the vast Fulani emirates by Sir Frederick Lugard (later Lord Lugard), governor of northern Nigeria at the turn of the nineteenth century, this system of

---

11. Mahmood Mamdani, *Citizen and Subject: Contemporary Africa and the Legacy of Late Colonialism*, (Princeton, NJ: Princeton University Press, 1996).
12. Ibid., 87.
13. Ibid., 89.
14. See for example, Terence Ranger, *Peasant Consciousness and Guerrilla War in Zimbabwe* (Berkeley: University of California Press, 1985) David Lan, *Guns and Rain: Guerrillas and Spirit Mediums in Zimbabwe*,(Berkeley: University of California Press, 1985).

colonial local administration drew heavily on conflicting interpretations of pre-colonial sociopolitical structures for the purpose of colonial rule. By embracing indigenous sociopolitical structures as the legitimate form of political authority, British colonialism sought to appropriate the prevailing political arrangement as the means of colonial rule. The most enduring legacy of this colonial practice was apparent in contentious notions of chieftaincy rules and customary laws.[15] Indirect rule as a strategy of colonial rule was an elaborate process of discovering the virtues of "custom" and "tradition." Colonial authorities attempted to defend what they conveniently interpreted as customary practice and traditional authorities.[16] Given the complex nature of African societies, such subjective interpretations of hierarchical traditional authorities, motivated largely by political expediency, generated serious contestations for power among African rulers and their communities. In this rigidly structured system, major city-states, especially those with long-standing monarchical traditions, assumed greater political significance in the years immediately after the imposition of colonial rule. These colonial policies and the complex indigenous sociopolitical environment from which British administrators and chiefs constructed new political arrangements were complicated by Christian missionary activities, Islamic influences, and rapid social change.

With the rapid social change that accompanied colonial rule, modernizing elites, the driving engines of political transformation, emerged as intermediaries between British administrators and traditional chiefs. In the evolving political climate of the 1930s and 1940s, these Western-oriented elites had to embrace traditional doctrines that extolled the corporate character of communal identities, while projecting their expertise in modern development and democracy.[17] Nevertheless, chieftaincy still thrived in most African societies because chiefly incumbents attempted to integrate the legitimating ideologies of tradition into the decolonization process. Furthermore, while modern local government structures eroded chiefly power, traditional rulers and chiefs still managed to retain considerable influence by projecting themselves as custodians of cherished local values amidst rapid social and political transformation. Finally, the pivotal role of chieftaincy structures was sustained by the calculations of the new holders of state power, who sought to co-opt the chiefs for legitimization and mobilization purposes within the evolving political dispensation. Illustrations of the impact of colonial rule on chieftaincy in Nigeria, with references to chieftaincy and colonial administration in Ghana, Uganda, and South Africa, will reveal the complex consequences chieftaincy's incorporation into the colonial structure and the decolonization process.

As I mentioned earlier, the indirect rule system was introduced into northern Nigeria by Lugard as a strategy of local administration for the Fulani emirates following their conquest between 1897 and 1903.[18] The system, which adapted

---

15. See Martin Channock, *Law, Custom, and Social Order: The Colonial Experience of Malawi and Zambia* (Cambridge: Cambridge University Press, 1985).

16. Terence Ranger, "Tradition, and Travesty: Chiefs and Administration in Mkoni District, Zimbabwe, 1960–1980," *Africa* 52 (1982).

17. See, for example, Peter Ekeh, "Colonialism and the Two Publics in Africa: A Theoretical Statement," *Comparative Studies in Society and History* 17 (1975).

18. Risto Marjomaa, *War in the Savannah: The Military Collapse of the Sokoto Caliphate under the Invasion of the British Empire, 1897–1903* (Helsinki: Finnish Academy of Sciences and Letters, 1998).

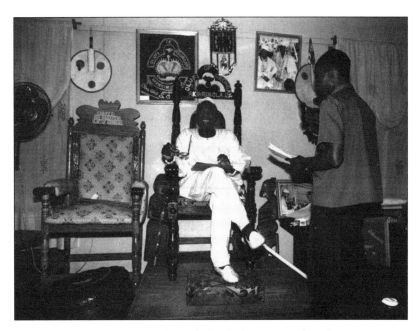

Figure 11.2. King Olufi of Gbongan, Nigeria.

"indigenous" political institutions to British colonial control, was subsequently imposed on the Southern Provinces in the early 1900s. Given the diversity of social formations and the prevailing political arrangements in the Nigerian region, this strategy of colonial control met with varying degrees of success in the Northern and Southern Provinces. While it achieved relative success in the Northern Provinces and the Yoruba region, with their monarchical institutions and centralized sociopolitical formations, it failed in the eastern region, where the British imposed a hierarchical chieftaincy structure called the "warrant system" on what were acephalous societies.[19] Starting with the 1901 reform introduced by Sir William MacGregor (governor of Lagos from 1899 to 1904), which reduced the role of the resident in the native authority (NA) councils from an executive to an advisory capacity and appointed "paramount rulers" as executive presidents in the residents' place, the colonial authorities imposed a rigid system of government at the turn of the century. Since provincial and divisional councils had extensive authority over local administration, the new ordinance established a centralized structure of local administration under the authority of a "supreme" traditional ruler. By establishing a centralized system of local administration under a traditional ruler, MacGregor's ordinance enhanced the power of monarchs considered historically significant while eroding the authority of major chiefs without royal claims.

It was shortsighted to expect this imposed traditional political arrangement to create order among competing traditional rulers, chiefs, educated elites, and local people. A neo-traditional structure that embraced specific "supreme" traditional

---

19. A. G. Afigbo, *The Warrant Chiefs: Indirect Rule in Southeastern Nigeria, 1891–1929*, (London: Longman, 1971).

rulers as preeminent kings naturally distorted preexisting nineteenth century political arrangements. It also created new political relationships among leaders and their communities within specific colonial jurisdictions. To legitimate this arrangement, the colonial authorities had to invest considerable resources in historically intelligible, but highly contentious, interpretations of traditional African monarchs as royal potentates. This arrangement required constant intrigues and the arbitrary use of colonial state power. Given the inconsistencies between the new colonial order and the previous political relationships among provincial towns, indirect rule failed to construct a stable mechanism for mediating conflict. Furthermore, it relied heavily on excessively authoritarian measures and the persistent manipulation of local interests.[20] Nevertheless, this policy sanctioned the authority of "paramount rulers" and senior chiefs over Native Authority structures, the native courts, and tax collection. But while major rulers in specific colonial jurisdictions competed for power and prestige, colonial rulers extended their influence beyond what it had been in the precolonial period, in which the configuration of power had depended on shifting political developments within the polity. Not surprisingly, this new political arrangement resulted in an inefficient and corrupt system of local administration.

Taxation was also an important aspect of the colonial system of indirect rule. Since taxes had to be generated locally, "paramount rulers" and their subordinates were charged with the task of collecting taxes in local communities. Because chiefs received a portion of the tax proceeds, they became aggressive tax collectors. Given the arbitrary and exploitative nature of tax collection, acceptance of the legitimacy of chieftaincy institutions eroded significantly among local people.

With the rapid social transformation of colonial Nigeria in the 1930s, this hierarchical political arrangement had to concede to reforms that reorganized provincial, district, and city administrations. The highly centralized indirect rule system erected at the turn of the century was clearly inadequate to meet the challenges of an increasingly complex colonial environment. Moreover, the apparent failure of this system in the Eastern Provinces, along with an unstable political environment in other parts of colonial Nigeria, prompted the introduction of reforms in the 1920s and the 1930s. For indirect rule to continue as a viable system of local administration, it had to adapt. Reformers like Sir Donald Cameron, governor of Nigeria from 1931 to 1935, contended that it was time that British tradition was utilized in this respect. The 1933 Native Authority Ordinance expressed this new official attitude, requiring that "paramount rulers" consult councils of chiefs on all matters affecting the welfare of local communities. While they still retained their executive powers under the supervision of the resident and the district officers, "paramount rulers" now had to recognize their councils' advisory and consultative roles. This historic provision, which was popularly described as "chiefs and council," was a major departure from the autocratic Native Authority system.

The reforms of Governor Cameron were carefully implemented by his successor, Sir Bennard Bourdillon, governor of Nigeria from 1935 to 1939. For the first time in four decades of colonial rule, British authorities had curtailed the centralized power of local potentates. Furthermore, the reform enhanced the influence of

---

20. J. A. Atanda, *The New Oyo Empire: Indirect Rule and Change in Southeastern Western Nigeria, 1894–1934* (London: Longman, 1973).

the emergent Western-oriented elite, whose complaints over inefficient colonial administration were voiced increasingly.[21]

The introduction of the post-World War II policy of the new British Labour government accelerated the pace of change. Initially, in the celebrated 1947 Local Government Dispatch, the British government underscored the disenchantment of the Western-oriented elite and some progressive colonial administrators with local administration and community development. This general statement of policy was centered on what British Secretary of State for the Colonies, Creech Jones, referred to as the "modified traditional machinery." In short, by emphasizing the importance of community development, responsive local government, and the participation of educated Africans, the new policy sought to marginalize traditional titleholders in local administration.[22]

Despite their ambitious claims, the reforms proved less radical than their proponents had anticipated. In reality, the policy simply replaced the chiefs with Western-oriented elites who, because of their formal educations, insisted on the right to govern.[23] Conversely, with limited ties to grassroots forces, the educated elite co-opted the assumed legitimacy of chiefs, whose fortunes were now on the wane. The policy set the stage for the decolonization process in the 1950s. With the fissure that accompanied the sociopolitical and economic pressures of this great period of transition, decolonization unleashed a complicated process of alliances and conflicts. Using a straightforward anticolonial ideology, nationalist leaders successfully mobilized urban workers, teachers, petty traders, artisans, and others against British colonial rule. Yet, the initial success against British colonialism precipitated a more complex trend arising from the exigencies of local power relations, the historical processes of state formation, and the complex nature of society. As local power brokers mobilized their followings, collective political action engendered intense centrifugal forces among competing communal groups. Preoccupied with modern constructions of ethnicity, rising political elites emerged as ethnic power brokers as ethno-regionally based politicians struggled for state power. In this evolving political arrangement, politicians forged political ties with chiefs around mutually intelligible cultural expressions in order to expand, strengthen, and consolidate their bases. As collective political action crystallized around the intense competition among regional and communal power brokers for scarce resources, the emergent postcolonial state simply could not mediate the conflicting interests of competing classes and communal groups. The struggle for state power was promptly reduced to a zero-sum game among the dominant political elites.

With the regionalization of state power in the constitutional reforms of the Macpherson and Lyttleton Constitutions, chieftaincy structures once again became vital to the political strategies that sustained evolving regional power configurations. In addition, since decolonization consolidated state power in the hands of Western-educated elites, the reforms of nationalists rapidly eroded chiefly authority. Chiefs that were marginalized by the ruling nationalists collaborated with

---

21. A.H.M. Kirk-Greene, *The Principles of Native Administration in Nigeria, Selected Documents, 1900–1947* (London: Oxford University Press, 1965).

22. Arthur Creech Jones, *Dispatch from the Secretary of State for the Colonies to the Governors of the African Territories*, 25 February (London: HMSO, 1947).

23. Richard C. Crook, "Decolonization, the Colonial State, and Chieftaincy in the Gold Coast," *African Affairs* 85 (1986).

opposition politicians to mobilize support for and safeguard their interests. The politics of decolonization in Nigeria emerged, in part, from precolonial notions of traditional authorities, the indirect rule system, and the colonial reforms of the 1930s and 1940s.

In the Gold Coast, the initial success of the Convention People's Party (CPP) was reflected in the implementation of Kwame Nkrumah's insistence on progressive change and the CPP's appropriation of traditional practices during decolonization.[24] Paradoxically, the opposition that was mounted against the CPP in 1954 by the National Liberation Movement was rooted in Asante tradition. Ultimately, it was a strong appeal to Asante nationalism under the leadership of the *Asantehene* (chiefs and elders), which was consolidated by Asante disaffection with Nkrumah's radical nationalist policy.[25] Similarly, in Uganda, it was the threat of Buganda nationalism, under the leadership of the *kabaka* (the Bugandan king) and a local Buganda party, *Kabaka Ya* (the kabaka's party), that prompted northern district chiefs and Acholi and Lango politicians to establish local political parties promoting their communal interests in the late 1950s.[26] These ambiguous political alliances suggest that, with the need to outmaneuver their opponents — whether these were the British colonial authorities or their fellow politicians — nationalist movements had to politicize and mobilize networks of local interests under the leadership of chiefs and elders and infuse them with their own values.[27]

In colonial Nyasaland, for instance, the Nyasaland African Congress, the major nationalist party in the region, was an alliance of several organizations, each with its own specific local concerns. With overlapping interests during decolonization, the leaders of these groups brought their grievances to senior chiefs. They then focused their energy on what they all considered the menace of federation.[28] In Kenya, local chiefs provided moral leadership for the welfare organizations from which the Kenya African Union (later the Kenya African National Union) drew its legitimacy.[29] Conversely, in many other anglophone African colonies, notably Tanganyika, Uganda, and Kenya, nationalist leaders confronted chiefs who had collaborated with colonial administrators. The removal of traditional chiefs from local administration led to the emergence of new communicators: the Western-oriented elite. The new leaders emerged as "coordinators" of the grassroots revolution that set the decolonization process in motion.[30] In colonial southern Nigeria, urban social welfare organizations with strong communal ties forged alliances with major regional parties.[31]

---

24. Maxwell Owusu, *The Uses and Abuses of Political Power: A Study of Continuity and Change in the Politics of Ghana* (Chicago: University of Chicago Press, 1970).

25. William Tordoff, *Government and Politics in Africa* (Bloomington: Indiana University Press, 1984).

26. Cherry Gertzel, *Party and Locality in Northern Uganda* (London: Athlone Press, 1974).

27. Immanuel Wallerstein, "Ethnicity and National Integration in West Africa," *Cahiers d'Etudes Africaines*, 3 (1960).

28. R. Rotberg, "African Nationalism: Concept or Confusion?" *Journal of Modern African Studies* 4 (1964) 44.

29. George Bennett, "The Development of Political Organizations in Kenya," *Political Studies* 5 (1957).

30. J. M. Lonsdale, "Some Origins of Nationalism in East Africa," *Journal of African History* 9 (1968).

31. P. C. Lloyd, "The Yoruba Today," *Sociological Review* (1957).

Even in the Union of South Africa, with its entrenched racist institutions and European domination—whether British or Afrikaner in the colonial or postcolonial period, respectively—was derived from the indirect rule system. While there was no decolonization project, European domination promoted deep communal loyalties among the indigenous African population. Using the platform of indigenous African custom, British and Afrikaner domination intensified the centrifugal pressure among South Africa's black population. Political scientist Mahmood Mamdani notes:

> The Bantu Authorities Act ([number] 68 of 1951) claimed to restore "the natural native democracy" to the reserves by creating a system of councils controlled by chiefs and headmen. For the first time, an autonomous Native Treasury and a Native Administration that paid from it—with powers to make rules in a native legislature—were added to the administration of customary law, in Zululand (Natal) and in other homelands. The pace was set in the Transkei in 1956, when the Transkeian Territorial Authority was created, growing over the next twenty years from "self-government" (1963) to "independence" (1976). The Transkeian example was emulated in three other instances—Siskei, Venda, and Bophuthatswana—whereas developments in Zululand stopped at the establishment of an autonomous indirect rule regime.[32]

The constitutional reforms that ushered in the decolonization process did not constitute a neat break from the preceding era of indirect rule. As the political transformation of the late colonial period witnessed the emergence of entrenched communal identities, local and national power brokers drew extensively from the legitimating influence of chiefs and elders.

Conclusion

At the imposition of colonial rule in the late nineteenth century, varying effects of the British system of indirect rule and the French, Portuguese, and Belgian systems of direct rule transformed the prevailing indigenous political structures in African colonies. Given the dynamic social, political, and economic conditions in which colonial policies were implemented, general statements of colonial policy could not be expressed as simple theoretical formulations; rather, preoccupied with issues of political expediency, colonial administrators had to adapt to rapidly shifting sociopolitical and economic conditions in Africa's diverse societies. Within these complex social and political formations, colonial administrative strategies massively distorted the political arrangements of nineteenth century Africa. Furthermore, as the chiefs and the emergent Western-oriented elites collaborated in appropriating neo-traditional ideologies in their attempts to mobilize political support, they also had to confront the pressing demands for development and democracy that decolonization created. The trend toward re-constructed notions of tradition and communal alliances

---

32. Mamdani, *Citizen and Subject*, 89.

**Figure 11.3. Sir Abubakar Tafawa Balewa with Princess Alexandra
at the Nigerian Independence Ceremony, 1960.**

clearly indicated that African societies lacked a viable civil society that was capable of sustaining broad-based national ideologies and legitimate modern state structures. The political arrangement prevailing at the dawn of independence weakened the progressive values of local development that had thrived in the late colonial period.

The vulnerability of the African state and society during the decolonization process gave the imperial powers considerable influence following the attainment of independence in the 1960s. In these evolving political arrangements, the trans- fer of power led to the imposition of constitutional reforms reflecting the bureaucratic, political, and legal traditions of the imperial powers. In economic production and exchange, the imperial powers retained their prevailing economic relations with African states. Thus, rather than provide a progressive alternative, decolonization encouraged conflicting communal loyalties affirmed by chiefs, emerging political elites, and local power brokers. A direct product of a fractured decolonization process, the imposed postcolonial state was massively incongruent with the natural structures of African society. The colonial state, therefore, shifted from the legitimating system of indirect rule to the legitimating system of nationalist democratic reform. Responding to these shifts, the nationalist movements themselves assumed ambiguous colorations.

Review Questions

1. Critically examine the role of chiefs in the French system of direct rule.
2. Analyze the evolution of the indirect rule system in colonial Nigeria.
3. Explain the processes of state formation in African colonies during decolonization.
4. Identify and discuss the role of chiefs in the struggle for liberation in anglophone and lusophone southern Africa.
5. Explain the interaction between chieftaincy, communal identities, the modernizing elites, and colonial policy during the decolonization process.
6. What role did chieftaincy structures play in British strategies of colonial administration?

[handwritten note in left margin: Social transform]

Additional Reading

Busia, Kofi. *The Position of the Chief in the Modern Political System of the Ashanti.* London: Oxford University Press, 1951.

Jones, Creech. *The Future of African Colonies.* Nottingham: Nottingham University Press, 1951.

Crowder, Michael. *Colonial West Africa: Collected Essays.* London: Frank Cass, 1978.

Crowder, Michael and Obaro Ikime, eds. *West African Chiefs: Their Changing Status under Colonial Rule and Independence.* New York: Africana Publishing, 1970.

Hobsbawm, Eric and Terence Ranger, eds. *The Invention of Tradition.* Cambridge: Cambridge University Press, 1988.

Hodgkin, Thomas. *Nationalism in Colonial Africa.* London: Muller, 1956.

Low, Anthony and Cranford Pratt. *Buganda and British Overrule, 1900–1955.* London: Oxford University Press, 1960.

Mair, Lucy P. *African Kingdom.* Oxford: Clarendon Press, 1977.

Mare, Gerhard. *Brothers Born of Warrior Blood: Politics and Ethnicity in South Africa.* Johannesburg: Raven Press, 1987.

Mamdani, Mahmood. *Citizen and Subject: Contemporary Africa and the Legacy of Late Colonialism.* Princeton: Princeton University Press, 1996.

Suret-Canale, Jean. *French Colonialism in Tropical Africa, 1900–1945.* London: Hurst, 1971.

Whitaker, C.S. *The Politics of Tradition: Continuity and Change in Northern Nigeria, 1946–1966.* Princeton: Princeton University Press, 1970.

Chapter 12

Cities and Urban Life

Steven J. Salm

African cities and their residents embarked on a period of immense change during the last few decades of colonialism. Shaped by the outbreak of World War II, changing demographics, and dynamic economic and political conditions, African cities experienced a rapid rise in population, increasing class and social divisions, and a growing availability of internal and external cultural stimuli. Urban residents needed new mechanisms to adapt to the changing environment and found those in new techniques of association and a burgeoning popular culture scene. Music, dance, cinema, and sports contributed to the identity formation of city dwellers and reflected the changing nature of urban life.

* * *

From the beginning of World War II to the dawn of independence, external influences, population shifts, and changing economic and political conditions helped to create new cultural and social movements that had a profound impact on the complexion of African urban environments. The war brought a strong Western military presence to many African cities. Thousands of Africans also joined the Allied forces, fighting in East and North Africa, Asia, and Europe. They returned with new experiences, and the population of cities exploded with the influx of ex-servicemen and massive rural-urban immigration. The economic situation, even at the best of times, could not keep pace with this rapid increase in population. An economic slump began to affect the everyday lives of Africans, but the excitement of city life continued to attract more people. Urban residents formed new social networks and developed new forms of entertainment and leisure to help them cope with the changing environment. In the years following the war, the vitality of the cities surged as independence movements grew stronger and Africans gained legislative power. By the early 1960s, most Africans had earned their independence from colonial rule. The last two decades of colonialism made a permanent imprint on the character of that independence, and African societies entered the next stage with a new euphoria. Urban areas experienced the full extent of these changes at a high and hurried level.

How do we define a city? There are many different types of cities throughout the world. They may be classified by population, geographical location, or a number of other variables. Aidan Southall defined two distinct types of towns and cities in Africa.[1] Type A cities were old, established, slowly growing towns of in-

---

1. Aidan Southall, "Introductory Summary," in *Social Change in Modern Africa*, Aidan Southall (ed.) (London: Oxford University Press, 1961).

digenous origin, or at least closely integrated with indigenous society. They were more common in West Africa and some parts of East Africa. This chapter focuses on a second category, type B cities. These were relatively new urban centers that grew rapidly during the twentieth century, especially from 1939 onward. Colonial governments established cities or expanded existing cities as administrative, economic, and political centers for individual colonies. The cities, often anchored by a viable port, became the major point of entry for European goods and the outlet for African raw materials. Exploiting African labor, colonial governments created roads, railroads, and improved other means of transport to connect these cities to the non-urban areas. These improved routes carried both goods and people into and out of the cities. Early type B cities, therefore, often had a multi-ethnic and multi-racial population, experienced sharp racial and class differences, and showed a propensity for an increased rate of change within the political, economic, social, and cultural spheres.

Why do we study urban history? It is an important element in understanding the development of both rural and urban African societies. Cities played an important role in the drive toward independence, not only political independence, but the struggle to obtain greater freedom in deciding important matters in every aspects of life. We cannot study the city in isolation from the rest of the population. During the late colonial period, change was pronounced for all African peoples, but urban societies experienced a variety of factors at a more intense level. Urban history must explore the interactions between the urban and non-urban areas. Migration, for example, increased the connections among people in very different places. It created links between people in the cities and their friends and families in the rural areas.

Within an urban environment, the diversity of people and interests coming together in a densely populated area demands that urban history address relationships ordered along ethnic, occupational, religious, recreational, and other lines. Urban history cannot focus on only one stratum of the population. It must probe the personalities and interactions within law courts, nightclubs, marketplaces, palm wine bars, and entertainment venues. Ideally, it must include a picture of the entire urban political, economic, and cultural hierarchy.

This chapter focuses on the development of major African urban centers from 1939 to the era of independence and explores the following themes: (1) urban expansion and World War II; (2) economic decline and protest from 1945 to independence; (3) voluntary associations and networks of change; and (4) developments in urban popular culture and changing technology. Though there are certainly many other areas of interest that could be addressed, these themes have been chosen to illustrate the underlying conflicts of the era and present a picture of the overall urban environment and everyday life in a variety of African cities.

Urban Expansion and World War II

World War II provided the impetus for rapid change in African urban environments. The presence of Western soldiers in African cities contributed to economic growth, shifting perceptions of race, and developments in popular culture. This, in part, stimulated rural-urban migration, bringing many new people into the cities in search of employment within the wartime economy. This section looks at the changes that occurred between 1939 and 1945, focusing on the effects of the war on the overall social and economic complexion of African cities.

Only since the mid-1930s and early 1940s have African cities experienced urban expansion on a large scale. Before 1939, most African colonial cities had small populations and undeveloped infrastructures focused on providing services related to colonial administrations and economies. Africans were not encouraged to come to the cities, but rather to stay in the agricultural and mining areas, thus contributing to the export resources of the colonial economy. Rural-urban migration always existed, but the number of migrants was small and colonial cities developed slowly. People indigenous to the regions where the cities grew worked as traders and laborers within the colonial economy and often remained part of the lower class. Educated people born in the cities, as well as immigrants, assumed roles within the colonial civil service and formed a middle-class African elite. In the late 1930s, however, the population began to expand rapidly, African social class divisions became more pronounced, and every facet of urban life experienced a corresponding change.

With the fall of France in 1941 and the establishment of the Vichy regime, the strategic importance of Africa for the Allied powers increased. Many cities experienced an economic upsurge resulting from the arrival of overseas troops and infrastructural renovations and improvements. Airport and port facilities, in particular, became crucial to provisioning the Allied war effort in North Africa and the Middle East and were upgraded. Roads, bridges, and army camps were constructed to support new technology and house Western troops. In the Gold Coast (now Ghana), for example, the United States military undertook major improvements to the Accra airport and used it as a base beginning in 1941. They also built a new bridge over the Korle Lagoon, and in the following year, Accra became the headquarters for the West African military command. New military quarters were opened at the Giffard and Burma Camps, and Western officers, technicians, and soldiers arrived.

Other cities experienced similar developments. Freetown, Sierra Leone, which served as a strategic port for the British Navy, saw a great deal of new investment. Early in the war, a British observer asserted that "since the European crisis [began] more money and staff have gone to fortifying the harbour and strengthening the garrison than have been spent on developing the colony in all the years we have held it."[2] The urban environment underwent rapid infrastructure changes and the effects were felt by many different strata of the population.

Business in hotels, shops, bars, and brothels increased dramatically. A new nightlife developed and generated new forms of popular culture. Nairobi, although a land-locked city, housed military camps for the King's African Rifles, the Royal Air Force, and the Gold Coast Regiment in its environs. In 1941, the American consul in Nairobi, Kenya, described the impact of the war on that city:

Nairobi is enjoying the greatest boom in its history. Within the last few months two new night clubs have been opened for the entertainment of the troops chiefly and canteens and other places for the troops are numer-

2. W. M. Macmillan, *Daily Guardian*, June 19, 1939.

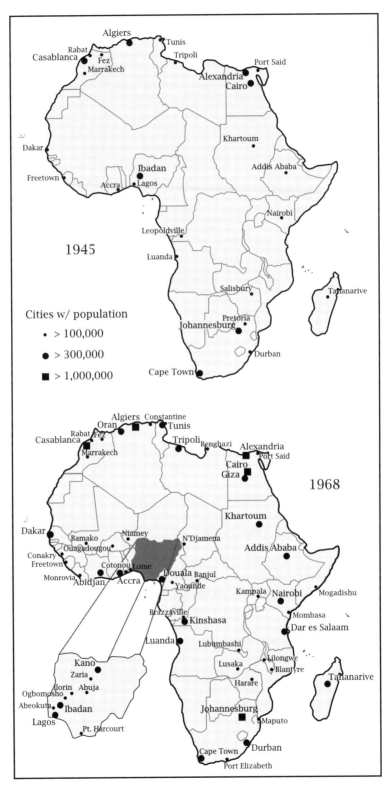

Urbanization in Africa, 1954–1968.

Figure 12.1. Downtown Nairobi.

ous. Hotels which were before the outbreak of war heavily in debt are now well out of the red; and shops of all kind are prospering.[3]

In Mombasa, Kenya, where considerable numbers of troops and naval forces were stationed, it was difficult to secure hotel accommodations, and many other services were scarce. The Mombasa district commissioner reported in 1940 that:

> War conditions and the presence of military forces on the island have opened up many new sources of employment.... There has been a large demand for servants created by the many newcomers to Mombasa and at the end of the year they were most difficult to obtain and wages tended to rise.[4]

The demand for labor, the increased opportunities for employment, and the attraction of the cultural climate encouraged thousands of rural Africans to make their way to the city. Urban populations throughout Africa exploded. In Nairobi, the population increased from 49,600 in 1936 to more than 300,000 in 1962. Brazzaville went from 23,436 people in 1937 to almost 128,000 in 1961. Though many factors contributed to the rapidly increasing population in African cities, a significant percentage of that growth was due to rural-urban immigration.

Scholars have argued that "push" and "pull" factors are the two basic motives for migration. "Push" factors are a response to conditions that *push* mi-

3. Quoted in Karim K. Janmohamed, "A History of Mombasa, c. 1895–1939," (Ph.D. diss. Northwestern University, 1978), 523.

4. Kenyan National Archives, Mombasa District Annual Report, 1940, 1–2. Quoted in Janmohamed, "A History of Mombasa," 524.

grants into moving from their homes. Some migrants saw the focus on wealth, generation, and gender status within traditional systems as a hindrance to young men and women with ambitions. The city, then, provided the means to better themselves and to escape from what they viewed as a position of confinement within rural society. In Freetown, for example, migrants to the city expressed this attitude in the slogan, "Mek a go Fritong mek I go fri" ("Let me go to Freetown, let me be free").[5]

"Pull" factors, on the other hand, involve conditions that exist in the destination city, or at least in the migrants' perceptions of the city, and *pull* them in that direction. Economic betterment was definitely important. Wages were much higher in the urban areas. Money earned was used to purchase new consumer goods or to secure resources to initiate the traditional marriage process. Some came to the city because they believed that they could become wealthy and buy fine things, thus increasing their social prestige. Others were enticed by cultural developments, such as the developing nightlife and increased diversity others described. Some of the immigrants, especially males, had at least a middle-school education and thought they were now too educated to work in agriculture or mining. They felt that they deserved jobs in the civil service, and the colonial administration in the city was the logical place to go. Though people migrated for a variety of reasons, it is safe to say that all of their motives involved a rational search for a better place in which to live and work.

If migrants' aims were to improve their standards of living by moving to urban areas, the economic reality they found often proved disappointing. Many migrants did not find employment in their desired fields, and many more found no jobs at all. Immigrants had to rely on the kindness of friends and family to survive even for a short time in the city. Rapid population growth, caused largely by continued rural-urban migration, and the inability to maintain the growth of the economy to match that of the population, resulted in widespread unemployment and underemployment.

New urban immigrants did experience something, however, that they would not have experienced had they remained in their villages. Urban residents of the World War II era began to see very the different faces of white people who, before this time, had protected their images carefully. One observer remarked: "When the Americans came we learnt a lot of things. It was the first time that I personally saw a white man holding a pick-axe and digging. Up to then it hadn't been natural to see a white man doing this."[6] "This" being hard, physical labor, which colonialism had stressed as a job for Africans, with whites acting as supervisors. Images like this contributed to changing conceptions of whites at all levels of African societies.

The sailors and soldiers associated with the Allied military presence also contributed to changing race relations, but in far different, less positive ways. Many of the troops that disembarked or were stationed in African cities demonstrated little respect for African people and their cultures. One observer, discussing soldiers in local bars during the war, said that "the effect of the Americans on the

---

5. See Kenneth Little, "The Role of Voluntary Associations in West African Urbanization," *American Anthropologist*, 59, 4 (1957), 579.

6. John Collins, *King of Highlife: ET Mensah*, Accra: Anansesem Publications, 1996 (first published by Off the Record Press, London, 1986), 6.

local women was appalling, they were free with them and thus encouraged prostitution."[7] Led to places for a small fee by young male guides, sailors flooded the restaurants, bars, hotels, and brothels of the cities. In Freetown, young people created a song in pidgin English about the negative effects of relations between sailors and prostitutes (also known as raray girls):

Ark Royal oh.
Ark Royal oh.
Sailor man don cam nar ton
Raray girl go die lek dog.[8]

The guides, or "pilots," as they were called, saw a side of Europeans that they had not seen before, at least not to quite the same extent. The rowdy and illicit behaviors and the level of racial arrogance of the European and American troops affected the attitudes of these young people and increased their racial animosity. The war helped shatter the myth of the superiority of the white race, a myth carefully constructed in the course of formal and informal colonialism by strict racial separation in all spheres of life, a myth that in its very essence helped maintain colonial rule.

Urban Lives from
1945 to Independence

The end of the war did not slow the process of change in African cities, but it did change its dynamics. Vast numbers of returning soldiers and additional rural immigrants brought new cultural stimuli into the urban arena. The population swelled, creating new problems for colonial administrations. Unemployment, huge increases in the cost of living, and housing problems became prevalent, stirring urban populations to active protest. As general economic conditions deteriorated and colonial power came under immense strain, Africans assumed higher roles in government, and a distinct class system developed. This section focuses on several postwar changes: growing divisions within urban societies, declining socioeconomic conditions, and increasing protests against colonial rule.

The divide between urban and rural areas in terms of the availability of goods and earning potential grew more pronounced after the war. People continued to move to cities in search of better job opportunities and higher wages. Few found them, however, and this resulted in a growing rift between social and economic classes within the urban environment.

Social Divisions

Social roles in African cities were determined largely by three factors: race, education, and wealth. These were all interdependent and could not easily be separated. For instance, most of the white population had both education and

---

7. Collins, *King of Highlife*, 7.
8. In F. R. Anthony, *Sawpit Boy* (London: 1980), 57.

wealth. Africans were divided according to their economic and employment levels. First, there was an elite class that included the senior branch of civil servants, those with professional qualifications, and those important in the commercial world. Secondly, there was a middle class consisting of those who held positions in the junior levels of the civil service or similar posts in the commercial world. This also included most of the Indians and Lebanese, as well as a few Europeans. The third and largest class consisted of laborers and small traders, mostly uneducated, and all African.

Though colonial governments began to inwardly admit that independence was inevitable, their ultimate goal was to retain their power in the African colonies for as long as possible. The propaganda of the war, however, meant a change in the techniques of rule. Realizing the need for reform, the British introduced new measures through the Colonial Development and Welfare Acts and offered some improvements in education, labor, and medical policies; yet the masses saw little real progress. At the other end of the social spectrum, however, the African elite, consisting of African civil servants and the rest of the Western-educated group, began to assume greater social prominence in the 1940s. A European settler who returned to Nairobi in 1946 after a seven-year absence spoke during a broadcast on the "new" African elite and the barriers that existed in race relations: "It struck me very much that a whole new generation of Africans had grown up, and the Europeans seemed as a rule to know all too little about them."[9] The social and economic factors that gave rise to the development of Nairobi were under the control of the colonial authorities and subject to the strong influence of white settlers. In the urban scheme of colonialism, Nairobi was a city created by Europeans, primarily as a place for Europeans and laborers in European enterprises to live and for others to provide services for the growing number of white settlers in the surrounding areas. During the late colonial period, Nairobi served as the center of British administration for East Africa as a whole and housed the main offices for many commercial and financial houses. Under this strong European dominance, the rise of the "new" African elite was not insignificant.

Colonial cities were segregated along racial and class lines. Arrangements were made to prevent the necessary interaction between settlers and Africans in the economic sphere from encroaching on the boundaries of social separation. Strict segregation in housing helped to ensure these divisions. In Freetown, the prejudice inherent in the colonial system exposed itself from early in the twentieth century with the establishment of Hill Station. Hill Station was a segregated settlement reserved for whites and built, ostensibly for health reasons, about four miles from the center of Freetown, in the mountains. It was established in 1904 with twenty bungalows for Europeans and a residence for the governor. The government even constructed an expensive railroad to transport white residents to and from the town each day. Racial prejudice was not confined to housing alone. In one case, a barrister and member of the Freetown elite was told that he could not be served a meal at the Freetown YMCA reserved for whites and that he should, instead, dine at the other, which was intended for use by Africans.[10]

---

9. Richard Frost, *Race Against Time: Human Relations and Politics in Kenya before Independence* (London: Rex Collings, 1978), 38.

10. See "Colour Bar in Freetown," *Sierra Leone Daily Mail*, February 11, 1946, 1.

When an African elite began to emerge in Brazzaville, the colonial state attempted to segregate the races by separating residential quarters. Rather than openly express the desire to maintain a separate existence, they invoked cultural reasons, saying that excessive drumming and dancing infringed on the rights of whites. The state controlled this by introducing laws that restricted African drumming and dancing to certain areas of the city, areas that later became two prominent suburban settlements for Africans.

To maintain Nairobi as a white-controlled town, colonial administrators introduced strict residential policies there as well. Africans were viewed mainly as people who could provide cheap labor on the farms in the surrounding highlands and as domestic workers in white households in the city. The continued population growth in the suburban areas created a fear of unrest in the government, which responded by proposing measures to slow the increase in population. The 1949 Vagrancy Bill, for example, gave the police powers to repatriate Africans who had not been in formal employment for the previous three months and introduced pass laws to reduce the number of "vagrants" in town and limit the movements of the poorest members of the population. Subsequent attempts to control the population and deal with Mau Mau insurgents included "Operation Anvil," launched in spring 1954. This was designed to rid the city of "undesirables" and resulted in the removal of more than twenty-four thousand residents, while denying entry to thousands more people.

Even elite gains in economic and political power were undermined by the continued social prejudice of colonialists, although some educated Africans and others working in the colonial government did mix with the colonizers on a social level. In Nairobi, for example, the colonial government promoted such interactions through the operation of the Kenyan National Theatre, but it is clear that these efforts did not reach the African masses. The site selected for the establishment of the National Theatre was in a section of the city far from the African areas, in a section where no Africans were even allowed to live, a section which was referred to by one author as the "snob" center of town.[11] This example illustrates the fact that attempts by colonial administrators to integrate their social lives with those of the African elite were minimal and that they failed to include the mass of the population in any such interactions.

Declining Economies

On the surface, urban economies appeared to be booming. Shops were filled with imported consumer goods such as radios, bicycles, sewing machines, and gramophones. The youthful members of the urban society embraced new social values that emphasized money and Western goods as measures of personal worth. This attitude was best summarized in the words of the Congolese musician Mwenda Jean Bosco:

> In the big cities you have to be rich to be appreciated and to have prestige
> in the public eye. If you cannot obtain wealth, you will not be noticed

---

11. Richard Frost, *Race Against Time: Human Relations and Politics in Kenya before Independence.* (London: Rex Collings, 1978), 70.

and, often enough, you will be treated with contempt. In our villages, on the other hand, you have to till the fields to satisfy your basic needs: otherwise you would be condemned to a slow death.[12]

Though racial animosity was still prevalent and the economy was beginning to idle, cities still bustled with youthful energy. The increasing political power of Africans appeared to be a step in the right direction. In some cases, there was growing collaboration between members of the African elite and colonial administrators to increase African representation in government. Tensions rose quickly, though, as the economic pinch began to take hold. Animosities were most pronounced between the lower classes and colonial governments, because the economic downturn was removing income opportunities and deteriorating the quality of life for the lower classes and the quality of life was deteriorating at a rapid pace.

The end of the war resulted in a rising rate of unemployment as various war-related manufacturing and infrastructure improvements were scaled down. The demobilization of soldiers who fought for the Allied forces coupled with continued migration posed new problems. When the war ended, the issue of repatriation came to the forefront. In Sierra Leone, for example, a total of 17,418 servicemen had been demobilized by the end of 1946. It is impossible to know the exact number of veterans who stayed in Freetown, but in a city with an estimated population of eighty thousand, even a small percentage would be significant. From January 1945 to February 1946, the Freetown Employment Exchange registered an increase from 524 to 4,121 in the number of people seeking work. In the Gold Coast, almost seventy thousand people returned after the war and were disappointed by food shortages and inflated prices for basic food items, low wages, and high unemployment. The colonial powers, preferring to keep the urban population at a minimum level, promoted agriculture and mining for export. Using resettlement allowances and pension offers, they encouraged soldiers to return to their villages, but many inevitably drifted back to the "bright lights" of the city. Prospects in the city were becoming bleak, but decreasing prices for agricultural exports hardly made living and working in the rural areas a better option.

The cost of living also began to escalate after the war. Despite government efforts to control them, prices continued to rise; the cost of common food items doubled in many cities. In Nairobi, for example, food prices increased by 79.5 percent between 1945 and 1948. The rising cost of living had its greatest impact on those in the lower classes with little or no income. The situation made one observer in Freetown note that "the low-waged earner is compelled to subsist only on minnow and mallet, underdeveloped species of fish which are devoid of any nutrition whatsoever."[13]

The decline in the economy was also reflected in deteriorating housing conditions in African cities. New slums sprang up everywhere. Although indicators of economic decline had been clear since the early 1940s, the issue of substandard housing became critical by the latter part of the decade. In the most prominent

---

12. In Wolfgang Bender, *Sweet Mother: Modern African Music* (Chicago: University of Chicago Press, 1991), 50–1.
13. "The "Rising Cost of Living Goes on Apace," *Sierra Leone Daily Mail*, June 21, 1952, 2.

"slum" areas of major cities, overcrowding, poverty, and lack of sanitation were rampant. A Freetown report in 1948 found an average occupancy of twenty-three persons per house, while only nine years earlier it had been eight persons per house.[14] Class divisions became more prominent. The African elite and the Europeans despised these developments. In the *Sierra Leone Daily Mail*, for example, one writer commented that "the city is ridden with awful slums.... As a matter of fact they almost outnumber the better half of the city. THE SLUMS MUST BE CLEARED."[15]

There was, however, no place to which urban residents could move. Segregation and lack of available housing made it difficult to find accommodation in the city without sharing overcrowded rooms. In 1947, Nairobi officials determined that it would require 23,300 houses or rooms to remedy the housing shortage in Nairobi, but six years later the improvement was negligible.[16]

Extreme housing shortages created a number of problems, especially for those in the lower wage groups. The lack of rental accommodation, the segregation, and the scarcity of land in urban areas resulted in the establishment of squatter settlements and locations on the outskirts of many African cities during the late 1940s and 1950s. These suburban settlements grew into small cities in themselves, but as African cities continued to expand territorially, they were eventually linked to the central urban environment.

Despite the recognized hardships in the cities, people continued to immigrate, and colonial administrations failed to facilitate the construction of new housing facilities. Recommendations were made to build thousands of new houses, but rarely did these plans come to completion. When they did, they often reflected poor planning. Such was the case with the people in central Accra. After a devastating earthquake in 1939 that destroyed many buildings in the central area, new housing estates were built, but they were far from the sea. For the Ga, a society centered culturally and economically on its relationship with the sea and its byproducts, moving to such estates was not an option. Many chose to remain in the central and quickly deteriorating part of the city.

By the end of the 1940s African cities were generally unstable, composed largely of recent immigrants, predominantly male, poorly housed, and existing on wage levels insufficient to support a family. It was not uncommon for African males to outnumber females by ratios as high as 4 to 1 at this time. Immigration during the 1950s, however, began to reveal demographic changes. The new immigrants still included male, temporary wage-earners, but they also included a more reactive group of younger, single men and women who came to the city with plans to live there on a more permanent basis. As housing and general living conditions deteriorated and the level of unemployment increased after the war, it became clear that colonial administrators had little interest in urban improvement. By the end of the 1940s, tensions in the urban environment had soared and strikes and rioting were common.

---

14. "Report of the Interim Town Planning Committee, Freetown, 1948." Cited in Michael Banton, *West African City: A Study of Tribal Life in Freetown*. (London: Oxford University Press, 1957), 84.

15. "Appalling Slums of Freetown," *Sierra Leone Daily Mail*, March 31, 1955, 5.

16. Colony and Protectorate of Kenya, *Report on Native Affairs, 1946–47*. Nairobi: Government Printer, 1949, 88.

Urban Protests

Rapidly declining economic conditions, the inactivity of colonial administrations, and changing attitudes led to increased protests for improvements in the quality of urban life. While the elite fought the battle against colonialism in the courts and through negotiations, the masses expressed their growing discontent on the streets. This was not, in most cases, a direct call for an end to colonialism, but was more closely related to the people's day-to-day activities and standards of living. Unrest took the form of strikes, boycotts, and riots throughout urban Africa.

In 1948, the tensions erupted into violence in Accra. This began at the end of January with a boycott of European goods. It ended in March with twenty-nine people dead and more than two hundred injured. On February 28th, a group of unarmed ex-soldiers embarked on a planned march to the colonial administration headquarters to present a petition to the governor protesting their current conditions. On the way, they were met by a group of police officers. After warnings, threats, and some stone throwing, the European superintendent grabbed a rifle from his men and opened fire, killing two of the ex-servicemen and injuring a number of others. Already tense Accra residents reacted quickly to this atrocity. Widespread rioting and looting erupted. Within a few hours, a number of European businesses had been looted and set on fire. The following morning, the rioters broke down the gates of the prison, setting a number of inmates free. The unrest soon spread to other major towns in the Gold Coast. The British declared a state of emergency and brought in troops from Nigeria to help quell the riots.

In 1951, an estimated twenty thousand Freetown women marched to protest the high cost of living. They carried placards that read, "Life is hard in Sierra, we go naked"; "Cost of living don monna we" ("The cost of living is bothering us"); and the straightforward plea, "We are starving." This march was a strong indicator of the severity of the economic conditions in the city. A large-scale strike, led by the Joint Industrial Council for Artisans and Allied Workers and the Transport Industry, began in February 1955 and quickly turned violent. Attacks against individuals, looting, and burning of shops and automobiles became common. People availed themselves of the opportunity to fill their pockets with looted goods. A group of young people even tried to set fire to the Eastern Police Station, but a contingent of the Sierra Leone Regiment forced them to flee before their work was complete.

Throughout Africa, the strikes, riots, and rebellions of the late 1940s and 1950s established the futility of sustaining the colonial system for any extended period of time. Discontent was widespread. A union or association often initiated a strike or boycott, but undercurrents of tension quickly attracted others. Memories of the violence lingered long after the disturbances were quieted, exacerbating animosities between urban Africans and colonial governments. During the 1955 Watch Night celebration in Freetown, a night when the youth created elaborate lanterns and paraded through the streets, depictions of the riot were prominent. One of the lanterns carried the words "I Shot To Kill," a reference to a statement that a police officer had made to the commission of inquiry after the riots. Government reports examining the causes of the urban disturbances invariably pointed to the deteriorating urban environmental conditions, unemployment, housing problems, and rising cost of living as the major contributors to the unrest. In African

Figure 12.2. Urban protest in Lagos.

urban centers, the first decade after World War II was filled with growing economic tensions and social divisions. Urban residents survived by employing adaptive techniques to increase connections with particular groups and by generating a new, urban culture capable of relieving the stress of everyday living.

Voluntary Associations and Networks of Change

As young immigrants continued to flow into the cities in great numbers and felt the pain of declining economies, class and generation differences became more exaggerated, and social roles were changed. This section discusses the outlook and aims of older generations versus those of the youth and highlights the changes in the urban environment by describing the various techniques of social organization that Africans employed as adaptive mechanisms.

Urban societies were involved in a dynamic process of adaptation to new circumstances and conditions. The influx of migrants into the cities brought together people of diverse backgrounds who shared similar experiences in a new environment. More often than not, new migrants maintained contact with their extended families and their wider communities, both as an adaptive technique and also to keep the option to return home if or when they were ready to leave the city. Many migrants remained firmly rooted in the rural community in which they were raised. They stressed that they were strangers to the city and tended to identify with their community of origin and their close family relationships. Spouses and children who had to be left behind, members of the extended family, and other village contacts continued to define the image of home for these migrants. They visited their communities, contributed to their development efforts, and built houses there. Commitments to the extended family and rural village were not un-common, even among permanent migrants. Even in the most extreme circumstances, urban immigrants continued to be influenced by the cultures from which they came, but the unique conditions of urban life also brought changes in social patterns.

The differences between generations were more profound in the urban areas. A large percentage of immigrants was made up of younger men and women who came to the city to escape the problems of age and generational status in the rural areas. Their presence and attitudes symbolized a growing age gap. The youth accepted changing cultural inputs at a faster pace, but they did not abandon their past. Without the social restrictions exerted by the older generations, young men and women were more apt to attend foreign films, dance to new Western forms of music, and adopt new fashions. As in any society, older generations viewed such behaviors as contrary to the overall interests of society and marked them as the worst signs of modernity. The youth, however, were not deterred, and they continued to find solace and independence from such judgments by bonding together in new associations.

One of the most significant social consequences of rural-urban migrations during and after World War II was the proliferation of new urban voluntary associations. The roots of these associations could be traced far into the African past, but the influx of new immigrants enhanced their meaning in the urban environment. As more people came to live in the city for longer periods, these associations helped people adjust to city life by providing funds to open businesses, help members cope with sickness or death, or providing a focus for their leisure time activities.

The choice of membership in a voluntary association was linked to the process of identity formation for many new immigrants. Virtually every social group within the city was represented in some sort of association. They were often organized around factors such as class, occupation, religion, ethnicity, music, or leisure time activities. They included groups of unemployed young men, new to the city and looking for a place to meet others in a similar situation, groups of traders, and elite social clubs. Many had some form of savings plan, a provision that was common in rural associations as well. Members made contributions regularly and were then allowed to draw from the group fund when necessary.

One type of association for new immigrants was based on ethnicity. A good example was the Igbo State Union in Lagos. Migrants to urban areas where other ethnic groups formed a larger percentage of the population formed this union to provide members with financial support during unemployment or in case of death. This union also provided a means for members to maintain their cultural heritage in a foreign environment by publicizing Igbo songs, history, language, and beliefs. Members collected money to support these activities and funded education. Some of the money was sent to the members' hometowns to improve amenities there. It was not uncommon for such unions to organize dances and sports competitions. Some of them also produced an annual magazine recording their members' whereabouts and activities.

Another type of association had an occupational basis. Market women formed these associations to finance individual business activities, open group-run enterprises, or control the prices of important goods. Other types of occupational

Figure 12.3. Modern Lagos, Nigeria.

associations included unions of drivers, artisans, and craft workers. They existed
to protect the interests of members through financial assistance. Drivers' unions,
for example, offered legal and financial help if a driver was arrested or fined. They
also contributed money to the family if a member died. Artisan and craft associations served similar functions but also regulated the apprenticeship system and
ensured an acceptable quality of work.

The activities and responsibilities of many associations included entertainment and leisure events as well. There were also groups whose main emphasis
was entertainment and leisure but who provided other services as well. These
ranged from music and dance societies to women's institutes and soccer clubs.
Groups revolved around a variety of themes. Members of religious associations
met to discuss their beliefs or plan charitable events. Sports clubs organized
weekly competitions to showcase the skills of their members and to strengthen
bonds of friendship between clubs. Young men and women, influenced by the
dancing in 1950s rock and roll movies, formed clubs, bought gramophones, organized dance lessons, and performed at social functions around the city. Social
clubs consisting of the most Westernized and elite section of a population came
together for lectures, tennis, and weekly ballroom dances. Regardless of the type
of association, the organization was usually highly developed. From president,
treasurer, doctor, secretary, and a host of other possible offices, each club chose
appropriate titles and assigned particular roles to each.

The existence of a diverse, largely immigrant, urban population encouraged
urban residents to seek familiar networks of association. Voluntary associations
assisted many immigrants in adapting to their new environment. They helped
maintain ties to rural areas, built and reinforced values and norms of behavior
suitable to city life, and provided networks of supporting relations. The workings
of these associations, as well as the forms of popular culture that were generated

within them, were influenced not only by the culture brought into the urban areas, but also by the historical legacies of the cities themselves.

Growth of Urban Popular Culture

The changing demographics of urban areas, growing class divides, and new social roles and technologies provided the impetus for the development of new urban popular culture forms. This section discusses a few of the many types of urban culture created during the period, and illuminates the rift between elite and mass culture in the areas of music and dance, cinema, and sports and leisure. It looks at the creation of new cultural forms as an expression of continuity, adaptation, and identity, as a statement on the new roles of youth, and as an indication of a changing worldview.

Leisure time in the city revolved around entertainment in open squares, outdoor bars, dance-halls, and cinemas. The development of elite society resulted in the development of new clubs, usually charging admission prices high enough to exclude much of the population. Before World War II, the most common types of dances at these clubs were based on Western styles like the waltz, fox-trot, and quick step. The dramatic increase in population and the external and internal influences introduced during the war years, however, attracted a younger, more dynamic group of people to the urban environment. The excitement of city life continued to attract additional immigrants in the years following the war. Many of the voluntary associations discussed in the previous section focused on leisure activities such as sports, music, or dancing.

Popular culture was sometimes subjected to official attempts to control it. The colonial elite tried to structure time and space as a means to control the workforce, train Christians, or affirm the correctness of Western culture. In 1947, the British Council organized the first public concerts in Nairobi in which Europeans and Africans appeared on the same stage. Two African choirs were joined by the director of the East African Conservatoire of Music and other European musicians. The audience consisted of both Europeans and Africans of the middle and upper classes. The cultural base was decidedly British-the only African thing about it was the people involved. In Freetown, also, there was a prevailing colonial conviction that scorned local music and praised only Western styles. A Sierra Leone musician, returning from London in 1957, complained of a lack of folk songs for him to take back:

> Our musicians have either been too occupied with foreign music that they have no time for local music or... [they have been] taught to look down on our native music as the rest of Sierra Leoneans have been.[17]

The dominance of European culture in Freetown permeated other aspects of life as well. For example, the "highlight" of Sierra Leone's first Festival of the Arts

---

17. *Sierra Leone Daily Mail*, October 1, 1957, 3.

in 1957, was a pageant of the most "important" events in Sierra Leonean history. The pageant included vignettes of the naming of Sierra Leone by a Portuguese seaman, the visit of Sir Francis Drake, the coming of the Jesuits, the slave trade, the reign of King Niambana, the coming of the settlers, the attacks by the French, and the colonizing of the country.[18] From this list, the emphasis is clear. Except for the scenes of King Niambana's reign and the slave trade, the vignettes were all focused on external influences and their role in the development of Sierra Leone.

It is important to mention such attempts by the colonial institutions to control leisure time and popular culture and the influence they had on the urban culture, especially that of the elite, but it is even more important to recognize that leisure time and popular culture also existed outside, independent of colonial influence and regulation. Active techniques of adopting and adapting external and internal cultural stimuli produced new, uniquely urban genres of entertainment.

A wide array of recreational activities, from football and fashion to music, dance, drinking, and nightlife, helped build social networks, humanized daily life, and forged new identities. Older traditions from both inside and outside Africa were carried into the cities along with new technologies and beliefs. Urban Africans took what was useful from these influences and adopted them, not by eliminating older traditions and values, but by adapting and remaking them into new cultural forms that better represented the uniqueness of city life.

Music and Technology

The arrival of foreign troops during World War II, coupled with technological changes, enhanced the exchange of musical influences between Africa and the West. The proliferation of bars and nightclubs continued long after Western soldiers had withdrawn. The population of the cities continued to rise quickly and the need for places of entertainment increased accordingly. New places served as gathering points to meet people, talk about the news, and hear the new music coming out of and into the cities. With the arrival of foreign servicemen, larger dance band orchestras began to replace smaller bands in the Gold Coast. One of the first such bands was E. T. Mensah and the Tempos playing their new style of highlife music. Influenced by swing, Afro-Cuban percussion, and calypso, highlife became popular throughout West Africa during the 1950s and 1960s.

E. T. Mensah:
"The King of Highlife"[24]

Emmanuel Tetteh Mensah (1919–1996) was born in the central part of Accra, in the Gold Coast. His mother was a cloth trader and his father was a full-

---

18. "Sir Maurice Opens First Festival of the Arts," *Sierra Leone Daily Mail*, December 9, 1957.
24. For more on E. T. Mensah and the evolution of highlife music, see Collins, *King of Highlife*; and Collins, *Highlife Time*, (Accra: Anansesem Publications), 1996.

time goldsmith and part-time guitar player, stimulating his musical interests at a young age. From his early musical days until the time of his death, he influenced the evolution of music in West Africa and beyond. He and his elder brother, Yebuah, went to elementary school in Jamestown, Accra and studied music under Joe "Teacher" Lamptey. Both played in the school orchestra and joined Lamptey's Accra Orchestra in 1933, E. T. playing flute and piccolo. The orchestra was a large dance band playing contemporary music standards from the repertoire of fox-trot, quickstep, waltz, samba, rumba, and early highlife. Though the orchestra played at many different types of functions, the required dress was always European apparel, with the men in ties and women in dresses. The orchestra broke up in 1936 and a few months later many of its members emerged with the Accra Rhythm Orchestra under the leadership of Yebuah.

In 1940, E. T. met Jack Leopard, a Scottish sergeant with the British Army who was interested in forming a dance band in Accra. Leopard chose the name, "Leopard and his Black and White Spots," to reflect the mix of African and European members in the band. Playing for European audiences at the army camps and European clubs in town, the band earned considerably more than they would have with the Accra Rhythm Orchestra, but they also played considerably less highlife music, focusing instead on jazz, swing, and ballroom styles. Leopard was transferred in 1942, but the band continued as the "Black and White Spots" for another two years before breaking up when E. T. was transferred to the north.

He returned to Accra in 1947 and joined the already established Tempos, playing both trumpet and saxophone. The Tempos first played at the European Club but soon became the house band for one of the first nightclubs in Accra, Weekend-in-Havana, where they played many more highlife numbers. By 1950 the band was traveling as far as Nigeria, playing its highlife music for new listeners. But success bred conflict and the band split again. This allowed E. T. to form a new band under the name "E. T. Mensah and the Tempos," a band that played more South American rhythms, calypso, and highlife. This type of music caught on very quickly and the band's popularity spread. The new Tempos made the first of their many recordings with Decca in 1952 and, after splitting again and reforming with new members, registered as the first professional dance band in Ghana in 1953. At the time of independence, E. T. composed a song that celebrated the event called "Ghana Freedom Highlife." The Tempos inspired many new dance bands in Accra and, after numerous trips through West Africa and Europe, E. T. certainly deserved his name, the "King of Highlife."

Due to their high price, gramophones remained out of the reach of all but the elite until the mid-1950s, but their impact was felt at all levels. Their sounds could be heard drifting out of shops, attracting customers to buy goods and introducing them to new music. Voluntary associations pooled their money to buy or rent gramophones for outdoor trips to the beach or other functions. The introduction of cheaper transistor radios and an increase in the playing time of African music on radio stations also meant that more people could hear more new music. The expanding recording industry, both within and outside Africa, and the increasing availability of gramophone records meant that Western and African musical forms could be disseminated more quickly. New music was being played live and on gramophones in bars and in other entertainment settings throughout African cities.

Figure 12.4. A highlife musician in Lagos.

Another technological change that affected the development of African urban music was the introduction of amplification. It is ironic to think that amplification allowed African bands to become more African, but it is true. The use of amplifiers meant that bands could now introduce more traditional African drums into their ensemble without drowning out the sounds of voices, guitars, wind instruments, and horns.

Juju music gained popularity in Nigeria during the 1940s and 1950s. Its development illustrated many of the major changes discussed above. Juju music was a popular urban guitar style that grew out of the palm-wine styles that were popular in Lagos in the early 1930s. Early juju groups typically consisted of a leader, who played banjo and sang, a tambourine player, and a *sèkèrè* (a gourd covered with beads). During the World War II era, a second vocalist was added, and by the time of independence, musicians had incorporated a variety of other instruments, including the Yoruba pressure-drum, accordion, electric guitar, vocals, and additional African drums. Tunde King was the first musician to commercially record juju music (Parlophone, 1936) and develop a widespread following. He combined imported styles, like the Kru and Ghanaian influenced palm-wine styles, *ashiko* music, and Yoruba praise music to produce a new, unique style. Two of the early innovators in juju music were the ukulele and banjo player, Ojoge Daniels, and the guitarist Ayinde Bakare, the leader of the Inner Circle Orchestra during the 1950s. The most famous juju musician before independence was I. K. Dairo, leader of the Blue Spots Band, established in 1957. Juju music permeated all levels of Lagos society. Musicians frequented elite "parlor parties," lower-class bars, and social gatherings naming ceremonies, weddings, funerals, and housewarming celebrations. Juju music developed into a social form of dance

Figure 12.5.   View of Abidjan, Côte d'Ivoire.

music with ten or more musicians on stage. Performed by international stars like King Sunny Ade and Ebenezer Obey, it continues to play an important role in the Yoruba music scene today.

Inspired by new technologies, Ghanaian highlife also began to take root in Nigeria in the 1950s. As long distance transportation became easier and musicians began to undertake international tours, the music and the artists became more widely known. Music also spread rapidly and over greater distances via transistor radios and gramophones. In Nigeria in the early 1950s, many dance bands still played mostly Western-style ballroom and swing music. When E. T. Mensah and the Tempos visited Lagos in the early 1950s, their popularity soared and they influenced the development of dance music there. By the middle of the decade, dance band highlife was well established.

The spread of musical influences, however, depended on a number of factors. The evolution of popular music in Sierra Leone, where the influence of the British was more prevalent among the Krio and class divisions were rampant, was different than in Lagos and Accra. Mensah, who toured the country in 1958, described the music scene:

> There were no dance bands in Sierra Leone and at the clubs they danced to gramophone records.... Another thing we noticed during our stay was that there was class distinction, with the upper class consisting of lawyers and doctors who did not like to mix with the working class. If we wanted this upper class to attend our dances we had to raise our entrance fee or charge two separate fees and provide two separate dance floors.[19]

In French West Africa, the African music and entertainment culture was slower to develop than in the British colonies. Touring in Abidjan in 1955, Men-

---

19. Collins, *King of Highlife*, 28.

sah described the effects of French colonialism on the night-life and music: "The French were treating the country as their own.... They ran the nightclubs and were importing European musicians and actors.... When I went there I never saw an African [dance] band."[20]

In the British-controlled territories, the policy of indirect rule tolerated and even promoted a certain amount of adoption and adaptation of Western music forms. In the French-controlled, direct-rule territories, on the other hand, there was a clear distinction between French and indigenous culture; the former was promoted while the latter was dismissed. It was much later, therefore, that hybrid music forms began to take a strong hold in the French territories.

By the mid-1950s, African music from francophone areas was receiving increasing attention. New, Congo-based record companies and Radio Brazzaville helped to disseminate the music throughout Africa. Congo music was based in the traditions of Luba music, but it incorporated elements of Latin American rumba. It utilized a percussion section of trap drums, congas, bongos, clips, and maracas, a horn section of trumpets and saxophones, and multiple guitars. The first musician to gain renown with this style was Mwenda Jean Bosco. He released *Masanga* in 1952 and it received the Osborne Award for the best African record of the year. By the end of the decade, Congo music was known from South Africa to Senegal, and its rhythms and melodies made an impact on the wider African music scene. Indeed, this music became so popular that by the end of the 1950s, bands like O. K. Jazz, Orchestre Bella Bella, Orchestre Veve, and Doudi Daniels and his Orchestre Mando Negro had sold hundreds of thousands of albums.

The use of the word "jazz" in band names was not uncommon amongst the Congolese bands. It reflected the influence of American soldiers stationed in Léopoldville during World War II, not the American musical genre itself. Congo music developed in and around the social life of urban gatherings. Young musicians sought engagements at wedding receptions, festivals, and other urban entertainment functions. If it was the urban social clubs that provided opportunities for many of the young Congolese rumba musicians, it was the Léopoldville recording industry that provided the spark for the further spread of the music and the popularity of the musicians. "Come to Brazzaville and See," a cha-cha composed by André Nkoura Courant which tells his girlfriend of urban problems, is representative of the syncretic music styles of the period and emphasizes the lyrical focus on everyday problems:

Brazzaville is so beautiful
But there is no job, what can we do?
Come to Brazzaville and see the Congo
Thérèse I will die for you
I'm lost, I'm lost
There's plenty of food in the market
But there's no money to buy it
When I put my hand in my pocket
I only feel the tailor's thread
Money is one's cushion dear,

---

20. Ibid., 32.

Money solves everything
So what shall we do?[21]

Throughout urban Africa, music served as an expression of city life. It not only reflected the process of cultural exchange through the adaptation of new styles, instruments, and technologies, but it influenced the process of urban identity formation that became so marked during the last two decades of colonialism.

Cinema

Though films arrived in Africa even before the turn of the century, colonial administrators began to play closer attention to the effects of cinema in the 1930s. Complete control over film distribution and exhibition was exercised by foreigners until independence. This affected the types of films that became popular and restricted the development of a truly African film industry. Close censorship was used to restrict the screening of films that might diminish the myth of white superiority, encourage the "wrong" behaviors in colonial subjects, or present scenes of immorality that would tarnish the inflated ideal of Western civilization. For example, the Film Board of French Equatorial Africa banned the showing of *Tempest over Asia* because it showed scenes of abuses against colonial subjects by whites.

By the start of World War II, colonial governments recognized the potential of cinema as an instrument of propaganda to promote the Allied mission. The British established the Colonial Film Unit in 1939 with the immediate aim of garnering African physical and monetary support for the war effort. Using radio broadcasts, newspaper media, films, and mobile cinema trucks, propaganda encouraged enlistment, appealed for contributions, explained recent events, and emphasized the threat presented by the Axis powers.

After the war, the emphasis shifted to films that colonial governments deemed to be of educational value. They made films to demonstrate British etiquette, promote basic health and education, and encourage people to adopt new agricultural techniques. Unsurprisingly, the Colonial Film Unit was a paternalistic institution, its main goal being to maintain control over what it saw as inferior Africans. The aim was to develop a different style of cinema for Africans, a style rooted more in teaching European ideals than in entertaining its clientele. By 1955, the Colonial Film Unit declared that it had fulfilled its goals and requested that the colonies finance their own film production. The dissemination of films outside cities decreased, but the development of urban cinema advanced rapidly as the availability of new foreign films increased.

By the 1950s, cinemas had opened in every major African city and with them came an expanded repertoire of films. In the English-speaking areas, imported films from the United States became popular. The *Tarzan* movies, westerns, and gangster films were very common. Indeed, they reinforced the dominance of white men and Western civilization by projecting stereotypical images of Africans and others as savage and cannibalistic; but the action and adventure films, in general,

---

21. A. Moundanda and A. C. Nkouka, *Biakongo-Chansons Congolaises*, (Brazzaville: mimeographed, n.d), 31. In Phyllis Martin, *Leisure and Society in Colonial Brazzaville*, (Cambridge: Cambridge University Press, 1995), 151.

were enticing, and their popularity soared. Members of urban youth groups assumed nicknames that reflected attachments to these films. It was not uncommon to meet a person who went by the name of John Wayne, Jack Palance, Lash La Rue, or even James Dean. Colonialists, religious leaders, and members of the African elite were quick to blame the influence of popular Hollywood films for the rise in juvenile delinquency and general decline in societal values, but the generational differences became more pronounced and youth groups continued to embrace aspects of foreign culture by adapting them to their own circumstances.

Sports

Throughout the world, sports have allowed people to come together, often in ways not otherwise possible. In late-colonial Africa, urban sports afforded great opportunities to forge new friendships and relationships important in the development of city life. Although sports like cricket, boxing, and polo were introduced to Africa with colonization and are still played today in many cities, there is no doubt that soccer made the biggest impact. Soccer was introduced early in the colonial era. At first, it was a game played by white men, but it was quickly taken up by Africans, sometimes with the cooperation of colonial elites. Soccer did not, however, become a widespread, popular sport until after World War II, when the quality of play and sports facilities advanced dramatically. By the 1950s, it was played at all social levels, and increasingly by well-organized teams and in larger, more modern stadiums.

Before the war, sports teams were sponsored by missions, schools, and colonial governments, all attempting to impose some structure on "carefree" Africans. Following the war, however, neighborhood associations and individuals became sponsors of African soccer teams, successfully taking at least partial control of the sport away from white society. The urban population increase during and after the war fueled a surge in interest, propelling soccer to the prominent level it holds in Africa today. By the mid-1950s, soccer was a mass phenomenon. It was more than just a sport, defining the changing face of cities. Phyllis Martin described the high position that soccer occupied within the larger urban experience of Brazzaville:

> No other form of popular culture could rival the excitement generated by [soccer] matches. To be part of the crowd was to be at the heart of a city experience. Nowhere else could one encounter drama on such a large scale and share it with old and new friends.[22]

Soccer matches reflected larger urban popular culture characteristics. The displays of live music, dancing, and team colors gave a match the appearance of a festival. In the cities, where identities were often linked to class, occupation, and ethnicity, allegiance to a particular football club helped create and reinforce bonds between groups of urban residents.

Colonial administrators attempted to harness the energy of the urban youth by not only co-opting them into organizations such as the Scouts, but also by building new sports stadiums and sponsoring teams. Such attempts were part of the larger colonial endeavor to regulate time and space, which was thought necessary to pro-

---

22. Ibid., 118.

duce a more orderly and efficient population of laborers. Félix Eboué, governor-general of French Equatorial Africa, wrote in his 1941 *La nouvelle politique indigène* that discipline among Africans must be obtained, and one of the ways to do this was through government control of "sports clubs, Scouts, paramilitary groups and recreational organizations." He added that he was "counting on all of these to offer the rootless native the structured life which is indispensable."[23]

The colonial powers, despite their efforts, were seldom in control of leisure and popular culture activities. Urban culture took on a life of its own, independent of colonial control. The continuing expansion of entertainment attractions such as open squares, bars, beer-gardens, dance-halls, and cinemas drew more immigrants to town. The increased entertainment structures provided new networks of association, essential to the forging of sub-communities.

The development of leisure in African urban centers might be characterized as a struggle to create a congenial environment to suit African needs beyond the reach of colonial attempts to impose colonialist and capitalist structures. By the time of independence, it was not uncommon to see younger men and women in African cities acting out roles they saw on cinema screens, listening to American and Latin American popular music on the radio and on gramophones, or cheering on their favorite international sports stars. They adopted these styles but adapted them to fit their own needs. They employed them in their search for new forms of relationships and changing identities in the urban environment.

Conclusion

The 1940s and 1950s were exciting times in African urban centers. Politically, the streets were being prepared for the procession to independence, and the elite class strengthened its hold on power. Economically, imported goods were abundant, and there was hope for improvement in general living conditions. Socially and culturally, the rapid growth of cities encouraged new networks of association and developments in popular culture. These were also difficult times to be urban residents. With urban growth came increasing poverty, unemployment, and housing problems; but the rate of change did not slow and the excitement was not quelled. Independence brought a new, short-lived optimism for many Africans, but the creation of unique adaptive techniques continued.

The research opportunities provided by the urban milieu are endless, and each study opens new avenues of research. More in-depth inquiries into sports, cinema, popular music, and other leisure activities, some of the most vibrant areas of urban cultural life, are necessary. It is essential, however, to incorporate economic and living conditions; age, class, and racial divisions; and technological changes into any investigation. None of these factors can be examined in isolation without missing an important element of their development. A major focus of colonial African urban history has been, and should continue to be, the struggle between the colonial or "official" sphere and the African, non-elite population for control over time and space. Whether struggling to establish control over resi-

---

23. Martin, *Leisure and Society*, 83.

dential localities or control over leisure time, the colonial state was not able to impose its will. Strikes and boycotts were obvious elements of resistance, but popular culture should also be given its due.

Finally, the emphasis on interactions between the urban and non-urban spheres presents us with the problematic conception of invoking such categorical oppositions as "traditional" and "modern," "rural" and "urban." Within each opposition, there are many permutations that have developed because of constant interactions between environments and communities. It is impossible to understand the changing constructs of the city without also taking into account changes in the suburban and rural settlements that interact with it on many different levels, and of course the opposite is also true. Yet, it is not the terms themselves that need to be removed from our lexicon; it is the use of them in binary opposition to one another that must be questioned and carefully reworked to create a more accurate picture of the relationship between economics, politics, and culture in African cities. We must look at cultural developments as part of a horizontal continuum that links the past with the present and draws lines toward the future.

Review Questions

1. You are a young African living in the rural areas between 1940 and 1960. Would you migrate to the urban centers? Why or why not?
2. Discuss the economic, social, and cultural impact of World War II on African cities.
3. What conditions affected the development of the urban environment following the war? What mechanisms did urban Africans employ to adapt to them?
4. What factors contributed to the development and vitality of urban culture during the last two decades of colonial rule? How did the life and music of E. T. Mensah reflect this vitality?
5. In what ways did colonial governments attempt to regulate urban lives, and how did Africans respond?

Additional Reading

Banton, Michael. *West African City: A Study of Tribal Life in Freetown.* London: Oxford University Press, 1957.

Bender, Wolfgang. *Sweet Mother: Modern African Music.* Chicago: University of Chicago Press, 1991.

Collins, John. *Highlife Time.* Accra: Anansesem Publications, 1996.

Diawara, Manthia. *African Cinema: Politics & Culture.* Bloomington: Indiana University Press, 1992.

Little, Kenneth. *West African Urbanization: A Study of Voluntary Associations in Social Change.* Cambridge: Cambridge University Press, 1970.

Martin, Phyllis. *Leisure and Society in Colonial Brazzaville.* Cambridge: Cambridge University Press, 1995.

Waterman, Christopher. *Juju: A Social History and Ethnography of an African Popular Music.* Chicago: University of Chicago Press, 1990.

Suggested Recordings

E. T. Mensah & the Tempos. *All for You*. Retroafric, B00000JLE4.

Franco's O.K. Jazz. *Originalite*. Retroafric, B00000JCWX.

King Sunny Ade and his African Beats: *Live Live Juju*. Rykodisc, RCD10047.

Jean Mwenda Bosco. *Mwenda Wa Bayeke*. Rounder Records, B0000003A8.

Various Artists. *Before Benga, Vol. 1: Kenya Dry*. Original Music, OMCD021.

Various Artists. *Before Benga. Vol. 2: The Nairobi Sound*. Original Music, OMCD022.

Various Artists. *Money No Be Sand: Afro-Lypso/Pidgin Highlife/Afro-Rock/Afro-Soul*. Original Music, OMCD031.

Various Artists. *Juju Roots 1930s–1950s*. Rounder Records, B00000038C.

Chapter 13

Westernization of Health Services

George Ndege

This chapter examines the nature, context, and consequences of the Westernization of health services in Africa. It broadens the traditional mainstream definition of health services to include the many and varied contestations, negotiations, and adaptations that have influenced not only the development but also the delivery of health services in Africa. The discussion is organized into three sections. The process of Westernization of health services is outlined in the first section. The challenges faced by the postcolonial governments during the first two decades of independence in democratizing health services by making them more patient-centered are examined in the second section. The final section assesses the effectiveness of Westernized health services against the backdrop of internal economic constraints, the onset of the AIDS pandemic, and the rise of opportunistic infections.

* * *

Traditionally, authors have defined the Westernization of health services in terms of European agency by emphasizing the colonial governments' efforts to develop medical facilities and their attempts to contain the spread of many diseases in Africa. In this approach, the African is presented as the consumer of health services with insignificant input into the process of health service delivery. The traditional narrative, therefore, is neatly packaged in an organized, linear fashion to reinforce the notion that the Westernization of health services is synonymous with progress and success. The number of health facilities, inoculation campaigns, new drugs and equipment, and medical personnel reveal the success of health services.

In recent decades, this construction of health services has been the subject of some criticism. Although traditional histories usually include Africans and their health and healing traditions, they do so only peripherally. Modern scholarship has rehabilitated this peripheral area. Most scholars now accept that a study of the Westernization of health services must transcend statistics to encompass a complex set of contestations, negotiations, and adaptations with which Africans have had to contend over the past century.

Nature and Context of the Westernization of Health Care Services

The Westernization of health care services was a natural outgrowth of the colonization of Africa, proceeding from the premise that African health and healing traditions were insignificant compared to the power of science and could neither reinforce nor replicate the objectivity of scientific medicine. Africans' loss of autonomy and independence during the colonial period adversely impacted the development and nurturing of knowledge that was considered inconsistent with mainstream thought in scientific medicine. Indeed, colonial health care services presumed the integrity of biomedicine because of laboratory-based and clinical methods. What could not be determined through an array of tests on bodily fluids, sensed by stethoscope, or diagnosed by the physician was considered irrelevant to the patient's treatment and recovery. The Westernization of health care services hardly accorded any place to traditional therapeutic practices.

The colonial state projected the Westernization of health services as the only route to social betterment for Africans. Yet in the theory and practice of Western biomedicine in Africa, the role of the African remained vague, and indigenous knowledge was rendered irrelevant. Instead, hospitals, dispensaries, and laboratories, albeit unevenly distributed in the countries, not only manifested the presence of colonial health care but also symbolized institutions of progress. The problem lay in the fact that such institutions were outside the reach of the majority of Africans. Through much of the colonial period, health care was not only urban focused; it also emphasized curative services over preventive ones. Hospitals and health centers were unevenly distributed, with the majority of them located either in urban places or in areas of European settlement. Health services were provided in the context of the colonial economy and racial preferences.[1] Colonial health care was anything but a social welfare scheme.

The colonial medical profession's enormous faith in scientific investigation, hospitals, and laboratories meant that it mainly catered to those who were able to reach the hospitals. Medical personnel hardly ventured into educational programs that would help prevent disease. The concerns and lifestyles of their local constituents were not considered critical to the primary agenda of preventing disease outbreaks. Even where attempts were made to involve the community in disease prevention campaigns, the stereotypical notion of the "diseased African" undermined meaningful dialogue between medical personnel and local populations. By and large, the local populations were regarded as inconsequential until a major disease outbreak occurred, and particularly until the sick went to seek treatment in the health centers.

Health services were thus limited in scope and impact, at least until after World War II. Although Africans reacted to their alienation from mainstream health care in a number of ways, it is safe to assert that their purpose was neither the acceptance nor the rejection of Western biomedicine per se. They sought to reconcile Western health care services with their situational reality because Western biomedicine was unable to meet all epidemic challenges. This was due to

---

1. Maynard W. Swanson, "The Sanitation Syndrome: Bubonic Plague and Urban Native Policy in the Cape Colony, 1900–1909," *Journal of African History* 17, 3 (1977): 387–410.

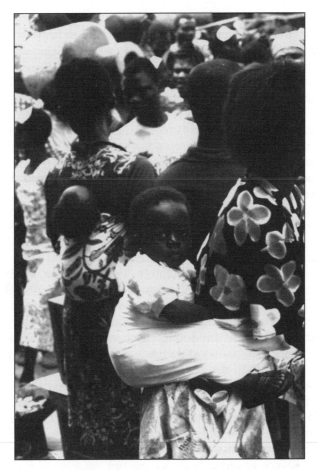

Figure 13.1. Growing up in Africa.

practitioners' limited knowledge of the disease regime in Africa and the less developed infrastructure, set priorities, and elitist nature of Western health care services. It is not surprising, therefore, that maternal and child care services were peripheral in the colonial scheme of health care delivery.[2] Indeed, standardized and professional midwifery training in Africa was slow to develop in mainstream colonial health care.[3] Maternal and child health care remained largely within the domain of traditional health and healing, which operated outside the orbit of the Westernized health services.

This is not to suggest that traditional health and healing practices were more effective against the many and varied diseases that predated colonialism or those

---

2. Even in the Belgian Congo, which had the most extensive medical infrastructure in maternal health care, the number of medically supervised deliveries in 1935 was estimated at only one percent. This rose to about twenty-eight percent in 1952. Indeed, the incorporation of maternal and child health care into the mainstream health services was a gradual and uneven process. See Nancy Rose Hunt, *A Colonial Lexicon: Of Birth Ritual, Medicalization, and Mobility in the Congo* (Durham, NC: Duke University Press, 1999), 3.

3. Ibid., 256–62.

that arrived with the onset of colonialism. The fact is that Africans did not see the route to social betterment totally in terms of Westernized health services or totally in terms of traditional therapeutic practices. They saw the two systems as coexisting with and supplementing each other. Thus, a major development arising from the introduction of Western health services was medical pluralism and the development of "double lives," in which patients visited traditional healers as well as colonial health centers and Western-trained physicians. While Western health services were separated from mainstream African therapeutic systems, which were holistic and embraced an entire framework of interrelations between humans and their natural and supernatural environments, African therapies were not rendered irrelevant.[4] The Westernization of health services did not supplant African health and healing strategies. It was not uncommon to find patients moving from traditional healers to hospitals and vice versa, depending on the nature of the ailment, the mind-set of the patient, the cost, and the availability of the service required. Thus, medical pluralism made perfect sense because of the limitations associated with both traditions.[5]

After World War II, serious attempts were made to institutionalize and streamline health services in Africa. In this regard, World War II constituted a major benchmark in the development of health care services. In the postwar environment, issues pertaining to education, health care, housing, and sanitation, particularly in urban areas, could hardly be dealt with outside the political circumstances of the times. The issues collectively constituted what Cooper has aptly described as the "burden of the declining empire."[6]

After the war, social medicine in colonial Africa was redefined in terms of ultimate rather than immediate causes.[7] In this regard, initiatives began to be directed at the domestic level, which had hitherto been ignored. The focus on ultimate causes signified a philosophical shift from the medical paradigm to a blend of the medical and materialist paradigm. In the medical paradigm, health care is primarily the province of physicians, nurses, and other "health personnel."[8] The thrust of health care policy is a disproportionate focus on the training of more and better skilled personnel, as well as on the construction of hospitals and clinics. In contrast, the materialist paradigm sees health care as a collective enterprise that has to be socially and collectively produced.[9] The materialist view is that good health care has to transcend the existence of hospitals, clinics, and skilled personnel. It has to be linked with the general need for a more equitable and humane society.

---

4. David Nyamwaya, "Causation of Illness in African Traditional Medicine," *Mila: A Biannual Newsletter of Cultural Research* 6, 2 (1983): 1–18.

5. C. MacCormack, "The Articulation of Western and Traditional Systems of Health Care," in *The Professionalization of African Medicine*, ed. G. L. Chavunduka and L. Murray (Manchester, England: Manchester University Press, 1986), 35–67.

6. Ann Laura Stoler and Frederick Cooper, *Tensions of Empire: Colonial Cultures in a Bourgeois World* (Berkeley, CA: University of California Press, 1997).

7. "On the Implementation and Interpretation of Social Medicine in the Native Reserves." Memorandum by Director of Medical Services, May 16, 1950, Kenya National Archives (KNA), Public Health (PH)/76/8/22/109.

8. S. Ogoh Alubo and Franklin Vivekananda, *Beyond the Illusion of Primary Health in an African Society* (Stockholm, Sweden: Bethany Books, 1995), 5–51.

9. Ibid., 50–1.

The path that the colonial state began to pursue after the war was one that blended these two paradigms. It was an attempt to strike a balance between the expansion of health care institutions and facilities on the one hand and an emphasis on a management strategy that would focus on the community and the prevention of disease outbreaks on the other. However, in expanding health care institutions, the state focused on the establishment of dispensaries to avoid a situation whereby health centers would be forced to cater to a large number of patients. Patients were to first visit dispensaries and then be referred to the health centers. Health centers would be referral institutions at the local level. The state sought to avoid health centers from being turned into enlarged outpatient departments. This shift in state policy was also motivated by political considerations.

Throughout the 1950s, the pace of decolonization quickened and urban social projects, such as the provision of education, health, and housing, were no longer considered peripheral issues. The nationalists interpreted the inadequacy of these developments as the clearest reflection of the social organization that had been nurtured by the colonial state. Thus, Africans became increasingly politicized.[10] It is against this setting that the African nationalists looked beyond colonialism into the postcolonial period when they would redress the imbalances and inequities in the delivery of health services.

Health Care Services After Independence

The African leadership promised to provide basic services to the citizenry by reforming the colonial health care system, which was still quite elitist in orientation, curative in emphasis, uneven in geographical distribution, and fragmented into two sectors, private and public or government. Indeed, most African governments began to emphasize preventive and rehabilitative health care with the hope of bringing the majority of people within the orbit of mainstream health care. Primary health care, with its emphasis on immunization programs, was aimed at reducing infant mortality rates, training nurses who could communicate directly with the local populations, and expanding health facilities to accommodate a wide range of people. This composed a major policy initiative taken by most postcolonial governments in the period immediately after independence, although its implementation and results varied.

African governments followed various developmental paths in promoting access to health care services. In this endeavor, a number of considerations, such as the political ideology of the government, the health of the economy, and the role of international agencies—particularly their financial support for various programs—were all crucial. Countries such as Kenya and Nigeria, which pursued liberal capitalist policies, maintained the colonial urban-based curative services. These governments were unwilling to go the full stretch to embrace socialized medicine. The attainment of universal free public health care was to be a gradual process dictated by the availability of financial resources. Private health care

---

10. Stoler and Cooper, *Tensions of Empire*, 34–5.

providers, trusts, missionaries, and individuals were allowed to be partners in the provision of health care services.

Meanwhile, the populist socialist states including Tanzania, Zambia, and Zimbabwe appended the basic and primary health care services model to the existing colonial model. The basic and primary health care services model operated on the premise that health care should reflect the economic, sociocultural, and political characteristics of a community. Preventive medicine was emphasized, and priority was given to those in greatest need. Thus, emphasis was placed on developing rural health care services by stressing local, rural-based development in place of colonial health care's trickle-down approach. The purpose was to bring health care services closer to the people by involving them in the development and expansion of health care facilities. It is therefore not surprising that the Afro-Marxist states including Mozambique, Angola, and Guinea-Bissau, all of which sought fundamental political, economic, social, and economic solutions to health care, embraced this patient-centered approach as well.

At the international level, the consensus on the broad parameters of primary health care for all helped mobilize financial resources, allowing for expansion in the treatment of infant and communicable diseases. The devoted involvement of international agencies such as the World Health Organization (WHO), the United Nations International Children's Emergency Fund (UNICEF), the United Nations Development Program (UNDP), and the International Parenthood Planning Federation (IPPF), among many others, provided the much-needed financial, human, and material support for a wide array of programs ranging from combating specific diseases such as measles, whooping cough, and smallpox to major preventative projects that would provide clean water and train personnel for the promotion of primary health care.

Yet the new focus in mainstream health care failed to define the place of traditional healers, as well as traditional health and healing practices, in the delivery of services. There were hardly any attempts to harness the resources of the traditional sector despite the fact that many respected members of the society, educated people, church leaders, and ordinary Christians visited them. Just as colonial laws had been used to subvert traditional knowledge, the policies of African governments stifled the knowledge of the pharmaceutical properties of items utilized in traditional healing systems. This transpired through their inability to revise the medical curriculum bequeathed by the colonial powers. Thus, the detailed knowledge of African herbalists on the pharmaceutical properties of items utilized in the traditional healing systems did not begin to engage the attention of Western-trained pharmacologists until much later in the post-colonial period.[11]

All in all, the health care projects and initiatives launched by most postcolonial African governments from the late 1950s to the mid-1980s were remarkably successful, if the number of hospitals and personnel are the measuring sticks of success. In Ghana, for example, the number of medical and nursing personnel in government service more than doubled between 1957 and 1963.[12] During this

11. Ali A. Mazrui, et. al., "Trends in Philosophy and Science in Africa," *in General History of Africa Volume 8*, ed. Ali A. Mazrui (Berkeley, CA: California University Press, 1999), 636–7.

12. Patrick A. Twumasi, "Colonial Rule, International Agency and Health: The Experience of Ghana," in *The Political Economy of Health in Africa*, ed. Toyin Falola and Dennis Ityavyar (Athens, OH: Ohio University Press, 1992), 114–5.

Table 1 Changes in Life Expectancy and Infant Mortality Rates in Selected Countries, 1960 and 1982

Country	Life Expectancy at Birth		Infant Mortality (per 1000)	
	1960	1982	1960	1982
Algeria	47	57	165	111
Chad	34	44	210	161
Ethiopia	37	47	172	122
Kenya	47	57	112	77
Nigeria	39	50	190	109
South Africa	53	63	92	55
Tanzania	42	53	144	98
Democratic Republic of Congo (Zaire)	40	51	150	106

Source: *Review of African Political Economy,* 36, (1986): 48.

same period, the number of physicians nearly tripled from 330 to 904, and the number of nurses increased from eight hundred to 2,366.[13] The number of trained midwives also increased from 616 to 1,235. The Ghanaian case is typical of African nations in the period between 1960 and 1980. The development of health services was also manifested in the increase in life expectancy and the decrease in infant mortality rates in postcolonial Africa, particularly between 1960 and 1982 (see Table 1).

The table shows that, in 1982, life expectancy at birth in the selected countries had increased by at least ten years since 1960. Similarly, infant mortality rates had declined sharply since 1960. These developments are manifestations of the concerted effort of the postcolonial governments to streamline the delivery of health care services to the citizenry. In addition, increased access to education, clean water, and state subsidies helped African governments make marked gains during the first three decades of independence, and thus to recast the image that was associated with the colonial state in the provision of health care. The critical factor in all this was the vibrant state of African economies, particularly during the 1960s and 1970s. Thus, when an economic downturn began to plague Africa in the late 1980s, the gains of the previous decades began to unravel. The situation was exacerbated by the onset of the AIDS pandemic.

Health Care Services and Well-Being in the Time of AIDS

In the early 1980s, the industrialized countries began to argue the benefits of free enterprise as the only mechanism that would help African countries free

---

13. Ibid., 114–5.

themselves from their debt burden.[14] African countries were advised to restructure their economies and to embrace and institutionalize the magic of the marketplace in the form of structural adjustment programs as invaluable means of curing their economies from the persistent ailment of underdevelopment.[15] As a result, debate began to revolve around fiscal discipline, particularly the role of market forces in determining the direction of the economy.

The structural adjustment programs were introduced without investigating the historical experience of African countries or the domestic constraints and challenges in the key social sectors of education and health care for the vulnerable sections of the population. African governments were advised to remove subsidies from health and educational services or lose external funding and aid. The programs were not homegrown; they were dictated by the Bretton Woods institutions. The result was severe and relentless suffering for the majority of the citizenry who had no safety net.[16]

Health care, therefore, became one of the areas heavily impacted by deep cuts in spending. As revenues dwindled because of the weakening economies of African states, governments were forced to adopt and implement the prescribed policies. Cost-sharing was introduced into the health care sector. Due to a lack of sufficient funds, the preventative, curative, and rehabilitative services that the governments had provided before the structural adjustments programs period were drastically reduced. Most dispensaries and hospitals lacked basic drugs. Meanwhile, the non-state health care providers, churches and private trusts, did not deliver services free of charge. Private hospitals were fairly expensive and outside the reach of most patients. Yet, the economic crunch hit the poor more than any other group, since these adverse developments occurred against the backdrop of retrenchment, a key demand of the IMF and World Bank as a condition for aid provision. Thus, even though the private hospitals continued to be enclaves of excellence in the midst of an ailing public health care system, only a small fraction of the population was capable of paying for treatment. The public health care system was, and continues to be, trapped in an all-embracing economic crunch and by the politics of external funding.

It is not surprising, therefore, that the gains of the first twenty-five years of independence are under siege, threatened mainly by poverty and AIDS. Table 2 shows that African countries experienced very low Gross National Product per capita growth for the decade ending in 1995. During the same period, the AIDS pandemic emerged as the one of the major challenges in the continent. The sub-Saharan countries have been worst hit. Table 2 shows that the adult HIV prevalence percentage in the fifteen to forty-nine age group is quite high, particularly in

---

14. John Toye, "Structural Adjustment: Context, Assumptions, Origin and Diversity," in *Structural Adjustment and Beyond in Sub-Saharan Africa,* ed. Rolph Van Der Hoeven and Fred Van Der Kraaij (Portsmouth, NH: Heinemann, 1994), 18–35. World Bank, *World Bank Report: Sub-Saharan Africa-From Crisis to Sustainable Growth, 1989* (Washington D.C: World Bank 1989).

15. Toyin Falola, "The Crisis of African Health Care Services," in Falola and Ityavyar, eds. *The Political Economy of Health in Africa,* 6.

16. Tiyambe Zeleza, "The Global Dimensions of Africa's Crisis: Debts, Structural Adjustment, and Workers," *Transafrican Journal of History,* 18 (1989): 3–7. Also see Kighoma Malima, "Structural Adjustment: The African Experience," in Van Der Hoeven and Van Der Kraaij, ed. *Structural Adjustment and Beyond,* 9–15.

Table 2 Selected Countries by Stage of the Epidemic, Adult Prevalence, Number of People Infected and Selected Economic Variables

Country	1997 Adult HIV Prevalence (% Population, 15–49)	1997 Number of People Currently Infected	Population Mid-1995 (Millions)	GNP Per Capita 1995 (Dollars)	Economic Growth: Average GNP PerCapita Growth (% 1985–95)
Nascent Epidemic					
Algeria	0.07	—	28.0	1,600	-2.4
Madagascar	0.12	8,600	13.7	230	-2.2
Mauritania	0.52	6,100	2.3	460	0.5
Mauritius	0.08	—	1.1	3,380	5.4
Morocco	0.03	—	26.0	1,110	0.9
Concentrated Epidemic					
Angola	2.12	110,000	10.8	410	-6.1
Cameroon	4.89	320,000	13.3	650	-6.6
Ethiopia	9.31	2,600,000	56.4	100	-0.3
Nigeria	4.12	2,300,000	111.3	260	1.2
Senegal	1.77	75,000	8.5	600	—
Generalized Epidemic					
Botswana	25.10	190,000	1.5	3,020	6.1
Burkina Faso	7.17	370,000	10.4	230	-0.2
Democratic Republic ofCongo	7.78	100,000	2.6	680	-3.2
Kenya	11.64	1,600,000	26.7	280	0.1
Uganda	9.51	930,000	19.2	240	2.7
South Africa	12.91	2,900,000	41.5	3,160	-1.1
Zimbabwe	25.84	1,500,000	11.0	540	-0.6

Key: ———— No statistics available.
Source: World Bank, *Policy Research Report, Confronting AIDS* (Oxford: Oxford University Press, 1999), 320–338.

Table 3 Infant and Child Mortality Rates in Selected African Countries

Country	Infant Mortality rate		Child mortality (Less than 5 Years of age)	
	Aids	No Aids	Aids	No Aids
Botswana	55.2	26.3	19.5	38.3
Burkina Faso	86.6	73.7	144.7	108.7
Burundi	79.6	66.3	128.6	90.9
Cameron	63.8	52.9	108.3	78.0
Cote d'Ivoire	74.8	61.8	120.9	84.2
Ethiopia	112.4	95.4	183.4	136.7
Kenya	53.9	32.9	105.2	45.4
Nigeria	57.4	41.4	112.7	68.2
South Africa	50.7	32.3	99.5	48.5
Tanzania	77.8	65.2	131.3	95.8
Uganda	68.6	58.5	120.6	92.2
Zimbabwe	53.7	24.0	115.6	31.8

Source: U.S. Government, *The Official Statistics* (Washington D.C.: Census Bureau, 1999).

the countries of eastern and southern Africa. Health and well-being have eluded the majority of the people. It is not surprising that infant and child mortality rates have begun to soar (see Table 3).

The sharp increase in infant and child mortality rates is due to many factors. The economic crunch has forced many African governments to reduce their expenditure on health services as well as other basic services, such as access to clean drinking water, immunization programs, and maternal and infant care.[17] HIV infection is also a critical factor because over fifty percent of new HIV infections occur among women, and mother-child transmission is an increasing problem.[18] Besides infant and child mortality rates, life expectancy is on the decline (see Tables 4 and 5). Table 4 shows that the AIDS pandemic is reducing the life span in some countries by as many as twenty years. Equally significant is the impact of AIDS on the economy as workers succumb to the pandemic and as it reduces the number of years of productive life. Table 5 shows the urban HIV prevalence in some selected African countries.

The important point, however, is that the combination of economic recession and the AIDS pandemic has severely strained health care in Africa. The reduced expenditure on health care services as a result of dwindling revenues has coincided with the resurgence of opportunistic infections, such as tuberculosis and pneumonia, which had been on the decline by the late 1980s. Immunization coverage of diseases such as polio, measles, tetanus, and tuberculosis has declined. Since the

---

17. Jealous Chirove, "Midwifery Goes Mainstream as hospitals Expand Options and Cut Costs," *Hospital Topics* 75, 3 (1997): 17.

18. UNAID, *HIV/AIDS Epidemiology in Sub-Saharan Africa* (Geneva, Switzerland: 1996),1–4.

Table 4 The Impact of Aids on African Life Expectancies

Country	Before the Pandemic	After the Onset of the Pandemic
Botswana	62	40
Burkina Faso	55	46
Burundi	55	46
Cameroon	59	51
Central African Republic	56	49
Democratic Republic of Congo	57	47
Congo	54	49
Ethiopia	51	41
Ivory Coast	57	46
Kenya	66	48
Lesotho	62	54
Malawi	51	37
Namibia	65	42
Nigeria	58	54
Rwanda	54	42
South Africa	65	56
Swaziland	58	39
Tanzania	55	46
Uganda	54	43
Zambia	56	37
Zimbabwe	65	39

Source: U.S. Government, *Official Statistics* (Washington, D.C.: Census Bureau, 1999).

health care system is still largely based on the availability of hospital-based facilities and services, a disproportionately large number of medical hospital beds are occupied by AIDS patients. Indeed, the strain on the health care system is evident in the drastic decrease in the number of physicians per person, which has been on the decline since 1993 in the countries that have been devastated by the AIDS pandemic.[19]

The quickened pace of the development of health services that characterized the two decades after independence has not been continued. The ambitious agenda of "Health for All" that African countries set to achieve by the year 2000 through comprehensive primary health care programs has given way to pessimism and doubt because of the adverse consequences of economic recession and the AIDS pandemic.

The foregoing discussion of the AIDS pandemic evokes a number of issues that have, by and large, been ignored in official discourses on health and healing. While many people succumb to AIDS, an equally large number still die from eas-

19. Carol Ezzell, "Caring for a Dying Continent," *Scientific American* 282, 5 (2000): 96–105, United Nations Development Program (UNDP), "SADC Regional Human Development Report," in *United Nations Development Program* (New York: Oxford University Press, 1998).

Table 5 Worker Attrition in Ghana, Kenya, Tanzania, Zambia, and Zimbabwe, Totals and by Sickness or Death, 1994

Country	Urban HIV Prevalence	Total in Sample		% Of Workers Leaving Firm	
		Firms	Workers	Due to all Causes	Due to Sickness or death
Zambia	24.7	194	14, 582	20.8	2.5
Zimbabwe	20.5	199	59, 210	9.1	1.2
Kenya	17.1	214	17, 126	7.7	0.9
Tanzania	16.1	197	14, 611	19.3	0.6
Ghana	2.2	188	9, 602	11.6	0.3
Total		992	115, 136	11.9	1.15

Source: World Bank, *Policy Research Report, Confronting AIDS* (Oxford: Oxford University Press, 1999), 320–338.

ily preventable and curable diseases such as malaria and cholera. As a result, many victims of AIDS succumb to death sooner than their counterparts in the developed world because of the inability of governments to provide the necessary resources for fighting opportunistic infections. Thus, the availability of services and drugs at local health facilities is a critical factor in the war against the pandemic, because many patients still see the hospital as a site where they can be provided with the necessary relief.

In the midst of this crisis, it is important that home treatment be positively reexamined. The home is the site where patients are first provided with medical treatment, whether traditional or biomedical. Traditional medicine is provided by family members or, in case of their failure to provide relief, a specialist. There are also itinerant "doctors" who readily administer a wide array of injections as part of home treatment and also sell an array of medicines, particularly antibiotics. The majority of such "doctors" are retirees from the private and public medical service, such as enrolled or community nurses and auxiliaries. However, it is not unusual to find those apprenticed through the "participant-observer" method administering injections without having undergone formal medical training. Maintaining good health entails more than the management of disease and illness by one method in one specific site—the hospital. While traditional healers are not precise in their diagnosis, they nonetheless play an important role in providing relief to properly diagnosed patients. This is one area in which their expertise can be harnessed to reinforce governmental as well as nongovernmental activities in coming to grips with not just AIDS, but other diseases as well. There is no doubt that herbalists provide effective cures for a host of opportunistic infections such as diarrhea, sore throats, and skin infections. Indeed, traditional medicines are becoming frequently used alternatives.

Maintaining good health also entails a role for family and community in providing home-based care programs, which can ease the congestion that currently characterizes hospitals. The extended family and community can provide immeasurable comfort and service to people living with HIV or AIDS, particularly provided with adequate resources and referral networks for medical, nursing, and counseling services. Home-based care should be seen as a vital ingredient in the extension of health services to patients.

Conclusion

The Westernization of health services was a function of the colonization of Africa, which influenced the development of health services during the colonial period. In their growth and expansion during the colonial period, health services were provided according to political and economic considerations. Their impact was unevenly distributed. The process of Westernizing health services also entailed relegating African traditional health and healing practices to the periphery of health care. The irony, however, was that the inadequacies and inequities of the mainstream health services undermined the attempts to supplant traditional medicine. In the 1940s and 1950s, the colonial regimes were forced to redress the imbalances and shortcomings that plagued the delivery of health services. The colonial state made attempts to improve preventive measures and to quicken the pace of delivery of health services to the citizenry.

After independence, the development of health services in Africa depended on complex interactions between colonial health care structures, the political ideologies of independent governments, and the availability of economic resources. The postcolonial governments infused life and compassion into a public health care system that had hitherto been defined primarily in economic terms. Indeed, within a relatively short period of time, many improvements resulted: increases in life spans, declines in mortality and crude death rates, more available hospital space for patients, and increases in the numbers of medical personnel.

Since the late 1980s, economic recession and the AIDS pandemic have adversely impacted the provision of health services, reversing the gains of the first few decades of independence. Life expectancy is falling back to preindependence period levels, preventable diseases are wreaking havoc, and the ailing health care system is underfinanced and ill-equipped to meet the health care needs of the citizenry. The role of the state in the health sector has been diminished by the insistence of the World Bank and the International Monetary Fund that African governments must reduce their expenditure on social welfare programs to induce the citizenry to assume some financial responsibility in matters of health and education. Since African economies have been underperforming in the 1990s due to internal as well as external constraints, however, governments have been forced to rely on scanty revenues and external aid that is hardly sufficient to meet the enormous economic and health challenges that exist.

Review Questions

1. Discuss the nature and consequences of the Westernization of health services.
2. Outline the major initiatives taken by postcolonial governments to redress the imbalances and inequities of the inherited colonial health care system.
3. Discuss the impact of the AIDS pandemic on the health care system.

4. Critically examine this statement: "Traditional therapies, home-based care programs, and family and community support are all crucial in this era of economic recession and AIDS."
5. Argue a case for or against collaboration between biomedical practitioners and African traditional healers.

Additional Reading

Cunningham, Andrew and Bridie Andrews, eds. *Western Medicine as Contested Knowledge*. Manchester and New York: Manchester University Press, 1997.

Falola, Toyin, and Dennis Ityavyar, eds. *The Political Economy of Health in Africa*. Athens, OH: Ohio University Press, 1992.

Feierman, Steven, and John M. Janzen, eds. *The Social Basis of Health and Healing in Africa*. Berkeley, CA: University of California Press, 1992.

Hunt, Nancy Rose. *A Colonial Lexicon: Of Birth Ritual, Medicalization and Mobility in the Congo*. Durham, NC: Duke University Press, 1999.

Janzen, John M. "The Comparative Study of Medical System as Changing Social Systems." *Social Science and Medicine* 12 (1978): 121–9.

Last, M., and G. Chavunduka, eds. *The Professionalization of African Medicine*. Manchester, England: Manchester University Press, 1986.

Turshen, Meredith. "The Impact of Colonialism on Health and Health Services in Tanzania." *International Journal of Health Services* 7, 1 (1977): 7–35.

Vaughn, Megan. *Curing Their Ills: Colonial Power and African Illness*. Stanford, CA: Stanford University Press, 1991.

Wallman, Sandra. *Kampala Women Getting By: Wellbeing in the Time of AIDS*. Athens, OH: Ohio University Press, 1996.

World Bank. *Confronting Aids: Public Priorities in a Global Epidemic*. Oxford: Oxford University Press, 1999.

World Health Organization. *The Promotion and Development of Traditional Medicine*. Geneva: Technical Report Series No. 622, 1978.

Chapter 14

African Environments

Christian Jennings

In this chapter, I examine the complex debates concerning African environments during the late colonial era, introducing several key issues that occupied African communities, environmentalists, and policy planners during the 1940s and 1950s. First, I provide a brief introduction to African environmental history, including some fundamental ecological terms and concepts. Then I turn to the late colonial era, tracing the rise of a particular idea in colonial environmental policy, which I call <u>development as conservation</u>*. This ideology grew out of the worldwide depression and soil erosion scare of the 1930s, leading colonial administrations to rely upon scientific expertise as a solution for perceived environmental crises. The resulting colonial policies, geared towards modernization and development, often lacked a thorough grounding in local ecological knowledge, but they nonetheless imposed heavy-handed measures on African farming communities. Finally, I offer a detailed examination of one particular environmental problem, that of the apparent conflict between* <u>Maasai pastoralists</u> *and wildlife conservation in East Africa. A closer historical inquiry reveals that the presumed conflict has very shallow roots indeed, and that pastoralists in East Africa have coexisted with wildlife for thousands of years. The perceived conflict which developed during the 1940s and 1950s, then, must be considered in a broad social and political context.*

* * *

The Environment in African History

Environmental history combines the techniques of two academic disciplines, history and ecology (or biology in a broader sense), using the data of "hard" science to interpret the past as it relates to humans' interactions with the diverse landscapes they inhabit. Environmental historians try to "read" landscapes; that is, they try to collect information about humans and their environments at given points in time and then detect the historical dynamics affecting these ecological relationships. During much of the twentieth century, the debate on African environmental history alternated between two extremes. On one side were scholars who conceived of a primitive precolonial Africa, where humans lived in a constant state of war against nature until they were introduced to modern agriculture and industry through the imposition of Western science and technology. Others argued that precolonial Africans lived in harmony with their surroundings and

Figure 14.1. Gurara Falls, Nigeria.

that colonialism robbed them of their natural wealth and abundant resources. But most scholars now agree that both of these views are simplistic, because they neglect the fact that humans have always lived in constantly changing relationships with their environments. Learning how to "read" landscapes properly, then, requires both an understanding of ecological relationships and an ability to interpret them within a dynamic historical context.

Ecology is the study of relationships between organisms and their surroundings, or environments. Ecologists previously regarded "good" environments as having some sort of internal balance or stability, but these days it is widely accepted that all environments are constantly changing, and not necessarily in one particular direction or toward any culminating "climax" state. A crucial component of current ecological thinking is biodiversity, meaning the number and variety of species and habitats in an environment.

Biodiversity involves both the total number of species in an area and their complex interactions; like the environment itself, biodiversity is constantly changing. Biodiversity is an elusive idea, impossible to measure with any sort of definitive standard, but ecologists generally agree that greater biodiversity is an important indicator of a healthy environment.

Human beings are an integral part of this biodiversity. We now know that humans have dramatically modified their environments for thousands of years, in ways that both positively and negatively affect biodiversity. Human activity makes a significant impact on soil composition and vegetation patterns, as well as the distribution and diversity of animal populations. Humans modify their environments through subsistence practices such as hunting, gathering, fishing, herding, and farming; through increases in population size and density; and through technological development, such as the introduction of iron tools. Many landscapes once considered "natural" are actually the result of human modification: the great African savannas, for instance, would simply be overgrown woodlands without the continual grazing of cattle and the occasional brushfires set by human inhabitants to maintain the rolling grasslands.

Environmental history in Africa involves changes within different time frames, from very long-term climate variation to very short-term human decisions, such as those made by individual farmers or herders. Over very long time spans, Africa, like other continents, has been subject to slow fluctuations in the earth's climate, which have produced major changes in African landscapes. For example, more than four thousand years ago, the Sahara was a rolling grassland which supported substantial populations of humans, cattle, and wildlife; the vast Sahara desert we see today is largely a product of climate change which unfolded over millennia, slowly but significantly altering the human history of the area. In contrast to such long-term changes, there are important short-term climate variations that can be detected by and adapted to by humans. Most of the African continent, for example, is characterized by a "bimodal" seasonal pattern: the year is divided into wet and dry seasons rather than the four seasons of the earth's temperate zones. This bimodal pattern means that much of Africa is particularly susceptible to drought, forcing humans, as well as plants and animals, to adapt.

African communities have adapted to these dry conditions in creative and diverse ways. Agriculturalists rotate their crops in a careful pattern to conserve water and soil, and pastoralists maintain a high level of mobility in order to make use of a wide zone of watering points and grasslands. Such human adaptations are usually the result of individual decisions in response to immediate concerns. Over the long term, a series of such decisions often develops into a noticeable historical trend, a process that can be thought of as "incremental adaptation." Incremental adaptation, or the accumulation of individual decisions in the context of long-term or widespread environmental patterns of which humans may be only partially aware, is a primary way in which humans modify their landscapes and affect biodiversity. In fact, evidence of incremental adaptation can be seen as a fundamental component of environmental history, providing many of the small pieces of information that historians put together to tell a larger story.[1]

In considering the background to twentieth-century environmental history, it is essential to remember that Africa was not an isolated continent before the era of European colonialism, but, rather, had been interacting with the broader world for an extraordinarily long time. This interaction involved not only the exchange of trade items and intellectual ideas, but also an ecological exchange of plant and animal species dating back at least thirty million years. Africans incorporated many species from elsewhere and made them their own. Domesticated cattle were adapted to local African environments perhaps seven thousand years ago, and not long after that wheat and barley were worked into African agriculture. Perhaps two thousand years ago, Africans borrowed bananas from southeast Asia and made them a staple of many African diets. More recently, important crops such as manioc (cassava) and maize (corn) were brought to Africa across the Atlantic Ocean. African peoples used all of these ecological exchanges to modify their landscapes and the biodiversity of their environments.[2]

---

1. William Doolittle, "Agricultural Change as an Incremental Process," *Annals of the Association of American Geographers* 74 (1984): 124–37.
2. James C. McCann, *Green Land, Brown Land, Black Land: An Environmental History of Africa, 1800–1990* (Portsmouth, NH: Heinemann, 1999), 12–5.

Africans also interacted with their environment through the different ways in which they organized their social and economic lives. Precolonial Africa consisted of a vast network of communities in diverse environmental settings, linked together by markets, urban centers, and far-flung trading routes. In addition, communities were often linked by ties of "reciprocal obligation," through kinship or marriage alliances. All of these economic, political, and social connections provided ways by which Africans could cope with environmental adversity and shape the landscapes they inhabited. During times of severe ecological stress, such as famines or outbreaks of disease, these complex networks of human interaction were often disrupted and restructured so that environmental history was closely intertwined with the history of African political and social institutions. Historians have even suggested that the development of many of Africa's powerful empires, such as Mali, Aksum, and Great Zimbabwe, was deeply affected by the influence of long-term climate changes. At the same time, these societies played a large part in modifying, sometimes dramatically, the environment of precolonial Africa. Pastoralists in East Africa, for example, practiced sophisticated range management techniques, helping to maintain the broad savannas which support both their cattle and a spectacular diversity of wildlife.[3]

During the colonial era, Africans throughout the continent continued to interact with and modify their environments as they had before. Yet they were now acting within the overarching political context of colonial administration, and this new center of authority began to dictate the shape and dynamics of African landscapes in new and often radical ways. European imperialists came to Africa with their own ideas of what Africa should look like, and when reality didn't meet their expectations, measures were often enacted to reshape Africa into the romantic image of the continent held by Europeans. At the same time, colonialism had a driving motive, economic profit, and environmental policy had to be crafted to best suit maximum production. As a result of the new structure of power created by colonial occupation, Europeans were able to take over the role of modifying African landscapes, but without the benefit of the detailed environmental knowledge and experience Africans had gained during previous centuries. The results of such policies, often based on superficial knowledge, continue to affect Africa's environments to the present day. In the following section, I will examine several of the environmental issues that emerged during the late colonial era in Africa, paying special attention to the links they share with the events and landscapes of the African past.

Development and Conservation in Late Colonial Africa

During the 1930s, environmental policy became a matter of international concern. The combined effects of the worldwide economic depression and the U.S. "Dust Bowl" crisis, which spawned a voluminous literature on soil erosion,

---

3. David Anderson and Richard Grove, "Introduction: The Scramble for Eden," in *Conservation in Africa: People, Policies and Practice*, ed. David Anderson and Richard Grove (Cambridge: Cambridge University Press, 1987), 6–10; McCann, *Green Land*, 23–51.

led many government officials to worry that the land under their supervision was being overworked. In African colonies, it became fashionable for officials to "see" soil erosion at work everywhere they looked, and popular colonial writers such as Elspeth Huxley trumpeted soil erosion as the foremost problem facing Africa. Europeans were quick to scapegoat African farming practices as the main culprit in soil erosion, especially on the crowded reserves to which many Africans had been confined, despite the fact that most colonial administrators and settlers had little expertise in farming themselves. At the Kenya Land Commission hearings in the mid-1930s, one witness charged that Africans had "never established a symbiotic relationship with the land. They are, in the strict scientific sense, parasites on the land, all of them."[4] The appeal to scientific reasoning was no accident. The soil erosion scare brought to prominence a new class of conservation experts, most of whom agreed that the proper way to curb the effects of soil erosion was to modernize farming through the application of scientific methods. By the end of the 1930s, colonial officials could accurately be said to have adopted an ideology of _development as conservation_ in their efforts to craft environmental policy.[5]

The colonial ideology of development as conservation rested on two assumptions about the proper way to develop African landscapes, inherited in part from earlier colonial administrations and strongly influenced by ecological problems and responses in the United States and Europe. First, administrators generally took for granted that Africa's landscapes were rapidly deteriorating in terms of soil quality, forest cover, and wildlife populations and that Africans themselves were incapable of managing their own resources. Secondly, they believed as a matter of faith that the proper response to these conditions was conservation through scientific management and technological progress, using coercive measures when necessary. Before World War II, however, most colonial administrations lacked the resources and the manpower to implement such technically complicated policies in rural areas. This would change after the war. Colonial administrations found that former soldiers could easily be incorporated into their bureaucracies, whether as forest rangers, policemen, or clerks. Naturally, the Forestry Services and Parks Departments, staffed with veterans of the war, were modeled along military lines. Further, the new, highly regimented system of agricultural production and distribution, which had been forged to support the war effort, now provided colonial administrations with an effective means of supervision and control over rural farming communities. At the same time, scientists began to take a more prominent role in the formation of colonial policy.[6]

Administrators looked to science as a guide in their difficult task of modernizing the economies and agricultural systems of the colonies, and conservation-minded scientists, who had come to public prominence during the soil erosion scare of the 1930s, seemed to possess an attractive quality of confidence and moral

---

4. A.T. Grove, "The African Environment, Understood and Misunderstood," in _The British Intellectual Engagement with Africa in the Twentieth Century_, ed. Douglas Rimmer and Anthony Kirk-Greene (Royal African Society, 2000), 182.

5. A.T. Grove, "African Environment," 181; David Anderson, "Depression, Dust Bowl, Demography, and Drought: The Colonial State and Soil Conservation in East Africa during the 1930s," _African Affairs_ 83 (1984), 321–43.

6. James Fairhead and Melissa Leach, "Dessication and Domination: Science and Struggles over Environment and Development in Colonial Guinea," _Journal of African History_ 41 (2000), 44–5.

authority. In the years following World War II, scientific issues continued to become a matter of international, or even global, concern, and Africa was no different. In 1948, scientists met in Goma, Zaire for the first inter-African conference on soil conservation, and in 1951 a conference in Abidjan drew scientists from across Africa to discuss forest policy. In an administrative context, the new prominence of science in public affairs led to a tentative melding of development policy with environmental concerns. The two concerns sometimes clashed, but they nonetheless shared a top-down approach that at best ignored the local African context and at worst dictated sweeping changes that often seriously undermined the capacity of African communities to make their own environmental decisions. The ideology of development as conservation (and vice versa) would underpin a whole range of sweeping colonial policies, and, as before, colonialists reserved for themselves the right to decide what African landscapes should look like. In general, colonial conservation and development policy tended to fall into two categories: large-scale agricultural schemes, which involved massive amounts of capital investment and labor mobilization, and smaller-scale projects aimed at the conservation of resources or the "improvement" of peasant farming in rural communities.[7]

The large-scale agricultural schemes, more often than not, were spectacular failures. They relied upon faith in the superiority of science, even when the scientific bases for the projects were superficial and lacked any detailed knowledge of local conditions. One such example was the East African Groundnut Scheme, which was implemented from 1947 to 1952. Responding to a global shortage of fats and oils, colonial administrators hoped to ease Britain's nearly total reliance on imports while at the same time demonstrating the benefits of science and market production to African farmers. The plan, crafted by Sir Frank Samuel, managing director of the United African Company, called for three million acres in Tanganyika and Kenya to be set aside for groundnut production and forecast a ten million pound profit for the British government in return for a twenty-four million pound investment. The scheme, in keeping with the contemporary trend, was organized as a military operation: many of the laborers were ex-soldiers, the project was supervised by a British general, and the plan even called for converted tanks to be used as tractors. However, the entire operation lacked any foundation in detailed environmental research or local planning. From the start, there were massive supply and transport problems, and the equipment that did arrive tended to be second-hand military surplus in less than perfect condition. The harbor and railways of Dar es Salaam became severely congested with the sudden infusion of equipment, while on the work sites, terrible labor conditions led to conflict between the workers and their managers. Not surprisingly, the tanks proved to be ineffective tractors. In the end, only a small fraction of the planned acreage was ever farmed, and most of the crops that were planted were lost to drought and insects. By the time the groundnut project was finally abandoned, the British government had lost more than thirty-five million pounds on the scheme.[8]

---

7. David Anderson, "Depression, Dust Bowl," 321, 339; Fairhead and Leach, "Dessication and Domination," 44–5; McCann, *Green Land*, 75.

8. Jan S. Hogendorn and K.M. Scott, "Very Large-Scale Agricultural Projects: The Lessons of the East African Groundnut Scheme," in *Imperialism, Colonialism and Hunger: East and Central Africa*, ed. Robert I. Rotberg (Lexington, Massachusetts: Lexington Books, 1983); Grove, "African Environment," 183–4.

Colonial officials also took measures to develop or "improve" peasant farming at the local scale, usually by imposing some form of conservation measure or European-derived farming technique. In the French colony of Guinea, administrators launched a wave of forest reservation policies in the decade after World War II, based upon an ideal of keeping twenty percent of Guinea's forest in reserve. Colonial forest guards patrolled a broad area, penalizing farmers who cleared reserved land, set unauthorized fires, or used the plant and animal resources of the forest without permission. Coercive measures such as these were often met with unenthusiastic responses from local communities, and on some occasions dissatisfaction with an administration's environmental policies boiled over into demonstrations of anger. In 1955, for example, four thousand farmers in central Tanganyika rioted against the British colonial administration's heavy-handed soil conservation measures, which included the imposition of labor-intensive terracing schemes that seriously disrupted traditional patterns of land use and labor. The anti-terracing riot in Tanganyika provides a striking example of how intrusive meddling in African agricultural and economic life by colonial administrations could provoke many Africans to rethink their situation through the lens of a new political consciousness. Similar protests against unpopular colonial conservation measures contributed to the movement for independence that swept across the continent after World War II. [9]

Local communities were not the only ones to question the colonial ideology of conversation through development; there were dissenting voices from within the ranks of the colonial administrations, as well. As early as 1938, Sir Frank Stockdale, the Agricultural Adviser to the British Colonial Office, warned that the wholesale adoption of "modernization" techniques, especially those involving heavy machinery, was inappropriate for African agriculture and might actually cause further damage to fragile African soils. Similarly, M.D.W. Jeffreys, a District Officer in Nigeria, complained in 1945 that colonial scorn for African farming practices was not supported by any scientific evidence; Jeffreys went on to cite several examples of African agricultural practices which demonstrated a thorough understanding of ecology and conservation. Regardless of dissenting official voices and unenthusiastic local responses to heavy-handed colonial policies, however, the idea of conservation through development became the primary influence in shaping ecological policy in late colonial Africa. This ideology would then be inherited, often uncritically, by the independent governments after 1960. In the next section, I will examine the historical roots of one particular conflict between colonial environmental policy and the interests of an African community, in this case the perceived conflict between wildlife and Maasai pastoralists of East Africa.[10]

9. Fairhead and Leach, "Dessication and Domination," 46–47; Pamela A. Maack, "We Don't Want Terraces! Protest and Identity under the Uluguru Land Usage Scheme," in *Custodians of the Land: Ecology and Culture in the History of Tanzania*, ed. Gregory Maddox, James Giblin, and Isaria N. Kimambo (London: James Currey, 1996).

10. Grove, "African Environment," 182–3.

Case Study: Pastoralists, Wildlife, and Conservation in East Africa

The annual migration of wildebeest into Maasai Mara Game Reserve in Kenya has long been a highlight of safaris for tourists visiting East Africa. Every July, the savanna becomes spotted as far as the eye can see with millions of wild animals, including the wildebeest and the zebra, the antelope, and the predators that follow them, all trekking northward from the Serengeti plains in Tanzania. This spectacle is one of the few truly staggering sights left in the world for those who want to see wildlife outside of a zoo. But astute observers will notice an unusual trend in the migration. From atop a boulder in the Maasai Mara, one can plainly see that the migrating animals make every effort to avoid traveling in the tall grass of the reserve itself. Instead, they skirt the edges of the park, moving in thin lines until they reach the well-grazed grasses of the private "group ranches" owned by Maasai pastoralists on the northern boundary of the reserve. Every morning, Land Rovers packed with tourists roll through the empty tall grasses of the reserve to take pictures of the animals grazing on the land outside the park. Many visitors seem unaware of this paradox: the reserve itself seems unattractive to the animals it ostensibly protects, while the Maasai grazing lands are preferred by the wild herbivores. How did this contradictory situation arise? The answers can be found in the intertwined histories of colonial policy toward wildlife and pastoralists and the gradual development of ecological knowledge of rangelands.

Pastoralists and wildlife have lived together in East Africa for several thousand years. A diverse array of recent archaeological studies has demonstrated that domesticated livestock have been in East Africa since at least 4,000 BP (before the present); at the same time, all of the species of wild fauna that have been found in the studies, dating as far back as 2,600 BP, were still in existence at the time of European colonization in the late twentieth century. This evidence seems to indicate that East African pastoralists have been highly successful in conserving wildlife, including large mammals such as elephants, during the past four millennia. By contrast, Europe, Asia, and the Americas suffered mass extinctions of large mammals during the past forty thousand years, a trend that runs roughly parallel to the appearance of humans in each area. Eastern and southern Africa are the only areas on our planet that survived these "late Pleistocene extinction events," with most of their large mammal populations intact. Whether by accident or design, humans and wildlife have been coevolving in East Africa for quite some time.[11]

The Maasai pastoralists are relatively recent arrivals in East Africa, but they, too, have lived alongside wildlife for hundreds of years. Their ancestors migrated south from the Nile Valley during the past millennium, arriving in the Rift Valley of East Africa perhaps a few centuries ago and displacing the earlier pastoralist populations who inhabited the area. Through warfare and assimilation, Maasai pastoralists expanded their influence during the nineteenth cen-

---

11. David Collett, "Pastoralists and Wildlife: Image and Reality in Kenya Maasailand," in Anderson and Grove, *Conservation in Africa*, 130–136; D. A. Burney, "Paleoecology of Humans and their Ancestors," in *East African Ecosystems and Their Conservation*, ed. T. R. McClanahan and T. P. Young (New York: Oxford University Press, 1996), 32–33.

Figure 14.2. Farming communities in northern Tanzania. Colonial officials doubted the ability of Africans to manage their own farms.

tury, effectively occupying a vast area stretching from the Laikipia plains in northern Kenya to the Maasai Steppe in central Tanzania. During the late nineteenth century, however, British colonialists quickly realized that the highland savannas of Maasailand included some of the best ranching and farmland in the world. The Maasai pastoralists of Kenya were pressured into treaties in 1904 and 1911 that dramatically reduced their land claims and eventually crowded them onto an arid, tightly controlled Maasai Reserve in southern Kenya. Mobility and access to dry season grazing reserves, two crucial features of pastoralist practice, were all but stripped from the Kenyan Maasai. On the Tanzanian side of Maasailand, German colonialists arrived in the wake of a devastating "Triple Disaster" of bovine pleuropneumonia, rinderpest, and smallpox, which temporarily forced many Maasai to abandon pastoralism. German visitors at the turn of the twentieth century mistakenly saw this depopulated landscape as a kind of primordial Eden. A German geographer described the Serengeti as

**Figure 14.3. The Serengeti Plains. In the background,
the escarpment of the Great Rift Valley.**

"grass, grass, grass, grass, and grass. One looks around and sees only grass and sky."[12]

The European perception of East Africa as a utopian wilderness full of exotic animals developed into a cultural phenomenon between the World Wars. During this "Golden Age" of hunting safaris, writers such as Isak Dinesen and Ernest Hemingway popularized the image of the hunting sportsman, and high-profile travelers such as Theodore Roosevelt helped to make the hunting safari an elite status marker. Yet the safari craze soon took a noticeable toll on East Africa's wildlife; in 1928, Dinesen's companion, Denys Finch Hatton, was one of the first well-known hunters to speak out publicly against the sheer volume of the killing. Early advocates of the establishment of a park system in East Africa were primarily concerned with protecting wildlife, not from African pastoralists such as the Maasai, but from European hunters and plantation owners. Tellingly, the first designated game reserve in Kenya was drawn to have nearly the same boundaries as the newly created "Masai Reserve." In 1930, the Society for the Preservation of the Fauna of the Empire sent R.W.G. Hingston to evaluate the state of wildlife in East Africa; his report called for the separation of humans and wildlife in a national park system but explicitly noted that this separation should not apply to the Maasai, who posed no threat to wildlife. When the Serengeti Plains and Ngorongoro Crater were designated as the first national park in East Africa in 1940, the resident Maasai pastoralists were allowed to stay and move freely within the park. Likewise, on the Kenyan side of the border, when national parks were established in 1952, Maasai were permitted to graze their cattle as they wished.[13]

12. Quoted in Jonathan S. Adams and Thomas O. McShane, *The Myth of Wild Africa: Conservation without Illusions* (Berkeley: University of California Press, 1996), 37.

13. Raymond Bonner, *At the Hand of Man: Peril and Hope for Africa's Wildlife* (New York: Alfred A. Knopf, 1993), 43, 167–168, 170; Adams and McShane, *The Myth of Wild Africa*, 28–30; W. K. Lindsay, "Integrating Parks and Pastoralists: Some Lessons from Am-

Conservationists began to question this laissez-faire policy during the years following World War II, and soon a combination of "scientific" theory, popular conservationism, and political expediency began to marginalize the pastoralists living on the reserves. This new, negative attitude toward the Maasai had an influential theoretical grounding in the work of anthropologist Melville Herskovits, who had published an essay, "The Cattle Complex in East Africa," in 1926. Herskovits had argued that East African pastoralists were focused on an irrational accumulation of cattle as a form of wealth, without any cultural checks to impede the process. Conservationists adopted this idea, often uncritically and out of Herskovits' intended context, and used it to argue that Maasai overstocking and overgrazing posed a serious threat to the rangelands. During the early 1950s, conservationists began to notice that, during the dry season, Maasai cattle appeared to displace wild herbivores at key watering points in the parks, trampling the fragile grass as well. Despite a lack of systematic research into the problem, an informal consensus began to develop, now seeing Maasai pastoralists as a threat to wildlife.[14]

The colonial governments of Tanganyika and Kenya were somewhat more skeptical about the perceived effects of Maasai pastoralism on the wildlife of the reserves, but the considerable political pressure brought to bear by well-known conservationists and their allies simply outmatched any resistance that the Maasai could muster. For example, in 1954 the governor of Tanganyika publicly promised Maasai pastoralists living in the western plains of the Serengeti that their land rights would be firmly upheld. Yet, even as he spoke, respected scholars were sounding the alarm, warning that Maasai cattle competed with wildlife for water and grass and that the Serengeti environment was too fragile to withstand the pressure. Famed researcher Louis Leakey wrote several papers and memoranda declaring that the Maasai had no legal right to be in the Serengeti. After all, Leakey reasoned, the Serengeti was a British colonial property, and the rulers could do with it as they wished; preferably, they could allow Leakey's archaeological digs to continue without the annoying presence of local Maasai. Sure enough, in 1958, twelve Maasai elders were pressured into signing an "Agreement by the Maasai to Vacate the Western Serengeti." In exchange, the Maasai were to be allowed to remain in the Ngorongoro Conservation Area to the east of the Serengeti, but this promise, too, would soon be broken.[15]

The conservationist movement in East Africa gained an immense boost with two influential publications: Bernhard Grzimek's *Serengeti Shall Not Die* in 1959 and Julian Huxley's UNESCO report in 1961. Grzimek, the president of the Frankfurt Zoological Society, was the preeminent international advocate for the preservation of wildlife. *Serengeti Shall Not Die*, which chronicles the conservation efforts of Grzimek and his son Michael, reads much like an adventure novel as the two men hop across the savanna in their propeller airplane. Like many Europeans in East Africa at the time, Grzimek did not feel that Africans were ready

---

boseli," in Anderson and Grove, *Conservation in Africa*, 152; Collett, "Pastoralists and Wildlife," 140–142.

14. Melville Herskovits, "The Cattle Complex in East Africa," *American Anthropologist* 28 (1926): 230–272, 361–388, 494–528, 633–664; Lindsey, "Integrating Parks and Pastoralists," 154.

15. Bonner, *At the Hand of Man*, 170–174; 177–178.

**Figure 14.4.   An elephant lunches in Ngorongoro Crater, where
Maasai pastoralists often clash with conservationists.**

for independence from colonial rule, especially when it came to the issue of managing their wildlife. For the Maasai in particular, Grzimek felt little admiration, declaring that these pastoralists had no reason to be in the Serengeti, which he felt could not support wild and domesticated grazing animals at the same time. The best Grzimek could say about the Maasai was that they were the lesser of the indigenous evils, since they evidently did not poach animals as other communities did. Following the publication of Grzimek's book, UNESCO chief Julian Huxley spent three months touring Africa in 1960, and his subsequent report, along with a series of articles in the *London Observer*, proclaimed in urgent terms the "grave" threat posed to wildlife by the "rapidly increasing" herds of the Maasai. Both Grzimek and Huxley neglected to provide detailed evidence to support their claims, but, of course, the growing sentiment toward separating wildlife from pastoralists had been fueled by partisanship rather than scholarship.[16]

---

16. Bernhard and Michael Grzimek, *Serengeti Shall Not Die* (New York: Ballantine, 1973), 191–192, 200; Bonner, *At the Hand of Man*, 60–61.

Researchers eventually did advance a "scientific" explanation to support the conservationists' assertion that Maasai pastoralism was environmentally unsound. Ecologist Lee Talbot carried out five years of research in Maasailand between 1956 and 1967 and came to the conclusion that Herskovits had indeed been correct in postulating a cultural bias among pastoralists leading to constantly increasing herds of cattle. Talbot felt that this emphasis on accumulation was built into the structure of Maasai society, and was in fact necessary for the reproduction of their communities, but that it resulted in an endless cycle of migration and land degradation by the pastoralists, who never achieved a "balance" with their environment. According to Talbot, this pattern had been relatively harmless during precolonial times, but the advent of Western science and policy in East Africa had removed the natural constraints previously imposed by the harsh environment of Maasailand. With their new access to European ranching methods, tsetse fly clearance, veterinary services, and water projects, the Maasai had been able to increase their herds far beyond the "carrying capacity" of their rangelands. Talbot recommended that wildlife tourism replace nomadic grazing in Maasailand, based upon the assumption that wildlife made "more productive use" of the rangelands and were a more stable economic resource.[17]

Leslie Brown, who had been a prominent agricultural administrator in Kenya before its independence, offered a similar point of view in an essay published in 1971. Brown saw the conservation of wildlife as essentially an issue of countering habitat destruction caused by African mismanagement. He felt that pastoralists were especially blameworthy and that their "biological needs" and "dietetic habits" damaged more acreage per person than their agricultural neighbors. Like Talbot, Brown was convinced that the Maasai and their herds had far exceeded the "carrying capacity" of their environment. Brown proposed that the Maasai be converted into agriculturalists, or at least be encouraged to give up their "ecologically unwise" dependence upon milk rather than meat. Further, he demanded that conservationists who insisted upon allowing a few "picturesque" Maasai to remain within the parks must still be prepared to advocate the removal of most of the cattle and humans. Brown did not explain where these "excess humans" should go or how they should survive once they got there.[18]

By the end of the colonial era in East Africa, then, a basic set of ideas had been formed about pastoralists and their interactions with the environment. Ecologists James Ellis and David Swift have referred to this set of ideas as the "dominant paradigm" and identified three of its main assumptions: first, that East African rangelands and their pastoralist human populations were potentially "stable" or "equilibrial" systems; second, that these systems had been destabilized through the improper practices of pastoralists; and third, that reforms needed to be imposed upon pastoralists to restore "equilibrium" and boost productivity. These concepts are still found in some ecology textbooks today. Recently, Katherine Homewood and W. A. Rodgers have noted that this "dominant paradigm" closely resembles a "tragedy of the commons," in which ecologists see

17. Lee M. Talbot, "Ecological Consequences of Rangeland Development in Masailand, East Africa," in *The Careless Technology: Ecology and International Development*, ed. M. Taghi Farvar and John P. Milton (Garden City, NY: Natural History Press, 1972), 703, 709.
18. Leslie H. Brown, "The Biology of Pastoral Man as a Factor in Conservation," *Biological Conservation* 3 (January 1971): 93, 97–99.

Figure 14.5. Maasai community, Kenya.

overgrazing as the result of misguided "traditional" patterns of land use by pastoralists. Homewood and Rodgers also suggested that social scientists, such as anthropologists and sociologists, were better prepared than ecologists and biologists to take into account the external political and economic pressures that often influence pastoralist decision-making in modern contexts. For example, the ever-shrinking land base available to pastoralists in East Africa and the strict limits on movement between critical water and pasture sources are not elements of "traditional" Maasai pastoralism, although they definitely contributed to the likelihood that Maasai communities would inhabit areas which could not support them. Unfortunately, social scientists were much less likely than ecologists to catch the attention of conservationist organizations.[19]

In 1961, Edward ole Mbarnoti offered this assessment of the impact of conservationists on his Maasai community:

> It is we Maasai who have preserved...our land which we were sharing with the wild animals long before the arrival of those who use game only as a means of getting money. So please do not tell us that we must be pushed out of our land for the financial convenience of commercial hunters and hotel keepers. And do not tell us that we must live only by the rules and regulations of zoologists....If Uhuru [freedom] means any-

---

19. James E. Ellis and David M. Swift, "Stability of African Pastoral Ecosystems: Alternate Paradigms and Implications for Development," *Journal of Range Management* 41 (November 1988): 451; Katherine Homewood and W. A. Rodgers, "Pastoralism, Conservation and the Overgrazing Controversy," in Anderson and Grove, *Conservation in Africa*, 111.

Figure 14.6. Roan antelopes in West Africa.

thing at all, it means that we are going to be treated like human beings and not like animals.[20]

From the preceding discussion, it seems clear that, at the very outset of independence in East Africa, ecology, democracy, and policy failed to find the common ground necessary to give Maasai pastoralists and East Africa's magnificent wildlife the respect they both deserved.

Conclusion

To summarize our current discussion, we have seen that environmental issues in late colonial Africa involved a complex array of ecological and political relationships which were further complicated by the sometimes jarring contrasts between "modern" attitudes toward conservation and development and "traditional" adaptations by Africans to their dynamic landscapes. Of course, the distinction between "modern" and "traditional" is usually useless in practice: most African communities did adopt certain aspects of modernization and development which they saw as beneficial, while, at the same time, environmentalists and policy planners often insisted on clinging to outdated and incorrect assumptions about African ecology. As we saw in the case study on Maasai pastoralists and wildlife in East Africa, sifting through the maze of contradictory evidence and opinions surrounding any environmental issue in Africa can be a daunting task in itself, not to speak of finding a common ground on which to discuss solutions. To

---

20. Jacobs, "Pastoral Maasai," 296.

come to any sort of deeper understanding of African environmental issues, however, it is precisely this sort of careful, detailed analysis which is required. Environmental historians can play an important role in placing these socially relevant environmental issues into a helpful, broader context.

Review Questions

1. What do we mean when we say that colonial officials adopted an ideology of *development as conservation* during the late colonial era? How did this ideology affect African communities and landscapes?
2. How did colonial officials in East Africa come to see Maasai pastoralists as a threat to wildlife?

Suggested Reading

Adams, Jonathan S., and Thomas O. McShane. *The Myth of Wild Africa: Conservation without Illusions*. Berkeley: University of California Press, 1996.

Anderson, David and Richard Grove, eds. *Conservation in Africa: People, Policies and Practice*. Cambridge: Cambridge University Press, 1987.

Bonner, Raymond. *At the Hand of Man: Peril and Hope for Africa's Wildlife*. New York: Alfred A. Knopf, 1993.

Maddox, Gregory, James Giblin, and Isaria N. Kimambo, eds. *Custodians of the Land: Ecology and Culture in the History of Tanzania*. London: James Currey, 1996.

McCann, James C. *Green Land, Brown Land, Black Land: An Environmental History of Africa, 1800–1990*. Portsmouth, NH: Heinemann, 1999.

Chapter 15

African Art

dele jegede

African art encompasses a diversity of objects that range from architecture to sculpture, from body arts to mural paintings, all of which are expressed in a wide array of media and performances. Although we refer to these objects generally as African art, their purposes, use, and histories are as rich and varied as the styles in which they are made. African art is an expression of the soul and spirit of the cultures that produce it. It is the physical expression of a people's worldview, occupying important junctures and playing significant roles throughout life. This chapter is concerned with an examination of some of these roles. Its primary focus will be on traditional African art.

* * *

I refer to the items discussed here as art. In reality, they are not "art" in the Western sense of that word. Frequently, art in Africa is used as a means to an end, like commemorating mythical forebearers or ancestral heroes. It may be necessary to invoke deities in ceremonies for societal purgation or immolation. The goals of art may be gestural or symbolic: a dead member may be honored through the observance of time-honored rituals or, depending on the member's status in the society, the convocation of masquerades. In instances where the rule of law is to be maintained and sanctions imposed, art becomes emblematic of collective power, exercised by recognized authorities. Art objects are also used as group emblems around which members rally whenever the need arises. These emblems include masks and staffs carved according to socially accepted styles.

Are these truly works art? Is the *Kifwebe* mask of the Songye in the Federal Democratic Republic (FDR) of Congo, with its impressive visual hauteur and expressive, mean posture, to be appreciated purely for its formal and aesthetic qualities? Are these aesthetic considerations merely an adjunct to its main purpose, the maintenance of social equilibrium?

What about the *Pwo*, a pristine, gracious, and serene mask produced by the Chokwe, who live in the FDR Congo and in Angola? (Figure 15.1) In its seductive, feminine elegance and postmodern presence, this mask indeed represents the quintessential ideals of Chokwe beauty. Does knowing its functions detract from or enhance our appreciation of the work itself? The Golden Stool of Ghana is perhaps one of the most popular visual icons of African art. Revered as a sanctified and sacred object because of its spiritual significance, the Golden Stool symbolizes the collective spiritual and political power of the Asante of Ghana. Embellished with repoussé—metal sheets with designs that are hammered in from the back—

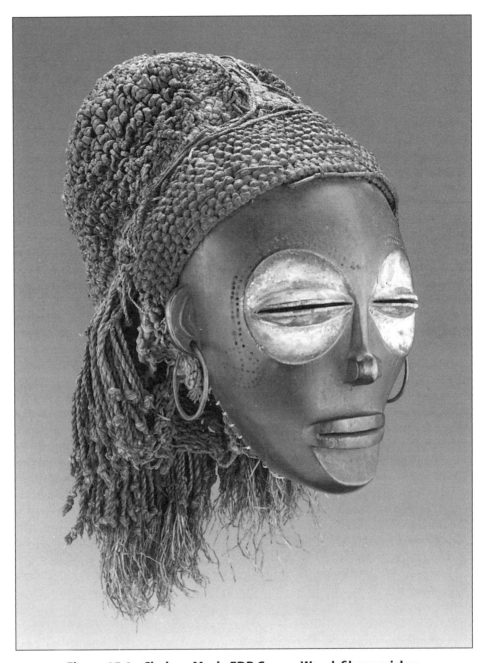

Figure 15.1. Chokwe Mask, FDR Congo. Wood, fibers, wicker.

and treated as much more than a simple, functional seat, the stool is blackened and retired to the shrine of the deceased leader.

Among the Igbo, the *ikenga* is testimony to a person's right hand: a symbol of hard work and success. Embodying the Igbos' quest for dominance in social, political, economic, and personal ventures, the *ikenga* symbolizes moral probity and physical and material success. It could be owned by an individual or by a community. An individual *ikenga* is consecrated and placed in a personal space where it is fed regularly with such items as kola nuts, palm oil, or the sacrificial blood of animals. Clearly, the *ikenga* is regarded first and foremost as a spiritual alter ego, not as art. Yet its form, even in its most primal, in which consists of a pair of ram horns, is intriguing. In all of these examples, it is possible for us to relate to the objects and respond to the magic and charm that they exude. We may confer on them the status of art: items to be savored for their aesthetic qualities and for the pleasure their forms communicate. However, our appreciation of these forms is enhanced when we learn of the social and cultural context in which they function.

If there is an African art museum in your neighborhood, the probability is high that it houses unfamiliar, even if striking objects like masks, sculptures, stools, textiles, and more. These items are often displayed in solitary confinement, within "sterilized" environments in which the spotlights directed at them make them look gorgeous but frozen. Some museums install protective beams that set off alarms once a visitor moves closer than is permitted. As a visitor, you are strictly forbidden to touch the objects; you may not even come close. Yet, the paradox is that, in their original cultures, these objects are meant to be used. Masks are worn and used in dances. Some are used to graze the ground and raise dust. Objects—as in the case of the Golden Stool and the *ikenga*, for example— are offered as sacrifices; they are fed with liquids and solids. This produces the patina and encrustations that are highly valued in traditional African works.

In African art museums, it is customary to see terse labels describing each item, listing not even the individual artist who made it, but the name of an entire group. This practice differs remarkably from the way Western art and artists are viewed. Euro-American art is valued for its individuality. The name of the artist is as important as the work itself. In Africa, art functions in a more interactive context. A mask, for example, is part of a panoply in which poetry melds into music and dance, while costumes complement sculptures during public performances.

Increasingly, African art museums in the United States and Europe are trying to provide their viewers with a sense of the cultural context in which the pieces they exhibit are used. Through creative displays, field photographs, videos, and interactive media, museums continue to make efforts to simulate the sense of performance that is associated with certain art works. Despite these strategies, African works of art in Euro-American museums remain no more than decapitated elements of expressive culture. Many who are privileged to view African art works in museums are touched by their visual presence, their aesthetic power, and their formal attributes. Yet there is nothing like seeing the works in their actual contexts. Masks are more than simple carvings, and masquerades embody much more than colorful costumes. In real time, masqueraders exude an impressive aura, particularly where music, dance, and poetry are invoked during performance.

Categories and Distinctions: Traditional and Contemporary

African art can be divided into two major categories: precolonial and post-colonial. Colonialism in Africa dates back to the mid-nineteenth century, when

European powers began a forceful occupation of Africa. By the second half of the twentieth century, African nations began to assert their independence. The 1960s marked a watershed in African political history; in that about two-thirds of African nations gained independence during this period. In the study of African art, the art produced before and during the colonial period is referred to as traditional art. Postcolonial art, or the art produced from the mid-twentieth century onward, is called contemporary art. Of course, this division is not as tidy as it may seem. As a result of the introduction of Western and Islamic cultures, Africa remains in a state of perpetual flux. It faces the challenge of knowing what to assimilate from other cultures. In the visual arts, this implies that there is a certain degree of overlap between traditional and contemporary arts. A myriad of objects made in wood, raffia, textiles, and some forms of architecture have been lost forever to termites, fire, humidity, humans, and other natural agents. As a result, it is very rare to find works in wood that are more than two centuries old. In its focus on traditional African art, this chapter is concerned with the body of work produced prior to, at the onset of, and during the colonial era.

Traditional art has a time-tested history: a style expectancy pattern with which patrons and artists alike comply. Three of the attributes of traditional art are style, use, and context. Although individual artists have their distinctive aesthetic peculiarities and the freedom to create, their work is expected to comply with the specific styles in which certain genres are rendered. Art works may be used in specified ways and within frameworks that are socially prescribed. Even where the art is used mainly to embellish and amplify, there are often symbolic gestures associated with such functions. There are situations in which the purpose of art transcends the prettiness of an object, where certain objects are created to project a hideous presence, to intimidate the observer or send chills down the spines of the uninitiated, and to deter those with malevolent dispositions toward society. In cases like these, the beauty of such objects lies in the extent to which they are successful at being repulsive. Since African art functions at various levels — for the living and the dead, physical and the metaphysical, secular and sacred, legislative and judicial, social and educational, symbolic and aesthetic — it is art for life's sake. While we may admire and appreciate its forms and expressive qualities, it has a primary function, which is often central to the social and religious values of the cultures that produce it.

This is quite different from contemporary art which reflects new trends, new materials, and new clients. Western education and a cash economy are two of the reasons for the creative shift that has occurred in the visual arts. The apprenticeship system is no longer prevalent: it has been replaced by a new educational system. In contemporary Africa, the emphasis on the visual arts is towards the exploration of new idioms and the determination to become a force in the international arena. Initiation rites are being replaced by college diplomas, while traditional medicine men have had to contend with hospitals that are staffed with trained medical personnel. Contemporary art is more vibrant, at least in terms of its scope and materials. The artist can express himself or herself in an assortment of modern media and styles — fiber glass, resin, synthetic paint, oil, photography and computer graphics among these. Whether they are self-taught or they are trained in art institutions that expose them to modern concepts and techniques, whether they learn art through brief workshops or through a modern apprenticeship system, contemporary African artists are like artists in other non-African cultures. They produce art that asserts its own independence: an art that is driven by the dynamics of contemporary society. Rather than cater to the needs of ancestors or function in initiations or other rites of passage, contemporary African art celebrates the independence of the artist, who is neither bound by group style nor by the dictates of priestly patrons. It meets the art-for-art's-sake doctrine.

History and Misconceptions

The history of traditional African art is as old and as rich as the African continent itself. It is a history that speaks of diversity of cultures and peoples, of languages and arts. It is also a history that was misunderstood and misinterpreted, initially at least, by European adventurers who often employed their own cultural yardsticks in trying to understand African art. Unfortunately, this initial arrogance has given room to a host of prejudicial attitudes, unwholesome assumptions, derogatory terms, and pejorative precepts. Based on the erroneous notion that Western societies were superior to those of the African continent and on conjectural, Euro-American mid-nineteenth century scholarship, the unhealthy notion that Africa was a dark, foreboding continent, a hostile jungle not fit for human subsistence, gained currency. Indigenous African religions were adjudged heathenish and their practitioners branded pagans, the warped assumption being that Christianity was the dominant and only acceptable form of religious expression. African art was considered primitive and uncouth, and its people were branded as savages.

It should be strongly asserted that African art is not primitive. Rather, it is one of the most profound and deeply intellectual arts of any civilization. The notion of African art as an embodiment of primitive civilization betrays ignorance, mischief, or prejudice. In contemporary society, vestiges of these stereotypical notions about Africa remain, thanks to mass media that appear fixated on the strange, the unfamiliar, and the exotic. Africa is a model for diversity. The multiplicity of cultures, languages, arts, and religions underline the necessity to develop a healthy respect for different perspectives, to avoid being judgmental, and to be receptive to others' views.

Africa, the world's second largest continent and birthplace of modern humans, has a population of about seven hundred million. In size alone, with over twelve million square miles, it is more than three times the size of the United States. The rain forest stretches from the westernmost coastal regions of Guinea to the lower central regions of Gabon and the Congo. It is bordered by other vegetation zones: the savanna woodlands, the savanna grasslands, and, of course, three major deserts, the Sahara, to the north and the Namib and Kalahari to the southwest. The relationship between geography and art makes the production of visual arts largely dependent on availability of materials. This explains, in part, why the profusion of masks and sculptures in wood, for which Africa is noted, comes from the western and central African regions—areas where there is a generous availability of timber. As Frank Willett has noted, when the abundance of media is coupled with elaborate socio-political institutions, the environment is just right for the qualitative production of art, often on a large scale.

The African continent has a prodigious variety of distinct languages, estimated at between eight hundred and one thousand. This situation appears to have spawned yet another stereotype: that the African continent is made up of "tribes," a term that has fallen into disuse. As employed in relation to Africa and, in particular, African art, tribe is considered derogatory and patronizing, more so since this nomenclature was imposed by early Europeans for whom Africa was nothing more than an agglomeration of simple-minded, childlike peoples. Others see this label as a continuation, at the intellectual level, of the same European hegemonic mind-set that led, in 1884 and 1885, to the partitioning of the continent into arbitrary colonies, an act that showed gross insensitivity to the cultural, linguistic, and ethnic affiliations of the African peoples.

Cross-Cultural Impacts

The arts of postcolonial Africa reflect the impact of Western cultures and two dominant external religious forces: Islam and Christianity. Beginning in the early seventh century, northern Africa came under the influence of Islam. Customarily, Africanist art historians exclude northern Africa from their area of interest, choosing to concentrate on sub-Saharan Africa, that is Africa south of the Sahara desert. One of the assumptions for this modern partitioning is that the association of northern Africa with Islamic religion prevents it from producing symbolic art. It is true that Islamic art is Arabesque—floral, decorative, ornamental, and largely non-representational. Its repertoire of intricately interlaced designs and curvilinear motifs is best appreciated in architectural and utilitarian decors. It is equally true, however, that this injunction against symbolic art applies mainly to Islamic religious art. As is apparent in the arts of numerous ethnic groups converted to Islam, living in regions from Mali to Nigeria in West Africa, the Islamic impact on the visual arts has not curtailed the creation of symbolic or abstract art. On the other hand, the missionaries who renewed their interest in penetrating Africa in the second half of the nineteenth century began by launching a series of vicious attacks on traditional African art which, because of its association with traditional systems of thought, was perceived as reprehensible and idolatory. A significant number of objects were burned by missionaries and local converts.

Just as it was affected by Islam and Christianity, African art also had a significant impact on Western art. In Paris at the turn of the twentieth century, European artists were fascinated by the quest for new creative horizons. Basking in the excitement and controversy that accompanied previous art movements—Realism, Impressionism, Post-Impressionism, and Fauvism among them—French artists strove to break new grounds. It was at this time that some artists, including Pablo Picasso, Georges Braque, Maurice Vlaminck, and Andre Derain, came under the influence of African art. This encounter led to radical stylistic changes in their work. An example is seen in Picasso's 1907 painting *Les Demoiselles d'Avignon*, in which the faces of the women are painted in a manner that recalls the styles of African masks. The resultant art movement, Cubism, was inspired not only by the abstracted, cuboidal features apparent in several African sculptures, but also by the African artist's conceptual approach, which did not aim at idealizing the human figure.

Masks and Masquerades

Numerous examples from various African cultures show that African art is an integral part of traditional societies. It is a required part of living, an indispensability rather than a habit which is peculiar to the elite class. I begin by looking at masking traditions in selected cultures. The use of masks and the convocation of masquerades by numerous ethnic groups in Africa underline the centrality of art to activities that range from the secular to the sacred, from law enforcement to entertainment.

Masquerades—regarded as reincarnated ancestors or heavenly beings—evoke total theater. There is considerable performer-audience interaction during masquerades. The beauty of masks can only be appreciated when they are used in the context of performance—when spectators, in droves, become an organic whole with the masquerades themselves, who are surrounded by acolytes, musicians, and supporters. For masquerades, the whole of the community becomes their stage, with crowds joining in or dropping out at every stage of the journey through the length and breadth of community streets. Masks are worn during initiation ceremonies, rites of passage, or obsequies. Some masquerades specialize in entertaining their audiences, while others are ferocious and, indeed, dangerous. In some societies, women are forbidden from seeing certain category of masks and masquerades.

People who have a limited understanding of Africa tend to associate the continent with masks. After all, these are perhaps some of the most common cultural symbols of the continent, thanks to the numerous flyers and relevant promotional materials advertising the continent to potential tourists. Besides, many specialty stores seem to have a special soft spot for masks, perhaps because they are seen as beautiful gift items. Added to this is the prominent display of masks in museums as well as in numerous glossy publications on Africa. The overall impression that has been created is that, upon arriving in Africa, the Western traveler cannot escape being drowned in a sea of masks and masquerades. The fact is that masquerades observe a cultural calendar, with appearances that are carefully planned and well coordinated. Even where they are summoned to make unplanned appearances, as during funeral ceremonies or in situations connected with the administration of justice, there are norms and rituals that must be observed.

Masks are made in a wide array of additive materials; bones, bells, buttons, mirrors, cowrie shells, feathers, animal parts, and other miscellaneous items are made into a composite and attached. Other materials may be removed, as with carved wood. Masquerades are fitted with costumes which are usually comprised of two parts: the top, which includes the mask, and the lower part, which is the costume proper. The costume may be made up of woven fiber, colorful appliqué, leaves, feathers, jute, raffia, rope, and similar materials, the main objective being that they are light and wearable and do not seriously impede mobility. Of course, there are instances in which there is no separation between the costume and the mask, just as there are cases where some of the basic categories are combined. Masks are not meant to be merely decorative. They are meant to be worn or, in rare cases such as with the Great Mask of the Dogon in Mali, set aside because of their distinct aura and power.

The Dogon have a plethora of masks whose spiritual forces (*nyama*), believed to be released at death, are harnessed in connection with the observation of various rites and ceremonies. Imperato has identified more than seventy-eight different types of masks, all of which are under the control of Awa, the society of masks. The Dogon believe that the spirit of the dead must be placated for the sustenance of social equilibrium. This is where the Awa exerts religious persuasion over the use of masks, which are owned by individual members. The Awa includes all circumcised males except those like blacksmiths and bards who, as members of a cast, belong in an endogamous group and live in separate quarters of their own within the village. The masks, which symbolize human, animal, and spiritual essences, are used as part of obsequies and also at Dama, which are special ceremonies commemorating the deaths of important personages. To watch any of these performances is to appreciate the totality of the arts, for what is at stake are not merely the sculptures, masks, or the headdreasses. There is the spectacle in which colors, dance, music, and the skills of individual performers are summoned. The Dama performances are rites that rehabilitate the soul of the deceased at the family altar, which is its final resting place. These performances also initiate the process of transforming the deceased to the hierarchy of ancestors. The Dama are performed every three years in honor of those who died in the intervening period, although the death of an important personage may warrant the convocation of a special Dama.

The ultimate masking performance among the Dogon is known as the Sigui, which occurs once every sixty years and marks the transition from one generation to the next. It is for this special occasion that the Great Mask, or Mother of Masks, is carved. The distinct feature of Great Masks is that, rather than being worn, they are kept with past Great Masks in a special place. Many Dogon masks are inspired by birds and animals—hornbills, antelopes, buffalo, hare, rhinoceros, monkeys, and hyenas, among others. Two of the most impressive masks are the *Sirige* and the *Kanaga*. A tall mask that is meant to depict a multi-story "house," the *Sirige* is carried by a dancer in full costume, who reenacts the Dogon creation myth. The *Kanaga*, which represents a bird, is a mask with a vertical projection and two horizontal arms that, together, evoke the effect of the Lorraine cross. The most numerous of all Dogon masks, the *Kanaga* is adorned with black, white, and red pigments that emphasize its energy, particularly when it is seen in motion.

Types of Masks

Masks can be divided into three basic types: face mask, cask or helmet mask, and headdress. The face mask comes in an assortment of sizes and may be carved in ways that allow the wearer to function maximally. Some face masks have a hollow interior into which the face fits snugly. Others have wooden bars or similar devices that the masquerader holds onto with his teeth. Rather than be attached to the face, some face masks are held by the wearer. Regardless of their shapes, face masks are a part of the larger costume, which completely covers the body, beautifully blends with the mask, and transforms the identity of the wearer. Some face masks have horizontal or vertical extensions. Perhaps the most notable example of a face mask with a vertical projection is found among the Bwa of Burkina Faso, whose remarkable plank masks, *Nwantantay*, are very tall and elegant. A peculiar stylistic characteristic of these masks is that the planks are divided into registers of geometric patterns—chevrons, checkers, lozenges, zigzags, and triangles, among others.

The iconology, or symbolic meanings, of these geometric designs are taught to Bwa youths during their initiation ceremonies. The top of the mask may terminate in a simple or complex crest, while the face is ovoid with a protruding beak issuing from the forehead. Often, concentric circles on the face serve as eyes, although the only hole on the face is from the mouth region. The range of colors that is used is limited: white, black, red, and umber. It is the way the colors are applied, as well as the repertoire of designs in which they are rendered, that gives Bwa masks their dominant visual distinction. The masks, which may appear as reincarnated ancestors, mythological heroes, or nature spirits, are used in a variety of contexts. They appear during the annual ceremonies for social renewal, a time when the society is cleansed of malevolent forces. They appear at funeral ceremonies to honor the dead, in rites of passage for young boys and girls, and in connection with agricultural rites and ceremonies. The traditional season for Bwa masks is at the beginning of the yearly rains, from early March to early May.

The Dan peoples in the neighboring countries of Liberia and Côte d'Ivoire produce a wide array of face masks, which are used in an equally diverse range of contexts. Some are used for enforcing laws, settling disputes, and promoting social interaction. The ruling body in every Dan community controls the use of the masks. When they are not engaged in dancing and entertaining people—or challenged to a race by daring men from the crowd who are convinced they can outrace the masquerade—they may be involved in teaching young initiates essential values cherished by the Dan. Masks have their origin in the Dan belief in reincarnation and in their ability to harness the spiritual power of *dü*, an invisible force that lives in all humans but is released after a person dies. *Dü* reveals itself in dream to a chosen member of the men's regulatory society, indicating the preferred visual form that it would like to assume. Once the mask is carved, it becomes empowered by *dü*, manifesting as *gle*, the most powerful of spiritual forces.

Most Dan masks fall into two broad *gle* categories: the peaceful, gentle *gle*, which is called *deangle*, and the fierce or warlike *gle*, *bugle*. In terms of visual representation, *deangle* or peaceful face masks have pronounced foreheads that terminate in pairs of slit eyes, with protruding lips that are sometimes parted to show teeth, although regional variations on this basic form have been noted. (Figure 15.2) During the critical transition phase when boys are secluded in the forest before they are initiated into men's society, it is a *deangle* mask that serves as the intermediary between the boys and the village, bearing messages and food from their parents. Contrasting with the gentle behavior of the *deangle* is the *bugle*, an aggressive and ferocious spirit with a complementary form that is equally assertive. *Bugle* masks originated with the idea that, in war, enemies had to be repelled and citizens had to be mobilized into action. The mask was conceived as a physical embodiment of these aggressive attributes. In peacetime, *bugle* masks direct their aggressive tendencies toward other entertaining, although no less fierce, roles. They are known to whip spectators and rip off their clothes with the sticks they carry. Should disputes arise amongst neighboring peoples or within a community, there are masks—*gle va*— with the responsibility for effecting armistice. In order to emphasize the enormity of its power and its superior status in its domain, *gle va* have highly abstracted and visually compelling features.

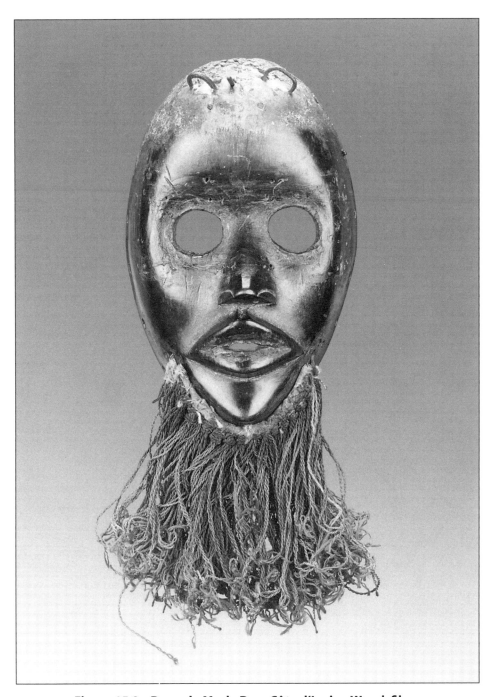

Figure 15.2. Deangle Mask. Dan, Côte d'Ivoire. Wood, fiber.

The cask or helmet mask, our second example, is worn over the head, completely covering the the face and neck areas. A costume, often of dyed or treated raffia, is attached to the mask through holes on its lower rim. A particularly exciting example of cask mask comes from the Mende in Sierra Leone, where the

Figure 15.3. Mende Helmet Mask, Sierra Leone. Wood.

Bundu, or Sande, society retains supreme control over a virile masking tradition. (Figure 15.3) It is exciting precisely because it is perhaps the only instance in Africa where women exercise such control over masks. Generally, wherever masks are employed, as among the Yoruba, whose *gelede* masking tradition is dedicated to the veneration of women, men are the principal decision makers and handlers. The situation among the Sande is different, however. Indeed, men risk considerable sanction who show any disrespect to women in the Sande society. As is the situation all over Africa, Sande masks are carved by men. Yet, the carving is done with the approval of Sande women initiates who alone have authority over the masks and who are the artists' sole patrons. The interior of the Sande mask is hollow and wide enough for the head of the wearer to fit inside.

Characteristic stylistic features of the cask mask include gorgeous hairstyles that are as numerous as they are unique. The Mende place considerable emphasis on orderly and resplendent hair styling, because of their belief that the way a woman wears her hair is indicative of her virtues, comportment, moral and emotional stability. This explains why, in most Sande masks, the hair—which the carver must take pains to depict as beautifully plaited or knotted—takes no less than one third of the total sculpture size. The eyes are veiled under a bulging forehead, itself considered as symbolic of integrity, honesty, success, and uprightness. The eyes are rarely ever depicted as wide or large, conforming with the Sande notion that the mask as a spiritual entity whose personality may not be scrutinized. This Sande ideal of the inscrutability of spiritual essences also affirms the power of the spirit to be introspective and to scrutinize human interactions without being examined. It is this same concept of spiritual authority that explains the small, often closed mouth of the typical Sande mask. The spirit does not communicate with mortals through the regular human channels; as such, small mouths are a demonstration of the virtues of self-restraint.

The neck of every Sande mask is composed of between two and three folds. These symbolize the ripples that accompany the emergence of the mask from its underwater abode. The Sande mask resides in water, the realm of the ancestors, from which its presence is invoked. The Sande mask is, therefore, more than a mere figural representation. It symbolizes the highest ideals of the Sande woman in addition to serving as the emblem of social and cultural identity. Every Sande woman is a potential initiate. The mask is used to teach girls between the ages of six and ten all the social, cultural and intellectual skills that will make them better citizens, making it an essential feature of the educational process. The girls undergo symbolic and physical metamorphosis at the school, where they are born again as enlightened and better equipped citizens. Additionally, the mask appears at funeral rites for important members of the Sande society and at other public events, where its presence exudes prestige and dignity.

Helmet masks are widespread across the continent. Among the Senufo of Côte d'Ivoire and Burkina Faso, *Kponyungo* masks are the embodiment of the organizational clout of the Poro, a male regulatory association that maintains educational, political, and social control over the society. The *Kponyungo* mask is designed to project the image of a ferocious animal. It is composed of a pair of fierce jaws with sets of ravenous teeth, antelope horns, bush pig tusks evoking aggression, and animals like chameleons or birds that prance gingerly atop the dome of the mask. Imbued with potent medicine and an accretion of sacrificial blood, the *Kponyungo* is a formidable agent against the malevolent forces in the society. Another helmet mask that shares similar attributes is the *Kòmò* mask of the Bamana in Mali. Endowed with powerful objects and magical substances, the *Kòmò* is a manifestation of the Bamana concept of *dibi*, or darkness and obscurity. The

Kòmò leader who wears the mask performs several agile dance steps before an appreciative audience.

Among the Yoruba of southwestern Nigeria, the Ekiti are noted for their *Epa* masks, which appear during the annual or occasional *egungun* (masquerade) festivals. In the northern parts of Ekiti, in such towns as Osi Ilorin, Opin, Oye, Erinmope, and Odo Owa, there is a vigorous tradition of carving that has earned the Yoruba a widespread reputation as perhaps the most prolific traditional art-producing group in Africa. *Epa* masquerades are celebrated with pomp and pageantry because the *egungun* congregation is rooted in the doctrine that ancestors, as powerful spirits, mediate the activities of the living for the benefit of society.

Scholars have disproven the notion that traditional African artists are anonymous. We know, for example, that in the northern part of Ekiti, the works of artists Areoogun, Bamgbose, and Bamgboye continue to generate considerable interest and admiration. In Odo Owa, Bamgboye's work is distinguished for its superb composition and its display of sheer artistry.

The *Epa* helmet mask consists of the head and a superstructure. The lower part fits into the masquerade's head, allowing him to see through an opening in the mouth. But it is the upper part of the *Epa* mask, usually a tableau of figures displaying a social hierarchy, that makes it the tour de force that it often is. This superstructure may be a composite of several figures surrounding a major one, or a central figure with a small supporting cast. Regardless of the complexity of the composition or the number of people or animals involved, *Epa* masks are carved straight from one log of wood without the use of nails, pegs, or adhesives. Some of them can be quite large and tall, reaching up to five feet or more and weighing up to sixty pounds. Among the popular themes for *Epa* masks are war generalship, royalty, and motherhood. The masks are used during the celebration of young men's transition from one age grade to another or in festivals honoring Ogun, the deity of iron implements. *Epa* may also be elevated to the status of a powerful spiritual entity, *imole*, in which case it receives periodic offerings and supplications.

The third type of mask is the headdress or crest mask, which may come in vertical or horizontal forms. As is the case with the few examples that we have examined above, the headdress is only a fraction of the entire package, which includes costumes of various media and amplification. Its uses also vary widely, depending on the ethnic group and the specific event. Our first example within this group is drawn from the Yoruba in Nigeria, where the fun, frolic, and banter that accompany *gelede* festivals mask deep philosophical beliefs, at the center of which is reverence for the awesome powers of womanhood. Confined to the southwestern extremes of the Yoruba country—in Ketu, Egba and Egbado areas—*gelede* masquerades are convoked as means of placating those powerful, elderly Yoruba women who are believed to have spiritual powers that can be used for good or ill. The objective of gelede festivals is to appease such women, believed to be *aje*—witches—and encourage them to use their power to the advantage of their communities.

The *gelede* is more than a headdress, however. It is an enchanting spectacle, colorful, boisterous, and interactive. Spectacular costumes that tickle and challenge the imagination add fun to performances that mirror womanhood by presenting and, indeed, exaggerating femininity. In the headdresses as well as in songs, gestures, and dance steps, *gelede* consistently draws attention to the necessity for conciliatory postures, for chastising and appeasing, for privileging and admonishing. The reason for this, according to Lawal, is predicated on the Yoruba view that the world is fragile and that existence should therefore be cognizant of checks and balances.[1] This is what *gelede* seeks to achieve: social equilibrium, the type that acknowledges the role—indeed, the primacy—of womanhood in a male dominated world. Although the *gelede* society is controlled and directed by males and post-menopausal women, *gelede* masquerades are a men's affair. The men are dressed in costumes that are deliberately provocative: women's breasts are often clearly depicted as ponderous or robust, or as sharp, pointed, and dangerous acccessories. The buttocks, which hold a particular fascination for Yoruba men, are prominently exaggerated.

One of the most celebrated headdresses on the continent is the *Tyi Wara* of the Bamana in Mali. (Figure 15.4) Like several other Bamana masks that are inspired by animals, the *Tyi Wara* is inspired the antelope. Several social associations exist among the Bamana, among which are the *N'tomo*, the *Komo*, the *Nama*, the *Kore* and the *Tyi Wara*. To ensure social mobilization and political equilibrium, each of these associations has economic, health, educational, judicial, and other responsibilities. Each association has its own visual symbol, in the same way that corporations have their own logos. The *Tyi Wara* belongs to a farmers' association. Thus, it is used to mobilize farmers during the planting season and to help ensure a bountiful harvest. Created in honor of the mythical figure that taught agriculture to the Bamana, the *Tyi Wara* are used in male and female pairs to the beat of drums and music. The symbolism of pairing underlines the importance of cooperation between the sexes for human growth. The male *Tyi Wara* symbolizes the sun, and the female the earth. Their fiber costumes symbolize water. In totality, the presence of these elements—earth, sun, and water—fulfils the basic requirements for fertility and increase, attributes that are desired not only in humans but also in agriculture.

Figural Art

Before I focus on a few examples of figural art, some general observations must be made. Unlike masks, which are used at specific times by certified personages with a wide range of specific performances and expectations, figural art is much too diverse to be easily categorized. There are totemic figures, heraldic statues, royal portraits, decorative and supportive house posts, protective and commemorative figures, just as there are numerous power figures that can be employed to meet a number of needs. From walking sticks to caryatids, door locks to palace or granary doors, sculptures in high or low relief or full three-dimensional form, pieces of figural art are as exciting as they are intriguing. Some are used pe-

---

1. Babatunde Lawal, *The Gelede Spectacle. Art, Gender, and Social Harmony in an African Culture*. Seattle: University of Seattle Press, 1996, xiii. Lawal's publication is the most recent in a field that has enjoyed robust attention from scholars. In particular, Henry John Drewal has published extensively on this topic. See *Gelede: Art and Female Power among the Yoruba*. Bloomington: Indiana University Press, 1983.

Figure 15.4. Bamana Mask, Mali. Wood, attachments.

riodically at important social occasions while others are left in the open. There are figures dedicated to personal, family, or community shrines; yet there are others that are exclusive to recognized community specialists—diviners, healers, and others with spiritual powers.

In the Federal Democratic Republic of Congo and in neighboring Angola, a wide variety of figures are devoted to common themes: seated royalty with crossed legs, maternity figures, prestige items, and an array of power objects. One of the most powerful figures in African art, the *Nkisi*, is found among the Kongo, who are partitioned into three countries: the Federal Democratic Republic of Congo, Angola, and the Congo Republic. The best known type of this figure is the *Nkisi Nkondi*, the latter word meaning "hunter." The *Nkisi* figure (pl. *Minkisi*) is intimidating, both in its appearance and in the power of the materials of which it is constituted. The *Nkisi* human figure is pregnant with a powerful medicinal preparation, *bilongo*, made by a ritual expert called the *nganga*. After the sculptor has completed carving the figure, the *nganga* goes to work. On top of the head, at the lower back, or in the abdominal pocket, a container is created. This can be in the form of a wooden box, a shell, a sachet, or a container with mirror as cover.

The container holds precious items—relics of the dead, clay from the cemetery that connects the spirit of the dead with the *Nkisi*, or any other powerful items that the *nganga* may place there—in packets that are sealed with resin. The chin and the rest of the body are also covered with an assortment of medicines. The figure may be seen holding a weapon, while its face has a disturbingly blank stare, the eyes having been made of shell, mica, metal, or even glass. Customarily, iron blades, screws, nails, and similar objects are driven into the body. A *Nkisi Nkondi* that is heavily covered in layers of iron blades and other metals simply indicates that it has been used frequently by those who desire its services. What are these services? If a person feels aggrieved and suspects witchcraft, if a village is suddenly afflicted by an inexplicable, fatal disease, if thieves invade the community and animals are being stolen, if someone has sworn false oaths, *Nkisi Nkondi* will be provoked into action. How do you provoke it? You do things to it that are considered uncomplimentary: gunpowder may be exploded right before it or insults may be hurled at it, not to mention the numerous nails and blades that are driven into it. It is these injuries and insults that provoke the *Nkisi Nkondi* into action, activating the *bilongo* in it to inflict the wrongdoer with similar injury.[2]

Many sculptures in Africa are votive; that is, they are used in ceremonies where deities or ancestors are supplicated for replenishment, blessing, or protection from malevolent forces like witches and sorcerers. Many more figures are devoted to issues of survival: fertility, increase, and productivity. Some are concerned with personal success, ancestral veneration, or personal embellishment. In the eastern parts of Gabon, the Kota peoples are known for their highly abstracted reliquary figures, which are placed on family heirlooms or held by the chief of the clan during communal rituals. The objects themselves consist of a wood core covered with sheets or strips of copper or brass. The conceptual and highly schematic nature of the reliquary figures found tremendous favor with modern artists in France at the beginning of the twentieth century, because it presented a radical view of the human body. The figures contain relics of a departed family member. As such, they are treated with reverence, and placed in spaces that are accessible only to initiated members of the family.

---

2. There are numerous publications and notes that deal with this exciting topic. I have drawn on the writings of Wyatt MacGaffey in *Africa: The Art of a Continent*, Tom Phillips, ed. New York: Prestel, 1995; Jacques Kerchache, Jean-Louis Paudrat and Lucien Stephan, translated by Marjolijn de Jager. *Art of Africa*. New York: Harry N. Abrams, Inc. 1993.

Figure 15.5. Nkisi Nkondi, Kongo.

In form and use, Kota reliquary figures manifest different realities from figures that, among the Baule of Côte d'Ivoire, represent nature spirits, or *asie usu*. While the reliquary figures are highly abstracted heads used by initiates, Baule na-

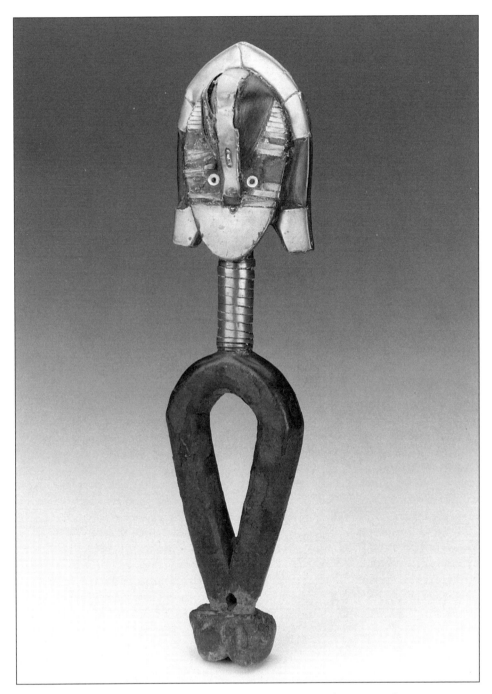

Figure 15.6. Kota Reliquary Guardian Figure, Gabon. Wood, copper.

ture spirit figures are often full representation of the human figure, although not done to actual human scale. They are used in a generic manner, depending on the nature of the problem. The Baule world acknowledges the power of spiritual beings whose activities may have positive or negative impacts on peoples' lives or may create social disequilibrium. The nature spirits play various roles, but their effect on individuals with whom they come in contact can only be positive or negative. When this is injurious to an individual (who, for example, is having mental problems), efforts are made to stem it. But when the effect of the contact is positive, as when one is blessed with the power of clairvoyance, then efforts are made to sustain that contact. Either way, the sculpture is covered in libations of blood and is used in sacrifices which are believed to empower it. Individual statues of "other-world men," *blolo bian*, or "other-world women," *blolo bla*, are also carved by the Baule to enable the concerned individual address life crises, like barrenness or sterility, that are believed to have been caused by one's otherworld sexual opposite. If your sexual opposite in the otherworld feels spurned or neglected, it may inflict all manner of disability, often of sexual nature, on you. Since fertility is central to the Baule conception of success, addressing the root of the problem begins at the diviner's place, ultimately resulting in the prescription that a carving be made to represent the otherworld spouse. This "spouse" will then be treated with offerings of food or money as part of the cure.

At the core of African thought systems is the family. Many of the initiation rites for boys and girls that are commonplace in Africa are aimed at emphasizing the centrality of family and the significance of fertility and children. These notions are widely amplified in the numerous figural sculptures of mothers and children. So widespread is the mother and child image that there is hardly any culture with a robust tradition of sculpture that does not have its own figural representation of motherhood. Among the Bamana in Mali, for example, the Gwan acts as a support group for women who are faced with barrenness. Where a woman finds difficulty in becoming pregnant soon after marriage, the diviner may be consulted. This was the case among the Asante in Ghana, whose *akua'ba* figures are credited with the power to bring about pregnancy as well as ensure successful delivery of the baby. (Figure 15.7) A woman who is desirous of becoming pregnant will, upon consultation with the appropriate expert and the observation of prescribed rites, carry the *akua'ba* and treat it like a real baby: bathe and clothe it, feed it, and cater to it.

Among the Yoruba, *ibeji* (twin) figures are take taken care of much like the *akua'ba* are by the Asanti. The essential difference between the two is that while the *akua'ba* is meant to induce pregnancy, the *ibeji* is a celebration of a child or of children that once lived. The idea behind *ibeji* figures concerns the Yoruba belief in reincarnation. This belief is seen in some of the names given to Yoruba children. A baby born to a family after the loss of the father or grandfather of the new baby is called Babatunde, or "father has returned." Similarly, a baby girl born following the bereavement of a female figure in the family—usually the maternal or paternal grandmother—is given the name Iyabo, "mother is back." For the Yoruba, who are reputed to have the highest numbers of twin births in Africa, twins are special children. If one of them dies, the mother commissions a sculpture, believed to be the repository for the soul of the departed one. It is treated with all the dignity and affection bestowed on the living twin. If, as often happens, the other twin dies, another sculpture is commissioned and accorded all the rights and honor given to the first. No one who has not given birth to twins or suffered a bereavement commissions an *ibeji* figure.

Let us focus on the figural sculptures of the Dogon in Mali to exemplify the thesis that, in traditional Africa, art is produced because it is tied to the history,

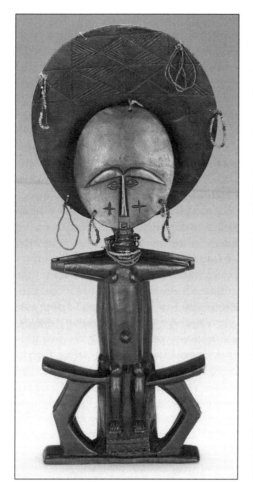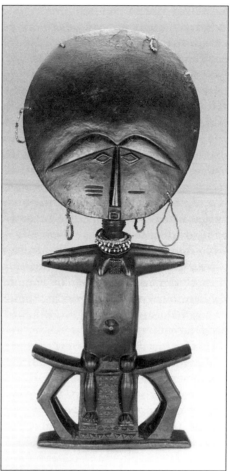

**Figure 15.7. Two *akua mma* (sing. *akua'ba*) figures,
Asante, Ghana. Wood, beaded strings, metal.**

the religious doctrines, and the cultural ethos of the people. Many studies on the Dogon—including those by Lieutenant Louis Desplagnes in 1907, Marcel Griaule between 1938 and 1965, Jean Laude and Pascal James Imperato in the 1970s, and Kate Ezra in the 1980s—demonstrate the extent to which Dogon art is immersed in Dogon cosmology. The collective deduction is that knowledge of Dogon religion and cosmology is a *sine qua non* for an understanding of the embedded message of Dogon art.[3] The profusion of masks and three-dimensional figures produced by the Dogon and, in earlier times, by the Tellem, and the multiple levels at which the figures intersect with history, myth, philosophy, and religion demand a contextualist approach to the study of Dogon art.

Numbering over 300,000, the Dogon people live in one of Africa's most enchanting topographical locations—the Bandiagara Cliffs in the southeastern part

---

3. See Pascal James Imperato, *Dogon Cliff Dwellers.* (New York: L. Kahan Gallery Inc/African Arts, 1978), 13.

of Mali. Their buildings, constructed of clay, seem to provide the observer with a hint of the form of Dogon art in general. Dogon architecture is heroic, schematic, blunt, and frugal—attributes that are also reflected in their sculptures, which are generally ascetic and tubular in form. Accounts of the Dogons' origin reveal that they were preceded in their current domain by the Tellem, who inhabited the cliffs from the eleventh through the fifteenth centuries. There, they built granaries that were used mainly for storing food and burying the dead. Scientific study carried out by a team of Dutch archaeologists in the 1960s and 1970s showed conclusively that the Dogon are not descendants of the Tellem. There are varying accounts of how the Dogon migrated to their current site. One account states that, following a severe drought, they migrated to the Bandiagara Plateau from their original settlement in the old Ghana Empire. They waged a battle with the Tellem, whom they drove into Yatenga, in what is now Burkina Faso. Another version states that the Dogon migrated from Mande around the fifteenth century.

In one of the varied myths of Dogon creation, Amma, the supreme creative force who inhabits the firmament, created earth, who bore him a pair of anthropoid twins, a male and a female, known as Nommo. This is the pair to which "Primordial Couple" figures allude. The male committed incest with his mother, upon which Amma decided to start afresh: he created another male and female pair of twins, Nommo, who procreated and begot three more pairs of twins. These were the eight original ancestors of the Dogon. One of them, the eighth Nommo, was the ancestor of Lebe, the oldest living Dogon, and the first *hogon*. The *hogon* is the religious and temporal head in every Dogon settlement. As the chief priest of the Lebe cult, the *hogon* is usually chosen from among the elders, and he occupies the position for life. Lebe is the order that is responsible for human and agricultural fertility. As in several African cultures, Dogon art celebrates the cyclic life of humankind.

Most Tellem pieces are swathed in the residues of sacrificial offerings: millet porridge, the blood of sacrificed animals, and crumbs of other edible items that have been sprinkled on the objects. ("Tellem" is used as a stylistic denominator for works that were produced by both the Tellem and the Dogon, since the Dogon used figures made by the Tellem, whom they succeeded). Tellem figures are carved from a single piece of lumber, are depicted in standing poses with arms raised, and have slim, tubular, schematized torsos and limbs. Some scholars have suggested that this stylistic index echoes the sinuous bodies of the Nommo—the eight original ancestors, who were water spirits. Because we do not have the luxury of written records about the Tellem, we can only hazard a guess as to the meaning of the raised hands. The standard rationalization is that this gesture is a form of supplication: asking the heavens for rain. While this may sound plausible in an environment where annual rainfall is not evenly distributed (the rainy season occurs between June and October), we must exercise caution in accepting this conjecture as fact. Put simply, there is no evidence to support it.

It is impossible in this brief chapter to do justice to the corpus of Dogon art, which includes decorated wooden pillars used to support men's meeting houses (*togu na*), door locks, masks, granary doors, horse riders, and mythical arks, some of which are over five feet in length. Added to these are single sculptures depicting both sexes, carved in the usual, schematized style characteristic of the Dogon. The "Primordial Couple" figure refers to the pair of twins that was born before the other four Nommo couples were created by Amma. It is in this regard that we must view Dogon art as essentially ideographic; the figures can be "read" as symbols of Dogon order. Several Primordial Couple figures are in existence, and, judging by subtle stylistic differences, they were made by various carvers. A stylistic homogeneity is easily identifiable, however. The figures are rendered either in seating or standing positions. Our example here comprises a standing couple, with features that are so clearly pronounced that the male cannot be confused with the female. Dogon carvers undoubtedly have their own creative canons. Their intent is not verisimilitude: they are not interested in realistic art. Instead, they aim at something much deeper—a timeless truth that reveals the essence of Dogon personality. The figures are tubular, with close attention paid to body adornment. From these figures, their cubical and abstracted forms, their elongation and schematization, we can see the antecedents of Cubism, a major twentieth century art movement that changed the course of modern art.

Conclusion

The traditional arts of African peoples are as diverse as the cultures that produce them. They are created and used not only as physical expressions of beauty, but often in conjunction with deeply entrenched cultural, educational, social, philosophical, and political values. Rather than the solitary, orphaned pieces that museums make them seem, they are part of a larger ensemble: an ensemble celebrating the various stations of the African life, from cradle to grave. It is an ensemble that vigorously mirrors the spectacle, the fun, the color, the vivacity, as well as the deep spirituality that Africa radiates. The arts are central to a worldview that seeks to empower African peoples to bring order to a universe in which malevolent and benevolent forces must be acknowledged to respect cosmological equilibrium. Traditional African art reflects the ethos of the African peoples at a particular period in the life and history of the African continent.

Review Questions

1. Compare and contrast the way African and Western societies perceive, use, and relate to art. What are the fundamental differences in the philosophical and religious approaches to art?
2. "African art is neither primitive not tribal." Discuss.
3. In what ways is the contemporary art of Africa different from the traditional art of Africa?
4. How have notions of the African continent impacted perception of traditional African art.
5. Explain the cross-cultural effects of Islam and Christianity on traditional African art.
6. What are the differences between mask and masquerades? Describe the form and context in which each functions.
7. Describe and compare the three categories into which masks have been divided.

8. Traditional African art addresses aesthetic and functional issues. Provide specific examples of works that support this statement.
9. Sande masks have stylistic, symbolic, and social attributes that set them aside from *gelede* masks. In what ways are these two masking traditions different? In what ways are they similar?
10. Discuss some of the ways in which Dogon art is a manifestation of Dogon cosmology.

Additional Reading

Dagan, Esther. *The Spirit's Image: The African Masking Tradition—Evolving Continuity*. Montreal, Canada: Galerie Amrad African Art Publications, 1992.

Drewal, Henry John, et al. *Yoruba: Nine Centuries of African Art and Thought*. New York: The Center for African Art, 1989.

Ezra, Kate. *Art of the Dogon: Selections from the Lester Wunderman Collection*. New York: Metropolitan Museum of Art, 1988.

Gottschalk, Burkhard. *Bundu: Bush-Devils in the Land of the Mende*. Dusseldorf, Germany: Africa Incognita, 1992.

Imperato, Pascal James. *Dogon Cliff Dwellers: The Art of Mali's Mountain People*. New York: L. Kahan Gallery Inc./African Arts, 1978.

Johnson, Barbara C. *Four Dan Sculptors: Continuity and Change*. San Francisco: The Fine Arts Museum of San Francisco, 1986.

Kerchache, Jacques, Jean-Louis Poudrat, and Lucien Stephan. *Art of Africa*. Trans. Marjolign de Jager. New York: Harry N. Abrams, Inc., 1993.

Phillips, Tom, ed. *Africa: The Art of a Continent*. New York: Prestel, 1996.

Chapter 16

Trends in African Literature

Adeleke Adeeko

This chapter surveys the dominant themes, narrative tendencies, and poetic styles of African literature since 1939. It demonstrates that the first major concern of African literature in the second half of the twentieth century was the rehabilitation of the cultural damage caused by colonialism and that coming to terms with the agonies of nation building became a central preoccupation of African literary work after formal decolonization. While the philosophy of Negritude guided writing in francophone countries, anthropological realism characterized literary activities in anglophone nations.

* * *

Rehabilitating the native consciousness that was severely undermined during colonial rule has been the major initial concern of African writing in the second half of the twentieth century. As perceived by writers and other intellectuals, Africa's loss of independent initiatives was glaringly obvious both in the European governance of physical space and in the dominance of the colonizers' views of the world in religion, education, high culture, and other means of social reproduction. To restore the equilibrium, thinkers and writers began to devise literary and cultural critiques to depict the European presence as a devastating interruption and to establish the validity of African civilizations. One statement that Chinua Achebe, the famous Nigerian novelist, made in a retrospective essay on his own writing expressed very concisely the predominant motivation of intellectual work in Africa in the mid-twentieth century: "I would be quite satisfied if my novels (especially the ones I set in the past) did no more than teach my readers that their past—with all its imperfections—was not one long night of savagery from which the first Europeans acting on God's behalf delivered them."[1] Condensed here are the defining concerns of African literature during the nationalism-dominated years that followed World War II and continued until independence in the 1960s. Achebe, like most of his contemporaries, presents his novelistic interpretation of the precolonial past as a means of modernizing African history and culture. Contrary to the instructions of colonial education, for instance, the palm tree is made a fit subject for poetry! While he does not use idioms of speculative philosophy like the French thinkers who theorized Negritude, Achebe is trying, like his contemporaries, to envision ways of repudiating the cultural myths that convinced Africans to accept their racial inferiority and made colonial conquest and domination palatable to its perpetrators.

---

1. Chinua Achebe, *Morning Yet on Creation Day: Essays* (London: Heinemann Educational Books, 1975), 44.

Among Francophones, Anglophones, and Lusophones, whether they were versed in speculative philosophy or ethnographic empiricism, locating where the rain of colonialism began to beat Africa (to use another apt Achebe image) was the overriding goal of literary and cultural production in the years following the end of World War II and the beginning of formal decolonization early in the 1960s. How this project is elaborated in cultural philosophy, poetry, and fiction is the subject of the first two sections of this chapter.

The chapter's third section addresses literary developments in the postindependence period. When African societies achieved independence, another set of political, economic, and cultural challenges soon arose because long-held positive expectations about the direction of African development began to disintegrate on all fronts. Political structures, perfected over centuries in Europe but fully introduced to Africa only a few years before independence, quickly collapsed in most countries. The predominantly capitalist economies soon proved inadequate to support the enormous demands of the populous and, for the most part, sparsely industrialized countries. Building a modern nation out of colonial political and economic structures created a daunting task—a task that frequently manifested as crisis—for African intellectuals. On the literary and cultural front, the inherent and not-so-inherent agonies of postcolonial nation building, manifested in economic and political crises, provoked acerbic criticism. From all possible ideological perspectives, analyses of the social dislocations fostered by the crises of governance and development dominated intellectual and literary production in ways that sharply contrasted with the high enthusiasm of the late colonial period.

The contribution of feminist critique to an understanding of African societies in the postindependence period is addressed in the fourth section. The fifth and final section comments on the state of African literary arts at the present time and makes brief projections about further developments.

Negritude

Contemporary African literature got its impetus in the decade preceding the outbreak of World War II, when young black men from Africa and the Caribbean studying in French universities seized the spirit of revolt of modernist European arts and politics and expressed their resentment of colonial ideologies. They resisted especially the representation of colonization as a means of civilizing culturally backward peoples. In journals and artistic manifestos, these men, led by Léopold Sédar Senghor, Aimé Césaire, and Léon-Gotran Damas, formulated some defining characteristics for black cultures, argued that black consciousness could only be understood within those parameters, and asserted the philosophical parity of their propositions with those of other world cultures, including those of Europe. The writers and philosophers named their movement Negritude, a term described by the Martinican Aimé Césaire as "the simple recognition of the fact of being black, and the acceptance of this fact, of our destiny as black people, of our history, and [of] our culture."[2] Senghor, the most prolific leader of the movement,

---

2. Quoted in Abiola Irele, *The African Experience in Literature and Ideology* (London: Heinemann Educational Books), 1981, 68.

Figure 16.1. Leopold Sédar Senghor of Senegal.

described Negritude as "the sum total of the cultural values of Africa."[3] Between the end of World War II and the attainment of independence in the 1960s, themes fostered by Negritude dominated philosophical inquiries and artistic production in francophone African countries.

The fundamental objective of Negritude was to show that African people, regardless of racist and colonialist notions about them, had developed their own particular culture, a notion Senghor defined as "a people's attitude to the world." Negritude writers also sought to outline the contours of the civilization underlying that African culture. Senghor asks in an essay on the movement's tasks: "Who would deny that Africans, too, have a certain way of conceiving life and of living it? A certain way of speaking, singing, and dancing; of painting and sculpturing, [*sic*] and even of laughing and crying?"[4] For Senghor, cultures operate civilizations, the operating cultural principle in African civilization is Negritude, and rhythm is its defining aspect. Unlike European civilizations which, since the Enlightenment at least, have relied principally on deadly, repressive, and ultimately superficial dissection of objects under the rubric of facts, matter, and logic, Africans, Senghor believes, have fundamentally viewed existence as an interconnected cosmos within which sympathetic interaction is the most fruitful way of

---

3. Quoted in Irele, *African Experience*, 68.

4. Leopold Sedar Senghor, "Négritude: A Humanism of the Twentieth Century," in *Colonial Discourse and Postcolonial Theory: A Reader* ed. Laura Chrisman and Patrick Williams, (New York: Columbia University Press, 1994,) 27.

knowing and living. Senghor famously summarizes the difference between European and African intellectual outlooks thus: "'I think, therefore I am,' wrote Descartes, the European par excellence. 'I feel, I dance the other,' the Negro African would say. He does not need, like Descartes, a 'tool-word'...a conjunction, in order to realize his being, but an object complement."[5]

Suffused by the principles of emotion and/or intuition (two human characteristics whose profundity, Senghor notes, even late-nineteenth century European rethinking of the Enlightenment has acknowledged), African cultures and civilizations reflect in their organizations the movement of excitement provoked by the object of use. It is in the nature of black thought to forge a unifying rhythm with the Other in the process of apprehending the world. Making critical discoveries and instituting ethical procedures that respect the Other, Senghor implies, are not mutually exclusive. Colonized peoples know very well that, on the contrary, European historical development shows little sympathy for the Other. That difference, urge Negritude thinkers, does not establish the superiority of European history. Emotion, rhythm, and sympathy with the object are themselves processes of knowing that are more effective, if only because they are more ethical, than the invasive dissection which the Enlightenment represented as the only means of true knowledge. At any rate, Senghor argues, the remarkable stylistic peculiarities of African arts, the deep sense of reciprocity that marks political organization in Africa, and the importance of amicability to the African definition of personality provide positive evidence for the prevalence of emotive interconnection in African culture and civilization. Poetry or rhythm, as mere signs or material artifacts, do not define the African worldview but reveal a deeper essence. Rhythm in Negritude "is simply the movement of attraction or repulsion that expresses the life of the cosmic forces; symmetry and asymmetry, repetition or opposition: in short the lines of force that link the meaningful signs that shapes and colors, timbre and tones are."[6]

Negritude's greatest literary achievement was in poetry. Here, as in its philosophical speculations, the ultimate mission was combating the alienation of consciousness brought about by colonialism. The Negritude writers belonged to a small but crucial class that had been trained to look up to Europe as the repository of reason and the bringer of progress. But the critical methodologies this class of writers learned in the process of their training also showed them that modern progress based on colonialist training would hinder their cultivation of the freedom of thought and action necessary to develop their native African environment. In revolt, the writers rejected colonialist programs, sought independence of thought and action, and created an African sensibility they could proudly claim. This is the spirit of resistance and rejuvenation recorded in David Diop's poem, "Waves": "The raging waves of freedom / Slap against the maddened Beast / Of yesterday's slave a fighter is born." The poem says that the colonized and the enslaved, "All who were drugged with fatality," from Suez to Hanoi, "Launch their immense song amid the waves / The raging waves of freedom / That slap slap against the maddened Beast."[7] In Negritude, poetry serves as the colonizeds' means of regaining freedom from the clutches of the Beast of imperialism.

---

5. Quoted in Irele, *African Experience* 77.
6. Senghor, " Négritude," 34.
7. David Mandessi Diop, *Hammer Blows: Poems* (London: Heinemann Educational Books, 1973), 15.

Negritude revolt also involves an inward journey, a "return" to Africa, often depicted as an abandoned, weather-beaten mother figure who is also a bastion of resilience, a distillation of essences, and a plentiful well of renewal. For example, the mother in David Diop's "To My Mother," relates to "*all* of the Negro who was blinded" but is now regaining the ability to "see the flowers again." The pleasant reminiscence about this mother, who shares in the reunion, helps the sons transcend the harsh inhumanity of the European environment in which they are living:

When memories rise around me
Memories of anxious halts on the edge of the abyss
Of icy seas where harvests drown
When days of drifting live in me again
Days in rags with a narcotic flavor
When behind closed shutters
The word turns aristocrat to embrace the void
Then mother I think of you.[8]

The journey back home in this poem, a return needed to confront the colonial Beast of "Waves," takes place psychically in the poet's memories.

Other major engagements of Negritude writing are outlined in Diop's "Africa," a poem dedicated, not surprisingly, "to [his] mother." First, the narrator confesses his alienation from his ancestral past: "Africa my Africa / Africa of proud warriors in ancestral savannas / Africa of which my grandmother sings / Beside her faraway river / I never knew you."[9] However, that a process to recover lost ground is already afoot is shown in the poet's taking stock of the land's brutal history under the recent back-breaking colonial domination that has almost emptied the people of the will to fight and reduced them to abjection.

Your beautiful black blood spilt in the fields
The blood of your sweat
The sweat of your toil
The toil of slavery
The slavery of your children
Africa tell me Africa
Can this be you the back that bends
And lies flat beneath the weight of humility
This trembling red-striped back
Saying yes to the whip along the roads of noon.

The predicatives of oppression—blood, sweat, toil, slavery, whipped bare backs—roll into one another like waves. But this realization, the poem avows, is useful only if it quickens the development of a new consciousness. Hence, in the concluding section, a voice calling the narrator an "impetuous son" indicates that the deplorable condition need not cause despair. A "young and hardy tree," that

---

8. Ibid., 3.
9. Ibid., 25.

voice says, can be seen growing amidst the "white and faded flowers" of wilting colonialism. A sure regeneration is taking place because the tree shall bear "fruits that take on little by little / The bitter taste of freedom." The poem moves from the despair of alienation to the paralysis of action caused by the enormity of colonialism's devastation. In the end, optimism arises in the reassertion of natural cycles which indicate that growth will inevitably supplant death.

Anthropological Realism

Aesthetic theories and cultural ideologies were not formalized in British colonies. Nonetheless, text after text demonstrates that anglophone writers and scholars, too, were anxious about colonialist cultural and political alienation. Jomo Kenyatta's preface to his 1938 *Facing Mount Kenya*, for instance, derided "'professional friends of the African'" whose goal was to repress the voice of the native African and "monopolise the office of interpreting his mind and speaking for him."[10] At the artistic level, anglophone writers echoed Kenyatta's concern by revealing different aspects of African cultures from which colonialist education and writing had estranged the world. Many stories and plays foregrounded lonely individuals dealing with the pain of seeking free life in a world in which the sensible pull of tradition and the strong lure of colonialist modernity exacted contradictory responses. A large number of anglophone texts, whether they were set in the distant precolonial past like Achebe's *Things Fall Apart* or in the more recent colonial moment like Ngugi's *The River Between*, and whether their protagonists were educated in European ways or not, showed that choosing existential directions in a colonialist epoch could not be a free choice because the options were not subject only to strict intellectual analysis but also tied to political questions.

Ngugi's *River Between* tells the story of two Gikuyu (Kikuyu) communities torn between a devotion to long-held ethnic social practices and an attraction to beliefs and behaviors clustered around Christianity and formal schooling. On opposite banks of the Honia river lie the Makuyu and Kameno communities, each espousing one position to the exclusion of the other. Joshua, the patriarch of a fiercely Pentecostalist group, lives in Makuyu where traditional Gikuyu rites like circumcision, initiation, and traditional feasts are considered pagan. Chege and others, who view Christianity as an aberration, live in Kameno. Kameno people troubled by the heavy hand of tradition usually seek refuge in Makuyu, while renegade Christian converts displeased with the radical rejection of Gikuyu practices preached in the church often go to Kameno. As time goes on, younger elements emerge who want to blend the social advantages of Christianity with the certainty guaranteed in Gikuyu traditions and to maintain a cordial social intercourse with those who disagree.

Spearheading the newer developments is Waiyaki, a Kameno youth whose traditionalist father sent him to a missionary school to make him "learn all the

---

10. Jomo Kenyatta, *Facing Mount Kenya* (New York: Vintage Books Edition, 1965), xviii.

wisdom and all the secrets of the white man."[11] His father, Chege, the last in a line of traditional seers and prophets, instructs his son to remain true, however, to the Gikuyu people and their ancient ways and to use his newly acquired knowledge to lead the people in expelling the Europeans. Waiyaki attends missionary schools and returns home to run independent schools that do not repudiate Gikuyu ways. He participates in circumcision ceremonies when his age mates are called. During his own circumcision rites he notes, however, that his enthusiasm for the ceremonies is dampened by the "ideas and notions" he had gathered in the missionary schools and that these ideas restrain him from "responding spontaneously."[12]

Among the Christians, dissent sprouts within Joshua's own immediate family when Muthoni decides to follow her fervent longing to be both a true Christian and a true Gikuyu woman. She rationalizes her thoughts thus: "Father and mother are circumcised. Are they not Christians? Circumcision did not prevent them from being Christians. I too have embraced the white man's faith. However, I know it is beautiful, oh so beautiful, to be initiated into womanhood. You learn the ways of the tribe."[13] Muthoni runs away from home and joins her age group for the female genital mutilation ritual. She dies as a result of complications from her wound. Because Muthoni's death is not mourned either in Kameno or Makuyu—the former has disowned her and the latter believes her Christian presence contaminated the ritual and her death was a sort of retribution from the Gods—Waiyaki becomes more determined to bring the two communities together. Anytime he goes to Makuyu he is rebuffed, and Kameno chastises him for the treachery involved in such cultural bridging. Meanwhile, Waiyaki discovers his love for Muthoni's only surviving sibling, Nyambura. The story outlines the growth of this love affair with the expansion of Waiyaki's role in the Gikuyu independent school movement. Echoes of the affair are exaggerated and distorted in the Gikuyu Cultural Association that sponsors the school movement. In the end, and to the utter surprise of the Kameno indigenist movement, Waiyaki asks for Nyambura's hand in marriage. The two lovers, simultaneously symbols and victims of the irreconcilable divisions in the land, are handed over to the elders who will judge their guilt or otherwise for polluting the land.

David Diop's Negritude-inflected poetry in French and Ngugi's ethnographic realism in English, as the above discussion shows, articulate the adequacy of African consciousness to the existential questions faced in each society. It is also apparent in the same texts that the traditional outlook is being reshaped fundamentally by colonialism. That the consciousness that will eventually emerge engages both writers is also noticeable in their foregrounding of the activities and thoughts of alienated characters who want to oversee the birth of a culture that will not repudiate the African past in order to embrace the modern present. Diop's poetic persona and Ngugi's Waiyaki, Muthoni, and Nyambura all want to create a consciousness that is modern and African.

While dealing with the agonies of colonialist modernity, the artists developed innovative conventions of writing about African subjects: the village became the *topos* of tradition even if colonialism had coerced it into changing; troubled

---

11. Ngugi wa Thiong'o, *The River Between*, (London: Heinemann Educational Books), 1965, 20.

12. Ibid., 39.

13. Ibid., 26.

modernity came to reside in churches and mission schools; and narrative tools like characterization assumed structural function and meaning within a story's local historical background. New rhetorical means of writing about Africa also emerged: figures of speech were drawn from the local environment and native speech patterns were foregrounded. A wedding was "as busy as an anthill," fame expanded "like a bush fire in the harmattan," and a young man grew "rapidly like a yam tendril in the rainy season." In conversations, characters used proverbs to facilitate discourse without sounding archaic or rustic—to introduce topics, to shift focus, to reiterate viewpoints, to invoke cultural precedents, and so on.

Chinua Achebe's "village" novels exemplify this new African narrative. For example, an understanding of *Things Fall Apart* requires that a reader pay attention to the story's details about the society, its openness to individual development, and the limits placed on successful individuals. Okonkwo, the novel's protagonist, rises and falls according to the extent to which he understands those rules and lives creatively within them. In *Arrow of God*, colonialism and Christianity wreak havoc on the community not because their harbingers own any superior intellect or means of coercion but because age-long social structures are stressed beyond recovery by the problems created under the new regime. Citizens convert to Christianity and the colonial administration expands at the end of *Arrow of God* because traditional political institutions give way under the weight of unprecedented problems. Epochal changes described in the two novels are attributed to the miscalculations of individuals so heavily invested in familiar ways of doing things that they are not able to negotiate a meeting of the emergent ways and the preexisting institutions and social visions.

The sense of a serious attempt to create new ways of depicting African subjects is most evident in Achebe's creation of a peculiar prose that reflects the difference between the world about which he is writing and the environments to which the English language is native. In a passage made famous by Achebe's comment on it as an example of his conscious effort to subordinate the English language to African concerns, Ezeulu, the protagonist in *Arrow of God,* says, "I want one of my sons to join these people and be my eyes there....The world is like a Mask, dancing....My spirit tells me that those who do not befriend the white man today will be saying *had we known* tomorrow." Achebe says he could have written the words as, "I am sending you as my representative among these people—just to be on the safe side in case the new religion develops. One has to move with the times or else one is left behind. I have a hunch that those who fail to come to terms with the white man may well regret their lack of foresight."[14] According to Achebe, the former is "in character" whereas the latter is not.

The years between the end of World War II and the attainment of formal independence were a period of intense nationalist politicking that questioned the presence of European powers in Africa and demanded their quick departure. The literary developments described above constitute the cultural wing of this movement even if the relationship is not always formalized. In ideology, poetry, and fiction the "dispossessed youth [writers] of Africa," to whom Jomo Kenyatta dedicated his *Facing Mount Kenya* in 1938, sustain the "fight for African freedom" and the struggle "to rebuild the destroyed shrines" as Kenyatta initially desired.

---

14. Achebe, *Morning Yet*, 61–62.

The Shock of Independence

In a 1971 poem titled "On African Writing," the Malawian poet Jack Mapanje, who was later jailed without trial by the government of Dr. Kamuzu Banda for the critical tone of his works, calls on African literature to rethink its unyielding attention to cultural restoration: "You've rocked at many passage rites, at drums / Mothers clapping their admiration of your / Initiation voices—now praises of decay." For Mapanje, cultural restoration, the dominant theme of the late colonial period, has become an empty rhetoric, or a "mouth-song" that pays only lip service to the nation. The words have failed to mature into yearnings for material rehabilitation or, in the poet's words, "hunting-marrying- / Fighting-killing praises." African writing remains "this nonsense about drinking / Palm wine from plastic tumblers" because the writers themselves remain inadequately self-critical and are unable to see that their audiences are "alert to all this / Absurdity about what you think they think!"[15] Mapanje's poem expresses the common critical stance of the most acclaimed African writing in the years after independence.

As early as 1957, the bloody ending of Peter Abrahams' *A Wreath for Udomo* expressed misgivings about the damage ethnic alliances would do to the newly independent African democracies. Around the declaration of Nigeria's independence in 1960, Wole Soyinka, in his play *A Dance of the Forests*, depicted the new nation as an *àbíkú*, a born-to-die-state. However, an episode in Ngugi's 1977 *Petals of Blood* captured the mood of postindependence African literature better than these early warnings. Toward the end of that novel, an old woman, well known for her radical political activism before tourism and brewing took over the soul of her town, is notified by the African Economic Bank that the piece of land she used to secure a loan will be confiscated because she has not fulfilled her mortgage obligations. Nyakinyua, who can not fathom how a faceless bank could have the power to take over her property, goes around the old neighborhoods to rally other little landholders threatened by the bank. To her surprise, she finds that the people have lost their willingness to fight: "they looked at her and they shook their heads: whom would they fight now? The Government? The Banks? KCO? The Party, Nderi? Yes who would they really fight?"[16] Nyakinyua dies a few days after her shocking realization. The old woman's fate symbolized new developments in the postindependent nation and the problem of how to confront them. To the masses, the promises of independence were unfulfilled and the sacrifices made for its attainment seemed to have not been worth the effort. The citizens seemed to be wary of carrying on a fight in which long-term victory was not assured.

In the postindependence years, the most important probe conducted insistently by writers was an investigation of the causes of the pervasive despair and disillusionment that killed Nyakinyua. Writers wondered if the origin of the social crises lied in the malformed capitalist structures handed down with independence that had been further damaged by large-scale mismanagement or in the personal

---

15. Jack Mapanje, "On African Writing (1971)," in *The Heinemann Book of African Poetry in English* ed. Adewale Maja-Pearce (London: Heinemann Educational Books, 1990), 107.
16. Ngugi wa Thiong'o, *Petals of Blood* (London: Heinemann Educational Books, 1977), 276.

Figure 16.2. Wole Soyinka, renowned African dramatist.

failings of the operators of the political economy, who were very timid about making radical changes that would open up a socialist path of development. Marxist writers pursued the latter cause, and liberal humanists favored the former line of thought. No longer content with describing the African condition to African citizens and sympathetic foreigners, liberal humanist writers satirized political corruption, decried the rapid decline of institutions, and highlighted the dispiriting effect all these had on citizens. Writers convinced that socialism might restore some of the vision that inspired the anticolonial struggles (anticolonialism, they held, was anticapitalism and socialism was the only logical step to take after independence) depicted postindependence failures as by-products of the class struggle insidiously concealed by nationalism.

Ayi Kwei Armah's first novel, *The Beautyful Ones Are Not Yet Born*, symbolizes the squalor of the early years of independent Ghana with the failure of the state to clear the garbage that has overtaken its city roads. The glossy lettering on garbage containers deployed citywide under an extravagant sanitation program gleams under piles of uncleared refuse. Staircase railings in government offices are re-varnished to cover up decades of grime. A railway clerk who will not take bribes from merchants who want to move their goods around is declared insane. To imply that surviving is easier in prison than on the outside, graffiti on latrine walls ask users to "pray for detention" because free food is readily available for the jailed. Processing food, which should be a means of nourishment, is shown everywhere as a means of corrupting the body. At the end of the novel, a military coup is announced and large portions of the population file into the streets to welcome the new leaders. But the unnamed protagonist, simply called "The Man," through whose eyes the surprisingly rapid aging and decay of the young country has been detailed, also shows readers that the saviors look very much like the old rulers. Within a few hours of coming to power, soldiers at road blocks commence their own "ingestion" of bribes as did the clerks in the deposed government. Gleefully unaware of the irony, the "revolutionary" soldiers extort gratuities from the driver of a lorry which bears the inscription "THE BEAUTYFUL ONES ARE NOT YET BORN". The soldiers notice neither the defective spelling nor the entire slogan's indictment of their own behavior. Not too far from where the soldiers carry on their corrupt operation, a corrupt minister in the old government, who has been forced out of hiding through the latrine hole of a tenement house, escapes in one of the powerboats he bought with his looting of government coffers. The ironic cleansing symbolized in the minister's passage through a latrine hole is quickly reversed in the soldiers' acts and in the minister's final escape. The cycle of corruption seems unbreakable.

Ngugi's Nyakinyua and Armah's "The Man" represent two different methods of literary reflection on the African condition in postindependence writing. One character seeks mass mobilization guided by a radical ideology while the other pursues the moral reformation of individuals. Nyakinyua, Bakayoko in Ousmane's *God's Bits of Wood*, and Idemudia in Festus Iyayi's *Violence* filter social events through their experience in mass movements, mainly labor unions and citizen's action groups, within which they have come to understand the class basis of oppression in colonial and postcolonial society. Their reflections also show that the disaffection caused by the postcolonial malaise will only be ameliorated with solutions designed to favor the working classes. The characters manifest the Marxist novelist's conviction that the conscientious artist in independent Africa cannot afford to be impartial with regard to all sections of society. Such objectivity, in their view, assumes that all social groups bear equal responsibility for society's condition. According to Ngugi, for instance, writers should make their work show the material causes of events and also reflect "the cause and the trends of a revolutionary struggle which has already destroyed the traditional power-map drawn up by the colonialist nations."[17] Armah's morally strict protagonist looks like the "objective" artist whom Ngugi considers inadequate. Like the story he dominates with his moral superiority, "The Man" surveys the society and decides how a correct national ethos could have changed individual and collective behavior. In The Man's world, appropriate political appointments and a sense of community could have altered things for the better.

The rampant repression of writers and other cultural leaders in the postindependent nations belies the atmosphere of free and engaging intellectual exchange that is implied in the writers' conflicting views on the most suitable ways of understanding the African predicament and the vision most adequate for transcending it. Works that favor mass mobilization and radical ideologies, besides putting

---

17. Ngugi wa Thiong'o, *Homecoming: Essays on African and Caribbean Literature, Culture, and Politics* (London: Heinemann, 1972), 65–66.

their authors at risk of fatal political harassment, may be removed from circulation. Ngugi's *Matigari* was banned in Kenya by the government of Arap Moi, and the novelist himself lives in prolonged exile. Texts whose satirical intent and subject seem to be identifiable, rightly or wrongly, are subject to a similar fate. For a long time, the novels of Nigeria's T. M. Aluko, perhaps the most prolific African satirical novelist, could not be sold in Malawi.

The poetry of Jack Mapanje and Frank Chipasula, two Malawians who were born after World War II and who both lived in exile for a good part of the long, repressive rule of Dr. Hastings Banda, reflect the ideological and material stresses of African writing since 1960. In the poem "Messages," the publication of the new songs Mapanje made a demand for in his poem "African Writing," discussed above, leads, as it were, to the poet's incarceration or exile. The African poet lands himself in jail for speaking against elders who inhale all the "free air" of the land, and elders who ban mini-skirts, which is done ostensibly to promote the nation's moral rectitude but actually turns young women into prostitutes. In addition, the chiefs who invoke tradition to take choice portions of the hunting party's kill but not to authorize the opening up of "more hunting bush," as tradition demands, publicly and maliciously vent their displeasure with the poet's outspoken speeches about the contradictions revealed. The nation has become a land of ruthless sychophancy, "Where you hack your own way single-handed / To make up anything up to the Shaka of / The tribe!"[18] Shaka's name here does not symbolize ingenious native African leadership as in Senghor's poem "Shaka the Great" but depicts a chief presiding over selfish national bloodletting. The mother in "Your Tears Still Burn at My Handcuffs" (1991),[19] not yet fully aware of the self-consuming destruction encouraged by the rulers, is introduced to the knowledge of sorrow pervading the country when her son is arrested. Some of Frank Chipasula's poems speak of handcuffs so many times that it feels as if they are the Malawian national jewelry of choice and the pain their wearing causes is a national experience. In "A Love Poem for My Country," the "streets are littered with handcuffed men / And the drums are thuds of the warden's spiked boots."[20] The macabre dance that accompanies the music is a "wriggle of agony" choreographed by "law and order." Images of lethal objects with pointed edges — "razor sharp barbed wire," "razor sharp knife," "hunter's dagger," "jagged rocks hurled at the enemy," and "axes" — pervade both the poet's observations about the virtual prison yard the country has become and the recollections conjured in exile.

---

18. Jack Mapanje, "Messages," in Maja-Pearce, *Heinemann Book of African Poetry*, 103–04.

19. Jack Mapanje, "Your Tears Still Burn at My Handcuffs" in *The Penguin Book of Modern African Poetry* ed. Gerald Moore and Ulli Beier (London: Penguin Books, 1998).

20. Frank Chipasula, "A Love Poem for My Country," in Moore and Beier, *Penguin Book of Modern African Poetery*, 178–179.

Feminist Critique and
the African Woman's Condition

The ever-increasing acceptance of the wisdom of feminist thought in African literature and criticism constitutes one other significant development in the critique of politics and culture in postindependence African literature. By 1966, when Flora Nwapa's *Efuru* was first published, set patterns of depicting African femininity and its place in culture and politics—filtered as they were through masculinist ideas about the nation—had become entrenched in African literature and would persist for a very long time thereafter.

Beginning with the Negritude era, the black woman has come to embody the enduring African experience and ethos. In her activities, demeanor, and moral tendencies are imprinted the character of Africa's embattled consciousness. That she still stands in spite of tremendous historical trouble, Negritude texts assert repeatedly, signifies the nation's tenacious will to survive and the reassurance that a defendable place and ethos still exist. In the more critical milieu that follows Negritude, actions of leading women in the literary texts are used to record the movement of history in such a way that they remind readers of traditional ethics bastardized in postcolonial society. The self-assured, although existentially ravaged, village woman is contrasted with the young, citified, restless, and lost woman who, not infrequently, turns to prostitution. In texts that promote radical ideologies, the prostitute is depicted as a sex worker who later alters her social consciousness. She may, as an omen of the liberating future, become pregnant.

Feminist African writing and criticism draw attention to the unjust gender politics embedded in making the woman's material shape carry cultural and historical continuity in the ways summarized above. Mariama Bâ, the Senegalese novelist, says, "We no longer accept the nostalgic praise to the African Mother who, in his anxiety, man confuses with Mother Africa."[21] In carrying out its project, feminist criticism uncovers the concealed cultural and political tendencies that usually render the African Mother and her daughter silent and the writing conventions that make women known only through men's inscriptions. Feminist literary production proposes different figurations of tradition and history in such ways that reveal the complexity of gender relations in precolonial African societies, foreground the activities of female-dominated sectors of social activities, and reevaluate the neutrality of the ostensibly universally liberating activities of the political and cultural movements preferred by men. As a result of the persistence of feminism, Efuru, in the novel Flora Nwapa names for her, now stands in the African literary canon beside the excessively manly Okonkwo in Achebe's *Things Fall Apart*.

Creating the speaking—indeed writing—female subject takes up the greater share of narrative space in Mariama Bâ's *So Long a Letter*. The story is composed as a series of autobiographical letters that the widowed Ramatoulaye will use as talking points when she meets her friend, Aissatou, who will be coming home from the United States to join her in marking the end of her seclusion after her husband's death. The letters, full of the reminiscences of a middle-aged woman

---

21. Quoted in Florence Stratton, *Contemporary African Literature and the Politics of Gender* (London: Routledge, 1994), 54–5.

who came to maturity during World War II, reflect African women's participation in the tremendous social changes of colonialism and independence. Ramatoulaye and Aissatou are among the first generation of Muslim women in their societies to receive a Western education in addition to Islamic schooling. "Being the first pioneers of the promotion of African women," Ramatoulaye remembers, "Men would call us scatter-brained. Others labelled us devils."[22] Like the men of nationalist novels, they straddled several traditions—indigenous African ways, Islamic customs, and colonialist French conventions—and blazed new trails in education and the professions.

The story's main conflict arises when Ramatoulaye's husband, who in earlier days wooed her in terms reminiscent of Negritude writing ("It's you whom I carry within me. You are my protecting black angel"), takes a second wife as is allowed by native and Islamic traditions. Modou's second marriage reflects a generational trend among the postindependence male elites who take selfish advantage of their knowledge of African traditions and the immense socioeconomic power of their Western education. But in their selective perpetuation of "tradition," the men, contrary to their clearly Western professions of love and respect to their first wives, do not consult their spouses. The men create tension in their first, second, and extended families and carry on as if nothing is amiss. The betrayal of their promises of undying love to their wives parallels the betrayal of the promises of independence. Gender relations in the postcolonial nation show, as Bâ's Ramatoulaye observes, that only a "slender liberty" has been "granted women."[23] To Ramatoulaye, Modou's second marriage is not merely tradition but a "betrayal" and an "abandonment of his first family"[24] and, if Modou's letters are to be believed, of his "protecting black angel." In Negritude logic, that means the African motherland.

The novel's most acute critique lies in its depiction of the activities of a wide spectrum of women. Women unaffected by elitist missionary and colonialist schooling—the typically illiterate village matriarchs—play crucial roles in complicating the lives of the middle class women whose marital problems dominate the story. The deeply religious and conservative Aunty Nabou, representing the mothers of the nationalist men who rule in the independent nation and who detest the ways of their sons' wives, maneuvers her son, Dr. Mawdo Fall, into polygamy. The royal Nabou, carrying traditional social class divisions into the modern age, believes his son must not entrust his family's future to the goldsmith's daughter he has taken for a wife, whether she is educated or not. Lady Mother-in-Law practically forces her daughter Binetou to become Modou's second wife, not believing that a second marriage can wreck a home. Moreover, marrying young Binetou to the trade unionist-turned government technical adviser opens an avenue of upward social mobility for both her and her daughter. In effect, *So Long a Letter* rewrites several of the basic ideological and representational strategies of male-authored texts. The older woman, the Mother Africa figure, lives in cities and not villages, and she protects only her son's interests. While she acts on behalf of her daughter, she has no regard for other people's daughters,

---

22. Mariama Bâ, *So Long a Letter,* trans. Modupe Bode-Thomas, (London: Heinemann Educational Books, 1981), 14–15.

23. Ibid., 51.

24. Ibid., 9.

and her actions create tension in the family. The hope for a less conflictual future seems to lie in the actions of the children nurtured only by the women abandoned by male nationalists. The nation represented here is divided by male-dominated social classes, which are themselves already split by gender affiliations further complicated by religion and tradition.

Conclusion

Four decades after independence, African literature faces the crisis of production that confronts other aspects of national life. Economic production in most economies is far less robust than it was a decade ago. Democratic political institutions are in varying states of collapse in many countries. Literary and cultural production have not, surprisingly, declined in proportion to the economic downturn and the demise of democratic institutions. It is true that the best-known writers and critics emerged in the relatively brighter economic and political climes that predated the incursion of the International Monetary Fund and the World Bank into African economies. It is also true that successors are not emerging in numbers that match the earlier generation of writers. But this is not because literary production has stopped in African countries, but because the forums that facilitate intra-continental exchange have collapsed. For instance, Heinemann Educational Books, which almost single-handedly created the canon of anglophone African literature, has broken up into spasmodic national units. The once prolific East African Publishing House suffered a similar fate. The publication of new titles in Heinemann's African Writers Series has been severely curtailed. While the collapse of distribution and production channels is, of course, intimately linked to the precipitous drop in the purchasing abilities of the reading public, the contents of the revived *Okike*, the literary journal founded by Chinua Achebe, show that literary creativity perseveres. Soon, I believe, the terms of discussing African literatures will, as they have in South Africa, assume national dimensions sufficient to complement this development.

At this moment, African texts that are circulated internationally deal with topics that are easily assimilated into large global concerns, like feminism and transnational migrations and their repercussions in the politics of multiculturalism. Works that deal with national issues like development, social dislocation, problems of democratic institutions, and so on will have to be written in postmodern styles with which cosmopolitan critics can easily identify in order to enter the international circuit. The reception and assimilation of the works of Tsitsi Dangarembga (*Nervous Conditions*), Ben Okri (*The Famished Road*), Biyi Bandele-Thomas (*The Sympathetic Undertaker*), and J. M. Coetzee, the South African author of novels too numerous to list, into feminist, postmodern, and postcolonial categories represent this tendency.

Review Questions

1. Is Negritude an antiracist racism? Justify your response with a reading of Senghor's "Negritude" essay.
2. Compare the use of language in Achebe's *Things Fall Apart* and Nwapa's *Efuru*.
3. Select two female characters each from Bâ's *So Long a Letter* and Nwapa's *Efuru* and describe the effect of historical changes on their concepts of womanhood.
4. Discuss the use of black and white images in Armah's *The Beautyful Ones Are Not Yet Born*.
5. Comment on the tone of Mapanje's "On African Writing." Relate his views to the writings of two other postindependence poets.

Additional Reading

Abiola Irele. "African Letters: The Making of a Tradition," *Yale Journal of Criticism 5*, 1 (Fall 1991): 69–90.

Mary E. Modupe Kolawole. *Womanism and African Consciousness*. Trenton: Africa World Press, 1997.

Emmanuel Obiechina. *Language and Theme: Essays in African Literature*. Washington, DC: Howard University Press, 1990.

Oyekan Owomoyela, ed. *A History of Twentieth Century African Literatures*. Lincoln: University of Nebraska Press, 1993.

Florence Stratton. *Contemporary African Literature and the Politics of Gender*. London: Routledge, 1994.

PART B

CASE STUDIES

Chapter 17

North Africa

Edmund Abaka

Forcible conquest, land expropriation, and debilitating economic policies led to anticolonial militancy in North Africa in the years preceding World War II. The defeat of the French in 1940 shattered French invincibility and increased nationalist agitation in Morocco, Algeria, and Tunisia. Britain's empty recognition of Egyptian "independence" in 1922, the economic crisis caused by World War II, and controversy over British occupation of the Suez Canal Zone hastened Egyptian independence. Whereas the colonial powers pursued modest reforms, North Africans demanded outright independence.

* * *

World War II profoundly affected Africa's decolonization process, accelerating the nationalist agitation that had begun in the years preceding the war. The postwar period was characterized by demands for a "new world order" in which the more than 160,000 Africans recruited from North and West Africa played an important part. In European settler territories like those in North Africa, most economic and social investments went to the European colonists, which frustrated Africans. The illusion of French omnipotence in North Africa was shattered by the apparent disparity between the drained French forces and the powerful British and American armies that invaded North Africa in 1942. In the wake of France's unveiled weakness, African nationalists increasingly agitated for independence. In Morocco, Sultan Muhammad V increasingly sided with the Muslim nationalist independence movement. In Algeria, the Front de Libèration Nationale (National Liberation Front, or FLN) launched a war of independence which tied up about half a million French troops by 1958. Faced with a three-front war, the French granted Tunisia and Morocco independence in order to concentrate on their major settler colony, Algeria. In the end, however, all North African countries won independence one after another.

This chapter examines the political, economic, and social impact of World War II on the European colonies in North Africa. In particular, it discusses the roles religious groups, educated elites, workers, and peasants played in agitating for independence after the war. It notes that the immediate postwar years represented a period of some détente and modest reform in some North African countries. Even as the colonial powers attempted to impose a system through which they could retain local control, North Africans sought total independence. Finally, the chapter analyzes the responses of the various colonial powers to the demands for and the march toward independence.

Some North African countries broke free from colonialism earlier than other parts of the continent. However, the struggle for independence, as epitomized by nationalist activities in the Maghreb (Algeria, Morocco, Tunisia), was long, violent, and bloody. By 1945, many North African countries were settler colonies with substantial and often violently racist European populations who were determined to stay in power at any cost. Hence, the path to independence was strewn with blood, misery, and tears.

Algeria

The great French demand for North African products during World War I enabled the settler population in Algeria to accumulate an abundance of credit and, in the postwar period, made them unwilling to change the political structure that let them control the country and its natural resources. European landownership increased from 1.6 million hectares (3.52 million acres) in 1890 to 2.7 million hectares (5.94 million acres) by 1940. A mere two percent of Algeria's population, mostly European immigrants, controlled approximately one-third of Algeria's profitable agricultural land. On the other hand, some 173,000 Muslim Algerians (eighty-seven thousand of whom fought in combat and twenty-five thousand of whom died) fought for France during World War I. Although the French government tried to reward them, the settlers forced Paris to retract its offer.[1] Settlers and colonial power alike, therefore, largely ignored Algerian demands for equal rights and treatment. All privileges went to the settlers, who also largely controlled Algeria's government.

Scholar Jamil Abun-Nasr argues that Ferhat Abbas (an Algerian scholar who, between 1922 and 1926, wrote numerous articles denouncing colonialism as a revolution to overthrow Algeria's ancient beliefs and ideas), did not personify Algerian nationalism as others had previously claimed. Indeed, Abun-Nasr notes that Abbas favored federation with France and was ready to distinguish between a trustworthy metropolitan France and a vengeful and implacable settler population.[2] Nonetheless, Abbas became a reluctant spokesman for the nationalist cause after the death of Shaykh Ahmed Ibn Badis, founder of a reformist religious movement with a nationalist leaning in 1928,[3] and the imprisonment of Massali al-Hajj, leader of the Algerian People's Party (Parti du Peuple Algérien, or PPA).

---

1. Jamil M. Abun-Nasr, *A History of the Maghrib in the Islamic Period* (Cambridge: Cambridge University Press, 1987), 317. For the contribution of North Africa (and Africa in general) to the war effort, see also John Reader, *Africa. A Biography of the Continent* (New York: Vintage Books, 1999), 637–40. See also Kevin Shillington, *History of Africa*, rev. ed. (New York: St Martin's Press, 1995), 366–72.

2. Abun-Nasr, *A History of the Maghrib in the Islamic Period*, 324. See also Robin Halett, *Africa since 1875* (Ann Arbor: University of Michigan Press, 1974), 227. Ferhat Abbas was a prominent political figure among the évolués, the educated Muslim elite who favored collaboration with the French to achieve a gradual expansion of the meager economic and political opportunities granted to Algerians after the war.

3. For details see A. E. Afigbo, et. al., *The Making of Modern Africa. Vol. II. The Twentieth Century* (London: Longman, 1992), 141.

In the vacuum left by Badis's death and al-Hajj's imprisonment, Abbas became a nationalist leader *par excellence.*

Abbas petitioned Marshal Pètain in 1941 and later Governor-General Peyrouton, the governor-general appointed by the French Committee of National Liberation, demanding equality before the law for all Algerians. He also poignantly told the American envoy, Richard Murphy, that his people wanted a free "Algerian fatherland."[4] Together with fifty-five others, Abbas drew up the Manifesto of the Algerian People as grounds for negotiating with the French Committee of National Liberation. The manifesto demanded liberty and equality in Algeria, agricultural reform, free compulsory education, immediate, full Muslim participation in the country's government, and an Algerian state. The manifesto scathingly indicted French colonialism.[5]

Even though the French Committee of National Liberation, the provisional government, and the government of the Fourth Republic were committed to some kind of reform, the pace was too slow for the Algerian nationalists. Moreover, the French administration in Algeria thwarted all attempts at reform. Beginning in 1941, a "growing effervescence of nationalism" suffused Algeria, a product of France's 1940 defeat, news of Syrian and Lebanese independence movements, and the United States' new role in world politics.[6]

The first major French response, made by Charles de Gaulle in an *ordonnance* of March 1944, gave equal rights to Muslims and French, removed some discriminatory legislation, and made civilian and military careers available to all. These measures, in effect, satisfied the demands made twenty-five years earlier. But Algerian *colon* opinion so violently opposed the measure, known as the Blum-Violette Project, that it was ultimately shelved. Massali al-Hajj's skepticism about success in creating an Algerian state associated with France combined with Abbas's desires led to the March 1944 formation of the Amis du Manifeste de la Liberté (Friends of the Declaration of Independence, or AML) in Sétif. The AML sought to create an Algerian republic federated with France. In spite of Massali's absence from the 1945 AML Congress, the PPA rejected the notion of federation with France and forced the congress to pass motions calling for Massali's release (Massali was then under house arrest). Furthermore, they insisted on the formation of an Algerian government without ties to France. When Muslims demonstrated in Sétif on May 1, 1945, they were roughly and brutally pushed back into the crowded Casbah.[7]

The spontaneous and ill-coordinated insurrection at Sétif and its subsequent brutal suppression by French authorities became the symbols of Algerian nationalism. The Sétif disturbances arose when Muslims celebrated the Allied victory in World War II. Shots were fired when police tried to seize green flags bearing the crescent emblem and banners proclaiming Algerian independence. When the police used brutal tactics to disperse the crowd, Muslim demonstrators attacked the

---

4. Abun-Nasr, *A History of the Maghrib in the Islamic Period*, 323.

5. Wilfrid Knapp, *North West Africa. A Political and Economic Survey*, 3rd ed. (Oxford: Oxford University Press, 1977), 81–82; Abun-Nasr, *A History of the Maghrib in the Islamic Period*, 323–324; Hallett, *Africa since 1875*, 228–9. Ibn Baddis had declared in response to Ferhat Abbas' position "La France, c'est moi" (earlier in 1936), that "This Muslim Algeria is not France, cannot be France, and does not want to be France."

6. Knapp, *North West Africa*, 82.

7. Abun-Nasr, pp. 323–4.

armed garrison at Sétif. The violence spread to Annaba, Gulma, and parts of
Oran as Muslims committed murder, arson, and other forms of violence against
the French. Such manifestations were clear expressions of anger against those
whom the Muslims held directly responsible for Algerian poverty and misery. The
French responded by bombing villages and using their ships to bombard the outskirts of Kerrata. The high Muslim casualty figures in the uprising, ranging from a
total of fifteen hundred according to official sources to eighty thousand according
to Algerian nationalists, led to the arrest of Abbas and 4,560 others. The incident
at Sétif propelled Algerian nationalism on the road to independence.[8]

The end of World War II renewed Algerian enthusiasm for nationalism. As Ferhat Abbas noted, "The 8th [of] May brought us back to the crusades, with this
worsening feature that, as far as the French in Algeria were concerned, it was a part
of their elite which for weeks tortured in cold blood and murdered innocent
people. This was possible because the Arab had always been considered a different
being, an enemy, an inferior man."[9] Algerian nationalistic sensibilities grew particularly acute following the war, as many Algerians, who had enjoyed relative equality while defending France, returned home only to find subordination under an in-
transigent French colonial system. Thus, French hopes that a middle group of
Algerian moderates and French liberals would defuse violent nationalism were
dashed.

In 1945, Algerians won the right to elect thirteen representatives to the
French Constituent Assembly, the same number of representatives that the
French settlers could elect. When Abbas was freed in March 1946, he organized
the Union Démocratique du Manifeste Algérien (Democratic Union for the Independence of Algeria, or UDMA), which had a more subdued tone than the AML
and demanded an Algerian republic federated with France such that Frenchmen
living in Algeria could be Algerian citizens and Algerians residing in France
could be granted citizenship. Despite a large Muslim abstention of fifty-two percent, the UDMA won eleven of the thirteen seats in France's Constituent Assembly. [10]

Released after the 1946 election, Massali al-Hajj launched the Mouvement
pour le Triomphe des Libertés Démocratiques (Movement for the Triumph of Democratic Liberties, or MTLD) to demand an Algerian national assembly and the
removal of French troops from Algeria. While squabbles between Massali and his
central committee rendered the movement ineffective, the first National Assembly
of the Fourth French Republic passed the 1947 Algerian Statute, which permitted
fiscal autonomy in Algeria but left political and economic power unaltered and
discarded proposals by Abbas and six others for political participation. The
statute did nothing about the uneven distribution of political and economic capacities among French and Muslim communities.[11] The Organisation Secrète (Secret Organization, or OS) was formed in 1948 by Mohamed Belouizdad, Ahmed
Ben Bella, Aït Ahmed, Ali Mahnas, and others who responded to electoral fraud
during the 1948 Algerian assembly elections, the legal repression of the PPA, and
dissent among members of MLTD. Additionally, the OS advocated direct action

---

8. Abun-Nasr, p. 432–5; Hallett, *Africa Since 1875*, 229.
9. Ibid., 84.
10. Abun-Nasr, *A History of the Maghrib in the Islamic Period*, 326.
11. Ibid., 326–7.

against the French to resolve the Algerian problem.[12] With a leadership composed of young men in their twenties, the OS began to organize a force of resistance fighters. In 1948, Ben Bella and other OS leaders attacked the Oran post office and made away with three million francs. Ben Bella and some of the OS leaders were jailed, but Ben Bella escaped from prison and fled to Cairo. In the spring of 1954, the revolutionaries regrouped and formed the Comité Révolutionnaire d'U-nité et d'Action (the Revolutionary Committee of Unity and Action, or CRUA).[13]

In late July 1954, the group formed a "committee of twenty-two," and agreed that, notwithstanding a shortage of cash, arms, and popular support, they would organize a revolution. On October 10, 1954, CRUA's six directing members changed the movement's name to National Liberation Front (Front de la Libération Nationale, or FLN).[14] The birth of the FLN signaled a new approach to Algerian independence. Launching the revolution on November 1, 1954, the FLN proclaimed:

> After decades of struggle, the National Movement has reached its final phase of fulfillment. At home, the people are united behind the watch-words of independence and action. Abroad, the atmosphere is favorable, especially with the diplomatic support of our Arab and Moslem brothers.
>
> Our National Movement, prostrated by years of immobility and routine, badly directed, was disintegrating little by little. Faced with this situation, a youthful group, gathering about it the majority of wholesome and resolute elements, judged that the moment had come to take the National Movement out of the impasse into which it had been forced by the conflicts of persons and of influence and to launch it into a true revolutionary struggle at the side of the Moroccan and Tunisian brothers.[15]

The revolution initially succeeded as the FLN launched coordinated attacks throughout the country: north of the desert in Oran, Batna, Arris, Biskra, Kabylia, and the Algiers district. With some three hundred Italian rifles purchased at Libyan war dumps, the revolutionaries began to form an army. Led by men such as Ben Bella, who had fought with the Allies in North Africa, the revolution attracted mass support and numerous volunteers. The revolutionaries destroyed an electric transformer station in Khenchela, attacked police stations and barracks, cut telephone wires, incinerated tobacco and cork barns at Kabylia, detonated bombs in Algiers, and held up a bus on the road between Biskra and Arris. The French government responded with repression. Nonetheless, while MTLD leaders and militants were arrested almost immediately, it took three to four months for some of the FLN leaders to be arrested. Still, in the rural areas, especially the Kabylia and the Aurès, the guerrilla war continued unabated. French forces responded with punitive raids and indiscriminate killing of rural Muslims. The FLN also executed local people who were considered traitors.[16]

---

12. Abun-Nasr, *A History of the Maghrib in the Islamic Period*, 342; Knapp, *North West Africa*, 86.

13. Knapp, *North West Africa*, 87.

14. Ibid., 87–8.

15. Bruce Fetter ed. *Colonial Rule in Africa. Readings from Primary Sources* (Madison: University of Wisconsin Press, 1979), 203–204, for the Proclamation of the National Liberation Front, November 1, 1954.

16. Knapp, *North West Africa*, 88–9.

French attempts to find a political solution to the conflict were again scuttled by the French settlers in Algeria. Jacques Soustelle, who was appointed governor-general of Algeria, arrived with a plan of pacification which sought to apply the statute of 1947. But he was too late to turn the tide of revolution and reduce the appeal of independence. Throughout 1955 and 1956, the fighting in Alergia increased in ferocity. About fifteen thousand FLN fighters held their own against a French army of some 200,000, necessitating the airlift of reinforcements from France.[17]

A decisive moment in the Algerian crisis came in 1956, when a group of liberal Europeans and FLN representatives met to declare a truce to establish a community of understanding and protect civilians. However, French settlers intensified their resistance when French Prime Minister Guy Mollet visited Algiers in February 1956. After being pelted with tomatoes and anything else at hand by angry Europeans in Algiers, Mollet retreated from any reform policy that might undercut the FLN. On the political front, the FLN achieved some successes. In May 1955, Ferhat Abbas promised to support the revolution, and in July 1956, the FLN absorbed the Algerian Communist Party, which had joined the rebellion. In Algiers, Yacef Saadi and Amar Ali fought and won a fierce battle with the French and made the strategically important Casbah a fortress for the FLN.[18]

Beginning in the summer of 1995, the FLN made serious attempts to win the support of Algerian workers in France, who were mostly members of the MTLD. While Mourad Terbouche (a prominent member of the MTLD) was largely successful in this, the leaders of the FLN—Ben Bella, Aït Ahmed, and Mohammed Khider—established an office in Cairo to secure arms and get official recognition. Gamal Nasser's reservations about Ben Bella limited any initial success. Ait and Mohammed Yazid traveled to Asia to attend the Bandung Conference, but they failed to persuade India's Pandit Nehru or any other participant to include the Algerian question in their final policy statements.[19]

In both Algeria and Cairo, the FLN intensified its struggle for independence. Meanwhile, the French government sought to end the war through negotiation. This was due, in part, to the fact that the massive French force was tied down in Algeria by 1960. Algerian guerrillas, furthermore, had fought a long and punishing battle with the French, and their leadership was amenable to negotiations by that year as well. The Algerian war ended at the May 1962 Evian Agreements, during which it was decided, inter alia, that:

> While Algeria is to retain French cultural institutions, it is not bound to them indefinitely. Some radio broadcasts and official texts are to be made available in French and the European population will be able to conduct administrative business in French. French schools can be established in Algeria (following the French system); periodicals and newspapers will enjoy mutual free passage between Algeria and France; provisions will be made for the study of the culture of each nation in the other's territory; Algerian higher education, with French aid, will be modeled on the French system.[20]

17. Ibid., 90–1.
18. Ibid., 91–2.
19. Ibid., 92–3.
20. Bruce Fetter (ed.), *Colonial Rule in Africa. Readings From Primary Sources*, 211–2. See also *The Passing of French Algeria*, trans. David C. Gordon (London, 1966), 78.

Regarding citizenship, the Evian Agreements also stipulated that:

> Europeans (who can prove regular residence) will have three years to opt
> for Algerian citizenship or to be considered foreigners; the converse is
> true for Algerians in France. In the interim, each will enjoy civil rights in
> the other's country, but not political rights. Europeans will be given repre-
> sentation in the Algerian parliament in proportion to their numbers, but
> only in a single college in which each delegate will vote as a separate indi-
> vidual. An "Association de Sauvegarde" will function to represent the in-
> terests of the European community but will play no political role. Provi-
> sions are made to set up a Court of Guarantees for Europeans who feel
> discriminated against.[21]

The Evian Agreements realized the NFL's aims and Algeria's independence.

Tunisia

The forces that crystallized in a mass nationalist movement in Tunisia were
unleashed during the 1930 Eucharistic Congress at Carthage. The Archbishop of
Carthage, Monsignor Lemaître (who was also responsible for erecting Cardinal
Lavigerie's statue facing the old Muslim sector of Tunis), organized the congress
to celebrate a century of French and Catholic activity in Algeria.[22] Habib Bourguiba and other Tunisian university graduates viewed the congress as a crusade.
Bourguiba and his colleagues Mahmud Matiri, Tahir Sfar, and Bahri Guiga (who
were already members of the Destour, the Liberal Constitutional Party), launched
a newspaper called *L'Action Tunisienne*, which introduced a new political approach. Educated and firmly rooted in Islamic tradition, the leaders used Islamic
symbols to propagate their nationalist message. They became controversial when
they buried Tunisian Muslims who had been naturalized as Frenchmen in Muslim
cemeteries under the 1923 law, condemned the official *ulema* (religious leaders)
for being too accommodating to the French, and divided the Destour leadership.
When *L'Action* was banned on April 27, 1933, Bourguiba resigned, and together
with other *L'Action* leaders formed the Neo-Destour party in 1934.[23] The party
made little progress in the 1930s. French colonial authorities suppressed it, and
Habib Bourguiba was imprisoned when he was linked to disturbances at Bordj Le
Boeuf on the Tunisian edge of the Sahara. While Bourguiba languished in prison
between 1936 and 1938, the party was reorganized. Membership, which stood at
one-hundred thousand in 1937, rose to 106,000 in 1954.[24]

In January 1938, the Neo-Destour and the General Confederation of Tunisian
Workers (Confédération Générale des Travailleurs Tunisiens, or CGTT) organized riots in Bizerte over the dismissal of an Algerian workman. When demon-

---

21. Fetter (ed.), *Colonial Rule in Africa. Readings From primary Sources*, 78.
22. Abun-Nasr, *A History of the Maghrib in the Islamic Period*, 347.
23. Robin Hallett, *Africa Since 1875*, 224; Abun-Nasr, *A History of the Maghrib in the Islamic Period*, 347–8.
24. See Basil Davidson, *Modern Africa. A Social and Political History*, 3rd ed. (London: Longman), 1997, 117; Abun-Nasr, *A History of the Maghrib in the Islamic Period*, 362.

strators tried to free Ali al-Balhawan (a Neo-Destour activist who had been arrested), the police fired on the demonstrators, killing 112 and wounding sixty-
two. Bourguiba was arrested the same day and, together with other political prisoners, taken to France later that year. Repression stymied nationalist agitation
until June 1942, when Bourguiba and other political prisoners were relocated to
Paris. The nationalist agitation was taken up in 1942 by the new Tunisian ruler,
Munsif Bey, who renewed the bond between the throne and the people, received
nationalist leaders in his palace, and sent an order to the Pétain government demanding the establishment of a consultative assembly with a Tunisian majority
and the reorganization of the assembly under Tunisian control.[25]

When German troops arrived in 1942, Munsif Bey continued to act independently. He dismissed the existing government and formed a new one, which included a Neo-Destour sympathizer, Muhammad Shanniq, as its leader. Other
members of the Neo-Destour Party were invited to join the government. When
the Allies entered Tunis on May 14, 1943, Bey was deposed by the Free French
authorities for allegedly collaborating with the Axis powers, while in reality his
only crime was confronting the French administration. The Germans sent Bourguiba to Rome in 1943. When he failed to openly support the Axis powers, the
Germans sent him back to Tunisia, hoping that his activities would be hostile to
the French. However, Bourguiba issued a proclamation in May denouncing fascism and Mussolini's expansionist designs.[26]

In March 1945, Bourguiba secretly left Tunisia for Egypt to petition for aid
from the newly founded Arab League. He proceeded to Asia, Europe, and the
United States during the next two years. Meanwhile, in Tunisia, a Congress of the
Destour, Neo-Destour, and the Union Générale Tunisienne du Travail (UGTT)
met on August 23, 1946 to coordinate the action of various anticolonial groups in
a National Tunisian Front and was broken up by police. Facing demonstrations,
strikes, and other forms of agitation, the French conceded. In July 1947, a new
Tunisian government was formed with Mustafa Ka'ak as prime minister. Although French and Tunisian ministers ostensibly shared power, real authority still
laid in the hands of the French resident-general.[27]

The "co-sovereignty" question became a major sore-point between the French
and the Tunisian nationalists. In August 1950, Muhammad Shanniq formed a new
government comprised of nine Tunisians and three French members. The Neo-Destour Secretary-General Salih b. Yusuf became Minister of Justice. After the French
government upheld the settler view (espoused by the Rassemblement Français de
Tunisie) that only a joint Franco-Tunisian sovereignty was compatible with
France's interests in the country, Prime Minister Shanniq and three other Tunisian
ministers went to Paris to demand Tunisian independence and recognition of
Tunisian sovereignty while accepting the retention of close cultural, economic, and
military relations with France. Riots erupted in Tunisia on January 15, 1952, when
the French Resident-General Hautecloque demanded the dismissal of the Shanniq
government. Habib Bourguiba was arrested on January 18, 1952, and in March,
Shanniq and other Tunisian ministers were also arrested. Alarmed, Bey appointed
two successive prime ministers (in March 1952 and in March 1954) who were

---

25. Abun-Nasr, *A History of the Maghrib in the Islamic Period*, 348.
26. Ibid., 364.
27. Ibid., 364.

more amenable to French interests. Whatever reforms had been initiated since the declaration of co-sovereignty were upheld.

France's concessions were unacceptable to the nationalists, who dismissed any form of compromise after January 1952. When the police resorted to repression, strikes, and demonstrations to counter the nationalists' actions, the Neo-Destour party formed a united front with the UGTT. While most Neo-Destour leaders were arrested, the UGTT leader, Farhat Hashdad, could continue working because of his international connections.[28]

From their mountain bases, Tunisian guerrillas launched attacks against the settlers, who, in turn, formed the Red Hand (a settler terrorist organization) and attacked Tunisian political leaders. The Red Hand assassinated Farhat Hashdad on December 5, 1952. Although the violence eventually forced the French government to begin the process of granting autonomy to Tunisia, that process was interrupted when the government fell on February 5, 1955. An agreement to grant Tunisian autonomy was eventually forged with Bourguiba on April 22, 1955. Although Bourguiba accepted the agreement as a preliminary move toward complete independence, several Tunisian leaders denounced it, because it gave the French control over Tunisia's foreign affairs, army, police, senior administrative posts, and sectors of the Tunisian economy. In June 1955, Bourguiba returned from France to a hero's welcome in Tunisia. When he endorsed the agreement at a November 1955 congress, Salih B. Yusuf broke away and declared war on Bourguiba and his followers, although Yusuf's guerrilla organization was subdued by June 1956.[29] By reuniting his party and overcoming Yusuf's opposition, Bourguiba established a reputation as a moderate and astute leader. Hence, the French, having agreed to grant Moroccan independence on March 2, 1956, agreed to grant Tunisian independence on March 20, 1956.

Following the elections on March 25, 1956, the Neo-Destour Party won eighty-eight out of ninety-eight assembly seats. On July 25, 1957, the assembly abolished the monarchy, declared a republic, and installed Bourguiba as head of state.

Morocco

In Morocco, as in Algeria, Tunisia, and other North African countries, economic depression increased the support for anticolonial and nationalist demands. These demands gained momentum in 1934 and expanded when the French allegedly attempted to divide Moroccan Muslims.

While the Great Depression brought hunger and unemployment to the poor in Morocco, affluent Moroccan merchants and professional men, who had profited from limited reforms insititued after World War II, found themselves marginalized by French settlers and businessmen. The colonial government demonstrated concern for the French community's economic interests more than it did for those of Moroccans. Beginning in 1937, the French periodically "decapitated" Allal al-Fasi's Committee for Action (formed in January 1937 to champion Mo-

---

28. Ibid,. 366.
29. Ibid., 366–7.

roccan independence).[30] When Moroccan nationalists responded with violent, sometimes fatal demonstrations, the French occupied Medina, the Muslim quarter at Fez, and surrounded Qaraouiyine University. Some nationalist leaders, such as Allal al-Fassi and al-Wazzani, were forced into exile; and others, such as Omar Abdeljalil and Ahmed Balafrej, went into voluntary exile.[31]

The nationalist movement did not, however, collapse with the arrest and exile of its leaders. While nationalist opposition to the French had taken root in a country where local authority was weak, agitation was strengthened by the growing understanding between the sultan and the nationalists. At the same time, a particular nationalist movement, composed of Abderssalem Bennouna and Abdel Khaled Torres's National Reform Party and Mekki Nacri's Maghreb Unity Party, grew in strength. (The Maghreb Unity Party had moved in from the French zone of Morocco, which had been established by the Treaty of Fez on March 12, 1912. The treaty, signed by Sultan Mulay Hafiz, placed Morocco under French protection and partitioned Morocco into a northern French zone and a small, southern Spanish zone.)[32]

Before World War II, there was little cooperation between French nationalists in northern Morocco and their Spanish counterparts in the south. World War II had a significant psychological and social effect on this relationship. The Moroccan nationalists and the sultan declared their support for France in September 1939. Yet France's crushing defeat in 1940 and the landing of powerful British and American armies in 1942 destroyed the pro-Vichy (pro-Nazi) French administration in Morocco and strengthened the cause of Moroccan nationalism throughout the country. The unbending rule of the Gaullist General Puaux, who replaced the Vichy administrator General Noguès as resident-general, combined with a restrictive war economy led to immeasurable hardship. Added to this, the strains and stresses of war tore down traditional loyalties and propelled the nationalist cause.[33] The war in North Africa also led to a meeting between President Roosevelt, Sultan Muhammed Ibn Youssef, Crown Prince Mulay Hassan, and General Noguès (before his recall) at the 1943 Casablanca Conference. For the Sultan, the meeting demonstrated the possibilities that came with a world balance in favor of the Allied powers.

The rule of General Puaux and the hopes awakened by American victories in North Africa kindled nationalist aspirations in Morocco. Nationalist leaders Ahmed Balafrej and Mohammed Lyazidi renewed their anti-colonial efforts. By December 1943, a group of professionals and merchants founded a party called *Istiqlal* (Independence), and demanded an end to colonial government.[34] They made appeals to the people to join them, just as the Neo-Destour was doing in Tunisia. They collected signatures for an independence manifesto that they presented to the governments of France, the United States, Britain, and the Soviet Union on January 11, 1944. Referring to the Atlantic Charter and Moroccan contributions to the Free French cause, the manifesto demanded Morocco's territorial integrity under Sultan Mohammed Ibn Youssef's leadership. The nationalist

30. Wilfrid Knapp, *North West Africa*, 275.

31. Ibid., 275–6.

32. For details see Hallett, *Africa since 1975*, 209.

33. Knapp, *North West Africa*, 276–7.

34. Basil Davidson, *Modern Africa. A Social and Political History*, 3rd ed. (London: Longman, 1994), 118.

movement grew stronger, relying on the closer alliance with the popular sultan and the harsh actions of the French security services.[35] Here, too, the French answered with renewed oppression. But the sultan succeeded in winning concessions from de Gaulle and secured General Puaux's retirement. Erik Labonne succeeded Puaux even as nationalist leaders like Allal al-Fasi and al-Wazzani were permitted to return from exile.

Both the *Istiqlal* and the Sultan opposed the reform program proposed by the French. Notwithstanding his declared opposition to French reforms, the Sultan secured permission from the French, and later, British, Spanish, and American governments to travel through the Spanish zone of Morocco and visit Tangier in exchange for his signature on the reform decrees.

This visit was the first such journey by a Moroccan sovereign since 1899, and it boosted the nationalist cause in many ways. The journey received popular acclaim in the French zone. In a Tangier speech to Moroccan notables, French and Spanish officials, and the diplomatic community (April 10, 1947), the Sultan departed from the prepared text, which lavished praise on France's work in Morocco, opting instead to discuss the need for reform.[36]

As the southern nationalists gained momentum, their northern counterparts latched on, and in 1951, a National Front unified rival parties in both the north and the south. The Moroccan nationalist movement continued to grow with the sultan's active participation. It also received support from the international community, particularly the Arab League, Egypt, and the United Nations. The movement got mass support in cities like Casablanca, where workers organized strikes and acts of violence. In the countryside, the local population was willing to resort to arms to support the sultan if necessary. Here, too, the French answered with additional repression.

At the same time, trade union activity began in Casablanca, even though the law prohibited the formation of trade unions. Abderrahim Bouabid and Tayyib Bouazza started to organize a national trade union movement in 1949, but news of the fate of Ferhat Hashdad, the Tunisian trade union leader murdered at the hands of nationalists, caused angry outcries in Casablanca. The riot which followed on December 7 and 8, 1952 indicated the strength and magnitude of communal and national feelings. The local French administration exacerbated tensions through a gross miscalculation in 1953, deposing the traditional Muslim ruler of Morocco, Sultan Ibn Youssef, and replacing him with a puppet, Ben Arafa.[37] This gave fresh fuel to the nationalist cause, in as much as the French action was interpreted as an assault on Islam. Casablanca and other urban centers such as Fez, Port Lyautey, and Marrakesh were consumed by violence. From September 1953 to September 1955, Casablanca alone recorded 2,276 acts of violence and sabotage and the deaths of sixty-six Europeans and 406 Moroccans.[38] Mass protests shook Moroccan towns where new trade unions were now very active. Many activists died in clashes with French troops.

In 1955, at the moment when one guerrilla war had shown its power in Tunisia and a second was exploding in Algeria, a third guerrilla war began in Mo-

---

35. Knapp, *North West Africa*, 277–8.
36. Ibid., 278.
37. Ibid., 278–9.
38. Ibid., 280.

rocco. Acting on the inspiration of Abd al-Karim thirty years earlier, a people's army of guerrilla bands became active in the hills.

The French found themselves alone in Morocco. They had counted on the antinationalist support of several Berber chiefs, notably al-Glaoui of Marrakesh, and on Sultan Ben Arafa, but the latter had no power outside his palace walls. Both men proved useless to the French, and their support withered away. Under mounting pressure, the Fauré government in France arranged the Aix-les-Baines Conference to bring together Morocco's representatives. The Conference agreed on Ben Arafa's departure (without abdication), the formation of a throne council, and the establishment of a national union to negotiate with France.[39] The conference's success paved the way for negotiations with Sultan Mohammed Ibn Youssef. Conceding, the French restored him to his throne as Mohammed V, king of an independent Morocco, and opened negotiations with *Istiqlal*. Morocco became independent on March 2, 1956, just eighteen days before Tunisia also won its independence.

Libya

At the end of World War II, Libya was essentially a nomadic nation with a strong belief in particularism. Its inhabitants did not live under a political authority that unified the disparate elements of its polity. When nationalist movements arose in Libya, therefore, its various groups compromised with the colonial administration.

Following its 1922 fascist coup, however, Italy pursued an energetic policy on Libya, invading the territory with mechanized transport and aircraft from World War I. Rapid colonization followed. Most of the public lands owned by the previous Turkish administration were appropriated by the Italian colonizers, especially after General de Bono, the Italian governor of Tripolitania, drew up a program of demographic colonization.[40] Generous concessions to Italians and other Europeans were made to encourage agricultural investment. The plains of Tajura, the hills of Khums, the Tarhuna mountains, the central Jaffara plains, and, following the Italo-Sanusi war, the Sanusi estates were all seized for colonization. In a ten-year conquest, the Italians imprisoned and exterminated their rivals. As the war ended, Italy relegated numerous Bedouins to concentration camps. By 1930, the leader of the Cyrenaican resistance, the elderly Umar al-Mukhtar, was captured and hanged. Vast expanses of land were taken from people who did not know about an Italian proclamation that managed Libya's "public" lands.[41] Even when the Cyrenaican people taken to Sirta camps were allowed to return in 1932, they were kept under close surveillance.

Following the Italo-Sanusi war, the Italians proved themselves enterprising colonialists and transformed Tripoli into one of the Mediterranean's most beautiful cities. De Bono's fascist program of demographic colonization, continued by

39. Ibid., 282.
40. Abun-Nasr, *A History of the Maghrib in the Islamic Period,* 400.
41. Hallett, *Africa since 1875,* 236–7; Abun-Nasr, *A History of the Maghrib in the Islamic Period,* 401–2.

the Italian Marshal Italo Balbo, governor of Libya in 1934, and approved by Mussolini in 1938, provided for the settlement of carefully-selected Italian peasants. In 1938, twenty thousand colonists left Italy for Libya, and in 1939, twelve thousand more joined them. Conceiving its colonial enterprise in terms of national honor and strength, Italy invested in public works such as roads, railways, and ports. At the outbreak of World War II, 120,000 Italians lived in Libya, comprising twelve per cent of Libya's population.[42]

In October 1939, Tripolitanian and Cyrenaican refugees in Cairo urged closer cooperation with Sanusi leader Sayyid Muhammad Idris. While many Tripolitanians supported the Axis powers, Sayyid agreed to organize a force under British command in Cyrenaica in June 1940. This widened the rift between Tripolitanians and Cyrenaicans. A Tripolitanian offer to support the war against the Axis powers was ignored, because the Tripolitanians made the support conditional upon Tripolitania's independence after the war. After October 1942, the British pursued retreating Axis forces across North Africa. By February 1943, the British controlled both Tripolitania and Cyrenaica. The fall of Tripoli to the British in 1943 ended Italian rule in North Africa.[43]

Following World War II, British military administrators governed Tripolitania and Cyrenaica while the French controlled the Fezzan. In the immediate aftermath of the war, however, the great powers failed to agree on a trusteeship system. Instead, they called on the United Nations to resolve the issue. In November 1949, the U.N. General Assembly resolved that Libya should become independent in two years. With the help of a U.N. commissioner, Sayyid Muhammad Idris was accepted by the Tripolitanians and, later, by the Cyrenaicans as the leader of Libya. In December 1951, Libya became the first North African colony to achieve independence.[44]

Some people predicted that provincial disunity among Tripolitania, Cyrenaica, and the Fezzan would undermine Lybia's new federal structure. Instead, Libyan national consciousness steadily grew, as King Idris provided an effective focus for national unity. Unfortunately, Idris left most of the state's affairs in the hands of wealthy families who progressively lost touch with the people and used their positions for personal enrichment.

King Idris's tenure of office came to a sudden end when Colonel Muamar Al-Qadhafi led a military coup in 1969. The new ruling junta, composed of Colonel Qadhafi and a number of young army officers, abolished the monarchy and proclaimed a republic.[45] Inspired by the career of President Nasser of Egypt, they dismissed all state functionaries associated with the old regime, vigorously attacked manifestations of European influence, demanded the removal of the British and American bases at El Adem and Wheelus Field, and established cordial diplomatic relations with the United Arab Republic and the Sudan.

42. Abun-Nasr, *A History of the Maghrib in the Islamic Period*, 401.
43. Hallett, *Africa Since 1875*, 236–7.
44. Ibid., 238.
45. Shillington, *History of Africa*, 382; Davidson, *Modern Africa*, 116.

Egypt

While the interwar years witnessed imperialism's last push in northeast Africa, they also saw a rise in anticolonial militancy and effective political organization for independence in that region. Economic deprivation set the stage for the massive discontent that incited strikes and demonstrations in Egypt. This unrest was exacerbated by the arrest of the Egyptian leader Sa'd Zaghlul and two colleagues on March 8, 1919. The arrests led to the 1919 revolution in which students from Al-Azhar University, transport workers, judges, and lawyers participated. One major consequence of the 1919 revolution was that Britain abolished its protectorate and recognized Egypt's independence on February 28, 1922.[46] However, Egypt ceased to be a British colony in name only. In reality, Egypt became a "neocolony," because Britain was still guarding its imperial frontier in the Suez Canal zone even though Egyptians could now govern themselves. The British government recognized Egyptian independence subject to the following four conditions:

1. British armed forces would continue to guard imperial lines of communication through Egypt, between the Mediterranean Sea and the Red Sea
2. Britain would be responsible for defending Egypt against external attack
3. Britain would protect foreign interests inside Egypt
4. Egypt would accept British control of the "Anglo-Egyptian condominium" of the Sudan[47]

Egyptian nationalists accepted this partial independence, since their main party, the Wafd (formed in 1918 by Zaghlul Pasha), was still weak. It was disliked by Egypt's King Faud, however, who saw it as a rival power base. Popular discontent increased during the Great Depression and plunged Egypt into economic crisis. The crisis, growing civil strife, and Italy's 1935 invasion of Ethiopia made Britain's position in Egypt somewhat tenuous. A 1936 Anglo-Egyptian treaty between the British imperial government and the Wafd government under Zaghlul's successor, Nahas Pasha (1876–1965), made some concessions to Egyptian nationalists. But the concessions altered nothing of substance: only on the third and least important of the four conditions of 1922, the protection of foreign interests, did Britain give way[48].

Britain used Egypt as a military base from which to combat Italian and German attempts to occupy the country, and it successfully drove the Germans out of North Africa by 1943. Although Egypt's government did not declare war against the Italians and Germans, Wafd nationalists took a pro-British position, believing that a takeover by fascist Italians and Nazi Germans would be worse than contin-

---

46. Basil Davidson, *Modern Africa. A Social and Political History*, 110; H.A. Ibrahim, "Politics and Nationalism in North-East Africa, 1939–35," in *General History of Africa. VII. Africa Under Colonial Domination 1880–1935*, A. Adu Boahen ed. (Paris: UNESCO, 1985), 583–6.

47. Davidson, *Modern Africa. A Social and Political History*, 110; Ibrahim, "Politics and Nationalism in North-East Africa, 1939–35," in *General History of Africa. VII. Africa Under Colonial Domination 1880–1935*, A. Adu Boahen ed. (Paris: UNESCO, 1985), 583–6.

48. Davidson, *Modern Africa*, 111.

ued British occupation.[49] In 1942, the long-standing rivalry between Egyptian King Farouk (who succeeded to the throne in 1936) and the Wafd came to a head. The British settled the dispute by forcing King Farouk to accept another Wafd government under Nahas Pasha.

As it did elsewhere, the tide of nationalism in Egypt intensified after World War II. A new dynamic was introduced into Egyptian politics: the State of Israel was founded, despite Egyptian and Arab attempts to prevent it. In addition to this, Israel's expansion from its small initial base strained relations between Egypt and Britain, as the Arab world held Britain responsible for surrendering most of Arab Palestine to Israel. Egyptian guerrilla activity against Britain's continued occupation of the Suez Canal Zone continued in 1952.[50] The Muslim Brotherhood, which had become a significant mass movement since its foundation in 1922, peaked in 1948 and 1949, at about the same time as Israel's defeat of Egypt in Palestine. At the Muslim Brotherhood's core stood "new traditionalists" who believed in a glorified Muslim past. The Brotherhood became a strong force in Egyptian politics during the 1940s and 1950s, and with as many as 200,000 members, the organization resisted suppression until 1966.

Egypt's defeat by Israel in 1948 and 1949 in the struggle over Palestine discredited both the Egyptian monarch and Nahas Pasha and created a leadership vacuum in Egypt, which was exploited by a group of young military officers in 1952. The officers opposed the monarchy and Egypt's old regime on the one hand and Britain's military presence in Egypt and the Suez Canal Zone on the other. Favoring economic and social justice for all Egyptians, these young army officers, led by Lieutenant Colonel Gamal Abdel Nasser, seized control of Cairo in a bloodless coup d'etat and gradually established control over the country. Since the old nationalists and the Wafd seemed unable to win real independence, the government's overthrow received wide support.[51] The young officers formed a new government under General Muhamed Naguib and declared Egypt a republic on February 10, 1953. The deposed King Farouk went quietly into exile.[52]

The progressive young army officers who played a vital role in the 1953 revolution found General Naguib too conservative and ousted him in a 1954 palace coup d'etat. The dynamic and popular Gamal Nasser became president. Responding to these new circumstances, the British agreed in July 1954 to evacuate their forces within twenty months. They kept this agreement, but the United States and other Western European powers grew increasingly hostile to Nasser's rhetoric and policies, which they viewed as antithetical to Western influence. In a sort of rapprochement, Nasser requested American and British financial aid to build the Aswan Dam across the Nile to improve agricultural production in Egypt. When the United States and Britain agreed to help and later retracted their offer in July 1956, Nasser constructed the dam with Soviet aid and turned the foreign-owned Suez Canal into Egyptian national property.[53]

---

49. Philip Curtin, Steven Feierman, Leonard Thompson, and Jan Vansina, *African History* (Boston: Little Brown and Company, 1978), 493–4.
50. Davidson, *Modern Africa*, 111.
51. Davidson, *Modern Africa*, 111; Philip Curtin et al., *Modern Africa*, 494.
52. Davidson, *Modern Africa*, 111–2.
53. For details, see Scott Lucas, ed. *Britain and Suez, The Lion's Last Roar*, (Manchester, Machester University Press, 1996); Davidson, *Modern Africa*, 112.

Nasser's actions galvanized Britain's determination to get rid of Nasser by any possible means. In the context of the Cold War, Nasser's radical nationalism seemed, to the West, to represent some kind of communism, and therefore, a threat to Western supremacy. At the same time, the Western powers were attracted by an Israeli leadership eager to cripple Egypt's new-found pride.[54]

A joint British, French, and Israeli invasion of the Suez Canal Zone was secretly planned. In November 1956, Israeli and allied troops invaded the Canal Zone. The invasion was ostensibly aimed at destroying Nasser's regime and replacing it with one more amenable to Western and Israeli interests. The Suez invasion met with worldwide condemnation. When the United States declared its opposition to it, the Israeli, British, and French invaders quickly withdrew from Egyptian soil. In the wake of the Suez Crisis, Egypt emerged as a truly independent state for the first time in modern history.[55]

Conclusion

North African nationalist agitation garnered greater strength after World War II, fueled in part by European land appropriations, a lack of access to political and economic participation, perceived assaults on Islam, and attempts at stifling trade union activity, among other factors. Whatever recovery followed the great Depression hardly trickled down to North Africans, and demands for the amelioration of their condition fell on deaf ears.

In Algeria, Ferhat Abbas and other leaders drew up the Manifesto of the Algerian People as a blueprint for Algeria's nationalist struggle. However, frustration at the lack of progress in political and economic equality occasioned the birth of the National Liberation Front, which launched the 1954 revolution and eventually won Algeria's independence.

In Tunisia, the January 1939 workers' demonstrations led to repression that crippled the nationalist movement. However, the activities of the Tunisian ruler Munsif Bey kept the nationalist flame burning. Police brutality and repression led to strikes, demonstrations, and the formation of a united front by the Union Générale Tunisienne du Travail and the Neo-Destour in 1952. From mountain bases, Tunisian guerrillas launched attacks against the settler population, and the increased violence forced the French to invite Bourguiba to the autonomy talks that eventually led to independence.

In Morocco, the French defeat in 1940 and the Allied landings in North Africa in 1942 led to the collapse of the pro-Vichy French administration. In 1943, a group of professionals formed the *Istiqlal* party and sent a manifesto to France, Britain, the United States, and the Soviet Union demanding independence. Violence, arson, sabotage, and guerrilla bands based in the hills ultimately forced the French to restore Mohammed Youssef as king of an independent Morocco in 1956.

---

54. Lucas, ed. *Britain and Suez, The Lion's Last Roar*, pp. 22–31. Davidson, *Modern Africa*, 112.

55. For details see Scott Lucas, ed. *Britain and Suez, The Lion's Last Roar*, (Manchester, Manchester University Press, 1996); Davidson, *Modern Africa*, 112.

In Egypt, the token independence granted by the British in 1922, continued British control of the Suez Canal zone, and Britain's surrender of part of Arab Palestine to Israel led to intense guerrilla activity. Egyptian anger over the creation of Israel on Arab land and Israel's defeat of Egypt in the 1948–1949 war eventually resulted in the 1952 revolution led by Lieutenant Colonel Gamal Abdel Nasser. When the Israeli-French-British invasion of the Suez Canal Zone (the 1956 Suez Crisis) met with wide condemnation, British, Israeli, and French troops withdrew, leaving Egypt as a truly independent North African state.

Review Questions

1. What role did Ferhat Abbas play in Algeria's struggle for independence?
2. Did the National Movement in Algeria reach its final phase of fulfillment with the formation of the National Liberation Front?
3. What role did economic factors, especially land appropriation, unemployment, and lack of economic opportunities after World War II play in the struggle for North African independence?
4. How and why did northern and southern Libyan nationalist movements unite to fight for independence?
5. What was the Suez Canal Crisis of 1956? How did it hasten Egyptian autonomy from Britain?

Additional Reading

Hoisington, William A. *The Casablanca Connection: French Colonial Policy, 1936–1943*. Chapel Hill: University of North Carolina Press, 1984.

Lucas, Scott., ed. *Britain and Suez: The Lion's Last Roar*. Manchester: Manchester University Press, 1996.

Salem, Norma. *Habib Bourguiba, Islam and the Creation of Tunisia*. London: Croom Helm, 1984.

Smith, Tony. *The French Stake in Algeria, 1945–1962*. Ithaca, NY: Cornell University Press, 1978.

Stephan, Bernard. *The Franco-Moroccan Conflict, 1943–56*. New Haven: Yale University Press, 1968.

Chapter 18

West Africa

Akanmu G. Adebayo

This chapter examines the last years of colonialism in West Africa. It focuses on the factors responsible for decolonization and the paths to independence in the territories under British, French, and Portuguese rule. It answers two main questions: Why was nationalism delayed in the areas under French and Portuguese rule? What consequences did the different methods of decolonization in anglophone, francophone, and lusophone countries have on postcolonial economy and politics? Finally, it discusses the legacies of colonialism in West Africa.

* * *

The Setting

Decolonization varied from colony to colony. In some, it was swift and peaceful; in others, it was a protracted process that ended in violence. In West Africa, with the exception of Portuguese Guinea, decolonization was achieved through peaceful and constitutional processes. One major reason for this was the absence, in any significant numbers, of European settlers in the region. Compared to other parts of Africa, such as Kenya, Algeria, Zimbabwe, and South Africa, West Africa was spared the complications that the political and economic provisions that were made for sizable European settler populations often brought to the politics of decolonization. Another reason for the peaceful process was the non-strategic nature of West Africa during the Cold War: the region offered no attraction for the superpowers. Most West African countries did not have (and were not located near) strategic waterways such as the Suez Canal in Egypt or the Gulf of Aden in Somalia. There were no compelling reasons for any colonial power to tarry longer in West Africa than the 1960s. In Nigeria, petroleum, a mineral of great economic and possibly strategic significance, had not been discovered in commercial quantities before the decision was made to transfer power. Portugal was the only colonial power that refused to leave and did so for other reasons than the Cold War.

Decolonization was, first and foremost, a process that ended in the transfer of power from Europeans to African leaders. This transfer did not favor the traditional elite, who were defeated by Europeans at the onset of colonialism. Instead, the European rulers chose an entirely new elite, made up of those educated in Christian and secular institutions. Furthermore, through the method of decolonization, many European powers ensured that *political* independence was granted while they still held the key to economic control. Thus, decolonization has come to be seen as "strategic withdrawal."[1]

Many factors, both internal and external, promoted the development of a nationalist consciousness in West Africa. Internal factors included the legacies of protest in the period prior to 1939, the increased radicalization of the West African press, and the expansion of educational opportunities that broadened the base of the educated elite. Others were the growth of cities through rural-urban migration, subsequent social and political problems, and the grievances against colonialism which existed in every class of society. External factors included Pan-Africanism, which awakened political consciousness among West Africans, the Italian invasion of Ethiopia, which outraged all nationalists, and the success of Asian and Arab nationalists, which gave West African nationalists a sense of optimism. Others were the effects of World War II, the international outcry against colonialism after the war, and political changes in Britain that brought a Labour Party that was sympathetic to decolonization into power. In this section, I look at some of these factors closely and explain how they affected the development of nationalism in West Africa. I begin with the grievances against colonialism.

All Africans had grievances against colonialism, but not all of them were able to express them in the form of nationalist agitation. Farmers endured forced labor, police and court brutalities, conscription during the World Wars, land alienation in settler colonies, and direct taxation and other levies, which drove many into debt. Muslim farmers also endured religious persecution. The working class was small but it was growing in membership as a result of colonial policies and programs. It included industrial, mine, railway, and port authority workers who were subjected to severe working conditions, earned low wages, were separated from their families for varying lengths of time, lacked high-level training and adequate protection on the job, and were conscripted into the military.

The business class was also small but growing. It consisted of men and women who engaged principally in the transportation business and in retail trading. The members of this class made some profit but could not significantly increase their wealth because they had little access to investment capital. Most banks were owned by expatriates, and there were allegations of discrimination against the African business elite in the granting of credit facilities. The colonial state and merchant companies monopolized the lucrative import-export trade business, although the growing elite would have liked nothing better than to replace the expatriate executives.

West African intellectuals and professionals were highly educated, but they suffered from salary discrimination and from a color bar in some colonies. They were alienated from the majority, and, as a result, colonial governments believed that they did not represent the people. In Nigeria in 1922, Governor Hugh Clifford berated the members of the Lagos elite and dared them to show why they should be regarded as spokesmen of the illiterate masses in the villages and small towns.

The traditional rulers also had grievances. They had lost power to the colonizers. Many religious leaders had been forced into hiding by a combination of

---

1. Readers are encouraged to read original articles and lively debates on decolonization in the following journals: *Journal of African History*, *Journal of Imperial and Commonwealth History*, and *International Journal of African Historical Studies*.

the Christianization movement, which drew many away from traditional worship, and colonial policies that abolished certain traditional practices and fetishes. Traditional political leaders, such as kings, chiefs, and headmen, found their positions either downgraded or eradicated in many colonies. In British colonies, where they exercised some power, such rulers lacked final authority.

Of all these categories of people, it was the educated elite who had the opportunity to translate their grievances into nationalist agitation. Generally, there were two phases of unrest, separated by World War II. By 1957, the winds of change that blew fiercely in West Africa during and after the war had produced independence for Ghana. Three years later most of West Africa had achieved independence. Although West Africa was not a battlefield, World War II had a significant impact on the region and on the advancement of nationalism, an impact that can be appreciated by comparing nationalism in the prewar and postwar eras.

Nationalism in British West Africa was strong before 1939, although most nationalist groups only demanded reforms in the colonial system and did not challenge the basis of colonialism. The most active groups were the National Council of British West Africa (NCBWA), the West African Student Union (WASU), the Nigerian National Democratic Party (NNDP), the Nigerian Youth Movement (NYM), and the West African Youth League (WAYL).

These parties were founded at different times between 1919 and 1938, often for specific purposes. For example, the NCBWA was established in 1919 by the Gold Coast attorney J. E. Casely Hayford. Its members were the educated elite of the coastal cities and their demands focused on matters of interest to their class. In effect, they demanded the expansion of the membership of the Gold Coast Legislative Council and protested against discrimination in the colonial civil service. They also called for the establishment of a university in West Africa. Although the NCBWA enjoyed pan-West African membership, its objectives were limited to seeking reforms in the colonial administration.

The NYM was a more radical organization. It was founded in 1934 primarily to protest, albeit unsuccessfully, the establishment of Yaba Higher College as a non-degree-awarding institution. Its membership was more national in character than that of any previous organization, it and included such men as H. O. Davies, Obafemi Awolowo, and Ernest Ikoli. These leaders interpreted British policy as racist. They reasoned that since Yaba College was not affiliated with a British university, the diplomas it granted would be inferior to any awarded by British institutions and that its African graduates would always be considered inferior to British officials. The movement received a boost when Nnamdi Azikiwe returned to Nigeria in 1937: it was transformed into a national organization with branches all over the country. It established a newspaper, the *Daily Service*, to disseminate information and to serve as the mouthpiece of national protest. The party was so popular that in 1938 it won election into the Lagos Town Council and won all three Lagos seats in the Legislative Council, thus ending the monopoly of Herbert Macaulay and the NNDP. Unfortunately, the party was soon torn apart by rivalries among its leaders.

In comparison to that in the British colonies, nationalist political consciousness before the war was limited in areas under French rule. This was due partly to the opportunity for the educated elite in French territories to participate in local and even in French politics. As a result, Blaise Diagne was elected into the French parliament as early as 1914.

World War II and
West African Nationalism

Despite their limitations, the political parties of the prewar era served as a rallying focus for the educated elite. They also grabbed the attention of the colonial powers whenever they linked forces with labor unions and grassroots organizations. Postwar nationalism built upon these prewar traditions of organization and protest. The war seemed to have supplied the missing pieces in West African nationalism.

World War II contributed to the growth of nationalism and also changed the character of protest in West Africa. First, it broke the myth of European superiority. Colonial officials had created the image of a superior race in Africa; in their deportment and through their isolation from colonial populations, they had presented themselves as demi-gods. The war burst this bubble. Under Nazi pressure, British and French imperialists recruited large numbers of Africans for their militaries. Different figures have been given for the number of African recruits, but J. B. Webster and Adu Boahen estimated that the number of men in the Royal West African Frontier Force increased from 7,000 to 176,000 during the war. About 100,000 returned to Nigeria and 65,000 returned to Ghana after the war. Thousands more were recruited for the Free French force from French West and Equatorial Africa. Military training and service was an immediately enlightening experience for these soldiers, many of whom got the opportunity to visit places outside West Africa and observe, first hand, the progress and development colonialism had denied them. They enjoyed a relatively high standard of living in the military. Their outlook on life and politics had changed by the time the war ended, and back home they became staunch supporters of urban nationalists, spreading news and information about their military service to rural areas.

However, it was the combat experience that was the most eye-opening for the African recruits. Fighting beside Europeans in North Africa, Asia, and Europe, African soldiers were able to see Europeans at close range. They saw the weak and the strong, the cowardly and the brave. They saw Europeans cry, laugh, and show emotion. These were situations in which they had never seen Europeans before. Mingling with the white soldiers in hotels, bars, and dance halls changed African soldiers' perception of white men. A few months of shooting Germans in combat, unfortunate as it may seem, did more to break the myth of European superiority than did years of colonial education. Ex-servicemen came back to tell their stories to all that cared to listen. The war was a leveler.

Secondly, Germany's defeat of France early in the war humiliated a principal colonial power in West Africa. French colonial rule was undermined, and the French government in exile, led by General Charles de Gaulle, lacked the resources necessary to prosecute the war. Ironically, France depended on African soldiers, workers, and resources to continue fighting. French West Africa did not declare independence at this time partly because the educated elites were loyal to France and partly because the British moved quickly to provide much-needed support for the French administration in the region.

Thirdly, harsh programs introduced under the general umbrella of "war efforts" caused suffering and shortages of essential commodities in the colonies. Taxes were increased while the cost of living rose. The hardships caused by these "war efforts" led to protest. Workers went on strike and colonial administrations put down their protests with severity. Nationalists joined workers in these protests and were able to transform labor unrest into agitation for self-government.

Furthermore, news of political changes in Asia filtered into West Africa, particularly news of the defeat of the Euro-American imperial powers by the Japanese. In addition, the Japanese slogan of "Asia for Asians" found echoes in West Africa.

Yet perhaps the most significant contribution of World War II to the development of nationalist activities in West Africa was U.S. pressure for a free, democratic world order.[2] The Atlantic Charter (see Appendix), issued jointly by the U.S. and Britain, declared the two countries' respect for "the right of all people to choose the form of government under which they will live; and the wish to see sovereign rights and self government restored to those who have been forcibly deprived of them." Britain became a victim of its own wartime propaganda. The Atlantic Charter was a statement the British obviously did not intend to honor; but the US, itself a colonial power in Asia and the Pacific, continued to encourage the British and the French to plan for decolonization after the war because of pressure from African and African American leaders.

Finally, the charter of the United Nations (UN) gave hope to colonial subjects everywhere. The UN, which was formed at the end of the war, was an anticolonial body that made the eradication of colonialism one of its major principles. It gave the African leaders a forum in which they could criticize colonialism and attack colonial powers.

The period between 1940 and 1960 is often called the age of decolonization in West Africa. The question is: did the colonial powers leave of their own free will or were they pushed out by their colonial subjects? Writings sympathetic to British and French interests tend to suggest that the colonial powers left and were not expelled. Those sympathetic to African interests indicate that colonialism was flushed out by the rising protests of the people. A consensus is emerging on the subject. It seems more profitable to see decolonization as both pull and push: colonial powers pulled out partly because colonial subjects pushed them out and partly as a result of their own volition.

It is probably fair to say that colonialism could have continued for a prolonged period after World War II if three conditions had been met: if the colonized people had not protested, if public opinion in the metropolitan countries had favored continued colonial commitments, and if imperialism had continued to receive international recognition. These conditions were not met. In postwar international politics, the imperial nations lost their domination of the world balance of power. And, according to Wm Roger Louis and Ronald Robinson, at both the metropolitan and colonial levels "attitudes hardened as ideologies changed and political movements and parties became assertive."[3] As the war was coming to an end, British and French public opinion was against continued colonial engagements, and West African elites in British colonies began to gear up for what they considered the final showdown with imperialism.

---

2. For more information on the role of the U.S. in the decolonization of West Africa, see Ebere Nwaubani, *The United States and Decolonization in West Africa, 1950-1960* (Rochester, NY: University of Rochester Press, 2001).

3. Prosser Gifford and Wm Roger Louis, eds. *The Transfer of Power in Africa: Decolonization, 1940-1960*. New Haven, CT: Yale University Press, 1982, p. 53.

We may use the idea that decolonization was a pull-push affair to explain the differences in the approach to decolonization by the French and British in West Africa. In terms of pull, the two colonial powers were faced with three questions in the postwar era: who would inherit power among the competing nationalist groups; how soon could these leaders be trained to take over; and who should rule and according to what principles?[4] Similarities and variations in French and British responses to these questions made French and British decolonization similar or different. For instance, the British had come to see the end of colonialism as inevitable, while the French, with their belief that Africans would become assimilated into French culture, did not believe that colonialism would wither away. Moreover, it would seem that the British were better prepared to answer these questions than the French: the British had had to deal with decolonization more frequently, and British relations with the US, decreased Britain's dependence on its colonies for postwar economic recovery.

In terms of push, we also see significant differences. West African leaders in French territories were less desirous of independence than their counterparts in British lands. This has often been explained as a result of the success of assimilation: African leaders were content with their roles in the French government. After all, Léopold Senghor and Félix Houphouët-Boigny, two French West African leaders, were ministers in the French government.

The success of assimilation alone, however, cannot sufficiently explain the slow pace of the anticolonial struggle in French West Africa. Indeed, British and French colonial education policies were comparable, and radical leadership in British West Africa emerged mainly among those educated abroad (particularly in the United States) and among those influenced by the Black politicians of North America and the Caribbean, men such as Nnamdi Azikiwe and Kwame Nkrumah. Therefore, it is probably more correct to argue that by their diffidence in seeking immediate independence, French West African leaders were only being pragmatic. It was inconceivable that France would have let them go before or immediately after the war, given the French experience in Vietnam, Lebanon, and Algeria. Moreover, given their weak economies and the possibility that French West Africa would be balkanized with independence, Senghor and Houphouët-Boigny probably reasoned that independence would further weaken their countries and place them in positions that were no better than those they held during colonialism. Thus, they supported the federation and were reluctant to press for independence until the emergence of Sekou's radical leadership.

Broadly speaking, there were two kinds of nationalism in West Africa. Both were present in each country to varying degrees, and both contributed either positively or negatively to the pace and style of decolonization. They also influenced the makeups and policies of postcolonial governments. The first type was ethnic nationalism. It was most notable in Nigeria, Côte d'Ivoire and Sierra Leone. Here, political parties were either ethnically based or had emerged from ethnic or cultural improvement associations. For instance, in Nigeria, the Action Group emerged from Egbe Omo Oduduwa, a Yoruba cultural and improvement association. In ethnic nationalism, political leaders saw themselves first as champions

---

4. For more details on this theme, readers are encouraged to see Tony Smith, "Patterns in the Transfer of Power: A Comparative Study of French and British Decolonization," in Prosser Gifford and Wm Roger Louis, *op. cit.* pp. 87–115.

Figure 18.1. Félix Houphouët-Boigny of Côte d'Ivoire.

and defenders of the interests of their ethnic group vis-à-vis other competing ethnic interests. Thus, leadership of anticolonial protests was diffused among ethnically based parties, and there were constant power struggles and petty quarrels among the ethnic leaders. This type of nationalism played into the hands of the colonial powers, delayed dates of independence, and continued to haunt the countries involved, sometimes leading to civil war. Unlike in North Africa, religion did not play a direct role in West African nationalism. However, in Nigeria, Mali, Guinea, and Senegal, religious and ethnic affiliations were sometimes coterminous, and aspects of anticolonial protests were based on religious affiliation.

The second type was the multiethnic nationalism typical of Ghana and Senegal. Here, political parties were established with a national mandate. Members and leaders of the parties came from various ethnic groups. Differences were often based on ideologies or principles rather than ethnic affiliations. In Ghana, for instance, although the Akan-speaking group formed a slight majority in the population, an Akan nationalism did not develop to oppose the non-Akan.

Four major tools were used by West African nationalists in their anticolonial protests. These were constitutional conferences, political parties or organizations, labor activities such as strikes and sit-ins, and political mobilization through a widely circulating press and yellow journalism. Constitutional conferences deserve a few words of explanation. Constitutions are the organic law of the state. They give official legal backing to negotiated arrangements and compromises.

They pass down written, shared, and sacred traditions from one generation to another. Constitutional arrangements were a required part of the decolonization process because they established the legal basis of the state at independence. In studying decolonization, therefore, attention must be paid to constitutional processes and provisions.

There were many deterrents to nationalism. They included ethnic politics, the readiness of some leaders to accept the dictates of colonial powers, and safeguards deliberately erected in new constitutions so that metropolitan capital could continue to be used to exploit West African resources after independence.

In the rest of this section I will examine the processes leading toward independence in West African states, beginning with Ghana in 1957 and ending with Portuguese Guinea in 1974.

Table 1 Independence in West Africa				
Year	Date	Country Name	Colonial Power	Leader at Independence
1957	March 6	Ghana	Britain	Kwame Nkrumah
1958	October 2	Guinea	France	Sékou Touré
1960	April 27	Togo	France	Sylvanus Olympio
1960	June 20	Mali	France	Modibo Keita
1960	August 1	Benin	France	Hubert Maga
1960	August 3	Niger	France	Hamani Diori
1960	August 5	Burkina Faso	France	Maurice Yameogo
1960	August 7	Côte d'Ivoire	France	Félix Houphouët-Boigny
1960	August 11	Chad	France	Ngarta Tombalbaye
1960	August 20	Senegal	France	Léopold Senghor
1960	October 1	Nigeria	Britain	Abubakar Tafawa Balewa
1960	November 28	Mauritania	France	Mukhtar Ould Daddah
1961	April 27	Sierra Leone	Britain	Milton Margai
1965	February 18	Gambia	Britain	Dawda Jawara
1974	September 10	Guinea Bissau	Portugal	Luis Cabral

Paths Toward Independence: British West Africa

Many factors contributed to Ghana's becoming the first country to achieve independence in all of sub-Saharan Africa. The first was the long tradition of anticolonial protest, dating back to the protest against the poll tax in the 1860s, the land rights protest in the 1890s, and the youth movement in the 1930s. The second was the relative economic prosperity of the country, which resulted partly from the export of gold, cocoa, and other raw materials and led to the construction and expansion of socioeconomic services such as schools, roads, hospitals, railroads, and harbors. The expansion of educational opportunities, of course, led to a rise in the membership of the educated elite, a pool that swelled the ranks of

Figure 18.2.   Tafawa Balewa and Kwame Nkrumah.

nationalist leaders. The third was the relative absence of ethnic nationalism. From the very beginning, Ghanaian nationalism had been Pan-African, pan-regional, or multiethnic. From Casely Hayford to Kwame Nkrumah, Ghanaian leaders strove to build bridges across ethnic divides.

Postwar political activity in Ghana began in 1947 with the formation of the United Gold Coast Convention (UGCC). Founded by Dr. J. B. Danquah and other leaders, the aim of the UGCC was encapsulated as "self-government within the shortest possible time." In 1948, Kwame Nkrumah was invited home from the United States to be its general secretary.

One major event that rallied the people around the UGCC was the colonial administration's order that the farmers cut down cocoa trees that were certified as diseased. This bred disaffection among the Gold Coast farmers whose major economic activity was cocoa farming. Another grievance against colonialism that the UGCC exploited was the high price of imported consumer goods, against which a boycott was organized in 1948. A third grievance was that of the ex-servicemen who had become unemployed since their return. They organized and staged a protest march against the government in 1948. Rioting, looting, and destruction became widespread in the colony, and the colonial government blamed the UGCC for all these disturbances. J. B. Danquah and five others were arrested and jailed. The people hailed their jailed leaders as heroes and urged more radicalism. Realizing that the UGCC leaders could not meet this demand, Nkrumah began the groundwork for the formation of another party.

The new party was the Convention People's Party (CPP), which was formed in 1949 by Nkrumah, K. A. Gbedemah, and Kojo Botsio, all breakaway leaders of the UGCC. It was an instant success. The first objective the party pursued toward the realization of the ultimate goal of "self-government now" was coined "positive action." This was a nonviolent form of resistance characterized by general strikes, boycotts, and demonstrations.

In January 1950, the CPP organized a nationwide strike and boycott. As a result, party leaders, including Nkrumah, were arrested and jailed for sedition. The *Accra Evening News*, the party's newspaper, was also banned. This did not diminish the mass popularity of the party, as demonstrated in the 1951 elections in which the CPP won thirty-three seats against the UGCC's three. While in prison, Nkrumah was elected as honorable representative for Accra. He was released to form the government. In June of 1953, the CPP continued its nationalist agitation by submitting a set of proposals for a new constitution to the assembly. On the basis of these proposals, the 1954 constitution, which provided for an unofficial all-African cabinet, was written and adopted. In the election following the constitution's introduction, the party won seventy-nine out of 104 seats. This paved the way for internal self-government in 1954. In 1956, the CPP tabled a motion calling for complete independence. It was passed. On March 6, 1957, Ghana gained its independence and became the first West African country to do so.

As in Ghana, the postwar independence movement in Nigeria utilized political parties and constitutional talks. However, the Nigerian story was not as straightforward. The first political party in the postwar era was the National Council of Nigeria and the Cameroons, NCNC. By this time, the NYM was moribund, although its newspaper, the *Daily Service*, continued to enjoy a wide readership. Inaugurated by Dr. Nnamdi Azikiwe on August 26, 1944, at Glover Memorial Hall in Lagos, the NCNC began as a multiethnic party. Herbert Macaulay was elected president while Azikiwe became general secretary. Among the party's objectives were the achievement of national unity and the spread of political awareness aimed at realizing self-government, economic and political security, and social equality for Nigeria and its peoples. The party was made up of affiliated groups including trade unions, ethnic organizations, and social clubs. It supported the 1945 General Strike and rallied trade unions solidly behind itself through Azikiwe's paper, *The West African Pilot*. NCNC's support of the strike and its leaders' tour of the country, aimed at making the people aware of the issues involved in the struggle, made the nationalist leaders known and accepted by Nigerians.

In 1948, the party adopted its Freedom Charter, which asserted the people's right to independence and self-government. But the party soon faced a series of dilemmas. There was a quarrel among the leaders about the expenditure of £13,000 collected for the purpose of sending a delegation to London. The new governor, Sir J. Macpherson, also contributed to the lull in the pace of NCNC activities by promising to review the Richards Constitution, one of the principal targets of agitation.

Despite these difficulties, until 1951, the NCNC paraded an all-Nigerian membership. After 1951, Nigerian nationalism became almost wholly regionalized. The Richards Constitution, which partitioned Nigeria, had introduced regionalism into the country. Apart from the constitutional basis for regionalism, there was also an ethnic reason, as the Yoruba-Igbo rivalry in Lagos had almost torn the NCNC apart.

In December 1949, the first specifically regional party in Nigeria was formed. This was the Jama'riyah Mutanen Arewa, which transformed itself into the Northern Peoples Congress (NPC) in 1951. Its leaders were the Hausa-Fulani, the most prominent of whom were Ahmadu Bello, the *Sardauna* of Sokoto, and his

Figure 18.3. Chief Obafemi Awolowo of Nigeria.

able lieutenant Abubakar Tafawa Balewa. In the 1951 elections, the NPC won a majority of the northern seats, and in the 1954 elections, it gained the largest number of seats in the Federal House of Representatives.

The Action Group was another regional party formally founded in 1951. It was an outgrowth of the Egbe Omo Oduduwa, a cultural association of the Yoruba. Its founder and leader was Chief Obafemi Awolowo, and its primary objective was to contest and win elections in the Western Region. Together with the NPC, the Action Group did much to promote regionalism and ethnic nationalism in Nigeria. Before long, the Azikiwe-led NCNC became fully regionalized and supported by the Igbo. The result was that it became impossible for any party to be "national" enough to win a clear majority at the federal level.

Other parties formed in the north and in the Middle Belt had significant impacts on Nigerian nationalism. These included the Northern Elements Progressive Union (NEPU) and the United Middle Belt Congress (UMBC). NEPU was established by a dissident, socialist faction of the NPC, while the UMBC was a multiethnic party formed to protect and advance the interests of the people of the Middle Belt, a zone of territory and ethnic groups located in the southern parts of Northern Nigeria.

One major problem of the ethnic nationalism in Nigeria was that the parties involved often failed to cooperate with each other, which the British administration exploited to prolong its rule over Nigeria. For instance, in 1953, when the Action Group introduced the motion that would have made Nigeria independent by 1956, the NPC opposed it. Their explanation was that NPC leaders were not consulted before the motion was proposed, although another explanation was that the Northern Region was not yet ready for self-government. The opposition to the motion occasioned a major constitutional crisis when Action Group ministers resigned their posts. Constitutional conferences were held in 1953 and 1954, and the result was a federal constitution with which all parties seemed pleased.

After the 1953 constitutional crisis, the parties began to put aside their ethnic and regional differences when issues affecting the whole country were at stake. Although elections continued to be won or lost based on ethnic affiliations, the central government remained a coalition (implying varying degrees of cooperation) because no party could win a clear majority. Matters concerning national unity, independence, and economic development were debated with passion. In January 1960, a formal motion for independence was presented and passed unanimously. October 1, 1960 was set as the date of Nigerian independence.

A major feature of the path to Nigerian independence was constitutional revision. Between 1946 and 1960, the leadership elite and the British tinkered with the constitution so frequently that, by the time of independence, Nigerians were inclined to think that the solution to all their problems was to write a new constitution. Yet the British used those constitutions as a tool to transfer power to the Nigerian elites piecemeal. The Richards Constitution of 1946, for instance, established three regions: the Northern, Eastern, and Western Regions. Its main goal was to grant Nigerians political powers at the regional level while the British could continue to dominate in the center. As the system of government was still unitary, the regional governments were not autonomous. These governments were designed to give Nigerian politicians some training in parliamentary procedure and give the traditional rulers a significant say in the political process. The Richards Constitution was unsatisfactory to the elite and therefore severely criticized. As mentioned above, J. Macpherson, the new governor, tried to macromanage the debate and undercut the elites' protests by calling for a revision of the constitution.

The result was the adoption of the Macpherson Constitution in 1951, which retained the regional structure established by the Richards Constitution and gave Nigerians some representation in the central government. In other words, the new constitution permitted the limited selection of Nigerians into the central executive council. It encouraged the organization of ethnic political parties, led to an election into the House of Representatives, and preceeded the appointment of representatives of the major parties as ministers. Then, in 1953, the motion for self-government occasioned the constitutional crisis previously discussed and made the Macpherson Constitution unworkable. The revisions undertaken in 1953-1954 produced the Lyttelton Constitution, under which the autonomy of regional governments was recognized. It was clear to the elites where political power resided. The three leaders—Ahmadu Bello in the North, Nnamdi Azikiwe in the East, and Obafemi Awolowo in the West—became premiers of their regions and sent their deputies to the federal level. Thus began what was probably the most enterprising era in Nigerian history. The leaders started to implement political, social and economic reform programs mandated by their parties' ideologies and campaign promises. Among other things, the North embarked on *Shari'a* legal reforms, the East introduced oil palm mills, and the West began free education programs and rapid industrialization.

Yet the year 1954 did not mark the end of constitutional revision in Nigeria. Revisions in 1957 and 1959 preceeded the independence constitution of 1960, which retained the three-region federal structure but increased the power of the federal government. The country would have a parliamentary system patterned after that of the British. The president, who would also be the commander-in-chief of the armed forces, would represent the British Crown. Governmental powers would, however, be in the hands of a prime minister. As no party won a clear majority, the NPC and NCNC established a coalition government, leaving the Action Group in opposition. Thus, at independence, Dr. Azikiwe emerged as president, Sir Abubakar Tafawa Balewa as prime minister, and Chief Obafemi Awolowo as leader of the opposition in the House of Representatives.

Nationalism was delayed in the other two British colonies, Sierra Leone and the Gambia. In Sierra Leone the anticolonial movement suffered from one major problem: the relationship between the Creoles, who had dominated the country since its establishment by British abolitionists in 1787, and the indigenous peoples of the colony. The development of nationalism after World War II led to the establishment of democratic institutions in Sierra Leone. The Creoles had high hopes that they would be favored in the transfer of power, but the British decided on majority rule in the constitution introduced in 1951. As a result, Dr. (later Sir) Milton Margai, a Mende, formed the Sierra Leone People's Party (SLPP), the party that won the first elections held under the new constitution and led the country to independence in 1961. Margai was challenged by Siaka Stevens, who had established the All People's Congress, the party that won the elections held in 1967.

The problem in the Gambia was mainly fear of its neighbor, Senegal. The British had long been protective of the narrow strip of territory called the Gambia. Constitutions were written for the country in 1954, 1960, and 1962. Political parties were formed, the most prominent and popular being the People's Progressive Party (PPP) of Sir Dawda Jawara. Eventually, in February 1965, the Gambia achieved independence.

Paths toward Independence: French West Africa

One of the most interesting features of nationalism in French West Africa was the role of the educated elite, who had become assimilated into French nationality and culture. In this regard, nationalism reflected the role played by one particular school. The students at the William Ponty School in Dakar, Senegal came from all over French West African territory. They discussed colonial policies. Graduates of the school formed alumni associations and introduced programs of political education. It is not surprising that this school produced many of the leaders of the anticolonial movement in French West Africa after World War II.

Another interesting feature of French West African nationalism was the formation of local branches of French political parties in the colonies. In 1920, for

Figure 18.4. Coastal site, West Africa.

instance, a branch of the French Socialist Party was established by Lamine Gueye in Senegal. The movement began to gain popularity and local branches sprang up in Guinea and Sudan in the 1930s. When compared to British West Africa, there is no doubt that these were humble beginnings. It should be understood, however, that the educated elite in French West Africa had more obstacles to the development of nationalism than those in British territories.

First, while the system of indirect rule in British West Africa favored traditional rulers at the expense of the educated elite, even the limited application of the system of assimilation in French West Africa favored the employment of educated Africans in the French administration. Operating from narrow class perspectives, these men probably saw nothing wrong with the colonial administration. As citizens of France, they were free from the forced labor and arbitrary arrest from which colonial subjects suffered.

Secondly, while the British regarded their territories in West Africa as colonies to be relinquished some day when they were ripe for independence, the French viewed the colonies as extensions of France and the colonists as black French citizens or subjects. They attempted to make their colonies as "French" as possible except in color. The idea that they were a part of French civilization produced in the elite a pride in their French heritage and, at least in the pre-World War II era, precluded any burning desire for independence.

Thirdly, while Britain allowed the formation of political parties in West Africa (especially to contest elections provided for by newly introduced constitutions), this was not the case in French West Africa. There, the laws governing the colonies were French laws, and the people had no authority to debate any matter or form a pressure group. Persons deemed vocal or active in condemnation of colonial rule or bold enough to openly challenge the French administration were arrested, imprisoned, or exiled. This was the experience of Louis Hunkanrin of Benin (formerly Dahomey). A political follower of Blaise Diagne of Senegal and a veteran of World War I, Hunkanrin returned home after the war and founded the Dahomean branch of the French Ligue des Droits de l'Homme (League of the Rights of Man). The colonial government closely monitored Hunkanrin's activities. Not surprisingly, the administration connected him to the Porto Novo riots of 1923, and he was promptly exiled to Mauritania. Situations like this underscored the point that political survival was only for those who cooperated with the French, placed their French citizenship above their African heritage, and were prepared to defend even the worst colonial policies. One such person was Blaise Diagne, who was elected repeatedly to the French parliament from 1914 through 1934 and who defended forced labor before the International Labor Organization (ILO). Radical leadership in French West Africa had to wait.

World War II produced similar effects in French West Africa as in the British colonies. The French nation lost prestige when it was defeated in the early stages of the war by Germany. The Atlantic Charter raised the hope of colonial subjects everywhere. There was opposition to imperialism in America and in the United Nations, and the Pan-African Congress of 1945 received representation from French West Africa.

In addition to these effects, the war had other economic, social and political ramifications which directly impacted nationalism in French West Africa. First, the social discrimination that divided colonial peoples in West Africa into citizens and subjects was seriously challenged. Secondly, as a gesture of gratitude to the colonies for their loyalty and steadfast support for France during the German occupation, France reformed the colonial administration. General de Gaulle summoned the Brazzaville Conference of colonial governors in 1944. The conference adopted a set of resolutions, including the elimination of the *indigénat* (arbitrary arrest and detention) and forced labor. The resolutions also decentralized French administration and granted greater participation in the administration to Africans, including a promise that Africans would be represented in the postwar French Constituent Assembly which would draw up the new French constitution.

In the end, nationalism took a reformist course because French postwar reform policies were not far-reaching. The French Constituent Assembly that met in 1945 extended citizenship to all colonial peoples and recommended self-government within the French Union to any colony that wished it, but these reforms and recommendations were withdrawn by the post-de Gaulle, 1946 Constituent Assembly. Nationalist leaders' efforts to prevent the nullification of the 1945 Gaullist-era provisions led directly to the first organized political action in French West Africa. The leaders succeeded in reestablishing the reforms concerning citizenship, forced labor, and the *indigénat*. They also won a territorial assembly for each colony and representation in the French National Assembly, Senate, and French Union Assembly. But they lost autonomy, and this loss was responsible for the formation of indigenous nationalist political parties.

The first truly nationalist and African party in French West Africa, the Rassemblement Démocratique Africaine (RDA) or African Democratic Rally, was formed in 1946. This was a single party covering all the territories under French administration in West Africa. It was founded in Bamako, Mali, at a conference attended by representatives from all of the territories. Its leader was Félix Houphouët-Boigny of Côte d'Ivoire. The RDA was interterritorial in structure. Its leadership hierarchies included representatives from the component parts of French West Africa. The membership also included groups like labor unions, tribal unions, elite associations, cooperative unions, and women's organizations. Although it was allied with the French Communist Party—the only party with an anticolonial stance in France—and although it adopted the techniques of the

Communist Party in organization and propaganda, the RDA rejected the communist ideology for African communities. Its membership grew so rapidly that in 1950 it had 700,000 members from all over the French territories. It was the major party in Côte d'Ivoire, Guinea, Mali, Burkina Faso, and Niger. It did not have a branch in Mauritania.

The RDA began 1946 with victory, winning six seats in the French National Assembly, five seats in the Senate, and seven seats in the Territorial Assemblies. The French quickly resorted to repressive measures against the party because of its growing popularity. Its leaders were arbitrarily arrested, its supporters were persecuted, and its newspapers were banned. Election results were falsified and party meetings were outlawed, and the French encouraged the formation of rival parties that would not be as radical or influential.

Meanwhile, another party—the Indépendents d'Outre Mer (IOM) or Overseas Independents—fought for reform and independence in French West Africa. IOM was founded in 1948 by a group opposed to the linkage between the RDA and the Communist Party. Léopold Sédar Senghor was its most prominent leader and Senegal was, therefore, the party's major base. The French government collaborated with the IOM from 1948 to 1951, the "anti-RDA" period. It was during this time that the IOM won elections into the French National Assembly.

In addition to the problems caused by French repression, cracks began to show in the RDA along ideological lines and over the French proposal to organize the territories into a federation. There were leaders and members of the RDA who wanted the party to break its alliance with the Communist Party and work out compromise with the government. Through this change of tactics, it was reasoned, the RDA would become an entity acceptable to the French. The conservatives in the party were led by Houphouët-Boigny, who was appointed a minister in the French government in Paris. Radicals in the party, led by the secretary-general Gabriel d'Arboussier, preferred a policy of defiance.

Eventually, a split occurred over the issue of the *loi cadre* in 1956. Sponsored in 1956 by Houphouët-Boigny, the *loi cadre* was the French version of internal autonomy, which had already been granted in the British colonies of Nigeria and Ghana. Under this law, the power of the territorial assembly of each colony would increase and the powers of the governor-general at Dakar would be curtailed. Each colony would have direct links with France, bypassing the governor-general in Dakar. Each territory would be self-governing, except in defense, foreign affairs, and economic development policies. Houphouët-Boigny favored decentralization, it was thought, for selfish reasons. His country, Côte d'Ivoire, was the richest in French West Africa, and decentralization would guarantee that Côte d'Ivoire did not have to share its wealth with smaller, poorer countries in the region. It turned out that the French government also favored decentralization, for it guaranteed easier control of smaller, individual countries by France. The *loi cadre* created more controversy than the French or Houphouët-Boigny had anticipated. A small but articulate group, led by Léopold Senghor of Senegal, Sékou Touré of Guinea, and Modibo Keita of Mali, opposed the law. They favored a stronger federation, which they believed would ensure greater stability and development over the entire region.

In the midst of the rather complicated debate over federation, Charles de Gaulle came to power in France and ordered the writing of a new constitution for the colonies. An astute politician and an arch-imperialist, de Gaulle intervened in the ongoing debate in order to serve the interests of France to the fullest. Three standpoints on the issue emerged: a faction of the RDA led by Senghor favored a *strong* federation and links with France, another faction led by Houphouët Boigny favored a *loose* federation and links with France, and a third faction, led by Sékou Touré Toure, favored federation with total independence. De Gaulle favored federation and links with France, but he leaned towards Houphouët Boigny's position rather than Senghor's. A referendum was held in 1958 to determine the outcome of the debate.

The question French West African leaders were asked in the September 1958 referendum was simple enough, and its phrasing clearly revealed de Gaulle's objectives. French West Africans were asked to vote "yes" if they wanted a loose federation of the separate territories and links with France through the French Community (Houphouët Boigny's idea) and "no" if they wanted total independence without any links with France. De Gaulle did not entertain any other options. Many leaders were unsure of what life would be without the umbilical cord attaching their countries and communities to France, and this was exactly the fear on which de Gaulle had predicated his referendum. Divisions among the leaders were apparent at the conference Senghor convened in Cotonou in July of 1958. The Cotonou Conference favored federation and independence, but to vote "no" would mean to sever relations with France. In the end, Senghor urged the leaders to vote "yes" to de Gaulle, believing that independence would come later. Only Sékou Touré of Guinea voted "no" (that is, for independence); the others voted "yes," to the dismay of the whole world. De Gaulle had won, but only temporarily.

Guinea became independent,[5] but de Gaulle showed that independence would be costly. French connections were severed immediately and completely. Departing French administrators destroyed records and infrastructure. For Guinea, therefore, the opening years of independence were difficult, save for a generous £10 million in aid from Ghana.

Meanwhile, those who voted "yes" began to work toward creating a federation. Senghor formed the Mali Federation, with Senegal, Burkina Faso (then called Upper Volta), Mali (then called Soudan), and Benin (then called Dahomey) as members. He urged de Gaulle to grant independence to the federation. Afraid of losing influence, Houphouët Boigny created the Entente Council comprising Côte d'Ivoire, Burkina Faso, Niger and Benin. He also requested independence. His Entente Council was a loose economic community rather than a state, and each member state would achieve independence separately. In the end, neither the Entente Council nor the Mali Federation survived. Hoping to divest France from the troubles in West Africa and concentrate on the Algerian War, De Gaulle decided to dismantle the federations and grant the colony independence in 1960. The dates of independence are available in Table 1.

---

5. In order to differentiate French Guinea from Portuguese Guinea, the former is often called Guinea or Guinea-Conakry and the latter is always called Guinea-Bissau.

Figure 18.5. Marketplace in Côte d'Ivoire.

Paths toward Independence:
Guinea-Bissau

The last West African country to achieve independence, Guinea-Bissau, did so through an all-out war. This was not surprising, as Portugal, its colonial master, had the longest and worst record in European colonization in Africa. Owing partly to its minimal role in European affairs and the underdevelopment of its own economy, Portugal depended so heavily on its colonies in Africa that it was almost inconceivable for the Portuguese government to let them go after World War II. Given the small size of the educated elite in these colonies, furthermore, the struggle for independence was slow in developing: literally, it awaited the achievement of independence in other parts of West Africa.

Amilcar Cabral was at the center of the independence movement in Guinea-Bissau. An immigrant from Cape Verde (which was also under Portuguese rule), Cabral was educated in Portugal and brought in contact with like-minded people from other Portuguese colonies. He struck up a lifelong friendship with Agostino Neto of Angola, and together they immersed themselves in the study of Marxism. After his education, Cabral returned to Guinea-Bissau and went into the colonial service as a field officer charged with conducting an agricultural survey of the colony. In this position, Cabral was able to learn about the country and establish contact with farmers. He formed a nationalist movement in 1953 called the Movimento de Independência Nacional da Guiné Portuguesa (Movement for National Independence of Guinea, or MING). MING was transformed three years later into the Partido Africano da Independência da Guiné e Cabo Verde (African Party for the Independence of Guinea and Cape Verde, PAIGC). These were all underground political groups, but PAIGC surfaced in the dock workers' strike of 1959. The Portuguese put down the strike violently in the hopes that Cabral's party, which had supported the workers, would be militarily defeated in the process. Instead, Cabral and the PAIGC embarked on what turned out to be a prolonged war, using their knowledge of the land and familiarity with the people to carry out guerrilla warfare and acts of sabotage.

In this all-out war for independence, three factors favored the PAIGC. The first was the party's effective organization. The second was international support, not only from independent West African countries but also from China and the Soviet Union as a result of the Cold War. Invaluable diplomatic support also came from the Organization of African Unity and the United Nations. The third reason for the PAIGC's success was that Portugal was faced with similar crises in other parts of Africa. The PAIGC continued the struggle throughout the 1960s against Portugal's superior military forces. In 1973, when the party proclaimed Guinea's independence, it was not surprising that international recognition came quickly. The final acts of the struggle occurred in 1974. In January, Cabral was assassinated; in April, a military coup occurred in Portugal and the new government decided to withdraw from the conflict in Africa; in September, Portugal recognized the independence of Guinea-Bissau.

Liberia

It is important to discuss the situation in contemporary Liberia. Having achieved its independence in 1847, Liberia was often described as the lone star of West Africa—not only because its flag carried one star but also because it was the only independent country in the region. Although it was spared the agonies of twentieth-century colonization, the country still suffered under an imperial system of one sort or another. In the period covered by this study, the most persistent problems in Liberia were the economic and financial crises that had engulfed the country since the Great Depression. And so it happened that while other, colonized countries were gaining their independence with struggles of one kind or another, the only hitherto independent country, Liberia, was still struggling.

Throughout the 1930s, Liberia's government unsuccessfully attempted to get assistance from foreign governments and companies. In frustration and anger, the country declared a moratorium on its debt to Firestone and suspended its diplomatic relations with Britain and the U.S. Eventually the Liberian government entered an agreement with Firestone for the exploitation of its rubber resources. (This turned out to be a timely agreement, for the country became crucial during World War II, when its rubber plantations were the only source of natural latex rubber accessible to the Allied Powers.) Liberia signed a defense agreement with the United States in 1942. Together with the economic boom from rubber, the strategic geographical importance of Liberia during the war led to intense activity in the construction of infrastructural facilities such as roads, an airport, and a harbor. The U.S. dollar became Liberia's legal currency in 1943, the same year of William Tubman's election as president. In 1944 Liberia entered the war and was counted among the victorious Allies. It was the only West African nation that signed the declaration of the United Nations autonomously. More prestigious still, it became a member of the UN Security Council in December 1960. Even as a non-permanent member of the council, Liberia was actively involved in African issues and debates over decolonization.

Economic Legacies of Colonialism in West Africa

While African nationalists concentrated on their political struggles in West Africa, the colonial powers were making plans to entrench the colonies in specific economic roles in the international division of labor. Under colonial rule, West African economies had existed for the benefit of the metropolises. Each colony was expected to be self-sufficient; in other words, African peoples were supposed to finance their own subordination. One way of doing this by raising revenues through direct and indirect taxes and using the returns to pay the salaries of expatriate administrators (roughly fifty percent), to repay loans raised to build railways, and so on (twenty percent), and to finance minor capital projects (thirty percent).

After World War II, under pressure from the United States and the United Nations, colonial powers made conscious efforts to introduce development projects as their colonies prepared for independence. There were short-term and long-term development plans, ranging from five to ten years and financed by the colonial powers. The projects were developed with the assumption that the postcolonial economies would be capitalist. Thus, policies were written into the plans and programs to induce the emergence of a capitalist class. Loans were given to entrepreneurs for the first time and were designed to enable them to establish medium-sized businesses and thereby gain management experience. The plans varied from colony to colony. In British Africa, for example, about seventy-five percent of the funds for the development plans came from Britain; in the French colonies, only about twenty-five percent of the funds came from France.

The theme of economic decolonization is a recurring one. Many scholars point to the inadequacy of colonies' preparation, as supported by metropolises, for the change. African leaders also tended to blame their failure on their countries' lack of economic independence. Kwame Nkrumah provided the most articulate critique of colonial economic plans and coined the term "neocolonialism" to describe the condition of African economies at independence.

The colonial economic legacies in West Africa were not very numerous and not very positive. This could be seen in five major areas. The first legacy was that the economies of the countries continued to be dominated by agriculture. Up to seventy-five percent of the labor force, composed mainly of illiterate men and women residing in villages, was engaged in this sector. Agriculture was not mechanized; it largely retained precolonial tools and land tenure systems. Research into export cash crops such as cocoa, groundnuts, and coffee progressed faster than research into food crops consumed in the region. Above all, very little was done during colonial rule in the areas of agribusiness and irrigation. Thus, agriculture continued to rely on nature, to exploit nature by extensive rather than intensive cultivation (putting more land under cultivation rather than increasing the productivity of that already being cultivated), and to harm nature through deforestation.

The second colonial economic legacy was monoculture, also involving the export of raw materials. Each country produced one or two crops for export and the entire region was dominated by the export of cocoa (in Ghana, Nigeria, and Côte d'Ivoire), groundnuts, cotton, and palm oil. Mineral extraction was similar: gold in Ghana, iron ore in Guinea and Mauritania, and petroleum in Nigeria were mined and exported.

The third legacy was the absence of a vibrant industrial sector at independence, which demanded that West Africa's produce and minerals be processed abroad. Traditional handicraft industries continued to meet the needs of the people for simple tools. Machinery and processed goods continued to be imported.

The fourth legacy was the structure of international trade. Independent West African states engaged in bilateral trade with their former colonial powers. Prices and markets continued to be determined by European powers. Inter-African and interregional trade was not encouraged.

The fifth legacy was that, at independence, West African countries were still tied to the currencies of their former colonial overlords: the pound sterling, or the franc. The French introduced the CFA franc and fixed its rate of exchange.

Appendix

The Atlantic Charter, August 14, 1941

The President of the United States of America and the Prime Minister, Mr. Churchill, representing His Majesty's Government in the United Kingdom, being met together, deem it right to make known certain common principles in the national policies of their respective countries on which they base their hopes for a better future for the world. First, their countries seek no aggrandizement, territorial or otherwise; Second, they desire to see no territorial changes that do not accord with the freely expressed wishes of the peoples concerned; Third, they respect the right of all people to choose the form of government under which they will live; and they wish to see sovereign rights and self government restored to those who have been forcibly deprived of them; Fourth, they will endeavor, with due respect for their existing obligations, to further the enjoyment by all States, great or small, victor or vanquished, of access, on equal terms, to the trade and to the raw materials of the world which are needed for their economic prosperity;Fifth, they desire to bring about the fullest collaboration between all nations in the economic field with the object of securing, for all, improved labor standards, economic advancement and social security; Sixth, after the final destruction of the Nazi tyranny, they hope to see established a peace which will afford all nations the means of dwelling in safety within their own boundaries, and which will afford assurance that all men in all lands live out their lives in freedom from want and fear; Seventh, such peace should enable all men to traverse the high seas and oceans without hindrance; Eighth, they believe that all of the nations of the world, for realistic as well as spiritual reasons, must come to the abandonment of the use of force. Since no future peace can be maintained if land, sea or air armaments continue to be employed by nations which threaten, or may threaten, aggression outside of their frontiers, they believe, pending the establishment of a wider and permanent system of general security, that the disarmament of such nations is essential. They likewise aid and encourage all other practicable measures which will lighten for peace-loving peoples the crushing burden of armaments. FRANKLIN D. ROOSEVELT WINSTON S. CHURCHILL

Source: Franklin D. Roosevelt and Samuel I. Rosenman, *The Public Papers and Addresses of Franklin D. Roosevelt*, New York: The Harper Brothers, 1950. Vol.10, p 314.

Review Questions

1. Discuss the impact of World War II on decolonization in West Africa.
2. How was nationalism in French West Africa similar to and different from nationalism in British West Africa?
3. Why was decolonization delayed in Portuguese West Africa? Describe the struggle for independence in Guinea-Bissau.
4. Citing relevant examples and case studies, explain the role of ethnic politics in the decolonization of West Africa.

Additional Reading

Ajayi, J. F. Ade and Michael Crowder, eds. *History of West Africa*, Vol. 2. New York: Columbia University Press, 1971.

Cabral, Amilcar. *National Liberation and Culture*. Syracuse, NY: Syracuse University Press, 1970.

Hargreaves, John D. *Decolonization in Africa*. London: Longman, 1988.

Nkrumah, Kwame. *Neo-colonialism: The Last Stage of Imperialism*. New York: International Publishers, 1966.

Nwaubani, Ebere. *The United States and Decolonization in West Africa, 1950-1960*. Rochester, NY: University of Rochester Press, 2001.

Wilson, H. S. *African Decolonization*. London: Edward Arnold, 1994.

Chapter 19

East, Central, and Equatorial Africa

George Ndege and Chima J. Korieh

The nature of African societies in the decolonization period depended largely on colonial authorities' strategies for the domination of African peoples; that is, it depended on African-European relations in Africa on the one hand and relations between the colonies and the empire on the other. The nature of African societies in this era also depended on economic systems and on the position of the African population in the colonial state structure. The history of East, Central, and Equatorial Africa in this period reveals the emergence of new forces and elements of continuity. The economic and political conditions of African societies in this period and the large-scale inequality created by colonial structures had already resulted in profound economic and social changes by the outbreak of World War II. In order to begin assessing the history of East, Central, and Equatorial Africa during decolonization, we must understand the nature of these societies before 1939.

* * *

Colonial Societies Before 1939

For the agricultural and pastoral peoples of East and Central Africa, access to land was essential to their way of life. In fact, before Europeans arrived, significant transformations in land use had taken place among those who grew millet, sorghum, maize, cotton, and tobacco and grazed cattle in Nyasaland and Northern Rhodesia. The presence of Arabs and newly arrived immigrants and contestation over land within African societies was evident by the middle of the nineteenth century. The arrival of David Livingstone, white missionaries, traders, planters, hunters, and concession seekers in Trans-Zambezi further upset preexisting land use systems.[1] The conflicting land claims and counter claims that followed European penetration in East, Central, and Equatorial Africa and the alienation of African-owned lands brought whites into conflict with Africans, a conflict that characterized black-white relations throughout the colonial period.

---

1. See, for example, Robert I. Rotberg, *The Rise of Nationalism in Central Africa: The Making of Malawi and Zambia 1873–1964* (Cambridge, MA: Harvard University Press, 1965), 29.

As in many other parts of Africa, the European administrations in East, Central, and Equatorial Africa were expected to raise most of their revenue within their territories. The resulting imposition of hut and poll taxes transformed rural life. Like their counterparts in other parts of Africa, colonial subjects in Nyasaland and Northern Rhodesia endured arbitrary rule. In Equatorial Africa (except for the coastal areas of Cameroon, most of Gabon, and the Congo rainforests, which contained natural products sellable on the European market such as wild rubber, tropical timber, and oil palms), the colonial administration systematically attempted to extract the cost of administration from local peoples. Colonial rule led to the decimation of villages, excessive and forced labor extraction, famine, and decreased population, especially among those who lived in territories granted to concessionaire companies or to planters.

Several features are important in understanding the colonial situations, the peculiar nature of resistance movements, and the decolonization processes in East, Central, and Equatorial Africa. They include large-scale land alienation, particularly in East and Central Africa, the predominance of settler communities in the region, the weak African peasant economy, and segregation. The history of East, Central, and Equatorial Africa is quite different from that of the British West African territories because of the larger white settler population and presence of an economy heavily dependent on mining or European commercial agriculture in the former. Both these sectors of the economy relied heavily on African labor. In Southern Rhodesia and the Belgian Congo, for example, mobility was controlled through registration and pass laws.[2] As a result, the British authorities saw the problem of devolution in East and Central Africa rather differently from the way they saw it in West Africa or the Sudan.[3] The absence of a large, educated African elite in most colonies of East and Central Africa made colonial authorities believe African independence in the territory was remote, and they held onto their power tenaciously. The dilemma the British faced was how to make concessions to Africans while supporting white settler groups.

Circumstances in Africa and the strategies of the imperialist powers also shaped the situation in Equatorial Africa. In French Equatorial Africa (AEF) and the Cameroon in particular, the interaction between those forces had effects ranging from the unremarkable to the disastrous.[4] The situation in AEF proved problematic for colonial administrators, although it was certainly more so for the African population, as it threatened their livelihood, their health, and sometimes their lives.[5] Except for the Cameroon, most of Equatorial Africa lacked the rich mineral deposits, agricultural potential, and precolonial trading networks that characterized most other colonial possessions in Africa.

By the 1930s, the contradictions of the colonial political economy had become apparent. One constant demand throughout most of the colonial period was

---

2. See Bogumil Jewsiewicki, "Rural Society and Belgian colonial economy," in *History of Central Africa*, vol. 2, ed. David Birmingham and Phyllis M. Martin (London: Longman, 1983), 95–125.

3. Bill Freund, *The Making of Contemporary Africa: The Development of African Societies since 1800* (Boulder, CO: Lynne Rienner Publishers, 1998), 189.

4. Ralph A. Austen and Rita Headrick, "Equatorial Africa under colonial rule" in *History of Central Africa*, vol. 2, ed. David Birmingham and Phyllis M. Martin, (London: Longman, 1983), 27.

5. Austen and Headrick, "Equatorial Africa," 27.

that for African labor, although individual colonies differed in their labor policies. African family life suffered as a result of imposed labor regimes in many parts of Central Africa. Marriages became difficult to sustain with men's prolonged absences from villages.[6] After 1930, the concept of "stabilized" labor in the Belgian Congo enabled workers to obtain a permit to have their families join them. In British Central Africa, it was quite difficult for migrant laborers to do this even in the late 1950s. In Angola and Mozambique, harsh labor policies, reminiscent of slavery, continued into the 1950s. The deteriorating quality of life in the colonies raised a new consciousness among workers and peasants, especially in the Belgian Congo system and on the Rhodesian mines.[7] The situation also led to the formation of new, syncretic churches and mutual aid associations and raised ethnic consciousness on the eve of the nationalist struggle for independence.

In the 1930s, colonial officials struggled with the economic and financial crises caused by the global depression amid growing uncertainty and concern over the future of the environment.[8] In East Africa, settlers' need for cheap labor and fear of competition from successful African farmers and officials' growing concern with overpopulation and environmental degradation combined to boost the issue of soil erosion to the fore of imperial policy.[9] Increased governmental intervention in African agriculture via marketing boards heightened political consciousness among Africans in Kenya.[10] What is often ignored, however, is the fact that the intervention largely resulted from the entrepreneurial production already set in motion by peasants. In Kenya, for example, the acreage of wattle planted by Africans increased from six thousand to one hundred thousand between 1925 and 1936, while the acreage planted by Europeans increased only from 8,830 to 16,681 over the same period.[11] Meanwhile, in Tanganyika, sisal exports increased, the cotton industry was revived, and tea and sugar were introduced with some success.[12] In Uganda, the growing success of peasant cash crop production was a marked trend. In Northern Rhodesia, both the colonial government and officials of the British South Africa Company imposed controls on African settlement patterns to gain administrative leverage, prevent deforestation, and improve agricultural practice.[13] Yet, conservationist concerns and forced relocations led to anticolonial sentiment in the settler colonies as the politics of soil conservation took center stage.

Colonial administrations sought to alter the perceived deterioration by embarking on de-stocking campaigns, forcing Africans to build terraces and regulat-

---

6. Phyllis M. Martin, "The Violence of Empire," in *History of Central Africa, vol.2,* ed. David Birmingham and Phyllis M. Martin (London: Longman, 1983), 16.

7. See, for example, Allen F. Isaacman, *The Tradition of Resistance in Mozambique* (Los Angeles: California University Press, 1976). See also Martin, "The Violence of Empire," 22–3.

8. Sara Berry, *No Condition is Permanent: The Social Dynamics of Agrarian Change in Sub-Saharan Africa* (Madison, WI: The University of Wisconsin Press 1993), 48.

9. Ibid., 48.

10. David Anderson, "Depression, Dust Bowl, Demography, and Drought," *African Affairs* 83 (1984): 321.

11. Robert Tignor, *The Colonial Transformation of Kenya: The Kamba, Kikuyu and Maasai from 1900 to 1939* (Princeton, NJ: Princeton University Press, 1976), 186.

12. Robert M. Maxon, *East Africa: An Introductory History* (Morgantown, WV: West Virginia Press, 1994), 184.

13. Berry, *No Condition is Permanent,* 49.

ing African production systems. The problem with the states' approaches to environmental degradation was that they ignored the roles of their own policies in creating environmental disasters. Land alienation resulted in congestion in some areas designated as "African" and aggravated the problem of soil erosion, as more people and livestock were forced to contend with shrinking land space. A number of communities challenged the colonial discourse on environmental degradation by demanding that more lands, particularly those that had been lost to European settlement, be added to the African reserves to ease the congestion. The settlers' neglect of the fundamental issue of land distribution led to conflict between Africans and the colonial state. The Africans saw conservation measures as a development that was not in their best interest, since the measures were considered likely to lead to more land alienation and since most of fertile land had been appropriated to European settlers.

The regulation of African production systems received strong support from both the colonial authorities and the settler community, while African reactions to the soil conservation measures were many and varied. Africans protested, defied the imposed regulations, and formed associations to protest the adverse colonial policies.[14] Thus, rural areas became fertile grounds for nationalist party organizers. By the outbreak of World War II, seeds that would define the contours of African nationalism had been planted by the colonial state.

World War II and Nationalist Movements

By the late 1930s, Europeans were no longer strangers waiting at the gate of the African continent. Except for Ethiopia and Liberia, which maintained some form of independence, all areas of the continent had been colonized by different European powers or were under minority white rule. To a much greater extent than any other event, however, the worldwide depression of the era had far-reaching socioeconomic and political implications for the history of Africa. The depression exposed the limits of the development policies Europeans were pursuing in Africa. The decline in state revenue and the low prices African products attracted in this period were fundamental to the local response to colonial rule from the late 1930s onward.

World War II facilitated the rise of nationalist movements. Europeans needed Africans to fight with them in World War II but did not think Africans would challenge them to get their independence. The weakened position of the United Kingdom and France, the primary colonial powers in East, Central, and Equatorial Africa, in world affairs strengthened the resolve of the new dominant international powers, the United States and the Soviet Union, to challenge the colonial system.[15] The new international environment and developments within the conti-

---

14. George Ndege, "History of Pastoralism in Kenya, 1895–1980," in *An Economic History of Kenya,* ed. William R. Ochieng and Robert M. Maxon (Nairobi: East African Publishers, 1992), 93–107.

15. The humiliation of France and Belgium during World War II undermined their military prestige. In France in particular, the struggle between Pétain and de Gaulle caused bitter rivalries in the French overseas territories and split them into two factions, the French North

nent provided the impetus for nationalist agitation throughout colonial Africa. A colonial official remarked in 1939, "At any rate, in Africa we can be sure that we have unlimited time in which to work."[16] This assumption was proven wrong, as the next two decades witnessed the liberation of many former colonial territories in Africa.

In economic terms, as a result of the war, African societies benefited from an increased European demand for their exports and from Britain's most ambitious efforts at colonial development through investment, an attempt to give colonialism a facelift at a time when it was being rendered irrelevant by the emerging postwar order.[17] Britain released the Colonial Development and Welfare Funds, "granted in aid of Ten-Year Development plans devised by local bureaucracies."[18] The relative prosperity of the period, therefore, led to the growth and development of three East African economies. The marked increase in the value and volume of sisal, coffee, and cotton production illustrated the development of the peasant sector in these territories (see Table 1). Though accelerated, the pace of economic development in East Africa was not fast enough to satisfy many Africans.[19]

In Uganda, for example, 398,000 bales of cotton were exported in 1954, up from five hundred in 1906. However, by 1960, coffee had surpassed cotton as the protectorate's most important export. By 1962, coffee accounted for nearly half the total value of Uganda's exports.[20] As Table 2 illustrates, the estimated value of mineral exports as a percentage of total exports remained fairly small. Agriculture continued to be the major sector from which most Africans derived their livelihood.

Established in 1948, the East Africa High Commission formulated and administered rules of import duty and excise and income taxes. All the three territories did not receive the establishment of the East African Common Market warmly, however. Uganda and Tanganyika complained about the disproportionate benefits that went to Kenya. Indeed, after the war, Kenya's contribution to the total value of the East African inter-territorial trade increased from 36.0% in 1945 to 60.4% in 1960 (see Table 3).

The irony, however, is that beneath these developments lay economic frustration and discontent. After the end of the war, those displaced from the rural areas as well as many young, unskilled, and undereducated people formed a vast pool of unemployed Africans in towns. Even those who were lucky enough to secure employment earned wages that could hardly sustain an acceptable standard of liv-

---

and West African territories on one side and Equatorial Africa on the other. See Crawford Young, "Decolonisation in Africa," in *Colonialism in Africa, 1870–1960: Volume 2, The History and Politics of Colonialism 1914–1960*, ed. L. H. Gann and Peter Duignan (Cambridge: Cambridge University Press, 1970), 454.

16. Margery Perham, *The Colonial Reckoning: The End of Imperial Rule in Light of the British Experience* (London: Collins, 1961), 114.

17. D. A. Low, *Eclipse of the Empire* (Cambridge: Cambridge University Press, 1993), 173; Maxon, *An Introductory History*, 209–10; Bill Freund, *The Making of Contemporary Africa: The Development of African Society since 1800, 2nd edition* (Boulder, CO: Lynne Rienner Publishers, 1998) 168–75.

18. Low, *Eclipse of Empire*, 174.

19. Maxon, *Introductory History*, 210.

20. Ibid., 230.

**Table 1 Selected East African Exports,
1938, 1946, 1952, and 1953**

Selected Exports: Value and % of Total Exports
Volume of Selected Exports

Kenya	Maize £m %	Sisal £m %	Coffee £m %	Maize Cwt Ô000	Sisal tons Ô000	Coffee cwt.Ô000
1953	0.3 2	2.5 13	6.7 34	215	315	296
1952	2.4 9	4.5 17	7.1 28	1, 368	35	338
1946	0.2 2	0.9 12	0.9 13	348	24	191
1938	0.3 9	0.4 11	0.8 20	N. A.	28	339
Uganda	Cotton 400 lb. bales	Sisal	Coffee	Cotton	Sisal	Coffee
1953	16.8 50	NIL	11.5 35	334	NIL	714
1952	29.9 63	NIL	12.3 26	378	NIL	789
1946	5.7 59	NIL	1.8 18	219	NIL	611
1938	3.4 73	NIL	0.3 7	432	NIL	280
Tanganyika	Cotton	Sisal	Coffee	Cotton	Sisal	Coffee
1953	4.8 14	12.7 37	5.8 17	80	171	305
1952	4.7 10	21.7 46	5.5 12	62	158	372
1946	0.4 4	3.9 44	0.7 8	22	111	200
1938	0.4 10	1.4 38	0.4 10	49	101	274

Source: Great Britain, *East Africa Royal Commission* 1953–1955 Report, Cmd. 9475

ing.[21] As the discontent among the urban population grew, the colonial state was forced to contend with militant trade unionism as well as a very restive population.[22] As migrant labor "stabilized," the demand for better wages and working conditions gained momentum, and the opportunity cost of ignoring such demands was high. Strikes became an important avenue for expressing dissatisfaction with the colonial states' labor policies and their insensitivity to the plight of African workers.[23]

The rural areas were undergoing major changes as a result of the overly interventionist policies of the state. In Kenya, for example, the Swynnerton Plan was implemented to facilitate land consolidation and "concentrate land ownership in the hands of a few peasants who would become transformed into an 'African middle class' [that would] act as a collaborator-buffer class between the impoverished militant and landless peasants and the colonial government."[24] The plan

21. Claire Robertson, *Trouble Showed the Way* (Bloomington, IN: Indiana University Press, 1997), 141.
22. Frederick Cooper, *Decolonization and African Society: The Labor Question in French and British Africa* (Cambridge: Cambridge University Press, 1996), 352–5.
23. Ibid., 352–5.
24. Tabitha Kanogo, *Squatters and the Roots of Mau Mau* (Athens, OH: Ohio University Press, 1987), 164.

Table 2 Value of East African Exports, Imports, Revenue, and Expenditure

	Value of Domestic Exports	Estimated Value of Non-Mineral Exports	Estimated Value of Mineral Exports	Value of Net Imports	Revenue	Expenditure
	£m	£m	£m	£m	£m	£m
Kenya						
1953	19.5	18.6	0.9	51.7	21.3	22.8
1952	25.8	24.4	1.4	59.3	20.5	18.8
1946	7.1	6.4	0.7	16.4	9.0	7.7
1938	3.8	3.2	0.6	6.4	3.8	3.6
Uganda						
1953	33.4	33.2	0.2	25.7	17.7	17.4
1952	47.2	47.0	0.2	24.7	17.3	15.9
1946	9.6	9.5	0.1	5.3	4.0	3.6
1938	4.7	4.5	0.2	2.5	1.9	2.0
Tanganyika						
1953	34.5	30.9	3.6	28.4	14.7	14.7
1952	47.0	40.8	6.2	37.5	16.4	15.8
1946	8.8	7.4	1.4	8.1	5.1	5.1
1938	3.7	3.1	0.6	3.4	2.1	2.2

Source: Great Britain, *East Africa Royal Commission 1953–1955 Report*, Cmd. 9475, 460–461.

Table 3 Percentage of Total Value of the East African Inter-Territorial Trade, 1945–1960				
Year	Kenya	Uganda	Tanganyika	Total
1945	36.2	41.0	22.8	100
1948	37.2	45.6	16.9	100
1951	50.8	33.5	15.7	100
1954	47.1	44.0	8.9	100
1957	60.7	26.9	12.4	100
1960	60.4	29.5	10.1	100

Source: Van Zwanenberg, Roger with Anne King, *An Economic History of Kenya and Uganda 1800–1970* (Atlantic Highlands, NJ: Humanities Press, 1975), 242.

furthered the privatization of land ownership, thereby rendering thousands home-less[25] and failing to attain the desired primary objective of stabilizing the restive population. Instead it produced disgruntled individuals and feelings of hostility that soon found expression in a new political organization called the Kenya Land and Freedom Army. The struggle for land, freedom, living wages, and better working conditions coalesced to incite one of the bloodiest wars of decolonization in Africa, the Mau Mau uprising.

The counter-insurgency measures adopted by Britain were severe and brutal in the extreme. Following the declaration of a state of emergency in 1952, the colonists banned African political parties. Thousands of Kenyans, particularly members of the Kikuyu community, were killed, and many more were detained under very harsh conditions. The Kenya African Union, which had been formed in 1944, was banned, and its leaders—including Jomo Kenyatta, Kungu Karumba, Paul Ngei, Achiengí Oneko, Bildad Kaggia, and Fred Kubai—were arrested. They were sentenced to long periods of imprisonment for their involvement in Mau Mau. It was not until 1960 that the two nationwide multi-ethnic political parties, the Kenya African National Union (KANU) and the Kenya African Democratic Union (KADU), were formed.

In the years between 1952 and 1960, Kenyan trade union leaders articulated African political grievances. Trade unionism and nationalist politics coalesced, and new African leaders entered the political arena. One of the most able trade union leaders was Tom Mboya, who emerged as the most outspoken trade union leader-cum-politician during the emergency period. Meanwhile, while pursuing counter-insurgency measures to defeat the Mau Mau freedom fighters, the colonial state was forced to accept that independence could not be postponed indefinitely. The ban on political parties was lifted in 1955, but with a caveat: the new parties had to be district-based. There would still be no nationwide political parties.

The encouragement of district-based political parties was inimical to the development of mass Kenya-based nationalism. Thus, the eventual formation of nationwide political parties in 1960 occurred against a backdrop of ethnic and parochial nationalism. On the constitutional front, the British government in-

25. Ibid., 164–165; Robertson, *Trouble*, 141.

creased the number of Africans in the Legislative Council. The first African elections, based on educational and property qualifications, took place in 1958, a development that saw the election of eight Africans to the Legislative Council. These were, however, modest gains. It was not until the 1960 Lancaster Conference in London that Kenyans were on the sure road to independence, which they achieved in 1963.

In the neighboring territory of Uganda, the critical issue was Buganda separatism, with the kabaka (king of Buganda) becoming what Robert Maxon has aptly described as "the focal point of a very dynamic but insular nationalism."[26] Following the Buganda Agreement of 1900, the Baganda enjoyed a special status in the Uganda Protectorate. Thus, as the march to independence gained momentum through the 1950s, the British were forced to address the issue of Buganda's special status in the envisioned unitary postcolonial state. The Baganda had their own legislature, which largely served to further their special status within the protectorate. Attempts by British Governor Sir Andrew Cohen to institute radical changes based on a strongly centralized system of administration and elected representation in 1952 were, therefore, considered an affront to the Buganda Kingdom. In a sense, the governor's vision of a unitary Ugandan state was quite revolutionary to the Baganda, a denial of what they believed was their special place in the protectorate. The kabaka of Buganda, Mutesa II, protested against what Mazrui described as the "Cohenist unitarism"[27]

In the same period, the British secretary of state for the colonies suggested the formation of an East African federation similar to that in Central Africa. Kabaka Mutesa, supported by the Buganda legislature (the *Lukiko*), protested the move and requested that control of Buganda be transferred from the colonial office to the foreign office and that the kingdom be granted independence as a separate state.[28] The kabaka and, indeed, the Ugandan population felt uneasy about the East African Federation because of the strong settler community in Kenya. The strong opposition of the kabaka to Sir Andrew Cohen's "unitarism" agenda finally led to his exile to London in 1953.

The formation of Ugandan political parties reflected the shifting nature of political loyalties and alliances based on religion, region, and ethnicity.[29] Bugandan separatism was a consequence of the British divide-and-rule strategy, where preferred communities were pitied against other, "less sophisticated" communities. The British were therefore confronted with a problem that they themselves had created and nurtured in the nearly seven decades of their governance in the protectorate of Uganda. Uganda's attainment of independence in October 1962 did not end the dispute that surrounded the special place that the kingdom of Buganda desired in the postcolonial state.

The triumph of mass nationalism in Tanganyika was largely a result of the organizational efforts of Julius Nyerere, who was instrumental in founding the Tanganyika African National Union (TANU). Nyerere made TANU a mass political party that included local political leaders in rural areas and the masses of unedu-

26. Maxon, *Introductory History*, 227.
27. Ali A. Mazrui and Michael Tidy, *Nationalism and New States in Africa* (Portsmouth, NH: Heinemann, 1986), 101.
28. Maxon, *Introductory History*, 225.
29. Ibid., 226–230, Mazrui and Tidy, *Nationalism*, 102–3.

Figure 19.1. Patrice Lumumba and Kwame Nkrumah, 1960.

cated peasants. TANU capitalized on urban and rural discontent and even called for *uhuru* (self-government). By using *uhuru* as the clarion call for the people of Tanganyika to unite, Nyerere framed the nationalist struggle in terms of the advantages of independence. Self-government was envisioned as a panacea to the many and varied economic problems the peasants and workers in colonial establishments faced. TANU was non-ethnic and multiracial, characteristics that further contributed to its dominance. The nationalist movement in Tanganyika was fairly peaceful, at least in comparison to the volatile decolonization processes in Kenya and Southern Rhodesia (now Zimbabwe). While this has been largely attributed to Tanganyika's lack of an entrenched European settler community (rightly so in our view), it is also necessary to underscore the role of Governor Richard Turnbull, who had been chief secretary in the Kenya government at the height of the Mau Mau uprising. Governor Turnbull sought to avoid confrontation, and he cooperated with Nyerere to effect a fairly peaceful transition to independence, which was attained in December 1961.[30]

The history of the nationalist struggle during the decolonization era has been presented as a predominantly male affair with heroes and no heroines. This conspicuous omission has led Susan Geiger to ask, "Where are the women?"[31] Yet, the colonial system impacted the entire society, albeit in different ways in various places and times. Research conducted over the last decade by Cora Presley, Susan Geiger, and Claire Robertson has greatly illuminated women's contributions to the nationalist struggle.

Geiger has shown that without the active role of women TANU would not have developed into a mass party.[32] The women's wing of the party was active in gathering information and disseminating it to the nationalists who were under constant state surveillance. Women also organized meetings where they popularized the party's policies. Presley has argued that in Kenya, where the nationalist struggle was violent, women were not just informants and food suppliers for men fighting in the forests; they also fought, risked their lives, and bore the brunt of Britain's brutal counter-insurgency measures.[33] Women's active roles in the na-

---

30. Maxon, *Introductory History*, 220–221; Mazrui and Tidy, *Nationalism*, 100.
31. Susan Geiger, *TANU Women: gender and Culture in the Making of Tanganyikan Nationalism, 1955–1965* (Portsmouth, NH: Heinemann, 1998), 9–10.
32. Ibid., 1–17, 66–9, 90–104.
33. Cora Presley, *Kikuyu Women, the Mau Mau Rebellion, and Social Change in Kenya* (Boulder, CO: Westview, 1992).

Figure 19.2. Julius Nyerere and Tafawa Balewa.

tionalist campaign stemmed from the fact that women, perhaps more than men, were victims of the colonial state's policies that restricted access to education, the economy, employment, and freedom of relocation.[34] Women were not passive victims waiting to be liberated by men from the clutches of colonialism. They were compatriots in the fight for a better postcolonial order.

As it did in East Africa, the political economy of industrialization and settler-controlled agriculture intensified the prejudice and discrimination to which the people of Nyasaland and Northern Rhodesia were subjected before World War II.[35] African experiences in the copperbelt added to the discontent that ultimately expressed itself with violence.[36] By 1945, African mine workers had noticed few improvements in their working conditions despite two strikes and a generally heightened appreciation of the critical role they played in industrial life. The inability of the colonial administration to act decisively on these issues led to the emergence of nationalist movements in the copperbelt and in Central Africa generally. In Equatorial Africa, the colonists were disappointed by their failure to manage the territories through the private sector. The system of concessionaire companies proved to be an economic failure and raised the political cost of local rule by provoking African resistance, especially in French Equatorial Africa (AEF), until the 1930s.[37]

World War II was a catalyst for fundamental changes in Central and Equatorial Africa, especially in the political realm. In Nyasaland and Northern Rhodesia, both white officials and indigenous leaders, albeit for different reasons, sought to involve Africans more intimately in the political process than they had hitherto been.[38] While nationalist agitation in India and Palestine produced unrest in Africa, many Africans expected their political fortunes to improve as a result of the Atlantic Charter, agreed upon by Roosevelt and Churchill in 1941. The charter stated that the leaders' motivation for fighting stemmed from a respect for the right of all peoples to choose the form of government under which they would live. For colonized people, especially the educated elite, the implementation of the

---

34. Also see Robertson, *Trouble*, 138–145.
35. Rotberg, *The Rise of Nationalism*, 156.
36. Rotberg, *The Rise of Nationalism*, 156.
37. Austen and Headrick, *Equatorial Africa under Colonial Rule*, 39.
38. Rotberg, *The Rise of Nationalism*, 179.

charter in the colonial territories was fundamental to their pursuit of freedom and self-determination.

Of course, there were those within the imperial humanitarian and parliamentary circles who were interested in genuine political and social reform in the colonies.[39] Yet colonial officials, despite the urges to allow African participation in national affairs, were not willing to concede more than nominal power to Africans. On the copperbelt, the government of Northern Rhodesia established an Urban Advisory Council as early as 1938. This council, which at first consisted of members nominated by the administration and was allowed to meet four times a year, neither exerted significant influence nor accomplished any meaningful result for the African population.[40] Though the council achieved little of significance, colonial apologists erroneously believed that the "formation of councils had prevented the development of a national African political consciousness."[41] By 1948, Africans themselves had already began to organize the movement with which they would eventually seize independence.

Until the 1930s, France's policies and involvement in its African territories was minimal, except in the area of basic transport infrastructure. The French showed more commitment to their African colonies from the mid-1930s onward. However, the new French commitment stemmed from external circumstances of French decline rather than from a desire for positive development within Africa. In addition, France's neo-mercantilist stance, aimed at integrating the colonies into the metropolitan economy, was incompatible with the liberal impulse to grant local populations greater opportunities for self-determination.[42] French colonial policy in Equatorial Africa necessitated changes under a new generation of administrators who demanded reforms with the support of the left-wing Popular Front government in France, which took office in 1936.[43]

While self government was explicitly excluded from French policy outlined at the Brazzaville Conference of 1944, France's condition at the end of the World War II provided for considerable change.[44] Its weakened economic and political position after the war led its government to incorporate its African colonies into a self-sufficient economic unit and to experiment with the liberal ideology of the Gaullists and their left-wing allies in France. Such experiments included granting citizenship to Africans under the 1946 constitution of the Fourth French Republic and launching a series of development projects within the African territories under the auspices of FIDES (Fonds d'investissement et de Developement Economique et Social des Territoires d'Outre-Mer).[45] Despite these advances, the

---

39. For example, Lord Hailey's investigations into the discharge of Britain's colonial responsibilities and the passage of the colonial Development and Welfare Act, Rotberg argued, echoed Lord Passfield's earlier concerns and indicated a widespread sensitivity to the overseas climate of opinion. Such sentiments, Rotberg maintains, helped to shape the report of the Bledisloe Commission. The lessons of the copperbelt strikes of 1935 to 1940 also influenced the official mind. Rotberg, *The Rise of Nationalism*, 179.

40. Ibid., 180.

41. Ibid., 181.

42. Austen and Headrick, "Equatorial Africa under Colonial Rule," 82–3.

43. Catherine Coquery-Vidrovitch, "Colonisation ou imperialisme: La politique africaine de la France entre les deux guerres," *Le Mouvement Social* 107, (1979): 51–76.

44. Austen and Headrick, "Equatorial Africa under Colonial Rule," 83.

45. Ibid., 83.

fact that France still wanted control over the colonies was revealed by France's attempt to retain political control over Indo-China and Algeria. Developments within the British West African territories forced France to rethink its policy after 1955. French policy in Equatorial Africa became both economically and politically liberal.

Within Equatorial Africa, economic efforts revolved around the bureaucracy's efforts to increase African economic growth as a means of solving financial problems at home. Increased growth during the late 1930s and expansion in the immediate post-World War II period bolstered the government's confidence in the economy. Yet, economic growth did not translate into increased social welfare. Peasant production in the Cameroon and the AEF savanna remained the main source of export goods. In the AEF in particular, France's attempt to organize settlement schemes (*paysannats*) following Belgian models in the Congo was unsuccessful as a means of increasing peasant investment in agriculture. Although the French version was less oppressive than the Belgian system, Africans in the AEF saw it as an additional tax burden.

Postwar developments witnessed increased African participation in the overall economy of the AEF, however. African participation in commerce, transport, and timber cutting increased, but increased competition between African and Europeans brought them into conflict.[46] Africans suffered from a decline in export prices and were threatened by the growing concentration of capital and modern enterprises in state and private enclaves.[47] The Cameroon Development Corporation, formed in 1946 by the British administration, never returned the plantations confiscated from German owners to the private sector. Private firms and capital dominated the timber industry and mining sector in Gabon, a situation that prevailed until the emergence of political parties and the achievement of independence.

The formation of the Nyasaland African Congress in 1944 marked the beginning of modern nationalism in Central Africa. The Nyasaland African Congress was formed by a number of Africans and a few Europeans. James Frederick Piagusi Sangala was its most prominent leader; another leader was W. H. Timcke, a British South African who had settled in Nyasaland after World War I and was the leader of the white farmers' cooperative organization in Cholo until it failed in 1929. Sangala appealed to the people of Nyasaland for support in his effort to include African voices in ongoing political discussions.[48] The Nyasaland African Congress was not to achieve political independence but rather to be a mouthpiece for Africans, with the idea that it would cooperate with governmental, commercial, planter, and missionary bodies, and with native authorities so as to speed up the progress of independence for Nyasaland.[49] In later years, a nominated missionary's rejection of the representation of African interests in the Legislative Council[50] marked a departure from the traditional search for economic betterment and the cooperationist stance.

In Northern Rhodesia, the move to have African interests represented in the Legislative Council led to the nomination of Colonel (later Sir) Stewart Gore-

---

46. Ibid., 85; Pierre-Philippe Rey, *Colonialisme, neo-colonialisme et transition au capitalisme: Example de la "Comilog" au Congo-Brazzaville* (Paris: F. Maspero, 1971), 476–92.
47. Austen and Headrick, "Equatorial Africa under Colonial Rule," 85.
48. Circular letter of 1 October, 1943, Zomba Archives, Malawi, la/1423, Cited in Rotberg, *The Rise of Nationalism*, 183.
49. Ibid., 184.
50. Ibid., 190.

Browne to the council. Gore-Browne was ahead of his time in urging the government to give Northern Rhodesians a greater sense of participation in the affairs of their country. Gore-Browne realized that the views of educated Africans deserved equal recognition with those of the chiefs and elders who generally accepted the maintenance of the colonial *status quo*.[51]

Pressure from Gore-Browne resulted in the creation of new provincial councils. After 1943, these new councils and preexisting urban advisory councils formed the avenue through which African leaders achieved a sense of involvement in Northern Rhodesian politics. Ironically, some envisaged the councils as insurance against indigenous nationalism, theoretically providing a sufficiently meaningful alternative to satisfy the political passions of refractory Africans.[52]

Unable to secure any redress for their grievances through the provincial councils, educated Africans revived the urban and rural welfare associations that had been important in past politics. The various welfare associations provided them with alternative channels of communication after the 1940 strike.[53] By 1943, for example, the Lusaka African Welfare Association was meeting regularly. It agitated against racial discrimination and regarded itself as the mouthpiece of the African community in the Lusaka district. Hitherto, African organizations had not been expected to discuss political issues, but to cater exclusively to the non-political interests of African residents in townships.[54] Yet, Archibald H. Elwell, a colonial social welfare officer on the copperbelt in Kitwe, showed Africans ways they could support their cause. His address to the Kitwe African Society one evening was fundamental in raising issues that the government could no longer ignore.

Times were changing rapidly and, in May 1946, representatives from fourteen welfare associations met at Broken Hill and created the Federation of African Societies of Northern Rhodesia with Dauti Yamba as president and W. Charles Kulawa as secretary. The federation and other groups capitalized on the deterioration of race relations to advance their political activities, which prompted the administration to form an African Representative Council in 1946 in Northern Rhodesia.[55]

Despite this concession, the administration in Northern Rhodesia wanted to restrict the Representative Council to an advisory role.[56] By 1948, Africans became aware that the achievement of their political goals would require a new means of expression. Indeed, Gore-Browne's call for a "responsible government" for the unofficial (settler) majority in the Legislative Council alarmed Africans, who had hitherto regarded Gore-Browne as an ally.[57] To the Africans, the imposition of "responsible government" amounted to the imposition of white settler rule and a threat to Africans' rights as protected persons. The result was the transformation of the Federation of African Societies into the Northern Rhodesian

---

51. Ibid., 200.

52. Ibid.

53. Ibid., 202–3.

54. Ibid., 204–6.

55. Nyasaland followed with a similar council headed by the secretary for native affairs.

56. See address of the acting governor of Northern Rhodesia in *African Representative Council Proceedings*, 1 (1946): cc. 3–4.

57. Although Gore-Browne was convinced that his proposal would place Africans in a position sufficiently strong for them to resist white domination, the African population felt betrayed. See Rotberg, *The Rise of Nationalism*, 210–1.

African Congress by the end of 1948 and the demand for wide-ranging social and political reforms. The prospects of white settler rule placed Northern Rhodesians in a dilemma over whether to support the existing colonial structure or to ask for home rule. Horrified by the idea of settler rule, they desired to retain their positions as protected persons and to gradually obtain political control over the areas in which they lived, a right that protection had, in their eyes, always implied.

The debate over the federation of Nyasaland and the three territories of North and South Rhodesia altered the nature of earlier protests and African reactions to white rule in Central Africa. The success of the Afrikaner Nationalist Party in the South African elections of 1948 heightened the fear that an Afrikaner-style racial political ideology might spread to Central Africa. Thus, a memorandum from a small group of Central Africans in London in 1949 to the colonial office opposing federation joined other objections emanating from Central Africa. Yet the support of industrial, business, and humanitarian interests sustained the movement toward federation. African nationalist activity in Nyasaland and Northern Rhodesia gained strength from the British government's decision to impose a federal system on the people of Central Africa. Indeed, the ratification of the federation marked the beginning of the struggle for independence in Nyasaland and Northern Rhodesia.

The failure of the Federation of Rhodesia and Nyasaland to create an environment conducive to racial harmony strengthened the nationalist movement for independence. The first few years of federal rule witnessed no fundamental relaxation of the color bars that segregated the races. The settlers and the governments of both Northern Rhodesia and Nyasaland worked in concert to counteract the effect of African opposition to federalism. The new structure deprived Africans of any meaningful representation, and taxation siphoned money from their pockets. Africans now distrusted the ability of the British to safeguard their interests.

Within the federation itself, the envisaged partnership between Africans and white settlers did not work. Moreover, events in other parts of Africa, including Ghana's achievement of independence in 1957, affected Rhodesia and Nyasaland in the late 1950s. Indeed, through the activities of the Nyasaland African Congress and the Zambia (Northern Rhodesia) African National Congress, Africans began to assert themselves in ways that alarmed the Europeans living throughout Central Africa. The leadership provided by Kenneth Kaunda and Dr. Hastings Banda vigorously challenged white authority, despite the white establishment's use of intimidation, detention, and bans on political activities. The detention of Kaunda and other nationalist leaders could not prevent the tide of change that was sweeping through the region. The banning of the Nyasaland and Zambia Congresses led to the formation of new political parties. To a large extent, it was the Africans' persistence that led to the dismantling of the federation by the end of 1963, leading to the independence of Nyasaland, renamed Malawi, in July 1964 and the independence of Northern Rhodesia, now the Republic of Zambia, in October 1964.

The French colonial territories in Equatorial Africa followed a different path toward independence. The mid-1940s witnessed the emergence of nationalist leaders and constitutional changes. Indeed, political reforms had started in the late 1930s when, "amid liberalizing economic and social policies, Africans were allowed broader participation in territorial administrative councils."[58] The re-

---

58. Austen and Headrick, "Equatorial Africa under Colonial Rule," 87.

Figure 19.3. Kenneth Kaunda of Zambia.

forms in the 1930s did not lead to autonomous political activities in the AEF. Un-like British West Africa, the AEF was isolated from the external ideological influ-ences that impacted many European-African relations in the era of decoloniza-tion. Yet significant changes followed the end World War II, with government support for development projects within African countries and the extension of French citizenship to Africans in the 1946 French constitution.

In Equatorial Africa, political changes in the decolonization years were deter-mined by four related factors: the metropolis, the colonial state, the white settlers, and the politicized Africans.[59] The metropolis initiated constitutional changes, usually in response to pressure from outside equatorial Africa. Metropolitan groups such as the Gaullists and the Catholics, although identifying with African aspirations, were less successful in advancing African interests because they iden-tified with right-wing settlers and were conservative in orientation. The contradic-tion in the reforms of the period was that local colonial administrations as well as metropolitan groups, while seeking African support, also encouraged the settler political participation that limited Africans' progress. This limitation provoked radical anticolonial sentiment among Africans. The white settlers sought to pro-tect their economic interests and improve their political position. Their limited number and short history in the region significantly reduced their importance in the steady progress toward independence. In the end, Africans became the focus of the new political systems under the auspices of the newly created parties and trade unions.[60] Unlike in West and East Africa, where trade unions played a major role in the decolonization process, however, the unions' role was limited in the AEF by the absence of large groups of unionized industrial workers.

The structure of the colonial state and the relationship of the African elite with the official bureaucracy influenced the decolonization process in Equatorial Africa. African leaders there had closer ties with Europeans and more defined eth-nic loyalties than the elite in other parts of Africa. Nevertheless, the largest politi-cal movements in Equatorial Africa, the UPC (Union des Populations du

---

59. Ibid., 88.
60. Ibid., 88–9.

Cameroon) in Cameroon and Barthelemy Boganda's MESAN (Mouvement pour l'Evolution Sociale de l'Afrique Noire) in Ubangi-Shari, made attempts to cut across ethnic loyalties and free themselves of European influence.[61] The radical stance of the UPC invited the wrath of the French government, and it was banned in 1958. The failure of radical nationalism in Equatorial Africa was a victory for France and shaped the nature of the postindependence relationship between France and its former colonial territories. Unlike leaders in other parts of Africa, many of the nationalist leaders that emerged with anticolonial sentiments sought accommodation with France to assure continued aid. Indeed, the states that emerged in equatorial Africa came to "formal independence not just under pro-French governments, but with stronger political and economic ties to the former metropolis than to one another."[62]

Conclusion

The era of decolonization was a complex period in African history. Just as the processes of conquest, partition, and administration differed throughout the continent, so did the processes of decolonization. While it is difficult to view the experiences of any African territory during this era as isolated from those of the others, many historians have noted that the extent and influence of colonial encounters and the nature of African responses to them varied from colony to colony.

In East, Central, and Equatorial Africa, the trajectory of the decolonization era was informed by internal developments within Africa, the presence of European settlers, and the nature of African responses to colonial domination. Two important factors, international capital and settler colonization, shaped the response of the metropolis and the white settlers to the agitation for independence. White settlers and metropolitan leaders fought between retaining political hegemony and granting some forms of participation to Africans in national politics. The ambivalent nature of colonial imperial policy in the region gave the decolonization process its unique character.

Review Questions

1. Explain the factors that led to the development of nationalism in East, Central, and Equatorial Africa in the period after World War II.
2. Outline the role of women in the decolonization process.
3. Discuss how and why the decolonization process differed from one country to another in East, Central, and Equatorial Africa.
4. Explain the role of international capital and white settler politics in shaping the response of the metropolis to the Africans' agitation for independence.
5. Why did the formation of African political parties reflect the shifting nature of loyalties based on region and ethnicity?
6. What role did trade unions play in the decolonization process?

---

61. Ibid., 90.
62. Ibid., 92.

Additional Reading

Barber, James. *Rhodesia: The Road to Rebellion.* Oxford: Oxford University Press, 1967.

Berger, Elena. *Labor, Race and Colonial Rule.* Oxford: Clarendon Press, 1974.

Birmingham, David and Phyllis M. Martin. *History of Central Africa, vol. 2.* New York: Longman, 1983.

Clough, Marshall S. *Mau Mau Memoirs: History, Memory, and Politics.* Boulder, Colorado: Lynne Rienner, 1998.

Cooper, Frederick. *Decolonization and African Society: The Labor Question in French and British Africa.* Cambridge: Cambridge University Press, 1996.

Epstein, A. L. *Politics in an Urban African Community.* Manchester: Manchester University Press, 1958.

Falola, Toyin. *Nationalism and African Intellectuals.* Rochester, NY: University of Rochester Press, 2001.

Fetter, Bruce, ed. *Demography from Scanty Evidence: Central Africa in the Colonial Era.* Boulder, CO: Lynne Rienner Publishers, 1990.

Joseph, Richard. *Radical Nationalism in Cameroun.* Oxford: Clarendon Press, 1977.

Mackenzie, A. Fiona. *Land, Ecology and Resistance in Kenya, 1880–1952.* Portsmouth,

NH: Heinemann, 1998.

Mamdani, Mahmood. *Citizen and Subject: Contemporary Africa and the Legacy of Late Colonialism.* Princeton, NJ: Princeton University Press, 1996.

Maxon, Robert M. *East Africa: An Introductory History.* Morgantown, West Virginia: West Virginia University Press, 1994.

Mazrui, Ali, and Michael Tidy. *Nationalism and New States in Africa.* Portsmouth, NH: Heinemann, 1986.

Palmer, Robin, and Neil Parsons, ed. *The Roots of Rural Poverty in Central and Southern Africa.* Portsmouth, NH: Heinemann, 1977.

Ogot, B. A. and William R. Ochieng', ed. *Decolonization and Independence in Kenya, 1940–1993.* Athens, OH: Ohio University Press, 1995.

Parsons, Timothy H. *The African Rank-and-File: Social Implications of Colonial Military Service in the King's African Rifles, 1902–1964.* Portsmouth, NH: Heinemann, 1999.

Rotbert, Robert I, ed. *Imperialism, Colonialism and Hunger: East and Central Africa.* Lexington, MA: Lexington Books, 1983.

_____. *The Rise of Nationalism in Central Africa: The Making of Malawi and Zambia 1873–1964.* Cambridge, MA: Harvard University Press, 1965.

_____. "The Rise of African Nationalism: The Case of East and Central Africa." *World Politics,* 15 (1962): 75–90.

Wills, A. J. *An Introduction to the History of Central Africa: Zambia, Malawi, and Zimbabwe, 4th ed.* Oxford: Oxford University Press, 1985.

Chapter 20

Portuguese Africa

Edmund Abaka

Portuguese rule in Africa in the twentieth century was defined by pride and the illusions of a bygone era. The attempt to fuse Africans and Europeans into a multiracial empire, as was done in Brazil, did not work. Portuguese rule in Angola, Mozambique, Guinea-Bissau, and Cape Verde involved forced labor, land confiscation, and excessive taxation, due in part to the fact that Portugal was a poor country. These policies, coupled with wage discrimination and "Portugalization," brought together disparate groups in a long tradition of resistance to Portuguese activities in Africa. The nationalist struggle and its attendant wars (1960s and 1970s) were waged in the context of the Cold War, and the support of the Soviet Union and of Cuba was instrumental in the eventual victories of the nationalist forces.

* * *

Portuguese Colonial Enterprise in Africa

The fundamental principles of Portuguese rule in Africa were devised by António de Oliveira Salazar, dictator of Portugal from 1928 to 1968. He incorporated these principles into the Colonial Act of 1930, and they became part of the 1951 Portuguese constitution. Articles 133 through 136 of that constitution stated, inter alia, that:

> It is intrinsic in the Portuguese Nation to fulfill its historic mission of colonization in the lands of the Discoveries under their sovereignty and to diffuse among the populations inhabiting them the benefits of their civilization, as well as to exercise the moral influence enjoined on it by the Patronage of the East.
>
> The Overseas Territories of Portugal shall be known as "provinces." Their politico-administrative organization shall be on lines best suited to their geographical situation and their social standards.
>
> The Overseas Provinces, as an integral part of the Portuguese State, are united among themselves and with Metropolitan Portugal.[1]

---

1. Ronald H. Chilcote, ed. and trans., *Emerging Nationalism in Portuguese Africa: Documents* (Stanford, Calif., 1972, 18); Bruce Fetter, ed., *Colonial Rule in Africa. Readings From Primary Sources* (Madison: University of Wisconsin Press, 1979), 106.

This forlorn appeal to the hopes, pride, and illusions of a bygone era defined Portuguese rule in Africa in the twentieth century. They saw Britain and France's abandonment of their colonies as a failure of their brand of colonization; Portuguese colonialism, in contrast, was a " a transcendent campaign, a sharing of values."[2] Nonetheless, the attempt to fuse Africans and Europeans into a multiracial empire as in Brazil eventually floundered. The major elements of Portuguese rule in Africa—especially forced labor, assimilation or "Portugalization," land confiscation, and tax policies—were major sources of the grievances underlying the nationalist struggle for independence in the 1960s and 1970s. This chapter discusses the Portuguese presence in Angola, Mozambique, Guinea-Bissau, and Cape Verde since the Scramble for and partition of Africa. The activities of various organizations, nationalist groups, and political parties that participated in this struggle against the Portuguese African "empire" constitute the essence of the chapter.

Portuguese Contact

Portugal's earliest explorations of Africa resulted in a few settlements on the Gold Coast in the fifteenth century and in towns on the Indian Ocean coast of Mozambique, in Luanda (Atlantic coast), and near a few trading posts in the Kwanza and Zambezi river valleys in the sixteenth century. These settlements became centers for a profitable slave trade to the New World. In 1500, the Portuguese also seized the island of São Tomé (200 miles west of Gabon) in the Gulf of Guinea and utilized slave labor imported from the adjacent African coast to produce sugar for European markets. Modeled after similar plantations in Madeira and southern Portugal, the São Tomé experiment provided a template for plantations in Brazil in the sixteenth century and the Caribbean in the seventeenth and eighteenth centuries.[3] The British, French, and Dutch eventually superceded the Portuguese in Africa.

Portuguese trading stations and later colonial possessions were weak because no economic base for administrative maintenance replaced the slave trade, and Portugal was too poor to support its colonies. Its average per capita income was very low (no more than £95 as late as 1962, compared with £224 in Belgium and £240 in France). Portugal also suffered from high illiteracy rates and relied heavily on foreign investments. During the colonial Scramble for Africa and during the continent's partition, memories of the "great century" and desires for prestige, laced with talk of a "civilizing mission," were swept along by a powerful ideological tide championed by the "new imperialists." João de Andrade Corvo typified this group when he asserted in the 1870s that "only through colonies, will Portugal be able to take the place she deserves in the concert of nations; only on their

2. Rupert Emerson, "Foreword," in *Angola in Ferment. The Background and Prospects of Angolan Nationalism,* Thomas Okuma, ed. (Westport, CT.: Greenwood Press, 1974), vii.

3. Philip Curtin, Steven Feierman, Leonard Thompson, and Jan Vansina, *African History* (Boston: Little, Brown and Company, 1978), 215. For early settlements, see also David M. Abshire and Michael A. Samuels, ed. *Portuguese Africa. A Handbook* (New York: Praeger, 1969), 33–7; David Birmingham, *The Portuguese Conquest of Angola* (London: Oxford University Press, 1965). For Mozambique see Allen F. Isaacman (in collaboration with Barbara Isaacman), *The Tradition of Resistance in Mozambique. The Zambesi Valley 1850–1921* (Berkeley: University of California Press, 1976), 1–5.

preservation and prosperity does her future greatness depend."[4] Riding this new wave of imperialism and propelled by an appeal to the past, to faith, and to duty, Portugal laid claim to large parts of Central Africa (about 750,000 square miles) between 1875 and 1900.[5]

Portugal had difficulty getting other powers to recognize its claims in Africa during the European Scramble for colonies. The Anglo-Portuguese Treaty of 1884, in which the British government agreed to recognize Portuguese claims to sovereignty over the coast on either side of the mouth of the Congo in return for certain commercial privileges, aroused a fierce storm of protest in Britain, France, and Germany and had to be abandoned. At the Berlin Conference of 1884–1885, Portugal secured the small enclave of Cabinda north of the Congo, a recognition of its claim to the coast south of the Congo River, and an agreement with the newly-created Congo Free State on the northeastern boundary of Angola. Additionally, in 1886–1887, Portugal persuaded France and Germany to recognize its control over the territory separating the Portuguese possessions of Angola and Mozambique; the government demarcated these territories on a map with a rose pink color to signify Portuguese rights.[6]

By 1890, Portugal controlled only about one-tenth of Angola and had only a tenuous hold on Mozambique, but it conducted punitive expeditions in both countries over the next thirty years, spurred on by a new colonial mystique that was fomented by a group of young colonial army officers. On the eve of World War I, Portuguese rule in Angola and Mozambique centered on the coastal towns of Luanda, Benguela, Beira, and Lourenço Marques and their immediate hinterlands.[7]

Portuguese Africa, 1900–1950

In 1910, a republican administration replaced the Portuguese monarchy. During the next sixteen years, Portugal went through some forty-five governments before the republic was overthrown in a military coup. Beginning in the late 1920s, the authoritarian *Estado Nova* ("New State"), led by Dr. António Salazar and his associates, utilized censorship, informants, secret police, and the military to perpetuate colonial rule. Indeed, Salazar's ideology transformed Portuguese imperialism. One newspaper editor summed it up in 1935: "Africa is for us a moral justi-

---

4. Quoted in Fetter, *Colonial Rule in Africa. Readings From Primary Sources*, 5; J. Duffy, *Portugal in Africa* (Harmondsworth, England, 1962), 107. Robin Hallett, *Africa since 1875* (Ann Arbor: University of Michigan Press, 1974), 490. For João de Andrade Corvo's views and activities see David M. Abshire, "From the Scramble for Africa to the 'New State,'" in *Portuguese Africa: A Handbook*, in David M. Abshire and Michael A. Samuels, ed. (New York: Praeger, 1969), 68–70.

5. For the boundaries of Portugal's territorial claims in Central Africa see Eric Axelson, *Portugal and the Scramble for Africa 1875–1891* (Johannesburg: Witwatersrand University Press, 1967), 1–90.

6. Ibid., 1. See also Ronald H. Chilcote, *Portuguese Africa* (Englewood Cliffs, NJ.: Prentice-Hall, 1967), 117–9.

7. Axelson, *Portugal and the Scramble for Africa*, 232–58.

fication and a raison d'être as a power. Without it we would be a small nation: with it we are a great country."[8] This appeal to the past, to faith, and to duty became the underlying principle of Portuguese imperialism in Africa.

Migration from Portugal to Angola and Mozambique in the early twentieth century changed the face of the two African societies. Angola's European population numbered just over nine thousand in 1900, about forty-four thousand in 1940, and eighty-eight thousand in 1951. Many of the migrants were poor whites, lacking in both skill and capital. Although they often could not find suitable work, they were too proud to return to Portugal, and so drifted to the villages and cohabited with African women.[9]

Mozambique's climate, less salubrious than that of Angola, prevented excessive migration. Nonetheless, between 1928 and 1951, the country's European population grew from eighteen thousand to fifty-two thousand. Most of Africa's Portuguese population was concentrated in Luanda (Angola), Lourenço Marques, and Beira (Mozambique), all of which were port cities, railroad terminals, and tourist resorts. Eventually Luanda (with a population of 200,000) became the third largest city in the Portuguese empire after Lisbon and Oporto. By 1950, the Portuguese had created an administrative service proportionally larger than the size of its territory and population.[10] Like the British and the French, the Portuguese used African chiefs and headmen in the lower levels of colonial administration as intermediaries between the colonial officers and the people and quickly deposed those who failed to perform their duties faithfully.

The absence of a legal color bar, the acceptance of mixed marriages, the *mestiço* (Afro-European) presence, and a provision allowing Africans to achieve literacy in Portuguese, to obtain a reasonable income, and the ability to become *assimilados* and enjoy the full rights of citizenship with "good conduct" masked some insidious dimensions of Portuguese rule in Africa. *Assimilados*, numbering only about 4,500 in Mozambique and thirty thousand in Angola in 1950, and *mestiços*, numbering about sixty thousand in the two colonies, constituted a small proportion of the total population. By 1963, only twenty-six thousand children, no more than a fifth of which were Africans, attended primary schools in Mozambique, and only 332 pupils attended secondary school.[11] Hence, the much-touted policy of assimilation, which depended on education, was ostensibly pursued at a time when educational facilities were extremely limited.

Added to the limited access to education and other forms of discrimination was the widespread and indiscriminate use of forced labor. Forced labor became the "flywheel of the whole economy."[12] Accustomed to regarding Africans as fit only to be slaves, the Portuguese used them in the post-slavery period as "contract laborers," which meant, in reality, virtual slaves. Recruiting agents used bribes and threats to force chiefs to supply them with laborers, who were sent to plantations in São Tomé and Principe under an1889 labor code—a devious piece of leg-

---

8. Quoted in J. Duffy, *Portuguese Africa* (Cambridge, MA.: Harvard University Press, 1959), 277.

9. Hallett, *Africa since 1875*, 511. See also Duffy, *Portugal in Africa*, 204.

10. Duffy, *Portuguese Africa*, 288.

11. Axelson, *Portugal and the Scramble*, 18.

12. B. Davidson, *The African Awakening*. (London, 1955, 197); Hallett, *Africa since 1875*, 513.

islation used to justify lifelong labor in place of of what was supposed to be a five-year contract.[13]

Importance of African Colonies to Portugal

The unprecedented economic boom of the 1920s gave way to the economic crisis of the 1930s and led to increased economic integration between the colonies and Portugal. Portugal was a poor country, and trade policies that subordinated the colonies' economies to that of Portugal were vigorously pursued. Beginning in the 1930s, the colonies were exploited for Portugal's benefit. Portugal bought sugar at prices well below the world market price and enjoyed a fifty percent tariff advantage on goods imported into the colonies until the 1950s. The colonies could import goods from other countries only if the cost was fifteen percent less than that of Portuguese imports. Seventy-five percent of all cotton textiles and fifty percent of all building materials had to come from Lisbon. Likewise, Portuguese industry was protected through administrative action, and foreign exchange was provided only for goods sanctioned by the Lisbon authorities. All in all, Angola and Mozambique contributed twenty-five percent of Portugal's total revenue during this period, even while colonial importers faced problems trying to obtain import licenses from Lisbon.[14]

Taxation

Portugal levied a ten percent industrial tax on the gross profits of joint stock companies and private firms in Africa. Agriculture, forestry, cattle ranching, fishing, mining, and most industries developing natural resources paid an exploitation tax, although this tax was low. The colonial government of Angola had the power to grant agricultural concessions of five thousand hectares (1 hectare = 2.471 acres) and could give three such concessions to any individual or firm. The minister of the colonies in Lisbon could grant up to 100,000 hectares for an annual rent of 0.8 escudos per hectare (17 escudos = $1.00). Ranching concessions were fixed for seventy years and timber concessions for twenty-five, with a possible ten-year extension at a rate of 0.15 escudos per hectare for ten years. The concessions could be increased by twenty-five hectares every tenth year up to the sixtieth year.[15]

---

13. Chilcote, *Portuguese Africa*, 12–13.

14. C. Coquery-Vidrovitch, "The Colonial Economy of the Former French, Belgian and Portuguese Zones, 1914–1935," in UNESCO *General History of Africa. VII. Africa under Colonial Domination 1880–1935*, A. Adu Boahen, ed. (Paris: UNESCO, 1985), 354–7; K. Madhu Panikar, *Angola in Flames* (New York: Asia Publishing House, 1962). See also Andrew Wilson Green, "Portugal and the African Territories: Economic Implications," in *Portuguese Africa. A Handbook*, David M. Abshire and Michael A. Manuels, eds. (New York: Praeger), 345–63.

15. K. Madhu Panikar, *Angola in Flames*, 31.

Mining

The most important economic activity in the Portuguese colonies was mining. Lisbon granted exclusive privileges and tax exemptions to the Diamond Company of Angola and to petroleum companies. Intent on counterbalancing the economic interests of Britain in Rhodesia and Belgium in the Congo, Portugal induced large international businesses with interests in Angola and Mozambique, such as Tanganyika Concessions and the the American oil companies (Standard Oil and Gulf Oil), to invest heavily in the colonies. In this way, the companies could use their influence with their home governments to mobilize public opinion against African opposition to European activities in Angola and Mozambique.[16]

Discrimination and Land Policy

Decree Law Number 3983 of March 16, 1918 gave Portugal all land not belonging to individuals or corporate bodies, thus essentially depriving Africans of their property. Furthermore, under the Portuguese Native Statute of 1954, no "native" (defined as any black person or person of black descent who was born in or resided in a province and did not have the knowledge and social habits considered prerequisites for Portuguese citizenship), could acquire property.[17] Though Africans and Portuguese could attend school together, there were only ten Africans in a class of eight hundred at the only *Liceu* (secondary school) in Mozambique. Portuguese citizenship could be revoked by a judge despite the insistence, according to one author, that "One State, One Race, One Faith, and One Civilization" were the building blocks of the Portuguese empire. Portugal tried to create in Africa the mixed society it had created in Brazil, but, in sexual matters, so-called freedom was a one-way street, with frequent liaisons between Portuguese men and African women, but not vice versa.[18]

Wage Discrimination

Even though the Portuguese attributed the lack of African political participation to a dearth of educated Africans, those who were educated and assimilated still faced discrimination. African economic mobility into the class of artisans and skilled laborers was very limited. Rigid barriers to promotion and unequal pay scales for Africans and Portuguese were common. For example, while an African in a furniture factory in Luanda was paid seventy cents day making legs for chairs, his Portuguese counterpart received three dollars for the same work. Likewise, while African waiters in mining towns earned twenty-five dollars a month, Portuguese waiters took home fifty dollars. In Luanda, a Portuguese painter, stone mason, or carpenter received twice the wage of his African counterpart. In other districts the income gap between Portuguese workers and their African counterparts was even wider.[19]

---

16. Ibid., 31.
17. Panikar, *Angola in Flames*, 33.
18. Panikar, *Angola in Flames*, 38–9.
19. Peter Shapiro, "Report from Angola," *Issue: A Quarterly Journal of Africanist Opinion* 2, 3 (Fall 1972): 38–9; Duffy, *Portuguese Africa*, 205.

Labor Policies

Another odious dimension of Portuguese rule in Africa was forced labor. Africans were an important labor source for Portuguese farms and plantations in Angola, Mozambique, and São Tomé. The exploitation of Africans through forced labor occurred in all colonies: French, Portuguese, English, and Belgian. But with an economy teetering on bankruptcy, the success of the Portuguese colonial enterprise came to depend on its ability to mobilize and control free labor. An 1899 government commission declared:

> We need native labor, we need it in order to better the conditions of these laborers, we need it for the economy of Europe and for the progress of Africa.... The capital needed to exploit [tropical Africa], and it so needs to be exploited, lies in the procurement of labor for exploitation.[20]

The first article of the labor code intimated that:

> All natives of the Portuguese overseas provinces are subject to the obligation, moral and legal, of attempting to obtain through work the means that they lack to subsist and to better their social condition. They have full liberty to choose the method of fulfilling this obligation, but if they do not fulfill it public authority may force a fulfillment.[21]

Hence, under this code, Africans were sent to work on Portuguese plantations. From the interwar years onward, Africans represented a labor pool — an instrument for the development of Portugal and its colonies — to the Portuguese colonial administration.

In Angola, forced labor was used for work on roads and plantations until the 1950s. An American journalist, writing in 1948, provided a succinct account of the methods employed:

> When an Angolan plantation owner requires labor, he notifies the government of his needs. The demand is passed down to the village chiefs, who are ordered to supply fixed quotas of laborers from their communities. If the required numbers are not forthcoming, police are sent to round them up.[22]

To escape these demands, many Portuguese Africans moved into neighboring British or Belgian territories, causing serious depopulation in parts of Angola.

In Portuguese Africa, the law compelled every African to work for Portuguese farmers or the colonial government for six months, a requirement that was often extended to eighteen months. This policy was allegedly designed to teach Africans responsibility. By using the whip, so the argument went, administrators might in-

---

20. Quoted in "Politics and Nationalism in Central and Southern Africa, 1919–1935," in Boahen ed., *General History of Africa*, 697; Panikar, *Angola in Flames*, 41–7.
21. Duffy, *Portuguese Africa*, 155.
22. Quoted in Davidson, *The African Awakening*, 203. See Portuguese labor policy or practice. See also James Duffy, *Portugal in Africa* (Cambridge: Harvard University Press, 1962), 184–6.

culcate the dignity of labor. It was a nightmarish experience working on government projects, because workers engaged in back-breaking work and received no wages.[23]

In exchange for an agreement to reserve 47.5 percent of South African traffic for the Lourenço Marques railroad, some 250 recruiters were required to supply eighty thousand Africans a year to the mines in the Transvaal, South Africa. Approximately 900,000 Mozambicans—only 740,000 of whom returned in satisfactory health and thirty-five thousand of whom died—were sent to the Transvaal, constituting one of the colony's major revenue sources. Between 1938 and 1948, over one million people migrated from the two colonies to escape such forced labor.[24]

In Mozambique, the colonial state also resorted to coercing labor to work on settler estates, build roads, expand the ports of Lourenço Marques and Beira, construct railroads, and work as domestic servants. Even though women were legally exempt, they were increasingly recruited; even pregnant women were recruited for forced labor and road construction. In remote places, workers were housed together in barracks and made to work for up to six months or more. After 1926, Mozambican peasants were forced to cultivate cotton and sell it at deflated prices to European companies.[25]

Resistance to Colonialism
Before 1950: Angola

The nationalist movements that wrested control from the Portuguese emerged from several threads of resistance to colonial activities, especially Portugal's dominance in the slave trade and its penetration of local markets. Initially sporadic and geographically scattered, such resistance preceded the more organized movements of the 1960s and 1970s. In northern Angola, between 1913 and 1915, Alvaro Tulante Buta led a revolt to protest the deportation of Congolese laborers to São Tomé.[26] From 1872 to 1919, Africans in the Dembos region revolted against the Portuguese. In the Benguelan highlands, the Cuanhama people also engaged in a lengthy rebellion against the Portuguese between 1904 and 1915.[27]

---

23. Coquery-Vidrovitch, "The Colonial Economy of the Former French, Belgian and Portuguese Zones, 1914–35," in *General History of Africa, VII: Africa under Colonial Domination 1880–1935*. A. Adu Boahen, ed. (Paris: UNESCO, 1985), 364. For details about forced labor in Mozambique see Allen Isaacman (in collaboration with Barbara Isaacman), *The Tradition of Resistance in Mozambique. The Zambesi Valley 1850–1921* (Berkeley: University of California Press, 1976), 84–7.

24. Ibid. 364. See also Panikar, *Angola in Flames*, 43.

25. A. B. Davidson, A. Isaacman, and R. Pélissier, "Politics and Nationalism in Central and Southern Africa, 1919–1935," in *General History of Africa. VII. Africa under Colonial Domination 1880–1935*. A. Adu Boahen, ed. (Paris: UNESCO, 1985), 697–8.

26. Chilcote, *Emerging Nationalism in Portuguese Africa*, xxvi–xxvii.

27. Isaacman (in collaboration with Isaacman), *Tradition of Resistance in Mozambique*, 107–10.

In an atmosphere of corporal punishment and arbitrary and venal treatment by recruiters and colonial authorities alike, migration became a means of revolt. Entire villages abandoned their homes and fields and withdrew to areas further away from the colonial administrative control in northern and eastern Angola. There was also clandestine emigration through harsh terrain to the Belgian Congo, Zambia (then Northern Rhodesia), and Namibia (then South West Africa). [28]

While these events were occurring in rural areas, assimilated intellectuals and journalists railed against colonial abuses in Luanda and Lisbon. The *assimilados* welcomed the collapse of the monarchy and the advent of a republic. In 1912, African expatriates in Lisbon formed the Junta de Defensa dos Direitos de Africa, and in Angola, though Liga Angolana gained recognition in 1913, its Cuanza Norte "conspiracy" of 1916–1917 linked alienated intellectuals with Mbundu peasants in the Lunda hinterland and posed a serious threat to the colonial administration. Led by António de Assis Júnior (1887–1960), the group condemned colonial oppression and the preferential treatment given to the settler community. Concern over rebellions and a fear of an *assimilado*-peasant alliance led to a swift repression of the group. In 1922, High Commissioner Norton de Matos clamped down on the Liga Angolana and the Gremio Africana (the African Union), ordered Assis arrested, and deported many of the group's other leaders. He also banned local newspapers and curtailed opportunities for *assimilado* civil servants, thus crushing intellectual resistance to the colonial regime and driving the resistance underground. Even though the Liga Angolana reappeared in 1929–1930 as the Liga Nacional Africana and the Gremio Africano resurfaced in the 1920s as the Associação dos Naturais de Angola (ANANGOLA), Salazar's stranglehold on Portugal and strong opposition to resistance movements rendered them ineffective. They eventually merged to become the Movimento Nacionalista Africano but were forced to suspend their activities from 1925 to 1945.[29]

Resistance Against Colonialism in the 1960s: Angola

The African colonies were vital to the Portuguese economy, and, therefore, Portugal was determined not to make any concessions to African demands for independence. Resistance to Portuguese colonialism in the 1960s stemmed from the weakness of the colonial state, its increasing authoritarianism, its use of forced labor as a centerpiece of development, and its policy of assimilation. The wave of nationalism that swept across the African continent in the 1960s had important repercussions in Portuguese Africa, highlighting its political and economic powerlessness. One external event that had repercussions for the Angolan struggle was the hijacking of a Portuguese luxury liner, the *Santa Maria* (January 1961), by

---

28. Ibid. 107–10.
29. Davidson, Isaacman, and Pélissier, "Politics and Nationalism in Central and Southern Africa, 1919–35," 699–702.

Henrique Malta Galvao, a former colonial high inspector and a Salazar opponent. Galvao and sixty armed men seized the liner with six hundred passengers and three hundred crew members off the Curaçao coast and set off for Angola to establish a rebel Portuguese government. Engine trouble and problems with passengers and crew members forced Galvao to land at Recife, Brazil. The incident drew attention to the Angolan issue and on February 4, 1961, several hundred Africans and mulattos raided Luanda's main political prison. Forty Africans and seven policemen were killed in the raid. In the riotous climate that followed the incident, many Africans were killed (about three hundred in the first three days, according to one estimate). Though the fighting subsided at the end of the month, the atmosphere in Luanda was poisoned, a harbinger of the violence to erupt in the 1960s and 1970s.[30]

Resistance Against Colonialism: Mozambique

In Mozambique, documented worker and peasant opposition was common, albeit uncoordinated. Powerless to resist on a large scale, peasants minimized the disruptive effects of Portuguese domination through tax evasion, withdrawal into the interior, and flight across the permeable African boundaries to neighboring countries.[31] In a few instances, refugee communities sprang up in rugged mountain zones and coastal swamps that defied easy penetration. Likewise, some peasants withheld their labor, planting cotton fields after the designated time, cultivating the minimum acreage, and burning the fields after the harvest. Even though rural protest hardly ever took the form of organized resistance, peasants in the Zambezi valley, angered by forced labor, mandatory cotton production, and sexual abuses, joined a rebellion directed by descendants of the Barue royal family and Shona spirit mediums (1917) to liberate their homelands and overturn the oppressive colonial system.[32]

Rural peasants also utilized cultural symbols in their hostility toward the colonial regime. While the workers of the Sena Sugar Estates described European overseers in unflattering sexual terms, the Chope in southern Mozambique denounced tax collectors and other colonial officials, particularly in songs. Makua and Makonde artists ridiculed state officials in highly stylized carvings that distorted their features and eliminated their humanity.[33]

Urban resistance, initially sporadic due to the prohibition of African unions and facing a white labor movement imbued with the state's racial and cultural prejudices, gradually began to coalesce around African workers. There were

---

30. Shapiro, "Report from Angola," 39.
31. Isaacman, *Tradition of Resistance in Mozambique*, 86–9.
32. Davidson, Isaacman, and Pélissier, "Politics and Nationalism in Central and Southern Africa, 1919–35," 704.
33. See E. Mondlane, *The Struggle For Mozambique* (Harmondsworth, England: Penguin, 1969); Davidson, Isaacman, and Pélissier, "Politics and Nationalism in Central and Southern Africa, 1919–35," 705.

strikes and work stoppages by African workers of the Merchants Association (1913), tram workers (1917), and railroad technicians (1918). Workers organized through informal grassroots networks. Port and wharf workers were harassed by troops, undercut by strikebreakers, and sometimes surrounded by police who forced them to unload ships. In this climate, independent churches again offered an institutional framework for workers to vent their grievances against the colonial administration. Alienated, migrant Mozambican mine workers joined churches or formed autonomous sects modeled after the Ethiopian movements in South Africa and Rhodesia. In these churches, Mozambicans elected their own officials, controlled their own budgets, drafted their own constitutions, and chose their own flags, thus acquiring "free space" in an enclosed authoritarian regime.[34]

Urban intellectual protest in Portuguese colonies, though relatively small-scale in comparison to that in other parts of Africa, began slowly in 1908. A Lourenço Marques newspaper, O Africano (the mouthpiece of the Germino Africano, and its successor O Brado Africano (the African Voice) highlighted recurring abuses by the colonial regime. These newspapers attacked poor working conditions, the lack of educational opportunities, brutal forced-labor tactics, and the practice of seizing women to work on road construction projects without food or wages.[35] They also decried the custom of forcing Africans to work on European estates from sunrise to sunset for roughly a shilling a month, the use of strikebreakers to replace African workers, and the informal color bar which froze Africans on the lower rungs of the occupational ladder. Beginning in cautious and reformist tones and appealing to goodwill and a sense of justice, newspaper editorials took on a defiant, angry tone during the Salazar period (1928–1968).[36] For all their criticism of the colonial abuses, however, these spokespersons for the resistance lived in a social and cultural milieu far removed from the shanty towns and barracks that dominated the countryside. Moreover, rivalry between African and mulatto segments of the colonial elite eventually contributed to the demise of the African union in the 1940s. A small number of African intellectuals were linked to the broader African struggle in the diaspora through W. E. B. Du Bois's Pan-African congresses.[37]

The Militant and Final Phase of Nationalist Agitation for Independence

Salazar's Portugal was convinced that its national identity was organically linked to its past, and, therefore, any transfer of power to Africans was inconceivable. Salazar resisted pressure to transfer power from moderate reform groups led

---

34. Ibid., 706–8.
35. Chilcote, Portuguese Africa, 77–8.
36. Davidson, Isaacman, and Pélissier, "Politics and Nationalism in Central and Southern Africa, 1919–35," 709–10.
37. The Pan-African Congresses were held in 1900 (London), 1919 (Paris), 1921 (London, Brussels and Paris), 1922 (London). These congresses helped to publicize the demands of Africans and people of African descent for an end to discrimination and colonialism throughout the world.

by African *assimilados*, the Organization of African Unity (OAU), and Portugal's American ally to provincial Africans. Neither the government nor Portuguese capitalists were prepared to relinquish political power over the colonies, because the colonies were evidence that the small, weak state of Portugal was once a world power. Portuguese politicians had long sought to maintain patriotic credibility by defending the colonies. The colonies, especially Angola and Mozambique, supplied raw materials to Portuguese industry and offered preferential markets for Portuguese goods (over forty percent of Angola's imports and about thirty percent Mozambique's were from Portugal). In addition, nascent Portuguese multinational enterprises such as the Companhia Uniao Fabril took advantage of preferential legislation to invest in industry and mining in Africa, particularly in Angola. During the 1940s and 1950s, earnings from overseas trade with the colonies counterbalanced deficits in the Portuguese balance of payments.[38]

Beginning in 1954, Salazar made it easier for qualified Africans to exercise their civil rights. Some have argued that Portugal was thinking of an eventual "Brazilian solution" by which the colonies would become self-governing states, possibly led by settlers and *assimilados*, and be closely bound to Portugal by economic and cultural ties. However, any thought of transferring power, even to a settler elite, evaporated after 1961 as Lisbon became more determined to stifle independence and armed resistance movements. Portugal relaxed the detested labor laws and allowed some social reforms, especially after M. Caetano succeeded Salazar in 1968, but it was too little, too late. The Portuguese reforms failed to satisfy the members of nationalist movements who had lived through the whole gamut of previous colonial policies. To stifle the political dissent, the Portuguese administrators and secret police (PIDE) increasingly used their power to repress the protesters.[39]

The 1960s marked the high point of nationalist agitation in the Portuguese African colonies. Many resistance movements, both regional and national, emerged and were supported financially and materially by independent African states and the international community. A few major revolutionary parties emerged from the many movements of the 1960s and became the focal points of resistance to the Portuguese in Africa.

The Portuguese administration faced mounting nationalist resistance from guerrillas of the Popular Movement for the Liberation of Angola (Movimento Popular de Libertação de Angola, or MPLA), founded clandestinely in 1956, and of the Front for the Liberation of Mozambique (Frente de Libertação de Moçambique, or FRELIMO), founded in 1962.[40]

Hence, beginning in the 1950s, the situation in the Portuguese African colonies was characterized by political dissent led in a large part by *mestiços* or *assimilados*, resident Portuguese, and men whose citizenship and, in many cases, overseas educations allowed some limited range for action. It was this group that began to look at the struggle in terms of national rather than local resistance, and thereby transformed the fight from one of localized active or passive resistance to one of national guerrilla warfare.

---

38. John D. Hargreaves, *Decolonization in Africa*, 2nd. eds., (London: Addison Wesley Longman, 1996), 229.
39. Ibid., 230.
40. Duffy, *Portugal in Africa*, 213–4.

The War for Independence in Guinea-Bissau and Cape Verde

Militant nationalist resistance began in the small West African colonies of Guinea Bissau and the Cape Verde Islands (to which the Portuguese desperately clung) when the African Party for the Independence of Guinea-Bissau and Cape Verde (Partido Africano de Independência de Guiné e Cabo Verde, or PAIGC), led by Amílcar Cabral (1924–1973), was clandestinely formed in 1956.[41] These wars of counterviolence against a particularly retrograde Portuguese colonialism were long, tedious, and painful. The nationalist movements waged guerrilla warfare against a ruthless colonial system that was supported by a strong alliance with the industrial powers of the North Atlantic Treaty Organization (NATO).[42]

In 1956, a small group of clerks and civil servants, many from Cape Verde, founded the PAIGC under Amilcar Cabral, and, three years later, instigated a major dock workers' strike at Bissau. When colonial police brutally suppressed the strikers, the PAIGC responded by launching a full-scale national liberation war. By 1966, the PAIGC controlled a substantial portion of Portuguese Guinea, having driven the Portuguese from their fortified positions.[43] Cabral's career as an agronomist helped him understand and appreciate the needs of rural Africans and facilitated PAIGC efforts at mobilizing rural areas. The PAIGC built schools, health clinics, roads, and agricultural projects in the liberated areas in conformance with grassroots socialist ideas. By September 1973, a large portion of the country had been liberated and the PAIGC had declared the independence of both Portuguese Guinea and Cape Verde. However, Cabral was assassinated in January 1974, before the Portuguese withdrawal in September 1974.

Angola's Independence War

In Angola, a brutal, thirteen-year guerrilla war started in the cotton fields, where compulsory cultivation, low prices, and delayed payments led to an outbreak of violence in January 1961. Portuguese Air Force planes strafed Angolan villages in response to this initial flare-up. Violence then erupted in the Angolan capital, Luanda. Agostinho Neto founded the Popular Movement for the Liberation of Angola (MPLA) in December 1956, largely as an urban working-class movement. However, while most of the MPLA leaders awaited trial in 1961, Angolan peasants, stirred by events across the Congolese border, revolted against forced cotton cultivation and the Portuguese administration's forced labor practices. In February, unidentified leaders directed a crowd of urban poor in an attack on the prison where the MPLA leaders were being held. Armed groups of

---

41. See Gérard Chaliand, *Armed Struggle in Africa with the Guerrillas in Portuguese Guinea*. David Rattray and Robert Leonhardt, trans. (New York: Monthly Review Press, 1969).
42. Basil Davidson, *Africa in History*, revised edition. (New York: Touchstone, 1995), 340.
43. Chaliand, *Armed Struggle in Africa with the Guerrillas in Portuguese Guinea*. David Rattray and Robert Leonhardt, trans. (New York: Monthly Review Press, 1969), xiii.

whites, influenced by recent atrocities in Angola, ran amok through black slums, killing hundreds of people.[44]

In March, violence spread to the north, where the colonial administration had seized lands of the Kongo people and redistributed them to poor, unskilled Portuguese immigrants attracted to the prospect of making a fortune in coffee cultivation. To supply the immigrants with a labor pool, the government subjected the Kongo to forced labor. As the northern white population increased from eighty thousand in 1960 to 300,000 in 1970, ethnic tensions began to boil. When workers on one plantation demanded six months overdue wages, violence erupted. Hundreds of white settlers, Ovimbundu workers (who had been sent to the area as forced laborers), and thousands of Kongo people died in the aftermath. The disturbances in the coffee region were further exacerbated when white farmers withheld the wages of African conscript laborers.[45]

The leaders of the major liberation movements in Portuguese Africa saw the liberation struggle as a battle for the "hearts and minds" of their people. If they were to succeed in winning independence, they would have to channel local grievances into national agendas and found independent, modern states. Hence, these liberation movements focused on freeing and modernizing the people through a revolution against both traditional structures and colonial rule.[46]

Many of the resistance leaders, mainly of the MPLA, left Luanda for Angola's coffee-growing region. In March 1961, another resistance group, the Union of the Populations of Angola (UPA) called for massive destruction of property and crops in the northern coffee-growing regions. The attacks came at a time when the United Nations was debating the future of the Portuguese colonies. They targeted Portuguese settlers in the northern coffee-growing areas and were led from across the border by the UPA, which later became Holden Roberto's Bakongo-based Frente Nacional de Libertaçao de Angola, or FNLA. Although he had once dreamed of restoring the old Kongo kingdom, Roberto now professed broader Pan-African aims. Portuguese police and soldiers responded to the uprising through indiscriminate attacks on Africans around Luanda, a reaction that won Holden Roberto support in many African states and even in the United States, where he was regarded as less dangerous than the radical ideologues in Luanda. Yet, disunity among nationalist groups militated against any early success. While the UPA concentrated its efforts in the north (and won Zaire's support), the MPLA operated in the vast, underpopulated area of eastern Angola (and was supported by Zambia). UNITA, formed in 1967, was based in the east and south. Fratricidal war between various groups further characterized the initial phase of the revolution.[47]

This phase of the revolution witnessed a shift from traditional, rural revolts to a politically-based mass rebellion. The initial clashes resulted in Portugal's attempt to reconquer the territory and led to the flight of over 100,000 people to neighboring Zaire (now the Democratic Republic of Congo).[48]

---

44. See Chilcote, *Portuguese Africa*, 75–6.

45. Ibid., 77.

46. This plan, rigorously carried out, explains the success of the liberation movements, most especially that of the PAIGC in Guinea-Bissau and Cape Verde, in mobilizing the rural areas in the struggle against the Portuguese army.

47. Chilcote, *Portuguese Africa*, 79–81.

48. A. E. Afigbo et al., *The Making of Modern Africa. Vol II. The Twentieth Century*

The Cold War's contribution to the complex independence story unfolding in Africa was particularly striking. The liberation wars of the 1960s drew international powers into the fight. The MPLA, pursuing a socialist policy of reform, secured Soviet aid in the form of training and weapons. Convinced that the country needed a socialist transformation, the MPLA developed a sophisticated, operational, and revolutionary platform. However, it was plagued by ideological, ethnic, and personal internal divisions and by external rivalry, both with the FNLA and, beginning in 1966, with UNITA, a group that benefited from Zambia's support.[49]

The FNLA, based in Zaire, played a minor role in the war's initial phase. As the end of the war approached, however, the FNLA became very active, enjoying support from Zaire and the United States as a counterweight to the pro-Soviet MPLA. Significantly, the FNLA's activities were aimed more at the Soviet-backed MPLA than at the Portuguese colonial authorities. Similarly, Jonas Savimbi's UNITA (based among the Ovimbundu in the south east) was also more concerned about the MPLA than about the Portuguese.[50] UNITA received financial and material help from the apartheid South African government, which feared that the MPLA would support the South West African Peoples' Organization (SWAPO), a group already fighting for Namibia's independence. (Given its military—especially naval—facilities, South Africa was not ready to relinquish Namibia.) In 1974, UNITA formed an anti-MPLA alliance with the Portuguese, plunging Angola into civil war as the Portuguese departed.[51]

The MPLA controlled Luanda and had support in rural areas. In the early 1970s, the MPLA also received material and moral support from its socialist counterpart, the newly independent Guinea-Bissau. Fearing the MPLA would assume control after independence in November 1975, South Africa invaded Angola from Namibia and pushed toward the capital.[52] From the north, the FNLA, equipped by the United States and supported by troops from the self-proclaimed anticommunist government of Zaire, Portuguese irregulars, and mercenaries, also moved toward the capital. As Agostinho Neto proclaimed Angolan independence in 1975, he appealed to the Soviet bloc for aid to defend the capital against the invading armies. Cuba obliged, sending about thirteen thousand Soviet-equipped Cuban troops.[53] The Cuban-MPLA forces (now the national army) defeated a crack South African force at the strategic junction of Cuito Carnavale and, in early 1976, flushed UNITA and its South African allies out of central Angola.

(Essex, England: Longman, 1986), 350–1. See also Kevin Shillington, *History of Africa* (New York: St. Martin's Press, 1995), 398.

49. Arthur Jay Klinghoffer, *The Angolan War: A Study in Soviet Policy in the Third World* (Boulder, CO.: Westview Press, 1980), 9–12.

50. For more on UNITA see John A. Marcum, " 'UNITA': The Politics of Survival," in *Angola, Mozambique and the West*, Helen Kitchen, ed. (New York: Praeger, 1987), 4–16.

51. Hargreaves, *Decolonization in Africa*. 230–231; Shillington, *History of Africa*. 399. For the civil war see John A. Marcum, "A Quarter Century of War," in *Angola, Mozambique and the West*, Helen Kitchen ed. 17–35.

52. John A. Marcum, "United States Options in Angola," in *Angola, Mozambique and the West*, Kitchen, ed. 36–53.

53. See Gillian Gunn, "Cuba and Angola," in *Angola, Mozambique and the West*, Kitchen, ed. 71–80.

This enhanced Cuba's image as a defender of Angolans from a racist South African regime.[54]

The War for Independence in Mozambique

In Mozambique, as in Angola, nationalist forces were initially disunited. In 1962, however, two major exiled organizations, the Mozambique African National Union (MANU), and União Democrática Nacional de Moçambique (UDENAMO) united to form the Frente de Libertaçao de Moçambique (FRELIMO) in the Tanzanian capital of Dar es Salaam, propelled in part by the June 1960 massacre of several hundred protesting peasants in northern Mozambique. FRELIMO was formed to unite all the Mozambican political parties, associations, and leaders in a single movement to spearhead the liberation of Mozambique from Portuguese rule.[55] Under Eduardo Mondlane and his deputy Samora Machel, FRELIMO launched the militant phase of the independence struggle in 1964 with military campaigns aimed at securing control of Mozambique's two northern provinces. By 1968, FRELIMO had also established bases in Tete Province.

Mozambique's liberation struggle, like that of Angola, was influenced by the Cold War. U.S. policy makers in the Nixon administration were increasingly worried by signs of growing Communist influence in Southern Africa's leading liberation movements.[56] The MPLA had access to Soviet and Cuban financial, material, and ideological support. Just as the United States supported Zaire as an anticommunist bastion against Angola, it now discretely increased its economic and military cooperation with Portugal within the NATO framework, hoping to engender reform in Portuguese labor practices and to encourage a liberal policy under Salazar's successor, Marcelo Caetano. However, the resistance leaders' continued struggle against and frustration with hostile external intervention prevented the attainment of these goals.

Henry Kissinger's assessment of the Mozambique situation in 1969 was that "the outlook for the rebellions is one of continued stalemate: the rebels cannot oust the Portuguese and the Portuguese can contain but not eliminate the rebels."[57]

Independence in Portuguese Africa

Long, drawn-out guerrilla wars strained Portugal's fiscal and material resources to the breaking point. Portugal maintained large conscript armies in

---

54. Ibid., 74. See also Shillington, *History of Africa*. 399.

55. Chilcote, *Emerging Nationalism in Portuguese Africa*, 495.

56. Marcum, "United States Options in Angola," in *Angola, Mozambique and the West* Kitchen, ed. 36–53.

57. Quoted in B. Cohen and Mohamed El-Khawas ed., *The Kissinger Study of Southern Africa* (Nottingham, 1979), 87.

Africa, with up to forty thousand men in Guinea-Bissau and more than sixty thousand each in Angola and Mozambique, severely straining the Portuguese population and economy. Between 1960 and 1971, Portuguese military expenditure rose from 4.6 to 8.3 percent of Portugal's gross national product and came to consume forty-six percent of government expenditure. The loss of over 7,674 Portuguese during fourteen years of colonial war was not as problematic as the stalemate in the military campaigns. The wars dragged on interminably and inconclusively, demoralizing conscripts and frustrating commanders. In April 1974, the Portuguese army revolted in Portugal itself, overthrew the ruling dictatorship, and began a series of social and economic reforms, including decolonization.

Portugal's military junta was headed by General Spinola, a veteran of the wars in Guinea-Bissau. Spinola promised a speedy transfer of power within a continuing federal framework for the colonies. The revolution in Lisbon destroyed all of the colonial armies' willingness to continue fighting, and on July 27, 1974, Spinola announced that negotiations for an early power transfer would start immediately.

Negotiations began with Cape Verde and Guinea-Bissau, and Portuguese forces withdrew from the territories in September 1974. Discussions with Luiz Cabral (Amilcar Cabral's brother and successor) resulted in the declaration of the colonies' independence.[58]

In Angola, Spinola hoped to establish a coalition government in which all three liberation movements were represented in preparation for a two-year transition to independence. In this way, Spinola hoped to prevent the MPLA from holding the dominant political position in the country. However, his efforts were frustrated partly by Zairean President Mobutu Sese Sekou's patronage of FNLA and UNITA, and, more importantly, by the groups' friendship with South Africa and the United States (the CIA assisted Savimbi's UNITA in securing arms and intelligence in 1974). The United States increasingly worried about Soviet and Cuban aid to the MPLA. Cuban troops began training and arming MPLA troops in Congo during the late 1960s, and, in 1975, a massive airlift of troops and supplies to Angola enabled the MPLA-Cuban-Soviet faction to stop an FNLA-South African incursion into Angola. This major victory, followed by a United Nations Security Council condemnation (March 31, 1976) of the South African invasion of Angola, enabled the MPLA to maintain its control over Luanda and large parts of the country.[59]

In Mozambique, Eduardo Mondlane was killed by an assassin's bomb in February 1969, but his deputy, Samora Machel, led FRELIMO to victory and to independence. FRELIMO agreed to a cease-fire and to the transitional government that led the country to independence in July 1975.

Portugal also conceded independence to its small island colonies. The PAIGC negotiated the separate independence of the islands in July 1974, and São Tomé and Príncipe became independent under the Movimento de Libertação de São Tomé e Príncipe (MLSTP), hitherto a party of exiles. The newly elected Constituent Assembly proclaimed the Democratic Republic of São Tomé and Príncipe the day after the last Portuguese troops withdrew on July 11, 1974. Pinto da Costa was elected as the republic's first president.[60]

---

58. Hargreaves, *Decolonization in Africa*. 233.

59. For details see Klinghoffer, *The Angolan War: A Study in Soviet Policy in the Third World*, 9–29, 43–59.

60. Hargreaves, *Decolonization in Africa*. 233–4. For São Tomé and Príncipe see Tony

Conclusion

During the Salazar dictatorship, Portugal's colonial system provided the country with a sense of national greatness. Portugal gradually extended and solidified its previously tenuous hold over Angola and Mozambique and pursued a colonial policy characterized by limited access to education, forced labor, wage discrimination, and generous land and mining concessions to Portuguese and European individuals and firms. As a poor country, Portugal subordinated the economics of its African colonies to those of its own economy. It bought colonial produce at prices well below those of the world market and enjoyed a fifty percent tariff on goods it exported to the colonies.

Portuguese activities incited geographically scattered individuals and organizations in Angola, Mozambique, Guinea-Bissau, Cape Verde, and São Tomé to work together for independence. Whereas migration offered one form of resistance (especially against forced labor), urban workers, independent churches, and nationalist movements such as the MPLA and FNLA in Angola, FRELIMO in Mozambique, and the PAIGC in Guinea-Bissau and Cape Verde became the focal points of nationalist agitation against Portuguese rule. In the bipolar world of the 1960s, some of these nationalist movements received support from the Soviet Union and Cuba, while others received support from the West to counter Soviet influence.

The nationalist wars waged interminably and resulted in a change of leadership in Portugal. In 1974, the Portuguese military junta under General Spinola negotiated a transfer of power to the PAIGC, the MPLA, and FRELIMO, thereby ending some of Africa's longest colonial wars.

Review Questions

1. Why did Portugal retain its African possessions for such a long time?
2. Outline the main grievances of the independence movements in Portuguese Africa.
3. What role did Amilcar Cabral play in Guinea Bissau's independence?
4. Identify the roles of the MPLA, FNLA, and UNITA in Angola's independence struggle.
5. What roles did the United States and Cuba play in the independence of the Portuguese African colonies?
6. How did Mozambique attain independence?

Additional Reading

Chaliand, Gérard. *Armed Struggle in Africa With the Guerillas in "Portuguese" Guinea*. New York: Monthly Review Press, 1969.

Hodges and Malyn Newitt, *São Tomé and Príncipe: From Plantation Colony to Microstate* (Boulder, Westview Press, 1988).

Hodges, Tony, and Malyn Newitt. *São Tomé and Principe. From Plantation Colony to Microstate*. Boulder: Westview Press, 1988.

Isaacman, Allen, and Barbara Isaacman. *Mozambique. From Colonialism to Revolution*. Boulder: Westview Press, 1983.

Kitchen, Helen, ed. *Angola, Mozambique, and the West*. New York: Praeger, 1987.

Klinghoffer, Arthur J. *The Angolan War: A Study in Soviet Policy in the Third World*. Boulder: Westview Press.

Chapter 21

Southern African States, 1939 to Independence

Funso Afolayan

This chapter examines developments in the southern African states between 1939 and 2001. The states discussed in this chapter are Botswana, Swaziland, Lesotho, Zimbabwe, Namibia, Madagascar, Comoros, Seychelles, and Mauritius. Beginning with the impact of World War II, the chapter examines the development of nationalism, the process of decolonization, and the achievement of independence in these states. Among the issues to be explored will be the development of royalty politics and decolonization in Botswana, Swaziland, and Lesotho, the emergence of a small but active Western-educated elite across the sub-region, colonial reforms and their consequences in Madagascar and other island nations of the Indian Ocean, and the tortuous and violent roads to independence in Namibia and Zimbabwe. Relations with apartheid South Africa, with all their pains, twists, and devastations will also be explored.

* * *

World War II: African Participation

The outbreak of World War II had major repercussions for the states of southern Africa. The need for men and other resources ensured that virtually all South African states would be sucked into the war effort. Colonial officials from British-ruled Southern Rhodesia (later Zimbabwe) to French-ruled Madagascar enjoined local African rulers to mobilize their people for the war effort. Botswana, in spite of its small population, supplied ten thousand men for the war effort. Commanded by officers, drawn from the Protectorate Administration, and regimental sergeant majors, appointed from members of the indigenous chiefly families, the new recruits received elementary military training at Lobatse before being shipped to the front. Tswana soldiers served with distinction as anti-aircraft gunners, as infantry-men, and in various other capacities in the Middle East, Italy, Austria, and Yugoslavia. At the victory parade in England in June 1946, a party of fifteen Tswana soldiers graced the occasion and represented their country.[1] Similarly, in Swaziland, to demonstrate his loyalty to the British administration, King Sobhuza mobilized nearly four thousand men, calling them by their regiments and sending them to the war front. As members of the African Pioneer Corps, their conspicuous bravery in battle did not go unnoticed.[2]

The outbreak of hostilities was viewed with considerable concern in Southern Rhodesia, which was ruled and dominated by white settlers. The Prime Minister, Sir Godfrey Huggins, promptly informed his fellow European settlers that the colonies would be lost and the settlers' dominance and way of life destroyed if the Allies were defeated. To avoid such an eventuality, Sir Huggins asserted, no effort would be spared in aiding the Allies in their war effort. Consequently, he put Rhodesia on a war footing and ordered general mobilization. Europeans volunteered enthusiastically, though there were fears over creating new labor shortages in the industries that were stimulated by the demands of the war and the need for substitutes for imported British goods no longer available because of British concentration on war production. What was even more limiting, however, was the small size of the British settler population, which stood at sixty-four thousand in 1939. The white settlers were determined not to conscript and arm their black subjects; but, as efforts to mobilize a mass white army faltered and as the need for more soldiers increased, the government finally relented. Beginning in 1940 and continuing throughout the war years, the Rhodesian African Rifles began to enlist black volunteers. By the end of the war, 14,302 Africans and nearly ten thousand whites had fought in the war on the British side in lands as far apart as North Africa, Italy, Burma, and elsewhere.[3]

Mauritius and Seychelles

In Mauritius, an island colony off the coast of the Indian Ocean, the outbreak of the war coincided with a period of labor militancy. In 1938, the British firmly suppressed a dockworkers' strike organized by the Labour Party, threatening peace on the island. While the exigencies of war slowed political activity, the end of the battles inaugurated a new era of constitutional change that would set Mauritius on the road to eventual independence. Under the guardianship of Governor Donald Mackenzie-Kennedy, widespread consultations resulted in the adoption of a new constitution in 1947. This constitution was a compromise between the demands of the Indian majority who wanted universal suffrage and the demands of the Creoles and the Franco-Mauritians who opposed it, as they believed it would deliver Mauritius to Indian domination. Preoccupation with alleviating the fears of the minorities and resolving the problems of power transfer consumed so much of the attention and energy of the Mauritians and their British rulers during these years that no one grappled with the growing demographic and unemployment problems that were beginning to confront the country during this last phase

---

1. Anthony Sillery, *Botswana: A Short Political History* (London: Methuen & Co., 1974), 143–4.
2. Alan R. Booth, *Swaziland: Tradition and Change in a Southern African Kingdom* (Boulder, CO: Westview Press, 1983), 42.
3. Lewis H. Gann and Thomas H. Henriksen, *The Struggle for Zimbabwe: Battle in the Bush* (New York: Praeger Publishers, 1981), 15–7.

of colonial rule. The years between 1948 and 1968 were years of political activism in which concerns for religion and culture, communal power and privileges overshadowed those of race and class. The fact that the Mauritians were able to resolve this potentially explosive situation in an amicable and remarkably democratic manner prepared the way for the emergence of Mauritius, after its independence in 1968, as an island of political stability, economic progress, and ethno-sectarian tolerance in a sea of political chaos and economic crises that would characterize much of postcolonial African history.[4]

On the neighboring islands of the Seychelles, World War II also signaled a new direction in colonial development. Until August 1903, the British had administered the Seychelles as part of Mauritius. In 1921, the British rejected a petition submitted by a group of influential Seychellois requesting the re-amalgamation of Seychelles with Mauritius on the basis of the former's lack of economic viability. With the end of World War II and the nationalists' agitation for reforms that followed in its wake, elected representation was introduced into the Legislative Council of the Seychelles in 1948. However, property and literacy qualifications would ensure that only about two thousand citizens would be eligible to vote. The formation of two major political parties in 1963 and the granting of a universal adult franchise in 1967 increased the level of political participation in the final countdown to full independence in 1976.[5] African participation as fighters in World War II and their contributions as food producers in support of the war efforts were crucial factors that impelled the British and the other colonial masters to become more favorably disposed towards granting many of the demands of the nationalists for political representation and accelerated economic and social changes during the post-World war II colonial period.

The High Commission Territories: The Road to Independence in Botswana, Lesotho, and Swaziland

Botswana: Royalty Politics and Decolonization

Tshekedi Khama and Colonial Reforms

At the outbreak of World War II, the protectorate of Bechuanaland was engrossed in reforming its Native Administration. In 1934, five years before the outbreak of the war and at the insistence of the resident commissioner, the Native Advisory Council had enacted the Native Administration Proclamation and the Native Tribunals Proclamations. Both were directed at regulating, formalizing, and thus modernizing the administrative and judicial systems, especially with the

---

4. On the history of Mauritius during these years, see Larry W. Bowman, *Mauritius: Democracy and Development in the Indian Ocean* (Boulder, CO: Westview Press, 1991), 8–42. See also Adele Smith Simmons, *Modern Mauritius: The Politics of Decolonization* (Bloomington: Indiana University Press, 1982), 71–189.

5. On the Seychelles see Marcus Franda, *The Seychelles: Unquiet Islands* (Boulder, CO: Westview Press, 1982).

accession of inexperienced, yet educated, young chiefs, many of whom had been educated outside the protectorate and as such had very little exposure to indigenous traditions and values. As the High Commissioner explained in a carefully worded memorandum, the two proclamations were framed:

> with the intention of preserving...the exercise of tribal authority by the chiefs, preserving native law and custom, and preserving the administration of justice by native courts or *Kgotlas*, through making it possible for them to function satisfactorily under changed and changing conditions.[6]

Thus, though it did not appear that these measures were enacted to further erode the declining power of the chiefs, this was the way most of the chiefs perceived the legislation. Tshekedi, the most senior of these chiefs and the regent of the Ngwato, and Bathoen II, the young ruler of the Ngwaketse, challenged the validity of the proclamations in court. They argued that the laws changed aspects of native laws and customs which the high commissioner was bound to respect by the Order in Council of May 9, 1891. The chiefs lost the case. In ruling against their petition, Mr. Justice Watermeyer stated that the word "respect" did not mean that the high commissioner could not change native laws and customs, but that he should endeavor to treat them with consideration.

In the end, the implementation of the proclamations was not as vexatious as the chiefs had anticipated. Consequently, they received the enactment of another law reforming the Native Treasury System more positively. The new law exposed members of the Native Advisory Council to the many possibilities of a regulated and service-oriented financial system. In 1943, after six years of consultation and positive debates in which both Tshekedi and Bathoen cooperated enthusiastically, the 1934 laws were replaced by two new proclamations. While these preserved the prerogative of the high commissioner, the features of the 1934 laws most objectionable to the chiefs did not appear in the new laws. These new developments were facilitated by the pragmatic and tactful policies of the resident commissioner, Aden Clarke, who went to great lengths to cultivate the friendship and loyalty of Tshekedi, having come to the conclusion that, more than anyone, this regent held the key to the peaceful and successful governance of the Tswana.

Tshekedi's succession to the regency of the most populous of the Tswana groups was accidental. In 1923, Khama III of the Ngwato died. His son, Sekgoma, succeeded him but died two years later, leaving behind Seretse, a four-year old boy, as heir to the throne. Serestse's uncle, twenty-one year old Tshekedi, terminated his studies at South Africa's Fort Hare College to become regent. In spite of his youth, Tshekedi soon proved himself a capable and effective ruler. British officials soon discovered that this young man would not be manipulated and could not but be impressed by his intelligence, imagination, and vitality. Determined, against all odds, to seek and induce developments that would benefit his people, the regent left exhausted colonial officials panting, unable to match his drive and energy. His commitment to protecting the power and independence of the Ngwato chieftaincy brought him into regular conflict with exasperated protectorate administrators. He never hesitated to appeal to or to go to London if the authorities in Africa were not sufficiently responsive to his demands. His firm re-

---

6. Quoted in Anthony Sillery, *Botswana: A Short Political History*, 143.

pression of a 1931 royalist rebellion fomented by dissident members of the Bamangwato clan—who had their properties confiscated, their houses burnt, and their ringleaders banished—and his whipping in 1933 of a white boy for assaulting a Tswana girl were clear indications of how far he was prepared to go to preserve the prerogatives of his office. In 1947, with the aid of a military regiment, he forcefully extracted outstanding dues and taxes from a group of Kalaka people ruled by Mswazi, a man who had for many years resisted Ngwato's rule through tax evasion, the flouting of royal orders, and violence. Consequently, many members of the recalcitrant group fled across the border to Rhodesia, creating diplomatic complications that the resident commissioner had to settle.[7] One year later, Tshekedi was confronted with a serious dynastic crisis which would not only shake the Ngwato chieftaincy but would have major national and international repercussions. This was the Seretse Affair.

The Seretse Affair

After becoming the chief-designate in 1925 at the age of four, Seretse embarked on an extended program of Western education which took him to Lovedale College, Fort Hare University College, the University of the Witwatersrand, Balliol College, Oxford, and the Middle Temple in London. In September 1948, Tshekedi, who was busy building what he considered his major bequest to his people, a new secondary school in Moeng Valley, received a telegram from Seretse informing him of his imminent marriage to an English girl, Ruth Williams. For Tshekedi, who had worked steadfastly to defend and protect the integrity and traditions of his people, this was a devastating blow. That his nephew, his adopted son, and the heir to the throne should so flout traditional customs in contracting a marriage without consulting his people and that the prospective bride was neither a Tswana nor even an African, but a European, was simply scandalous. In spite of Tshekedi's efforts to stop it, however, the marriage took place as scheduled in late September of 1948. Seretse flew to Serowe to reconcile with his uncle and reconnect with his people, but the damage had been done. The Ngwato became polarized into two groups. Those who supported Tshekedi insisted that Seretse's English wife should not be permitted to come into Bechuanaland, although no one questioned Seretse's right to the throne. As the rift deepened, the majority of the younger generation gradually shifted their support to Seretse. Without evidence, they accused his uncle of trying to win himself a permanent position of power by exploiting the marriage to banish his nephew from the throne. Finally, after a series of abortive efforts, a great meeting of the leaders of the Ngwato voted decisively for the installation of Seretse as chief with his English wife as his consort. Tshekedi resigned his regency and proceeded with many of his leading supporters to settle in the Kwena country. However, before his departure, he called on the colonial administration to set up a judicial enquiry to decide whether Seretse should succeed to the kingship and what the status of his European wife and their children would be if he did become king.

Walter Harragin, chief justice of the high commission territories, presided over the enquiry. In its report, submitted toward the end of 1949, the tribunal advised against the recognition of Seretse as chief. Meanwhile, across the border, Daniel

---

7. On Tshekedi, see Mary Benson, *Tshekedi Khama* (London: Faber and Faber, 1960).

Malan, the first prime minister of apartheid South Africa—where miscegenation would soon be ruled a serious crime—warned the British of dire consequences should Seretse be installed as chief. Seretse was summarily recalled from Bechuanaland to London for "consultations." What followed was, in the words of Winston Churchill, "a very disreputable transaction."[8] In London, he was told by Patrick Gordon Walker, the Labour Party commonwealth secretary, to renounce his right to the kingship; when he refused, he was promptly informed that he was banned from returning to his homeland and consigned to a life of exile with his English wife in Britain for at least five years. To pacify Seretse's angry supporters and avoid a breakdown of law and order, Tshekedi was also banished from the Ngwato country until 1952. A series of riots in Serowe signaled the resolution of the Ngwato not to elect an alternative chief. The report of the tribunal was never released; the colonial government was neither brave nor honest enough to admit before a watching and critical world that the main reason why it would not recognize Seretse as chief was its reluctance to offend the racial sensibilities of white South Africans, who in 1948, the year of Seretse's marriage, had instituted what would turn out to be the most racist and repressive political system in the European colonial enterprise in Africa.

As a former resident commissioner in the protectorate noted, the Commissioners, who were themselves resident in South Africa and were closely involved in South African affairs and society, did not have the freedom and will to take any decisive action that might be viewed with misgivings by their South African hosts. Official recognition and acceptance of Seretse's marriage by the colonial administration would have saved everybody a lot of trouble, especially after the Ngwato people themselves voted almost unanimously that the race of Seretse's wife was irrelevant to their acceptance of Seretse as their ruler. Sanity was somewhat restored in 1956, when Seretse was reconciled with his uncle and returned to the protectorate. Both renounced all their personal claims to the chieftaincy. In 1956, Seretse became the vice-chairman of the Ngwato Traditional Council, which had been chaired since 1953 by Rasebolai Kgamane, a war veteran and respected third senior member of the Ngwato royal clan. Tshekedi served as secretary of the council from 1957 until his death two years later, when Seretse succeeded him as secretary of the Bamangwato Council.[9]

The Road to Independence

Though the Seretse affair was the major issue that preoccupied the minds of the people of Botswana during these years, preparations were also being made for independence. A Joint Advisory Council made up of African and European members was established in 1951. In 1959, the council recommended that it be reconstituted as a legislative council mandated to decide a new constitution for the country. Its decisions were enacted into a new constitution in 1960, a fateful year for the advent of African independence: Nigeria as well as the majority of the francophone African countries would secure their liberation from imperial tutelage that year. In South Africa, intensified repression following the police massacre at Sharpeville

---

8. Churchill, quoted in Thomas M. Callaghy, ed., *South Africa in Southern Africa: The Intensifying Vortex of Violence* (New York: Praeger, 1983), 358.

9. On Seretse and the marriage imbroglio see Gys Dubbeld, *Seretse Khama* (Cape Town: Maskew Miller, 1992); and Michael Dutfield, *A Marriage of Inconvenience: The Persecution of Ruth and Seretse Khama* (London: Unwin Hyman, 1990).

would send a stream of refugees fleeing into Botswana, where their presence would provide a stimulus for Tswana nationalism. In 1959, the African elite in Botswana, most of whom had worked and studied in South Africa, formed the short-lived Federal Party. The party gave way to the establishment, in 1960, of the Bechuanaland People's Party (BPP) led by K. T. Motsete, a Church of England minister and schoolteacher who had returned from London University after gaining four degrees; P. G. Matante, a vigorous preacher from Johannesburg with close links to Robert Sobukwe's Pan Africanist Congress (PAC); and Motsamai Mpho, who had only recently experienced and survived a treason trial in South Africa. The radicalism of the BPP and its call for immediate independence gained it widespread support. However, the BPP's close association with South African political groups such as the PAC and the ANC would prove to be among its major liabilities. Its enemies feared a specter of foreign domination should the group come to power.

In the meantime, alarmed by the radical demands of the BPP and its potentiality for creating public chaos and disorder, Seretse, by then a member of both the Legislative Council and the Executive Council, entered the fray. In 1962, along with Quett Masire, Seretse formed the Bechuanaland Democratic Party (BDP). Known as the "uncrowned king" of the Ngwato, with a solid reputation as a highly educated and selfless prince (had he not renounced the kingship for the sake of his people?), Seretse was able to secure the support of the chiefs, who in turn drew their followers into the new party. By adroitly cultivating a moderate image, preaching and practicing racial tolerance, defining his party's agenda to incorporate the interests of farmers, herdsmen, and others, and carefully distancing himself and his party from the South African political groups, Seretse not only secured the support of the majority of the population, but he also gained the tacit support of the colonial administration, who were no doubt alarmed by the stridency of the BPP. In spite of opposition from the BPP, a constitutional review began in July 1963. In November, the British accepted the BDP's proposal for a progressive and amicable transfer of power. The adoption of a nonracial constitution in 1965 led to a general election in which the BDP won twenty-eight of the thirty-one seats. Seretse, who had suffered the indignity of banishment from his throne and country, was knighted by the queen of England shortly before he assumed office on September 30, 1966 as the head of state and first president of the Republic of Botswana.[10]

From Basutoland to Lesotho: The Politics of Independence

In many ways, political developments in Basutoland paralleled those in Botswana. In 1938, the British administration issued two proclamations that followed the pattern previously discussed with regard to Botswana. The intention was

---

10. On the history of Botswana during this period see Sillery, *Botswana: A Short Political History*; Richard Stevens, *Lesotho, Botswana and Swaziland: The Former High Commission Territories in Southern Africa* (New York: Praeger, 1967); and F. Morton and J. Ramsay, [eds.], *The Birth of Botswana: A History of the Bechuanaland Protectorate from 1910 to 1966* (Gaborone: Macmillan, 1987).

to streamline the Native Administration and adapt it to the demands of modern times. The proliferation of chieftaincies and the administration's ill-advised recognition of them had made the administration of native courts a cumbersome and inefficient undertaking. By 1939, there were 1,340 recognized chiefs, all of whom exercised judicial functions. Efforts to discourage many of the chiefs from holding court yielded limited results; thereafter, some were expressly prohibited from doing so. It took seven years before the number of chiefs with native courts could be drastically reduced to 122. By 1949, the number had been reduced to 107, and eight years later it was reduced to sixty-three. Though many of the chiefs thus "demoted" or no longer recognized were unhappy with their loss of status and influence, the 1938 proclamations inaugurating reforms in the Native Administration were better received in Basutoland than they had been in Botswana four years earlier. One reason for this was the limited influence and lack of popularity of chiefs in Basutoland that resulted from their high-handedness. The support of the paramount chief, Griffith, was also decisive in securing the acceptance of the proposed reforms.

The succession dispute following Griffith's death in 1939 also played into the hands of the British. Mantsebo, Griffith's widow, became the queen regent, pending the selection of a substantive chief. In the meantime, and before Mantsebo could effectively consolidate herself in office, the British took advantage of the vacuum created by Griffith's death to weaken the power of the paramount chief, who lost the ultimate power to appoint and dismiss subordinate chiefs. The other recognized chiefs were also brought under close supervision. Placed on government salaries, they lost their control over court fines and fees, which were thenceforth transferred to district "National Treasuries" to be used for the support of health, educational, and welfare services. The 1945 introduction of district councils, which included elected members and were overseen by the colonial district commissioner, further eroded the chiefs' power. In 1948, an Advisory Council composed of three chiefs to be nominated by the National Council (a board of leading chiefs and headmen) was established to monitor the expenditures of the National Treasuries and approve local taxes imposed by the paramount chief. A spate of witchcraft accusations and ritual killings during the 1940s implicated many chiefs whom the council had not chosen and showed the extent of the discontent created by these reforms.

In 1952, the Basutoland African Congress (later renamed Basutoland Congress Party, BCP) was formed by Ntsu Mokhehle, a graduate of Fort Hare, schoolteacher, and former ANC activist. Drawing the majority of its active members from among Basuto who had worked in South Africa, some of whom were also active in the ANC, the BCP was able to quickly consolidate its hold on Basuto politics. Constitutional changes were introduced under pressure from the BCP as well as from the Basutoland National Council. In 1959, the National Council was transformed into a Legislative Council of eighty nominated members. As in other commissioned territories, the high commissioner retained control of external affairs, defense, and internal security. The British attempt to entrench special privileges for the non-Basuto (mostly white settlers) in the territory and to deny the council control over them was firmly resisted by the Basuto, who pressured the British to grant a single franchise and equal rights for all persons in the territory. As Jack Halpern noted, this was the best possible course of action in the prevailing circumstance, because "acceptance of the British conditions..."

would have formalized legal apartheid in Basutoland."[11] The chiefs and other traditional members of society became alarmed at the militancy and growing popularity of the Congress Party in the countdown to the 1960 elections. To make matters worse, the BCP had become openly hostile in its attitude toward the chiefs. Its 1960 party manifesto expressly demanded that the role of the paramount chief be limited to that of a ceremonial head of state. To counter the influence of the BCP, one of the chiefs, Lebua Jonathan, formed the Basutoland National Party (BNP). Its attempt to brand the BCP as a communist organization and win support from the traditionally minded Basuto could not shake the influence of the BCP, which, in spite of divisions within its ranks, was still sufficiently popular with the Basuto commoners to win twenty-nine of the forty elective seats in the 1960 National Council and seventy-three out of 162 in the district council elections. But the royalist-backed National Party was not finished; it held the last card in its hands. With the support of the forty members nominated by the chiefs and headmen, Jonathan's BNP's minority of eleven elected members soon gained overall control of the council. In July 1960, Jonathan became the first prime minister of Basutoland.

In the meantime, the BCP's association with South African nationalist movements, Mokhehle's strictures against the apartheid regime, and the leader's authoritarian style continued to create tension and division within the party while scaring many who feared the military designs of the racist state. To upstage the BCP, Jonathan skillfully played on these divisions and on the fears of Basuto women, who thought that an open break with South Africa might jeopardize their main source of subsistence: the regular flow of remittances from their migrant-worker husbands in apartheid South Africa. Jonathan urged the women, to think of their stomachs before casting their vote for the BCP in the 1965 General Election. The strategy worked: the BNP narrowly won the election, gaining thirty-one out of the sixty seats. The BCP gained twenty-five seats while the Marema-Tlou Freedom Party, a monarchist group which had broken away from the BCP, won the remaining four. On October 4, 1966, Basutoland became the independent Kingdom of Lesotho. The paramount chief, Motlotlehi Moshoeshoe II, became the nominal head of state with the title of King of Lesotho, though real power was vested in the National Assembly and in the office of the Prime Minister, the redoubtable Chief Lebua Jonathan.[12]

---

11. Jack Halpern, *Basutoland, Bechuanaland and Swaziland, South Africa's Hostages* (London: Penguin Books, 1965), 128.

12. On the history of Lesotho during this period, see J. E. Spence, *Lesotho: The Politics of Dependence*, (London: Oxford University Press, 1968); Halpern, *Basutoland, Bechuanaland and Swaziland, South Africa's Hostage*; Stevens, *Lesotho, Botswana and Swaziland: The Former High Commission Territories in Southern Africa*.

Swaziland: Colonialism, Tradition, and Change in a South African Kingdom

Sobhuza and the Consolidation of Royal Authority

At the outbreak of World War II, the most compelling issue confronting the Swazi people was that of regaining much of their most fertile land, which had been forcefully and improperly appropriated early in the century by European settlers and other concession seekers, especially from South Africa. Sustained efforts by the queen mother and regent, Gwamile Labotsibeni, between 1903 and 1921 had borne little fruit in the face of determined British colonial opposition to any attempt to challenge the increasingly entrenched white settlers' interests in the protectorate. On his accession to the kingship in 1921, Sobhuza increased the pressure. In 1923, he led a deputation to London to demand redress of the land inequities. The delegation was curtly rebuffed by the Colonial Office. The following year, Sobhuza employed the service of Dr. Pixley Ka Izaka Seme[13] to file a land grievance lawsuit before the Special Court of Swaziland. When the suit was dismissed, he followed it with an appeal to the Privy Council in London, but this was also denied in 1926.

In 1941, the combination of overpopulation, continued land dispossession, overstocking, and growing poverty among peasants impelled Sobhuza to petition the British king for immediate redress of the land inequities. The appeal was timely. Embroiled in a mortal combat with Germany, Britain needed all the support and resources it could get. Colonial Welfare and Development funds were made available for the repurchase of European-held lands, including the remaining crown lands, that were earmarked for Swazi use. In 1946, a Native Land Resettlement Scheme made a total of 350,000 acres of land available to relieve the pressure of overgrazing and land exhaustion. In 1912, the queen regent up a national fund to buy back land from the government and the settlers. To complement these efforts, Sobhuza established the Lifa Fund in 1944, to be financed through a levy on Swazi cattle and migrant workers' wages for the repurchase of additional land. By the declaration of independence in 1960, fifty-six percent of the land was in Swazi hands.

In the meantime, Sobhuza continued to consolidate his power and influence in Swaziland. Ruling in a much more centralized political system than either Botswana or Bechuanaland, Sobhuza was able to exploit Britain's use of the indirect rule system to strengthen and further consolidate the power of the kingship,

---

13. A Tonga, with close Zulu associations (he married the daughter of Dinuzulu, the Zulu paramount chief), Dr. Izaka Seme was a principal founder of the African National Congress. He gave the keynote address at its inaugural meeting in 1912. After earning degrees from Columbia University and Oxford, he was called to the bar at the Middle Temple in London in 1910 before returning to South Africa where he set up a law practice in Johannesburg. Between 1930 and 1937, he served as the ANC president. His political activism and his large legal practice brought him into contact and collaboration with many distinguished Africans, such as King Sobhuza of the Swazi. On Seme, see Thomas Karis and Gwendolyn M. Carter, *From Protest to Challenge: A Documentary History of African Politics in South Africa, 1882–1964, Volume 4: Political Profiles* (Stanford, CA: Hoover Institution Press, 1977), 137–9.

or the *ngwenyama*. With considerable dexterity and decisiveness, Sobhuza employed a wide variety of traditional and modern strategies to increase the power and prestige of his office well beyond the circumscribed boundaries prescribed for Native Authorities by the colonial master. His creative use of the elaborate annual *Incwala* ceremony as a symbolic and practical means for the ritualization of the *ngwenyama* was decisive. Through this most sacred of all rituals, the king's vitality as the soul of the nation, his prerogative as the rainmaker and guarantor of the prosperity of his people, and his possession of medicinal powers for their well-being and protection were annually reinforced and reaffirmed. As the repository of the nation's traditions, the king alone had the power to perform the *Incwala*; two princes who had dared to trespass on this royal prerogative in earlier times had paid with their lives. In a series of interconnected ceremonies spanning three weeks every year, queens, princes and princesses, councilors and commoners, age regiments, and ritual specialists competed to outdo one another in ritualizing and strengthening the virility of the king. Through its assignment of specific ritual functions to every significant individual and group in its performance, the *Incwala* became a unifying force in the state.[14]

British attempts during the 1940s and 1950s to weaken Sobhuza and take away the power of the Libandla, the Swazi General Assembly, to appoint and remove local chiefs and headmen failed.[15] In contrast to Basutoland, the establishment of district councils did not threaten chiefly powers in Swaziland. In 1954, forty district councils (*tinkudla*) were established and given jurisdiction over the local development of educational, health, and welfare services. Made up of local members of the Libandla and governed by officials (*induna*) appointed by the king, these councils became local expressions of royal control and chiefly power. The already considerable power of the monarchy was further reinforced by its control of Swazi Nation Land (SNL), which the king held in trust for the nation and distributed to the people through the chiefs. By placing a premium on the loyalty of the chiefs and thus of their people to his person, the king reinforced his image as the fount of honor and endowment in the state.[16]

Interest Groups, Party Politics, and the Path to Independence

The gradual but progressive consolidation of royal power in the Swazi Protectorate was challenged by two emergent interest groups, the European settlers and

---

14. On the *Incwala* and the rituals of royalty among the Swazi see Hilda Kuper, *The Swazi: A South African Kingdom* (New York: Holt, Rinehart and Winston, 1963); Hilda Kuper, *An African Aristocracy: Rank Among the Swazi* (London: Oxford University Press, 1980).

15. The Libandla was one of two principal councils composing the Swazi traditional administration. Comprised of every adult male, it met about once a year. The other council was the Liqoqo. Smaller in size, it consisted only of the king's principal advisers and key members of the royal family.

16. On Sobhuza, see Hilda Kuper, *Sobhuza II: Ngwenyama and King of Swaziland* (London: Duckworth, 1978).

the Swazi petit bourgeoisie. By the beginning of World War II, European settlers, in spite of their small number, controlled the bulk of Swaziland's arable land. Thus the colonial irrigation schemes of the 1950s, made possible by the influx of development money after the war, benefited the settlers disproportionately, further increasing their power and influence. Successive attempts by the monarchy, first under queen regent Gwamile and later under Sobhuza, to curtail the settlers' influence and reclaim Swazi lands were consistently frustrated by a British colonial authority accustomed and committed to defending and extending settlers' interests, often at the expense of the indigenous population.

Like the settlers—though they were by no means their allies—the emergent elite also mounted a definite challenge to the autonomy of the monarchy. Educated in colonial and mission educational systems, this group was composed of teachers, clerks, artisans, civil servants, and professionals. Landless and often lacking in royal pretensions, they defined themselves and their interests as occupying a position midway between the settlers and the monarchy, despising the former for their racist and condescending attitudes and the latter for its conservatism and uncompromising hold on power. In 1929, a group of educated elite came together to form the Progressive Association (PA). However, for much of the colonial period, the members of the petit bourgeoisie were too few in number and too preoccupied with issues related to wages and conditions of service to have much time for either politics or nationalism. World War II would signal a new direction for this class. Participation in the war front overseas and exposure to European societies and to new ideologies of liberation would result in new ways of thinking about the situation at home.

In 1944, John Nquku and other nationalists resolutely resisted the new Native Administration Proclamation, which attempted to establish the king as the sole Native Authority in Swaziland. Taken aback by the opposition the proclamation engendered, the British adopted a more modern approach through the creation, in 1950, of the Swazi courts and the Swazi National Treasury, both of which brought some accountability and devolution of power to the Swazi administration. In 1945, the PA was transformed into the Swaziland Progressive Party (SPP) with John Nquku as its president. A teacher, school inspector, and journalist, Nquku had traveled extensively in Europe and America. In 1960, he committed his party to a program of internal self-government as the first step toward full independence and the rejection of any form of incorporation into the apartheid republic of South Africa. That same year, Sobhuza took the initiative to suggest to the protectorate administration that a legislative council made up of equal numbers of elected Europeans and nominated Africans be established to prepare the kingdom for independence. The fact that the African members would be nominated using traditional Swazi methods would guarantee complete royal control over which Africans would sit on the council. This was unacceptable to the Progressive Party, which promptly rejected the proposals and proposed the establishment of a completely nonracial council elected on the basis of universal suffrage.

To serve as a counterweight to the SPP, European settlers supported the establishment, in 1962, of the Swaziland Democratic Party (SDP), which accepted the principle of a nonracial parliamentary democracy but with specific guarantees for private property in the form of, for example, land or white business investments. The party was short-lived; its close association with settlers' interests did not, apparently, endear many Swazi, royalists, and nationalists, most of whom resented the settlers' privileges and pretensions. Meanwhile, the SPP was embroiled in an internal crisis which would eventually divide it and deprive it of electoral advantage it derived from being the first major nationalist party. In 1963, one of its leaders, Dr. Ambrose Zwane, broke away to establish the Ngwane National Liberatory Congress (NNLC), which espoused a more radical agenda and called for universal suffrage and immediate independence. To upstage both the SPP and the SDP, demonstrate its strength, and increase the pressure for independence, the NNLC organized a series of strikes among blue-collar workers in the mines and sugar plantations, calling for higher wages and improved conditions of service. With the support of Sobhuza, the British flew in troops from Kenya to break the strikes and restore order.

Suspicious of settlers' intentions, critical and even resentful of the claims and lofty airs of the nationalists, and uncertain of the designs of the British—whom he sensed would not grant independence except through a form of electoral transitional program—Sobhuza decided to form his own party. Taking advantage of the *ngwenyama*'s popularity, his benevolent land policy, and his extensive influence among the rural population, the new party, the Imbokodvo National Movement, soon established itself as a leading contender in the struggle for rulership of the Swazi. In the 1965 Legislative Council election, the Imbokodvo won all twenty-four elected seats. It repeated this feat during the 1967 elections for the National Assembly. On September 6, 1968, Swaziland gained full independence from Britain. Sobhuza became the head of state and king. Prince Makhosini Dlamini, the leader of the Imbokodvo, became prime minister. The establishment of a small Senate, with half of its members nominated by the king and with power to veto laws passed by the lower house, ensured that ultimate authority rested with the *ngwenyama*.[17]

Colonialism, Resistance, and Decolonization on the Indian Ocean Islands: The Case of Madagascar

World War II and Colonial Reforms

World War II had consequences for the southern African states other than pulling their populations into active service. In Madagascar, the French governor-general Marcel de Coppet took advantage of the wave of patriotism that greeted the outbreak of the war to mobilize local resources in support of the war effort. However, Germany's defeat of France led to a major disruption in French rule. Coppet was recalled by the Vichy regime. His replacement was Leon Cayla, who, as a former governor-general (1930–1939), had established a reputation for being ruthless and for stifling voices of opposition. His suppression of political activities

---

17. On the progress toward decolonization in Swaziland see Booth, *Swaziland*; Christian P. Potholm, *Swaziland: The Dynamics of Political Modernization* (Berkeley: University of California Press, 1972).

and trade unionism, arbitrary arrest of critics, and banning of antigovernment
newspapers ensured that he was both feared and loathed by the Malagasy educated elite, who saw his reappointment by the German-controlled Vichy regime as
a sign of worse days to come. Having reached the mandatory retirement age,
Cayla remained only nine months. However, his replacement, Armand Annet,
was no better; Annet simply followed in Cayla's footsteps, repressing all opposition. His contempt for the Malagasy led him to abolish the Délégations
Economiques et Financières, a consultative body created in 1924 in response to
years of agitation by the Malagasy urban elite for civil and political rights. The
close alliance between the local colonial administration and the Vichy regime was
irksome for the British, who would not countenance the control of this strategic
island by the German-controlled French government. Consequently, the Allies
blockaded the island in late 1941, forcing it to surrender to a British invading
force in November 1942. The Malagasy nationalists were disappointed when the
British handed over the island to the Free French in January 1943.

Under the Free French, the extraction of resources increased as Madagascar
became a supplier of men and of raw materials for the war effort. Rising inflation,
stagnant wages, and acute and widespread shortages made life unbearable. Constant official intervention in daily life, through rationing and price control, did
not help matters. For instance, in 1944, the government compelled farmers to sell
their entire crops at a low, fixed price, while it sold rice and other food products
at a high price. In spite of intense pressure, reforms were few and far between.
Notable among such reforms were the increased responsibilities granted to village
councils (fokonolonas) and the establishment of a central or national representative council. The new council was an improvement over the ill-fated Délégations.
Its major limitations included a lack of control over budget matters and an over-
representation of settlers, who, with only one percent of the population, secured
half the electoral representation. In addition, the governor-general retained the
power to dissolve the council at will. Taking advantage of the principles of colonial representation articulated at the Brazzaville Conference, Malagasy voters
sent their two leading nationalists, Joseph Ravoahangy and Joseph Raseta, to the
first Constituent Assembly of the Fourth French Republic in Paris. Inspired by the
principles of self-determination enshrined in the Atlantic and United Nations
Charters, the nationalists demanded autonomy for their country. As one nationalist stated in 1945:

> The great powers have resolved to create a new order...in which force
> will no longer dominate the world...a new order in which people will be
> sovereign and free to govern themselves. A new order that will respect the
> dignity and rights of human beings without distinction of race, color, or
> religion.[18]

While in Paris, the nationalists attempted to work with friendly French parties,
but they discovered that none of the French parties were enthused about the

---

18. J. Tronchon, *L'Insurrection malgache de 1947* (Paris: Maspéro) 134, quoted in
Maureen Covell, *Madagascar, Politics, Economics and Society* (London: Frances Pinter Publishers, 1987), 25.

prospect of full independence for Madagascar; they were all committed to the maintenance of the French Union and empire. To bypass this obstacle, the two nationalists joined Jacques Rabemananjara, a Paris-based poet and a Catholic Betsimisaraka from the east coast of Madagascar who had recently been elected to a third Malagasy seat, to form the Mouvement Democratique de la Rénovation Malagache (MDRM). Though their attempt to introduce an independence bill in the assembly failed, they secured other concessions. In October 1946, Madagascar became an overseas territory, which implied that all Malagasy became French citizens, even though only ten thousand people could vote. Forced labor was abolished and most restrictions on political activities were lifted. The subsequent division of the island into five provinces, each with its own budget and assembly, was viewed by the MDRM as part of the French strategy to keep the island divided and set the Merina against the *côtiers* (coastal peoples). This was not a baseless allegation.

From Resistance to Rebellion: The Nationalist Revolt of 1947

The French administration resented the MDRM, which it regarded as a separatist movement committed to the restoration of the Merina monarchy, which the French had terminated following their conquest in 1895, and its dominance over much of the island. The French attempt to favor and exploit the *côtiers* while discriminating against the Merina could not break the Merina's dominance on the island. Since the Merina were the most educated, the most populous, and the most westernized ethnic group in the colony, the French were compelled to rely on them to fill the senior positions in the civil service, in trade, and in the military. Besides securing widespread support among the Merina, the MDRM also received the support of two "secret societies," the Jeunesse Nationaliste (JINA) and the Parti Nationaliste Malgache (PANAMA), both of which emerged as anticolonial movements during the war. Composed of extremists who were more radical and more anticolonial than the moderate and apparently levelheaded leaders of the MDRM, the two groups spurned the MDRM's readiness to accept autonomy within the French union. Instead they demanded complete independence from France. In addition, the MDRM received the allegiance of the majority of the returned *anciens combattants* (ex-servicemen), who became many of the middle-level activists for the party.

The combination of all these forces, especially the militancy of JINA and PANAMA, greatly alarmed the French administration. To counter the popularity of these groups, the French supported the formation of an anti-MDRM party, the Parti des Désherités de Madagascar (PADESM). The use of the term "disinherited" in the party's name showed the administration's deft attempt to exploit the fear of those groups and peoples who considered themselves socially and politically underprivileged under the old order that there would be a return of the "Merina oligarchy." None of these official maneuvers could deter the MDRM, however; it continued to win every election to the French Senate, the Council of the French Union, and the National Representative Assembly. With its electoral mandate, the MDRM and its associated groups became bolder in their demands for liberalization and autonomy. Early in 1946, sensing trouble brewing, the administration arrested several MDRM leaders. However, by that time, resentment to

French rule had spread widely among the elite, peasants, and ex-servicemen, espe-cially along the east coast, where colonial exactions in the forms of enforced cash cropping and illegal labor exploitation were rampant.

Unusually low wartime export crop prices combined with the abuses and racism of French settlers and colonial officials to provoke the outbreak of an anti-European rebellion on March 29, 1947. Though the revolt was poorly coordi-nated and badly executed, it succeeded temporarily in dislocating the administra-tion and creating a general sense of unrest. In addition to killing twenty-eight European settlers and scores of Malagasies perceived as French collaborators, groups of armed Malagasies severed communication links and destroyed several government and mission buildings. In spite of their rhetoric, and even though they knew, as did the administration, that some form of uprising was being planned, the leaders of the MDRM were not directly involved in the revolt, and the three MDRM deputies promptly dissociated themselves from it. With their close con-nections to France and paid residencies in Paris, the deputies had much to lose through revolt. Hence, on March 27, two days before the revolt, they sent a mes-sage to their followers ordering them to resist any provocation. The initiative for the revolt lay with the leaders of JINA and PANAMA, namely Rakotondrabe, Ravelonahina, and Betrevola, all of whom were skeptical of the prospects of achieving Malagasy independence by parliamentary means and, as such, were more willing to resort to militant measures. Though the revolt was widespread and fighters came from all over the island, it was most pronounced in the east coast areas, where the geography was best suited to guerrilla warfare and where the secret societies were most established. That these were also areas where land appropriation, labor expropriation, and rice exploitation were most rife revealed the economic nature of the revolt. The fact that the hardest fighting took place among groups such as the Tanala, well-known for their avowed opposition to the restoration of the Merina monarchial hegemony, disproved the French claim that this was a Merina-led MDRM rebellion.

The revolt shocked the French, who reacted fiercely. French troops were rushed to the island, and by the end of 1948, the revolt had been crushed ruth-lessly and brutally. French soldiers wrought havoc among the Malagasy popula-tion, while many died from starvation, and exposure to diseases as they fled into the forest to escape the wrath of the French army. The official statement of the colonial administration—that only 11,200 people died in the clash—has been consistently rejected by others who have described that figure as a gross underes-timate. The commander of the French forces on the island put the number of ca-sualties at eighty-nine thousand. The French Communist Party published a list of ninety thousand casualties, while the high commissioner scaled the figure to over 100,000, out of which fewer than six hundred were non-Malagasy. Determined to use this revolt as an opportunity to emasculate their enemies, the French branded all nationalists traitors to the noble cause of the French Empire. Under the succes-sive governor-generalships of De Coppet and Pierre de Chevigne, surveillance of opponents, arbitrary arrests, imprisonment without trial, and other forms of in-timidation became the order of the day. Even the three deputies, in spite of their parliamentary status, were not spared. Two of them, Raseta and Ravoahangy, were sentenced to death; the third, Rabemananjara, was sentenced to life impris-onment. In addition, the government put much of the coastal region under mili-tary occupation. This state of siege would continue until 1956, when new domestic and international developments would lead to a gradual relaxation of the repressive apparatus of the state.[19]

The Countdown to Independence

The new direction in colonial policy was heralded by the appointment of two successive liberal-minded governor-generals. The first of these, Robert Bargue (1950–1954), adopted a policy of bridge building between the administration and the nationalists. By focusing on socioeconomic issues, channeling funds to Malagasy farmers, and addressing many of the grievances harbored against the administration and the settlers, Bargue took the thunder out of the political agenda and agitation of the nationalists. To demonstrate government sensitivity to the needs of the coastal groups, geographical quotas were introduced to govern the award of scholarships to universities and for study abroad programs in France as well as to determine appointments to the civil service. Bargue's successor, Andre Soucadaux (1954–1960), was even more receptive to working with the Malagasy nationalists. He actively supported the nationalists' petition to Paris asking for amnesty for the nationalist leaders whose death sentences had been commuted to life imprisonment. Sensing the changed atmosphere and the new spirit of cooperation on the island, Paris granted the request, pardoning and releasing the three ex-deputies, though immediately exiling them to France.

Determined to keep the initiative in its hands or at least not lose control of events on the island, the administration became more proactive in encouraging the spirit of political participation and self-government (though only within the French Union), both of which the French had reluctantly come to accept as inevitable steps in the future of their colonial enterprise. Following and as a result of the 1947 revolt, the MDRM was banned and PADESM simply disintegrated. Elections to local assemblies and to the French National Assembly continued, though candidates ran as independents, focusing on local issues and depending on their personalities and supporters to ensure their elections. In 1956, Soucadaux became instrumental in the establishment of a new nationalist party, the socialist Parti Social Démocrate (PSD). The leadership of the new party fell to Philibert Tsiranana, a côtier with credentials the French considered impressive and reliable. An intelligent and energetic man, Tsiranana had been a founding member of PADESM. While studying in France, he dissociated himself from the Malagasy student organization, which he considered too radical and too Merina to cater to the interests of the côtiers. Since he was in France during the 1947 revolt, he could not be accused of being a party either to the revolt or to its repression. His membership in the French Socialist Party brought him into close relation with influential individuals in French politics. One of these was Soucadaux, the socialist governor-general of Madagascar. Tsiranana's open opposition to immediate independence as against the interests of the côtiers and his proposal of a twenty- to thirty-year program of gradual transition under French tutelage were sufficiently reassuring to the French administrators, who reposed their confidence in him.

---

19. For a fuller discussion of the causes and consequences of the 1947 revolt, see Covell, *Madagascar, Politics, Economics and Society*, 9–50; and Mervyn Brown, *Madagascar Rediscovered: A History from Early Times to Independence* (Hamden, CT: Archon Books, 1979), 257–72.

With official support, Tsiranana was elected to the French National Assembly in 1956 along with other leading nationalists in exile. One of his first parliamentary acts was to vote for the passage of the *loi cadre*.

This new law defined the relationship that would exist between France and its former colonies. Under it, the colonies became overseas provinces with a degree of internal autonomy and a citizenry enjoying universal suffrage. A common electoral role and unified system of ministerial government were also created for the new French Union. In the preindependence election that was held in 1957 and contested by thirty-seven parties, the PSD secured a decisive electoral victory. The division among the opposition parties, especially that among the Merina-based groups, benefited the PSD. On May 1, 1958, Tsiranana became the head of the government. Three months later, he received Charles de Gaulle. De Gaulle was touring the colonies to campaign for his constitutional proposals granting full internal autonomy (not independence) to the colonies as republics within a larger French community. Paris would still have a measure of control over defense, foreign relations, civil liberties, education, and finance in these republics. A vote for independence would mean an end to all French aid and services. The referendum that followed was a resounding victory for Tsiranana. As in virtually all the French colonies except Guinea, seventy-seven percent of the Malagasy electorate voted for de Gaulle's proposals and against full independence. Following the trend in other French colonies in Western Africa, further negotiations resulted in full independence in 1960. To win the support of the Merina and strengthen his hand, Tsiranana succeeded, with the permission of the French, in returning the three exiled deputies to Madagascar and appointing two of them to key ministerial positions in his government.

The forms, structures, and euphoria of independence should not let us forget the limited and conditional nature of Madagascar's liberation. A series of cooperative agreements signed with the French ensured that, in spite of formal independence, the essentials of French hegemony would be preserved. The defense agreement stipulated that the new Malagasy army would be trained, equipped, and partially financed by France. France would be free to station its troops in Madagascar and have free and ready access to Malagasy territory, waters, and air space in addition to retaining control of its military base at Antseranana. In foreign policy, the two countries agreed to exchange information and grant each other's citizens the rights of citizenship. The French ambassador would remain the permanent head of the Antananarivo diplomatic community. To ensure that the future Malagasy elite would remain imbued with and committed to French values and culture, close relations would be maintained in education: France would continue to finance higher education while appointing the head of the University of Madagascar. On the economic front, Madagascar, like most of the former French colonies, would remain within the franc zone, meaning fiscal policies would be determined by the Bank of France. The wholesale end of the export-import trade continued to be dominated by a tripod of French oligopolies, the Marseillaise, the Lyonnaise, and the Société de l'Emyrne, whose reputation for sharp practices gave them the title of "the three crocodiles of the island."

For Tsiranana and his *côtier*-dominated ruling elite, these agreements, carefully selected and prepared by the departing colonial master, did not represent last minute backdoor concessions to a reluctant patrimonial taskmaster determined to take with one hand what it had given with the other. With Tsiranana's tenuous political hold on the country and with the Merina still dominant in the civil service and the professions, the perpetuation of French neocolonial influence would serve as a useful counterweight to the growing cooperation of domestic and international Communist opposition. As Maureen Covell aptly put it: "Sober calculation of the requirements of survival, a real Francophilia and personal links between Tsiranana and de Gaulle all lay behind the accords."[20]

Between Madagascar and the French: The Politics of the Comoros Islands

To the northwest of Madagascar was the four-Island nation of Comoros, comprised of Grande Comore, Anjouan, Mayotte, and Moheli. By-products of volcanic eruptions, these Islands and their numerous adjacent coral islets enjoyed a warm tropical climate which permitted the cultivation of rice, maize, and tropical fruits as well as fishing and inter-island trade. Organized into autonomous, but constantly warring, sultanates, the islands were dominated by the Swahili-speaking Muslim settlers, rulers, and landowners who maintained a rigid caste-like distinction between themselves and their serf-like peasants and servants. From its base in Madagascar, the French obtained the island of Mayotte in 1841 through a treaty with the local sultan. More treaties of protection with the other sultans soon brought the other islands under French control. French colonization had three major repercussions. First, it opened the islands to large-scale immigration as many Christianized Malagasies came to settle on the islands, inaugurating an era of major sociocultural transformation. Secondly, the French introduced new cash crops, such as spices, copra, cloves, vanilla, cinnamon, perfume essences, and oils, greatly increasing the islands' prosperity.

Finally, for administrative convenience, the French administered the Comoros as part of the colony of Madagascar between 1916 and 1946. The French, however, continued to rule through the indigenous Muslim rulers. They made little effort to transform the society culturally, since their rule remained distant and indirect. In 1946, the Comoros became a Territoire d'Outre Mer of France (French Overseas Province or Department). Since the Comoros already enjoyed considerable internal autonomy, during the referendum of 1958 they voted to retain their status as an autonomous state within the French Empire. This gave them self-government within a global French community but also guaranteed continued French aid, protection, and influence. However, in 1974, three islands of the archipelago voted for full independence (the highly Christianized Mayotte voted overwhelmingly against independence as part of a muslim-dominated Comoros state). Independence for these islands came on June 5, 1975. Ahmed Abdallah became the president of the new state, but his government lasted for only two months. On August 3, 1975, a left-wing coup led by Ali Soilih overthrew Abdallah and plunged Comoros into a period of political instability that would last for decades after its independence. The continued attempt to recover Mayotte from the French was abortive, first because the Mayotte continued to vote against reunification, and second because the strategic location of the island on

---

20. Covell, *Madagascar, Politics, Economics and Society*, 34.

the routes of the oil supertankers had made Mayotte a significant location for French military deploymen.[21]

Under the Shadow of Apartheid
Relations with South Africa: The Struggle
for Incorporation

For much of the present century, South Africa cast a long shadow over its subregional neighbors. The areas most affected by this were the high commission territories. One of these, Lesotho, is entirely geographically enclosed by South Africa, one of two countries in the world to be completely situated within another country. The second, Swaziland, is partially encircled by South Africa, while the third, Botswana, is surrounded on nearly all its frontiers by South Africa or states under direct or indirect South African control. During the European Scramble for and partition of Africa in the late nineteenth century, the three countries accepted British protectorate status in an attempt to avoid annexation by the Cape Colony or any of the Boer republics. At the conclusion of the Anglo-Boer war in 1902, South Africa demanded the incorporation of at least two of the territories in one or two of its Afrikaner republics. Since the two parties could not agree on how the nonwhites in the territories should be treated, no headway was made in this regard, and the Peace of Veereeniging war was signed without a resolution of the transfer issue.

Following the 1910 Act of Union, South Africa accelerated its efforts to annex the three states. Initially and in principle, the British were not averse to this idea, and indeed were committed to granting South Africa's request provided that sufficient safeguards could be established to protect the indigenous populations of the states. Gradually, however, as racialism became entrenched in South African policy, it became clear that South African whites could no longer be trusted to respect and protect the rights of Africans either in South Africa or in the high commission territories. This realization made the British reluctant to grant outright incorporation. Instead they argued that before any transfer could occur, the African inhabitants of the high commission territories would have to be duly consulted to ascertain their desire and interests in the matter. In 1913, General Botha requested the transfer of two of the states. The British gave an evasive answer to the effect that the request would be considered though the possibility of transferring Bechuanaland in the near future was viewed as being very remote. The South African Native Land Bill of 1913 was promulgated with the expectation that only with the incorporation of the three protectorates would enough land be available for the African population.

Successive attempts by Premier Smuts and General Hertzog to annex the territories foundered on the British government's skepticism about the trustworthiness of South Africa's purported safeguards for the rights of the said indigenous populations. In exasperation, Herzog resorted to blackmail, threatening the territories

21. Jocelyn Murray, ed., *Cultural Atlas of Africa* (New York, N.Y: Facts on File, Inc., 1981, 218–9. See also A. Bourde, "The Comoro Islands: Problems of a Microcosm." *Journal of Modern African Studies*, 3, 1, 1965, 91–102.

with severe consequences for not embracing the generous invitation being offered by South Africa. "If the Natives," he warned, "do not want to come in...[but] hold themselves apart, then they must realize that the markets of the Union will no longer be open to them.... The longer they try to remain outside the more they will have to pay the penalty for it."[22]

Preoccupation with World War II ensured that there would be a lull in the demand for the transfer of the territories. With the end of the war in 1945, the issue came into the limelight again and was made more acute by developments in the territories. The first of these was the support Tshekedi Khama, the paramount chief of the Ngwato, gave to the demand of the Herero of South West Africa to be transferred as a mandated territory to Britain. South Africa regarded this support as an intolerable interference in South African internal affairs, in spite of the fact that Bechuanaland shared an extensive (1,300 mile) frontier with South West Africa. The second event that generated much uneasiness and controversy in South Africa was the marriage of Seretse Khama, heir apparent to the Ngwato throne, to an English girl in 1948. For South Africa, which had just institutionalized apartheid and would outlaw interracial marriage and criminalize interracial sex in the following year, this was completely unacceptable. South Africa could not have the future chief of one of its potential future provinces married to a white woman. This would run counter to all its doctrines of racial separation and set a bad example to blacks in South Africa. Consequently, South Africa put considerable pressure on the British government to stop the marriage, and if that proved impossible, it would pressure Britain to debar Seretse from succeeding to the kingship. To demonstrate its unwillingness to budge on this point, South Africa threatened Bechuanaland with a total blockade and economic sanctions and possibly seizure and forced incorporation. As noted earlier, not willing to offend the racial sensibilities of South African whites, the British Labour Party gave in to the apartheid state's pressure. Seretse was summoned to London and banned from returning to his homeland.

Pleased with the turn of events, the new Afrikaner Nationalist government in Pretoria heightened the pressure. The new prime minister, Dr. Daniel Malan, expressed resentment at the British claim that the apartheid government could not be trusted to protect the interests of nonwhites in the territories. He regarded it as a grievous injustice that South Africa was, unlike other Commonwealth states, compelled to harbor, "within her embrace, and even within her borders...territories entirely dependent on her economically, and largely also for their defense, but belonging to and governed by another country." He added, "So long as this is tolerated...there can be no real equality nor even full independence for her."[23]

Efforts made by J. G. Strydom, who succeeded Malan in 1954, to achieve transfer yielded no dividends. By now it had become evident that, in the changed atmosphere of post-World War II politics, decolonization and self-determination had become the vogue. Under the watchful eyes of the United Nations and other international organizations, colonial masters like Britain could no longer dispose of their colonies as they deemed fit without courting international censure and opprobrium. Furthermore, Africans' contributions to the war effort in human and

22. William Hailey, *The Republic of South Africa and the High Commission Territories* (Oxford: Oxford University Press, 1965).

23. Hailey, *The Republic of South Africa and the High Commission Territories.*

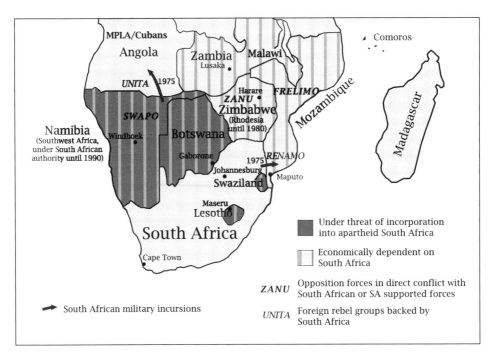

South African colonialism in southern Africa.

material resources also demanded that they be treated with dignity and rewarded with self-determination. South Africa's racial ideology and its repression of the African population within its territory, which reached an explosive point in the Sharpeville massacre of 1960, also began to give the apartheid state a terrible reputation before the world. In 1954, Churchill informed the South African government that Britain had no intention of changing its mind on the territories. He advised the South African Government to desist from needlessly pressing "an issue on which we could not fall in with their views without failing in our trust."[24] Seven years later, in 1961, South Africa severed its last formal relations with Britain by becoming a republic, bringing the possibility of a territorial transfer to an end.

Under Verwoerd, who succeeded Strydom as prime minister in 1958, South Africa gradually reconciled itself to the possibility that the transfer would not happen. Thus, it adopted a new policy of coexistence in which the high commissioned territories' economic dependence on South Africa would give the latter a great deal of political influence. Addressing this in June 1964, Dr. Verwoerd informed the South African parliament that even though:

> the gradual process of independence in the territories may cause difficulties...if this is their place of employment, if this is the source of their revenue, if our co-operation in connection with customs revenue is in their interest, then any individual government that is established there must

---

24. Churchill, quoted in N. E. Davis, *A History of Southern Africa* (Harlow, England: Longman, 1978), 168.

maintain friendship with its neighbor [i.e., South Africa] in the interests of its own people.[25]

Verwoerd's statement underlined the economic dependence and vulnerability of the territories. Britain's failure to develop the territories during the colonial era, preserving them instead as reservoirs of land for white settlers and of cheap labor for the South African mines, had set the stage for a state of dependency on their worst enemies, the whites of apartheid South Africa. As Basil Davidson noted, "the Basuto, if he wants to get into the modern world, is given only one road to follow—the road to white South Africa."[26] This vulnerability would also ensure that the newly independent states would be in no position to play any active role in the struggle for liberation in apartheid South Africa without incurring the military reprisals and economic destabilization that came to mark their relation with the apartheid state during the 1970s and 1980s.[27]

The Last Colonial Frontiers: Decolonization, Cold War, and Independence in Namibia and Zimbabwe

Namibia: From Mandated Territory to Independence

South Africa's involvement in developments in South West Africa (Namibia) and Southern Rhodesia (Zimbabwe) also brought it into conflict with the international community. In 1920, Namibia was taken from Germany and transferred to South Africa to be administered as a mandated territory on behalf of the League of Nations. With the end of the League and the formation of the United Nations in 1945, the old mandated territories became trust territories of the UN. South Africa, however, refused to accept the UN's authority over Namibia. Instead, it demanded that the territory be incorporated into South Africa as its fifth province. A series of apparently conflicting rulings by the International Court of Justice between 1950 and 1966 did not help matters. While affirming that South Africa still had international responsibility for the territory and should submit annual reports on the area, the court held that South Africa had no legal obligation to place Namibia under UN trusteeship. Finally, in 1966, the UN General Assembly removed South Africa's right to administer the territory, and in 1971, the International Court ruled that South Africa should withdraw from Namibia. South Africa, of course, ignored the ruling as well as other UN resolutions, confident that none of the major powers was sufficiently committed to African libera-

---

25. Quoted in Halpern, *Basutoland, Bechuanaland and Swaziland, South Africa's Hostages,* 437.

26. Basil Davidson, *Report on South Africa* (London: Jonathan Cape, 1952), 213.

27. On South Africa's foreign relations and the quest for incorporation, see Sam C. Nolutshungu, *South Africa in Africa: A Study of Ideology and Foreign Policy* (Manchester: Manchester University Press, 1975); Ronald Hyam, *The Failure of South African Expansion, 1909–1939* (London: Macmillan, 1972), and Joseph Hanlon, *Beggar Your Neighbours: Apartheid Power in Southern Africa* (Bloomington: Indiana University Press, 1986).

tion to risk going to war with South Africa over the matter. Thereafter, South Africa continued its introduction of the policies of apartheid into the territory. As in South Africa, a 1968 act created six *bantustans,* or African homelands, in Namibia. The whole apparatus of the South African apartheid system creating different levels of economic development as well as social and political statuses for the different races in the area began to be established. Through forced relocation, inferior education, job discrimination, and a whole series of apartheid laws, Africans were ejected from "white areas" and consigned to unskilled and semi-skilled work.

The consistent failure of the United Nations to deal effectively with the defiance of its resolutions convinced the Africans of Namibia that their salvation would not come from the world community. UN resolutions in New York had to be matched by an active resistance movement on the ground in Namibia. In 1957, the Ovamboland People's Organization (OPO) was formed; it became the South West African People's Organization (SWAPO) in 1960. Meanwhile, a largely Herero-backed organization, the South West Africa National Union (SWANU), was formed. SWANU was especially critical of SWAPO's over-reliance on the UN and other outside help. In 1960, the two groups joined forces to launch a sustained campaign of armed resistance against the army of apartheid South Africa. The struggle would last for twenty-six years, resulting in countless casualties, especially at the hand of South African death squads operating in Namibia. The defeat of the South African army by the Cuban-backed Angola army at the southern Angola town of Cuito Cuanavale in 1987 pushed the apartheid state to the negotiating table. In their first instance of post-Cold War cooperation, the United States and the Soviet Union forged a cease-fire and made negotiations that resulted in the independence of Namibia in 1990. Sam Nujoma, leader of SWAPO, became its first president.[28]

From Southern Rhodesia to Zimbabwe

As in Namibia, the struggle for independence would follow a tortuous path in Zimbabwe. Under the imperial designs of Cecil Rhodes, the British arch-imperialist, the lands of the Shona and the Ndebele soon came under the effective control of Rhodes's British South Africa Company (BSACO). Company rule continued until 1924, when Southern Rhodesia became a self-governing, white settler-controlled British Crown Colony. In 1954, Southern Rhodesia federated with the British colonial territories of Northern Rhodesia (Zambia) and Nyasaland (Malawi) to form the Central African Federation. The federation was short-lived. Perceiving it as a means of perpetuating white minority domination, its black majority populations opted for separate independence, which was granted to Malawi and Zambia in 1963. In Southern Rhodesia, black nationalists' expectations that independence would soon be achieved were shattered in 1962, when the white electorate voted the Rhodesian Front (RF), a party with an unswerving commitment to maintaining white supremacy, into power.

---

28. On Namibia, see Alfred T. Moleah, *Namibia: The Struggle for Liberation* (Wilmington, DE: Disa Press, 1983); Peter Katjavivi, *A History of Resistance in Namibia* (London: James Currey, 1987); and D. Herbstein and J. Evenson, *The Devils are Among US: The War for Namibia* (London: Zed Books, 1990).

Figure 21.1 Sam Nujoma of Namibia.

In 1965, to further consolidate white control in the territory, the RF government led by Ian Smith announced its Unilateral Declaration of Independence (UDI), thus severing any ties with the British crown. Though Britain refused to approve the new measure, it did little to counter it. Under pressure from the newly independent African states, the United Nations imposed mandatory economic sanctions against the "illegal" RF regime in 1967. However, the support of South Africa and of the Portuguese authorities in Mozambique and Angola enabled the ostracized state to break many of the sanctions. Cold War politics complicated the situation. The United States openly flouted the UN sanctions by continuing to purchase Rhodesian chrome for many years.

With the failure of the UN sanctions and the international community's unwillingness to more forcefully confront the racist regime, the burden fell on the shoulders of the African nationalist groups. The most important of these were the Zimbabwe African People's Union (ZAPU) and the Zimbabwe African National Union (ZANU). In the face of intense repression by the RF regime, the two groups went underground, but they declared an all-out war against the illegal regime beginning in 1966. The exit of the Portuguese from their southern African colonies in 1974 intensified the pace and effectiveness of the guerrilla campaign, as the nationalists were able to establish bases in and launch attacks from Zambia and Mozambique. In 1976, ZAPU and ZANU joined forces as the Patriotic Front (PF). The RF's efforts to stop the developing, massive white exodus by forging a power-sharing arrangement that would give a semblance of power to moderate blacks while keeping real control in white settlers' hands failed to stem the mili-

Figure 21.2. Cecil Rhodes.

tary advance of the Patriotic Front. In 1979, after a major showdown between Britain and other Commonwealth nations at the Commonwealth meeting in Lusaka, Britain was pressured to invite all the belligerent groups to London, where a comprehensive peace was forged, resulting in Rhodesia's independence as Zimbabwe in 1980. Robert Mugabe, leader of ZANU, became its first prime minister.[29]

Conclusion:
The Challenges of Independence

The achievement of independence left the southern African states with many challenges. In Namibia and Zimbabwe, land remained a contentious issue, with the bulk of the arable land under the control of a minority white population numbering less than one percent of the population. In the Comoros, the prosperity of

---

29. On Zimbabwe, see Gann and Henriksen, *The Struggle for Zimbabwe*. See also Robert Good, *UDI: The International Politics of the Rhodesian Rebellion* (London: Faber and Faber, 1973; and Elaine Windrich, *Britain and the Politics of Rhodesian Independence* (London: Croom Helm, 1978).

Figure 21.3. Robert Mubabe of Zimbabwe.

a small elite of local landholders and cash crop producers could not hide the desperate poverty of the majority of the population. In Mauritius, the challenges of ethnic and racial diversity had been effectively contained and channeled toward making the country a model of social tolerance, democratic stability, and economic development. In Africa's smallest country, the Seychelles, post-independence political leaders managed to combine a record of bitterly polarized political experience with an impressive program of economic growth and improvement in social services. On the other hand, the high commission territories emerged from British rule among the poorest nations in the World. Breaking out of this state of vicious poverty would tax the ability of the leaders and the limited resources of these states.

   More than any other region of the continent, the history of the Southern African states has been dominated by a long struggle for freedom from the tentacles of imperialism and the racial hegemony of European settlers in the region. The limited resources and lack of colonial development in most of these states rendered them particularly economically dependent on South Africa, a vulnerability the apartheid state did not fail to exploit in order to weaken and destabilize the frontier states, thus ensuring that none of them would be able to pursue an activist and independent policy in the struggle for liberation from white minority domination in the region. The end of apartheid and the negotiated settlement that resulted in a transition to nonracial government in South Africa in 1994 should signal the beginning of a new era of peace, stability, and cooperation in the region.

Review Questions

1. With reference to the Southern African states, how accurate is the view that World War II was a watershed in the sociopolitical transformation of Africa in the first half of the twentieth century?
2. With reference to the high commission territories, assess the significance of the institution of chieftaincy in the social and political development of southern Africa during the colonial period.
3. What were the major challenges that faced the movements for national liberation in the southern African states between 1945 and 1990?
4. "The last colonial frontiers." Why did the struggle for independence in Zimbabwe and Namibia last for so long?
5. With particular reference to Madagascar, account for the relative significance of internal and external factors in the decolonization process in the African island-states of the Indian Ocean.
6. Account for the failure of South Africa's expansionist policy and politics in Southern Africa. What were the major consequences of the policy?

Additional Reading

Booth, Alan R. *Swaziland: Tradition and Change in a Southern African Kingdom*. Boulder, CO: Westview Press, 1983.

Callaghy, Thomas M. ed. *South Africa in Southern Africa: The Intensifying Vortex of Violence*. New York: Praeger, 1983.

Covell, Maureen. *Madagascar, Politics, Economics and Society*. London and New York: Frances Pinter Publishers, 1987.

Franda, Marcus. *The Seychelles: Unquiet Islands*. Boulder, CO: Westview Press, 1982.

Herbstein, D. and J. Evenson. *The Devils are Among US: The War for Namibia*. London: Zed Books, 1990.

Sillery, Anthony. *Botswana: A Short Political History*. London: Methuen & Co., 1974.

Spence, J. E. *Lesotho: The Politics of Dependence*. London: Oxford University Press, 1968.

Chapter 22

South Africa: The Rise and Fall of Apartheid

Funso Afolayan

On June 1, 1948, Daniel Malan, the leader of the Herenigde ("Reunited" or "Purified") National Party (HNP), arrived in Pretoria to take control of the reins of government. Addressing a tumultuous crowd of Afrikaner enthusiasts who had come to welcome him at the train station, the new leader declared:

> In the past we felt like strangers in our own country, but today South Africa belongs to us once more. For the first time since the union, South Africa is our own. May God grant that it always remains our own.[1]

The triumph of the Afrikaner nationalists and their formal institutionalization of apartheid as a policy of governance and of social and human relations ushered in a new era in South African history. It was an era characterized by political repression, economic deprivation, and social injustice as well as sustained and vigorous domestic resistance and sporadic, though ultimately effective, international opposition that eventually effected the demise of the apartheid state during the last decade of the twentieth century. This is the story of this chapter.

* * *

The Triumph of Afrikaner Nationalism

The triumph of the Herenigde National Party (NP since 1951) in the 1948 election was not a forgone conclusion; it was a product of many years of hard work, tenacity, and dedication by Malan and other Afrikaner nationalists. After decades of rebellion, resistance, defeat, humiliation, and collaboration, the forces of Afrikaner nationalism were finally gaining strength. The nineteenth century had ended with a major contest, the South African or Anglo-Boer War between descendants of the Dutch settlers (Boers) and English settlers, over who would control the destiny of South Africa and its warring peoples. Though the British won the war, the Afrikaners never gave up their claims to the ownership of South Africa, a land over which their forbearers had fought and died for over three centuries. Britain's exit with the establishment of the South African Union and the

---

1. *Rand Daily Mail*, June 2, 1948.

427

achievement of independence in 1910 brought Afrikaner generals, who had crossed swords with British imperial commanders during the war, to the helm of affairs. The governments of Generals Louis Botha, Jan Smuts, and Brian Hertzog did much to consolidate white control and racial segregation in South Africa. Though committed to white supremacy, their cautious approach to the issue did not endear them to the most ardent of the Afrikaners, who resented their patronizing attitude toward blacks and Asians, their warm relations with Britain, their liberal outlook and cold contempt for the racist ideology of the *volk*, their brutal repression of Afrikaner-inspired revolts and strikes, and their reluctance to go to the limit to enthrone Afrikanerdom in South Africa. Accumulated grievances and growing resentment led Malan, one of the most rabid Afrikaner nationalists, to break away from the United South African National Party government of Smuts and Hertzog to form his own "Purified" (Herenigde) National Party in 1934. That same year, the Volkkas Bank was established to provide credit facilities to Afrikaners. Four years later, in 1938, the centennial celebration of the Great Trek took place.[2] A year later, World War II started, creating what the *Johannesburg Star* described as a "grave crisis in South Africa."[3]

World War II and the Reawakening of Afrikaner Militancy

With the active support of five of his eleven cabinet members, Prime Minister Hertzog wanted South Africa to either support Hitler or remain neutral. Smuts, his coalition partner, had the support of the remaining six ministers in arguing that it was in South Africa's best interest to enter the war on the British side. Unable to dissuade the parliament with his defense of neutrality and further estranging the wavering members with his ill-advised defense of Adolf Hitler, Hertzog resigned the premiership. Three days later, on September 8, he was warmly received into the "Purified" National Party by Malan, who evoked the spirits of the Boer ancestors, the Great Trekkers: "In spirit, I see the figures of Piet Retief, Andries Pretorius, Sarel Cilliers, Hendrik Potgieter....it is as though I hear them saying: 'Even when you were divided we loved you, but now that you are one, our love for you is doubled.'"[4] This apparent unity of the *volk* (nation) was short-lived, however. Encouraged by Hitler's early successes, Afrikaner nationalists began to demand that Afrikaans be made the only language of instruction in South African schools. This was too much for Hertzog, who had spent most of his career pursuing a more inclusive white South African policy. With his life's work in ruins, Hertzog retired from public life, dying in early 1942.

Malan became the leader of the opposition, but his major battles during these early years would be fought not in parliament but outside it, where Afrikaner loy-

---

2. On the development and the eventual triumph of Afrikaner nationalism, see Thomas D. Moodie, *The Rise of Afrikanerdom: Power, Apartheid and the Rise of the Afrikaner Civil Religion* (Berkeley: University of California Press, 1975); and William H. Vatcher, Jr., *White Laager: The Rise of Afrikaner Nationalism* (New York: Fredrick A Praeger, Publishers, 1965).

3. *The Star*, September 4, 1939, front page reprinted in *Illustrated History of South Africa: The Real Story* (Pleasantville, NY: Reader's Digest Association, Inc., 1988), 345.

4. Quoted in *Illustrated History of South Africa*, 348.

alists, impatient with the pace and direction of change, were taking to extra-parliamentary measures to achieve their goals of racial purity and exclusiveness. As
German propaganda streamed into South Africa through a local German station,
Radio Zeesen, several pro-Nazi groups sprang into being. The most influential of
these was the Ossewabrandwag (OB, or Ox-wagon Sentinel), established in 1939
to give cultural expression to the new Afrikaner nationalism that the 1938 centennial celebration of the Great Trek had engendered. Its fortune oscillated with the
progress of the Germans in the war. By 1941, it claimed a national membership of
400,000, nearly twice the total number of volunteers that Smut was able to put
under arms in support of Britain. To become a member of its military wing, the
Stormjaers (Storm troopers), a recruit, with his hand on the Bible, a loaded re-
volver pointing at his chest and another at his back, would take a solemn oath declaring: "If I advance, follow me. If I retreat, shoot me. If I die, avenge me. So help
me God."[5]

Others were more effusive in their admiration for Hitler and his vision for
Germany. Speaking before a student group in September 1940, the Reverend
Koot Vorster of the Dutch Reformed Church declared:

> Hitler's *Mein Kampf* shows the way to greatness—the path of South
> Africa. Hitler gave the Germans a calling. He gave them a fanaticism,
> which causes them to stand back for no one. We must follow this ex-
> ample because only by such holy fanaticism can the Afrikaner nation
> achieve its calling.[6]

As the movement quickly transformed itself from a mere cultural organization into a distinctly military one and its members began to amass arsenals of
hand grenades and guns in readiness for acts of sabotage, the government swung
into action, cracking down on the movement. Koot Vorster, his brother John,
who would later become prime minister of apartheid South Africa, and up to two
thousand OB members, many of whom would later become prominent members
of the National Party government, were arrested and interned by Smuts at Koffie-
fontein in the northern Cape for the duration of the war.[7]

"All Roads to Johannesburg": Rural Poverty and Urbanization

In the meantime, South Africa became actively engaged in the war, taking its
stand, as Smuts put it, "for the defense of freedom and the destruction of Hit-
lerism and all that it implies."[8] By the end of the war, 218,260 South Africans
were in uniform. Of this number, 46,627 were Africans, while, of the 5,500 South
Africans killed in the war, more than a quarter of them were black. While Smuts

---

5. *Illustrated History of South Africa*, 349.
6. Koot Vorster, quoted in *Illustrated History of South Africa*, 349.
7. On the development of these extra-parliamentary groups as the vanguard of
Afrikaner nationalism, see Hermann Giliomee, *Ethnic Power Mobilized* (London: Yale University Press, 1979); and Dan O'Meara, *Volkscapitalism: Class, Capital and Ideology in the
Development of Afrikaner Nationalism, 1934–1948* (Cambridge: Cambridge University
Press, 1983).
8. Smuts, quoted in *Illustrated History of South Africa*, 350.

was not averse to putting blacks under arms, Malan, the leader of the National Party, railed endlessly against arming the "kaffirs" (an Arabic term for "infidels" or "pagans") and warned of dire consequences for whites. The Government relented and desisted from using blacks in combat. South African contributions to the war effort took other forms. The closure of the Mediterranean to Allied shipping by the Axis in 1941 made the sea route via the Cape of Good Hope vital for Allied forces operating in Asia and North Africa. Durban and Cape Town flourished as major provisioning ports supplying Allied merchant ships and warships with munitions, food, water, clothing, and other items.

No effort was spared to ensure an Allied victory, as thousands of South African women knitted furiously, producing thousands of pullovers, mittens, balaclavas, and socks for "the boys at the front." In addition, South Africa became a major source for the supply of strategic minerals such as gold, platinum, uranium, and steel to the Allies. The South African Iron and Steel Industrial Corporation (ISCOR), established in 1928, produced a record 866,107 metric tons in 1945. A plethora of posters and stamps urged South Africans to play their part by guarding against unwittingly giving information to the enemy and avoiding the overuse of strategic resources such as steel, cloth and gasoline. One poster advised: "Don't buy new clothes needlessly. Don't be afraid of wearing old clothes in wartime."[9] Another advised whites not to keep more servants than they really needed in order to free up labor for more useful purposes.

The demands of the war also stimulated rapid expansion in the mining and manufacturing industries. The number of employees in the coal-mining and garment industries nearly doubled. Gold mining actually witnessed a slight decline from about 1941 onwards but remained South Africa's greatest industry, with 370,959 employees, of which 328,335 were black, in 1946.[10]

Urbanization was a major development during the 1930s and 1940s. Inspired partly by the economic expansion, it was fueled largely by gnawing rural poverty. As a noted South African historian put it in 1930, rural Africans were "dragging along the very lowest level of bare subsistence," living in "poverty, congestion and chaos," blighted by "ill-health and starvation, endemic typhus and almost chronic scurvy," suffering an "appalling mortality rate among infants," dwelling in "heavily over-populated," "grossly neglected," and generally barren reserves, and "utterly dependent on wage-earning outside" that is by migrant workers, to relieve "a dead level of poverty" inside.[11] Further, since white farmers owned all the best land, for the majority of the rural Africans, survival depended on securing labor jobs on the white farms where the pay was low and often insufficient for subsistence, making employment in the burgeoning industries in Johannesburg the only lifeline left for displaced Africans. By 1936, conditions in the rural areas had deteriorated to such an extent that the choice before the majority of rural

---

9. For samples of such posters, see *Illustrated History of South Africa*, 350–1, the major source for much of this section.

10. For details of these developments in the industries, see Leonard Thompson, *A History of South Africa* (New Haven, CT: Yale University Press, 1995). On life in South Africa during World War II, see *South Africa's Yesterdays* (Cape Town: Reader's Digest, 1981); Edward Roux, *Time Longer than Rope* (Madison: University of Wisconsin Press, 1964); and Kenneth W. Grundy, *Soldiers Without Politics* (Berkeley: University of California Press, 1983), 63–89.

11. W. M. Macmillan, quoted in *Illustrated History of South Africa*, 354–5.

Africans was brutally simple: migrate to the towns or stay and starve to death. Most chose to join the exodus to the cities. The African Great Trek had begun.

By 1946, the African population of Johannesburg was 400,000, representing a one hundred percent increase in ten years. Every effort made by the government to confine Africans to the reserves and keep them out of town, unless they had special permission to work, failed. Neither the urban authorities, who claimed not to have money, nor the industries, which had the cash but not the will, did anything to provide housing for this avalanche of immigrants. By 1944, the situation had reached an explosive point. Homeless and desperate, thousands of destitute (for there is hardly a better term to describe these throngs) people organized around notable leaders began to move out of their overcrowded hovels, setting up homes made of sacks, wood, discarded corrugated iron, and cardboard on any vacant piece of land on the outskirts of the cities. By 1948, close to 100,000 Africans were living in squatter settlements on the southwestern borders of Johannesburg in an area later known as Soweto, an acronym for "southwestern township."

One of the most celebrated of the new squatter leaders was the Zulu-speaking James Mpanza, who had been jailed for killing an Indian trader but was spared the gallows through his conversion to Christianity. Claiming to have messianic visions like Jesus Christ, he drew thousands to his Sofasonke (meaning "we shall all die together") Party. In March 1944, with hundreds of his followers, he seized control of a piece of land located between the railroad line and the communal hall and instructed his excited followers to begin to mark out plots on which to erect their shelters. While the Smuts government wavered on how to deal with this new trouble, the squatters consolidated their hold. By the first week of April the number of squatters on the new land had reached eight thousand. By the end of 1946, there were twenty thousand people dotting on the site. James Mpanza proclaimed himself the king of Orlando, the name for the location. Thereafter, he proceeded to draw up laws to govern the "kingdom." He imposed an entry fee of six shillings and collected weekly taxes to run the day-to-day administration while a "police" force was established to deal with problems of law and order. Mpanza legalized the brewing of native beer in defiance of government prohibition. In January 1946, after the authorities had failed to persuade him to disband his movement peacefully, they decided to expel Mpanza to Natal and crush his movement by force. Mpanza took his case all the way to the Appeal Court, which ruled in his favor. As Oriel Monongoaha, leader of the Primville squatters, put it in 1947:

> The government is beaten, because even the government of England could not stop the people from squatting. The government was like a man who has a cornfield, which is invaded by birds. He chases the birds from one part of the field and they alight in another part.... we squatters are the birds. The government sends its policemen to chase us away and we move off and occupy another spot. We shall see whether it is the farmer or the birds who get tired first.[12]

---

12. Quoted in A. W. Stadler, "Birds in the Cornfield: Squatter Movements in Johannesburg, 1944–1947," *Journal of Southern African Studies* 6, 1(1979): 93.

For the Africans, life in the urban centers was a grim struggle for survival. However, out of the misery, violence, drunkenness, prostitution, squalor, and disease developed a new urban culture, known variously as *Marabi*, *I-Tswari* or *Mabokwe*. This culture of the slum yard, believed by its followers to be both "black and beautiful," thrived on its own distinctly African music, a vibrant blend of Negro spirituals, Boer beats, and traditional rural African rhythms.[13] Presided over by women known as *shebeen* queens and serviced by "exquisite ladies of the night," *shebeens* were the most important avenues of recreation for the slum dwellers, serving at the same time as "a drinking hole, an all-night restaurant, a dance hall and a brothel."[14] Stressed by the decay and poverty of the rural areas, new migrants quickly found themselves sucked into this violent but throbbing life of illicit home beer-brewing and police raids for illegal liquor gang fights and street muggings, weekend *shebeen* parties, and *isiqataviku* ("kill me quick") drinking. In Peter Abraham's *Mine Boy* (1946), a woman advises a newcomer from the rural areas to prepare for a tough existence:

> In the city it is like this: all the time you are fighting. Fighting. Fighting! When you are asleep and when you are awake. And you look only after yourself. If you do not you are finished. If you are soft everyone will spit in your face. They will rob you and cheat you and betray you. So to live here you must be hard, hard as a stone. And money is your best friend. With money you can bribe a policeman. With money you can buy somebody to go to jail for you. That is how it is, Xuma.[15]

The African's struggle was not limited to the slums alone. He had other battles on other fronts, namely with his employers and the governing authorities. To cope with the high cost of living, low wages, and other deprivations caused by the war, Africans organized themselves into trade unions through which they organized bus boycotts and strikes, even though strikes were illegal. The most successful of the bus boycotts was in protest against increased fares, and it occurred in the Alexandra township northeast of Johannesburg in August 1943. For ten days, twenty thousand workers decided to wake up at three in the morning and walk to work, returning home at nine in the evening. In 1943, the mines were plagued by a spate of work stoppages, forcing the government to establish the Lansdowne Commission of Enquiry to investigate the working conditions of African miners. In August 1944, the African Mine Workers Union (AMWU) denounced the commission's recommendations as being hopelessly inadequate and unsatisfactory. Two years later, in August 1946, in one of the biggest strikes in South African history, seventy-four thousand mine workers went on strike, demanding improved working conditions and a minimum wage of ten shillings a day, the pay white workers received. This was too much for Smuts, since it posed an intolerable threat to the very basis of the country's segregation policies — the cheap labor sys-

---

13. On South African music, theater and performance, see David B. Coplan, *In Township Tonight! South Africa's Black City Music and Theartre* (London: Longman, 1985); and Veit Erlmann, *African Stars: Studies in Black South African Performance* (Chicago: University of Chicago Press, 1991).
14. *Illustrated History of South Africa*, 358.
15. Peter Abrahams, *Mine Boy* (1946; reprint, London: 1963), 75–6.

tem. Within five days, the strike, in which twelve miners were killed and one hundred people were injured, had been crushed.[16]

Countdown to Victory:
The National Party and the 1948 Election

In the wartime "khaki" election of 1943, Smuts led his United Party (UP) and won a major victory, but his popularity had started to wane. His failure to check African urbanization, curtail the squatter movement, stop urban crime, and strictly restrict Indian trade and property rights alienated many whites who saw his liberal and centrist policies as inimical to the protection of their group interests. Smuts did not help matters when he attempted to grant Indians limited political representation and called for a retreat from segregation and for the arming of blacks in readiness for a possible invasion of South Africa by Japan. The support of a handful of whites who had fought for democracy in Europe and who now felt that African aspirations must be accorded some respect would not be enough to help him. Groups that had previously supported the government began to waver in their loyalty. Farmers were suffering from an acute shortage of labor, which, in spite of mechanization, remained vital. Since they were unable to compete with the wages paid by the mines and since the government was helpless to reverse the continuing drift of potential laborers to the cities, the farmers began to doubt the United Party's commitment to their interests. Afrikaners, who dominated agriculture, were also resentful of the fact that they continued to play second fiddle to English-speaking whites in trade and business and that, on average, an English-speaking white was twice as wealthy as an Afrikaner. Critics of the government pointed to strikes, rural protests, and the influx of Africans into cities to arouse white fears of *swart gevaar* ("black peril") and *oorstrooming* ("swarming") and to raise the specter of black revolution.

As the 1948 election drew closer, the nationalists began to assail Smuts, castigating him as being too old (he was seventy-eight) for the challenges of the time, too preoccupied with international affairs (he was a member of the Allied Command Council) to have a grip on internal South African problems, and too uncertain and ambiguous in his policies, which attempted fruitlessly to please whites while trying not to push blacks to revolt. In contrast to the United Party's obfuscated vision of a liberalized though segregated society, Malan's HNP presented a clear agenda that would entrench white supremacy and ensure racial "purity." Malan promised to check Africans' influx into the cities, restrict blacks' political rights to their reserves, stop mixed marriages, scrap African electoral representation, ban black trade unions, halt Indian immigration, and control the white immigration, which was threatening Afrikaner jobs and reducing Afrikaners to a minority white group in their own nation. This was the promise of "apartheid" or apartness, which meant each race should develop separately and along its own lines. This promise appealed to the Afrikaners, who rallied actively behind Malan to give him the lead he needed in the 1948 election.

---

16. On African workers' militancy in the townships during the 1940s, see M. Stein, *Black Trade Unionism during the Second World War: The Witwatersrand Strike of December 1942;* and Tom Lodge, *Black Politics in South Africa since 1945* (London: 1983).

With forty-eight seats to the United Party's eighty-nine in the 153-seat House of Assembly, a National Party victory in 1948 would require a net gain of twenty-eight seats, a swing unprecedented in South African electoral history. Everyone expected the NP to make some gains, but victory was regarded beyond the realm of possibility. Yet it happened: the NP had won seventy seats to the UP's sixty-five. The Afrikaner Party, an ally of the NP, won nine seats, giving the NP the majority it needed to control both parliament and the government. Though narrow, it was a stunning victory for the NP, made sweeter by the fact that it was made possible by a recent delimitation commission, ironically supported by Smuts, that made it easier to win rural votes. This constitutional amendment created rural constituencies containing far fewer voters than those in the urban electoral divisions. In the rural areas, the NP won a number of seats with few voters, compared to the far larger number of voters per constituencies in the urban areas, where the UP dominated. The NP had won the majority in the National Assembly without winning the majority in the popular vote. Smuts, the beleaguered prime minister, was beaten by only 224 votes in his Standerton constituency by Wentzel du Plessis, a renegade civil servant and a member of the officially discredited Afrikaner Broederbond (brotherhood). A new era had dawned in the history of South Africa.[17]

The Apartheid State

Though the National Party's leaders and supporters were surprised by their victory in the 1948 election, they were not unprepared for it. Within days, they left no one in doubt of what the new policy of government and racial relations would be in South Africa—the preservation of white supremacy and, most especially, of Afrikaner power in a nation they defined as synonymous with the Afrikaner race and identity. "Today," Malan told his cheering supporters, "South Africa belongs to us once more." In this new South Africa, there would be no blacks, except as temporary migrants or as workers in servile positions performing duties that whites considered too menial for their race. In this new South Africa of the *volk*, Afrikaner Nationalists (National Party supporters and Broederbonders) would lead, other whites would follow; nonwhites would function only as implements of labor, not as citizens. The advent of Malan brought the age of the generals (Botha, Hertzog, and Smuts) to a dramatic close; the age of the ideologues, the racial purists, the technocrats, and the social engineers was beginning.

Apartheid:
Defining a New Social and Political Order

With ruthless determination and unapologetic self-righteousness, the National Party proceeded with its agenda and consolidated its power. Building on

---

17. On the vote for apartheid see Vic Alhadeff, *A Newspaper History of South Africa* (Cape Town: Don Nelson, 1976) and David Harrison, *The White Tribe of Africa* (Johannesburg: Macmillan, 1981)

the segregationist foundations already established by previous rulers from Cecil Rhodes to Alfred Milner and from Hertzog to Smuts, the Nationalists enshrined racial distinctions in all spheres of South African life. Apartheid was the instrument for bringing this new policy into reality. Defined variously as apartness, separateness, and distinctness, it was meant to ensure the natural rights of whites to land ownership and to supreme rulership in a South Africa composed of distinct races, where the supremacy of white interests over all others would remain unquestioned. What was unique about apartheid was not that it was new. Segregationist attitudes and racial prejudices were features of life in other European colonies in Asia and Africa as well as in the post-civil war and post-Reconstruction United States. What was anathema was that the Nationalists were enshrining racialism in an age of decolonization and majority rule, when Nazism and its attendant Jewish holocaust had given the doctrine of racial superiority a bad name. Though not always explicitly stated, the language of biological racism and social Darwinism was at the core of Afrikaner discourse during these years. Nationalist politicians continued to play on white fears of racial mixing, or miscegenation. As William Beinart put it, "The killing blow in a political argument was, put delicately: would you let your daughter marry a black man?"[18] Writing on the same theme, Thomas Moodie reported the case of an Afrikaner republican who admitted "that he was better able to raise money for the party by mentioning the fact that white women were dancing with black men in Cape Town, than by stressing the republican issue."[19]

For the next forty years, as the world moved away from racialism, apartheid would remain the dominant feature of life in South Africa, casting a long shadow over its society and giving its Government a distinct notoriety in the world. The new technocrats at the helm of affairs were well prepared for their mission. Groomed in the inter-war years—an era characterized by economic depression and political extremism—they brought a single (though skewed) sense of purpose, a fierce determination to their task. At the head of the pack was Daniel Malan, a solid nationalist and consistent opposition leader who became the indomitable architect of the new and resurgent Afrikanerdom. At his death in 1956, his Deputy, J.G. Strydom, a shrewd politician and popular speaker who was even more rabid in his commitment to the creed of Afrikaner domination, succeeded Malan. However, the Golden Globe Award for the successful articulation and ruthless implementation of the nationalist programs should go to Hendrik Frensch Verwoerd. Born in the Netherlands in 1901 and educated in Germany, Verwoerd migrated to South Africa with his pro-Boer parents in 1903, where he became a professor of psychology at the University of Stellensbosch before resigning his post and moving north in 1937 to edit the newly established *Die Transvaler*. Known as a fiery republican, Malan appointed him as a senator in 1948. As minister of native affairs from 1950 to 1958, and prime minister between 1958 and 1966, Verwoerd dominated South African policy toward Africans. In April 1961 he was shot twice in the face by a would-be-assassin, but he survived to forge ahead with his apartheid programs and intensify his repression of the African nationalist movement before a deranged attendant stabbed him to death as he pre-

---

18. William Beinart, *Twentieth-Century South Africa* (Oxford: Oxford University Press, 1994), 141.
19. Moodie, *Afrikanerdom*, 250.

pared to make a major speech to the South African parliament in September 1966.[20]

Creating the Apartheid Society
Legislations and Reactions: Securing an
Electoral Autocracy

Unusually preoccupied with issues of nationhood, identity, and culture, the nationalists took steps to create a society in which their own, exclusive form of *baasskap* (supremacy) would be permanent. The new order was built on seven foundational pillars. The first of these can best be characterized as electoral autocracy, defined in South Africa as the principle of white participation and control of all central and major political institutions. There were two aspects to achieving this goal. The first involved the seizure of absolute power by the National Party, through gaining virtually total control of parliament. Within weeks of its ascension to power, worried about the tenuous nature of its narrow majority, the National party government created ten new parliamentary seats for white voters in South West Africa (Namibia) and won all the seats. Other maneuvers were employed to entrench Afrikaner control, such as denying or delaying citizenship rights to white immigrants to deny oppositional, potential voters. In addition, the government successfully Afrikanerized all key institutions of the state, such as the civil service, the police, the army, and other government institutions.

After attending to the white votes, the government neutralized whatever residual electoral influence non-whites still had. The first to fall under the sledgehammer was the token enfranchisement of Indians granted by Smuts in 1946, which had been rejected by the Indians themselves as inadequate. Next on the list was the Native Representative Council (NRC), created by the Smuts Government in 1937 as a means of pacifying African opinion but was, under the leadership of notables such as Albert Luthuli and Z. K. Matthews, developing into a platform for the articulation of African opposition to unpopular government measures. Z. K. Matthews described the Nationalist victory as a "great disappointment" and pledged with other members of the NRC not to do any business with the new government.[21] The government abolished the council in 1951.

Thereafter, the government directed its artillery against colored voters. Colored voters, by virtue of their "kinship" and cultural relations with whites, could have been allies of the government if well-treated or granted full citizenship rights, but the Afrikaner racial purists would not countenance such a possibility.

---

20. On Verwoerd, see Alexander Hepple, *Verwoerd* (Harmondsworth: Penguin, 1967); Jan Botha, *Verwoed is Dead* (Cape Town: Books of Africa ltd., 1967); Henry Kenney, *Architect of Apartheid: H. F. Verwoerd—An Appraisal* (Johannesburg: J. Ball, 1980). Writing on Verwoerd, Leonard Thompson noted that though he was charming in private life, in public life he was "dogmatic, intolerant, domineering and xenophobic." See Thompson, *A History of South Africa*, 189.

21. On Zachariah Keodirelang Matthews, see his *Freedom for My People: the Autobiography of Z.K. Matthews, Southern Africa 1901 to 1968; Memoir* by Monica Wilson. (Capetown: D. Philip, 1981).

Thus, for years, the nationalists agitated for the spatial and residential segregation of coloreds from whites and white neighborhoods. However, attempts to abrogate coloreds' voting rights met with considerable resistance from opposition parties as well as from Havenga, the leader of the Afrikaner Party. Other advocates for the rights of colored voters included the War Veterans' Torch Commando, an ex-servicemen's extra-parliamentary movement established in 1951. Another was the Women's Defense of the Constitution League (known as Black Sash), established in 1956. After four years of fruitless efforts and relentless opposition, the government decided that the higher morality of its popular mandate should take precedence over strict conformity to the rules and principles of the constitution. In two daring moves that clearly violated the principles of equal and proportional representation, the government expanded and packed both the parliament and the Appeal Court with new members known to be government loyalists. In 1956, it finally passed a bill removing black people from the common voters' roll. Henceforth, four elected white representatives would represent colored people. When told of the drastic reduction in representation that this new rule meant for them, Donges, the minister of the interior, replied with characteristic insensitiveness (bearing in mind how serious a problem alcoholism had become among the Cape coloreds), that four full bottles of wine were better than fifty-six empty ones.[22]

The Population Registration Act: Keeping the Races Apart

Next on the Nationalist agenda was a program to ensure a clearer definition of races. In 1950, the government passed the Population Registration Act, which sought to classify everyone living in South Africa according to his or her race based on physical appearance, general acceptance, and social recognition. Henceforth, everyone had to carry an identity card with his or her race clearly marked on it. Amended several times to plug loopholes, this law created considerable hardships, especially for those of mixed race, and most especially in a society in which generations of white masters and rulers had sired numerous children by black and Asian women, their slaves and servants. White officials were given a wide degree of latitude in determining the races of individuals brought before them. A Race Classification Board was set up to adjudicate disputed cases. Purifying the white race involved the use of procedures that, apart from being highly subjective, were crude in the extreme. One of the procedures involved pushing a pencil into the hair. If the pencil stayed in the hair after the head was shaken, the subject would be classified as African or colored, since he must have had *kroes* (frizzy) hair. Should the pencil drop out, the subject could be accepted as being white or colored, meaning having straight hair. With a stroke of the bureaucrat's pen, thousands of people suddenly found their identities changed overnight. Thousands who thought they were white were degraded in social status and classified as colored, acquiring all the indignities associated with that status. "Indi-

---

22. On the government assault on the Cape Colored franchise, see Rodney Davenport and Christopher Saunders, *South Africa: A Modern History* (New York: St. Martin's Press, 2000), 379–396; and Beinart, *Twentieth-Century South Africa*, 142–4.

ans" became "Malays," "Japanese" became "Whites," and so on. Changes in racial status meant changes in job opportunities, compensation, civil and political rights, residential locations, which class one could ride on the train, which parks or beaches one could visit, and many other things besides.

Invariably, the colored population was most affected by the new direction in racial policy. In many cases, people were ejected from their houses, husbands were forced to separate from their wives, and children were expelled from their schools to ensure racial purity. In one celebrated case during the 1960s, in the eastern Transvaal town of Piet Retief, parents of pupils from an Afrikaner school complained that one of the children, Sandra Laing, looked colored, and as such should not be allowed to stay on in the school. After some controversy, and in spite of the fact that the biological parents were certified, upright, and well-respected Afrikaners, the law had to take its course. Sandra Laing was reclassified as "Colored" and expelled from the school. After a great local and international outcry, she was reclassified as white, but no white school would admit her. Rejected by her community and her people, she married an African, moved away, and severed all ties with her parents. Years later, when the producer of the film *The Search for Sandra Laing* visited her parents, the humiliation and anguish they had gone through were still palpable in their speech. While her mother spoke of her experience and anger, the subject was still too painfully fresh for her father to talk about it.

Prohibition of Mixed Marriages and Immorality Acts: Apartheid in the Bedroom

Considered vital to keeping the white race pure, the next item on the Nationalist agenda was to bring an end to its "defilement" and "bastardization" through mixed marriages and sexual relations across racial lines. By 1948, an average of one hundred "mixed" marriages per year within a population of several million might not have appeared to pose any immediate danger to the survival of the white race. However, for the racial purists, even one mixed marriage would be enough to imperil the white race and put it on the road to extinction. It is not surprising that the Prohibition of Mixed Marriages Act of 1949 was the first significant legislation introduced by the new government. The most revealing aspect of its passage was that, unlike the other bills, the opposition members of parliament joined the NP parliamentarians to actively support this bill. The only serious criticism of the bill came from Sam Kahn, a native representative and the lone Communist in the parliament. Amidst jeers and interjections from the Nationalist benches, Kahn denounced the bill as "the immoral offspring of an illicit union between racial superstition and biological ignorance."[23] He told his fellow parliamentarians that there was nothing inherently or biologically inferior or morally wrong about mixed marriages, and that what was evil was a constructed and perverse social system that doomed them to a life of debasement and degradation. Kahn's intervention was fruitless; white parliamentarians on both sides of the

---

23. Kahn, quoted in *Illustrated History of South Africa*, 375. On the spate of laws creating the apartheid society, see Gwendolen M. Carter, *The Politics of Inequality* (London: Thames and Hudson, 1958); and Thompson, *A History of South Africa*, 187–220.

aisles were united in their resentment to mixed marriages. The bill passed by an overwhelming majority.

When the Nationalists saw that the new bill was not strong enough to stop white men from having sex with black women, they rushed another bill, the Immorality Act, through parliament in 1950, which outlawed all sexual relations across racial boundaries, especially those between blacks and whites. Nonwhites were not impressed by either of these bills. For them, the bills were symptoms of whites' failure to discipline their sexual appetites, especially as most whites involved perceived such liaisons as marks of patriarchal domination over subordinate women rather than as the results of mutual affection. No one was surprised when the first person to be tried and sentenced under the new bill was a northern Cape Dutch Reformed Church minister caught in the act with a domestic servant in a garage next to his house. Black women, mostly servants, who were the usual objects of white sexual adventures, were not spared. Many received harsh and unfair sentences. Court cases received wide publicity, as the topic was symptomatic of South Africa's most dramatic and traumatic tension: racism. As enforcement of the Immorality Act reached a passionate peak in the 1960s, opposition newspapers ridiculed snooping policemen with binoculars, cameras, and listening devices, hiding in trees and other dark places, and peeping through keyholes to observe, photograph, and arrest couples caught in the act. Other measures included late night and early morning raids to feel bed sheets for warmth and check the underwear of suspects for "blots" or other signs of sexual intercourse. For whites who could not resist the temptation of black flesh and who were not daring enough to break the law—many of whom were Afrikaners—occasional forays into neighboring countries of Lesotho, Botswana, and Swaziland became the norm. By the time the Immorality Act was scrapped in 1985, it had created enormous trauma for those caught in its web, resulting in many split families, shattered lives, and frequent suicides.[24]

Residential and Cultural Apartheid: Group Areas and Separate Amenities Acts

To ensure that the races would be kept biologically and socially separate, they would need to be kept physically and socially apart. As one politician argued, allowing frequent mixing of the races at railroad stations and other places might produce consequences that would one day make South Africa become like Brazil, with its variegated diversity of racial types. Nationalist politicians frequently denounced mixed suburbs as the deathbeds of the white race. Consequently, in 1950, the government passed the Group Areas Act. The act was meant to strengthen and widely extend residential segregation, a practice that had been in existence in some areas of Africa since the 1920s and in some places in India since the 1940s. Under the act, land ownership, purchase, and occupancy were to be strictly controlled to restrict each race to its own residential and trading sections of towns and cities. Responding to critics of the act, P. W. Botha (later prime minister), argued that in order "to gain a clear view regarding fair treatment and the

---

24. *Illustrated History of South Africa*, 375–76; Carter, *The Politics of Inequality*.

rights of non-Europeans, we should first answer another question, and that is: do we stand for the domination and supremacy of Europeans or not? For if you stand for the domination and supremacy of the European then everything you do must be in the first place calculated to ensure that domination."[25]

However, effective enforcement of this act was hampered by two problems. The first was a loophole in the act that required segregation but did not compel people in charge of public facilities to enforce it. To plug this hole, the government passed a number of provincial ordinances to compel "liberal" municipalities such as that of Cape Town to toe the party line. The second problem was a series of legal challenges coordinated by the African National Congress (ANC). The court ruled against the government on the grounds that while the separation of facilities was legal, it should not result in substantial inequality. But this anti-apartheid victory was short-lived. In 1953, the government successfully passed the Reservation of Separate Amenities Act, making the maintenance of separate and unequal public amenities legal.

The implementation of these acts created considerable hardship and suffering for all the people affected. In 1951, to manage the lingering problems caused by squatting in the cities, the government passed the Prevention of Illegal Squatting Act. Destroying settlements, expropriating properties, refurbishing and reselling seized cottages to whites, and moving people from place to place became major preoccupations of the apartheid technocrats, especially during the 1950s. Major cities such as Cape Town, Durban, and Johannesburg were pulled apart and dramatically reconfigured to conform to the new order as mandated by the acts. In Cape Town, the centrally located District Six was destroyed, resulting in the displacement of nearly sixty thousand colored people to make way for proposed new roads, commercial zones, and housing for whites. In Johannesburg, Sophiatown as well as Martindale and Newclare, which by the early 1950s had collectively become the "Harlem" of South Africa and a crucible of black culture and music, with a burgeoning population of eighty thousand, was destroyed by bulldozers. Its inhabitants were violently removed and scattered to African locations and reserves. The majority relocated to Meadowlands, a town twelve miles from Johannesburg. On the ruins of Sophiatown, a new brick-bungalow white suburb—significantly named Triomf (Triumph) by the government—developed. According to a study by the Surplus People Project, the white planners, to reduce friction between the races, uprooted nearly four million people over a period of three decades. Out of these, less than two percent were white.[26]

Equally galling was the introduction of racial segregation in all spheres of South African life. Railroads, ticket offices, platforms, subways, bridges, and carriages were all racially segregated. Signs with the ubiquitous phrase, "whites only/*blankes alleen*" became visible everywhere, extending the new "petty apartheid" to buses, park benches, cinemas, park benches, post office counters, churches, restaurants, liquor outlets, swimming pools, and beaches.

However, while the passage and enforcement of these laws intensified the population problems of the African homelands, it could not arrest the continuing and rapid increase of the African population in the cities. By 1980, the population

---

25. Botha, quoted in *Illustrated History of South Africa*, 377.
26. Thompson, *A History*, 193–5. See also Laurine Platzky and Cherryl Walker, *The Surplus People: Forced Removals in South Africa* (Johannesburg: Ravan Press, 1985).

of urban South Africa was made up of four million whites, seven million Africans, two million colored people, and 700,000 Indians.[27] Working mainly in the mines and industries and servicing white domestic needs, the black urban settlers lived in the many new and expanding townships adjacent to the major cities, such as Orlando and Soweto in Johannesburg. Slums, poverty, malnutrition, and diseases, especially tuberculosis and kwashiorkor, were common features of these towns.

Nevertheless, in spite of the demographic realities, the government continued to treat Africans living in the cities as visitors with no citizen rights whose real homes were in their homelands led by their "tribal chiefs." To confirm this, the government passed the Native Laws Amendment Act of 1952, which gave it the power to monitor and control the movement of Africans in all urban areas of South Africa. The act extended the carrying of passes to African women and it ruled that Africans who failed to obtain valid jobs or had their pass books disqualified must not remain in the urban areas for more than seventy-two hours. Local authorities were empowered to remove, deport, imprison, or punish "idle or undesirable natives." Many such "vagrants" were promptly arrested, tried, and sentenced to hard labor on white potato farms without pay or compensation besides the food needed to keep them fit to work. Similarly, also in 1952, the government passed the bizarrely named Abolition of Passes Act, which replaced the pass with a newly consolidated ninety-six page reference book. The new book provided officials with ready access to an African's life history and rights of movement and of work. To be caught without this book, anywhere and at any time, could land the defaulting Africans from university professors to mine laborers in jail. To strengthen its hand, the government passed another law in 1956, which abrogated the rights of Africans to appeal against their forced removal from urban areas. Two years later, another law empowered police and local authorities to invade, raid, and search (without a search warrant) any dwelling for illegal residents and for the purpose of maintaining law and order.

Myths of Separate Development: Verwoerd, Homelands, and "Bantu" Education

Maintaining racial segregation and white supremacy also required that all vestiges of African political power and autonomy be removed and replaced by a new system of tribally-based local and regional native authorities. As Malan argued, "We have the choice of giving whites their own territory and the Bantu theirs, or of giving everybody one state and seeing the Bantu govern."[28] The Bantu Authorities Act of 1951 became the instrument of this new policy. Its guiding principle was "separate development," under which all Africans would be categorized according to their tribal antecedents and assigned to specific "homelands", within which they would exercise their citizenship and political rights and

---

27. For these statistics see Thompson, *A History of South Africa*, Appendix: Statistics, tables 1 and 2, 278–9.

28. Malan, quoted in Beinart, *Twentieth-Century South Africa*, 154.

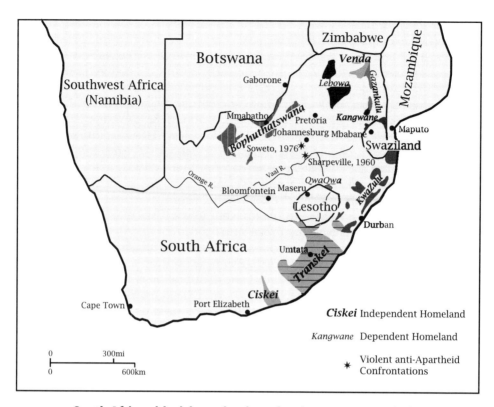

South African black homelands and resistance to apartheid.

beyond which they would have no such rights, would be treated as alien visitors, and would have to carry passes at all times. Whites, though from a wide variety of backgrounds, became members of a single nation occupying the best and the bulk of South African land. Africans, on the other hand, were splintered into isolated and fragmented minority nations. White-owned firms were precluded from investing directly in homelands, in deference to critics' fear that this might undercut the profits of similar industries established in white areas. To show its determination to restore and elevate tribal chieftaincy, the administration instructed officials to stop shaking hands with chiefs, since it was believed that Africans did not traditionally shake hands. Henceforth, chiefs were not to be addressed or saluted as "Dear Mr.," or "Dear Sir," but by their African praise names.[29]

Some of the chiefs and local elite members welcomed the new policy, though often with reservations. They saw the limited opportunity it offered as a means of autonomy and self-realization in a highly restricted social and political terrain. For others, however, the homeland policy was a sham. Its balkanization of Africans into fragmented territories was meant to keep them weak and divided; its consignment of Africans to virtually barren and perennially insufficient land was meant to make the homeland a reservoir for the recruitment of cheap black labor for white establishments; its elevation of tribal chiefs was directed at abort-

---

29. Beinart, *Twentieth-Century South Africa*, 154–8.

ing the emergence of a Western-educated ruling elite; its promise of self-govern-ment was aimed at forestalling the rising tide of African nationalism and denying Africans their inalienable rights as citizens of South Africa. Nevertheless, the gov-ernment remained undeterred, working with those who cooperated and ruthlessly crushing those who dared to stand in the way of the Nationalist cause.

One important area of conflict and controversy concerned control over the educational system. By 1948, African education was largely in the hands of Christian missions, which operated 4,500 schools. With the Nationalist victory, these schools came under increased scrutiny and suspicion. Nationalist ideo-logues began to criticize the missions for inculcating dangerous liberal ideas into the untamed minds of Africans, giving them a bloated idea of their own impor-tance and turning them into farcical caricatures of Westerners. Under the Bantu Education Act of 1953, the government transferred control of African public ed-ucation from the provinces to the central government and drove the missions from the educational field by starving them of funds and official support. In ad-dition, African children were to be taught in their vernacular languages instead of English until after the eighth grade, when both English as well as Afrikaans would be used. Technical rather than liberal education would be emphasized. African children would be taught to know and accept their "proper place" in life. "What is the use," Verwoerd asked his critics, "of teaching a Bantu child mathematics when it cannot use it in life?"[30] Native education, he insisted in his characteristic and devious fashion, "should be controlled in such a way that it should be in accord with the policy of the state....If the native in South Africa today in any kind of school in existence is being taught to expect that he will live his adult life under a policy of equal rights, he is making a big mistake....There is no place for him in the European community above the level of certain forms of labor."[31]

Horrified by the new, sustained assault on African education, the ANC an-grily denounced the government program as "education for barbarism" and vowed to campaign for an African boycott of the new schools. To prevent the ANC or aberrant missions from establishing alternative schools, the law stipu-lated that no schools could be established without the express permission of the government, permission that was rarely, if ever, given. In 1959, in the face of large-scale student and faculty protests, the parliament passed the Extension of University Education Act, which extended racial segregation to higher education, prohibiting white colleges from accepting black students and forbidding inte-grated classes. Black students already attending white colleges were to be sum-marily transferred to black colleges (within two years). During the 1960s, govern-ment control was extended to cover the education of colored and Asian children as well. By 1978, out of the 150,000 students enrolled in universities in South Africa, only twenty percent were nonwhites. Nevertheless, the consequences of the Bantu education policy were not all negative. The number of African children attending school rose from 800,000 in 1953 to 1,800,000 in 1963, though the majority never went beyond the elementary grades. While the quality of educa-tion and levels of literacy declined sharply, some went on to secondary schools,

30. *Illustrated History of South Africa*, 379.
31. Verwoerd, quoted in Roger Omond, *Apartheid Handbook* (New York, N.Y.: Viking Penguin, 1986), 80.

while a few obtained degrees from the few black universities or through correspondence courses from the University of South Africa.[32]

Protest Politics and African Resistance Cracks in the Monoliths: White Opposition to Apartheid

Opposition to the apartheid state was not limited to Africans. Whites, who were the principal beneficiaries of the apartheid system, were by no means unanimous in their support of it. A few, though unfortunately too few, were prepared to break ranks and damn the consequences. Some of the earliest opposition to apartheid came from churches. This was surprising, since religion was regularly used by the Nationalists to justify apartheid. Nevertheless, opposition from the churches was neither pronounced nor united. The Dutch Reformed Church remained unshaken for many years in its support for the apartheid state. In 1948, it refused to join the other white South African churches in issuing a statement condemning apartheid. The first break occurred in 1962, when C. F. Beyers Naude, a prominent Broederbonder and Afrikaner clergyman, left to establish the Christian Institute, which, in defiance of state laws, began to bring black and white Christians together. His sharp and radical criticisms of official policies became too irksome for the government, which banned him and abolished his institute in 1977. But the damage to the church-apartheid-state marriage had been done. A year later, in 1978, a group of Afrikaner clergy issued a scathing critique of apartheid.[33]

Opposition also came from South African English-speaking Universities, most notably the Universities of Cape Town and the Witwatersrand. In 1959, the National Union of South African Students (NUSAS), which had been established in 1924, organized a series of major demonstrations against the closure of white universities to black students. A giant protest billboard at the University of Witwatersrand expressed their sentiments:

> We affirm in the name of the University of the Witwatersrand that it is our duty to uphold the principle that a university is a place where men and women without regard to race and color are welcome to join in the acquisition and advancement of knowledge; and continue faithfully to de-

32. On the apartheid educational policies, see South African Institute of Race Relations (SAIRR), *Survey of Race Relations in South Africa, 1980* (Johannesburg: SAIRR, 1981), 458–500; Mokubung Nkomo, ed., *Pedagogy of Domination: Towards a Democratic Education in South Africa* (Trenton, NJ: African World Press, 1990); and Thompson, *A History of South Africa*, 195–8.

33. See "The Koinonia Declaration," *Journal of Theology for Southern Africa* (September 1978); Frank Chikane, *The Church's Prophetic Witness against Apartheid in South Africa* (Johannesburg: 1988); Louw Alberts and Frank Chikane, eds. *The Road to Rustenburg: the Church Looking Forward to a New South Africa* (Cape Town: Struik Christian Books, 1991); and J. de Gruchy, *The Church Struggle in South Africa* (London: Collins, 1986).

fend this ideal against all who have sought by legislative enactment to curtail the autonomy of the university.[34]

In 1966, NUSAS invited Senator Robert Kennedy to South Africa and arranged for him to give a series of rousing speeches denouncing apartheid. In 1973, eight NUSAS leaders were "banned" for endangering state security.[35] A year later, NUSAS was officially prohibited from receiving funds from abroad.

Comprised predominantly of English-speaking, middle-class white women, the organization known as Black Sash developed an effective strategy of embarrassing Nationalist politicians and attracting media attention. They regularly delved into major public issues, such as the defense of the colored franchise. Wearing white dresses adorned with black sashes, they waylaid politicians, standing silently with their heads bowed at the entrances to public buildings, such as the parliament building, where they could not be ignored. In exasperation, the government finally banned such demonstrations in 1976, but Black Sash remained active in providing legal aid for those who fell afoul of the apartheid state.[36]

The most perceptive and enduring criticisms of the apartheid state, however, came from liberal authors and activists, who were mostly English speaking. In 1947, the year before the Nationalist victory, Alan Paton published his best seller, *Cry the Beloved Country*, in which he spoke of "the sickness of the land," "the broken tribe." The tragedy, he said, "is not that things are broken. The tragedy is that they are not mended again. The white man has broken the tribe."[37] His cautious optimism and hope for humane racial relations and reconciliation were soon shattered by the Nationalists' victory one year later, when caution, morality, and liberalism were thrown to the dogs. After years of frustrating and fruitless liberal politics, Paton's hope in the future of South Africa turned to disillusionment. "God save us," he prayed in 1958, "from the South Africa of the Group Areas Act, which knows no reason, justice, or mercy."[38] Other notable authors included Athol Fugard, Andre Brinke, and Nobel laureate Nadine Gordimer, whose works reveal the cruel dilemmas of race, class, and gender in the apartheid state. A few Afrikaners also dared to become traitors to their *volk*. One was Rian Malan, who in fear for his life, fled into exile, only to be driven back by his anguished conscience to write *My Traitor's Heart*, a blistering critique of the apartheid state in its dying years.[39] Among the notable white activists who stood solidly behind the

---

34. *Illustrated History of South Africa*, 379. See also Hendrik W. van der Merwe and David Welsh, eds., *The Future of the University in South Africa* (Cape Town: D. Philip, 1977).

35. To be "banned" means, among other things, to have one's movement restricted, be put under surveillance, and be restricted from meeting with more than two people without express state permission and from being quoted in speech or in writings within South Africa.

36. On Black Sash, see Cherry Michelman, *The Black Sash of South Africa: A Case Study in Liberalism* (London: Oxford University Press, 1975).

37. Alan Paton, *Cry the Beloved Country* (New York: Schribner, Simon & Schuster Inc., 1995; first published in 1948) 52, 56.

38. Alan Paton, *The People Wept: Being a brief Account of the Origin, Contents, and Application of that Unjust Law of the Union of South Africa known as the Group Areas act of 1950, since Consolidated as Act no. 77 of 1957* (Kloof, Natal: Alan Paton, 1958) 44.

39. Rian Malan, *My Traitor's Heart: A South African Exile Returns to Face His Country, His Tribe and His Conscience* (New York: Vintage Press, 1991).

African cause were Ruth First and Helen Joseph, who marched with African demonstrators and spent time in jail. Another was Helen Suzman, the lone Progressive Party Member of parliament from 1961 to 1974 who championed the African nationalist cause, visited Mandela in prison, advocated prison reform, and vigorously, though often futilely, opposed every racially oppressive bill.[40]

The ANC and the Defiance Campaigns

However, the most sustained and, ultimately, the most effective opposition to the apartheid state came from Africans. As early as 1912, the South African Native National Congress (the SANC, which became the ANC in 1921) had been organized to coordinate African resistance to the Land Act of 1913, which appropriated eighty-seven percent of South African land for the exclusive use of the white minority population. During the 1930s and 1940s, the ANC pursued nonviolent, constitutional means of achieving its goals. It made no headway. By 1948, racial oppression had become a permanent feature of the South African landscape. Few Africans paused to ponder what a nationalist victory in the election of that year would mean. As Albert Luthuli, Nobel laureate and later president of the ANC, wrote in his autobiography, *Let My People Go,*

> For most of us Africans, bandied about on the field while the game was in progress and then kicked to one side when the game was won, the election seemed largely irrelevant. We had endured Botha, Hertzog and Smuts. It did not seem of much importance whether the whites gave us more Smuts or switched to Malan. Our lot had grown steadily worse, and no election seemed likely to alter the direction in which we were being forced.[41]

He admitted that even though most expected a nationalist victory to intensify African hardships, "very few (if any) of us understood how swift the deterioration was to be."[42] This was precisely what happened: the Nationalist government immediately tightened the noose around the Africans' neck.

As Africans came under the sledgehammer, pummeled by one law after the other, reduced to a level of servitude and indignity unprecedented in South African history, the ANC quickly recovered from its shock to organize resistance to the new order. The draconian nature of the apartheid legislation and the intensification of state repression convinced many young African activists that the time for talking and rational negotiation was over. A more militant program of action was needed. Encouraged by the success of the squatter movements, the global triumph of nationalism over colonialism, and the progress being made toward decolonization in places like India, Ghana, and Nigeria following the end of the

---

40. See Joanne Strangwayes-Booth, *A Cricket in the Thorn Tree: Helen Suzman and the Progressive Party in South Africa* (Bloomington: Indiana University Press, 1976); and Helen Suzman, *In No Uncertain Terms: A South African Memoir* (New York: Alfred A. Knopf, 1993).

41. Albert Luthuli, *Let My People Go* (New York, McGraw-Hill, 1962), 107.

42. Luthuli, *Let My People Go,* 107.

Figure 21.1. Dr. James Moroka, ANC President.

World War II, a radical wing emerged within the ANC Youth League in the late 1940s. In 1949, determined to jostle the moderate and hesitant ANC leadership, the Congress Youth League (CYL), a radical group within the ANC, maneuvered Alfred Xuma, ANC president since 1940, out of office. James Moroka, who promised more militant, mass action, replaced him. The next challenge was forging a united front among the various opposition groups. After much hesitation and tension, coloreds, Indians, and Communists, all of whom were already imperiled in one way or another by the apartheid state, were admitted into the fold of the ANC to forge a united and coordinated mass movement against an increasingly repressive government.

In June 1951, a meeting of representatives from all the leading antiapartheid groups devised a program of action to achieve political liberation and end racial segregation through civil disobedience and work stoppages. The representatives sent a letter to the government, signed by Moroka and Walter Sisulu, leader of the ANC delegation to the meeting, asking for the scrapping of all unjust laws by February 1952. The letter warned the government that failure to comply would result in a defiance campaign beginning on April 6, 1952 and culminating in a general workers' strike on June 26. The government replied, warning that it would use all the resources at its disposal to quell any disturbance. The ANC then issued a pamphlet proclaiming in both English and Afrikaans, "We stand on the eve of a great national crisis. We call on every true South African to support us."[43]

On April 6, 1952, addressing a crowd of fifty thousand people gathered at Freedom Square, Fordsburg on the outskirts of Johannesburg, Moroka spoke about the historic significance of the campaign. Whites, he said, "cannot escape the fact that whatever page they turn in the history of South Africa they find it red with the blood of the fallen, with ill-will and insecurity written across its pages."[44] Alarmed by the resurgence of opposition, the government took steps to crush its opponents. Several leaders were arrested and banned, but this did not stop the major strike slated for June 26, 1952. Amidst much chanting and cheering, groups of protesters deliberately contravened selected laws and regulations around the country, courting arrest to flood the jails and thus overburden the state's law enforcement machinery. By the end of the year, nearly eight thousand people had been arrested, but this was not enough to break the movement or the ANC. The ANC finally stopped the campaign following the outbreak of violence and shooting by police in East London and Port Elizabeth.

Nevertheless, the demonstration showed the great potentiality and effectiveness of united efforts by oppressed groups. The campaign increased the ANC's credibility and boosted its paid membership from seven thousand at the beginning of the campaign to 100,000 by the time it ended six months later. The new spirit of cooperation soon bore fruit. In June 1955, a Congress of the People met at Kliptown near Soweto to draft, in the words of Z. K. Matthews, the Cape ANC leader who proposed the meeting, a freedom charter for the democratic South Africa of the future. This was an extraordinary meeting with representatives drawn from a broad spectrum of South African society. Of the nearly three thousand delegates that attended, two thousand were Africans, 320 Indians, 230 colored, and 112 whites. Though the police, who declared that everyone present was under arrest for treason, eventually broke up the meeting, the congress succeeded in drafting and adopting its Freedom Charter. The charter opened with a firm declaration that "South Africa belongs to all who live in it, black and white, and that no government can justly claim authority unless it is based on the will of the people." Thereafter it set out a list of basic rights and freedoms, such as equality before the law; freedom of speech and assembly; the right to vote and to work; equal pay for equal work; unemployment benefits; and free medical care as well as free, compulsory, and equal education. Though the charter was criticized by liberals and the government for promoting socialist ideas and by radicals for conceding too much to "national groups," it endured as the basic policy statement of the antiapartheid struggle for many decades to come.[45]

In the meantime, rural and urban protests against the state and its acts were increasing. The Federation of South African Women (FSAW), formed by Lilian Ngoyi and other women, organized a series of demonstrations against the decision of the government to extend the carrying of passes to African women, culmi-

---

43. *Illustrated History of South Africa*, 383.
44. James Moroka, quoted in *Illustrated History of South Africa*, 383.
45. On the Freedom Charter, see Lodge, *Black Politics in South Africa since 1945* (New York: Longman, 1983), 68–74; T. Karis and G. Carter, *From Protest to Challenge: Documents of African Politics in South Africa, 1882–1964 Vol. 3: Challenge and Violence, 1953–1964* (Stanford, CA: Hoover Institution Press, 1977), 56–69.

nating, on August 9, 1956, in a gathering of twenty thousand women in front of the national administrative headquarters in Pretoria. After presenting a petition to the prime minister's office, the women stood in silence for thirty minutes before dispersing. Their demonstrations continued, however, resulting in the arrest of two thousand women in 1958 for failure to carry passes. Successful bus boycotts in the townships of Johannesburg and Pretoria by African workers fighting for fare increases preoccupied everyone during the early months of 1957.[46]

Enraged by the content and intent of the Freedom Charter, the government enacted more repressive legislation to stem the rising tide of resistance, signaling the beginning of an unprecedented crackdown on the black liberation movement. In September 1955, the police raided the homes of five hundred activists to confiscate documents related to the charter. In the early hours of December 5, 1956, 156 leading activists were arrested and put on trial for high treason. Though the government was unable to prove its case that the men were planning to overthrow the state by violence and replace it with a communist one, the trial dragged on for too long, preoccupying the ANC leadership at a crucial time in the evolution of the liberation movement. By the time the last thirty defendants were discharged by the judge for want of credible evidence, the liberation struggle had taken another decisive turn.

From Sharpeville to Robben Island: Violence and Repression

By 1958, radical elements within the ANC had become dissatisfied with its moderate and nonviolent approach under the leadership of Luthuli, Mandela, and others. They were especially convinced that cooperation with whites was impeding the progress of the liberation movement. The most articulate of the radicals was Robert Sobukwe. Born in the eastern Cape in 1924, he was educated at Fort Hare before becoming a Bantu language instructor at the University of the Witwatersrand. Though by no means an extremist, Sobukwe agreed with the ideas of Anton Lembede, the theorist of Africanism and founder of the CYL, that the liberation struggle in South Africa was fundamentally racial and not class-based. Whites, he said, could become genuine Africans, but not yet; they were too inherently identified with the existing oppressive order (whose rallying ideology was whiteness) to be trusted to wholeheartedly fight for the African cause.

Unable either to gain control of the ANC or to persuade its leaders to adopt a more militant posture, the Africanists under Sobukwe broke away in 1949 to establish the Pan-Africanist Congress (PAC). When resigning his university post so that he could present himself for arrest for not carrying passes, Sobukwe had accused the authorities of "fighting to entrench an outworn, anachronistic, vile sys-

---

46. On rural and urban protests during these years, see Lodge, *Black Politics in South Africa*; Karis and Carter, *From Protest to Challenge: Documents of African Politics in South Africa, 1882–1964 Vol. 3: Challenge and Violence, 1953–1964.* On women and the struggle against apartheid, see Hilda Bernstein, *For Their Triumphs and Their Tears: Women in Apartheid South Africa* (London: International Defence and Aid Fund for Southern Africa, 1985); Cherryl Walker, *Women and resistance in South Africa* (New York: Monthly Review Press, 1991); and Diana E. H. Russell, *Lives of Courage: Women for a New South Africa* (New York: Basic Books, 1989).

Figure 22.2. Nelson Mandela.

tem of oppression." "They represent decadence," he told his listeners, "We represent the fresh fragrance of flowers in bloom; they represent the rancid smell of decaying vegetation.... We have history on our side. We will win."[47] On March 21, 1960, upstaging the ANC, the PAC launched a major campaign against passes. Though Sobukwe had pledged that the campaign would be conducted in a spirit of absolute nonviolence, police in the small town of Sharpeville panicked at the sight of the crowd and opened fire, killing sixty-seven people and wounding 186. The majority of them were shot in the back. Government reaction to the disturbances was swift, sweeping, and fierce. The government declared a state of emergency, called out the army reserves to deal with the insurgents, outlawed the ANC and the PAC, and arrested ninety-eight whites, ninety Indians, thirty-six coloreds, and 11,279 Africans. Six thousand eight hundred people were sent to jail, while hundreds of others were beaten by the police and compelled to return to work.[48]

The year 1960 marked a turning point in the history of South Africa. It convinced Africans that nonviolent methods would achieve nothing for them but defeat, arrest, jail, and death at the hand of a violent state. As Mandela put it at his trial in 1964:

---

47. Sobukwe, quoted in *Illustrated History of South Africa*, 400. On the PAC, see Gail M. Gerhart, *Black Power in South Africa: The Evolution of an Ideology* (Berkeley: University of California Press), 124–251; and Lodge, *Black Politics*, 201–30.
48. Thompson, *A History of South Africa*, 210.

We of the ANC had always stood for a non-racial democracy, and we shrank from any policy which might drive the races further apart than they already were. But the hard facts were that fifty years of non-violence had brought the African people nothing but more repressive legislation, and fewer and fewer rights....It would be unrealistic and wrong for African leaders to continue preaching non-violence at a time when the Government met our peaceful demands with force.[49]

Since the liberation organizations could no longer operate openly and legally, they went underground.

At the center of this transformation was Nelson Mandela. Born into the Thembu royal family of the Transkei in 1918, Mandela went to Fort Hare in 1938 but was expelled for political activism two years later. After obtaining his B.A. and law degrees by correspondence, he practiced law with Oliver Tambo in Johannesburg. Actively involved with Tambo and Walter Sisulu in the foundation of the ANC Youth League, he became its national secretary in 1948 and a member of the ANC's national executive committee in 1949. The following year, he was elected the national president of the Youth League, becoming the brain behind the Defiance Campaign of 1952. In 1961, repeatedly banned, hunted, and chased by the police, he went underground, eluding his pursuers for seventeen months, during which he slipped out of the country to visit and make speeches in several African and European countries and to seek support for the liberation movement before returning, unnoticed, to South Africa.[50]

In the meantime, militant groups such as the Umkhonto we Sizwe ("The Spear of the Nation") in the ANC, Poqo ("Pure") in the PAC, and the African Resistance Movement, organized by young white professionals and students, emerged to meet state violence with revolutionary violence. Between them, the three groups and others succeeded in carrying out over two hundred bomb attacks on selected and strategic government targets. However, these new efforts yielded little fruit. In July 1963, the government arrested and subsequently put on trial seventeen Umkhonto leaders. By the end of 1964, Mandela, Walter Sisulu, and others were serving life sentences on Robben Island. Sobukwe also spent six years on Robben Island. Upon his release in 1969, he was kept politically impotent by the government, which banned him from South Africa until his death in Kimberley in 1978. Indeed, in the decade after 1963, everything appeared quiescent. It was, so it seemed, high noon for the apostles of Afrikaner nationalism. The years that followed Rivonia would usher in an era of economic boom unparalleled in the nation's history. Nevertheless, developments during these years began to prepare the way for a major outburst of resistance in 1976.

The first major impetus for this outburst was a vibrant intellectual ferment, especially in the arts. Novelists, playwrights, and poets mingled with jazz musicians, singers, and dancers to bring a strong message of hope and liberation to the townships. Subversive books and records on South Africa, produced abroad, such

---

49. Nelson Mandela, *I Am Prepared to Die* (London: International Defense and Aid Fund for Southern Africa, 1979), 32–3.

50. On Mandela, see Mandela, *Long Walk to Freedom: The Autobiography of Nelson Mandela* (Boston: Little, Brown and Company, 1994); Anthony Sampson, *Mandela, The Authorized Biography* (New York: Alfred Knopf, 1999).

as Bloke Modisane's *Blame Me on History*, Alex La Guma's *Walk in the Night*, the poems of Dennis Brutus, and the many records of Miriam Makeba, evaded official censors, circulating widely as veritable vehicles of confrontation with the apartheid state.[51] Secondly, the rapid expansion of the economy that characterized these year resulted in the emergence of a black middle class comprised of semi-skilled and unskilled workers, whose incipient class consciousness would lead to the establishment of an effective black trade union movement. A spate of strikes that began in 1973 and disturbed the stock market would signal their formal engagement in the battle for economic and political justice in apartheid South Africa.[52]

Thirdly, with virtually all the leading veterans of the liberation movement languishing in jail, silenced by banning, or driven into exile, the initiative in the resistance movement fell to the younger generation, especially to students. In 1968, Steve Biko, a twenty-year-old medical student from the University of Natal, and other black students broke away from the multiracial yet white-dominated and white-led NUSAS to form the South African Student Organization (SASO). The failure of mass confrontation with the state led to the emergence of the new ideology of Black Consciousness (BC). Black Consciousness developed as an attitude of the mind, a way of thinking. Years of white oppression and white liberal paternalism had combined to weaken Africans' self-confidence and pride in themselves as inherently equal to whites. For Biko and his followers, a major factor in the failure of earlier attempts by the ANC and PAC was their great hurry and impatience to achieve liberation, even when it was clear the people were neither psychologically ready nor politically conscienticized to make the necessary sacrifice and commitment. Before political liberation could come, Africans had to first be liberated from the fear and feelings of inferiority that had prevented unity and effective organization in the past. "Black is beautiful" and "I am black and proud" became fashionable slogans of BC advocates. As Biko stated in 1971,

> Black consciousness is in essence the realization by the black man of the need to rally together with his brother around the cause of their subjection—the blackness of their skin—and to operate as a group in order to rid themselves of the shackles that bind them to perpetual servitude. It seeks to demonstrate the lie that black is an aberration from the "normal" which is white.... It seeks to infuse the black community with a new-found pride in themselves, their efforts, their value systems, their culture, their religion and their outlook on life.... Blacks no longer seek to reform the system because doing so implies acceptance of the major points around which the system revolves. Blacks are out to completely transform the system and to make of it what they wish.[53]

51. Notable among such works are Ezekiel Mphahlele, *Down Second Avenue* (Boston: Faber and Faber, 1959); Miriam Tlai, *Amandla: a novel* (Johannesburg: Raven, 1980); and Mongane Serote, *To Every Birth Its Blood* (Johannesburg: Raven, 1981); and Mbulelo Vizikhungo Mzamane, *The Children of Soweto: A Trilogy* (Johannesburg: Raven, 1982).

52. John D. Brewer, *After Soweto: An Unfinished Journey* (Oxford: Clarendon Press, 1986) 326–328.

53. Steve Biko, *I Write What I like*, ed. Aelred Stubbs (London: Harper & Row, 1979). See also Anthony W. Marx, *Lessons of Struggle: South African Internal Opposition, 1960–1990* (New York: 1992).

Soweto and the End of Apartheid

Conceived and nourished within the atmosphere of the seemingly innocuous University Student Christian Movement, BC emphasized individual responsibility and self-help. The movement's liberationist ideology spread rapidly through South Africa's urban schools. In June 1976, already politically informed by BC ideas, thousands of black school children took to the streets in protest against the government's decision mandating that half of their courses be taught in Afrikaans, the language of their oppressor. The protest began in the black township of Soweto, which would soon give its name to the uprising. As the demonstration spread across the country, the government reacted fiercely. By the time the dust settled nine months later, at least 575 people, most of them students, had been killed; only five of those killed were whites.

In 1977, SASO and all its affiliated organizations, such as the Black Parents' Association and the Union of Black Journalists, were disbanded, and their leaders were sent to jail. That same year, police arrested Steve Biko. After interrogating and torturing him, four policemen (who later confessed to the crime) repeatedly smashed his head against the wall, fracturing his skull and damaging his brain before driving his blood-soaked naked body in the back of a van for a distance of 750 miles. Denied medical attention, Biko died the following day, still in police custody. Because of the brutal government crackdown, thousands of young black South Africans fled the country to study abroad or to swell the ranks of the ANC resistance fighters in neighboring countries. Many of those who remained abandoned schooling, chanting the slogan "liberation before education" and vowing to remain illiterate rather than become educated slaves in apartheid South Africa. In hindsight, as it turned out, this was an enormous price to pay for the cause of liberation. This group (collectively dubbed "the wasted generation") would soon come of age and constitute the bulk of the millions of unemployed and unemployable people that would come to task South African society after 1994.[54]

South Africa and the World: Collaboration, Defiance, and Sanctions

The government's apparent success in crushing the uprising did not mean that Soweto was a failure. Indeed it marked the beginning of the end for the apartheid state in South Africa. For the next seventeen years, South Africa would know no peace. Its troubles would not only be domestic; they would also be international. The triumph of nationalism in Asia and the rest of Africa after World War II brought South Africa under increased pressure. In 1963, newly independent African states established the Organization of African unity (OAU), which promptly established a Liberation Committee directed toward the eradication of apartheid and all other vestiges of colonialism in Africa. The OAU pledged its

---

54. On the Soweto uprising and its aftermath, see Baruch Hirson, *Year of Fire, Year of Ash: The Soweto Revolt: Roots of a Revolution* (London: Zed Press, 1979); Davenport and Saunders, *South Africa*, 432–54.

moral and material support for the African states bordering South Africa. Compared with South Africa, however, these states were militarily weak and vulnerable. States like Lesotho and Swaziland, small and landlocked and, in the case of the former, entirely surrounded by South Africa, could take no initiatives, since they were in many ways economically dependent on South Africa. Malawi's best air link to the outside world was through Johannesburg, while Zambia exported half of its copper—its principal foreign exchange earner—through South Africa's railroads and ports. Besides, for many of these countries, money earned through labor migration to South African mines remained the main source of income.

As for other African states to the north, including Tanzania, Ghana, and Nigeria, in spite of their strident antiapartheid rhetoric, they were too weak militarily and too preoccupied with the problems of economic survival and political stability to put any military pressure on South Africa. Nevertheless, the newly independent African states employed their growing numerical strength in the United Nations as well as in the British Commonwealth of Nations to put pressure on these world bodies to become proactive in the campaign against the apartheid state. In 1961, weary of criticisms from former British colonies like India, Canada, and Ghana, South Africa broke its remaining legal ties with Britain, becoming a republic and formally withdrawing from the Commonwealth. Similarly, beginning in 1952, the UN General Assembly passed annual resolutions condemning apartheid, in most cases overruling the objections and vetoes of the dominant Western nations: the US, Britain, and France. In 1967, the UN created a Special Committee as well as a Unit on Apartheid and began to issue publications exposing and denouncing the heinous practices of apartheid in South Africa. Four years later, the International Court of Justice declared South Africa's continuing occupation of Namibia, which was in defiance of a UN ruling, illegal. In 1973, the General Assembly declared apartheid "a crime against humanity." In 1977, following the Soweto uprising, the massacre of hundreds of school children, and the killing of Steve Biko, the UN Security Council, in an unprecedented decision, voted unanimously to impose a mandatory arms embargo on South Africa.[55]

Notwithstanding all these pressures, the apartheid regime saddled on. A number of factors combined to allow this, among which economic considerations were important. Until 1978, no significant white economic interests in South Africa opposed apartheid. Indeed, it would seem that industrial capitalism and apartheid were engaged in an embrace, as cheap labor and discriminatory practices brought huge profits to industries and ensured the dominance of white workers. And even when, beginning in the late 1960s, capitalists began to criticize aspects of the government's control of imports, the restrictions of the color bar, and the lack of skilled black workers, they remained solid in their cooperation with the apartheid regime. In the meantime, the South African economy began to expand; the 1960s were years of considerable economic boom, which attracted significant foreign investment to the country, mainly from Britain, the US, Japan, West Germany, France, and Switzerland. Britain, the former colonial master with racial and cultural ties to South Africa, had the largest stake (forty percent of all

---

55. On South Africa and the world, see Thompson, *A History of South Africa*, 213–20, the main source for much of this section. See also James Barber and John Barratt, *South Africa's Foreign Policy: The Search for Status and Security, 1945–1988* (Cambridge: 1990).

foreign capital). Consequently, both the British Conservative and Labour Parties were united in their opposition to the arms embargo on South Africa.[56]

The attitude of the other major economic power, the United States, was no different. Seizing the opportunity afforded by the quietude of the 1960s and the booming South African economy, American firms such as Ford, General Motors, Mobil, and Caltex Oil made significant investments in South Africa. By 1978, in addition to controlling twenty percent of the country's foreign capital, the US had replaced Britain as South Africa's leading trading partner. The returns on foreign investments remained at a fifteen percent high during the turbulent 1970s. Policy makers in Washington justified their continuing collaboration with the apartheid regime on at least two grounds. The first, and probably the most important, was economic. Apart from providing good returns on investments, South Africa was either the leading or a significant producer of numerous valuable minerals, such as gold (sixty percent of the world supply), platinum (forty-seven percent), vanadium (forty-three percent), chromium (thirty-three percent), and manganese (twenty-five percent), and of diamonds, uranium, and other products.

South Africa also adroitly exploited the power politics of the Cold War. It presented the ANC and its allied organizations as Communists and South Africa as the last bastion of Christian civilization to defend against the triumph of Communism in Africa. However, as a leading historian of South Africa contended,

> Pretoria's rhetoric against communism was a skillful attempt to divert attention from the domestic causes of black resistance in South Africa. Black South Africans needed no foreign indoctrination to oppose apartheid.[57]

For the policy makers in Washington, whose views of the world were bifurcated by Cold War rhetoric, the usefulness of South Africa as an ally in the war against the Red threat was a useful argument. In any case, from 1960 onwards, American policy towards the apartheid state was neither uniform nor consistent, except to the degree represented by the main political parties. Thus, while the democratic administrations of Kennedy, Johnson, and Carter tended to tighten the noose on the apartheid regime, the Republican administrations of Eisenhower, Nixon, Reagan, and Bush remained supportive of maintaining good relations with South Africa.

Reforms, Internal Combustion, Stalemate, and Negotiations

Meanwhile, the pressure on the apartheid state intensified. John Vorster resigned as prime minister in 1978 amidst a financial scandal and a party crisis. He was succeeded by Pieter Willem Botha, a hot-tempered, domineering, yet intelli-

---

56. Merle Lipton, *Capitalism and Apartheid* (Aldershot, England: Macmillan, 1985); Ann Seidman and Neva Seidman Makgetla, *Outposts of Monopoly Capitalism: Southern Africa in the Changing Global Economy* (Westport, CT: Zed Press, 1980); and Duncan Innes, *Anglo-American and the Rise of Modern South Africa* (New York: Monthly Review Press, 1984).

57. Thompson, *A History of South Africa*, 216. On U. S relations with South Africa during the apartheid years, see Barbara Rogers, *White Wealth and Black Poverty: American Investments in Southern Africa* (Westport, CT: Greenwood Press, 1976); and Ann and Neva Seidman, *South Africa and U.S. Multinational Corporations* (Westport, CT: L. Hill, 1977).

gent politician, whose main response to black resistance was a greater assertion of state power and a defiant attitude toward the world. Under him, South Africa became in essence a military state, and the State Security Council, created in 1972, became the *de facto* power. By the early 1980s, unable to crush internal resistance or stem the rising tide of international condemnation, Botha adopted a reformist approach that aimed to remove some of the nonessential symbols and practices of apartheid without endangering white supremacy. The labor laws were relaxed, permitting the organization of African trade unions. Color bars were removed from major occupations. In 1984, a new parliament, made up of three chambers, each consisting of 178 whites, eighty-five colored citizens, and forty-five Indians, was created. Blacks, constituting about seventy-five percent of the population, were not represented. In 1986, the government repealed the thirty-four acts that had established the pass laws. That same year, it decriminalized multiracial parties and interracial marriage and sex.[58]

For Africans, as well as for many colored citizens and most Indians, these reforms were too little, too late. From prison and from exile, ANC leaders called on the South African youth to embark on an organized, sustained program of resistance and civil disobedience to hasten the dissolution of the apartheid state. In essence, ANC leaders asserted, resistance fighters had to make South Africa ungovernable and continue battling until the regime was defeated or compelled to negotiate its own demise. Consequently, the 1980s marked a period of rampant violence, bloody demonstrations, numerous workers' strikes, rural disturbances, bus boycotts, and funeral marches. As workers united with peasants, the middle-class with the proletariat, and Africans with coloreds and Asians, school children abandoned their classes to scrawl antiapartheid graffiti on walls, fly ANC flags, and chant antiapartheid slogans at whites. Violence also increased in the black townships, as African policemen and government collaborators came under attack. In the rural areas, overpopulation, acute land shortage, institutional decadence, and widespread poverty combined to create tension and fear, sometimes expressed in civil unrest, witchcraft accusations, and burnings. As increasing numbers of South African whites began to sympathize with the liberation struggle, black youths lost their fear of whites and became resolute and defiant. Rural anger and urban frustration boiled over into sporadic attacks on whites, with fatal consequences. Visitors to South Africa in the mid 1980s could feel whites' fear and apprehension, as they slept with doors firmly barred, hounds ready to attack, and loaded pistols under their pillows, waiting restively for "the night of the long knives," which many believed was bound to come.[59]

In response, the state, now under the full control of hardliner-securocrats (made up of top military generals and other security chiefs), unleashed the full apparatus of its repressive artillery on the dissidents. Mass arrests, police beatings

---

58. See Robert M. Price, *The Apartheid State in Crisis: Political Transformation in South Africa, 1975–1990* (New York: Oxford University Press, 1991); R. Hunt Davis, Jr., ed., *Apartheid Unravels* (Gainsville, FL: University of Florida Press: Center for African Studies, 1991); and Josette Cole, *Crossroads: The Politics of Reform and Repression, 1976–1986* (Johannesburg: Ravan Press, 1987).

59. Stephen M. Davis, *Apartheid's Rebels: Inside South Africa's Hidden War* (New Haven CT: Yale University Press, 1987); Martin Murray, *South Africa: Time of Agony, Time of Destiny; the Upsurge of Popular Protest* (London: Verso, 1987). See also Malan, *My Traitor's Heart*.

and torture, and political assassination by "vigilantes" and hit squads, became commonplace within South Africa. Abroad, as the public became inundated with gory images of bloody demonstrations, South African police brutality, and daily funeral processions of slain young activists, the pendulum of opinion shifted forcefully to the antiapartheid movement. Poets, journalists, writers, tourists, and scholars wrote biting critiques of apartheid. Movie stars, leading musicians, and human rights activists organized concerts and fundraising campaigns in the leading Western cities, from Paris and London to New York and Los Angeles, which were supported by the millions now increasingly aware of the evils of apartheid. Time, it would appear, was running out for South Africa. The advent of the arch-conservative governments of Margaret Thatcher in Britain and Ronald Reagan in the US, both of whom advocated constructive engagement with South Africa and regularly vetoed strong antiapartheid UN Security Council resolutions, could not stem the tide of opposition.

In 1986, in response to intense and successful antiapartheid campaigns by African-Americans and other pressure groups, the United States Congress overturned President Reagan's veto and imposed economic sanctions on South Africa. As the prices of shares on the Johannesburg Stock Exchange plummeted, many whites began to flee the country, taking their money with them. The government passed laws severely restricting the amount of money that could be taken out of the country, but this only worsened the situation, as it discouraged foreign investment. In the past, the South African government had developed effective strategies for circumventing trade sanctions. However, capital flight, the brain drain, arms embargoes, tighter exclusion from the international capital market, and disinvestments were more difficult to counter.

On the military front, the news was not good either. In 1975, following the withdrawal of Portugal from its African colonies, South Africa, with the active support of the United States, invaded Angola to assist the pro-Western UNITA in its war against the OAU-supported and Communist-backed MPLA. Similar forays by South African forces into Mozambique in support of FRELIMO and against the legitimate government of Samora Machel and Chisano led to thousands of deaths and to the social and economic dislocation from which Mozambique is still trying to recover. However, in 1987, the South African Defense Force (SADF) suffered a major military defeat at the hands of a combined force of Cuban and Angolan soldiers in the Southern Angolan town of Cuito. As the death rate among white soldiers climbed, the Afrikaner press and Afrikaner intellectuals began to seriously question the invincibility of the SADF and its claim that it was winning the war. On the global scene, the collapse of the Soviet Union and the eclipse of Communism in Eastern Europe signaled a new era in international relations in which the "Communist menace" argument would no longer work. As internal and external pressures mounted, the South African government and Afrikaners' confidence in their ability to contain their enemies and to defy the trends of history and international opposition began to falter. By 1989, as William Beinart put it, "a stalemate had been reached in which the opposition could not unseat the government by force and the government could not reassert full control."[60]

---

60. Beinart, *Twentieth-Century South Africa*, 250. See also Robert Schrire, *Adapt or Die: The End of White Politics in South Africa* (New York: Hurst, 1991).

Long Walk to Freedom:
An End and a New Beginning, 1989–1994

The Nationalists, it would seem, were at their wits' end. The wheel had turned full circle. Forty years of daring, though rabidly racist, social engineering had brought them back to where they had been in 1948: at the bar of history. Beginning in 1982, a series of secret meetings between government and business representatives and representatives of the ANC took place in Zambia, Senegal, the US, and elsewhere. These clandestine forums brought the two sides closer and strengthened the hope for a negotiated settlement but produced few concrete results. In 1987, P. W. Botha had warned his fellow Afrikaners that they must either "adapt or die," but he lacked both the imagination to discern what needed to be done and the will to carry it out. In 1989, two fortuitous strokes and a revolt within his party edged Botha out of power, bringing F. W. de Klerk, an astute politician and the erstwhile minister of education, to the negotiating table. Maneuvered into power by reform-minded party supporters already disenchanted with the mindless and costly repression of Botha and his securocrats, de Klerk was sure the moment was ripe for decisive action to resolve the stalemate. Twenty years younger than Botha, he was convinced that the best hope for his people was to negotiate from their current position of strength rather than wait for the final showdown—if not the apocalypse—which was bound to come if the stalemate continued. The pace of his actions and the extent of his concessions and success would surprise both his supporters and the opposition at home and abroad.[61] Within months of his ascension to power, he unbanned the ANC, the SACP, and the PAC. On February 2, 1990, after twenty-seven years, the most famous prisoner in the world, Nelson Mandela, walked out of the apartheid "gulag," tall, gaunt, and dignified, a man of destiny, carrying, and so it seemed, the promise of salvation under his belt. Apartheid would not die easily, however; its final days would be as bloody as its early years.

Continuing unemployment and economic hardship in the cities, especially among immigrant workers, created new social tensions that soon spiraled into ethnic mobilization and violence. Sporadic and organized clashes between supporters of the ANC and those of Mangosutho Buthelezi's Zulu-dominated Inkatha Freedom Party claimed thousands of lives, especially in KwaZulu-Natal and on the Rand. Buthelezi, in spite of his initial promise as a potential African-ist leader, was viewed with suspicion by the ANC for cooperating with the apartheid state (though he refused to accept an independent Zulu homeland). In any case, Buthelezi was determined to stake out his claim to a share in the political leadership of the new South Africa by successfully appealing to, mobilizing, and strengthening Zulu nationalism, though at a very heavy cost in human carnage.[62]

There were elements within the white establishment determined to stop the negotiations by launching random and unprovoked attacks on blacks wherever

---

61. On De Klerk, see F. W. de Klerk, *The Last Trek—A New Beginning: The Autobiography* (New York: St. Martin's Press, 1999).

62. On Buthelezi, see Mzala, *Gatsha Buthelezi: Chief with a Double Agenda* (Atlantic Highlands, N.J.: Zed Books, 1988); Jack Shepherd Smith, *Buthelezi: The Biography* (Melville, S.A.: Hans Strydom Publishers, 1988); and Mangosuthu G. Buthelezi, *South Africa: My Vision of the Future* (New York: St. Martin's Press, 1990).

they were most vulnerable. White rightist organizations such as the Afrikaner Resistance Movement (AWB) led by Eugene Terreblanche and the Volksfront commanded by retired General Constand Viljoen appeared determined to provoke an apocalyptic "Third Boer War" to preserve the racial distinction and political supremacy of the Afrikaner *volk*. In 1991, Magnus Malan, the defense chief, was forced to resign when it was revealed that the security force was providing financial aid and military training for members of the Inkatha Freedom Party in an attempt to destabilize the ANC and derail the negotiations. However, despite months of senseless violence and intemperate agitation for secession by extremist white Afrikaner groups, a negotiated settlement resulted in a general election in April 1994. On May 10, 1994, in the presence of scores of world leaders and as millions watched on television across the globe, following the swearing in of F. W. de Klerk and Thabo Mbeki as joint vice presidents, Nelson Mandela took the oath of office as president of a free, democratic, united and nonracial South Africa.[63]

Conclusion
A New South Africa: Challenges and Prospects

Though a new era has dawned in South Africa, no one should expect that the harsh and brutal legacies of apartheid will disappear overnight. Township civil war and state security violence have given way to urban and rural crimes, although these crimes are no less frequent than they were before 1994: whites, tourists, and other foreign visitors are only just beginning to notice them. Yet the main challenge remains economic. Seventy percent of blacks live below the poverty line, subsisting in "conditions of unacceptable poverty and deprivation," to use de Klerk's telling phrase.[64] In addition, forty-five percent of blacks are unemployed; seven million blacks are homeless (out of a total population of forty-four million); and sixty percent of blacks are illiterate while there is no illiteracy among whites. Though a few blacks are being gradually inducted into the commanding heights of the economy, the yawning gap between the rich and the poor remains one of the widest in the world, as eighty-eight percent of the nation's personal wealth is controlled by five percent of the population. The government's Reconstruction and Development Program, meant to redress some of the inequities of the apartheid years, promised more than available resources would allow it to deliver. A 1994 law encouraging white landowners to voluntarily part with land taken illegally from Africans produced little result. Sporadic attacks on white farmers and landowners and cases of squatters refusing to vacate occupied "white lands" have increased. A Truth and Reconciliation Commission (TRC), set up in

---

63. For the details of the negotiations, the fits and starts, that led to this "miracle" or negotiated settlement, see the fascinating account by Allister Sparks, *Tomorrow Is Another Country: The Inside Story of South Africa's Road to Change* (New York: Hill and Wang, 1995). See also Mandela, *Long Walk to Freedom*; Andrew Reynold, ed., *Election '99 South Africa: from Mandela to Mbeki* (New York: St. Martin's, 1999) and De Klerk, *The Last Trek — A New Beginning*.

64. De Klerk, *The Last Trek — A New Beginning*, 398.

1995 and chaired by Archbishop Desmond Tutu, gave amnesty to those who made full public disclosure of their crimes and human rights violations. While many questioned the wisdom of sacrificing justice for reconciliation, while others warned of the danger of entrenching a culture of impunity, and while notable offenders, like former President P. W. Botha (who was eventually convicted on contempt charges) refused to cooperate, the successful establishment and operation of the Truth and Reconciliation Commission was a major step forward in South Africa's tortuous attempt at creating a just, peaceful, and democratic society.[65]

Nevertheless, while the challenges are daunting, there are many reasons for optimism. Notable among these "countervailing factors," to use Allister Spark's phrase,[66] are the absence of racism among the vast majority of black South Africans; the strong mutual commitment to the beautiful land of South Africa by all its people, irrespective of their race; the inclusive nature of the ANC and the pragmatic character of its seasoned and tested leadership; the tried and proven culture of negotiation, compromise, and cooperation; the existence of a virile and vigorous civil society including the independent media, seasoned labor unions, the judiciary, the church, students, women, and cultural organizations; South Africa's sophisticated industries and economic infrastructure, the most developed in Africa; and finally its enormous wealth, not only in material but also in human resources. With regard to politics, the ANC has remained the majority party, but it has managed, through a careful and deliberate incorporation of all interest groups, to present itself and operate as a nonracial, nonsexist, egalitarian, and democratic organization, thus putting to rest many people's fear of a one-party dictatorship. Mandela's decision not to run for a second term, in spite of his immense popularity, and his replacement by Thabo Mbeki following a peaceful election in 1999 offer hope that South Africa might yet provide a model of good governance, racial reconciliation, and economic justice that will eventually begin to heal the deep divisions, malformations, abject deprivations, scarred psyches, and troubled memories of the past.

Review Questions

1. "Today, South Africa belongs to us once more.... May God grant that it will always remain so" (Daniel Malan, 1948). Account for the development and triumph of Afrikaner nationalism in South Africa between 1939 and 1948.
2. With reference to five key apartheid laws, show to what extent whites were prepared to go to ensure their continued domination over Africans in South Africa between 1948 and 1960.
3. "God save us from the South Africa of the Group Areas Act, which knows no reason, justice, or mercy" (Alan Paton, 1958). Against the background of

---

65. On the TRC see Kenneth Christie, *The South African Truth Commission* (New York: Palgrave, 2000).

66. For a fuller discussion of some of these factors, see Sparks, *Tomorrow Is Another Country*, 215–41. The phrase is from page 230. On the challenges ahead in the new South Africa, see Stephen J. Stedman, *South Africa: The Political Economy of Transformation* (Boulder CO: Lynne Rienner Publishers, 1994); Lindsay Eades, *The End of Apartheid in South Africa* (Westport, CT.: Greenwood Press, 1999), 101–22.

the worldwide triumph of nationalism in the twentieth century, account for the successful consolidation and long survival of apartheid in South Africa.

4. "During my lifetime, I have dedicated myself to this struggle of the African people.... I have cherished the ideal of a democratic and free society in which all persons live together in harmony and with equal opportunities. It is an ideal, which I hope to live for and to achieve. But if need be, it is an ideal for which I am prepared to die" (Nelson Mandela, First Accused, at the Rivonia Trial, April 20, 1964). What were the main features, major stages, and constraints involved in the development of African nationalism in South Africa between 1939 and 1976?

5. Account for the major social and economic consequences of the policy and the practice of apartheid in South Africa between 1948 and 1994.

6. "Our motto is to maintain white supremacy for all time to come over our own people and our own country, by force if necessary." (Hendrik Verwoerd, Prime Minister of South Africa, 1958–1966). Explain the collapse of the apartheid state between 1976 and 1994.

Additional Reading

Beinart, William. *Twentieth-Century South Africa.* Oxford: Oxford University Press, 1994.

De Klerk, F. W. *The Last Trek—A New Beginning: The Autobiography.* New York: St. Martin's Press, 1999.

Mandela, Nelson. *Long Walk to Freedom: The Autobiography of Nelson Mandela.* Boston: Little and Brown, 1994.

Moleah, Alfred T. *South Africa: Colonialism, Apartheid and African Dispossession.* Wilmington, Delaware: Disa Press, 1993.

Ross, Robert. *A Concise History of South Africa.* Cambridge: Cambridge University Press, 1999.

Thompson, Leonard. *A History of South Africa* New Haven, CT: Yale University Press, 1995.

Waldmeir, Patti. *Anatomy of a Miracle: The End of Apartheid and the Birth of a New South Africa.* New York: W.W. Norton, 1997.

PART C

REFLECTIONS ON COLONIALISM

Chapter 23

The Psychology of Colonialism

Ehiedu E. G. Iweriebor

This chapter examines the psychological aspects of colonialism in Africa. It identifies cultural imperialism as the general ideological framework through which the psychology of colonialism was implanted and propagated in Africa. The specific mechanisms of this domination included the falsification of African history, colonial education, missionary religious imperialism, and racial social stratification. While the colonialists probably expected a one-dimensional response of submission and surrender from the colonized to psychological programming, African responses were, in fact, complex and dialectical, with elements of both dependence and independence. The program was sufficiently powerful and enduring in its consequences that it continues to affect Africa's self-image, development choices, and decisions in the era of "neocolonial" independence.

* * *

Introduction

This chapter examines the psychology of colonialism that was imposed on Africans and African societies by the European colonial powers during the period of colonial domination from the late nineteenth century to the 1960s. The psychology of colonialism refers, on the one hand, to the colonial cultural mechanisms and processes, encapsulated in the ideology and practice of racism with which the colonizers attempted to justify their invasion, that led to the conquest and domination of Africa, and, on the other hand, to those mechanisms with which they attempted to create pathological societies in which Africans appeared as inferior defeated people requiring colonial domination for their propulsion into "civilization" and "modernity." More specifically, psychological colonization was the process by which the colonizers attempted to create colonized societies and peoples who were politically disempowered, culturally defeated, and programmed to feel inferior and deserving of domination. This entailed assaulting the key cultural props and belief systems of the colonized people and representing them as inherently inferior. The consequence of the successful inculcation of psychological colonization was the creation of peoples and societies that were disoriented, insecure, controllable, imitative and dependent on the dominators for approval and advancement.

This psychological colonization was one of the mechanisms colonizers used to maintain ideological control and the cohesion of their societies in Africa. Its objective was to create a new social order, the colonial order, in which the colonizers' power and authority represented the natural order and was unquestionable. The application of this ideology was to yield two new "species," the authoritative and omniscient colonizers as the "directors" from "director-societies" and the subjected and disempowered colonized as the "directed" from "directed-societies." The fundamental expectation and ultimate success of this process was the creation of a perfect, mutual understanding between the colonizers and the colonized of each others' places in the colonial order as the "directors" and the "directed," respectively.

The study of the psychology of colonialism is important for a complete appreciation of the colonial enterprise and experience in Africa in its own right, but it is also essential because it is a much neglected theme in the historiography of African colonialism. While several aspects of colonialism, such as the Scramble for and partition of Africa, systems of colonial rule, social change, economic exploitation, the upsurge of African nationalism, and the recovery of independence, have been studied, apart from a few studies by writers like Gustav Jahoda, Albert Memmi, and Frantz Fanon and the various commentaries on their works, the psychology of colonialism has not been studied very much.[1] Hence, it is necessary to examine and understand the phenomenon, its impact on the colonized, and their responses to it during and after the era of colonialism.

In addition, while the various colonial powers' political administrations differed in form, as did, for instance Britain's indirect rule and France's direct rule and its assimilation and association policies, European colonial governments, had fundamental similarities. They shared a negative ideological conception of African peoples and societies, the basic objective of economic exploitation, the aim of cultural aggrandizement, and the ideology and practice of racism as a mechanism for creating crippled colonized peoples and maintaining control over African societies. Consequently, it is possible to study the psychology of colonialism as a common phenomenon in all colonial situations on the continent.

This chapter is organized into four main sections. The first section outlines the colonizers' ideological construction of Africa and Africans. The second section examines the mechanisms of the implantation of psychological colonization and their impacts. As should be expected, the experience generated varied responses in the colonized including acceptance, alienation, subservience, self-abasement, acquiescence, and rejection. The failure of psychological colonization to totally disempower the colonized was reflected in the rise of nationalism as the fundamental political challenge to colonialism and the eventual attainment of independence, which is the subject of section three. While political independence re-

---

1. See, Gustav Jahoda, *White Man: A Study of the Attitudes of Africans to Europeans in Ghana Before Independence* (London: Oxford University Press, 1961); Albert Memmi, *The Colonizer and the Colonized* (Boston: Beacon Press, 1965); Frantz Fanon, *The Wretched of the Earth* (New York: Grove Press, 1968); Georges Balandier, *The Sociology of Black Africa* (New York: Praeger Publishers, 1970); Renate Zehar, *Colonialism and Alienation: Political Thoughts of Frantz Fanon*(Benin City, Nigeria: Ethiope Publishing Corporation, 1974); L. Adele Jinadu, *Fanon: In Search of the African Revolution* (Enugu, Nigeria: Fourth Dimension Publishers, 1980).

stored power to African leaders, it did not lead to Africa's recovery of complete ideological independence, freedom of thought and action, and capacity for autonomous development, as most postindependence African governments maintained colonial economic policies and structures. Africa thereby entered the phase of indirect African subjection to Western domination, that is, the era of neocolonialism, or independence without freedom. The manifestation of this was primarily and most prominently in the economic arena, sustained by the class interests of Africa's emergent ruling class and the relentless ideological propaganda, economic pressures, and financial blandishments of the former colonial powers and their new agencies of world domination, the World Bank and the International Monetary Fund (IMF), a new dependency that reflected the deep-seated nature of psychological colonialism's impact.

Thus, the psychology of colonialism survived and persisted in new forms in the era of neocolonial independence, giving birth to the psychology of neocolonialism as the new face of an old phenomenon. This is examined in section four. The chapter concludes with an assessment of the continuing challenge posed by psychological colonialism's legacy and the possibility of Africans' recovery of complete freedom and the autonomous initiative for political, social, and economic self-development on the one hand and ideological, cultural, and psychological liberation on the other.

The Ideological Construction of Colonized Africa and Africans

A monumental project like the European colonial enterprise, which sought to impose political domination over Africa and exploit African resources for the promotion of the economic development, industrial advancement, and social prosperity of the capitalist West, necessarily required an ideology to justify the necessity for its mission. Such an ideology was also required to convince the colonized that they were inferior peoples in backward societies who deserved to be colonized.

This was the context in which the intelligentsia of European imperialism — the journalists, scholars, missionaries, political activists, politicians, and administrators from the colonial powers — began to use racism to justify and facilitate the imposition and maintenance of colonialism. The Western colonial powers, in elaborating and executing this ideology, were armed with an ancient intellectual and popular tradition that demonized African peoples and societies.[2] Equipped with the racial confidence, cultural certitudes, and military power provided by the capitalist industrialization and economic development of their societies during the preceding two centuries, colonial powers created a Manichean ideology of racial domination in which the colonizers and the colonized were sharply differentiated as two incompatible groups or even two different species: the colonizers as human and the colonized as subhuman "natives."

---

2. For an effective summary of the demonization of African societies in Western thought and history, see Joseph Harris, *Africans and Their History* 2nd ed.(New York: Penguin, 1998), 1–19. A good source for the sampling of Western views on race and racism is Louis Snyder, *The Idea of Racialism* (Princeton, New Jersey: Van Nostrand, 1962).

While the primary objective of the economic exploitation of Africa was never in doubt, this aim was not usually blatantly stated. Instead, in varying formulations, through philosophical statements from the French or through general administrative policy statements and directives from the British, the objectives of colonialism were described as "civilizing mission[s]."[3] Such a conception necessarily implied that the prospective colonial subjects and societies were "uncivilized" an idea that became the basis of the colonizers' ideology of racial domination. The colonized and their societies were described in the Western language of domination in largely negative terms as "backward," "uncivilized," "primitive," "savage," "pagan," and "tribal": in short as inferior.[4] If Africans embodied all the negations of European-defined "civilization," they were therefore the polar opposites of the European people and societies which were constructed and projected directly and indirectly as "civilized," "advanced," "complex," "scientific," "technological," "sophisticated," and so forth. This was the classic formulation in Manichean fashion of the basis of the colonial ideology of racial domination: "We: superior" and "They: inferior."

In a corollary of this racist ideology, since African societies were "uncivilized" and "inferior" and therefore inherently incapable of self-propulsion to "modernity," it was the responsibility of the politically and culturally capable and industrially advanced Europeans to rescue the benighted ("dark") and stagnant continent. This was popularized in the age of colonial imperialism as the "White man's burden,"[5] through which exploitative colonial enterprises were cloaked in the garb of "civilizing mission[s]." This concept was propagated during the Scramble for African territories and resources. It was expressed in the Berlin Treaty drafted at the infamous Berlin Conference of 1884–1885, at which the aspirant Western colonial powers agreed on the terms for the partition, colonization and exploitation of Africa.[6]

By the time of the actual invasion, conquest, and imposition of colonial domination in the late nineteenth and early twentieth centuries, the ideology of colonial racism and the "mission to civilize" the "natives" had emerged as unquestionable certitudes in the political beliefs, cultural attitudes, and foreign policy orientations of the colonizing societies. Consequently, European participants in the colonial enterprise, from lowly clerks to military commanders, traders, missionaries, and senior administrators, were filled with a quasi-religious zeal for and absolute confidence in the historic necessity to dominate, exploit, and civilize

---

3. For examples of the view of colonialism as a civilizing mission, see the statements of various colonial administrators, scholars, and advocates: Emile Banning, "Le Partage Politique de l'Afrique d'apres les transactions Internationales les plus recentes, 1885 a 1888" *Colonial Rule in Africa: Readings from Primary Sources* ed. Bruce Fetter, (Madison: University of Wisconsin Press, 1979), 28–33; "The Fundamental Principles of Overseas Portugal: The Constitution of Portugal (1951) Articles 133 to 136," in Fetter, *Colonial Rule* 105–106 and excerpts from Frederick Lugard, "The Dual Mandate 1926" *Documents on Modern Africa* ed. T. Walter Wallbank, (Princeton, NJ: D. Van Nostrand, 1964), 40–1.

4. Ehiedu Iweriebor, *The Age of Neo-colonialism in Africa* (Ibadan, Nigeria: African Book Builders, 1997), 57–68.

5. For a summary of various views of Western imperialism as a "civilizing mission," see Snyder, *The Idea of Racialism* Chapter 5, 54–61.

6. For the Berlin treaty, see "Berlin Act. Trade and Civilization..." in Edward Hertslet, *The Map of Africa by Treaty* vol 1, (London: HMSO, 1896), 20–47.

Africa. Such an imperialist project definitely needed practitioners and participants who had no doubts about the sanctity and necessity of their design. This missionary outlook was an essential psychological and ideological garment for the colonizers, insulating them from any uncertainties about their superiority and assuring them of the rectitude of their mission.

Since it was the colonized peoples and societies who were negatively constructed and were the objects of the "civilizing mission," and since it was in their societies that this mission was to be performed mechanisms had to be created to implant and inculcate these ideas in the minds of the colonized peoples as well.

Mechanisms of the Implantation of Psychological Colonialism

While colonialism was established and maintained by military force, administered by authoritarian, bureaucratic colonial states, and exploited economically by colonial capitalist firms, the relative cohesion of the colonized societies was procured and maintained by the ideology and practice of racial domination and psychological colonization. As with other aspects of the colonial enterprise, mechanisms, institutions, and processes had to be created to implant and spread a psychology of domination among the colonized. This was necessary to procure their psychological disempowerment and ensure practical compliance with the new order, that is, the colonial situation.

The general ideological framework through which this was undertaken may be referred to as cultural imperialism, or the attempt of the colonial dominators to destroy the validity of the cultural conventions, values, norms, usages and institutions of the colonized people. These included political and social ideologies, belief systems, history, orature, performing arts like music, dance, and drama, marriage systems, fashion, and so on. These conventions, processes, and institutions give peoples their identities and social coherence as distinctive human societies. If these forces are challenged, undermined, and destroyed, societies are liable to become psychologically defeated, culturally disoriented, and socially unhinged and therefore easier to control and dominate.

Cultural imperialism was developed, propagated, and executed in Africa through various direct and indirect processes and institutions including historical falsification, colonizers' educational institutions and languages, European missionary activity, social services, mass media (newspapers, radio, films, books, comics), and racial stratification through social and residential segregation.

The Falsification of Africa's Historical Past

In the effort to disempower African peoples and program them to accept domination, the colonial powers and their propagandists generally attempted to falsify African history. They often proclaimed that Africa had no history or more specifically that it had no societies with organized political, social, and cultural systems and developed economies and technologies; they asserted that the societies had no arts, government, culture, science, or organized or settled existence or what in Western thought is called civilization.

This effort at eradicating African history required that all evidence of the existence of distinguished civilizations or advanced polities such as Egypt, Kush, Axum, Ghana, Kanem-Borno, Mali, Songhai, Kongo, Zimbabwe, and others had to be suppressed, minimized, ignored, or explained away as non-African or provided with an external push or initiative. Yet, since these advanced polities had existed and since their physical locations could not be altered, various methods were used to advance historical falsification. Here racism fully came into play. The creation of these advanced societies was ascribed to external, non-African (specifically non-Negroid) people. This approach was best captured by the "Hamitic Hypothesis," which was advanced by such colonial apologists as C. Seligman in the *Races of Africa* and others like Harry Johnston and Maurice Delafosse.[7] Its basic claim was that all evidence of advanced political and social systems with sophisticated cultural creations like monuments and artworks and the scientific knowledge and technological capacity to undergird their creation were the results of the intervention of a mythical, non-African Caucasian racial group called the "Hamites."

While this view of the emergence of African civilizations was clearly a fabrication, its effective refutation required investigations beyond nationalist assertions of their existence. Historical research especially from the 1940s to the present, has conclusively demonstrated that African civilizations were created by native African genius and that the impulse and motivation for their creation were internally stimulated.[8]

What remains important, however, is that during the colonial period the historical falsification and erasure of Africa's history was part of the success of psychological colonization. It was intended to persuade the colonized that they were without a history were incapable of self-propulsion, and therefore required Western colonial domination to achieve their entry into history. The basic claim here, which became the generalized perception of Africa in the colonial and even postcolonial periods, was that African development had always been the result of external impulsion, not native initiative. This was transmitted through school systems and, more practically through the media and other agencies. In the postcolonial period, psychologically colonized African politicians, academics, and journalists implicitly or explicitly continued to believe this anti-African falsehood and to consciously and unconsciously propagate it with all its damaging consequences. As part of procuring the subservience and submission of colonized Africans, this aspect of psychological colonization was a powerful tool for creating self-doubt and a sense of inadequacy and inferiority.

---

7. For summaries and critiques of these views, see J. Ki-Zerbo, "General Introduction" and J.D. Fage, "The Development of African Historiography," *UNESCO General History of Africa I:Methodology and Pre-history* ed. J. Ki-Zerbo, abridged ed. (Paris: UNESCO, 1989), 1–9, 10–5.

8. The academic study of African history has grown substantially since the 1940s and continues to grow. Numerous published works now exist on various regions and fields of African history. The most comprehensive surveys are the eight volumes of the *UNESCO General History of Africa*. For the civilizations, states and societies of Africaup to the eighteenth century, see vol. 1–5.

Colonial Education and the Creation of a Culturally Disoriented Elite

Colonial education systems formed the second major mechanism used for the psychological colonization of Africans.[9] These systems were established from the early colonial period onward by colonial governments and missionaries. Government schools were intended to create the low-level technical, clerical, and artisanal personnel who would be required by the colonial bureaucracies. The missionaries intended their schools to inspire new, native catechists and priests to convert Africans to Christianity.

Africans saw colonial education as an avenue for social and occupational advancement in a novel situation in which formal credentials provided by school-based education systems were required. Hence, those who had access to them eagerly enrolled in these schools. Relative to the populations of the African colonies, and despite the colonial claims of "civilizing mission[s]," the schools were actually sparse and inadequate.

Despite their small numbers, the schools were a powerful mechanism through which the psychology of colonialism was implanted in the minds of educated Africans. As formal institutions, the schools were advertised as superior to the preexisting African educational systems whose importance progressively diminished in colonial urban areas. Secondly, the new schools' curricula in areas like history and social studies aimed to propagate the claims of Western capitalist societies as civilized, advanced and superior. By the same token, African societies were usually denounced, diminished, and demonized as backward and inferior. The history taught in schools mainly focused on ancient Greece and Rome and more recent aspects of European history such as the Renaissance, the Reformation, the voyages of world "discovery," and industrialization. In this context Africa had no history; instead European activities in Africa—the slave trade, colonial invasions, conquests, and establishment of colonial rule—were presented as African history. In a word, African history began with European ingress.

Students subjected to colonial education were taught to question the validity of their societies' cultural institutions, conventions, and practices. These were often contrasted negatively with European cultural conventions. African students were programmed to doubt the normalcy and validity of their cultural heritage, and sometimes to despise and denounce it. Simultaneously, they were indoctrinated to accept colonialism as a civilizing mission and African societies as needing colonialism for their "modernization" or advancement out of "backwardness" into "civilization." The educated Africans who imbibed these views were already conditioned to depend on the West and on Western rationality, methods, and technology for "modernization."

Furthermore, while colonial education reached only a few Africans, those who received it were a sociologically important minority who would become teachers, journalists, priests, nationalists, politicians, lawyers, and other professionals. They exercised an impact which was far out of proportion to their num-

---

9. For a good pioneering exploration of the implantation of the psychology of colonialism through the colonial education system in the Gold Coast, see Gustav Jahoda, *White Man*.

bers. This was because as people who had been effectively subjected to psychological colonization, they became the "native" carriers of the colonizers' views about themselves and were therefore a very powerful local vanguard for the normalization and propagation of colonialist views of African societies as inherently backward, pathological, immobile, and in need of Western colonial domination.

Colonial Languages and Linguistic Disempowerment

An important aspect of the inculcation of psychological colonialism in the education system relates to the question of language. The new colonial situation effected a simultaneous advancement of European languages and diminution of African languages both practically and ideologically. In general, the languages spoken at school were those of the colonizers: English, French, German, Italian, Spanish, and Portuguese. Students had no choice but to learn these languages. Since they were also the languages of the colonial administrations, of economic transactions, and of advertisements for the fruits of Western science and technology, they came to provide high stature and power for colonized Africans who mastered them so as to be recognized and accepted by the colonizers. They were also seen as the keys to unlocking the mystery of white peoples' overt military power and economic and technological superiority.

At the same time, African languages were minimized. Ideologically, in colonial propaganda, African languages did not really exist. What existed as means of communication were "dialects," "vernaculars," and "native tongues." Colonizers so described African languages to deny that Africans had any capacity to express advanced political and philosophical thought or scientific and technological knowledge. Once the colonized accepted this belief in the inadequacy of their languages, they learned to despise their linguistic heritage as inferior to that of the colonizers' and as another example of their societies' inadequacies. Practically, since most African languages (though not all) were not alphabetized and in particular since they were not used in the formal arenas of the colonial situation (education, administration, and economic activities), they were rendered irrelevant.

As the African languages were neglected and increasingly despised even by the colonized as inferior and inadequate "vernaculars," the profile and stature of the colonizers' languages rose. As they became the means by which literate Africans advanced occupationally, acquired social status, and sought social acceptance from the colonizers, Africans were further disempowered linguistically and culturally. Thus those who had a worshipful regard for the colonizers' languages as those of high culture, rationality, technology, and power were psychologically conditioned to accept their own societies' linguistic traditions as inferior. The colonial languages, therefore, were powerful tools for the inculcation of the colonial psychology of subservience.

The Colonial Mass Media and the Advertisement of Western Power

The mass media represented by the print press (including newspapers, magazines, books, and comics) and by electronic media (such as radio, film, and later television), were another powerful mechanism for the psychological colonization of Africans. Despite the high level of illiteracy in European languages in much of colonial Africa, for those who were literate, the mass media served to routinely and regularly propagate the alleged virtues of the capitalist West and especially to advertise the products of capitalist industries. Since African societies did not at that time have their own mass media as a counter to the propaganda of the colonial media, the latter enjoyed monopoly power and a hegemonic position from which to publicize the cultural superiority and economic power of the colonizers.

Colonial books, comics, and films generally portrayed Africans and African societies as primitive, uncivilized, and backward. African audiences exposed to the constant reiteration of such views about their societies were again programmed to despise their societies and to accept the superiority of the West and the Western colonizers. For African audiences, therefore, the Western model became the ideal they pursued. The importance of the mass media in the dissemination of psychological colonialism stemmed from its prominence and its consistency in the delivery of its messages.

European Christian Missionaries and Religious Imperialism

Major agents that contributed to the implantation and dissemination of psychological colonialism were European Christian missionaries and churches.[10] Although the missionaries often came to Africa on their own accord and for the explicit purpose of gaining converts, their own assumptions, attitudes, and actions often coincided with and reinforced the objectives and processes of the colonialists.

In the first place, the ideological premise of European missionary evangelism was the assumption that Africa was a benighted continent and that Africans were pagan savages whose "evil souls" needed to be saved, purified and won for the European God.[11] According to this European Christian construct, Africans really had no indigenous religions and spiritual belief systems, worship forms, or liturgical systems. The missionaries demonized the religious and spiritual systems of Africans variously as "devil worship," "evil," "witchcraft," "shamanism,"

---

10. For a survey of Christianity in Africa during the early colonial period see, Asare Opoku, "Religion in Africa During the Colonial Period," *UNESCO General History of Africa V11: Africa under Colonial Domination, 1880–1935.* ed. Adu Boahen, abridged ed. (Paris: UNESCO, 1989), 217–28.

11. For a powerful exposition of missionary views and attitudes to Africans, their religions, belief systems, and African responses during the colonial period, see V.Y. Mudimbe, *The Invention of Africa* (Bloomington and Indianapolis: Indiana University Press, 1988), 44–64.

"juju," and so on. In this construct, Africans lacking the only "true" religion (Christianity) needed to be saved from the clutches of devil worship, evil witchdoctors, and shamans. The demonization of African religions and belief systems was a necessary preparatory basis for the project of evangelizing and converting "heathen" Africa to European Christianity.

With the political protection and support of their cohorts, the colonial administrators, the missionaries began their projects of demonization, iconoclasm, and Christianization. With the support of the colonial states and the participation of their African converts, the missionaries destroyed indigenous African religious symbols, places of worship, and sacred objects, which they demonized as "fetish" objects, "juju," and so on. They were often replaced with the grand physical symbols of African religious defeat: European Christian churches. Converts used new Christian fetish objects, rosaries and crosses, which were of course, not perceived or described as fetish objects but as sacred icons and instruments of prayer.

The missionaries were pioneers in providing Western education and health services to Africans. These were used to facilitate the process of conversion by providing evidence of the social benefits of Christianization. In so far as they propagated the superiority of Western religion, culture, and science, furthermore, these services were important additional instruments in the inculcation of psychological colonialism in Africa.

In their Christianization programs, European missionaries and churches sought to present African societies as pathological. African converts had to, at least, formally accept this characterization of their societies. Those who subscribed fully to the view became alienated from their societies' religious traditions and belief systems and denounced their own societies. Even those converts who did not fully accept the demonization and denunciation of their societies found themselves conflicted psychologically and in relation to their societies.

Social Distance in the Colonial Situation: Social and Residential Segregation

Racism, racial stratification, and psychological colonialism were also established and maintained through the social distance constructed between the European colonizers and the colonized subjects. This racial social segregation was institutionalized to ensure that the colonized natives knew their place in the social hierarchy of the colonial situation.

Social distance and segregation were manifested in two main spheres: interpersonal relations and residential segregation. In general colonizers endeavored to minimize contact with colonized Africans. There were few situations or contexts in which the colonizers and Africans interacted socially. In situations where contact was inescapable, for example, in the workplace, for political administration or during economic interactions, the colonizers generally adopted stiff authoritative postures and formal speech patterns which often consisted of barked orders or formal and stilted directives. In addition, when the colonizers wanted to procure forced labor or extort taxes, they often went through the police or the military; i.e., through a show or threat of force. In short, social relations in the colonial situation were an expression and reassertion of the European colonizers' racial power, distance and authority.

Social distance was also achieved by the maintenance of separate social arenas. Colonial societies usually had racially exclusive social clubs, theaters, dance halls, playgrounds, and churches. Residential segregation deepened the social distance and social isolation of the Europeans. The colonizers' residential spaces, usually called European reservations, were usually well-planned, well-appointed, low-density residential areas which were equipped with all the best types of infrastructure for commodious living, such as well paved roads, electricity, water supplies, gardens, playgrounds, garbage disposal facilities, African servants, and so on, all of which were provided and paid for by African resources. In contrast, the colonizeds' residences were unplanned, high-density, and overcrowded areas with unpaved roads and often with no electricity, potable water supplies, or garbage disposal systems.[12]

Confronted with this social distance, formal communication, commandist interaction involving shows and threats of force, and obvious contrast in residential quality, the colonized absorbed the impression that the colonizers were powerful and superior while they were powerless and inferior.

These were some of the mechanisms, processes, and institutions through which psychological colonialism was implanted in the colonial African psyche. While these mechanisms and processes were analytically separable, in practice they worked together to create crippled, racially stratified societies and to inculcate in the colonized a sense of their own difference, weakness, and inferiority and of the colonizers' power, authority and superiority.

Responses of Colonized Africans:
The Dialectics of Dependence and Independence

The African Context as a Constraint
on the Impact of Psychological Colonization

The colonizers' attempt to inculcate psychological colonialism through racist ideologies, the practice of racial discrimination, and the various agencies and processes outlined in the preceding sections inevitably generated complex responses from colonized Africans. While the colonizers might have expected a one-dimensional response of complete surrender to the dogmas of African inferiority and backwardness, countervailing forces ensured that actual responses were multidimensional, composed of elements of ambiguity, ambivalence, acceptance, acquiescence, rejection, and self-assertion. In short, these responses are best described as dialectical.

Among the countervailing circumstances which limited the impact of psychological colonization were the state of African societies and the limited reach of colonial administrative authority. Precolonial African societies, although under-

---

12. See, Frantz Fanon's powerful contrastive characterization of the two areas. Fanon, *The Wretched of the Earth* 38–40.

going profound transformations in the nineteenth century on the eve of colonization, were not the anarchic, simple, and backward societies of colonial propaganda, but politically complex and socially coherent civilizations, products of centuries of evolution. Their characteristics bore no resemblance whatsoever to the negative attributes ascribed to them by colonial ideologies. Africans did not perceive themselves as pathological or backward people that needed subjection to external powers in order to propel themselves into "modernity." They could not simply wipe out their existing cultural heritage and self-image and automatically adopt colonialist constructions. Hence, the reactions of colonized Africans to cultural imperialism were not simply those of surrender and submission, but were rather ambivalent or more accurately dialectical. Yet, because the colonizers now possessed and exercised power they systematically and consistently attempted to engender a belief in a "pathological" Africa, foisting this myth on the Africa that already existed.

Another limitation on the impact of psychological colonization should be noted. Although African societies were now administered by the colonizers, the actual political power and governmental reach of the colonial states was limited. The colonizers were mostly confined to the urban, administrative, commercial, and mining centers, areas where the colonizers had their greatest impact. Africans in rural and non-administrative areas did not experience direct cultural imperialism or manifest the kinds of self-perceptual confusion exhibited in the urban areas. In short, the reach and impact of colonialist psychological colonization was never total, universal, or uniform.

The Dialectic of Dependence

The colonizeds' response was dialectical and characterized by elements of dependence and independence. On the one hand, it was the Africans who were in closest contact with the colonizers through political administration, economic interactions (through mines, companies, railroads), educational institutions, and churches who were most intensely affected by the pressures of psychological colonization. They were the groups that most experienced the afflictions of and exhibited ambivalence toward psychological colonization, expressing alienation, estrangement, confusion, imitation, adoption, adaptation, acquiescence, and rejection. They would attempt to mimic and adopt the lifestyles of the colonizers, considering them representative of civilized forms. They usually sought the approval of the colonizers in personal and social conduct so as to be stamped as "civilized, detribalized natives." They were also at the vanguard of Africans' self-abuse and the denigration of aspects of African cultures as "backward" and "inferior." These reactions suggest that such Africans who had been subjected to psychological colonization and been successfully programmed had acquired deep dependency complexes and a colonial mentality.

The Dialectic of Independence

The reactions of the colonized Africans were often not unilinear, but multilinear and contradictory, however. While they sought to mimic the colonizers and "achieve" equality with them through Europeanization, they eventually realized that the colonizers would never treat or accept them as equals, whatever their educational attainment or level of social status. This experience generated ambivalence toward the colonizers.

In addition, while their colonial education and exposure to the colonizers' lifestyles made these colonized Africans more amenable to subservience and dependency, the same education exposed them to the exploitative nature of colonialism, the falsity of the European claims of superiority and the hypocrisy of the doctrine of the "civilizing mission" as a mere cover for rapacious economic exploitation. Their education in Western history also demonstrated that European economic and social transformation generated by capitalist industrialization was a historically constituted phenomenon and not an expression of the inherent racial superiority of Europeans.

Since educated Africans were closest in social class to the colonial officials and aspired to their social and occupational stations, their actual experience of the racial discrimination, social distance, and cultural arrogance inherent in colonial society engendered doubts about colonialists' disinterested claims of being on "civilizing mission[s]." The continuing resistance of African farmers and the emergent working class added to the critical attitudes of educated Africans. All this reflected the incomplete subordination of these elites to colonial psychological programming.

Educated Africans' experiences and reflections often moved them in the direction of independence of thought and action. This eventually led them to form or activate nationalist resistance movements, articulate ideological liberation statements, and participate in struggles for freedom. This represented the other dimension of the dialectical responses of the colonized: the quest for and assertion of independence. As a movement of resistance to psychological colonization, the response was best exemplified by the emergence of African nationalism, especially cultural and political nationalism.

African Cultural and Political Nationalism as Resistance to Psychological Colonization

African nationalism broadly defined was the attempt to throw off the yoke of colonial domination, achieve political, cultural, and psychological freedom and economic independence and build new nations from the varieties of people who comprised the colonial territories.[13] While groups like farmers, urban workers, market women, traders, merchants, professionals, and other activists resisted colonial domination and psychological programming in their own particular arenas, nationalism was a global territorial movement, organized and led by the nationalist intelligentsia who sought to terminate political domination, economic exploitation, cultural imperialism, and psychological colonialism at the colony-wide level.

---

13. For the classic study of the origins and development of African nationalism, see Thomas Hodgkin, *Nationalism in Colonial Africa* (New York: New York University Press, 1957); see also B.O. Oloruntimehin, "African Politics and Nationalism," in Boahen, *UNESCO General History of Africa VII* 240–8; and the various articles in section 2 of Ali Mazrui, ed. *UNESCO General History of Africa, VIII: Africa since 1935* unabridged ed. (Paris: UNESCO, 1999), 105–281.

The two dimensions of nationalism that were the most important responses to psychological colonialism were cultural and political. In general, cultural nationalism asserted the normalcy and validity of African cultural usages, social conventions, values, and institutions such as languages, orature, music, dance, art, religions, foods, dress styles, marriage systems, and political and social thought. In addition, cultural and religious nationalist movements arose at various periods to defend, promote, reform, and popularize the African cultural heritage. This was exemplified, from the late nineteenth century and recurrently throughout the colonial period, in the creation of independent African churches especially in the South, Central and West African regions. These institutions separated from European Christian churches or were formed independently of them. They were established to indigenize the practice of Christianity and to rid it of Western cultural baggage and the arrogance of the European churches. As in the religious sphere, this also occurred in other areas of culture such as in history, orature, philosophy, languages and so on.

All of these activities were intended to assert the normalcy of African culture and counter the negative portrayal of Africa created by colonizers' ideology and psychological programming. Although limited in its reach and impact to the acculturated African elite in the urban areas and by the context of colonial domination, cultural nationalism was crucially important in highlighting the empirical grounds (empires, kingdoms, religions, art works, architectural monuments) for African cultural self-worth.

African nationalism emerged to challenge, confront, and terminate the colonizers' psychological programming and political domination that made that programming possible. African political nationalism evolved throughout the colonial period and exhibited reformist and radical currents politically and ideologically. Despite major variations in ideology and strategy, African nationalism was tied together by a common quest to terminate colonial domination.

Colonized Africans responded to psychological colonialism in complex, ambiguous, contradictory, and dialectical ways, even though colonial psychological programming was a powerful force to which colonizers expected a one-dimensional reaction. Actual reactions reflected elements of dependence and independence. Yet, the psychology of colonialism had enduring, psychologically damaging and socially disorienting consequences for the colonized. As the next section will show, though it was significantly shaken by the nationalist cultural and political struggles, this psychology was not destroyed.

African Independence: Between the Psychology of Freedom and the Psychology of Neocolonialism

The various African nationalist struggles, reformist and radical, culminated in the recovery of political power by the African elite and the achievement of independence by African countries in the 1960s. This was a decisive historic achievement. Yet, independence posed a profound challenge to the new leaders, who were now confronted with the prospect of nation-building. Nations had to be established, despite all the damaging political, economic, cultural, and psychological legacies of colonialism, the complex heritages of the precolonial societies, the positive gains of nationalism and the ambiguous ideological orientations of the nationalist leaders and movements.

The Gains of Independence and the Psychology of Freedom

Independence opened a new terrain of contestation between the psychology of freedom and the psychology of colonialism. On the one hand, limited as African independence was, there was no question that it represented major gains for Africans in terms of the removal of the context in which psychological colonization thrived. If properly utilized, independence could be an opportunity to systematically build the political, economic, social, cultural, and ideological processes, institutions, and social forces to incrementally and effectively terminate the psychology of colonialism and enthrone that of freedom. The gains of independence had administrative, political, economic and cultural aspects which included the removal of colonial rulers and the environment in which colonial racism flourished, an effect most visibly expressed in the Africanization of the political and bureaucratic leadership of African states. Independence also provided the opportunity for the creation and expansion of educational facilities, social services, and economic development programs in order to address the social questions of mass poverty and social deprivation and the economic question of modern industrial and technological underdevelopment.

The complexity of the gains of independence was reflected in the expression of cultural rebirth. Independence enabled African politicians, activists, and intelligentsia to unashamedly and boldly proclaim the normalcy and achievements of African culture, history, and societies. The emergence of African literature, dance, music, arts, and other humanities was perhaps the most eloquent testimony of the benefits of independence to African cultural rebirth. This cultural renaissance was officially expressed in the various African Festivals of Arts and Culture held in Dakar in 1966, Algiers in 1969, and Lagos in 1977.

Yet, cultural reassertion was problematic because it was not grounded in the material realities of the newly independent societies. That is, African societies were not creating the economic systems and technological capacities that would be the indices of societal power to ground the rebirth in their political, social and economic terrains. Without autonomous domestic economic systems, technological capacities, social prosperity and military power, the cultural renaissances were in many ways empty shows. For, while the ancient African societies created the productive forces and capacities to support and execute their cultural creativity and construction, postindependence African societies were characterized by the absence of any domestic connection between the technologies of production and the expression of culture. Thus the software of culture was African but the hardware, purchased at great cost, was imported. To that extent, expressions of cultural revival and creativity were hostage to the dependency syndrome. This again expressed the existence of dependence in the context of independence.

In short, independence provided the context for the possibility and the capacity for African societies to transform and empower themselves. Fulfilling that capacity would mean the recovery of complete psychological freedom in which Africans had the exclusive right and responsibility to make societal choices without reference, direct or indirect to any external powers.

Compromised Independence and the Psychology of Neocolonialism

Yet, Africans' achievement of independence was not a total and absolute victory over the forces of domination, given colonizers' methods of psychological programming and their continuing quest for control and domination over Africa. In fact, to protect Western economic interests without their direct physical presence, during decolonization the colonialists directly and indirectly created institutions, beliefs, and processes that reinforced African dependency on the West. This led to the consolidation and persistence of psychological colonialism in what became the era of neocolonial independence.[14]

The general strategy was to create African ideological and economic dependence on Western models, institutions, and ideas. This was done in two major areas, the first of which concerned the choice of strategies for economic development. Western-dominated financial institutions such as the World Bank and the International Monetary Fund (IMF) and numerous bilateral aid agencies promoted the ideology and conditions of African dependence. These agencies projected themselves as omniscient in matters of economic development and dealt with African leaders who had been programmed to feel incapable of producing independent visions and strategies of development. The neo-imperialist multilateral and bilateral "aid" agencies advised African leaders and governments on what economic development policies, programs and strategies to adopt. Essentially, these policies promoted the maintenance and expansion of the colonial economic system of the exportation of raw materials and the importation of manufactured goods. In the context of independence this was slightly modified, with a new dependency-inducing economic development strategy known as "import substitution industrialization" whereby factories and assembly plants would be established with imported skills, machinery, equipment, and raw materials to produce or assemble imported consumer goods.

The economic advisory activities of the neo-imperialist agencies reconsolidated colonialists' hold over Africa on the eve of independence. They made African leaders and states dependent on the former colonizers' economic visions, ideologies, policies, programs, and strategies. To the extent that African leaders felt able, willing, or obliged to leave the visions and strategies of postcolonial economic development to agencies of the colonizers, it can be said that postcolonial African leaders and states were still entrapped by psychological colonialism, or what may be called in the postcolonial era the psychology of neocolonialism.

The second expression of the survival and even revival of the psychology of colonialism after independence was reflected in the general ideological and political orientations of African leaders in their choice of strategies, processes, and in-

---

14. For perspectives on the postindependence period as the era of neocolonialism in Africa, see Kwame Nkrumah, *Neo-colonialism: The Last Stage of Imperialism* (New York: International Publishers, 1966); Jack Woodis, *Introduction to Neo-colonialism* (New York: International Publishers, 1967); Iweriebor, *The Age of Neo-colonialism in Africa*.

stitutions for nation-building. In general, apart from a few bold and innovative leaders like Julius Nyerere of Tanzania, Kwame Nkrumah of Ghana, Gamal Nasser of Egypt, Ben Bella and Houari Boumedienne of Algeria, Modibo Keita of Mali, and later Samora Machel of Mozambique, Amilcar Cabral of Guinea-Bissau, Agostinho Neto of Angola, and Thomas Sankara of Burkina Faso, the majority of African leaders conceived of nation-building, quite prosaically, as the process of creating copies of Western societies in Africa complete with their political, social, and economic institutions and pathologies. Thus even after independence African leaders and elites still retained elements of psychological programming, and their political choices and ideological tendencies revealed a deep-seated dependency complex. African countries, while achieving political independence, were still in fundamental ways unfree.

This condition continued because African leaders and states did not embark on programs of cultural revolution to purge themselves of the sediments and complexes of dependency which had been scorched on their psyches by psychological colonization. Without such societal self-purgation, the task of postcolonial nation-building was virtually programmed to fail. Consequently, apart from the stock, tired explanations for the relative failure of African postcolonial nation-building—such as corruption, ethnic and other conflicts, mismanagement and instability—it is arguable that Africa's persistent underdevelopment, instability, and failures were partly the result of the survival of the psychology of colonialism. Such dependent psychological orientations have meant that African leaders have been largely unable to conceive the challenges of postcolonial nation-building as opportunities and responsibilities to autonomously envision their ideal societies, formulate ideologies, strategies, and programs, and then mobilize resources and people to bring such societies into being. For as long as the psychology of neocolonialism persists, Africa will remain entrapped in the vicious cycle of dependency, poverty, underdevelopment, lamentation and vulnerability to hostile external forces and be incapable of self-propulsion toward an autonomously designed free and self-advancing continent.

The dependency complexes plaguing the psyches of African leaders and elites must be dissolved through self-conscious programs of cultural purgation and reeducation in the ways of freedom. Only a monumental and clearly articulated effort of psychological deprogramming from dependency and re-empowerment will make it possible for African societies and peoples to restore themselves to power, authority, and the capacity for self-advancement. This will make it possible for Africa to enter the world again as a history-making subject rather than as the object of other societies' activities, a condition that will signal the final recovery of the psychology of freedom and genuine liberation.

Conclusion

This chapter has examined the various aspects of the psychology of colonialism that was imposed on African societies during the colonial period. It has outlined the various mechanisms through which the colonial powers pursued the project of psychological colonization. While the colonizers probably expected a one-dimensional response from colonized Africans, African responses were, in fact, varied, ambivalent, and dialectical and included elements of acceptance, acquiescence, submission, rejection and assertions of independence. The upsurge of African cultural and political nationalism and the attainment of independence provided the clearest evidence of the incomplete success of the program of psychological colonization.

But the chapter also shows that the colonial program was partially successful in creating deep-seated dependency complexes and a colonial mentality among African leaders and elites. This has been most forcefully manifested in the postcolonial period by the failure of African leaders to create autonomous visions, ideologies, and strategies for political and social transformation. Thus, in the era of neocolonial independence, African countries, burdened and incapacitated by the survival of psychological colonialism, have failed to create free, self-propelling societies and their leaders have retained strong propensities toward dependency on external models and directors. In order to terminate this condition, to enable Africans to regain the initiative for self-development that their forebears had exercised, it is imperative to devise well thought-out programs and strategies for the dissolution of psychological colonialism and the reprogramming of African leaders and peoples in the ways of freedom, empowerment and self-direction.

Review Questions

1. What is the psychology of colonialism? Why and how was it applied in the African colonies?
2. How did Africans respond to psychological colonization? How and why did the responses meet or fail to meet the expectations of the colonizers?
3. What mechanisms were used to implant the psychology of colonialism in Africa?
4. In what ways did the psychology of colonialism survive after independence, and what has been its impact?

Additional Reading

Balandier, Georges. *The Sociology of Black Africa*. New York: Praeger, 1970.
Fanon, Frantz. *The Wretched of the Earth*. New York: Grove Press, 1968.
Iweriebor, Ehiedu. *The Age of Neo-colonialism in Africa*. Ibadan, Nigeria: African Book Builders, 1997.
Gustav, Jahoda. *White Man*. London: Oxford University Press, 1961.
Mudimbe, V.Y. *The Invention of Africa*. Bloomington and Indianapolis: University of Indiana Press, 1988.

Chapter 24

Neocolonialism

Saheed A. Adejumobi

As the gap continues to increase between the rich and poor countries of the world, African nations face an arduous task in defining a new role that is not completely shaped and dictated by the disempowering characteristics of the colonial experience. Major developments in African history, such as the international slave trade, the introduction of development policies guided by religious and secular liberal principles, and the implementation of formal imperialism, all helped to consolidate European political and economic influence in Africa. A combination of domestic and international events concerning Africa culminated in decolonization and eventual political independence for countries throughout the continent beginning in the 1950s. The euphoria that accompanied this political development, however, gave way to despair as it became clear that a new form of dependence had replaced colonial rule. In essence, decolonization can be described as the co-optation of the "independent" African states and their political elite into a European-constructed neocolonial network.

* * *

With the failure of the postcolonial state in Africa, which emerged out of African nationalism and the decolonization initiatives of European powers on the continent, there have been calls for new methods of analysis to map the paths of modern nation-states. This chapter analyzes the postwar social, political, and economic underdevelopment of former colonies, especially those in modern Africa. It is argued that the roots of the myriad problems of underdevelopment, such as the lack of functional social welfare infrastructure and the political instability in Africa, could be placed under the rubric of one major historical phenomenon: neocolonialism. Many political and academic figures define Africa's problems as a result of centuries of exploitation. Particular emphasis is placed on foreign influence in the areas of politics, economics, and culture. Related theses also hold that modern African nation-states remain under the control of imperial powers, leading to economic and political systems that are directed from outside the continent.

Kwame Nkrumah (1909–1972) coined the term neocolonialism, or "new colonialism," which describes the features of the continued exploitation of colonies after independence has been achieved. Nkrumah was born in Nkroful in the British colony of the Gold Coast (now Ghana) and studied in local schools prior to obtaining his college degree in 1939 from Lincoln University, Pennsylvania. A leading exponent of the intellectual ideas of African nationalism and Pan-African unity, he rose to become the first president of the independent Republic of Ghana. The foundational politics of Pan-Africanism, as propagated by historical actors of African descent such as Henry Sylvester Williams, Marcus Garvey, and W.E.B. DuBois, among others, sought to connect the experience of Africans in the diaspora who emerged from slavery with that of Africans who lived under the political control of European colonialism.

Nkrumah's political philosophy aimed at finding solutions to the lack of individual and institutional access to social, political, and economic power in Africa following colonialism. He not only helped popularize the theory of neocolonialism, but he provided the intellectual temperament and organizational audacity that enabled the idea to advance beyond the evangelical and literary sphere and produce an embryonic movement which, in the long term, assumed worldwide significance. Nkrumah achieved similar success in representing the frustrations of African leaders as well as former colonial subjects who found it nearly impossible to shed the yoke and burden of imperial relationships. Although the Nkrumah-led movement was based on the idea of the common cultural and political objectives of people of color, Nkrumah always approached African-related international economic issues in light of the exploitation and abuses within the colonies. As with other modern African leaders, his ideas began as mere yearnings for social, political, and economic reform to be granted by European colonialist powers and evolved into an outright call for self-government for Africans.

Postcolonial theorists have expanded on the notion of imperialism after empire with an awareness that the end of empire has not signaled the opening of a new stage in the development of the Third World. Political independence brought neither an end to economic problems nor an end to economic dependency. On the contrary, some of the new states became more involved in and dependent on the Western-dominated world system than they had been under colonial rule. The ideas of "neocolonialism" and "dependency" were introduced to explain this new situation. They represented the imposition of the metropolitan powers' dominant cultural values through effective technological, bureaucratic, and moralizing avenues.

By the late 1950s, it had become clear to the surviving empires that formal colonialism had to be brought to an end. Only Portugal continued to resist this, since Portugal's politically isolated and marginalized metropolitan economy could not afford to put an end to formal colonialism. The Portuguese government needed to exploit its African resources, and since its economy was not competitive, it could do so only through direct control. The British and French, on the other hand, saw a great need to modernize the relationship between themselves and their colonies and to bring that relationship into line with the requirements of the new, multinational capitalism. According to Nkrumah, the neocolonial stage was the most dangerous and worst form of imperialism. He attributed this phenomenon to the fact that, for those who operated it, the new order meant power without responsibility. Those who suffered from it, the former colonies, would now experience exploitation without visible means of redress.

In a neocolonial context, the state is, in theory, independent and has all the outward trappings of international sovereignty. In reality, however, its economic system, and thus its political policy, is directed from outside. The practice of neocolonialism features foreign capital being used for exploitative rather than beneficial purposes in the less developed parts of the world. Investment under neocolonialism increases rather than decreases the gap between the rich and the poor nations. The system is often based on dividing large colonial territories into a number of small, nonviable states that are incapable of independent development and must rely upon the former imperial power for defense and even internal security. The economic and financial systems of the former colonies are linked, as in colonial days, with those of the former colonial ruler.

In neocolonialist territories, where the former colonial power is assumed to have relinquished political control, if the social conditions occasioned by neocolonialism cause a revolt, the local government can be sacrificed and another equally subservient one substituted for it. Since states are dependent upon each other, a revolt in a neocolonial state is often accompanied by threats to other underdeveloped nations who may have the potential to challenge the unequal relationship. Hence, the same social pressures which can produce revolts in neocolonial territories will also affect those states which have refused to accept the system. The imperial powers have a ready-made weapon for continual dominance.

European-African Relationship in a Colonial Context

The relationship between European and African coastal merchants began through the trade in and barter of agricultural products and mineral resources. In most cases, the relationship was facilitated by extended credit in cash or kind. The relationship was altered by the slave trade, a development which removed all equal dimensions of the economic situation and laid the foundation for new social and political dynamics between the West and Africa. Under the influence of Enlightenment tradition and later Victorian liberal developmental ideas, European Christian missionaries and officials introduced educational policies and the production of cash crops mainly for export purposes. They also promised improved welfare and Christian citizenship for African adherents to Christianity. The unbalanced credit relations between most Western traders and their African counterparts continued under colonial rule, with European merchants advancing money to African buyers who scoured the countryside making advances to African producers. With the consolidation of colonial rule in the late nineteenth and early twentieth centuries, the sense of partnership between European and African missionaries and traders gave way to policies geared toward maximizing the benefits of the colonial power under newly fashioned political and economic structures. African protest movements and the support of European humanitarian groups combined to help launch modern African nationalist and anticolonial movements.

Anticolonial activities reached their peak in the postwar era, while postwar colonial reforms were marked by the launching of new developmental regulations that upheld earlier policies of inequality. In spite of these limitations, the economic and political intelligentsia that emerged from the European-African encounter still expressed faith in the liberal projects of building nation-states and embracing modernization. Thus, decolonization reforms as configured by European powers and postwar African leaders did not focus on realigning the unequal economic relationship between Africa and the West. Rather, under the auspices of

Cold War political and economic policies, Africa was considered a potential "partner" and sphere of influence in the battle between Eastern and Western Europe. Nevertheless, several postcolonial African leaders, including Kwame Nkrumah, highlighted not only the contradictions but also the potential value of colonial economic, educational, and social welfare programs.

Imperialism by Other Means: Politics, Economics, Education

There are conflicting perspectives on the reasons for the enduring problem of neocolonialism on the continent of Africa. One school of thought highlights the complex and multivalent traditional African political structures as the most important deterrent to a viable postcolonial existence. Such scholars have emphasized how African politicians and cultural groups have exploited the transitional and unstable political atmosphere in Africa for parochial and ill-defined economic goals. Another school of thought argues that the combined implications of the slave trade and colonialism helped impose the stigma of inferiority on the African continent and its people from the fifteenth century onwards. Two fundamental factors also contributed to the way in which Africa and Africans were perceived and defined. First, the mechanism of colonial racism constructed the identity of European peoples in a dialectical opposition to African natives.[1] Secondly, the construction and nurturing of the notion of an absolute racial difference became, by extension, the essential ground for the conception of a homogenous national identity.[2] Theorists of colonialism argue that modern European nationalism is still very much influenced by the legacy of colonial racism and social Darwinism. For Etienne Balibar, the construction of a people is facilitated by the eclipse of internal differences through the representation of the whole population by a hegemonic group, race, or class. The representative group is the active agent that stands behind the effectiveness of the concept of nation. Hence, the ideas of nation, people, and race are never far removed.[3] It is also argued that the introduction of Christianity was Janus-faced, since, on the one hand, mission activities helped introduce Western education and liberal political and economic principles and, on the other hand, they undermined the legitimacy and relevance of traditional civil society. These developments compounded the desire to perfect the evolution of modern constitutions, a factor which has often been accompanied by social and economic revolution.

Postcolonial political and economic theorists agree, however, that the end of formal colonialism did not mark the end of imperial influence. They argue that

1. Michael Hardt and Antonio Negri, *Empire* (Cambridge, MA: Harvard University Press, 2000), p. 103.

2. For example, see Robert Young, *Colonial Desire: Hybridity in Theory, Culture and Race* (London: Routledge, 1995).

3. See Etienne Balibar, "Racism and Nationalism," in *Race, Nation, Class*, ed., Etienne Balibar and Immanuel Wallerstein (London: Verso, 1991), 37–67, cited in Michael Hardt and Antonio Negri, *Empire*, 103.

the problems associated with empire and economic dependency continued after many African countries obtained their political independence.

The Ideas of Kwame Nkrumah

In 1957, Ghana became the first nation in black Africa to obtain its independence. This achievement became a source of inspiration not only for people of African descent, but also for nations around the world which still bore the burden of imperialism. In spite of the country's new political status, the rulers of Ghana and the rest of the continent soon came to realize that, even though they had regained sovereignty, in many ways it was a Pyrrhic victory. With the attainment of independence from formal colonialism, most African intellectuals and political leaders desired Western technology and progress at all costs. Yet many also came to recognize the complexities of independence. In addition to Kwame Nkrumah, leaders like Nnamdi Azikiwe and Obafemi Awolowo of Nigeria, Sékou Touré of Guinea, Jomo Kenyatta of Kenya, and Julius Nyerere of Tanzania all welcomed Western innovations but saw the need for psychological and cultural emancipation from Europe. Some of these individuals emphasized the importance of reaffirming traditional African civilization, which they claimed had been eroded under the influence of colonialism. Most of the postcolonial leadership class, however, eventually succumbed to the pressures initiated from within by the masses who had been promised the benefits of a self-governing society and from without by former imperial overlords who clamored for the retention of old economic relationships. In this laid the major attributes of a neocolonial state.

In his influential book, *Neo-colonialism: The Last Stage of Imperialism* (1965), Kwame Nkrumah echoed the Russian political theorist Vladimir Lenin, who had described imperialism as "the highest stage of capitalism." Nkrumah identified neocolonialism as the final and most severe form of imperialism. He argued that the practitioners of neocolonialism wielded power without responsibility, while those who suffered from exploitation had no potential avenue for redress. In the days of old-fashioned colonialism, Nkrumah continued, the imperial power had to justify at home the actions it was taking abroad. In addition, within the colonies, those who served the ruling imperial power could at least look to the metropolitan power for protection against any violent moves by their opponents. In the days of neocolonialism, neither was the case.[4]

Most modern African countries, like other underdeveloped countries, continue to suffer from lack of development in three major spheres: (1) heavy industry and secondary industry, (2) infrastructure for such industries as transport, power, and communications, and (3) projects geared toward improving the welfare of the masses, including social services, health, education, and other necessities for modern living. The lack of well-tooled manpower and economic viability has also inhibited sustainable African development. Many African states remain unable to either conquer the forces of nature, which inhibit health and transporta-

---

4. Kwame Nkrumah, *Neo-colonialism: The Last Stage of Imperialism* (London: Nelson, 1965), xi.

**Figure 24.1. Patrice Lumumba, right, under arrest in the Congo, 1961.
Lumumba was one of the earliest victims of neocolonialism.**

tion improvements, or to tap or manipulate some of those forces in pursuance of social and economic development. The lack of a large-scale indigenous entrepreneurial class with access to credit, the shortage of capital, and the lack of technical know-how have forced African governments to turn to the former colonial powers, or to the developed world in general, for the skills and capital required to fill the material and fiscal void. The dilemma involved with inviting foreign investors into African countries is heightened by the fact that, since the economic sector is largely state controlled, the financing of public corporations and enterprise through foreign capital obtained as loans and grants results in neocolonial control. Although the economic power of the indigenous government could be consolidated through such devices as excise duties and taxes or the joint participation of public funds and foreign capital in a particular enterprise, the postwar bipolarization of global economic and political issues placed African leaders in a quagmire with regard to modernization and development. If a government welcomed foreign investors it was generally considered "pro-West," while the degree to which it objected to this external source of funding signified its "leftist" or even "communist" leanings. Many postcolonial African leaders understood that since there was little private indigenous capital available for investment, their governments had no choice but to accept partnership with foreign entrepreneurs.

Neocolonial theorists have argued that, under the guise of providing "aid" for development in the former colonies, the former colonial powers often achieved their old imperial objectives through new means. Kwame Nkrumah highlighted Latin America, Asia, the Caribbean, and Africa as sites where the flag of imperialism and the colonial presence were dispensed with but replaced by other methods of ascendancy. He argued that Western intelligence agencies not only helped to theorize and actualize neocolonialism, but they also helped to continually undermine the self-determination of "satellite states," or former colonial territories. Nkrumah also highlighted other methods by which neocolonialists often "slipped" past the guard of their former territories, giving the departing colonialists privileges that infringed on the colonized state's sovereignty. Examples included the establishment of military bases, the stationing of troops, and the supply of "advisers." Some also included requests for a number of "rights" to be granted to the imperial power by the new indigenous administrators, including land or maritime concessions, prospecting rights for minerals and or oil, and the rights to collect customs, perform administrative tasks, issue currencies, and be exempted from customs duties and/or taxes for expatriate enterprises. Above all, the prerogative of disbursing financial "aid" or loans has often been in the hands of the erstwhile colonialists. The loans were to be paid back at huge rates of interest. Some former colonial powers have demanded and been granted privileges in the arena of cultural engagement and the supply of informational or educational tools, which retain the connection to or reliance on the former colonial overlord. Former colonial powers have also tried to retain influence to the exclusion of rival powers.

Nkrumah believed that the postwar years marked—for the first time in human history—an era in which the potential material resources of the world were so great that there was hardly a basis for the large gap between the rich and poor nations. The major deficiency, he stressed, was the lack of any means to direct resources to the needy. He saw the solution to this problem in the provision of an effective means to force the redeployment of available resources. Nkrumah linked Africa's failure to make headway in purposeful industrial development to the fact that the continent's natural resources were being used for the greater development of the Western world. As a deterrent to the exploitation of Africa's resources, he called for a union government on a Pan-African level. Nkrumah scorned civil rights movements based on appeals and moralizing arguments, claiming that only "deeds" could secure world realignment. Nkrumah highlighted the need for "positive action," concluding that the failure to embark on such action could eventually culminate in a Third World War.

While other theorists on the colonial experience and Africa's undesirable economic and political condition, such as Frantz Fanon, Amilcar Cabral, and Samora Machel, advocated armed revolution as one of the most feasible solutions, Nkrumah believed that physical conflict would emerge only when progressive reforms were not enacted. He often couched his philosophy in utopian terms, emphasizing that the methods of neocolonialism were subtle and varied, and thus could only be countered by an African continent that was politically and economically united. When this occurred, he continued, those who monopolized economic resources that should have been utilized for the advancement of the poor would not only be forced to face a formidable partner in Africa, but also to face the working class in the metropolitan territories. Nkrumah believed that it was only out of such an experience that a new struggle could arise to complete the imperialism's liquidation. He thus called for a union government on a Pan-African level as the solution to Africa's exploitation.

Nkrumah and his followers argued that two principles inspired the launching of early capitalism: the subjugation of the working classes and the exclusion of the state from having any voice in the control of capitalist enterprise. The twentieth-century capitalist phenomenon, however, was characterized by the abandonment of these two principles and their replacement with the "welfare state" system. In the new order, the former colonial powers led a revolution aimed at the provision of higher working-class living standards within state-regulated capitalism at home. With the potential of social revolt tempered at home, Nkrumah stated, the developed countries—especially the former colonial powers—succeeded in exporting their internal problems and transferring the conflict between rich and poor from the national to the international stage. Nkrumah was very critical of foreign companies operating in Africa with the sole mission of exploiting mineral resources and paying little or no attention to the welfare of the African working-class population. He also indicted the Labour Party in Britain for failing to live up to its reputation as the friend of the underclass in local and global contexts. Through the activities of the social democratic parties of Europe led by the British Labour Party and various intercontinental trade unions, European interests perpetuated international monopolies in Africa, Asia, and Latin America.

Nkrumah condemned what he described as "Western propaganda" such as is often nurtured by Hollywood. He also saw elements of neocolonialism in the evolution of modern popular culture and its consumption both in the Western world and in Africa. The example of Africans who would cheer when their movie heroes slaughtered "Red Indians," Asians, or those who were oppressed in the global political and economic equation was identified by Nkrumah as evidence of the success of Western propaganda. By extension, he also condemned the fact that in antisocialist propaganda, members of trade unions, revolutionary politicians, or individuals with dark skins were often cast as the villains, while the white policeman or the Federal Agent was always the hero. Nkrumah stressed that this phenomenon was the ideological underbelly of political murders, which so often used local people as their instruments. The monopoly of the press, newspapers, and magazines through foreign correspondents exhibited the influence of imperial states over international capitalist journalism. Nkrumah indicted the radio and the Peace Corps, the United States Information Agency, and Moral Re-Armament as part of the plans to ideologically invade the so-called Third World. Nkrumah also indicted modern religious evangelism, which often inculcated anti-citizenship characteristics in colonized indigenous communities, stating that the policy of divide and rule perpetuated neocolonialism.

Nigerian nationalist Obafemi Awolowo provided a perspective similar to Nkrumah's on the neocolonial characteristics of the relationship between the West and Africa. In a lecture titled "Imperialist Agents in Dependent Countries," he argued that foreign power had to be removed before a country could be truly independent. Awolowo identified four "agencies" of imperialist aggression and domination:the political agencies made up of legislative, executive, and judicial officials, the economic agencies consisting of trading, industrial, and commercial classes, the "cultural and spiritual agencies" of education and religion, and the military.[5] Both Kwame Nkrumah and Obafemi Awolowo represented examples of postwar at-

---

5. Saheed A. Adejumobi, *Life More Abundant: Colonial Transition, the Yoruba Intelligentsia and the Politics of Social Welfare Reform in Nigeria, 1940–1970* (Ph.D. Thesis, The University of Texas at Austin, 2001), 340.

tempts by African leaders to forge an alternative mode of political and economic relationship between the former colonies and their erstwhile overlords.

Neocolonialism in Practice

Towards the end of the 1960s, Africanist historians sought to move away from excessive concentration on the political aspects of both the precolonial and the colonial African past. They felt that all the various facets of Africa's past had to be researched rigorously if the discipline was to attain true maturity. There was a particularly urgent need for research in the area of economic history. This perception came at a time when underdevelopment theory was being popularized in areas beyond its place of origin in South America.[6] African economic history, therefore, came to be studied in the context of the underdevelopment of the continent, and this approach was posed as an alternative to the notion of African political agency hitherto dominant in postcolonial African historiography. In *How Europe Underdeveloped Africa,* Walter Rodney argued that Africans lost their initiative for home-bred economic production and development with the onslaught of colonialism, and that the attempt to regain it would only come with independence. African responses in the colonial era, albeit vigorous, "were simply responses to the options laid down by the colonialists." True historical initiative by a people or by individuals required that they have the power to decide on the direction in which they want to move. In Africa, this would have to await the 1960s.[7]

The term neocolonialism continues to assume significance in light of all the former colonists' methods of control. It signifies the inability of the so-called Third World nations to develop an independent economic and political identity under the pressures of globalization. During the Cold War, the Soviet Union was seen as just as much a neocolonial power as the United States. Aid and development programs enacted during that era were almost always granted with strings attached. More recently, the term neocolonialism has been used to represent the role of the new powers of the "North," especially in the United States, whose colonial past has been replaced by its neocolonialist role in establishing a global capitalist economy over the "South."

Postcolonial scholars argue that the unequal relationship between advanced industrial nations and developing countries has continued beyond the period of traditional colonialism. Much of the analysis of the social, economic, and educational development of the "Third World" has ignored this basic aspect of the situation. Other scholars have stressed that Africa's cultural elite, many of whom live comfortably, like expatriates in First World conditions, continue to contribute to the solidification of neocolonial global relationships. Critics accuse some of these expatriate intellectuals of deconstructing the language needed to articulate modern demands geared toward countering "Northern" hegemony because of their apathy. In this regard, some scholars have reanimated ideas linking the poor so-

---

6. Arnold Temu and Bonaventure Swai, *Historians and Africanist History: A Critique* (London: Zed Press, 1981), 75.

7. Walter Rodney, *How Europe Underdeveloped Africa* (Washington D. C.: Howard University Press, 1974), 243.

cial and economic conditions of Africans to the experiences of other, various underclasses, or "subaltern" communities, which are found in urban centers around the world. Many such communities are defined by the way in which they suffer under the weight of material reconfigurations in the global economy.

Within the context of a new, liberal, revolutionary order globalized by Western financial analysts and advisers, parallels are also often drawn between the moralizing sermon of the need to adopt universal liberal democratic values and the attainment of true citizenship rights and sustainable economic development. Institutions such as the elite Bretton Woods and Paris Club often promote the fiscal values guided and operated by bureaucrats wielding externally sanctioned economic models as the solutions to the pressing need for a social welfare policy that caters to the needs of the citizenry of developing nations.[8] Such institutions, in recommending the privatization of failed state enterprises, have advised liberalizing economies to imbibe the lessons and values of the corporate world in order to find solutions to social problems. Today, the large transnational corporations have, in many cases, surpassed the jurisdiction and authority of nation-states. Nigeria, like many other African countries, faces the Bretton Woods-induced shock therapy package of price liberalization, stabilization, and privatization which aims to reform the postcolonial economic enterprises by the fastest means possible, regardless of its negative impact on the citizenry.

This new, liberal economic world order, which has the responsibility of addressing balance-of-payment problems, producing long-term international investments, and maintaining exchange stability, has launched a series of purely economic interventions that have undermined local African institutional frameworks of economic decision making. The Bretton Woods solutions often separate economic conditions from political and cultural conditions. The lack of a national consensus on the part of the African elite makes the process of privatization and liberalization a testy political affair. Marginalized groups often prefer the sale of state and private enterprises to foreign multinationals rather than to a privileged indigenous elite. As a result, the welfare of the citizens often remains in the hands of a foreign-oriented, primarily profit-driven enterprise. Frantz Fanon described the African national bourgeoisie as an appendage of multinational capital, a parasite feeding on its own people, mimicking the West rather than seeking its own innovative road. A few African elites attempted to find an alternative route towards sustainable growth but were either stifled by domestic and international forces or by overreaching or ambitious projects. Kwame Nkrumah articulated the need for strong industrial development to break the vicious cycle of poverty in Africa. The Cold War enabled Ghana to secure financial aid from the West for some of its major economic projects, but this was accompanied by a demand to curb Nkrumah's influence. In Nigeria, for a fleeting moment in history, the postwar Yoruba leadership realized that the culture upon which enterprise largely depends cannot rise and attain great success unless the people are in command of sufficient capital to allow them leisure, security, and command over nature. In Tanzania, attempts to mobilize mass support for self-reorganization were mocked by other African governments as utopian and were stifled in the end by

---

8. Adeleke Adeseri, "Senior Civil Servants to Undergo Training in Private Sector," *The Guardian Online*, http://www.ngrguardiannews.com/, Sunday, May 28, 2000.

the workings of global trade agreements. In a unipolar world devoid of the Cold War scenario in which West fought East for the terms of economic and cultural African nationalism, previously tepid liberal rallies for African rights were fully undermined.[9]

In addition to Kwame Nkrumah, scholars such as W.E.B. DuBois, Walter Rodney, C.L.R. James, Samir Amin, Eric Williams, and Obafemi Awolowo expounded the thesis of political and economic neocolonialism. Others, including Cheik Anta Diop, V. Y. Mudimbe, and Ngugi wa Thiongo, to name only a few, have also identified intellectual neocolonialism as a method by which African thought and intellectual practices were made dependent upon Western analytical and practical norms. The above named intellectuals/activists have often questioned the direction of African studies in many institutions. They claim that "facts" relating to the study of Africa were often "invented" and were also usually dehumanizing. The common thread among such theories is the argument that modern African states in their current form cannot finance governments capable of sustainable development.

While most Pan-African scholars have described African political and economic unity as the most important requirement for the restoration of growth and dignity to the continent, local ruling classes must be urged further to redefine the constitutions setting forth the meaning of political and social citizenship in Africa. Political systems must help inculcate a more sympathetic attitude toward the market system, rather than one in which the system marginalizes citizens lacking direct access to the seats of power. There is also a need to create a new incentive structure, as traditional social welfare systems are becoming overburdened and, in many cases, being abandoned. The postcolonial state remains over centralized; the need for the devolution of power and new political constitutions is urgent. The effects of international non-governmental organizations (NGOs) on health and social welfare issues are limited in Africa, as major political and economic limitations have, in many instances, been placed on the relationship between individual initiatives and the state's ability to provide social goods. According to historian Ebere Nwaubani, neocolonialism, more than colonialism, is a collaborative arrangement between the former European colonial rulers and the indigenous political elite. Thus, to function at all, neocolonialism requires flexible local mediators.[10] Its influence can, therefore, be undermined through the improvement of the relationship between African governments and their citizenry. Solutions can also be found in mediating forces, such as public opinion and the media, tools which can educate the public about issues so that citizens can exert direct pressure, not only upon the corporate forces operating in their societies, but also upon their local governments. Only if these measures are taken can there emerge a modern African state capable of actualizing mutual state and citizen obligations and reducing the need for dependence on international NGOs and monetary institutions.

---

9. See Gerald Horne, "Who Lost the Cold War? Africans and African Americans," *Diplomatic History, The Journal of the Society of American Foreign Relations* 20, 4 (1996).

10. Ebere Nwaubani, *The United States and Decolonization in West Africa, 1950–1960* (Rochester, NY: University of Rochester Press, 2001), 242.

Review Questions

1. Define neocolonialism. How is the theory relevant to modern African history?
2. Suggest methods by which African states can become truly independent.
3. Compare and contrast the experiences of postcolonial Africa with those of any other continent in the world.

Additional Reading

Falola, Toyin, ed. *Britain and Nigeria: Exploitation or Development?* London: Atlantic Highlands, 1987.

Hardt, Michael and Antonio Negri. *Empire.* Cambridge, MA: Harvard University Press, 2000.

Nkrumah, Kwame. *Neo-colonialism: The Last Stage of Imperialism.* London: Nelson, 1965.

Nwaubani, Ebere. *The United States and Decolonization in West Africa, 1950–1960.* Rochester, NY: University of Rochester Press, 2001.

Pomeroy, W. J. *American Neo-colonialism: Its Emergence in the Philippines and Asia.* New York: International Publishers, 1970.

Rodney, W. *How Europe Underdeveloped Africa.* Washington DC: Howard University Press, 1974.

Saini, M. K. *Politics of Multinationals: A Pattern in Neo-colonialism.* New Delhi: Gitanjali Prakashan, 1981.

Woddis, J. *Introduction to Neocolonialism.* New York: International Publishers, 1967.

Chapter 25

Africa and Europe: Anatomy of a Colonial Relationship

Ebere Nwaubani

We depend on France, through the strong historical ties between them and us—that is, since the colonial era. But even more important is the fact that we depend on [France] because of the political links between us.... French-speaking African countries are like little regions of France. And this is the reality.... We get our clothes from France, our food from France, our language from there! We are not now speaking in an African language. We are speaking the language of others, which also means that our thinking and thought processes are conditioned by them.[1]

This chapter is intended to assess Africa's relationship with Europe in the context of the thematic concerns of this volume, that is, colonialism, national-ism, and decolonization. At a basic level, colonialism involves the loss of sover-eignty by the colonized state. Political control paves the way for the imposition and penetration of aspects of the social, economic, and cultural norms of the col-onizing society. Consequently, colonialism resulted in the reordering of the colo-nized society as a caricature of the colonizer. There is, of course, great merit in arguing that at a more fundamental level, European rule saw to the integration of Africa into the Western world system. An assessment along these lines calls for a study of the more obvious institutions that have mediated relations be-tween Africa and Europe. The colonial administration itself must feature promi-nently in any such analysis, but so must its supportive structures—notably, the colonial economy, the church, the school, and even the physical infrastructure. These introductory remarks map out the contours of this chapter. Inevitably, I will touch on some of the major narratives and issues addressed in preceding chapters.

* * *

---

1. Thomas Sankara (late president of Burkina Faso) in an interview with *The Guardian* (Lagos), Sunday, March 24, 1985.

Before the Colonial Period

In discussing Africa's relationship with Europe, one would be mistaken to begin with the period of colonial rule. On account of their geographic proximity, North Africa and Europe have been in contact from antiquity. For sub-Saharan Africa, direct contact with Europe dates from the fifteenth century, when the Portuguese came to trade. The resulting relationship was not, for quite a while, asymmetrical in nature. For example, until the 1870s, the coastal West African traders in palm oil were able to impose their own commercial conventions on their British trading partners.[2] This leverage was possible because the terms of exchange favored West Africa in the period from about 1680 to 1870.[3] It is significant that the onset of the unfavorable terms of trade coincided with the beginning of the European Scramble for Africa.

The intervening period, from the arrival of the Portuguese in the mid-fifteenth century to 1870, prefigured the colonial period—whether one thinks in terms of the unequal development of capitalism or of its corollary, the integration of Africa into the Western-dominated world economic system. As an example of the unequal development of capitalism occasioned by the Atlantic slave trade, one can draw on the Asante experience. Asante gold was the basis of Asante trade, first with the Western Sudan, and from the mid-fifteenth century, with the Portuguese. Those Asante who became prosperous in the gold trade invested in agriculture and manufacturing. The economic activities thus generated gave rise to population growth, urbanization, and expansion in intra-regional trade. The picture changed dramatically in the mid-seventeenth century, when the Asante shifted to exporting slaves: there was widespread de-urbanization, depopulation, collapse of manufacturing, and decline of agricultural output, all of which had adverse impacts on intra-regional trade.[4]

If Asante furnishes an example of how the Atlantic slave trade retarded the development of capitalism, Kongo is a good example of how the trade initiated the European political, economic, and cultural domination of Africa. The Portuguese were influential in the Congo basin, where they were actively involved in the slave trade and slavery. Afonso Mbemba Nzinga, who usurped the kingship of Kongo in 1506, was deeply committed to Christianity and adopted Portuguese dress, titles, and etiquette. The capital city was renamed São Salvador.[5] In emphasizing the impact of the Atlantic trade, I am drawing attention to the fact that the colonial era was not an entirely new phase in African history: it merely accentuated preexisting processes in the relationship between Africans and Europeans. I now turn to examine the major features of that relationship, especially during the colonial period.

---

2. Martin Lynn, *Commerce and Economic Change in West Africa: The Palm Oil Trade in the Nineteenth Century*, Cambridge University Press, 1997.

3. D. Eltis and L. C. Jennings, "Trade between Western Africa and the Atlantic World in the Pre-colonial Era," *American Historical Review*, 93 (1988): 936–959.

4. R. A. Kea, *Settlements, Trade, and Politics in the Seventeenth-Century Gold Coast* (Baltimore, MD: Johns Hopkins University Press, 1982).

5. John Iliffe, *Africans: The History of a Continent* (Cambridge: Cambridge University Press, 1995), 130, 141.

The Colonial Period

A New Political Culture

Colonialism determined the political geography of contemporary Africa, in the sense that it introduced Western-type nation-states and political boundaries. The Europeans carved up Africa, drawing arbitrary lines that, in some cases, put members of the same kinship unit in separate colonial territories. In other cases, diverse and sometimes hostile peoples were lumped together in the same territory. This also means that from a political economy perspective, colonialism bestowed on Africa a dis-enabling framework of fragmented national economies (ministates such as Togo, Benin, The Gambia, Burundi, and Rwanda) that are too small to achieve economies of scale or specialization.

The new territories created by the Europeans, along with their designations, were, in general, entirely new creations. Nonetheless, from the era of the Scramble and the Partition, the colonial territories, which were later to become the modern African states, evolved as well-defined spaces for state actions. Even the missionaries and traders operated within these spaces. On the other hand, Africans did not initially accept that their fates were inextricably linked with the colonial "states" in which they found themselves. The Westernized African intellectual and political elite started by defining their political identity in pan-African terms. The formation of the National Congress of British West Africa in March 1920 symbolized a shift to a regional identity, but not the end of Pan-African loyalties. By the early 1930s, the National Congress and the Pan-African conferences were dead; territorially based political organizations were becoming more important. It was in the 1940s, when the colonial powers began making political concessions in the context of the territories they had created, that the elite finally accepted that their fate and future were tied to their respective colonial territories. By and large, independence occurred within the context of the individual territories, which meant that Africans inherited the colonial creations. This is not to say that even today, Africans readily identify with this colonial inheritance. The roots of African states are still too shallow and too fragile to command automatic loyalty. For many, the primary point of loyalty is still the ethnic group.

It has been argued that in the process of creating new territories, the colonialists also created "tribes," a word beloved by Westerners when talking about African ethnic groups.[6] Without doubt, ethnic groups — each as a distinct cultural group, and therefore with a cultural core (including a common language with dialectical variations, similar belief systems, and similar ethnographic practices) — antedated colonialism. However, the sense of shared identity and interest that define an ethnic group was often absent or fluid in the precolonial period. Christian missionaries played a pivotal role in the evolution of the contemporary expression of ethnic consciousness. More often than not, the missionaries were the first to codify African languages, initially, by translating the Bible, the prayer books, and the hymn books into African languages. A "vernacular" literature gradually emerged, a process that also standardized a common language (in place of dialects

---

6. See L. Vail, ed., *The Creation of Tribalism in Southern Africa* (Berkeley: University of California Press, 1991).

of varying degrees of mutual intelligibility) and fostered common cultural characteristics. The overall result, facilitated by expanding access to Western literacy, was that ethnicities which had been fluid and orally soft soon acquired "hard" identities.[7]

In a different way, the colonial administrations also helped reshape social (ethnic) identities. "Tribe" was the cornerstone of colonial hegemony. The British, for example, operated on the premise that Africans lived in "tribes" (which made for relative cultural homogeneity) and that these should constitute the basis for local administration. This premise informed the "native administration" (the territorial unit of indirect rule) system. With regard to other colonial powers, there were numerous instances in which, for administrative convenience, communities were divided or amalgamated. In these ways, the colonial rulers created, in many cases, entirely new sociocultural units with which the people gradually came to identify themselves. It is in this sense that some scholars claim that colonialism created "tribes" in Africa.

Ethnicity is a different matter altogether. Ethnicity does not refer to the affinity individuals feel for those from their own ethnic group; it refers to relationships between peoples from different ethnic groups. Ethnicity, in this sense, is also the creation of colonialism. To begin with, each of the colonial territories bunched together ethnic groups and peoples who scarcely had any common political relationship. "The foundations of ethnicity," Colin Leys has argued,

> were laid when the various traditional modes and relations of production began to be displaced by capitalist ones, giving rise to new forms of insecurity, and obliging people [from different ethnic backgrounds] to compete with each other [for the first time] on a national plane for work, land, and ultimately for education and other services seen as necessary for security.

This competition was occurring in a new (colonial) environment. Thus ethnicity has to do with "the fact that people identify other exploited people [those from other/more favored ethnic groups] as the source of their insecurity and frustrations, rather than their common exploiters," the imperialists.[8] Simply put, ethnicity was, in its origins, a system of scapegoating that kept oppressed groups (the colonized) from recognizing who (the colonizer), in fact, held power over them.

Colonial rule operated with African collaborators of all sorts. As a general principle, the Europeans had to rule through African intermediaries, generically known as "chiefs." The British system in this regard is known as "indirect rule." It is generally held that indirect rule was in a class of its own as a system of local administration, precisely because the chiefs in British territories actually ruled at the local level. The fact, however, is that any colonial authority is, by definition, an autocracy. By its very nature, autocracy cannot tolerate any authority outside itself and cannot allow any such authority to acquire the autonomy that a more democratic system would accept. For this reason, the chiefs—even in British territories—lost their sovereignty and independence of action as they became mere

---

7. On this, see Adrian Hastings, *The Construction of Nationhood: Ethnicity, Religion and Nationalism* (Cambridge: Cambridge University Press, 1997), 148–166.

8. Colin Leys, *Underdevelopment in Kenya: The Political Economy of Neo-colonialism, 1964–1971* (Heinemann Educational Books, 1975), 199, 252.

adjuncts, supervised, watched, and rigorously controlled by the colonial administration. More than anyone else, the chiefs themselves were well aware that if and when they deviated from expected behavior, they risked being dismissed from office. Expected behavior, of course, had to do with their job schedules: the collection of taxes, the conscription of labor, and above all, the coercion and intimidation of their peoples for the benefit of the colonial rulers. In this way, the colonial regime divorced the chiefs from their peoples.

There was a far more fundamental way in which colonial rule disrupted the organic relationship between the governed and the government. There were two broad types of political systems—acephalous and centralized—in precolonial Africa. In acephalous systems, politics was diffusionary in nature: through the kinship unit, open forums, professional units, women's organizations, age-grades, and village assemblies, the societies had viable channels for the popular expression and determination of political opinion. In centralized states, people were organically linked through the lineage, the village, and other social units to the seat of power. The result was that, in both systems, there were opportunities for the individual to feel and identify with the concreteness of power. In addition, government had a direct bearing on people's day-to-day life. Consequently, people cultivated an instinctive sense of commitment to the life and interests of the community.

By contrast, the colonial regime was distinctively alienating. First, it meant rule by foreigners. Second, with colonial officials located in the district, provincial, and central capitals, government was now distanced from the people, both physically and psychologically. Given this geographical remove, there was no dialogue between the people and the government; indeed, the government talked down to the people. "Government" became, both in practice and in concept, an impersonal, abstract, mysterious mechanism. As the government related to the people mostly through its excesses—forced labor, taxes, deportation, corporal and capital punishment, imprisonment, military action, and other forms of terror and violence—it conjured up only the negative. A sharp "them" (government) and "us" (the people) divide emerged. Consequently, the colonial regime could not generate an ethic of public service, in the sense of a public official seeing himself or herself (and being seen) as rendering service to his or her community. Instead, since one was serving a foreign regime that was removed from the people and their concerns, there was a general understanding that one need not put one's best efforts into "government" work. By the same token, public property, being "government" property, was nobody's and could therefore be used or rather misused in any way, even stolen; and if one stole or damaged "government" property, one was not looked upon with much disdain. It is no wonder that the "modern" public sector in Africa is still characterized by chronic truancy, lack of any sense of urgency and commitment, corruption, and low productivity.

Economic Changes

There are two paradigms, "market" and "underdevelopment," employed in discussing the colonial economy and its impact. The "market" approach is best illustrated by Anthony Hopkins's *Economic History of West Africa*. Hopkins traces the economic history of West Africa from precolonial times, through the trans-Saharan and Atlantic trading systems, to the establishment and development of the colonial economy. The concept of the market is the unifying theme of his study. Hopkins identifies the factors that made for changes in the size of the market. The Saharan and Atlantic trades were, he says, strong external inputs into the West African market. But the "legitimate" commerce of the nineteenth century was far more momentous as it established strong linkages between external trade and the domestic economy. Those linkages survived into the twentieth century and thus paved the way for the further structural transformation of the West African market. Hopkins stresses that this transformation stemmed from the efforts of the colonial administration, European traders and firms, and of course, Africans themselves, all operating in the colonial context.

Diametrically opposed to the market paradigm is the "development of underdevelopment" (*dependencia* or dependency) thesis which holds that the fundamental cause of Africa's "development crisis" stems from the nature of the continent's relationship with the global economic system. *Dependencia* insists that while Africa may have been *undeveloped* before the contact with the West, it only became *under*developed as a result of being locked into the Western international capitalist system. The seminal work in this regard is Walter Rodney, *How Europe Underdeveloped Africa*, first published in 1972.

To underdevelopment theorists (*dependencistas*), the world is divided into the "metropolis" or "core" (the advanced capitalist countries of North America and Western Europe) and the "satellites" or "peripheries" (Africa, the Caribbean, Latin America, the Middle East, and the "Third World" regions of Asia). Thus, rather than taking a particular country as the unit of analysis, these theorists regard national economies as integral units of an unevenly structured global capitalist system. This system, they say, is characterized by a chain of metropolis-satellite relations. This chain links the entire system, from the ultimate global metropolis (that is, the United States) via a series of intermediate units that are simultaneously metropolis and satellite (for example, African capital cities, which are both exploited by the metropolis and themselves exploiting their own hinterlands) right down to the ultimate satellite (for example, the landless rural laborer who has no one to exploit). In this setting, *surplus* is continuously expropriated from the many and appropriated by the few at all levels, from bottom to top. Consequently, "the satellites remain underdeveloped for lack of access to their own surplus."[9] In this way, the paradigm rejects the diffusionist model of international trade as an agency of economic development and argues that Western capitalism has blocked Africa's independent development.

According to *dependencistas*, the unequal and exploitative relationship between the Western capitalist countries and Africa has continued because "flag independence" did not alter the substance of the colonial relationship. Second, African countries remain highly dependent on the West for capital, technology, and markets for their products. Besides, the top public officials, being in league with Western capital, formulate public policy in a manner favorable to the West.

Dependencia has many antagonists. There is, however, much empirical evidence to substantiate it. In 1943, Franklin Roosevelt (the United States president at the time) paid a very brief visit to Bathurst (now Banjul), capital of The Gambia. He was horrified by what he saw:

---

9. A. G. Frank, *Capitalism and Underdevelopment: Historical Studies of Chile and Brazil* (New York: Monthly Review Press, 1967), 3. Also see A. G. Frank, *Capitalism and Underdevelopment in Latin America* (New York: Monthly Review Press, 1967).

It's the most horrible thing I have ever seen in my life.... With a little study, I got the point of view that for every dollar that the British, who have been there for two hundred years, have put into Gambia, they have taken out ten. It's plain exploitation of those people.

He found "no education whatsoever" and that "the agriculture there is pitiful." The "one main asset," he observed, "is peanuts, and the natives grow a lot of peanuts. How do they grow them? They have been growing them now for years, and they still use a pointed stick. Nobody ever saw a plow in Gambia. The British have not done a thing about it." Road development was no better: "The only road out of Barthust," to the airport, was built by the United States.[10]

Stephen Baier, a non-*dependencista* historian, reaches the same conclusions as the underdevelopment theorists in his *Economic History of Central Niger*, namely, that the colonial system dislocated African economies, and that it benefited the Europeans at the expense of the Africans. Baier's book clearly shows the precolonial economic dynamism of the Central Sudan (particularly, the present-day Niger Republic). This dynamism stemmed from the strong commercial links within the region, and especially from the location of the Central Sudan at the heart of the vigorous trans-Saharan trade. This geographical location enabled the region to play a lucrative intermediary role between North Africa and the West African savanna regions. Baier shows that within the first fifteen years of colonial rule (in Niger), the entire network was disjointed as the French severed the ancient links with North Africa by redirecting business to the coast. In other parts of Africa, colonialism ensured the same result: the economic unity that existed in precolonial times was shattered, with disastrous consequences for African interests.

Baier's book also shows that, by 1920, most of the large-scale African merchants of the precolonial Central Sudan were no longer active. Those still in business survived only as agents of a certain Dufour (a French army officer) or by relying on him as a source of capital. After he was discharged from the army because of his commercial activities, Dufour remained in Zinder (in Niger) and continued his business activities. Unlike the Africans, Dufour had access to vast capital, from his partners in France and European firms in Northern Nigeria. As a result of these contacts, Dufour easily dominated the commerce of Zinder from the 1920s until his retirement in 1935.

Dufour's story can be replicated in virtually any other part of Africa. It is, above all else, the story of the dominance of European entrepreneurship at the expense of the African, as the colonial system worked to the disadvantage of the latter. This European dominance of the economy had several implications. First, it meant that most of the surplus generated by the economy was repatriated to Europe, which meant that the colonial economy was unable to generate the savings essential for investment. Of course, the exported capital added to the accumulating surplus of the European countries. It was therefore no surprise that colonial Africa was very poorly served in terms of capital investment: S. H. Frankel's estimate of combined public and private overseas capital in sub-Saharan Africa in about 1936 suggests that the average per capita investment was generally under

---

10. Samuel Rosenman (compiler), *The Public Papers and Addresses of Franklin Roosevelt, Vol. 13, 1941–45* (New York: Russell and Russell, 1969), 68–69; Elliot Roosevelt, *As He Saw It* (New York: Duell, Sloan & Pearce, 1946), 75.

ten pounds sterling a head, and was, indeed, much less in many places: £4.8 in British West Africa as a whole; £2.1 in French West Africa; and £8.1 in British East Africa.[11] The European dominance of the economy, the capital flight, and the low level of investment all ensured a very low level of capital formation among Africans, and the concomitant underdevelopment of the indigenous social classes.

The mercantile system established by the Europeans was precisely that ran by Dufour: a rudimentary system of trade consisting of the assembly of raw materials, which were exported, for the most part, in their unprocessed form, and in exchange, the importation and distribution of a variety of manufactured consumer goods. By its very nature, this rudimentary export-import system meant the investment of as little capital as possible for generating optimum profit. For the Europeans, the weakness of this kind of exchange relations was compensated for by its high profit margins. On the whole, the operational philosophy of the export trade was to buy as much as possible and as cheaply as possible; that of the import trade was to sell little, but at a high price.

Except for the physical infrastructure (roads, railways, and ports) which were essential to the export-import colonial economy, colonial administrations did little to foster economic development. There was, for example, "no intention on [the] part of the [colonial] Government to cooperate in, or initiate" industrialization,[12] not even with respect to processing the cash crops which were shipped to Europe. Given this conscious determination not to promote or encourage industrialization, and given the very rudimentary nature of the merchant capitalism run by the Europeans, the production base of the colonial economy rested on the cultivation of cash crops. In more technical terms, this meant that it was only through the export of cash crops that the colonies could earn the foreign exchange (European currencies) they needed to pay for their imports (essentially, European consumer goods). As a result, the colonial administrations had every reason to emphasize cash crop production and to force the Africans into it.

In the white settler societies, notably, Algeria, Kenya, Southern Rhodesia (where the Africans hardly fared better than the blacks in apartheid South Africa), the Portuguese and Belgian colonies, and French Equatorial Africa to a lesser extent, capital was simply appropriated from the African through primitive accumulation, that is, through land alienation and forced labor. In Kenya, Africans were effectively prohibited from cultivating cash crops. For example, the 1918 Coffee Plantations Registration Ordinance required every coffee planter to buy a license, costing thirty shillings; but Africans were not even allowed to buy the license. They were equally excluded from rearing diary stock and tea cultivation.[13] In general, official policy in the white settler societies was focused on the expansion of European agricultural production and the consolidation of the position of the settlers.

In West Africa, cash crop production was in the hands of the Africans. But the colonial administration did little to qualitatively improve agricultural output.

---

11. S. Herbert Frankel, *Capital Investment in Africa: Its Course and Effects* (New York: Fertig, 1969); first published 1938.

12. Margery Perham, "Introduction," in *The Economics of a Tropical Dependency: Mining, Commerce and Finance in Nigeria*, ed., M. Perham (London: Faber and Faber, 1964), vii.

13. Regina Smith Oboler, *Women, Power, and Economic Change: The Nandi of Kenya* (Stanford, CA: Stanford University Press, 1985), 144.

Until the late 1950s, there were hardly any technical support services for the farmers. And throughout the colonial period, the technology changed very little. The colonial administration pushed up production levels through taxation, forced labor, forced cultivation of cash crops, and other coercive measures.

The single-minded concentration on cash crop production distorted African economies. For example, the French in Senegal pushed for the cultivation of peanuts, to make the colony pay its way. The focus on peanuts was, of course, at the expense of millet (the people's staple food). The result was that soon, the millet produced in a farming season was inadequate for the whole year. By the 1940s, it had become common to make up for this shortfall through the importation of millet (from other parts of Africa) and grains (notably, rice from the United States). In effect, the people of Senegal turned from producing what they consume (millet) to producing what they do not consume in any appreciable degree (peanuts). This production and consumption pattern has had an enduring impact on Senegal. In the 1960s, the surface area for the cultivation of millet averaged one-quarter that for peanuts.[14]

The French drive for an ever-increasing production of peanuts had environmental consequences: more and more land had to be brought under cultivation—trees and forests were recklessly cleared, resulting in "a steady degradation of the soil, falling productivity per acre, and the worst forms of desertification," as the land was increasingly exposed to wind erosion. Worse was the fact that peanut production did not improve the quality of life of the actual producers as they spent more on buying food than they earned from peanut cultivation; they had to borrow from the wealthy during "the hungry period each year" at exorbitant rates of interest.[15] Thus, just from the example of the French in Senegal, one sees the causal context of the distress of contemporary Africa: the fragile nature of the production base, rural poverty, environmental degradation, and food crisis, all arising from the commodification of agriculture for the European market.

Colonialism was thus paradoxical in its overall economic impact: at the same time that it expanded the base of the Africa market, it also failed, and indeed, inherently lacked the capacity, to constructively transform the societies to "create the material basis of the new world" of real capitalism, as canvassed by classical Marxism.[16] In the words of Kwame Nkrumah,

> It was when they [the colonial rulers] had gone that we were faced with the stark realities...there were slums and squalor in our towns...there was much ignorance and few skills....of industry we had none...we made not a pin, not a handkerchief, not a match.[17]

---

14. See D. B. C. O'Brien, *The Mourides of Senegal: The Political and Economic Organization of an Islamic Brotherhood* (Oxford University Press, 1971).

15. Ibid.

16. Karl Marx had hoped that British rule in India would, by unifying the country and through infrastructural development, shatter the earlier "stagnant Asiatic mode of production," thereby paving the way for the emergence of capitalism in India. See Karl Marx, "The British Rule in India," *The New York Tribune*, June 25, 1853, reprinted in E. Burns, *A Handbook of Marxism* (London, 1935), 182–187.

17. Kwame Nkrumah, *Africa Must Unite* (New York: International Publishers, 1963), xiii.

The economic system instituted in Africa by European colonial rule transformed Africa into a peripheral appendage of Western capitalism, with its attendant consequences. One consequence is an international division of labor that consignes Africa to the production of raw materials for the West (for which Africans receive inequitably low monopsonistic prices).[18] In 1980, a former chief of staff of the French Armed Forces, General Mery, gave expression to this outcome:

> Between France and this continent [Africa] there exists a unity of links established by geography and history which the complementarity of their economies, with one founded on raw materials and the other on the transformation of those raw materials serves only to reinforce.[19]

The fact that African economies are officially geared towards cash crop production means that they are so structured that they cannot function without very large imports of food, consumer goods, and machinery.[20] Colonialism also ensured the transfer of surplus value from the colonies to the metropolitan countries, a process that continued after World War II. It has been calculated that between 1945 and 1951, Britain, for example, extracted some £140 million from its colonies and put in only about £40 million under the Colonial Development and Welfare Acts.[21] Colonialism also created "dual economies," in which the "modernized" enclaves (mines, plantations, financial and industrial sectors) had—and still have—few backward or forward links with the indigenous economy. In these ways, Western imperialism ensured the total disarticulation of the inner essence and autonomous dynamism of the African economy. This disarticulation is evident in two ways: first, the commodification of African agriculture for the European market (through increased cultivation of cash crops) which steadily undermined the ability of Africans to feed themselves. Consequently, consumption became increasingly dependent on European manufactured imports as the colonial period progressed. Second is the redefinition of the essence of the African economies in a way that makes a fetish out of foreign exchange, balance of payments, terms of trade, and all the idioms of Western economic mythology. These distortions have persisted until today and explain why in 1983–1984, drought-stricken Burkina Faso, Chad, Senegal, Mali, and Niger produced a combined record harvest of 154 million metric tons of cotton and at the same time, had to rely on food imports of 1.77 million tons of cereals as well as food aid to feed themselves.[22] They also explain why, in 1980, sixty-one percent

---

18. It cost two tonnes of cocoa to buy a tractor in 1976, and twenty tonnes in 1989. See *African Guardian* (Lagos), March 20, 1990. This is a system of unequal exchange that compels Africans to work ten times as hard just to maintain the same consumption level over a ten-year period.

19. *West Africa* (London), September 15, 1980.

20. In turn, this means that African countries must continuously earn huge foreign amounts of exchange or borrow to finance their extensive import needs.

21. D. K. Fieldhouse, *Black Africa 1945–80: Economic Decolonization & Arrested Development* (London: Allen & Unwin, 1986), 6.

22. J. Giri, "Retrospective de l'Economie Sahelienne," Club du Sahel, Paris, 1984. Cited in World Commission on Environment and Development, *Our Common Future* (Oxford: Oxford University Press, 1987), 68.

of all the money loaned to Tanzanian farmers went into the cultivation of tobacco (a cash crop).[23]

Independence occurred within the unchanged framework of colonialism and therefore essentially amounted to change without change. The hegemonic structures and relationships persisted not only through the invisible linkages created by the very fact of colonialism itself, but through such explicit devices as the franc zone and the Lomé Convention.[24] Since the 1980s, the imperialistic structures and relationships have been reinforced by the World Bank and the International Monetary Fund, through their so-called structural adjustment programs. It is instructive that these programs emphasize cash crop production.

Cultural and Social Dimensions

In 1925, Carl Jung, the Swiss psychologist, visited Uganda, where he met a very elderly *laibon* (medicine man). When Jung asked him about his dreams, the old man answered with tears in his eyes, "In the old days the *laibons* had dreams, and knew whether there is war or sickness or whether rain comes and where the herds should be driven." But with the advent of the British, "no one had dreams anymore. Dreams were no longer needed because now the English knew everything!" Jung interpreted this reply to mean that the medicine man had lost his raison d'être:

> The divine voice which counseled the tribe [*sic*] was no longer needed because 'the English knew better.' Formerly the medicine man had negotiated with gods or the power of destiny, and had advised his people. He exerted great influence, just as in ancient Greece the word of the Pythia possessed the highest authority. Now the medicine man's authority was replaced by that of the D.C. [District Commissioner].

To Jung, this immense spiritual loss meant that "the value of the people's life now lay wholly in this world." Besides, Jung believed that the *laibon* "was the living embodiment of the spreading disintegration of an undermined, unrestorable world."[25] Colonial rule, especially through Christianity and Western education,

---

23. *Africa* (London), June 1985.

24. Most francophone African countries and even non-French-speaking Equatorial Guinea were members of the franc zone from 1960 until it was scrapped sometime in the 1990s. Their currencies, which looked like the French franc, could be exchanged for the latter at a fixed rate; national treasuries had to deposit a percentage of their foreign reserves in Paris (initially one hundred percent, reduced to sixty-five percent in 1981). The franc of the African countries was tied to and backed by the French, a relationship that ensured immense leverage by the Banque de France over the fiscal and economic policies of the African countries concerned.

Under the Lomé Convention, primary products imported into Western Europe enjoy preferential treatment in contrast to processed commodities which attract a variety of restrictions. A U.S. government study established that the "Lomé arrangements also provide a framework for European investment in Third World ventures which reinforces European access to Third World natural resources and markets." See Congressional Research Service, *Soviet Policy and the United States Response in the Third World*, report prepared for the Committee on Foreign Affairs, U.S. House of Representatives (Washington, DC: Government Printing Office, March 1981), 258.

25. C. G. Jung, *Memories, Dreams, Reflections*, trans. Richard and Clara Winston (New York: Pantheon Books, 1973), 265.

Figure 25.1. Colonial architecture.

Figure 25.2. House in a rural area.

eroded many aspects of African cultures, including the peoples' vision of how they fit into the cosmos.

Christianity and Western education were crucial in the configuration of new social identities. Christianity introduced into Africa new ideas about the supernatural world and new modes and rituals of worship—the church, the Bible, the sacraments. Christianity also meant the subversion of African religions: to the Christian, everything associated with African religions was irreligious and profane. Thus, all the symbols and expressions of African religions were not only condemned but also brutalized.

Christianity not only preached a new religion, it also preached a new, revolutionary ethic: the idea that life could be separated into the spiritual and the secular. This ethic was diametrically opposed to the general African social system, where the individual mattered only in relation to the community as a whole, and where life, even in its day-to-day manifestation, was a religious experience. Furthermore, by fragmenting the society into Christians and non-Christians, the new religions undermined the organic unity of African societies, a development captured in Chinua Achebe's *Things Fall Apart*: "The whiteman is very clever. He came quietly and peaceably with his religion. We were amused at his foolishness and allowed him to stay. Now he has won our brothers and our clan can no longer act like one. He has put a knife on the things that held us together and we have fallen apart."

In some cases, African Christians responded to the missionary intolerance of African cultures—and the monopolization of church leadership by Europeans—by forming their own churches. These churches, which began to emerge in the late nineteenth century, are collectively known as "Independent African Churches." In South Africa alone, their numbers increased from thirty in 1913 to 880 in 1948.[26] Except that they permitted polygny, the earliest African churches did not differ much from the orthodox Christian denominations. However, over the years, the African churches have forged their own distinct identity, through the incorporation of traditional practices such as drumming and dancing, prophet-leaders (who claim not only the ability to divine the supernatural world, but also the ability to heal), and belief in the existence of witches and similar metaphysical elements. The African churches point to the reality of Christianity in Africa today: a general pattern of adjusting new ideas to traditional practices. Many Christians today participate in traditional ceremonies of a kind and to a degree that would have been censured by many nineteenth-century missionaries. More significantly, at times of stress—such as prolonged illness, sudden death, and even unemployment—people still turn to oracles and diviners, demonstrating that the hearts of many who have formally adopted Christianity continue to harbor traditional beliefs.

Western education has proved to be the most radical and enduring of all the innovations introduced by the colonial powers. It was the most potent tool in the cultural conquest of the African. Western education was instituted as an alternative rather than as a complement to African educational practices. This ensured that, at all levels, the colonial educational system was European-oriented, whether one is talking of history, geography, music, or politics. The result was that the system produced people who knew European history, but no African his-

---

26. James W. Fernandez, "African Religious Movements," *Annual Review of Anthropology*, 7 (1978): 195.

tory; European geography, but nothing about African geography, and so on. Since whatever the schools taught had little to do with the society and culture of the African, Western education refocused Africans to a world totally different from the one into which they were born. In this sense, the schools served as mechanisms whereby the African could gain a new social place, a new culture, and therefore a new identity, which approximated that of the European colonizer. The French had the greatest success in this regard. In 1942, the U.S. State Department Intelligence Unit reported that:

> The French have consciously cultivated a native elite for use as auxiliaries in the administration of the French colonial domain. This select native group, well educated, and employed in the service of the government, is composed of the French assimilés — natives who are given French citizenship and who approach the status of equality with metropolitan Frenchmen. The special privilege and prestige given such French natives has induced them to orient their thinking and loyalties within the French rather than the native orbit.[27]

One feature of Western education during the colonial period was its very restricted nature. For example, in French West Africa, in 1947, only 12.4 percent of school-age children were attending school in Senegal, ten percent in Dahomey, five percent in Soudan (Mali), and 3.7 percent in the Ivory Coast.[28] Educational opportunities were even more limited for women: in 1934 in French West Africa, the government operated 265 village schools and thirteen urban schools, with 22,323 students who ranged between six and thirteen in age. Of this number, only 2,301 were girls. At the same time, there were seventy-five regional schools with 22,289 students of whom only 2,243 were girls.[29]

The restricted nature of Western educational facilities changed very little during the colonial period. Consequently, "the least promising aspect of the situation in about 1960," according to David Fieldhouse, "was the supply of educated and skilled people. Colonial states had been able to spend little on public education, relying heavily on mission schools." According to Fieldhouse's calculations, the average for all sub-Saharan Africa in 1960 was "36 percent of the age group in primary schools," but this varied very widely, being "under 10 percent" in poor countries such as Niger, Mauritania, and Burkina Faso. He also calculates that in Africa "as a whole only some 16 percent of adults were literate in 1960." The picture was far worse at the secondary and tertiary levels: in 1960, the average enrollment in secondary schools was "only 3 percent of the age group...Tertiary education was so rare that it produced few recorded statistics."[30]

27. Coordinator of Information, British Empire Section, Special Memorandum No. 27, "Native Manpower and Morale," 10 January 1942, in OSS/State Department Intelligence and Research Reports Part 13: Africa, 1941–61. A microfilm project of the Union of America Publications Inc., (Washington, DC., 1980), reel 1.

28. Robin Hallett, *Africa Since 1875: A Modern History* (Ann Arbor, MI: University of Michigan Press, 1974), 341.

29. Michael Crowder, *West Africa under Colonial Rule* (Evanston, IL: Northwestern University Press, 1968), 375.

30. Fieldhouse, *Black Africa*, 34.

In its origins, Western education was intended to produce the supporting staff—clerks, interpreters, and Christian evangelists—for the colonial system. Until the 1930s, a primary school education, even a basic proficiency in the three R's (reading, writing, and arithmetic), unlocked the door to a whole new world: to employment as a clerk or interpreter in the colonial administration or with a European commercial enterprise or as a schoolteacher, each of which carried a salary more substantial and more regular and a status more exalted than anything those without the benefit of Western education could ever hope to achieve. Thus in considering the impact of Western education, it is worth emphasizing that it opened the door not only to a new world of ideas, but to new tastes, aspirations, and values as well. At the same time, it created a wide array of new opportunities, thereby becoming an entirely new indicator of status, a new avenue for wealth accumulation and social mobility. In the process, a new, Westernized, social class quickly emerged.

The new class, especially its elite, was to be the medium through which Western culture was diffused to the mass of the population. This elite was also, to vary Karl Marx, the grave-diggers of colonialism, since African nationalism was essentially the turning of European ideas, instruments, and institutions against Europe. The earliest manifestations of this development are evidenced in the writings and careers of people such as Africanus Horton, George Johnson, and Edward Blyden, who made their mark in the late nineteenth and early twentieth centuries. This was the period when the Europeans were establishing their rule over Africa. In their writings, people such as Horton and Blyden tried to grapple with this tragedy and sought to reestablish the psychic and emotional security of the African. Blyden, for example, argued that races could not be regarded as superior or inferior to one another; on the contrary, each race had made its own unique contribution to universal civilization. The Negro race, Blyden argued, had been present in ancient Egypt—which he regarded as the world's first great civilization—and so could claim credit for its share in passing on to posterity "the germs of all the arts and sciences."[31] Emphasis on the cultural vitality of African peoples remained a key component of African nationalism.[32]

Reconstitution of Gender Relations

There is now a large body of literature addressing the question of how colonialism reconstructed gender relations. In 1923, Captain R. S. Rattray asked old Asante men and women why he did not know about the prominent role played by women in the political life of their society although he had been among them for so many years. The answer, Rattray wrote, was always the same:

> The white man never asked us this; you have dealings with and recognize only the men; we supposed the Europeans considered women of no account, and we know you do not recognize them as we have always done.[33]

---

31. For a good overview of Blyden's writings, see Robert W. July, "Nineteenth-Century Negritude: Edward W. Blyden," *Journal of African History* 5, 1 (1964): 73–86.

32. James S. Coleman made this point in 1954, in "Nationalism in Tropical Africa," *American Political Science Review* 48, 2 (June 1954): 409.

33. R. S. Rattray, *Ashanti* (New York: Negro University Press, 1969), 84; first published 1923.

The late nineteenth-century Europeans, it must be remembered, came from a Victorian background, which, by definition, subordinated women to men. It was against this background that they related to Africans. Consequently, colonial institutions, notably, the administration, the church, the school, the economy, the courts and the law, and the agricultural bureaucracies, had different impacts on women and men. More often than not, this led to a loss of status for the women, both as members of colonized societies and as women. For example, Elizabeth Schmidt's study of the Shona of Zimbabwe shows that the collaboration between Shona men and British colonial officials undermined the socioeconomic position of women. In the field of education, Schmidt found that the goal of missionaries was to create hardworking, virtuous Christian wives for the Shona male elite. Thus, women were not educated for employment or for economic independence; they were, instead, socialized into European housekeeping norms. Their school curriculum was rudimentary, mostly comprising of reading, writing, and arithmetic. Girls in the senior classes of primary school learned to keep house and raise children according to middle-class Western values. Much of this education, which was called "Domestic Science," took place outside the classroom. In big mission stations, the wives of the missionaries (European and African alike) took young African women into their homes to provide them with the practical training in housekeeping that would make them good Christian wives.[34]

In a number of instances women, like men, resisted the restrictions imposed on them by colonialism. One of the best-known cases is the 1929 Women's War in Eastern Nigeria. A good example of this dialectic of loss of status and constructive response is provided by the Yoruba of Nigeria. Traditionally, the Yoruba regard marriage as a union between two kinship groups, not two individuals. As a result, a Yoruba marriage embodies rituals which symbolize the unification of the two families. These include the giving of consent by both families and the payment of bridewealth. Traditionally, polygyny was the defining feature of Yoruba marriage. Husbands provided their wives with a place to live and contributed to the support of their children. Wives usually took turns cooking for their husband and also helped with his farmwork. Yoruba wives were also noted for their economic independence and high degree of mobility. It was, therefore, not uncommon to find wives who were richer than their husbands. Under normal circumstances, husbands gave their wives the initial capital to establish a business. But neither the husband nor the wife had a right to use or interfere in the management of the other's property. Husbands and wives did not even inherit from one another: the man's property passed to his children and younger siblings, while the woman's property passed to her children.[35]

Kristin Mann's study of the Yoruba Westernized elite (in late nineteenth to early twentieth-century Lagos) has revealed how Christianity altered this mar-

34. Elizabeth Schmidt, *Peasants, Traders, and Wives: Shona Women in the History of Zimbabwe, 1870–1939* (Portsmouth, NH: Heinemann, 1992).

35. Oyeronke Oyewumi, *The Invention of Women: Making an African Sense of Western Gender Discourses* (Minneapolis: University of Minnesota Press, 1998). In this study, Oyewumi revealed that among precolonial Yoruba (more precisely, Oyo Yoruba), the body (that is, the fact of being a man or woman) did not provide the basis for the organization of the social world, in terms of the roles, status, and expectations of men and women. Also see Kristin Mann, "The Dangers of Dependence: Christian Marriage among Elite Women in Lagos Colony, 1880–1915," *Journal of African History* 24 (1983): 37–56.

riage system. Many of the elite continued to regard consent and a modified form of bridewealth as vital preliminaries to Christian marriage. On the other hand, missionaries and the colonial administration insisted on monogamy as the ideal form of marriage and, along with it, the notion that marriage was a union between two individuals rather than two kinship groups. Men did not always live up to this ideal since some entered into extramarital relations, which often produced children. In addition, the missionaries socialized Yoruba Christians to subscribe to Victorian ideas which portrayed husbands as breadwinners and wives as mothers and home-makers. This meant that Victorianized Yoruba women did not work outside the home or play a part in public life. The result was that elite women became dependent on their husbands, and this placed a premium on the woman marrying a man who could support her comfortably. Another response to the changed times was that parents went to great lengths to provide Western education for their daughters:

> A thorough European education, including if possible a few years at an English boarding school, provided the best protection money could buy, because foreign-educated women were in great demand as Christian wives for elite men. A few parents worried so much about girls' marriage options that if forced to choose they sent daughters abroad for schooling instead of sons. One father maintained that his boys could succeed in trade or the colonial service with a local education, but his girls required an English education so that they could make good Christian marriages.[36]

Western education did not, however, make up for the loss of autonomy by elite women, including their economic dependence on their husbands. At the same time, the types of business which Yoruba women normally engaged in—trading or cooking and selling food—were out of the question for Victorianized women. And during the period which Mann studied, all the jobs in the colonial service were reserved for men. The women could teach, but only in the lowest grades. Given these frustrating conditions, by the beginning of the twentieth century, most elite women had begun to abandon some aspects of Christian marriage, especially those aspects that undermined their economic independence.[37]

The End of Colonial Rule

"Decolonization" and "independence" are used interchangeably as operational concepts in discussing the end of colonial rule. Some scholars, myself included, are dissatisfied with this conceptualization. To begin with, everyone now agrees that European interests remained paramount behind the façade of African rule, and therefore that independence was, in reality, a transition to neocolonialism. This agreement on the superficiality of independence informs the desire to disentangle the two concepts or processes. In this reconceptualization, "independence" is simply the transfer of political power from Europeans to Africans; "decolonization," on the other hand, is, in the words of John Darwin,

---

36. Mann, "The Dangers of Dependence," 45.
37. Ibid.

a partial retraction, redeployment and redistribution of European influences in the regions of the extra-European world whose economic, political and cultural life had previously seemed destined to flow into Western
molds.[38]

The beauty of this distinction is that we now have a concept, "decolonization," that
clearly accommodates the deep-seated colonial continuities of the post-colonial era.
Defined in this way, "decolonization" includes but goes beyond "independence."

Much of the literature on "independence" is in what I call the "nationalist"
category. This literature dwells on how the African political elite (the nationalists)
organized anticolonial movements, "demanded" or "struggled for," and "won"
independence from apparently reluctant colonial powers. Anthony Hopkins, for
example, holds that in the post-1945 era, African anticolonial movements "assumed a more organized and more overt political form." This development, according to him, had its antecedents in the 1930s, but "the years between 1945
and 1950 saw an upsurge of militant, anticolonial activities...in the Press, in
mass demonstrations and in confrontation between African leaders and colonial
officials." After 1950, however, the character of African opposition to colonialism changed "from that of bitterness and militancy" to "a more conciliatory and
cooperative mood." As an explanation for this change, Hopkins says that "the
colonial powers had started to make substantial concessions to African demands
by promoting a greater degree of self-government."[39] The nationalists, it is generally held, were helped by external factors such as World War II, in its various dimensions (especially the 1941 Anglo-American Atlantic Charter) and the anticolonialism of the United States.

Space constraints and the specific purpose of this chapter do not permit a detailed exploration of the explanatory limitations of this "nationalist" interpretation. First, let me acknowledge that, in varying degrees, this interpretation has
some validity when applied to the anticolonial movements in the former white
settler colonies (Algeria, Kenya, Namibia, Zimbabwe, and South Africa) and the
former Portuguese territories. With these exceptions, skepticism is a virtue when
employing the nationalist interpretation. It is clear to me that the literature in this
genre adopts as truths what are at best analytical assumptions. The first difficulty
with the interpretation is that it assumes a monolithic nationalist movement, and
therefore ignores the sharp ethnic feuds, which invariably meant competing agendas, amongst the African political elite in each colonial territory.

Little empirical evidence has emerged to support the idea of "mass demonstrations" and "confrontation between African leaders and colonial officials."
Leopold Sédar Sénghor told a Nigerian newspaper of his negotiation with Charles
de Gaulle for the independence of Senegal: "In 1959, I was the first member of
parliament to go and ask for independence from De Gaulle. Our discussion lasted
half an hour, and he granted it."[40] This was the general pattern of the so-called
struggle for independence in the French territories. According to Michael Crow-

---

38. John Darwin, *Britain and Decolonization: The Retreat from Empire in the Post-war
World* (London: Macmillan, 1988), 7.
39. A. G. Hopkins, *An Economic History of West Africa* (London: Longman, 1973),
260, 271.
40. *The Guardian* (Lagos), July 4, 1988.

der and Donal Cruise O'Brien, the African political elite in the French territories "formerly rejected independence in favor of a greater participation in the political process of a French Union or Community of which Africa would be a constituent part."[41] The result was that "the independence of the African territories in 1960 came more as a result of French 'goodwill' and 'magnanimity' than under the pressure of African nationalist movements."[42]

In much of British Africa, the nationalist anticolonial effort, at its best, consisted of writings in newspapers read by a tiny segment of the population, petitions and delegations to London and attendance of constitutional conferences. There was nothing in the form of the protest marches which characterized the civil rights struggle in the United States. Nor was there much of a civic education program aimed at the construction of a popular-democratic social order. The elevation of this "pen and paper" nationalism into a heroic struggle which ousted the British presumes an astonishing degree of cause and effect which has not been, and cannot be, convincingly demonstrated.

Recent scholarship makes it very easy to dismiss the causal relevance of external factors. It is now quite obvious that the Atlantic Charter was irrelevant in terms of changing British policy. One may recall the obtuse forthrightness of British Prime Minister Winston Churchill in 1942: "That there be no mistake about it any quarter. We intend to hold what we have. I have not become the King's First Minister to preside over the liquidation of the British Empire."[43] W. R. Louis shows that in the 1940s, in the face of U.S. anticolonial rhetoric, "Englishmen generally held strong feelings about Empire." Not only Churchill and the Conservatives, but "Members of the Labour Party also held strong convictions." Louis' work, like other recent studies, has established that there was no sustained effort on the U.S. side to uphold the Atlantic Charter.[44] More generally, I have demonstrated, elsewhere, that the U.S. was not a catalyst in the independence of African states; if anything, the U.S. endorsed European colonialism in Africa.[45]

In 1945, the three major British political parties, Conservative, Labour, and Liberal, separately gave public talks on the political future of Africa: none of the parties was, at the time, thinking of independence for Africa.[46] Similarly, a glance at the relevant secondary literature will show that the 1946 French constitution did not envisage statehood, even as a long-term goal, for the colonial territories; its essence was to achieve the integration of the territories into the French Union. Portugal and Belgium did not have independence on their agendas in the 1940s or

41. Michael Crowder and Donal Cruise O'Brien, "Politics of Decolonization in French West Africa, 1945–1960," in *History of West Africa, vol. 2*, eds. J. F. Ade Ajayi and Michael Crowder, (Essex, UK: Longman Group, 1987), 736. Also see Michael Crowder, "Independence as a Goal in French West African Politics: 1944–60," in *French-Speaking Africa: The Search for Identity*, ed. William H. Lewis (New York: Walker, 1965).

42. Guy Martin, "The Historical, Economic, and Political Bases of France's African Policy," *Journal of Modern African Studies* 23, 2 (June 1985): 191.

43. *The Times* (London), November 11, 1942.

44. Wm. Roger Louis, *Imperialism at Bay, 1941–1945: The United States and Decolonization of the British Empire* (New York: Oxford University Press, 1977).

45. Ebere Nwaubani, *The United States and Decolonization in West Africa, 1950–1960* (Rochester, NY: University of Rochester Press, 2001).

46. See "Africa and the British Political Parties," *African Affairs* 44, 176 (July 1945): 108–17.

even the 1950s. The unavoidable conclusion is that World War II, on its own, neither weakened Europe's imperial resolve in Africa nor compelled or induced the colonial powers to make political concessions.

Mostly written between the late 1950s and the 1970s, the nationalist literature did not benefit from the primary sources central to its discourse, notably the official files and the memoirs of the major African and European actors. Consequently, the literature could not come to grips with the motivations and broad dynamics of the process which they described. Historians are only beginning to study those files. From the little we know from such studies, the African political elite did, in some cases, play some part in the achievement of independence. So did the colonial powers themselves, especially in controlling the content and pace of the transfer of power. Beyond the role played by the African elite and the colonial powers, an adequate explanation must account for the pervasive imperialistic continuities in postcolonial Africa. From this perspective, the causal background of independence reflects a complicated array of factors that are difficult to tease apart.

Review Questions

1. Drawing on the experience of two colonies under different colonial powers, discuss aspects of the political culture ushered in by the Europeans.
2. It has been argued that ethnicity during the colonial period was a system of scapegoating that keeps oppressed groups (the colonized) from recognizing who (the colonizer), in fact, holds power over them. Examine this argument, with specific examples from two or three colonies.
3. Using one specific ethnic group as an example, discuss the ways in which colonial rule reshaped gender relations.

Additional Reading

A. Boahen. *African Perspectives on Colonialism*. Baltimore, MD: Johns Hopkins University Press, 1987.

D. K. Fieldhouse. *Black Africa 1945–80: Economic Decolonization & Arrested Development*. London: Allen & Unwin, 1986, chap. 2.

Adrian Hastings. *The Construction of Nationhood: Ethnicity, Religion and Nationalism*. Cambridge University Press, 1997, see esp. 148–166.

Terence Ranger. "The Invention of Tradition in Colonial Africa," in *The Invention of Tradition*, ed., E. J. Hobsbawm and T. Ranger. Cambridge University Press, 1983. Ranger has shifted from his argument in this famous essay.

Index